Legal Ethics

Legal Ethics

Jonathan Herring

OXFORD
UNIVERSITY PRESS

OXFORD
UNIVERSITY PRESS

Great Clarendon Street, Oxford, OX2 6DP,
United Kingdom

Oxford University Press is a department of the University of Oxford.
It furthers the University's objective of excellence in research, scholarship,
and education by publishing worldwide. Oxford is a registered trade mark of
Oxford University Press in the UK and in certain other countries

© Oxford University Press 2014

Published in the United States of America by Oxford University Press
198 Madison Avenue, New York, NY 10016, United States of America

British Library Cataloguing in Publication Data
Data available

ISBN 978-0-19-870345-7

Printed in Great Britain by
Ashford Colour Press Ltd, Gosport, Hampshire

Preface

It is astonishing that a student can go through his or her legal training with little or no understanding of professional ethics. It is all the more surprising given the major scandals in the financial sector leading to the economic collapse that has so characterised this century. Lawyers played no small role in these and the events have justifiably led to considerable soul-searching within the profession. But that is merely part of a broader crisis in the legal profession. As legal aid budgets are drastically cut, denying many access to justice, there is a discomforting truth in the cynics' claim that lawyers exist to make rich people richer. Lawyers need a clearer understanding of the ethical basis of what they do and the ethical restrictions on their behaviour if they are to regain the confidence of the public and confidence in themselves.

This book is firmly targeted at the student reader. It does not purport to give answers to all of the difficult issues raised. I hope that readers will gain an understanding of the different views that people take and be equipped to develop their own perspectives. There is plenty of further reading suggested at the end of each chapter for those wishing to find out more.

I am very grateful for the support of many people in the writing of this book. I am especially grateful to Anja Bossow, Louise Ferdjani, Xanthia Hargreaves, Daniel Perry, Sophie Scholl, and Ralph Spencer-Tucker for their help in recording the What Would You Do? podcasts which appear on the website associated with this book. The anonymous reviewers (both academic and student) have provided invaluable assistance. The team at Oxford University Press have been wonderful, especially Sarah Viner, who has been an outstanding editor with whom to work. I have greatly enjoyed the support of many friends and colleagues during the writing of this book, including Alan Bogg, Stephen Gilmore, George P. Smith II, Rachel Taylor, and Se-shauna Wheattle. Above all, I have been loved beyond measure by my family, Kirsten, Laurel, Jo and Darcy.

Grateful acknowledgement is made to:

- the Bar Standards Board for kind permission to reproduce sections of the Code of Conduct of the Bar for England and Wales; and

- the Law Society for kind permission to reproduce extracts from the Solicitors Regulation Authority (SRA) Handbook, Legal Practice Course Outcomes 2011, and Outcomes-Focused Regulation at a Glance © The Law Society.

Jonathan Herring
Oxford
1 October 2013

Guide to the features in *Legal Ethics*

Key issues

- What does it mean to be a pro
- What role do lawyers play in so
- What challenges are facing the

Key issues • Introduction

Each chapter begins by clearly identifying a list of the key issues covered and offering an introduction to the topic in question.

 Key case

Spaulding v Zimmerman, 116 N.W. 2d 704 [Minn. 1962]

In this notorious American case, a child was injured in a car accident. The drive obtained a medical report on the child, which disclosed that the child had a po heart condition (unknown by the child's family), which may have been caused The case settled and the defendant's lawyers never disclosed the report. The ma to court, where the judge found that the defence lawyers had not acted improp no duty to disclose the report and were acting in their client's interests.

Follow the Code • Key statute • Key case

Throughout the text, extracts from the professional codes of conduct and statutes are clearly highlighted in 'Follow the Code' and 'Key statute' boxes. 'Key cases' are similarly drawn out and explained in detail.

Digging deeper

The principle of confidentiality fits well into an adversarial model of justice, in which each s is seeking to win, by fair means or foul. Clients can be completely open with their lawyers a lawyers can select from what they are told the best pieces of evidence to present to the cou While, of course, a lawyer must never deceive the court or other lawyers, confidentiality alle the lawyer to keep hidden information that might affect the outcome of the trial. Those wh oppose the adversarial approach may question the significance of confidentiality. The mov the Civil Procedure Rules towards a less adversarial and more cooperative approach may n be entirely consistent with the traditional approach to confidentiality. We will discuss this r approach to litigation further in Chapter 9.

Digging deeper • Alternative view • Application

A variety of viewpoints and the application of theory to practice are brought out in 'Alternative view' and 'Application' boxes, which encourage students to think critically. 'Digging deeper' boxes allow students to delve into more complex issues and academic debates.

Scandal!

In 2013, a novel was published under a pseudonym (Robert Galbraith). Several months after publication, it was leaked to the press that the author was J. K. Rowling,[15] the author of the Harry Potter novels. It transpired that her solicitors had leaked her identity. She was reported as saying that she had assumed she could expect 'total confidentiality' from her lawyers and was 'very angry' at what had happened. Of course, the sales of the book rocketed, and so she could not expect legal damages and she had not lost financially. Nevertheless, the firm of solicitors was highly apologetic. One of its partners had told his wife's best friend, who had let it slip to a journalist.

Definition ● Example ● Scandal!

Key terms and ideas are defined and examples are provided throughout. Particularly thought-provoking or shocking examples are outlined in the 'Scandal!' boxes.

What would you do?

You are advising a company defending against a claim for sexual harassment brought by an employee who cannot afford a lawyer and so has brought the proceedings herself. It is clear from your investigations that the claim is justified and that a serious wrong has been done to the employee. However, you notice that, in the paperwork, the claimant has made a technical error on which the company could rely to make a legal defence.

What would they do?

This 'What would you do?' scenario is accompanied by a podcast in which current law students debate the issues and articulate their own responses to the ethical questions that it

What would you do? ● What would they do? podcasts

'What would you do?' scenarios appear throughout the textbook, providing fictional scenarios with which students can engage, encouraging them to consider how they would react to particular ethical dilemmas. Selected 'What would you do?' scenarios are accompanied by 'What would they do?' podcasts in which current law students debate the issues and articulate their own responses to the ethical questions raised.

Further reading

The detail on the law on confidentiality can be found in the following works:

J. Auburn, *Legal Professional Privilege: Law and Theory* (Hart, 2000).

M. Brindle and G. Dehn, 'Confidence, public interest and the lawyer', in R. Cranston (ed.) *Legal Ethics And Professional Responsibility* (Oxford University Press, 1995).

A. Higgins, 'Legal advice privilege and its relevance to corporations' (2010) 73 Modern Law Review 371.

A. Higgins, 'ECJ confirms no privilege for in-house counsel: *Azko Nobel v European Commission*' (2011) 30 Civil Justice Quarterly 113.

Conclusion ● Further reading

Each chapter ends with a conclusion and a list of further reading directing students to a wide range of books, articles, and websites.

An accompanying Online Resource Centre can be accessed online at:
www.oxfordtextbooks.co.uk/orc/herringethics/

Outline contents

Outline contents

Detailed contents

Table of cases

United States

Table of statutes and professional codes

Ethical theories

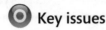

Key issues

- What are ethics?
- Is there a right answer to an ethical dilemma?
- How are lawyers' ethics different from general ethics?

Introduction

'Lawyers' ethics' has been described as one of the great oxymorons. Jokes about lawyers abound. Few are complimentary:

> The National Institutes of Health have announced that they will no longer be using rats for medical experimentation. In their place, they will use lawyers. They have given three reasons for this decision.
>
> 1. There are now more lawyers than there are rats.
> 2. The medical researchers don't become as emotionally attached to the lawyers as they did to the rats.
> 3. There are some things that even rats won't do.

At one time, three learned professions were seen as the pillars of society: doctors; clergy; and lawyers. While once the three most respected occupations in the land, a lively debate could now be had over which of these is held most in disrepute.

In a survey by the American Bar Association of public attitudes about lawyers, the following five were the most common responses:

- 'lawyers are too expensive';
- 'lawyers are greedy';
- 'lawyers are not honest';
- 'there are too many lawyers';
- 'lawyers are self-serving, don't care about clients'.

A survey in the UK found that only 42 per cent of respondents would trust a lawyer to tell the truth.[1]

---

[1] Legal Services Consumer Panel, *Annual Tracker Survey* (Legal Services Consumer Panel, 2013).

If lawyers seek to be held in high regard by society, it is crucial that there be a system of legal ethics that ensures that the public can have confidence in the legal profession. That is why the topic of this book—ethics for lawyers—is so important.

It is easy, however, to be starry-eyed about lawyers' ethics. Although people say that they want lawyers to be fair to both sides, to be scrupulously honest, and to put justice first, it is all rather different if they are talking about the lawyer who is representing them: in that event, they want their lawyers to do everything necessary to win the case. People want their opponent's lawyer to be fair and reasonable—but not their own!

Lawyers and legal ethics

As is well known, there are two primary branches of the legal profession: solicitors and barristers. Less well known is the fact that others play a crucial role in the provision of legal services, including legal executives, licensed conveyancers, will drafters, paralegals, and informal advisers. This book is primarily designed for law students who most commonly go on to seek work as solicitors or barristers, and so it will focus on these.

As we shall see later in this chapter, there has been a lively debate over whether or not legal ethics should be part of a law degree. We will explore the reasons for this later on. This book, however, will be designed to introduce students to the major issues around legal ethics. As well as setting out what are generally accepted as the ethical principles governing lawyers, it will also identify the different theories behind these principles.

The aim of this book is to introduce you not only to the rules of lawyers' ethics, but also, more importantly, to the principles behind the regulations. This is crucial because cases that can be dealt with under the rules are easy; hard cases are those in which it is not clear whether a rule applies or which of two rules apply. In these cases, it is necessary to know the principles behind the rules to assess the best way forward. Further, this book will explain alternative ways of examining ethical issues and criticisms of the current approaches. You should then be in a good position to take a sensitive and well-rounded approach to the rules.

Although the phrase 'lawyers' ethics' itself might bring a smile to the face of some, the issue is extremely important. The financial crisis of recent years can be blamed, in part, to ethical failures on the parts of the lawyers involved. Indeed, one of the major responses to the financial crisis has been to tighten the regulation and enforcement of ethics. If courts and the justice system are seen to lack an ethical foundation, society—that is, people—will lose respect for the law. A degree of respect for lawyers and the legal system is crucial for a well-functioning society.

This chapter will start by setting out some general theories about ethics. How do we judge what is the right thing to do? What makes a decision morally justifiable? What makes a person good? Of course, people disagree on these questions. There is no consensus on the correct answer to these questions and many books have been written on them.

It hardly needs to be said that lawyers are people and so are bound by these general principles just like anyone else. So lawyers must not kill innocent people—but that is true for everyone and so is not a special ethical obligation on lawyers. Because this book is about *lawyers'* ethics rather than general ethics, we need to go beyond the standard ethical rules and explore two questions, as follows.

1. Are there any additional ethical obligations that a lawyer has over and above the general ethical principles that apply to anyone else?
2. Are there circumstances in which lawyers are excused from the general ethical obligations that are imposed on others?

The first question considers whether, in addition to the general ethical principles (that is, 'do not kill', 'do not lie', among other things), there are special ethical obligations imposed upon lawyers. As we shall see, many people believe that lawyers have especial obligations to their clients that are more onerous than the normal obligations that people owe to each other.

The second question asks whether a lawyer may be excused from those ethical obligations that are imposed generally. A person who discovers that his or her friend is going to commit a crime may be under an obligation to report that friend to the authorities; a lawyer's special obligation of confidence may mean that the lawyer is not. Charles Fried, a leading legal ethicist, once asked: 'Can a good lawyer be a good person?'[2] The very fact that this question has been raised indicates that many believe that sometimes lawyers are asked to do things that, if they were done by a non-lawyer, would be seen to be wrong. A further interesting question is whether, in the interpretation and application of the law, lawyers have particular obligations. Lawyers are often called upon to interpret or apply the law. In cases in which the law is ambiguous, to what extent is the lawyer required to ensure that the law takes a moral approach?

These extra obligations arise because of the special position that lawyers have in relation to their clients, and in relation to society more generally. In relation to their clients, lawyers have a special relationship of trust. People will disclose to their lawyers highly personal information and give them highly valued property. There need to be legal and ethical obligations that protect those who put such trust in lawyers. This is important for clients, but also for lawyers. If lawyers cease to be trustworthy, people will no longer use lawyers in relation to their sensitive matters. This will be disastrous both for lawyers, who will lose business, but also for society more generally. It is widely thought to be beneficial that people can seek legal advice and engage in legal transactions. If people cannot find out what the law is and have no access to legal services to enforce their legal rights, the rule of law will break down.

---

[2] C. Fried, 'The lawyer as friend: The moral foundations of the lawyer–client relation' (1976) 85 Yale Law Journal 1060.

But there is a balance here. While we want people to have trust in their lawyers and to have an advocate who will represent them in legal proceedings, lawyers also have a special duty to courts and the justice system generally. If lawyers are seen to act immorally and to undermine the principles of justice underpinning the legal system, the legal system will fall into disrepute.

As we shall see as this chapter develops, many of the most difficult ethical issues for lawyers arise when there is a clash between their duties to their clients and their broader duties to the justice system, and to society more generally. Lawyers will disagree on where that balance should be and much academic debate centres on that question. It is one to which we will return repeatedly in this book.

The role of ethics

We need to say a little more about what is meant by 'ethics'. When we are undertaking an ethical analysis we are seeking to answer the question: 'What is the right thing to do?' Another way of putting the question is to ask: 'How would we want people to respond to this situation?'

Rosalind Hursthouse[3] has stated that there are no 'moral wiz-kids'. Her point is that while we might expect the very best physicist to discover the right answer to scientific questions, we do not expect the same of ethicists. Good ethicists are not necessarily correct, but should be able to explain their views in clear ways, with reasoned arguments. So we cannot expect ethicists to give us the 'right answer'; we have to work that out for ourselves. But we can expect ethicists to provide us with tools that we can use to reach reasonable answers. They can provide us with the tools to live good and virtuous lives. They can help us to understand which answers are consistent with certain values and which are inconsistent. Ethicists can therefore help us to find out the appropriate responses to dilemmas, once we choose which values we want to uphold.

The nature of ethics will become clearer if we distinguish ethics from some other things.

Norms and ethics

It is important to distinguish the 'norms' that govern lawyers and ethics. There may be certain norms that lawyers follow: they may wear suits; they may be in their offices by 9.30; they may like drinking coffee! But these are norms—that is, behaviour that is common, but which is not itself justified by an ethical principle. There is nothing unethical in not drinking coffee, even if it is uncommon.

Perhaps the best way of telling whether something is a norm or moral principle is looking at the reaction of others when the rule is broken. If a male solicitor were to turn up to work not wearing a tie, there may be a few eyebrows raised, but he would

---

[3] R. Hursthouse, *On Virtue Ethics* (Oxford University Press, 1999).

not be condemned—at least not in anything like the same way as he would had he revealed confidential information. This latter instance would lead to his investigation by the professional body and perhaps even by a court. It could lead to a punishment. His failure to wear a tie might, at most, lead to a quiet word in his ear. While breach of an ethical principle might indicate a character flaw, a breach of a norm would indicate only a need to be reminded of 'the way in which we do things'. It would be seen as a matter of ignorance or eccentricity rather than of immorality.

One way of determining the ethical obligations under which lawyers act is to look at what a lawyer did or did not do. In doing so, you might spot that, soon after meeting a client, the lawyer set out the arrangement for the payment of fees. But this, in itself, would not tell you whether this was because this was a norm or an ethical principle; you would also need to consider what would happen if the behaviour were breached. Who would respond to the breach and how? Social norms are typically enforced by people saying bad things about the transgressor or shunning him or her. Laws are enforced by courts by means of punishment. Professional regulations fall somewhere in between, with consequences that can be legal or professional, and which can ultimately result in the transgressor's removal from the professions.[4]

Law and ethics

Asking whether an action is 'legal' and whether it is 'ethical' are two very different questions. Something may be ethically, but not legally, required. Being polite to other people may be demanded by ethics, for example, but not by the law; adultery may be unethical, but it is not illegal. The law may require Person A to pay damages to Person B for a breach of contract or for causing Person B an injury, even though Person A is not morally to blame. Similarly, an act may be against the law even if it is not unethical. Such instances are rare, but a father who does not buy a parking ticket for a hospital car park because he has no change and has a seriously ill child whom he needs to take to the hospital may be behaving illegally, even if not unethically. Generally, however, the two are linked. It is relatively rare for people to be found to have breached the law in circumstances in which they have acted well in ethical terms. And most serious breaches of ethical standards will involve a breach of law of some kind.

The law tends to focus on matters that harm the public and are susceptible to proof. So a behaviour that is unethical, but does not cause a public harm (lying to a friend, for example) is unlikely to be unlawful. The harm is only to the other person and does not require societal condemnation by means of the law. Other behaviour that may cause a public harm cannot be readily susceptible to proof or definition. Malicious gossip might be an example. Even if we were to decide that gossip harmed the public good, it would be hard to define gossip in a way that would be sufficiently clear for the law. Also, the law tends to focus on behaviour that is seriously harmful.

---

[4] For more discussion, see H. Hart, *The Concept of Law* (Oxford University Press, 1961).

Unethical conduct that causes only minor harms may not be sufficiently serious to merit an official legal response.

Ethics and law are focused on different things. For law, the focus is on cases in which there is a sufficiently serious harm and a need for someone to be held to account in a public forum; for ethics, the focus is on whether the act is a good thing to do.

There is much more that could be said about the link between law and ethics, something that has generated substantial debate amongst legal philosophers.

Ethical disagreements

If you hope that ethicists and ethical analysis will provide you with the right answer to every difficult question, you will soon be disappointed. Ethicists disagree on what is ethical. This can be disconcerting. In this section, I will explore a little more why that may be and why it is that people disagree.

The overarching approach

As we set out some of the ethical approaches, it will be noted that they adopt a rather different style of approach to resolving ethical dilemmas and that this leads to different answers. Some of the different approaches are as follows.

1. *Rule-based approaches*—for example, deontology (considered later in the chapter)
   Some approaches seek to reduce ethical principles to a set of rules to follow. This has an appeal to lawyers, because they are familiar with the idea of applying rules to particular situations and following them. For supporters of this approach, the answer to the question 'What is the ethical response to this situation?' is 'Follow the rules'.

2. *Outcome-based approaches*—for example, utilitarianism (considered later in the chapter)
   Some approaches argue that the central issue in an ethical dilemma is to look to the consequences of the decision. To be ethical is to produce the best outcome. For supporters of this approach, the answer to the question 'What is the ethical response to this situation?' is 'Consider what will produce the best outcome'.

3. *Character-based approaches*—for example, virtue ethics (considered later in the chapter)

   Some approaches argue that ethics is about character. Ethics is about displaying certain virtues, such as honesty or kindness. So, for supporters of this approach, the answer to the question 'What is the ethical response to this situation?' is 'Act in a way that displays virtue'.

This book will not seek to judge between these general theories, which it will explore in more detail shortly. People will disagree strongly over which approach is preferable.

It is certainly not the purpose of this volume to persuade you of the benefits of one approach over another. It is hoped, however, that after reading this chapter you will be better equipped to explain your ethical reasons for acting in certain ways and to judge the decisions of others. It might also be that you will come to understand better why someone might take a completely different view from your own on what is ethically the appropriate thing to do in a given situation. It is not necessarily the case that the other person is wrong and you are right; rather, you might be asking different questions or starting from fundamentally different ethical points.

Minimum requirements or maximally ethical

One reason why people disagree on the answers to ethical dilemmas is that they may be asking different questions. When asking an ethical question, it is important to be clear whether we are asking 'What is the minimum standard that is ethically required?' or 'What is the best response?' Sometimes, an ethical dilemma raises two alternatives: action A or action B. However, more often there are a range of alternative courses of action. The answer is often far more nuanced than simply 'This is the ethical thing to do and that is not the ethical thing to do'. For example, it may be that there is an option that is ethically acceptable, but not as good as the ethically most desirable, or an option that is ethically good, but is not required. For example, if a lawyer engages in pro bono work, offering free legal advice to disadvantaged groups or charities, this may be required as an ethically good thing to do. But most people would not regard a lawyer who failed to engage in that work as acting in an ethically bad way. So it is important to be clear whether what is being asked is 'What is ethically acceptable?' or 'What is ethically the best?' When professional bodies set down ethical guidance, they are generally setting out the minimum requirements for lawyers.

Guiding me or judging others?

There is an important distinction between asking what is ethically the right thing for me to do and asking what is the ethically appropriate response to someone else's behaviour. 'Should I drop litter?' is a different question from 'How should I respond if someone else drops litter?', which is again a different question from asking 'How should the law respond if someone else drops litter?' In particular, it does not always follow from your own decision that it would be unethical for you to act in a particular way that you think that you and/or society should condemn a person who chooses to act in that way. There may be reasons peculiar to you that mean it would be wrong for you to engage in an action that would not be wrong for someone else. For example, if you were head of a campaign to encourage people to become vegetarian, that would give you a reason not to eat meat (that is, you would be being hypocritical if you were to do so) that would not apply to others. It is important to be aware of this distinction when reading academic writing. When lawyers discuss ethics, they are often discussing how the law should respond to the unethical behaviour of others, while philosophers are often discussing the way in which an ethical person should behave. These are different, although related, questions.

Ethics and regulation

In this book, we are talking about the ethical conduct of solicitors and barristers. In Chapter 3, we will be looking at how lawyers should be regulated in ethical matters. The issue of ethical regulation raises some special issues. The questions 'What is ethical?' and 'What should be included in ethical regulation?' are not the same, for two reasons.

First, ethical regulation must offer guidance. If we are to punish a lawyer for breaching professional ethics, that lawyer is entitled to know what the ethical requirements are. This requires the ethical guidance to be reasonably clear and capable of being applied. Consider, for example, a complex ethical dilemma involving a conflict of interest. A philosopher addressing the issue might produce a densely argued document covering many pages of analysis, teasing out numerous nuanced points that need to be put into balance. However, a lawyer in the throes of the ethical dilemma cannot be expected to undertake an analysis of that depth. This means that there is often a crudeness about the ethical guidance used in regulation. It offers clear concise guidance that can readily be applied, but it does so by sacrificing the sophistication that a deeply philosophical analysis would offer. Indeed, as we will discuss in Chapter 3, this leads to a lively debate over how detailed or how clear that regulation should be.

Second, the regulation must be capable of being enforced. Regulation would be a laughing stock if it were not enforceable. For example, let us say that you consider it to be unethical for a lawyer to look lustfully at a client. A regulation prohibiting lawyers from doing so would be impractical: we could never know what the lawyer was thinking. A better regulation might target matters capable of determination: whether the lawyer said anything inappropriate to the client, for example. So there may be some aspects of ethical behaviour that cannot be captured in a code of regulation because they could never be enforced.

People and acts

Codes of professional legal ethics focus mostly on acts, rather than character. They set out what actions are ethical or not. Not all philosophers agree with that approach. Some think that the better approach is to ask whether someone is a 'good person'— that we should be seeking to produce good lawyers, not only lawyers who do good things. Alice Woolley disagrees: '[L]egal ethics should never be concerned with the morality of *lawyers* or of *clients*; rather it should be concerned only with the morality of the acts lawyers or clients do (or propose to do).'[5]

[5] A. Woolley, 'Philosophical legal ethics: Ethics, morals and jurisprudence—Introduction: The legitimate concerns of legal ethics' (2010) 13 Legal Ethics 168.

The issue is not straightforward: what someone is and what someone does are closely related: you cannot really claim to *be* brave if you do not *do* brave things. Nevertheless, Woolley is right to emphasise that, generally, we are asking whether a particular act in a particular situation is justified, rather than making a general assessment of someone's life. In particular, if a lawyer has breached an ethical code, it will not be a defence to claim that, generally, he or she lives an ethical life.

General ethical principles

Here, we will describe some of the general ethical approaches that are taken to ethical dilemmas, before looking at some more concrete principles. We will start with perhaps the most popular ethical approach: **consequentialism**.

 ## Definition

> **Consequentialism** determines whether an act is morally justified or not, depending on whether it produces good or bad consequences overall.

Consequentialism

For a consequentialist, the key issue in determining whether an action is ethically appropriate is to consider its consequences. Quite simply, the action is right if, all things considered, the consequences are good; the action is wrong if, all things considered, its consequences are bad. This approach therefore tends to reject firm rules for ethics, such as 'Do not lie' or 'Do not kill', because it all depends on the circumstances. So if, in a particular situation, lying is going to produce an outcome that is more good than bad, then it is legitimate to lie.

Consequentialism requires a careful consideration of all of the consequences of an act. There may be some good and some bad consequences flowing from an act, in which case you need to determine whether, overall, more of the consequences are good or more are bad. So although it might be presumed that a particular lie will be good because it will make someone happy, a consequentialist would think about the possibility that he or she will be found out; in that instance, there will be more harm than good, and this will need to be taken into account.

It is not surprising that consequentialism is a popular ethical approach. It reflects how most people make many day-to-day decisions. When deciding what to watch on television, you are likely to think about which programme you will enjoy the most. If you are deciding what birthday present to buy a friend, you will consider what they will like the best. Most people want good things to flow from their actions, not bad.

◉ Application

You are acting for the prosecution of a man accused of murder. Conclusive DNA evidence has shown that he has committed the crime, but, owing to a technical violation of the rules, you cannot rely on that evidence and a conviction cannot be secured without it. A police officer offers to plant some incriminating evidence.

If you were a consequentialist, you might decide that the good of ensuring a conviction of a guilty person justifies planting the evidence.

Problems with consequentialism

At the heart of consequentialism is the claim that we must consider what will produce the most 'good'. But what does 'good' mean? One popular theory, known as 'utilitarianism', suggests that we should seek to increase the good. The greatest good is the largest amount of pleasure or happiness. But that may be problematic. Most people do not simply make decisions about what makes them happy: we may choose the television programme that is educational over one that is more fun; we may attend the lecture when we are tired, rather than sleep in late. Both of these may be seen as decisions to promote the 'good', but not necessarily happiness.

So perhaps consequentialism should not be restricted to happiness, but should include other kinds of goods? Suddenly, the approach becomes very vague. If I buy gym membership for my brother rather than buy him a cake, how can I weigh up the good of his health against the pleasure that the cake would have given him? Comparing the good of health with the deliciousness of cake is comparing incommensurables.

There are further uncertainties surrounding consequentialism. The approach all depends on predicting the consequences of our actions. But often we cannot do so. If I am not sure how people will react to my decision, it is difficult to work out whether it will produce good or not. Not only that, but how wide should the net of consequences be thrown? If I am considering driving to visit my mum next weekend, am I to consider the environmental consequences of the journey, or the impact on other road users of my erratic driving? And does a proper consequentialist analysis require me to compare the good produced by visiting my mum with the good that might be produced by visiting any of the other people whom I might see? A full consideration of all of the consequences might mean that I need to spend the whole weekend thinking it through! So the attractive simplicity of consequentialism becomes considerably more complex if we properly consider all of the outcomes of an action.

Others criticise consequentialism from other perspectives. One is that it places no weight on motivations. The act is justified under consequentialism if it produces good results, even if it is badly motivated. If a judge decides to acquit an innocent defendant because he finds her attractive, is that ethical? The result is good: the innocent defendant goes free, but has the judge acted ethically?

For others, the problem with utilitarianism is that it leads to unacceptable results. Imagine that a judge sentences an innocent, but unpopular, politician to prison for ten years. A utilitarian calculation might suggest that the joy caused to the public by the imprisonment is greater than the harm done to the politician and that the wrongful imprisonment is therefore justified. But is that right? Can good consequences (the happiness to the public) really justify injustice? Can a lawyer who runs off with his millionaire client's money really try to justify this by saying that he derived far more pleasure from the money than the millionaire would have done, and so has acted ethically?! Surely, the good consequences do not always justify the means?

 Scandal!

In 2010, the BBC[6] reported that a vicar, a lawyer, and a businessman had been convicted of helping people illegally to obtain permission to remain in the country in breach of immigration law. The vicar had undertaken 'sham marriages' to bypass immigration rules.

One can imagine, in cases such as these, defendants persuading themselves that they were doing good by helping those in a desperate situation. However, the courts will not allow a defence to a criminal offence to be based on a claim that, in this case, more good than bad was achieved.

These powerful concerns with consequentialism have led some commentators to develop an alternative approach: **rule consequentialism**.

 Definition

> **Rule consequentialism** promotes the following of rules that will normally overall produce good consequences.

Rule consequentialism

Rule consequentialists argue in favour of developing rules that, if followed, will promote the best outcomes over the long run. So rule consequentialism asks 'Which general rules will promote the best consequences in the long term, assuming that everyone accepts and complies with them?',[7] rather than what will promote the most good in this particular case. So we might decide that the rule that lawyers should not steal their clients' money is a rule that, if followed, will promote the good, even if we might accept that there can be individual cases in which that is not so. Lawyers should follow the rule that promotes good generally, even if it does not do so in a particular

---

[6] BBC News, 'Sussex vicar guilty of immigration marriage scam', 29 July 2010, online at www.bbc.co.uk/news/uk-england-sussex-10781151

[7] W. Glannon, *Biomedical Ethics* (Oxford University Press, 2005), 5.

case. This makes it easier for people to follow guidance because they need only to follow the general rule, rather than to assess its usefulness in any particular case.

One benefit of the rule consequentialist approach is that, sometimes, there is a difference between what is good for an individual lawyer and what is good for lawyers as a group.[8] A good example may be that if one lawyer were to refuse to represent a man charged with rape, that would probably not cause any harm—but if all lawyers were to refuse to represent men charged with rape, that could be problematic.

Problems with rule consequentialism

Although rule consequentialism is popular, it too has difficulties. It is problematic for individuals seeking guidance on what to do in their particular situations. Working out the consequences of alternative courses of action as required for 'act utilitarianism' is difficult enough; attempting to work out what general rule to apply in cases of this kind would be very complex. Further, there is the issue of whether, within 'rule utilitarianism', the rules have exceptions, and if so, how these exceptions are to be calculated.

Other criticisms can include that, as mentioned earlier in relation to consequentialism, no account is taken of motive in rule consequentialism; nor does the rule utilitarian take account of special duties that we might owe to our children, for example. It does not provide sufficient scope for an actor to say that although generally this is a good rule, in the circumstances of this case, it will be improper to follow it.

Deontology

Deontology provides a quite different approach to ethics from consequentialism. A deontological approach holds that certain actions are good or wrong *in or of* themselves. It is, they say, right to tell the truth not because doing so makes people happy or because of other good consequences, but simply because telling the truth is a good. Immanuel Kant is widely seen as a leading proponent of this approach. One of his fundamental principles is well known: you should never use someone simply as a means to an end. This is important for lawyers because it shows that lawyers should not use clients to achieve their own goals, even if they believe that doing so will create more good.

 **Definition**

> **Deontology** states that there are certain moral rules that must be followed, regardless of the circumstances.

---

[8] A. Ayers, 'The lawyer's perspective: The gap between individual decisions and collective consequences in legal ethics' (2011) 36 Journal of the Legal Profession 77.

It is crucial for deontologists that a breach of an ethical principle cannot be justified simply by referring to the consequences. Telling the truth might cause pain in some cases, but that is no justification for lying.

One of the great benefits of deontology is its clarity—at least as long as the rules are clear! There is no need to worry yourself about the consequences of your action; you simply follow the rule, come what may. Lawyers may be drawn to this approach because they are familiar with statutes or contracts setting out requirements that must be followed.

Deontologists often place much weight on duties. They emphasise the duties that parents owe to their children, or physicians to their patients, which are overlooked in utilitarian approaches. When making a decision about our children, we must take into account the duties that we owe them, not only the consequences for all children. Lawyers must acknowledge their special duties to clients and justice, and not consider only the consequences of their actions.

Problems with deontology

Consequentialists will question whether principles should be stuck to, come what may. Even if you are not an out-and-out consequentialist, you might ask: 'Should I not lie if doing so will save someone's life?' The classic scenario is the person in Nazi Germany, who is hiding a Jew escaping persecution, being asked by a soldier if he or she has any Jewish people in the house. In such a case, the deontologist must be truly committed to his or her principles to demand that the person should tell the truth despite the inevitable results.

Some deontologists are willing to give some flexibility. They accept that the principle must be followed unless there are overwhelmingly bad consequences that will flow from it. You should not kill, they say, although maybe if thousands of people were going to be saved as a result, it may be acceptable. Lawyers are familiar with this in terms of human rights. You must not discriminate against someone, but it might be possible to produce a very strong case for why discrimination might be justified. Those who are willing to accept this more flexible version of deontology face the problem that doing so renders their approach less clear-cut: inevitable uncertainty will surround precisely how bad the consequences must be to justify interfering with the principle. They also face claims that once they are allowing consequences to override the rule, they are consequentialists in disguise.

Perhaps the central problem facing deontologists is to explain where their principles come from. Why should we not lie? One argument is that deontological principles are derived from rationality. Our rationality is what distinguishes us from animals and provides us with the means to develop moral principles. The problem is that people's rationality leads them to different conclusions on difficult moral issues.

It is not surprising that many (but by no means all) religious people take a deontological approach. For them, there are certain things that God has declared wrong. No explanation or justification is needed: God has spoken. Deontologists seeking to explain their principles in a non-religious way usually suggest that there are certain self-evident goods that are part of human flourishing: truth, knowledge, friendship, among other things. The difficulty may be that what is self-evidently good to some is not so to others. Is it self-evidently good that a child should be raised by his or her biological parents? Some would say so, but others would not. Another possible source of deontological principles is public opinion—yet history teaches us that the majority of people have followed some very unpleasant principles in the past. Also, why should the fact that most people believe X to be true make X an ethical principle? This different source of deontological principles is a problem for lawyers and for drafters of legal ethical principles. If the law wishes to take a deontological approach, whose deontological principles should the law adopt? Having said that, whichever theory is adopted, there will usually be a debate over which version of the theory is to be applied.

Applying deontology: principlism

A popular way of applying a deontological approach is through an approach known as **principlism**.

 **Definition**

> **Principlism** involves applying a set of prima facie principles to an ethical dilemma.

Principlism avoids some of the grand themes that we have discussed so far and suggests that we can identify some key principles. Through considering an application of these to the issue at hand, the correct ethical approach becomes apparent. This approach has been particularly influentially put forward in a book by Tom Beauchamp and James Childress, *Principles of Biomedical Ethics*.[9] While written for medical law and ethics, it has been applied in a range of situations. It relies on four key principles:

- respect for autonomy;
- non-maleficence;
- beneficence; and
- justice.

If these were used more generally for legal ethics, they would require that, in any moral dilemma, a lawyer should consider the four principles to direct his or her action.
    The four principles need a little more explanation.

---

[9] T. Beauchamp and J. Childress, *Principles of Biomedical Ethics*, 7th edn (Oxford University Press, 2013).

Autonomy

Autonomy is about allowing people to make their own decisions, unless their doing so harms others or the common good. Applying this in the legal context, lawyers should respect the decisions that clients make about what they want to do. For example, if a client asks a lawyer to draft a will giving particular gifts, the lawyer should respect the client's decision. It is not for the lawyer to tell the client to give more money to charity. This is not to say that the lawyer should not provide information or advice, but that the lawyer should acknowledge that the decision is the client's own.

In favour of emphasising autonomy is the view that lawyers have a central role in society in terms of helping people to achieve what they want in life. Lawyers play a positive role in helping people to reach their aspirations: to set up a company; to buy a house; or to get married. They also have a role in protecting clients from oppression and ensuring that clients are free to make their own decisions. The primary job for a lawyer under the autonomy principle is to help clients to realise their objectives.

There is one aspect of the autonomy principle that might appeal to some lawyers: that the lawyer is non-judgemental. The whole point of autonomy is that people are free to pursue their own visions of the 'good life'. It is not for lawyers to tell clients whether they are making bad decisions. In the past, it may have been that doctors, lawyers, and other professionals were seen as the experts to whom ordinary people deferred. Now, the relationship between professionals and clients has changed. People consulting lawyers on divorce would be astonished to hear their lawyers suggest that they change their minds and be reconciled with their spouses. The lawyer's job is to help the client to obtain the divorce, not to question the client's decision.

Non-maleficence

Non-malificence is the principle that a lawyer should not harm a client. An obvious example is that the lawyer should not steal his or her client's funds. This is a *negative* principle: it tells a lawyer what they should not do.

Beneficence

Beneficence is the related principle that the lawyer should seek to promote the well-being of the client. It is a *positive* principle, requiring action from a lawyer. The lawyer should seek to do his or her best to advance the client's cause and do as well as he or she can for the client.

Justice

The requirement of justice means that the lawyer must act fairly as between different clients and also to promote justice more widely. This may involve a commitment to the well-being of the legal profession[10] and to the justice system as a whole. Few would disagree with that principle. More problematic is the question of what is meant by

---

[10] D. Brindle and P. Curtis, 'Fight for equality that could put jobs at risk', *The Guardian*, 2 January 2008.

'justice'. At the heart of most theories of justice is the principle of formal equality: all equals should be treated equally and unequals should be treated unequally. The principle, so baldly stated, is perhaps uncontroversial—but its application causes difficulties: how do we know if two people are equal; and how do we know if treatment is equal?

Justice can be a slippery concept and there is no clear agreement about what it contains or involves. It comprises three aspects: the procedural; the substantive; and the social.

- The *procedural* aspects of justice require a proper hearing for disputes and that judges be free from bias. There should be an opportunity for each side to present its case and for reasons to be given for a decision. Procedural justice is not uncontroversial. Lawyers can get a bad name if they are seen to use procedural justice arguments to undermine substantive arguments. Claims that a case must fail because a particular form was not lodged at an appropriate time or in the correct way can appear to put technical requirements over and above finding a fair solution to a dispute. Yet there need to be rules about how claims can be made and how evidence is presented if there are to be fair procedures to deal with disputes. The difficulty is striking the balance in ensuring that these are complied with in a way that ensures fair outcomes.

- *Substantive* justice requires that the outcomes of legal disputes are just. What is a 'just' law is a huge question and beyond the scope of this book. Some lawyers believe that it is the job of Parliament and the courts to ensure that the content of the rules is fair. The lawyer will use the existing legal rules to pursue a client's case. If the content of the law is unfair, the blame for that rests not with the lawyer, but with the Parliament or courts.

- *Social* justice takes a broader view. Justice, it is said by some, is not only about having a fair legal system, but also about ensuring that society, generally, is fair. John Rawls suggested two key principles as aspects of the social dimension of justice: that offices and positions should be open to all, with fair equality of opportunity; and that the social system should act for the greatest benefit of the least advantaged of society. Not everyone will agree with these, by any means: here, we are entering political questions about the kind of society and government that we want.

Applying the principles

Having now explained the four principles, let us consider how they work in practice. Beauchamp and Childress[11] promote these principles because they represent a 'common morality'—that is, a set of principles agreed by people around the world and from a broad range of perspectives. They hope that everyone will agree that these

---

[11] See n. 9.

principles are good ones to follow. They also acknowledge that these are prima facie principles. In other words, they accept that there may be particular cases in which there are very good reasons why the principles should not apply.

They argue that, in approaching an ethical dilemma, we should consider what each of these four principles would have to say about how to act. Crucially, they do not rank the four principles. Importantly, this means that their approach does not provide an answer to a difficult dilemma. It provides us with tools to help us look at the issue, but does not give us the answer. It is easy to imagine cases in which respecting autonomy (doing what the client wants) conflicts with non-maleficence (not harming the client). Where there is a conflict, Beauchamp and Childress hope that a careful consideration of the application of these principles will lead to the solution becoming apparent.

The popularity of their approach lies partly in the fact that it provides a workable way of thinking through the issues. By taking each principle one by one and thinking through its significance, one is likely to consider most, if not all, relevant moral issues. Further, it provides an accessible language and tools with which to talk through issues with colleagues and, in doing so, highlight why there is a disagreement. It might, for example, become clear that the difference of viewpoints arises because one person is emphasising autonomy and another is emphasising non-maleficence.

Critics of principlism

Critics of principles argue that, in difficult cases, it does not really provide a clear approach, especially in cases in which the principles suggest different answers.[12] Suppose a client instructs a lawyer to act in a way that the lawyer judges will harm the client. For example, he or she asks the lawyer to institute proceedings, even though the lawyer thinks the case has no chance of success. In this instance, we have a clear clash between autonomy (complying with the decision of the client) and non-maleficence (not harming the client). Principlism does not tell us which principle to follow. Indeed, nearly all ethical dilemmas come down to a clash between two or more of these principles. Without an indication of which principle is to trump the other(s), they provide little help. Critics argue that there is a need for a unifying moral theory to justify these four principles, which would then provide a way of reconciling them in the event of a clash. Beauchamp and Childress do not claim that the principles provide the answers; rather, they provide an effective way of analysing an issue.[13] It may therefore be that principlism provides tools with which to think through an issue, rather than indicates the answer to be reached.

[12] A. Campbell, 'The virtues (and vices) of the four principles' (2003) 29 Journal of Medical Ethics 292.

[13] T. Beauchamp, 'Principlism and its alleged competitors' (1995) 5 Kennedy Institute of Ethics Journal 181.

Intuition

So far, we have been looking at forms of ethical analysis that promote rational ways of resolving dilemmas. They provide ways of thinking through the issues to determine what is the right thing to do. But maybe these are mistaken. Should we place greater weight on intuition[14]—that is, a gut feeling that something is right or wrong? Whatever logic or argument may suggest is right, 'our hearts' sometimes tell us that 'our heads' have got it wrong. These arguments are often particularly prominent in medical ethics. For example, many people feel that creating animal–human hybrids is wrong. They may not be able to articulate in a rational way *why* they think it is wrong; it simply *feels* wrong to many people.

Moral intuition can be important in practice. It is often intuition that alerts the practising lawyer to an ethical issue. He or she may realise that something 'does not feel right' and will then analyse the issue more carefully. Indeed, without intuition alerting lawyers to a potential issue, it is not clear that carefully drafted ethical guidance will be of help: the lawyers simply will not realise that they need to refer to it.

Alice Woolley argues that lawyers should acknowledge the importance of moral intuition. She argues:

> Moral decision making relies significantly on our intuition and moral emotions, the unconscious cognitive processes through which we perceive and respond to moral problems. Intuition and moral emotions are affected by reason—by our moral commitments, by our reasoned exchanges with others, and by our own reflections on what reasons matter most. Intuition and moral emotions are, though, nonetheless distinct and are themselves the primary operative feature in moral decision making, rather than reason itself. Knowing what to do in any particular case is not normally the direct product of an ex ante reasoned analysis.[15]

This view should not be dismissed too easily. While people articulate reasons for their ethical analysis, it may be that deeply held intuitions underlie these. It may well be that this explains why, when there is a disagreement over a moral issue, people rarely change their moral positions however much they may trade arguments. In other words, it may be that while people like to pretend that their moral views are the result of rational thought, in fact emotional responses and personal history play a bigger part than they like to admit. Their response to lying, for example, may be affected by experiences in the past of being lied to.

There is a further important point that Woolley makes. Successful ethics means not only that people will come to see the correct response, but also that they will be able to see that decision through to action. Ethics that talks to the 'head', but makes no

---

[14] G. Kaebnick, 'Reasons of the heart: Emotion, rationality, and the "wisdom of repugnance"' (2008) 38 Hastings Center Report 365; J. Niemela, 'What puts the "yuck" in the yuck factor?' (2011) 25 Bioethics 267.

[15] A. Woolley, 'Intuition and theory in legal ethics teaching' (2011) 9 University of St Thomas Law Journal 285, 287.

sense to the heart, may not work to help to prevent the lawyer being tempted to do the wrong thing. Principles that accord with a lawyer's moral values and deeply held commitments are more likely to be understood and complied with. As Woolley points out:

> In order to act ethically, a person must first perceive that the ethical problem exists; she must have moral sensitivity.... She must also have the judgment to know how to appropriately respond to the moral problem, to know which values or principles are relevant to it and to know which values or principles should be given priority given the context and facts.... Moral sensitivity and moral judgment allow an individual to know the right thing to do in a given situation; however, she must also be able to act on that knowledge. This additionally requires that the individual have moral motivation and moral will.[16]

Indeed, David Luban has gone so far as to suggest that the 'most important' aspect of ethical decision-making by a lawyer is 'the lawyer's moral sentiments', arguing that:

> ... the vaunted 'artificial reason of the law' is no substitute [in ethical decision-making] for the emotional responses that a lifetime of moral education provides us ... no form of reasoning, artificial or not, can bear the burden of discerning right from wrong in particular cases. We just aren't that smart.[17]

Concerns with intuition

Many ethicists are sceptical of relying on intuition. Cynics may say that is because it would do them out of a job! More seriously, there is a concern that 'gut feeling' can simply be the result of prejudice or ignorance. History teaches us that what seemed in the past natural to some people, such as an opposition to mixed-race marriages, now looks like blatant prejudice. So while we should acknowledge the importance of intuition, we must make sure that this is justified on a rational and coherent basis. We cannot rely on intuition alone.

Further, our intuition is sometimes unclear. We may face a dilemma and have no clear intuition of what is the right thing to do. This might be because, for example, it is a brand new situation or a highly complex one that we have not come across before. Clearly, in such a case, an ethicist needs tools in addition to intuition on which to rely.

Hermeneutics

Hermeneutics provides a very different way of responding to ethical dilemmas from those discussed so far. At its heart is listening to the different points of view and the stories that people have to tell.[18] Through discussions with another and listening, the solution emerges. That solution will be the one that works for the parties involved.

[16] Woolley (n. 15), 295.
[17] D. Luban, 'Reason and passion in legal ethics' (1999) 51 Stanford Law Review 873, 876.
[18] K. Boyd, 'Medical ethics: Principles, persons and perspectives—From controversy to conversation' (2005) 31 Journal of Medical Ethics 481.

 **Definition**

Hermeneutics promotes listening and talking through problems. Through articulating the issues and discussing them, a solution will emerge.

Problems with hermeneutics

Hermeneutics can work well as an approach to resolving interpersonal conflict. Indeed, as we shall see in Chapter 10, it is at the heart of mediation. The approach, however, works less well when there are interests involved that are not restricted to the two parties. The lawyer and client may well reach agreement over how to proceed by means of a discussion, but that agreement may represent an unethical course of action, because of the impact of the decision on third parties. Further, hermeneutics is not an approach that provides a busy lawyer with clear, concise guidance about what to do in a particular dilemma.

Before dismissing the benefit of hermeneutics in the context of lawyers' ethics, however, it may be worth considering whether it could be seen as explaining the source of lawyers' codes. The different legal associations and organisations are forums in which professionals can discuss and debate issues before producing the codes that guide fellow professionals. That process of discussion and debate could be seen to be based on hermeneutic principles.

Casuistry

A defining feature of casuistry is that it avoids relying on grand principles and applying them to the facts of the case, as does, for example, principlism; instead, casuistry recommends dealing with cases one by one and relying on the agreed approach in other cases. Lawyers will feel familiar with this, because it has some similarities with the approach to precedent in common law countries. So, if faced with an ethical dilemma, a lawyer will ask how similar cases are dealt with and seek to find the correct solution in that way.

Problems with casuistry

The problem with the approach is that casuistry provides little guidance where there appear to be conflicting precedents or where there is a novel situation with no direct precedent. Without appealing to some kind of underpinning principle, it might be a difficult approach to take. Indeed, a danger with casuistry is that the result can be a set of inconsistent precedents that lack a logical basis.

 Alternative view

This criticism of the casuistry approach—that it can lead to a series of inconsistent rules with no logical basis—is generally assumed to be a bad thing. But that is not beyond doubt: many people hold a series of inconsistent political, religious, and immoral beliefs, which work for them, even if they do not fit together in an entirely logical way. If we were to produce a set of rules to govern lawyers' ethics that worked in the context of the chaos of everyday life in the lawyer's office, why should it matter so much if that scheme lacks intellectual coherence?[19]

Feminist ethics

Feminist approaches now play a major role in ethical analysis.[20] Although the issue is debated, it is probably incorrect to identify **feminist ethics** as offering a unified approach to ethical analysis.

 Definition

> **Feminist ethics** considers ethical dilemma within the context of gender. It is alert to ensuring that styles of thinking or outcomes do not disadvantage women.

Feminists fiercely disagree on the correct approach to some ethical issues, however. Two leading feminists have explained the major schools of feminist thought in the following way:

> Today, feminist legal theory has evolved into four major schools: formal equality theory, "cultural feminism," dominance theory, and post-modern or anti-essentialist theory. Formal equality theory, grounded in liberal democratic thought, argues that women should be treated the same as men, while cultural feminists emphasize the need to take account of "differences" between men and women. Dominance theory sidesteps both of these approaches, focusing instead upon the embedded structures of power that make men's characteristics the norm from which "difference" is constructed. Anti-essentialism, by contrast, contends that there is no single category "female," pointing instead to the varying perspectives resulting, for example, from the intersection of gender, race and class.[21]

Many feminists have been drawn to an 'ethic of care', which does provide a unified approach and which we will discuss later. However, not all feminists would support such an approach. What does unite the feminist approach is that it asks 'the woman question'.[22] It is highly aware that gender and sex play an important part in the distribution of power within society. Gender is often the basis of assumptions about and

[19] J. Dewar, 'The normal chaos of family law' (1997) 61 Modern Law Review 467.

[20] C. Grant Bowman and E. M. Schneider, 'Feminist legal theory, feminist lawmaking, and the legal profession' (1998) 67 Fordham Law Review 249.

[21] Grant Bowman and Schneider (n. 20), 250.

[22] K. Bartlett, 'Feminist legal methods' (1990) 103 Harvard Law Review 829, 837.

expectations of individuals. Feminism seeks to prevent the oppression of women and to promote equality regardless of a person's sex. That includes tackling not only practices that overtly disadvantage women, but also 'the gender implications of rules and practices which might otherwise appear to be neutral or objective'.[23]

Feminist analysis is therefore interested in how the regulation of the legal professions and their practice might work against the interests of women. It explores concerns over diversity among barristers and solicitors (see Chapter 14). But there is more to a feminist approach than pointing out examples of sexism within the legal profession.

Feminism also explores whether values are being promoted that reflect 'male' norms, which work against the interests of women or which do not reflect the values that women hold. Arguably, a culture of long working hours, an aggressive litigious attitude, and a strongly economic-based model might be seen by some as fitting that description.

Naomi Cahn, for example, has complained that standard approaches to legal ethics posit the lawyer as being separated from her client.[24] The debate then centres on whether the lawyer should act as simply giving effect to the client's wishes or direct the client what to do. These debates 'distance the lawyer from the client, they rhetorically exclude one of the two voices in the attorney/client relationship, and as a result, they limit the context in which to view the client's problems'. Cahn would prefer a more contextual approach, recognising the interests of both parties and their relationship, and encouraging them to work through these together. Such an approach would suggest, for example, that the lawyer disclose her own values and perspectives with a client just as the client does, and then find a way to move on. This kind of approach is based on an ethic of care, which will be explored shortly.

One issue on which feminists disagree, however, is whether female lawyers act differently from male ones.[25] This is something that we will explore further in Chapter 14.

Problems with feminist ethics

One concern is that not all ethical dilemmas contain a clear gender element. Is there a particularly feminist perspective on lawyers' fees or the law on confidentiality? Some feminist commentators will insist that gendered assumptions can be made even in relation to such apparently dry issues. Critics will argue that seeing gender inequality everywhere is a false picture of the world.

[23] Bartlett (n. 22), 837.

[24] N. Cahn, 'A preliminary feminist critique of legal ethics' (1990–91) Georgetown Journal of Legal Ethics 23.

[25] A. Bartlett and L. Aitken, 'Competence in caring in legal practice' (2009) 16 International Journal of the Legal Profession 241.

Even if one accepts that there is gender inequality inherent to a particular issue, feminists do not always agree on what is the correct response. If, for example, the reason why there are fewer women than men making the rank of partner in firms of solicitors is the caring responsibilities of women, is the solution to free women from their caretaking (for example by offering more childcare facilities) or is it to change the mindset among firms of solicitors so that someone undertaking care is not disadvantaged in her career? Feminists will not agree on that.

Ethics of care

Considerable attention has been paid to the **ethics of care** in recent years.[26] This approach is critical of traditional legal ethics, with its focus on rights, individual autonomy, and abstracted universal principles. Instead, it focuses on relationships and care. Rather than valuing individual freedom, it values the interdependency and mutuality in relationships.

 Definition

> The **ethics of care** sees care as the core ethical value. An ethical response to a dilemma is one that promotes good, caring relationships.

Susan Wolf has argued:

> By depicting the moral community as a set of atomistic and self-serving individuals, it [liberal individualism] strips away relationships that are morally central. This not only is impoverished, but may also be harmful, because it encourages disregard of those bonds. It is also inaccurate; developing children as well as full-grown adults are profoundly interdependent. Indeed, we are so interdependent that we cannot even understand the terms of moral debate without some community process and shared understanding.[27]

The ethics of care therefore tends to avoid using abstract principles as the primary tool of ethical analysis, seeking instead to find an approach that fits in with the needs and relationships of the individual case.[28] Hence the focus is less on questions such as 'What do I owe others?' and rather on questions such as 'How can I best express my caring responsibilities?' and 'How can I best deal with vulnerability, suffering and dependence?'[29]

---

[26] See, e.g., J. Herring, *Caring and the Law* (Hart, 2013); V. Held, *The Ethics of Care* (Oxford University Press, 2006); C. Menkel-Meadow, 'Portia Redux: Another look at gender feminism and legal ethics', in D. Carle (ed.) *Lawyers' Ethics and the Pursuit of Social Justice: A Critical Reader* (New York University Press, 2005).

[27] S. Wolf, 'Introduction: Gender and feminism in bioethics', in S. Wolf (ed.) *Feminism and Bioethics* (Oxford University Press), 17–18.

[28] J. Tronto, *Moral Boundaries: A Political Argument for an Ethic of Care* (Routledge, 1983), 21.

[29] J. Bridgeman, *Parental Responsibility, Young Children and Healthcare Law* (Cambridge University Press, 2009).

The following are some of the key themes that are found in much writing on care ethics.[30]

1. *The inevitability of interdependence* Caring is the essence of life. From the very start of life, we are in relationships of dependency with others. The law should therefore see caring relationships as of crucial social significance.

2. *The value of care* Care is not only an inevitable part of life; it is also a *good* part of life. The law should therefore value and encourage it.

3. *Relational approaches* The law should not treat us as atomistic individuals with individual rights and interests that clash with others. Rather, the focus should be on the responsibilities that flow from our relationship with others. Virginia Held makes the point by contrasting the ethics of care and an ethic of justice:

> An ethic of justice focuses on questions of fairness, equality, individual rights, abstract principles, and the consistent application of them. An ethic of care focuses on attentiveness, trust, responsiveness to need, narrative nuance, and cultivating caring relations. Whereas an ethic of justice seeks a fair solution between competing individual interests and rights, an ethic of care sees the interest of carers and cared-for as importantly intertwined rather than as simply competing.[31]

Applying this approach to lawyers is likely to lead to greater emphasis on developing a good relationship, based on mutual respect, between the lawyer and client in which care is emphasised as the good that we are aiming to promote. Such an approach will move away from general principles, considering instead what response will fit best in the context of the particular relationship between this lawyer and this client.

A care-based approach would challenge some key features of traditional ethics. Is the preference for clear general rules desirable, or should we find the solution that fits with the caring responsibilities and clients involved? Should the lawyer whose child is sick at home leave a client in the hands of a colleague while he or she meets these caring responsibilities? Does the notion of a 'caring lawyer' involve some element of emotional bond between lawyer and client? How should the lawyer balance a caring obligation to the client with others?

Stephen Ellmann argues:

> The lawyer must care for every member of the community, each person in the web of interconnection, including those people who have manifested indifference or antagonism toward this very idea of mutual responsibility—manifested it, perhaps, by frauds, or crimes, or simple lack of caring for their fellow community members. To say that the lawyer should care for everyone regardless of character or conduct is rather like saying that everyone is entitled to exercise his or her legal rights regardless of character or other conduct—a quintessential claim of rights morality.[32]

---

[30] Herring (n. 26), ch. 3.   [31] Held (n. 26), 94.
[32] S. Ellmann, 'The ethic of care as an ethic for lawyers' (1993) 81 Georgetown Law Journal 2665, 2684.

Ellmann goes on to argue that the ethic of care cannot require an equal caring for all, because that would be impossible; rather, it requires that people take on special obligations to individuals. This can apply to the lawyer. Abstract principles about what lawyers must do for their clients do not acknowledge the competing claims that lawyers may face in their everyday lives.

Problems with ethics of care

Ethics of care approaches have, inevitably, received their fair share of criticism. First, it has been argued by feminists that its glorification of caring and dependency is likely to be harmful to women. The role of women as carers and dependants has led to their oppression and subordination.[33] To elevate and promote such a role is therefore harmful. Supporters of ethics of care would reply that the way ahead for women is not to seek to live the lives of independent, autonomous, un-obligated individuals that some men appear to live, but rather to promote these values of care and dependency.

A second concern is that the notion of care is too vague.[34] It might be pointed out that not all caring relationships are good ones: some may involve manipulation and oppression. Without a far clearer concept of what 'good care' is, care cannot form the basis of an ethical approach. Many supporters of an ethic of care would accept that more work needs to be done to 'flesh out' the concept and that it is in its relatively early days of development.[35]

Virtue ethics

Virtue ethics goes back to the writings of Socrates and Aristotle. It emphasises that, in assessing what is the morally correct thing to do, it is not the consequences of your actions that matter, but rather the attitudes (virtues) motivating your actions.[36] It is the character of an individual, not the consequences of his or her actions, that is more important. Virtues are good habits that will direct human nature towards good actions. James Rachels suggests that a virtue is 'a trait of character, manifested in habitual action, that it is good for a person to have'.[37]

 Definition

> **Virtue ethics** promotes the development of good characteristics that are seen to promote human flourishing. Ethical analysis should encourage us to be virtuous people, rather than to seek the solution to particular dilemmas.

---

[33] Wolf (n. 27), 9.

[34] P. Allmark, 'Can there be an ethics of care?', in K. Fulford, D. Dickenson, and T. Murray (eds) *Healthcare Ethics and Human Values* (Blackwell, 2002).

[35] C. Smart and B. Neale, *Family Fragments* (Polity, 1999).

[36] P. Gardiner, 'A virtue ethics approach to moral dilemmas in medicine' (2003) 29 Journal of Medical Ethics 297.   [37] J. Rachels, *The Elements of Moral Philosophy* (McGraw-Hill, 1999).

This opens up an interesting way of approaching ethical questions. We can ask 'How would an honest lawyer act in this scenario?', 'How would a just lawyer respond?', and so forth. Some people find this way of asking ethical dilemmas more helpful than considering how abstract principles apply. A further advantage of this approach is that it reassures those nervous about whether they are acting in the right way. If they are motivated by compassion or justice, they are displaying these virtues and need not worry about the consequences. That can be reassuring. It acknowledges that while we may seek to do the right thing, sometimes bad things happen.

Virtue ethics provides a useful way of guiding lawyers. It seeks not only to produce lawyers who comply with the rules, but also lawyers who display good character. We seek the just lawyer; the caring lawyer; the devoted lawyer. We move from act criteria to character tests.

There is disagreement among virtue ethicists over whether the consequences of an action are relevant to its ethical value. Some argue that as long as the act is virtuously motivated, the consequences are irrelevant. Others disagree, believing that the bad consequences can render a well-motivated act unjustifiable.[38]

One concern with virtue ethics is how we should decide what are 'good virtues'. In such a diverse society, there is little agreement on what makes a 'good person'; there are many different ideas of what makes a 'good life'. It may be that, in Western society, keeping fit or eating moderately would be regarded as a virtue, but it is unclear whether in other societies this would be so. But virtue ethicists often argue that there are moral values that are essential for any decent society: love, friendship, truth-telling, faithfulness, and wisdom would be accepted around the world as virtues.

So which virtues might be included within virtue ethics? We might include politeness, fidelity, prudence, temperance, courage, justice, generosity, compassion, mercy, gratitude, humility, simplicity, tolerance, purity, gentleness, good faith, humour, and love.[39]

Problems with virtue ethics

Critics of virtue ethics complain that appalling activities can be justified under virtue ethics. Consider the wicked doctor killing lots of elderly patients, believing that they will be better off dead than infirm, or the suicide bomber killing many to show a love of God: both might be well motivated, but their actions are clearly immoral. Of course, others would say that they were not actually acting virtuously, but only *believed* that they were doing so.

There is also a concern that virtue ethics fails to provide clear guidance on what precisely to do in a given situation. True, we are told to behave as virtuous people do—but if it is a novel situation, such advice might provide little practical guidance.

---

[38] P. Foot, *Natural Goodness* (Oxford University Press, 2001), 43.

[39] A. Compte Sponville, *A Short Treatise on the Great Virtues* (Heinemann, 2002); A. Woolley and B. Wendel, 'Legal ethics and moral character' (2010) 23 Georgetown Journal of Legal Ethics 1065.

A further problem is that there is little consensus on what makes a virtuous character. Asking people who are their moral heroes might soon reveal diversity of opinion. In the context of legal ethics, there may be concerns that the approach fails to acknowledge how easy it is for people to delude themselves into thinking that they are acting virtuously when they are not. It seems to be human nature for people to pretend that they are acting virtuously when they are not. A clear set of regulations telling lawyers what they can or cannot do may therefore be needed, rather than general guidance that lawyers must 'act honestly'.

Relativism

It is quite common to hear people say that, on moral questions, there is 'no right or wrong answer' and that 'Your view is as valid as mine'. Sometimes, when discussing ethics, people may say something like 'Personally, I think X is wrong', indicating that they are simply making a claim about what is wrong for them and that they are not saying that those who disagree are necessarily wrong. This view of ethics is known as 'relativism'. It is a claim that there are no right and wrong answers to a moral problem. An extreme relativist view would claim that there are never absolute right or wrong answers to a moral dilemma. A more moderate view would be that there is nearly always a range of acceptable moral answers and that we cannot choose between them.

The issue has become more prominent with recognition of cultural diversity. Are ethics developed in the West also based on a 'Western mindset'? We in the West tend to focus on individual rights, while concepts of community, tradition, and relationships may be neglected. Are these ethical principles no more than a reflection of certain Western norms, based on an assumption that the individualist lifestyles of the West are best?[40]

This view, in effect, suggests that we should, in terms of professional guidance, place little weight on ethical dimensions, or least accept that the guidance represents a choice between equally valid perspectives. We cannot ascertain what is good or bad—indeed there is no 'good' or 'bad'—and so we should focus on producing guidance that promotes efficiency, rather than goodness.

Problems with relativism

Although this is a popular perspective, in fact very few people really are extreme relativists. Whether rape is wrong is not really a matter of opinion. More realistically, people might claim that although there are some general moral precepts on which we can all agree, there are plenty on which there is no consensus. On these, we might take a guess at what is morally right, while accepting that we might be wrong. A person

---

[40] K. Bowman, 'What are the limits of bioethics in a culturally pluralistic society?' (2004) 32 Journal of Law, Medicine and Ethics 664.

might decide not to drink alcohol, while not necessarily saying that he or she thinks others should not do so. But in a way, even a view such as this is not relativist, because it takes a distinct view on the moral issue—namely, that there is no right or wrong answer. Further, in the context of legal ethics, if part of their role is to instil public confidence in the legal profession and protect clients from being taken advantage of, we cannot simply say that all ethical views are equally valid.

Are lawyers' ethics special?

A key issue is whether lawyers' ethics are any different from others. This issue will become apparent when we look at four viewpoints.

1. Lawyers' ethics are no different from general ethical foundations. So the principle that lawyers should keep clients' information confidential is no different from that which applies to any person given private information in a confidential setting. It may be that lawyers are given confidential information more commonly than other people, but the basic moral principles governing lawyers are the same as others.

2. Lawyers apply the same basic principles as other people, but the role of the professional means that they are applied in a particular way. So although the basic idea of confidentiality applies to all, there is an enhanced obligation for lawyers. Similarly, everyone must be honest, but lawyers are expected not only to be honest, but also to appear to be honest and to have the highest standards of honesty.

3. Lawyers apply the same basic principles as others, but have special exemption by virtue of their professional status. So although, generally, people must tell the truth, the special requirement of lawyers to do all that they can to promote their clients' well-being means that they are permitted to subvert that principle if necessary.

4. Lawyers' ethics are independent of the principles that apply to most people. The special obligations that lawyers have reflect their unique position for society. Lawyers' ethics should not, then, be seen simply as an enhanced form of general ethics, but as having their own special basis.

The debates between these views will be explored next and will be returned to throughout this book. They underpin many of the debates around lawyers' ethics.

The role of the lawyer

At the heart of many debates over legal ethics is the role of lawyers. For some commentators, the notion of partisanship is central to the role of the lawyer. The lawyer must show 'hyper-zeal' in pursuing a client's case, even if that means acting in a way that might otherwise appear unethical.[41] For such commentators, it is the duty of the

---

[41] Fried (n. 2).

lawyer to do everything that he or she can for the client that is the central moral claim. For others, the lawyer has commitments to the overall legal system, and to moral principles generally, that severely restrict the extent to which a lawyer can exercise hyper-zeal. The debate between these perspectives is reflected in the debates over a large number of the ethical issues that lawyers face.

Partisanship

One of the more controversial principles highlighted is partisanship—that is, the idea that the lawyer's primary role is to defend a client's rights and to put forward the best case possible. This must be done with no consideration of the impact on others. The lawyer defending the hospital trust against a personal injury claim brought by the parent of a paralysed child, for example, must put forward the best arguments for the trust and not be swayed by sympathy for the condition of the child. It is the job of the other party's lawyer to put forward the child's case.

Quite how far partisanship takes us is a matter for debate. Clearly, it could never require the lawyer to engage in illegal activity. No one suggests that. However, whether it requires the lawyer to use arguments of little moral merit with all zeal may be more debatable. A good example might be whether a barrister representing a man charged with rape should cross-examine the complainant with full rigour, even if doing so will cause the complainant severe distress and serious harm. We will consider some of these views further.[42]

Hyper-zeal

The argument in favour of 'hyper-zeal'—that is, that the lawyer should go 'all out' for his or her client—is as follows. A client has legal rights, but typically lacks the knowledge to assert these rights. If we believe that people should have the ability to access their rights, then access to lawyers is crucial. If a client wants his or her rights enforced, the lawyer must help the client to achieve this, even if others might think that the client should not assert these rights. The man accused of rape has a right to cross-examine the complainant fiercely and the lawyer has the obligation to enable the client to exercise his right. Once we start to say that the lawyer should not do everything that he or she can do for a client, we are, in effect, depriving people of access to their rights. Perhaps worse: we may be allowing people to exercise only the rights that their lawyers think they should exercise.

Lord Brougham's ancient statement is often quoted as summarising the position:

> An advocate, in the discharge of his duty, knows but one person in all the world, and that person is his client. To save that client by all means and expedients, and at all hazards and costs to other persons...is his first and only duty; and in performing

[42] T. Schneyer, 'The promise and problematics of legal ethics from the lawyer's point of view' (2004) 16 Yale Journal of Law & the Humanities 45.

this duty he must not regard the alarm, the torments, the destruction which he may bring upon others.[43]

Supporters of this view will accept that this can involve lawyers acting in ways that may seem disreputable. However, if this is unacceptable, then the problem lies in the law, not with the lawyer. If we think that a company should not be able to impose a contract with unfair terms on consumers, then any complaint lies with contract law, not the lawyer who advised the company as to its legal rights and drafted the contract.

Daniel Markovits argues that at the heart of the legal system is the separation of adjudication and advocacy.[44] The role of the lawyer is not to judge the merits of a client's case; that is the job of the courts. The lawyer makes the case for the client and the court decides if it is legitimate. This leads to what Markovits sees as the fundamental obligations placed on every lawyer—namely, loyalty, respect for the client's determination of ends, and legal assertiveness on behalf of clients. He accepts that this might lead a lawyer to lie—defined as 'asserting a proposition that one privately (and correctly) disbelieves'—and to cheat—that is, 'to exploit others by promoting claims or causes that one privately [and correctly] thinks undeserving'. These are justified because the lawyer is playing a role in a legitimate process. Indeed, properly understood, the lawyer is not lying or cheating, but faithfully presenting what his or her client wants to say and pursuing the client's case in a non-judgemental way. Lawyers, Markovits argues, should be seen as 'self-effacing', in that they put the interests of clients and presentation of the clients' cases first. He is, however, concerned that lawyers are not understanding their role and not appreciating the justification for what they are doing.

A linked argument is that if lawyers start to fail to disclose certain parts of the law from their clients because they think that doing so will not promote justice, then, in effect, the lawyers are changing the law. If, for example, under contract law, a company is allowed to put a punitive exemption clause in its contracts with consumers, but the lawyer decides not to tell the company about the existence of such clauses, it would be, in effect, as though the law had prohibited the use of these clauses. That would be improper: it should not be for lawyers to fashion their legal advice based on their own perception of fairness.[45]

Moderate zeal

Other commentators argue for a 'moderate zeal'. Tim Dare argues that lawyers should act with zeal, but not hyper-zeal.[46] There should, he argues, be limits on how far a lawyer seeks to act for a client. W. Bradley Wendel draws an interesting distinction

---

[43] J. Nightingale (ed.) *The Trial of Queen Caroline, Vol. 2* (Albion Press, 1820–21), 8.

[44] D. Markovits, *A Modern Legal Ethics: Adversary Advocacy in a Democratic Age* (Princeton University Press, 2010).   [45] Markovits (n. 44), ch. 1.

[46] T. Dare, *Counsel of Rogues? A Defence of the Standard Conception of the Lawyer's Role* (Ashgate, 2009).

between a lawyer protecting a legal entitlement of a client and a lawyer promoting a client's interests.[47] While lawyers are entitled to do all that they can to protect clients' legal entitlements, they do not need to do all that they can to promote clients' interests. Wendel suggests that lawyers should be competent and diligent in acting for their clients, and not necessarily zealous.

Dare suggests that 'institutions may be justified by appeal to ordinary or general morality, but that the conduct of those within those institutions is to be governed not by the original moral considerations but by the rules of the institution'.[48] He is therefore clear that because the legal system that we have is legitimate and because it depends on lawyers zealously presenting their clients' cases, any apparent immorality is justified. He emphasises the importance of pluralism: the idea that, within the constraints of the law, people are able to pursue what they think is good. Lawyers are needed to allow clients to exercise their choices and to follow their consciences, even if others (even the lawyers themselves) disagree with what the clients wish to do. However, Dare accepts that there are limits on this: the lawyer can put the client's immoral case even without being required to do everything possible to promote it.

Criticism of zealousness

Critics of zealousness argue that the role of the lawyer does not justify engaging in lying, cheating, or trickery. We see people who exploit the ignorance, poverty, or weakness of others for gain as acting immorally. This should be the case whether it is in the context of litigation or not.

There are a number of ways of pursuing the objection. The first is that arguments made for zealousness assume the justifiability of the current legal system. It is because the current system is legitimate that the lawyers' role within it is justified. However, we may question whether our current legal system—which seems to privilege the rich, who can afford the best lawyers and protracted litigation; which seems often designed to protect the interests of the advantaged rather than the marginalised; in which access to justice is denied to many—is a legitimate one. If it is not, then it cannot provide a justification for the lawyers' role within it.

Even accepting the legitimacy of the current legal system, it may be argued that the conception of zealousness emphasises autonomy too much. Yes, we do treasure the ability of people to pursue their own values, but autonomy can be used for good and bad. It is one thing to say that we should allow someone to pursue an immoral lifestyle if he or she so wishes; it is another to say that we should help him or her to do so. The legal system may allow large companies to exploit consumers, but this is not the same as saying that the law should help them to do that. Further, we need to weigh up

---

[47] W. Wendel, 'Legal ethics', in H. LaFollette (ed.) *The International Encyclopaedia of Ethics* (Blackwell, 2013).   [48] Dare (n. 46), 24.

the autonomy of different people: allowing one person to exercise his or her autonomy should not be at the expense of restricting another's.

Charles Fried has supported the zealous role of a lawyer, arguing that the lawyer should be like a good friend.[49] Because friendship is regarded as an intrinsic good and friends are zealous in promoting their friends' interests, so should a lawyer. But many have questioned this: is not a role of good friends to question your judgement if they think that you have made a mistake and even to stand in your way? Loyalty to a friend does not mean blind or complete loyalty. In any event, the analogy between a lawyer and a friend does not convince everyone. For a start, lawyers would stop being a client's 'friend' pretty quickly if they were not being paid. If a friend were to give you poor advice, you might forgive your friend fairly quickly, but you would not forgive your lawyer. The idea that lawyers are driven by the kind of long-term relationship that friends have seems false.[50]

It is interesting that much of the writing in support of a zealous approach assumes that clients want to win their cases at all costs and that lawyers should help them to do so. In fact, it may be questioned how many clients take that view. Indeed, it may be the role of a lawyer to point out the disadvantages to the client of winning—at least if that can be achieved only by humiliating a rival, ruining the other party's reputation, or acting against the client's deeper values. In a divorce case, a client may feel like doing all that he or she can to humiliate and ruin the ex-spouse, but that may well be contrary to the client's long-term interests.[51]

A final concern has been voiced by Naomi Cahn, who is critical of the traditional approach, which sees lawyers as mere conduits of legal advices.[52] She argues that, in fact, lawyers are inevitably influenced by their own reaction to a case: 'By defining a legal role in which lawyers must be neutral partisans on their clients' behalf, legal ethics ignores the lawyer's legal and non-legal experiences that influence how she approaches any legal problem and represents a client.' It may therefore be more honest to encourage lawyers to be open with clients about their own reaction to cases than to assume a facade of neutrality.

Digging deeper

This debate reflects a wider argument over the nature of law. When a judge decides a case, is the judge only to apply 'the rules' or also to seek to draw on the broader principles underpinning the law? For some, the judge applies the rules, and should not seek to go beyond these and draw on grander principles. For others, it is proper for the judge to

---

[49] Fried (n. 2).
[50] E. Dauer and A. Leff, 'Comment on Fried's lawyer as friend' (1976) 85 Yale Law Journal 573.
[51] Cahn (n. 24).   [52] Cahn (n. 24).

develop the principles on which the law is founded and to rely on these, even if doing so requires stretching the rules or even bypassing them. This is similar to the debate over whether the lawyer, in upholding the law, is permitted to use the legal rules to a client's advantage, however much that might seem to undermine the fundamental values that the law protects.

In *Spaulding v Zimmerman*, the hyper-zeal approach was followed.

 Key case

Spaulding v Zimmerman, 116 N.W. 2d 704 [Minn. 1962]

In this notorious American case, a child was injured in a car accident. The driver's lawyer obtained a medical report on the child, which disclosed that the child had a potentially fatal heart condition (unknown by the child's family), which may have been caused by the accident. The case settled and the defendant's lawyers never disclosed the report. The matter later came to court, where the judge found that the defence lawyers had not acted improperly. They had no duty to disclose the report and were acting in their client's interests.

Neutrality

The principle of neutrality requires that lawyers should not prefer one client over another. All clients need lawyers and it would be undesirable if the man charged with child abuse could not find a lawyer to represent him. This is best represented by the 'cab-rank rule': the barrister must accept clients in the order in which their briefs are presented. This reinforces the idea that the lawyer must represent a client however much the lawyer may disagree with the case, and must do the best that he or she can. This will be explored further in Chapter 3.

There is another aspect to the principle of neutrality and that is that lawyers must give impartial advice. Their advice should not be tempered by emotion, but should be cool and dispassionate. It may be that the lawyer needs to tell the client what the client does not want to hear and that the client might even be upset by the lawyer's advice.

There is a third issue here that might be raised. As we have seen, it is sometimes said that lawyers must put aside their own moral views. They must present their clients' case forcefully, with no thought of their own views. There is, for example, no equivalent for lawyers of the conscientious objection protection that doctors have under the Abortion Act 1967, whereby the doctor can refuse to be involved in, for example, an abortion on account of a moral conviction. A lawyer does not have a statutory right to refuse to defend a doctor on the basis that the doctor engaged in abortions. Why this lack of regard for lawyers' moral sensitivities?

Others have suggested that, in fact, it is wrong to think that lawyers should set aside their own human or moral feelings. Indeed, a lawyer who does not deal on an emotional level with the issues that a client is facing may not be giving the best advice. It has even been suggested that the kind of neutrality traditionally advised has caused 'debilitating psychic tension',[53] and it has even been linked with high rates of drink and drug misuse among American lawyers.[54] Approaches based on an ethic of care would argue that good lawyer–client relationships must be built on honesty and mutual respect. Where a lawyer cannot relate to a client, they cannot enter into a good lawyer–client relationship and so the lawyer should be free not to act.[55] One concern about such an approach, however, is that it may mean that unpopular clients (for example people accused of child abuse) will not be able to find a lawyer to represent them.

Justice

For William Simon, the primary duty of a lawyer is to pursue justice.[56] Often, presenting a client's case will promote justice, but not always. If a lawyer is asked by a client to do something that will promote injustice, then the lawyer is not obliged to act. Some may go further and say that the lawyer *must* not act in a way that will promote injustice. However, Simon argues that this is only in cases in which there is clear injustice—and here lies the uncertainty: how is a lawyer to know what justice is? Supporters of the zealousness approach would say that the law provides the answer and that, as long as the client's request is compliant with the law, this should be sufficient.[57] Opponents argue that lawyers are moral agents and must justify their acts. They cannot justify promoting injustice by saying that they were simply following their clients' instructions. It was the 'following orders' mindset that explains the role that lawyers played in the financial crisis of the first decade of this century.[58]

Donald Nicolson has argued that this commitment to justice has a wide-reaching significance and is tied to the idea of being a professional:

> I ... ground this sense of professionalism in the personal ethical duties of practitioners and argue that individual lawyers have moral duties to ensure that legal services extend beyond those who can pay or qualify for legal aid. In other words, law involves a calling to devote one's training, skills and privileges to assist those

---

[53] L. Fisher, 'Truth as a double-edged sword: Deception, moral paradox and the ethics of advocacy' (1989) 14 Journal of the Legal Profession 89.

[54] P. Goodrich, 'Law-induced anxiety' (2000) 9 Social and Legal Studies 143.

[55] Cahn (n. 24).

[56] W. Simon, 'Legal ethics should be primarily a matter of principles, not rules' (2010) 15 Legal Ethics 200.

[57] B. Wendel, 'Razian authority and its implications for legal ethics' (2010) 13 Legal Ethics 191.

[58] K. Hall and V. Holmes, 'The power of rationalisation to influence lawyers' decisions to act unethically' (2008) 11 Legal Ethics 137.

who require law's benefits or protections, and hence a true legal professional is a lover of justice.[59]

We will be exploring in Chapter 13 the argument that lawyers owe special obligations to the justice system and to the broader social good.

 What would you do?

You are advising a company defending against a claim for sexual harassment brought by an employee who cannot afford a lawyer and so has brought the proceedings herself. It is clear from your investigations that the claim is justified and that a serious wrong has been done to the employee. However, you notice that, in the paperwork, the claimant has made a technical error on which the company could rely to make a legal defence.

What would they do?

This 'What would you do?' scenario is accompanied by a podcast in which current law students debate the issues and articulate their own responses to the ethical questions that it raises. The podcast is available online at www.oxfordtextbooks.co.uk/orc/herringethics/

Care

We have already mentioned the ethics of care. Various writers have sought to apply this approach to legal ethics. Christine Parker and Adrian Evans explain how this might work:

> [T]he ethics of care for lawyers focuses on trying to serve the best interests of both clients and others in a holistic way that incorporates moral, emotional and relational dimensions of a problem into the legal solution. It is particularly concerned with preserving or restoring (even reconciling) relationships and avoiding harm. It sees relationships, including both the client's network of relationships and the lawyer's own relationships with colleagues, family and community, as more important than the institutions of the law or systemic and social ideas of justice and ethics.[60]

In Chapter 3, we will explore further the potential implications of such an approach. One interesting aspect of it is that it opens up the idea that lawyers' ethics should focus

---

[59] D. Nicolson, 'Calling, character and clinical legal education: A cradle to grave approach to inculcating a love for justice' (2013) 16 Legal Ethics 36, 48.

[60] C. Parker and A. Evans, *Inside Lawyers' Ethics* (Cambridge University Press, 2009), 33.

not only on the obligations of lawyers, but also on the lawyer–client relationship as a whole. It is therefore arguable that clients should have obligations to their lawyers.[61]

◉ Application

Christine Parker and Adrian Evans helpfully set out a three-step process that can be used in address an ethical issue.[62] It involves asking three key questions and considering further questions in light of each of these.

The following is an adapted version of their process.

- *Step one*: What ethical issues have arisen or might arise in the future in this situation?

  Consider the following questions.

  - Whose interests are affected?

  - What values and interests are at stake for those affected?

  - Is there a conflict between these interests?

  - What are your own interest and values?

- *Step two*: What ethical principles should be used to resolve the issues in this scenario?

  Consider the following questions.

  - What do the codes of conduct say?

  - What general ethical principles apply to this scenario?

  - Are there any special responsibilities that lawyers have because of their role as lawyers?

  - How are the conflicts between these principles to be managed?

- *Step three*: How might the ethical thing to do actually be put into action in the current situation?

  Consider the following questions.

  - What actions can feasibly be done?

  - What will be the consequences of different alternatives?

  - What resources are needed from others to do the right thing?

  - How can we prevent this dilemma from arising again?

Should law degrees include ethics?

At the time of writing, legal ethics is not a compulsory part of the law degree. It is covered in the Legal Practice Course (LPC) and the Bar Professional Training Course (BPTC)

---

[61] D. Wilkens, 'Do clients have ethical obligations to lawyers? Some lessons from the diversity wars' (1998) 11 Georgetown Journal of Legal Ethics 855.   [62] Parker and Evans (n. 60).

to some extent.[63] In recent years, there has been an increased interest in making ethics part of the law degree. Kim Economides and Justine Rogers' 2009 report to the Law Society, *Preparatory Ethics Training for Future Solicitors*, recommended that 'awareness of and commitment to legal values and the moral context of the law, [be] mandatory in undergraduate law degrees.'[64] Professor Andrew Boon was then asked to produce a model curriculum.[65] The aim was to develop training to encourage students to learn about ethics, but also to reflect on the nature of legal ethics and to become involved in the formation of legal ethics in the future. These reports led to the Legal Education and Training Review (LETR),[66] which was set up by the Solicitors Regulation Authority (SRA), the Bar Standards Board (BSB), and the Institute of Legal Executives (ILEX).[67] The LETR report sees the need to 'strengthen requirements for education and training in legal ethics, values and professionalism, the development of management skills, communication skills, and equality and diversity.'[68]

The LETR is clear that achieving 'appropriate learning outcomes in respect of professional ethics, legal research, and the demonstration of a range of written and oral communication skills' must be part of legal education, training, and research.[69] Indeed, in its survey of lawyers asking what training was important, 'ethics and procedure came out above all other areas, having been rated "important" or "somewhat important" by over 95% and 94% of respondents, respectively.'[70] However, the LETR noted that there was 'no majority support for the introduction of professional ethics as a new Foundation of Legal Knowledge for the QLD [Qualifying Law Degree]/GDL [Graduate Diploma in Law]',[71] and so that was not recommended.[72] In short, although the LETR found it crucial that ethics should be a part of legal training, it did not make a clear recommendation as to where in the training process that should occur.

It is perhaps surprising that, in England, legal ethics are not yet an established part of a law degree. In other countries, notably the United States, the teaching of legal ethics is a standard part of a law degree. Why has there been a reluctance to include legal ethics in a law degree? There are a number of reasons, including, first, that academic lawyers have insisted that the law degree is not simply a preparation to be a lawyer. Only a minority of those completing law degrees become lawyers.[73]

---

[63] L. Webley, 'Legal ethics in the academic curriculum: Correspondent's report from the United Kingdom' (2011) 14 Legal Ethics 132.

[64] Law Society, *Preparatory Ethics Training for Future Solicitors* (Law Society, 2009), 3.

[65] A. Boon, *Legal Ethics at the Initial Stage: A Model Curriculum* (Law Society, 2010).

[66] P. Leighton, 'The Legal Education and Training Review (LETR), 2011–2012' (2011) 45 The Law Teacher 361.

[67] Law Society, *Response to Discussion Paper 02/2012* (Law Society, 2012).

[68] Legal Education Training Review, *Setting Standards* (LETR, 2013), ix.

[69] LETR (n. 68), xiv.   [70] LETR (n. 68), 33.   [71] LETR (n. 68), para 7.10.

[72] LETR (n. 68), para 7.89.

[73] S. Mayson, 'The education and training of solicitors: Time for change' (2011) 45 The Law Teacher 278.

Many law graduates do not go on to pursue a career as a solicitor or barrister and legal academics see themselves as not simply preparing students to be lawyers, but as providing a critical and philosophical approach to the study of law. This has meant that some academic lawyers are wary of teaching the law degree as simply a preparation to become a lawyer. Indeed, much research produced by legal academics is not read by practitioners, precisely because it is not seen as being directly relevant to the day-to-day practice of lawyers. Legal academics have been keen to assert their autonomy to decide the nature of law degrees and have resisted attempts by the professions to regulate too strictly the content of law degrees. On the other hand, it is important to law schools that the law degree is seen as a good first step towards the legal profession. There is no doubt that is what motivates many students to apply for a law degree in the first place. The tension between the academic aims of a law degree and the professional bodies is mitigated in part by the year of professional training at law school or Bar school, where the more practical skills—such as drafting, advocacy, and negotiations—are taught. Traditionally, many academics have felt that training on professional ethics fits into that part of the process better than the university part.

Second, there are few legal academics who feel equipped to teach legal ethics. There is a shortage of staff for many courses, and universities are under pressure to find staff to teach core subjects, or popular courses, rather than to create a new course on legal ethics.

A third argument that is sometimes put forward is that ethics 'cannot be taught'.[74] The basic principles of honesty and integrity are an ingrained part of character. In short, ethics are seen to be 'common sense' and there is little that one can do if a student has no appreciation of their significance. If a lawyer is corrupt, no amount of legal ethics training will change this.

A fourth concern that has sometimes been raised is whether it is possible to assess ethical reasoning. Ethical views may be seen as a matter of opinion and there are even concerns that lecturers may seek to impose their personal ethical opinions on their students.

None of these arguments are, I suggest, convincing.[75] As to the first, it will be clear that the role of lawyers and the regulations governing their behaviour are central to how the law operates in practice. A detailed academic study of the law must include a consideration of how the law works in practice, and that involves an investigation into the restrictions placed on and values found among lawyers. They play a central role in how law works in the real world.

As to the third and fourth points, there is plenty of academic writing on legal ethics in the United States and England showing that there is ample scope for reasoned academic debate and analysis. It is no more 'a matter of opinion' than many other areas of the law.

---

[74] A. Paterson, 'Legal ethics: Its nature and place in the curriculum', in R. Cranston (ed.) *Legal Ethics and Professional Responsibility* (Oxford University Press, 2006).

[75] Mayson (n. 73).

That leaves only the argument about resources. It is always difficult to know how law schools should focus their resources, but the study of the principles guiding lawyers as they negotiate on behalf of their clients and advise them in non-adversarial matters is essential, given that the vast majority of cases are resolved outside the courts, with legal advice.[76]

◉ Application

Professor Andrew Boon has drafted a list of what might be included in a legal ethics course as part of a law degree.[77] He defines the course as: 'The study of the relationship between morality and Law, the values underpinning the legal system, and the regulation of the legal services market, including the institutions, professional roles and ethics of the judiciary and legal professions.'

He proposes the following objectives for the course:

Objectives that are consistent with these aims are that the ethics curriculum should:
a) further appreciation of the relationship between morality and law
b) promote understanding of the role of the legal profession in supporting democracy and protecting justice and the rule of law
c) provide opportunities for ethical decision-making
d) promote understanding of the importance of values, including justice, honesty, integrity, critical self-reflection and respect for others
e) stimulate reflection on the ethical challenges of practice and lay a foundation for ethical behaviour[78]

Professional codes

It is one of the marks of a profession that it produces guidance for its members. The Bar Council has produced the Bar Council Code of Conduct (the Bar Code). The Law Society has produced the Guide to the Professional Conduct of Solicitors. These codes seek to set out how members of the profession ought to behave. They include general ethical principles, advice on the application of these to particular contexts, and an explanation of the particular legal obligations that are at play.

It is interesting to note that both of these codes came late to the professions. The Solicitors Regulation Authority (SRA) Code of Conduct was first produced in 1960 and the Bar Code in 1979. In part, the reticence was a feeling that the ethical principles

---

[76] R. Burridge and J. Webb, 'The values of common law legal education: Rethinking rules, responsibilities, relationships and roles in the law school' (2007) 10 Legal Ethics 72.

[77] Boon (n. 65).   [78] Boon (n. 65), 14.

could not be readily reduced to a single document. But perhaps there was also an assumption that the professional did not need to be told what ethical principles bound him or her because her or she knew that all too well. However, a range of pressures led to the production of these codes, including recognition of the complexity of work that lawyers had to enter into and of the ethical issues raised.

The codes have been controversial. One issue is that they tend to use vague language. In a way, this is inevitable. They are not, generally, setting down legislation that it is expected will be followed to the letter; rather, they are seeking to articulate principles. The professional bodies do not want someone who has clearly behaved in an inappropriate way to be able to claim to have complied with the letter of the code and so be blameless. However, this vagueness leads others to claim that what are left are statements of the obvious, or rules of etiquette.[79]

The status of the codes is somewhat ambiguous. At one level, they are not law as such. They are enforced by the professional bodies and sanctions are imposed by those bodies. However, a lawyer who breaches a professional code may find that fact being relied upon by a court. A client who claims that his or her lawyer was negligent would have the case greatly strengthened if it could be shown that the lawyer breached ethical codes. Similarly, a lawyer facing a criminal charge of fraud would face problems if it were established that he or she had breached a code. So even if the codes are not enforced by the courts as such, they will be taken into account when the courts consider how the general law applies to lawyers.

A crucial point is that few would see a professional code as saying all there is to say about ethics and lawyers. There are many things that the codes do not mention that lawyers would accept as being moral obligations. Inevitably, the codes cannot cover every scenario that a lawyer might face; in order to deal with such cases, a lawyer is likely to turn to some key values or ethical principles, described in this chapter.

We will look in detail at the form of regulation in Chapter 3, but some general points can be made now. The SRA Handbook took a new approach in its 2011 edition. It took an 'outcomes-focused approach' (OFA) to regulation.[80] The SRA explains that this OFA is 'a regulatory regime that focuses on the high level Principles and outcomes that should drive the provision of services for clients'. So rather than seeking to set out detailed guidance on specific issues, the SRA Code emphasises general points of principle, which it then leaves to solicitors to apply in the circumstances that they face.

The new Code focuses on ten key Principles.

---

[79] A. Ayers, 'What if legal ethics can't be reduced to a maxim?' (2013) 26 Georgetown Journal for Legal Ethics 1.

[80] Solicitors Regulation Authority, *Outcomes-Focused Regulation at a Glance* (Solicitors Regulation Authority, 2013).

Follow the Code

The following are the ten key Principles outlined in the SRA Code:

You must:
1. uphold the rule of law and the proper administration of justice;
2. act with integrity;
3. not allow your independence to be compromised;
4. act in the best interests of each *client*;
5. provide a proper standard of service to your *clients*;
6. behave in a way that maintains the trust the public places in you and in the provision of legal services;
7. comply with your legal and regulatory obligations and deal with your regulators and ombudsmen in an open, timely and co-operative manner;
8. run your business or carry out your role in the business effectively and in accordance with proper governance and sound financial and risk management principles;
9. run your business or carry out your role in the business in a way that encourages equality of opportunity and respect for diversity; and
10. protect *client* money and *assets*.

The Code states that it 'empowers' solicitors to determine the appropriate application of these Principles in the cases before them. Deliberately, there is 'more flexibility in how you achieve the right outcomes for your clients, which will require greater judgement on your part'.[81] This means that, rather than 'prescriptive rules', there are 'mandatory outcomes' and 'non-mandatory indicative behaviours'. The mandatory outcomes 'describe what you are expected to achieve in order to comply with the Principles in specific contexts, as set out in the different chapters in the Code'.[82] The indicative behaviours are not mandatory; they are 'examples of the kind of behaviours which may establish whether you have achieved the relevant outcomes and complied with the Principles'.

Because these indicative behaviours are not mandatory, it may be possible for a solicitor to demonstrate that he or she has not met the indicative behaviour, but has complied with the Principles by other means.

Digging deeper

The new SRA Code takes a particular stance over ethical issues, from which the following themes might be drawn out.

---

[81] SRA (n. 80), 2.   [82] SRA (n. 80), 2.

- The Code supports the use of general principles. There is therefore a degree of principlism indicated in the Code. However, these principles are mostly not abstract, but applied.

- The Code acknowledges that the application of principles might work out differently in different contexts. There is therefore an acceptance that the ethical approach must involve a careful appreciation of the particular set of facts. This might suggest support for those ethical approaches, such as the ethics of care, which seek to tailor the ethical solution to the facts of the particular case. However, there is a limit to that. The mandatory principles show that there are some bright lines that must not be crossed.

- The Code, interestingly, accepts that there is a degree of judgement involved in the application of the principles. This suggests that there is, in some cases, a range of acceptable views about what might be an ethical approach in a context and that the SRA will respect that. That is hardly full-blown relativism, but an acknowledgement that there is not always a single correct solution in ethically complex issues.

- The Code acknowledges that small firms and large firms, or solicitors with different kinds of clients, may respond differently to an ethical dilemma.

The Bar Code is, in some ways, more like the traditional approach to setting out ethical guidance in that it sets out what barristers must or must not do. It reads more like the traditional 'rule book' approach than does the SRA Handbook. That said, it would be wrong to exaggerate the differences between the two. The Bar Code is replete with sufficiently vague commands that leave quite some discretion to their interpretation. What is most notable is that the SRA Code is explicit about only providing general guidance.

Follow the Code

The key principles outlined in the Bar Code are that a barrister must not:

(a) engage in conduct whether in pursuit of his [or her] profession or otherwise which is:
  (i) dishonest or otherwise discreditable to a barrister;
  (ii) prejudicial to the administration of justice; or
  (iii) likely to diminish public confidence in the legal profession or the administration of justice or otherwise bring the legal profession into disrepute;
(b) engage directly or indirectly in any occupation if his [or her] association with that occupation may adversely affect the reputation of the Bar or in the case of a practising barrister prejudice his [or her] ability to attend properly to his [or her] practice.

Digging deeper

A couple of things to notice about the Bar Code principles: notice that these are a list of 'Thou shalt not's, rather than a list of things to which a person should aspire. Are ethics about not doing bad things or about doing good things? Further, the list seems to focus not on following ethical principles because they are good things to do in and of themselves, but on doing so because they produce bad consequences: discrediting barristers; prejudicing the administration of justice; or reducing confidence in the Bar or its reputation. Using the terminology considered earlier in the chapter, the Bar Code looks like a set of utilitarian principles, rather than deontological ones.

Conclusion

This chapter has introduced some of the key themes that will be explored in the book. It has sought to explain what ethics is: an attempt to find what is the right course of action. It has set out some general ethical theories that have been developed to resolve ethical dilemmas generally. It has then gone on to explore whether lawyers have special ethical obligations over and above the obligations of ordinary citizens. Finally, it has considered how legal training and legal practice has taken the ethical obligations of lawyers more seriously.

Some readers may feel frustrated that this chapter has not provided a single correct answer on how to resolve ethical dilemmas.[83] That is deliberate: there is no agreement over what is the best way in which to deal with ethical issues. You will need to develop your own way of thinking through the issues. Most commentators agree that there are some issues on which only one ethical response is justified: child abuse is wrong and there are no two ways about it. However, on other issues, reasonable people may disagree. This chapter has provided tools that you can use to find out what you think, but also to understand why other people may disagree.

 Further reading

The following are some books that are useful on general ethical issues:

T. Beauchamp and J. Childress, *Principles of Biomedical Ethics*, 7th edn (Oxford University Press, 2013).

P. Benn, *Ethics* (Routledge, 1997).

N. Biggar and L. Hogan, *Religious Voices in Public Places* (Oxford University Press, 2010).

---

[83] Ayers (n. 79).

R. Dworkin, *Taking Rights Seriously* (Harvard University Press, 1977).

J. Raz, *The Authority of Law* (Oxford University Press. 1979).

The following are some of the leading works on ethics as applied to lawyers:

R. Abel, *American Lawyers* (Oxford University Press, 1989).

A. Boon and J. Levin, *The Ethics and Conduct of Lawyers in England and Wales* (Hart, 2008).

T. Dare, *The Counsel of Rogues? A Defence of the Standard Conception of the Lawyer's Role* (Ashgate, 2009).

C. Fried, 'The lawyer as friend: The moral foundations of the lawyer–client relation' (1976) 86 Yale Law Journal 1060.

D. Luban, *Lawyers and Justice: An Ethical Study* (Princeton University Press, 1988).

D. Luban, *Legal Ethics and Human Dignity* (Cambridge University Press, 2007).

D. Markovits, *A Modern Legal Ethics* (Princeton University Press, 2009).

D. Nicolson and J. Webb, *Professional Legal Ethics* (Oxford University Press, 2000).

C. Parker and A. Evans, *Inside Lawyers' Ethics* (Cambridge University Press, 2007).

S. Pepper, 'The lawyer's amoral ethical role: A defense, a problem, and some possibilities' (1986) 11 American Bar Foundation Research Journal 613.

D. Rhode, *In the Interests of Justice* (Oxford University Press, 2000).

T. Schneyer, 'Moral philosophy's standard misconception of legal ethics' [1984] Wisconsin Law Review 1529.

W. Simon, *The Practice of Justice* (Harvard University Press, 1998).

K. Tranter, F. Bartlett, L. Corbin, M. Robertson, and R. Mortensen, *Reaffirming Legal Ethics: Taking Stock and New Ideas* (Routledge, 2010).

B. Wendel, *Lawyers and Fidelity to Law* (Princeton University Press, 2010).

A. Woolley and B. Wendel, 'Legal ethics and moral character' (2010) 23 Georgetown Journal of Legal Ethics 1065.

2

The social context of the legal profession

Key issues

- What does it mean to be a professional?
- What role do lawyers play in society?
- What challenges are facing the legal profession?

Introduction

This chapter looks at lawyers in the broader social context. Lawyers hold a position of privilege within society.[1] They hold a valuable resource: knowledge about the law. They therefore hold power. This chapter will explore why lawyers have this special status and the role that they play in the broader society. Much of the material on lawyers is written by lawyers and therefore offers an 'inside' perspective. However, it is important to see how others perceive lawyers and the place they hold in society.

Professionalism

Lawyers are seen as **professionals**. That is an important aspect of how they under-stand themselves and how they are viewed in society.[2] But what is a 'professional'?

Judges, lawyers, doctors, senior military officers, police chiefs, professors, teach-ers, architects, dentists, engineers, vets, and accountants are all typically included in a list of professionals.[3] The precise definition of a 'profession' is a matter of quite some debate. It seems that the notion of a profession involves a complex social, political, and economic process.[4] In 2012, a government report suggested that there were some

---

[1] S. Liu, 'The legal profession as a social process: A theory on lawyers and globalization' (2013) 38 Law and Social Inquiry 670.

[2] J. Evetts, 'Professionalism: Value and ideology' (2013) 61 Current Sociology 778.

[3] S. Lester, *On Professions and Being Professional* (Institute for Learning, 2013).

[4] D. Nicolson and J. Webb, 'Public rules and private values: Fractured profession(alism)s and institutional ethics' (2005) 12 International Journal of the Legal Profession 165.

13 million professionals in the UK, amounting to 42 per cent of all employment.[5] This figure suggests that the idea of professionals being an elite few has passed.

 **Definition**

Professionals are often characterised by the following features:[6]

- specialist knowledge;
- autonomy (freedom from intense regulation);
- social prestige;
- strict entry requirements (for example specialist training);
- commitment to codes of ethics and to core values;
- an acceptance of fiduciary obligations to clients;
- a sense of calling or vocation;
- an acceptance from the state of the special status of the profession; and
- community interest in the activities.

Some see this last factor as key: professionals work for the benefit of the public, rather than of themselves.[7] A common mark of professionals is that they will work longer than their fixed hours and go to great lengths to perform their duties to clients and to the public. If a client needs a professional's help outside standard office hours, that professional will feel obliged to help, in a way that other workers would not. Certainly, lawyers do regularly work long hours in order to ensure that the needs of clients are met.

It is somewhat ironic that lawyers, who are often portrayed as working to enrich themselves, rely on their dedication to the public good as the grounding of being a professional. Indeed, this has been the basis of a more critical assessment of professionalism as involving the maintenance of a social elite, entitled to substantial payment, rather than as actually reflecting genuine public benefit. Professionalism, critics say, is a mystique used to justify a privileged position and a monopoly on markets. Indeed, it has even been suggested that professional ethics is part of a smokescreen that involves 'a conspiracy against the laity'.[8]

John Leubsdorf promotes three models of professionalism, as follows.[9]

1. *Professionalism as helping the market* Professionalism enables clients to be informed about the services on offer, and ensures that there is a reasonable quality of service that is reasonably priced.

[5] HM Government, *Fair Access to Professional Careers: A Progress Report* (HM Government, 2012), 2.

[6] D. Sciulli, 'Why professions matter: Structural and institutional invariance in professions and professionalism' (2010) 9 Comparative Sociology 744.

[7] T. Parsons, 'The professions and social structure', in T. Parsons (ed.) *Essays in Sociological Theory* (Free Press, 1954).   [8] G. B. Shaw, *The Doctor's Dilemma* (1911), Act 1.

[9] J. Leubsdorf, 'Three models of professional reform' (1981) 67 Cornell Law Review 1021.

2. *Professionalism as promoting a public utility* This model sees professional services as being a matter of public good, and argues that we need professional regulation to ensure the efficiency and quality of these services.

3. *Professionalism as protection* This model recognises the dangers that exist in a relationship between a lawyer and a client, which can work against the interests of a client. Professionalism provides a means of ensuring that there is intervention to protect clients.

So is professionalism 'angel' or 'devil'? Is the lawyer a self-sacrificial servant of the good of the public and the justice system? Or a greedy, self-serving money-grabber? No doubt the answer lies somewhere in between. As Terence Halliday puts it, professional ethics holds 'in uneasy juxtaposition the two faces of professionalism—the one monopolistic, even narcissistic, and the other benign, even altruistic'.[10] While there are some aspects of legal ethics that seem designed to ensure that lawyers promote the interests of clients and justice more generally, there are other parts that seem to be designed to promote the interests of lawyers over the general good, such as the lack of regulation of fees (see Chapter 7) and the difficulties in pursuing complaints against solicitors (see Chapter 3).

A more generous view sees lawyers and other professionals as having struck a bargain with society.[11] Society gives lawyers prestige and allows them to charge high fees; in return, lawyers put the public good before self-interest. Lawyers must therefore regulate their behaviour by means of codes of ethics and must take out insurance to indemnify the public against any loss.[12] They must take on special obligations to their clients. These are set out in the professional codes, which acknowledge that regulation plays an important role in upholding the profession and protecting clients.

Follow the Code

The Solicitors Regulation Authority (SRA) Code of Conduct states that:

> The Handbook will, therefore, support not only consumers of legal services, but will also support the independence of the legal profession and its unique role in safeguarding the legal rights of those it serves.[13]

[10] T. Halliday, *Beyond Monopoly: Lawyers, State Crises, and Professional Empowerment* (University of Chicago Press, 1987), 3.

[11] A. Paterson, *Lawyers and the Public Good* (Cambridge University Press, 2012).

[12] D. Cooper, T. Puxty, K. Robson, and H. Wilmot, *Regulating the UK Accountancy Profession* (Policy Studies Institute, 1988).

[13] SRA Handbook, para 6.

The Legal Services Act 2007 created the Legal Services Board (LSB), which has included within its duties promoting professional principles within the legal profession.

Key statute

The Legal Services Act 2007, s. 1(3), reads:

The "professional principles" are:
  (a) that authorised persons should act with independence and integrity,
  (b) that authorised persons should maintain proper standards of work,
  (c) that authorised persons should act in the best interests of their clients,
  (d) that persons who exercise before any court a right of audience, or conduct litigation in relation to proceedings in any court, by virtue of being authorised persons should comply with their duty to the court to act with independence in the interests of justice, and
  (e) that the affairs of clients should be kept confidential.

The model of the altruistic lawyer seeking to promote the greater good—a bastion against individualism and materialism—is likely to produce a hollow laugh in most circles.[14] Andrew Boon and Jennifer Levin say that the new critical analysis argues that 'professions are joint enterprises aimed at securing material rewards and respect, their commitment to public service and ethics a sham and ideological propaganda'.[15] Ouch! However, it would be wrong to assume that all lawyers are champagne-swilling wheelers and dealers with multimillion-pound salaries. Many high-street solicitors, with some justification, believe that they could have obtained much higher salaries in other lines of work, but chose the legal profession—and a particular branch of it—as an act of public service. Nevertheless, there is no denying that one story of the development of the legal profession is of a struggle to maintain a monopoly over legal services, to exclude competition and thereby to maintain high salaries.[16]

Eliot Freidson sees this control over practice and employment as key to being a professional lawyer.[17] He argues:

I start by defining a profession as a kind of occupation whose members control recruitment, training and the work they do. This explicitly distinguishes occupational

---

[14] R. Rich, 'Sociological paradigms and the sociology of law', in C. Reasons and R. Rich (eds) *Sociology of Law* (Butterworths, 1978), 147–8.

[15] A. Boon and J. Levin, *The Ethics and Conduct of Lawyers in England and Wales* (Hart, 2008), 53.

[16] M. Larson, *The Rise of Professionalism* (University of California Press, 1977).

[17] E. Freidson, 'Theory and the professions' (1989) 64 Indiana Law Journal 1.

control from industrial or collective worker control, the former being limited to particular, demarcated tasks and the latter embracing the overall organization of a division of labor without controlling specialized tasks.[18]

 Alternative view

Not everyone finds it entirely convincing to define professionals as those who have control over their work, while others do not. Many self-employed people have broad control over the work that they do. Further, many lawyers will feel that, as individuals, they have little control over their work. The time sheets and the diktats of partners or chambers clerks rule. Lawyers, as a body, may have control over the work that they do, but individual lawyers may not see it that way. As to training, a wide range of jobs now require certain qualifications.

The power that lawyers have to control their recruitment and training may be questioned. In 2013, US President Obama suggested that, in the future, only a two-year law degree would be required for lawyers.[19] The professional status of lawyers in the United States did not prevent that. There is little doubt that if the British government were to take the same view, it would believe that it had the power to intervene. Arguably, the reason why the government has not intervened in lawyers' training is that it works reasonably well, rather than that the government is deferring to the professional status of lawyers. Perhaps all of this is to question the existence of a sharp divide between lawyers and other professionals as those who control their work and training, while other workers do not. It is a far blurrier line than is sometimes presented. It has been noted, for example, that car mechanics have many of the classic features of the professional, being able to claim specialised knowledge, technical training, and freedom from external supervision.[20]

These kinds of points have led some to question whether it is still helpful to distinguish between 'professionals' and 'non-professionals'.[21] Indeed, among the public, the word has come to mean little more than 'high quality',[22] with, for example, carpet cleaners and gardeners offering a 'professional service'. Some foresee the decline of the notion of the profession, with a realisation that all jobs have a degree of specialisation

[18] Freidson (n. 17), 2.   [19] *The Economist*, 'For many two years is plenty', 31 August 2013.

[20] M. Saks, 'Defining a profession: The role of knowledge and expertise' (2012) 2 Professionalism and Professions 151.

[21] R. Dingwall, 'Professions and social order in a global society' (1999) 9 International Review of Sociology 131.

[22] J. Montgomery, 'The virtues and vices of professionalism', in D. Bhugra and A. Malik (eds) *Professionalism in Mental Health Care* (Cambridge University Press, 2010).

and many require training, and that no clear divide can be drawn between the professional and the non-professional.

Not everyone accepts the inevitable demise of the term 'professional', however. Robert Dingwall suggests that increased globalisation will reinvigorate it.[23] This is because people seeking expert advice in another country will need reassurance that the person advising them is indeed an expert. This will create increased emphasis on training, qualification, and restrictions on who can call themselves 'qualified' in certain areas. In short, if lawyers and other experts are to operate in a global context, we need a way of assuring clients that the lawyers (and others) are indeed experts. Professional status provides a well-established way of doing this. Another point is that some groups still put considerable effort into being recognised as professions, for example midwives.[24] That suggests that the label is still seen as of value, at least in some contexts.

Certainly, those believing themselves to be professionals put much stock in retaining the status. Larson emphasises the value of being seen as professional:

> I see professionalization as the process by which producers of special services sought to constitute *and control* a market for their expertise. Because marketable expertise is a crucial element in the structure of modern inequality, professionalization appears also as a collective assertion of special social status and as a collective process of upward social mobility.[25]

As we have seen in the discussion so far, this assertion of power of a profession can be seen as a good, because it promises a high-quality service, or as a bad, privileging an elite[26] in a way that restricts access to the profession on the basis of race, gender, and class.[27] Whether, overall, the notion of professionalism provides benefit is much debated.[28]

Another issue is that the legal profession is becoming increasingly diverse. It will be interesting to see whether the power held by larger commercial firms leads to different forms of professional identity compared with that of smaller high-street firms. The differences in the kind of work done and the levels of remuneration may mean that there will be tensions over whether the solicitors can remain a single unified profession.[29] Further, large firms increasingly employ individuals with a broad range of skills so that they can offer their clients an extensive set of services. Legal, accountancy,

---

[23] Dingwall (n. 21).

[24] J. Evetts, *Professionalism in Turbulent Times: Changes, Challenges and Opportunities*, online at www.propel.stir.ac.uk/downloads/JuliaEvetts-FullPaper.pdf

[25] Larson (n. 16), xvi.   [26] T. Johnson, *Professions and Power* (Macmillan, 1972).

[27] Nicolson and Webb (n. 4); Dingwall (n. 21).

[28] J. Evetts, 'A new professionalism? Challenges and opportunities' (2011) 58 Current Sociology 406; S. Timmons, 'Professionalization and its discontents' (2011) 15 Health 377; Nicolson and Webb (n. 4).

[29] J. Flood, 'The re-landscaping of the legal profession: Large law firms and professional re-regulation' (2011) 59 Current Sociology 507; A. Francis, *At the Edge of Law: Emergent and Divergent Models of Legal Professionalism* (Ashgate, 2011).

public relations (PR), banking, financial, and media skills may all be offered by large firms. This will also challenge the extent to which it is clear which firms are law firms and which are not, which are professional or which are not, and who within a firm deserves the title 'professional'.[30]

The social place of lawyers

We will now explore a little further some of the themes surrounding the place that lawyers hold in society.

Their political role

For many people, the rule of law is central to a well-functioning society. Lord Bingham has set out eight aspects of the rule of law:

1. The law must be accessible, intelligible, clear and predictable.
2. Questions of legal right and liability should ordinarily be resolved by application of the law and not the exercise of discretion.
3. The laws of the land should apply equally to all, save to the extent that objective differences justify differentiation.
4. The law must afford adequate protection of fundamental human rights.
5. Means must be provided for resolving, without prohibitive cost or inordinate delay, bona fide civil disputes which the parties themselves are unable to resolve.
6. Ministers and public officers at all levels must exercise the powers conferred on them reasonably, in good faith, for the purpose for which the powers were conferred and without exceeding the limits of such powers.
7. Adjudicative procedures provided by the state should be fair.
8. The state must comply with its obligations in international law, the law which whether deriving from treaty or international custom and practice governs the conduct of nations.[31]

The notion of the 'rule of law' is covered in detail in books on constitutional law. We will not go into the concept now, but it should be clear that access to well-qualified lawyers plays a crucial role in achieving the rule of law. The law cannot be accessible to all or understood by all unless there are lawyers to advise people and to bring proceedings on their behalf. Lawyers do therefore play a central role in society.[32]

[30] D. Muzio, D. Brock, and R. Suddaby, 'Professions and institutional change: Towards an institutionalist sociology of the professions' (2013) 6 Journal of Management Studies 699.

[31] T. Bingham, *The Rule of Law* (Penguin, 2011), 5.

[32] A. Demack, 'Public interest or common good of the community? Bringing order to a dog's breakfast' (2003) 6 Legal Ethics 23.

It is important to recognise the political role that lawyers can play. Most obviously, this can be through 'cause lawyering'—that is, bringing legal actions for political purposes.[33] Lawyers can play an important role in holding the government to account and ensuring the protection of the rights of citizens. It is notable that, in recent years, lawyers have played a major role in political protests such as those in Turkey and in Pakistan. If the government were to have complete control over the legal profession and control who could or could not act as a lawyer, this would severely impact on the usefulness of the law as a control on government action and the effectiveness of human rights.[34] In the Marre Committee, it was stated that:

> The rights which can give rise to the strongest feelings usually concern a principle or cause, or involve a real or perceived oppression or abuse of power, either by the state or by a person or corporation which is more powerful and influential than the injured citizen. It is in these circumstances that the public needs an independent lawyer to ensure that justice is achieved...The public interest which requires that citizens are free to have access to, and protection for, their legal rights may transcend the interests even of government where those rights conflict with the wishes and interests of government.[35]

Lawyers also have a political role in public debates. Their contributions to proposals to change the law and in political debates are listened to seriously. Certainly, reform of legal procedures are heavily influenced by advice from lawyers practising in the area. However, lawyers need to be careful in political activism: if lawyers are seen to be pursuing their own interests, then their voices will carry less weight. Indeed, there is a danger of their involvement being counterproductive: 'the lawyers are against it' may even become an argument in favour of a proposal!

The Law Society has intervened in some political debates, proposing changes in the law. Indeed, it has had some tangible achievements in relation to mental health[36] and fraud.[37] That said, it is not difficult to find areas in which the Law Society has not been influential in its campaigns. The cutbacks in legal aid are no doubt the most significant failing. The Law Society was in a difficult position. The government was arguing that too much money was being paid to lawyers via legal aid and that the money could be better spent on disadvantaged groups from society. The Law Society, in campaigning against this, was easily open to the challenge that it was self-interested.[38]

---

[33] S. Scheingold, *The Politics of Rights: Lawyers, Public Policy, and Political Change* (University of Michigan Press, 2004).

[34] A. Boon, 'Professionalism under the Legal Services Act 2007' (2010) 17 International Journal of the Legal Profession 195.

[35] A. Marre, *A Time for Change: Report of the Committee on the Future of the Legal Profession* (Law Society, 1988), paras 6.8 and 6.7.

[36] Law Society, *Huge Success in Long-Running Law Society Campaign* (Law Society, 2005).

[37] Law Society, *Government Climb down over Abolishing Juries in Fraud Trials* (Law Society, 2006).

[38] See further Chapter 7.

Power

Lawyers hold power. Arguably, courts are the ultimate seat of power in the land. Even the government can be forced to act following a court ruling. Yet, for the vast majority of people, access to the ultimate seat of power is only available through a lawyer. Similarly, most people at a crisis point in their lives will require legal advice. Be they facing a criminal charge, in the midst of family breakdown, having lost their job, or buying a house, they need legal advice and the outcome of that advice will have a fundamental effect on their lives. Lawyers therefore enter people's lives often at highly sensitive times. This gives them considerable power in the personal context, as well as the political.[39]

A less direct way in which lawyers can exercise power is that the way in which lawyers advise clients and develop norms will influence the law itself. Of course, in a particular case, the advice given by a lawyer can have a strong impact on the outcome. If the lawyer advises the client to abandon a claim, the client is likely to heed that advice. But in a broader sense if, amongst lawyers, a particular approach is taken to a category of claims, then that is likely to become a legal norm, which will probably be upheld in a court.

Sometimes, there are 'turf wars' between the professions. For example, it has been suggested the insolvency market has seen a turf battle between the lawyers and accountants.[40] For a long time, there has been tension between solicitors and barristers over how to divide up legal work. Increasingly, there is also tension between law firms in different countries vying for international work.

Knowledge

For lawyers, the source of their power is their expert knowledge. Their understanding of the legal regulations and their application is a sought-after commodity. It is therefore crucial for lawyers that their knowledge remains valued. Two consequences in particular flow from this. The first is that the profession requires a person to complete rigorous training before he or she can practise as a lawyer. This reinforces the notion that lawyers hold expert knowledge that cannot readily be gained by the ordinary person. The second is that it is crucial that the law carries a mystique, so that the knowledge is not readily gained elsewhere.

A cynic might say that lawyers deliberately exacerbate this to enshrine their position. Strange words are used, obtuse forms must be submitted, and complex procedures followed. Lawyers may claim that the law deals with difficult issues and that complex regulations are unavoidable. For small matters, people can and do bring their

---

[39] A. Abbott, *The System of Professions: An Essay on the Expert Division of Labor* (University of Chicago Press, 1988).

[40] J. Webb, 'Turf wars and market control: Competition and complexity in the market for legal services' (2004) 11 International Journal of the Legal Profession 81.

own cases without undue difficulty. Nevertheless, critics will argue that, to maintain the power that lawyers' knowledge provides, it is important to them that the law is not seen as straightforward.

A further part of the 'mystique' of lawyering is the claim that law involves a degree of judgement. Law is not simply a set of rules that you learn and apply, as you might in mechanics or statistics; rather, there is an art in the application of the rules, which gives the lawyer applying regulations the edge over the person who has read the key rules on the Internet.

As Reza Banakar notes:

> [K]nowledge of legal rules and doctrine does not by itself provide a sufficient basis for legal practice. Much of lawyers' day-to-day work concerns dealing with clients, interviewing witnesses or drafting documents which require the use of non-legal knowledge and social skills. Also, practicing lawyers have a pragmatic understanding of law, which is aimed at settling cases to their advantage. Legal rules and doctrine are only two among a number of devices (or 'resources') that the practicing lawyer employs if, and in so far as, they serve to negotiate the boundaries of the law in his or her favour. Legal doctrine is abandoned in favour of other measures (for example delay tactics) when it no longer serves to bring about the desired end.[41]

As this quote indicates, lawyers draw on the law as only one resource when advising clients and seeking to resolve their problems.

Of course, this claim to specialist knowledge is open to challenge. Are the rules really as complex as lawyers pretend? To what extent do lawyers use Latin phrases and complex terminology simply to disguise a relatively straightforward matter? Is the art of 'application' simply a smokescreen for the fact that the laws are somewhat vague and that one person's interpretation is as good as another?

◉ Application

A good example of these issues is a recent proposal to replace the current legal procedures for obtaining a divorce with an online Internet application form. Rather than paying a lawyer to complete the divorce petition and the accompanying paperwork, a person would be able to fill in the form without expert advice.[42] As this shows (leaving aside a range of issues that the reform would raise), an argument can be made that apparently erudite areas of the law can, without undue effort, be reduced to a relatively straightforward procedure that all might understand. The do-it-yourself (DIY) forms for wills and conveyancing available at good bookshops also suggest that a member of the public with reasonable intelligence can complete the paperwork that he or she needs.

---

[41] R. Banakar and M. Travers, *Theory and Method in Socio-Legal Research* (Hart, 2005), 9.

[42] For the detail, see J. Herring, 'Divorce, Internet hubs and Stephen Cretney', in R. Probert and C. Barton (eds) *Fifty Years in Family Law* (Intersentia, 2012).

Social status

Another aspect of professionalism is the social position within society occupied by professionals. Interestingly, this might suggest that not all lawyers are equal:[43] lawyers dealing with clients of high social position themselves have a high social position; those dealing with clients of a low social position might have a lower social position within the legal profession. The senior partner of a large firm of solicitors can expect to socialise in high-society events. The legal aid immigration lawyer is less likely to be invited to join the golf club.

Solicitors are regularly consulted by people. A study conducted by the SRA in 2008 found that:[44]

- 41 per cent of people said that they had used a solicitor in the past five years;
- 21 per cent of those to whom the SRA spoke had used a solicitor for buying, selling, or remortgaging property, after which the most frequently used services were:
  - 14 per cent had used a solicitor for wills or probate matters;
  - 5 per cent had used a solicitor for personal injury services; and
  - after this, the remaining services that people said that they had used (in order of frequency) were matrimonial matters, employment claims, criminal defence, civil disputes, and asylum/immigration issues;
- 83 per cent of people who had used a solicitor in the past five years were satisfied with their overall performance (the most satisfied of these being those based in Wales); and
- 36 per cent of the general public were unlikely to seek information on solicitors' professional backgrounds before employing them.

Ethics

Part of what gives lawyers their particular social status is the ethical codes that bind them. Professional ethics can be seen as a building block in power. That is not immediately apparent—indeed, they might be thought of as an inhibition of power—but a code of ethics helps to make lawyers distinct and therefore protects them from threats to their monopoly. It is possible, therefore, to view ethical regulations in a more cynical light. Many lawyers would claim that ethical codes are there to protect clients from the few 'rotten apples'. Practising lawyers are more likely to see ethical codes as an inconvenience, rather than as a way of drumming up business.

Ross Cranston disagrees with the cynics: '[A]ny association with the profession dispels the suggestion that the profession's ethical codes are self-interest writ large.

---

[43] J. Heinz and E. Laumann, *Chicago Lawyers: The Social Structure of the Bar* (Russell Sage Foundation, 1982).

[44] Solicitors Regulation Authority, *Survey of Public Attitudes towards Solicitors* (SRA, 2008).

There is a genuine concern with high ethical standards, not least so as to maintain the profession's public standing.'[45] The rules of protection of confidential information and against conflict of interests are well known and enforced. Even if allowed to by a change in legislation, a member of the public who sought to set up as a legal adviser would face the difficulty of reassuring clients that he or she could offer the degree of protection guaranteed by the lawyers' professional codes of ethics. The idea that they are bound by a 'special code of conduct' also helps to promote a degree of mystique around the legal professions.

'The crisis of legal professionalism'

There was a huge growth in the legal profession in the latter half of the twentieth century. The greater availability of legal aid and increased access to higher education fuelled the increase in the number of people seeking to be lawyers. A growing rights culture and the complexity of legal instruments drew greater attention to the law and increased the market for legal advice. However, in more recent years, there have been challenges to the position of lawyers and few would paint as rosy a picture of the legal profession as they would have done, say, 15 years ago. Some say that the 'noble profession' is 'losing its soul'.[46] The legal profession is not, overall, as confident and as buoyant as it was at the end of the twentieth century.

The challenges to legal practitioners have come from several directions.

Legal aid

A major crisis for the legal profession is the withdrawal of legal aid over the past few years. This is discussed in detail in Chapter 7. As the costs for legal services have risen, so has the legal aid budget. Following the financial crisis and cutbacks in government expenditure, the legal aid budget was greatly reduced, posing a serious challenge to the profession in several ways.

Most obviously, there are lawyers whose livelihoods depended upon legal aid payment. For these, the restrictions on the number of people and kinds of cases for which legal aid is available, and a reduction in the amount paid, has had a significant impact on their incomes. One survey found that 32 per cent of firms that were in existence in both 2007–08 and 2010–11 reported an increase in monetary turnover during the period, while 41 per cent reported a decrease in turnover.[47] Many firms have had to close or refocus their businesses in an attempt to respond to these changes.

[45] R. Cranston, 'Legal ethics and professional responsibility', in R. Cranston (ed.) *Legal Ethics and Professional Responsibility* (Clarendon Press, 1995), 1.

[46] A. Kronman, *The Lost Lawyer: Failing Ideals of the Legal Profession* (Harvard University Press, 1995).

[47] P. Pleasence, N. Balmer, and R. Moorhead, *A Time of Change: Solicitors' Firms in England and Wales* (Law Society, 2010).

The longer-term consequences are potentially even more serious. As a result of the cutbacks, it is inevitable that people needing legal services will not be able to access them. If lawyers are seen to be charging so much that the ordinary person cannot afford their services or lawyers are interested only in acting for rich clients, a serious lack of trust in the legal procession will set in and, indeed, a lack of trust in the whole justice system. The full consequences of the cutbacks in legal aid are not yet apparent, but solicitors and barristers will need to think carefully about their responses.

It may also be that, in response to the cutbacks, alternative forms of dispute resolution will be developed. We will explore this further in Chapter 10. It is envisioned in family law, for example, that rather than using courts and lawyers, couples will use mediation. Other kinds of dispute may also explore using alternative dispute resolution (ADR). Given that the law is seen as slow, complex, and expensive, the creation of alternatives to legal advice and dispute resolution poses a further challenge to the profession.

One danger for lawyers is that their services will simply become too expensive, especially if, as suggested earlier in the chapter, questions are raised about the quality of their services and alternatives. Moorhead, Sherr, and Paterson, in their survey, accepted that, if one looks at the hourly rate for services, lawyers do indeed charge more than mediators or non-legal advisers.[48] However, their survey showed that non-lawyer agencies took up to two-and-a-half hours more per matter than did solicitors. This meant that the total cost for a case dealt with by non-lawyers was, in fact, sometimes more than twice as expensive as one dealt with by lawyers. This is surprising and the reasons are complex. In part, lawyers had an incentive to be quicker on the contracted cases, because they would be paid the same amount of money however many hours they put in. Significantly, the non-lawyer agencies were looking at issues in the round, offering a range of services for example and also taking on debt counselling when advising a client on a debt issue. Also, the authors found that lawyers were stricter about what time counted as billable time than were non-lawyers. Their conclusion is surprising: non-lawyers offered an improved quality of services, but at a greater cost. This is probably the opposite outcome to what most people would have expected.

Internationalisation

Legal work has become increasingly international. Commercial firms now compete for business not only with each other, but also with firms around the world. Increasingly, corporate clients are expecting advice from a range of experts, not only on legal matters, but also on issues ranging from PR to tax. They will expect a highly skilled, flexible, international service. This makes it particularly hard for smaller commercial

---

[48] R. Moorhead, A. Sherr, and A. Paterson, 'Contesting professionalism: Legal aid and non-lawyers in England and Wales' (2003) 37 Law and Society Review 765.

firms to survive. Significantly, there is increasing pressure on costs as competition increases. All of these factors lead to major challenges for large corporate firms.

Challenges to monopoly

The special position that legal professionals hold in our society is, in part, based on the monopoly that they have on access to legal advice. It is central to this that lawyers can claim to be able to provide legal advice of a higher quality and legal services that are more trustworthy than those of others. If people were to believe that accessing legal advice over the Internet would provide just as accurate advice as legal counsel or that asking a financial adviser to make financial arrangements was just as secure as asking a lawyer, the legal profession would be in trouble.[49] As already noted, cutbacks in legal aid are likely to produce a range of non-lawyer-based services, which may challenge the profession.

The Internet provides pages of information proffering legal advice. You can download a copy of a standard-form will and receive instructions on how to fill it in. The government offers pages giving legal advice that you can use to resolve family problems. Books are available on DIY conveyancing, divorcing, and the like. In the light of these, it becomes more important for lawyers to clarify the services that they offer. Moorhead and colleagues suggest that lawyers could refer to special skills, including the following:

- a 'craft approach,' treating every problem as unique and requiring customized service;
- putting the client's interests above the lawyer's own economic (or other) interests and guaranteeing independence from the state;
- substantial training in legal thought and the skills of legal practice, improving the capacity to perform high-quality legal work;
- breadth of knowledge ensuring that 'subtle and important issues and linkages' can be recognized, aiding appropriate/comprehensive diagnosis of the client's problems;
- the ability to pursue a case all the way through the courts, providing critical leverage in advancing the client's interests; and
- for dissatisfied clients, recourse to disciplinary bodies enforcing ethical codes.[50]

Whether these will be sufficient to persuade clients to prefer lawyers to the Internet or non-professional advice services remains to be seen.

There is little getting away from the fact that, for many routine legal transactions, specialist legal advice is not necessary. For example, for many people, a standard-form will may be appropriate. What lawyers would want to emphasise, however, is the

---

[49] Moorhead et al. (n. 48), 770.   [50] Moorhead et al. (n. 48), 771.

phrase 'most people'. There will be some for whom the standard form is not appropriate. The problem is that the public do not know into which category they fall. The lawyer has the skill to reassure people that they are receiving a personalised form.

One can understand that many clients will feel somewhat frustrated at paying large sums of money for a copy of, for example, a lawyer's standard form will, which may well be of the kind that they could have found on the Internet at no cost. But someone relying on the Internet form will be taking a risk. The challenge for lawyers is whether clients will be willing to take that risk in return for paying a significantly lower price. No doubt, large companies entering contracts worth large sums of money will; whether individuals will is a matter for debate.

The message from conveyancing is a salutary lesson for lawyers. In 1968, 55.6 per cent of solicitors derived income from conveyancing. Yet increasing concern that the legal monopoly on conveyancing caused increased costs led to a direct challenge to that monopoly. Licensed conveyancers can now perform this work, and less and less of it is performed by solicitors. The availability of standard forms and Internet packages means that, for most conveyancing transactions, a solicitor is not required. In the future, we may see similar moves in other areas of legal work.[51] It is not hard to imagine a large amount of work that currently takes lawyers significant amounts of time (such as drafting contracts, wills, and litigation forms) being completed by complex computer programs in the future.[52] Interestingly, Richard Susskind does not think that this is a bad thing. He asks:

> [W]hat if we could find new, innovative ways of allowing our clients to tap into our knowledge and expertise? In particular, what if we, as lawyers, could make our knowledge and expertise available through a wide range of online legal services, whether for the drafting of documents or for the resolution of disputes? If we can find online methods of enabling access to our experience and the service is thereby less costly, less cumbersome, more convenient, and quicker, then I suggest that clients...would welcome these services with arms flung open.[53]

Quality of service

Top-quality firms pride themselves on listening to their clients and finding a solution that is tailored to the individual needs of their clients. Not all lawyers succeed in doing this. Lawyers have a reputation for being arrogant: they see the client's views as 'vulgar' and their sense of fairness 'disqualified'.[54] For example, if a woman were to visit a lawyer seeking advice about a divorce, she might want to emphasise that her

---

[51] R. Susskind, *The Future of Law: Facing the Challenge of Information Technology* (Oxford University Press, 1998).

[52] R. Susskind, *Tomorrow's Lawyers* (Oxford University Press, 2013).

[53] Susskind (n. 51), 159.

[54] P. Bourdieu, 'What makes a social class? On the theoretical and practical existence of groups' (1987) 32 Berkeley Journal of Sociology 1.

husband had an affair and caused the family break-up. She might feel that he should 'pay' for his bad conduct. However, the lawyer is likely to tell her that the court will not be particularly interested in deciding who caused the break-up or who was at fault.

That example might show the problems. You might take the view that the lawyer is doing the right thing: the parties must look to the future, and must determine what will be best for the children and how the money should be divided fairly. Looking back at the past is not helpful. Using lawyers to fight over 'who said what to whom' is an expensive way to work out grief at the end of the relationship. Or you might take the view that this is the lawyer imposing the 'legal agenda' on the couple: the law should accept the problems and grievances that people have rather than force them to 'behave well'.

This perspective may be too kind to lawyers. There is some evidence that lawyers, when interviewing clients, seek to pigeonhole their clients and their problems, so that they can deal more easily with the legal issues.[55] This might be seen as efficient, but it can work against the claim, mentioned earlier, that lawyers treat their clients as individuals. Certainly, at their worst, the clients of lawyers can feel as though they have lost control of their case. They seek advice about a problem and, six months later, receive a packaged solution and a hefty bill, with little involvement. Criminal cases, in particular, are cited as examples in which the defence is prepared by the legal team and may have little in common with what the client seeks to present as his or her defence.[56] Again, the issue is not easy: the defence that the client seeks to run may be a hopeless one in the views of the legal experts—but the alternative defence might leave the client with no control over or understanding of what is being said.

This lack of effective communication between lawyers and clients, and a perception of arrogance among lawyers, offers those seeking to provide alternative services scope for offering a service that 'listens' and 'treats clients as people'. This is certainly something that family mediators, for example, emphasise when suggesting that clients may prefer mediation over seeking a lawyer. It is noticeable that lawyers now often emphasise the qualities of listening and communicating with clients.[57]

Trust

The legal profession has struggled in recent years to develop an image of trust. Lawyers are consulted because a person faces a risk and is seeking to reduce or mitigate that risk.[58] It is crucial that lawyers are seen as trustworthy.

---

[55] A. Sherr, 'Lawyers and clients: The first meeting' (1986) 49 Modern Law Review 323.

[56] M. McConville, J. Hodgson, L. Bridges, and A. Pavlovic, *Standing Accused: The Organization and Practices of Criminal Defence Lawyers in Britain* (Oxford University Press, 1994).

[57] Moorhead et al. (n. 48).

[58] J. Webb and D. Nicolson, 'Institutionalising trust: Ethics and the responsive regulation of the legal profession' (1999) 2 Legal Ethics 148.

Faith in the legal profession was seriously dented by the financial crisis, during which law firms were heavily involved in companies that collapsed, notably including Enron. These financial collapses have challenged the assumptions that professional status and self-regulation are part of bargain in which professionals have autonomy in organising their affairs, while guaranteeing quality and putting the interests of the public before their own.[59]

Digging deeper

As Julian Webb and Donald Nicolson suggest, we have seen a shift in recent years from personal trust in a particular lawyer to institutional trust in the profession of lawyers.[60] The days of seeing the 'family's lawyer' are, by and large, relegated to television costume dramas. Most people will rely on advertisements or recommendations from friends. However, as Webb and Nicolson acknowledge, the personal connection between lawyer and client has not been lost in the commercial world. Commercial lawyers spend much time developing personal connections and developing strong bonds with clients. However, most lawyers are trusted as members of a profession and lawyers will not be expected to earn trust on an individual basis. This may especially be so in large firms, in which the head practitioner deals face to face with the client, supported by a team of junior lawyers and other employees who may not interact directly with the client at all.

Too many lawyers

A common concern among the profession is that there are 'too many lawyers'. Certainly, there has been a sharp increase in the number of legal professionals in England and Wales, and indeed in most Western countries. This manifests in a number of ways. An increasing number of law graduates and even those completing the professional training are not able to find a job. Those who complete articles or pupillage can struggle to be kept on by their firms or chambers, or to find an alternative place of employment. There is considerable competition for work between firms of solicitors in some areas.[61]

There are three main issues to address: whether it is true that there are 'too many lawyers'; if so, why;[62] and if so, what can be done about it.[63]

Looking at the first question, Carrie Menkel-Meadow notes that much depends on who is asking the question.[64] A specialist practitioner seeing a drop in income as a result

---

[59] Flood (n. 29).   [60] Webb and Nicolson (n. 58).   [61] Webb (n. 40).

[62] R. Abel, 'What does and should influence the number of lawyers?' (2012) 19 International Journal of the Legal Profession 131.

[63] E. Katvan, 'The "overcrowding the profession" argument and the professional melting pot' (2012) 19 International Journal of the Legal Profession 301.

[64] C. Menkel-Meadow, 'Too many lawyers? Or should lawyers be doing other things?' (2012) 19 International Journal of the Legal Profession 147.

of other lawyers setting up in competition might look at the question very differently from an immigrant seeking legally aided advice who cannot find a lawyer in his or her area. Menkel-Meadow suggests that if we ask whether there are legal needs that are not been met, the answer is a resounding 'yes'. So it may not be a matter of there being too many lawyers, but rather too many seeking only a particular kind of work.

On the numbers of law graduates, if only the best law graduates are finding work, then the profession may not mind that the least able are struggling to find jobs. Indeed, the popularity of law as a career and the numbers willing to risk the efforts needed to obtain entry may be seen as a success story. What is interesting is that while there is evidence that law graduates are not finding it as easy to obtain employment as lawyers as they once did, they do not seem to find it unduly difficult to find employment elsewhere.

In relation to the second question, for Herbert Kritzer, the answer to the question of why there are too many lawyers is straightforward: 'It's the law schools, stupid!'[65] Having said that (and at the risk of being 'stupid'), it might be emphasised that, as already noted, most law graduates do not seek a career in law; the number of lawyers practising is therefore not necessarily dependent on the number of students studying law.[66] The number of firms offering pupillage or training contracts must also have an impact, along with the salaries on offer, the quality of life on offer for lawyers, and the range of alternatives for those law graduates who do not seek a career in the law.

Addressing the third matter, there are three main ways in which one might restrict the number of lawyers. The first is restricting entry to the profession through gatekeeping structures, for example simply restricting the places available on professional courses or even who can take a law degree, although in considering that option it should be remembered that plenty of people complete a law degree without planning to become a lawyer. Another way would be to raise the qualifications required, making it harder to qualify as a lawyer.[67] Another would be to restrict competition between firms and to restrict advertisements.[68]

Lawyers as servant

Some see a crisis in the legal profession in another way. Lawyers, it is claimed, are increasingly working as 'functionaries subservient to the dictates of their corporate clients'.[69] It is claimed that the balance of power has shifted in favour of corporate

[65] H. Kritzer, 'It's the law schools, stupid! Explaining the continuing increase in the number of lawyers' (2013) 19 International Journal of the Legal Profession 209.

[66] B. Green, 'The flood of US lawyers: Natural fluctuation or professional climate change?' (2012) 19 International Journal of the Legal Profession 193.   [67] Green (n. 66).

[68] E. Katvan, C. Silver, and N. Ziv, 'Too many lawyers?' (2012) 19 International Journal of the Legal Profession 123.

[69] J. Bagust, 'The legal profession and the business of law' (2013) 35 Sydney Law Review 27.

clients and away from law firms. The 'logic of the market'[70] has taken over legal practice in large firms. As Bagust argues:

> Within this logic, economic interests are favoured over the social realities of individual workers. Its effects, through the 'intrusive imposition of commercial values', have the propensity to condemn old solidarities—such as professional associations—to the margins, if elements of their practices, such as professional autonomy and altruistic service, threaten to subdue profit maximisation and economic efficiency.[71]

The emphasis on maximisation of profit impacts on workplace relationships.[72] The status of lawyers as professionals serving justice and the public good has been eroded by large firms offering clients services designed to increase profits.[73] This challenges the self-image of lawyers, especially those who have entered the profession as a result of a calling to work for the greater good, expecting a degree of professional responsibility.

One aspect of this is the importance for solicitors of timekeeping. Lawyers must record the time that they spend on files, typically in six-minute segments. We will explore this further in Chapter 7. Studies suggest that this leads to a commoditisation. Lawyers' work becomes assessed mechanically. Interestingly, in one survey, lawyers were found to be seeking to counter this by claiming an element of discretion in deciding, for example, not to record a piece of work done very quickly or even to charge more for work that is complex.[74] This discretion over how to record the time taken enables lawyers to keep some 'professional discretion' over billing.

It remains to be seen whether the changing nature of the work and values of lawyers cause disenchantment among solicitors or whether the focus on money-making inspires them.

Specialism

Increasingly, lawyers are becoming specialised. It is rare to find a firm that will offer advice on all areas of law. A recent study of the work of solicitors found that 27 per cent of firms reported that they conducted at least 90 per cent of their work in a single category.[75]

Even high-street law firms that used to offer all services to their clients tend now to emphasise one or two areas in which they claim especial skill. Certainly, at an individual level, nearly all lawyers will now specialise, sometimes with a very high degree of specificity. This poses a challenge to the coherence and legitimacy of professional ethics.

---

[70] P. Bourdieu, 'The essence of neoliberalism', *Le Monde Diplomatique*, December 1998, online at http://mondediplo.com/1998/12/08bourdieu [71] Bagust (n. 69), 39.

[72] H. Sommerlad, 'The commercialisation of law and the enterprising legal practitioner: Continuity and change' (2011) 18 International Journal of the Legal Profession 73.

[73] C. Seron, 'The status of legal professionalism at the close of the twentieth century: Chicago lawyers and urban lawyers' (2007) 32 Law and Social Inquiry 581.

[74] Seron (n. 73).   [75] Pleasence et al. (n. 47).

John Flood argues, with some justification, that there is a group of elite large law firms that dominate 'the 21st century legal profession'.[76] The largest law firms employ more than 3,000 lawyers, with offices in more 30 countries and revenues exceeding £1 billion. They are utterly different from the dusty high-street practices that can be found in towns around the country.[77]

The job of the partner in a firm of commercial solicitors in London is very different from that of a high-street criminal advocate. Their salaries, things that they do, ways that they dress, and values may all completely differ. It is hard, with such diversity, to maintain professional unity. The professional ethics codes are problematic given that lawyers working in different areas of law face very different kinds of ethical dilemmas.[78] Interestingly, city solicitors have formed their own group to represent their own interests, believing that the Law Society does not fully understand the world in which they work. Yet it can be argued that specialisation, while a threat to professional unity, is essential if lawyers are to claim to have particular skills or knowledge that cannot be acquired elsewhere.

Mental health

A somewhat under-discussed issue is the mental health of lawyers. This has received more attention in the United States, where there is evidence of high rates of anxiety, depression, and stress among law students and lawyers.[79] One study found 20 per cent of practising lawyers suffering depression—twice the rates among the public—and rates of alcoholism double the norm.[80] Goodrich notes that '[o]ther studies have indicated that lawyers are prone to workaholism, obsessive compulsive behaviour, hostility, interpersonal insensitivity, isolation and failed relationships'.[81] In a 2012 survey of 1,000 English lawyers, the organisation Law Care found that 74.7 per cent reported feeling more stressed than they had felt five years ago.[82] Explanations included overwork, poor management, lack of appreciation, and feelings of isolation. Some 19 per cent admitted drinking more than the recommended units of alcohol at least once a week.

---

[76] J. Flood, 'From ethics to regulation: The re-organization and re-professionalization of large law firms in the 21st century' (2012) 59 Current Sociology 152.

[77] M. Galanter and S. Roberts, 'From kinship to magic circle: The London commercial law firm in the twentieth century' (2008) 15 International Journal of the Legal Profession 143.

[78] R. Moorhead, 'Lawyer specialization: Managing the professional paradox' (2010) 32 Law and Policy 226.

[79] P. Goodrich, 'Law-induced anxiety: Legists, anti-lawyers and the boredom of legality' (2000) 9 Social and Legal Studies 143.

[80] C. Mauney, *The Lawyers' Epidemic: Depression, Suicide and Substance Abuse*, online at www.scbar.org/LinkClick.aspx?fileticket=rZNzWAnfCR4%3D&tabid=160

[81] Goodrich (n. 79), 144.   [82] Law Care, *Stress in the Legal Profession Survey* (Law Care, 2012).

Culture

Lawyers do not operate in a vacuum. They operate with others, in chambers or in firms, or in their dealings with other lawyers. This creates a professional culture that can impact on the way in which lawyers work and what they expect from each other.[83]

There is much debate over whether there is a distinctive legal culture. By 'culture' is generally meant a set of ideas, attitudes, and values that have come to shape a group's set of understandings about themselves and how they are expected to behave towards each other. Lawrence Friedman argues that there are two aspects to a culture: an external dimension, which affects how others see lawyers and legal institutions; and an internal dimension, which reflects how people see themselves.[84] Of course, these two dimensions affect each other: lawyers may become aware of how they are understood by others and that may affect their internal attitudes. Whether the legal culture is sufficiently distinct from culture generally to justify its own label is a matter for debate. Further, as discussed earlier in the chapter, given the broad range of work that lawyers do, it may be open to debate whether we can identify a specifically legal culture.

Lawyers are often firestorm adversaries in court, seeking to portray each other's arguments in a weak light and to pit arguments against each other. Clients are somewhat dismayed after a case to see their lawyers being friendly with their opponents. Lawyers realise that they may be fierce adversaries one day, but on the same side the next. They may be denigrating their fellow lawyers in the morning and negotiating a reasonable compromise that afternoon.

Some aspects of legal culture can be identified as a way of depersonalising the adversarial nature of law. The wearing of wigs and gowns, the use of formal language, and the formal procedures of the courtroom can ease the discomfort of arguing against someone whom a lawyer may know well. This depersonalisation also makes it clear that lawyers are acting in a role: representing their clients and, in a sense, not being themselves. This assists the lawyer who is, for example, defending a client whom the lawyer in fact believes to be guilty. This depersonalisation is criticised by those who seek to promote a more relational approach to legal ethics, such as supporters of an ethics of care (see Chapter 1).

Culture can certainly have an impact on disadvantaged groups within the legal profession. Women work hard at perpetuating a professional image to combat stereotypical assumptions made about them. This involves dressing in a 'professional' way, paying close attention to personal grooming and how they present themselves. This will be explored further in Chapter 14.

[83] D. Nelken, 'Using the concept of legal culture' (2004) 29 Australian Journal of Legal Philosophy 29.

[84] L. Friedman, *The Legal System: A Social Science Perspective* (Russell Sage Foundation, 1975).

What would you do?

You love your job, but feel out of place. You are expected to wear clothes in which you don't feel comfortable. You feel you must put on an act—to be 'posh'—and you can never really relax and be yourself. Because of your gender, you feel that you are expected to behave in certain ways—and so you do so, because it's simply easier. One friend recommends that you should leave the firm. Another friend says that it's worth acting the part because your pay is so good.

Legal executives

Legal executives are often overlooked when the legal profession is discussed.[85] In fact, much of their work is analogous to that of a solicitor and they are often employed as fee earners in their own right. Despite the attempts of legal executives to achieve full professional status, they are generally clearly subordinate to solicitors. To become a legal executive there is no need to have obtained a law degree, but a person must have passed two sets of examinations and achieved a qualifying period of employment.

Legal executives do have rights of audience in some courts and they are able to conduct litigation in certain kinds of case. This puts them on a higher playing field than that of a paralegal. Traditionally, they have not been able to be partners, but the Legal Services Act 1997 allows them to be partners in alternative business structures (see Chapter 3).

Legal executives do not fall under the remit of the Law Society, nor are they caught by the Solicitors Guidance.[86] Rather surprisingly, there is limited formal ethical guidance for legal executives. Many will follow the SRA Code, however, even if not officially bound by it.

The Chartered Institute of Legal Executives (CILEx) was formed from the Institute of Legal Executives (ILEX) in 2012. It has around 20,000 members, of whom 7,500 are Fellows and the remaining are trainee or qualified legal executives. Since 1989, there have been around 95,000 who have become legal executives. Some 74 per cent of the memberships are women and 38 per cent are black or ethnic minority (BME). These are surprisingly high figures, suggesting that the legal executive has been seen as a route by those who seek a career in the law, but who are not able to enter the profession. Only 9 per cent of members went to fee-paying schools and 81.5 per cent had parents who did not attend university. CILEx claims that it appeals especially to those who could not afford the university or Graduate Diploma in Law (GDL) routes into the profession.[87]

---

[85] A. Francis, 'Legal ethics, moral agency and professional autonomy: The unbearable ethics of being (a legal executive)?' (2007) 10 Legal Ethics 131.   [86] Francis (n. 85).

[87] Chartered Institute of Legal Executives, *Facts and Statistics* (CILEx, 2013).

Anti-lawyers

It was Dick the Butcher, in one of Shakespeare's lesser-known plays, who declared: 'The first thing we do, let's kill all the lawyers.'[88] There is no escaping the reality that there are some who oppose lawyers![89] The friendlier opposition complains that, in the past half-century, there has been a proliferation of law and lawyers. It sometimes seems that the response of governments to any problem is to pass legislation. In a wide range of areas of life, there is ever more law and regulations. As Goodrich puts it:

> In essence, law comes increasingly to dominate—to colonize—all aspects of the public sphere, it becomes the form of all political intervention in the social, and in consequence the social is depoliticized as the lifeworld comes to be structured overwhelmingly according to the agonistic and functional logic of the legal world. There is, in other words, a shift in representation of the social, a tendency to juridify all discourse and in consequence to reduce all discourse to the stable, singular and ugly reality of law.[90]

This discussion depends very much on your perspective. For the employer, the exponential growth in employment law leads to greater bureaucracy, even making employing people unattractive. For the employee, the law provides powerful protection from unfair dismissal or treatment. To the powerful, legal intervention is often an irritation that is a threat to power. For the weak, it provides hope for improvement in their position.

Some opposition to law and lawyers comes from a libertarian perspective, which at its most extreme sees government intervention through law or otherwise as an unwarranted intervention in individual liberty; at a more moderate level, it considers that any such intervention should be restricted to the minimum.

A different kind of claim may be made about the *form* of law: it is unnecessarily complex and fixated on technical details. We could produce a much simpler law, with directions that are comprehensible to the layperson. 'Do not hurt people' could, for example, replace a huge morass of complex provisions in the criminal law. The law could then be understood by the average person and we could escape the need for expensive lawyers to explain these provisions. While at first sight an attractive argument, it is misleading. Let us take the example of the simplified criminal law. Does the rule 'Do not hurt people' cover saying untrue things about them to others? Does it cover just touching someone's elbow? You would not know without... seeking legal advice. Indeed, you probably have a better chance of discovering the answers from a

---

[88] Shakespeare, *King Henry the Sixth-Part Two*, Act 4, Scene II, 71–78.

[89] P. Campos, P. Schlag, and S. Smith, *Against the Law* (Duke University Press, 2009); P. Campos, *Jurismania: The Madness of American Law* (Oxford University Press, 1998).

[90] Goodrich (n. 79), 153.

detailed and complex law than a simple one. The simpler the law, the greater the job of interpretation, because less is written down. However, even accepting the need for detailed law, we might still question whether enough is done to ensure that the law is made available in a clear and accessible way.

 Scandal!

Martha Derthick has undertaken a study of the tactics of lawyers working for tobacco firms in the United States.[91] One particularly pernicious tactic used was that tobacco firms would make sure that their lawyers commissioned reports into the health effects of smoking. If the reports were negative (that is, if they showed a link between smoking and ill-health), the report was said to be protected by legal privilege and could not be disclosed to anyone, even those suing the companies and seeking full disclosure. If the reports were positive, they were well publicised.

Conclusion

The practice of lawyers and the operation of legal ethics do not occur in a vacuum. The position that lawyers have in society, the way in which they are regarded by others, and the perceptions of lawyers of themselves all impact upon the lawyer's values. They also reflect the pressures that lawyers feel under and may explain some of the lapses in ethical practice. While lawyers, in some ways, have considerable power, as this chapter has shown the legal profession is under challenge from a number of directions. It is clear that the profession is undergoing some profound changes.[92] This is nothing unusual. In recent years, it has witnessed a huge increase in the numbers of women and BME lawyers; it has seen a reduction in the kind of work that can be undertaken only by qualified lawyers; it has seen severe cutbacks in legal aid. All of these have changed the profession already.

 Further reading

The following discuss the concept of professionalism:

A. Boon, 'Professionalism under the Legal Services Act 2007' (2010) 17 International Journal of the Legal Profession 195.

[91] M. Derthick, 'The lawyers did it: The cigarette manufacturers' policy towards smoking and health', in R. Kagan, M. Krygier, and K. Winston (eds) *Legality and Community* (Rowman and Littlefield, 2002).

[92] R. Abel, *English Lawyers between Market and State: The Politics of Professionalism* (Oxford University Press, 2004).

J. Evetts, 'Professionalism: Value and ideology' (2013) 61 Current Sociology 778.

J. Montgomery, 'The virtues and vices of professionalism', in D. Bhugra and A. Malik (eds) *Professionalism in Mental Health Care* (Cambridge University Press, 2010).

D. Sciulli, 'Why professions matter: Structural and institutional invariance in professions and professionalism' (2010) 9 Comparative Sociology 744.

This material is helpful on the legal profession:

A. Boon and J. Levin, *The Ethics and Conduct of Lawyers in England and Wales* (Hart, 2008).

J. Flood, 'From ethics to regulation: The re-organization and re-professionalization of large law firms in the 21st century' (2012) 59 Current Sociology 152.

A. Francis, *At the Edge of Law: Emergent and Divergent Models of Legal Professionalism* (Ashgate, 2011).

M. Galanter and S. Roberts, 'From kinship to magic circle: The London commercial law firm in the twentieth century' (2008) 15 International Journal of the Legal Profession 143.

R. Moorhead, 'Lawyer specialization: Managing the professional paradox' (2010) 32 Law and Policy 226.

D. Nicolson and J. Webb, 'Public rules and private values: Fractured profession(alism)s and institutional ethics' (2005) 12 International Journal of the Legal Profession 165.

H. Sommerlad, 'The commercialisation of law and the enterprising legal practitioner: Continuity and change' (2011) 18 International Journal of the Legal Profession 73.

R. Susskind, *Tomorrow's Lawyers* (Oxford University Press, 2013).

J. Webb, 'Turf wars and market control: Competition and complexity in the market for legal services' (2004) 11 International Journal of the Legal Profession 81.

J. Webb and D. Nicolson, 'Institutionalising trust: Ethics and the responsive regulation of the legal profession' (1999) 2 Legal Ethics 148.

3

The regulation of the legal profession

 Key issues

- How do the professions regulate themselves?
- What is the nature of the professional guidance?
- What consequences are there for breach of the guidance?

Introduction

The structure, organisation, and regulation of the legal profession, at first, appear a somewhat boring issue. Yet it tells us much about how the profession understands itself, is understood by society, and is able to exercise power. In this chapter, we will consider who is allowed to become a solicitor or a barrister and what training they must have completed. Further, we will consider the nature of the ethical guidance issued by the profession. Essential to any system of professional ethics is some form of enforcement and sanction. Of course, most lawyers will follow the guidelines using common sense and will not be tempted to act in an unethical way. However, if public confidence is to be maintained and the ethical principles are to be taken seriously, then there must be consequences for those who do breach the ethical codes.

The need for regulation

The regulation of legal services is central to a well-functioning justice system. In his influential review, Sir David Clementi identified six roles for regulation, as follows.[1]

1. *Maintenance of the rule of law* If we wish to have a 'predictable and proportionate legal system with fair, transparent, and effective judicial institutions', then it 'is essential to the protection of both citizens and commerce against any arbitrary use of state authority and unlawful acts of both organisations and individuals'.[2]

2. *Access to justice* Regulation should ensure that everyone has access to good legal advice and services.

---

[1] D. Clementi, *Review of the Regulatory Framework for Legal Services in England and Wales: Final Report* (Cabinet Office, 2004). [2] Clementi (n. 1), 3.

3. *Protection and promotion of consumer interests* Many clients are in a vulnerable position when seeking advice. They may be going through a difficult personal time (for example a divorce or an insolvency) or may be making a major decision (for example buying a house). The regulator must ensure that the lawyer does not exploit the vulnerable position of the client.

4. *Promotion of competition* The regulatory framework should promote competition for legal services. This should help to keep standards high and costs low.

5. *Encouragement of a confident, strong, and effective legal profession* The regulation can ensure that new members are appropriately trained and able to supply good-quality services, and that current members are kept up to date.

6. *Promoting public understanding of the citizen's legal rights*

Who can practise law?

In order to practise, a solicitor must:

1. have been admitted as a solicitor;

2. have his or her name on the roll; and

3. have a current practising certificate.[3]

The Legal Services Act 2007 lists reserved legal activities that can be undertaken only by solicitors or other approved persons.[4] 'Other approved persons' includes licensed conveyancers, patent attorneys, and costs drafters, who can undertake certain activities for which they have received specific training.[5] The reserved activities include the exercise of rights of audience, conducting litigation, and obtaining probate.

Key statute

Legal Services Act 2007, s. 12, offers the following definitions:

Meaning of "reserved legal activity" and "legal activity"

(1) In this Act "reserved legal activity" means—
    (a) the exercise of a right of audience;
    (b) the conduct of litigation;
    (c) reserved instrument activities;
    (d) probate activities;
    (e) notarial activities;
    (f) the administration of oaths.

---

[3] Solicitors Act 1974, s. 1.   [4] Legal Services Act 2007, ss 12, 13.
[5] Legal Services Act 2007, Sch. 4.

[...]
(3)   In this Act "legal activity" means—
    (a)   an activity which is a reserved legal activity within the meaning of this Act as origi-
        nally enacted, and
    (b)   any other activity which consists of one or both of the following—
        (i)   the provision of legal advice or assistance in connection with the application
            of the law or with any form of resolution of legal disputes;
        (ii)   the provision of representation in connection with any matter concerning the
            application of the law or any form of resolution of legal disputes.
(4)   But "legal activity" does not include any activity of a judicial or quasi-judicial nature
    (including acting as a mediator).
(5)   For the purposes of subsection (3) "legal dispute" includes a dispute as to any matter of
    fact the resolution of which is relevant to determining the nature of any person's legal
    rights or liabilities.
(6)   Section 24 makes provision for adding legal activities to the reserved legal activities.

This list of reserved activities is important because it sets out those activities that only an authorised lawyer can perform. But there are plenty of matters in which lawyers engage that are not regulated. These include many non-litigious commercial matters, claims management, and insolvency. These are often dealt with by lawyers, but need not be.

Regulatory bodies

In this section, we will describe some of the main bodies involved in regulating the legal profession.

The Legal Services Board

Overseeing all of the regulatory bodies is the Legal Services Board (LSB).

Key statute

Under the Legal Services Act 2007, s. 3(2):

The LSB has the job of promoting the regulatory objectives:

(1)   In this Act a reference to "the regulatory objectives" is a reference to the objectives of—
    (a)   protecting and promoting the public interest;
    (b)   supporting the constitutional principle of the rule of law;
    (c)   improving access to justice;

(d)   protecting and promoting the interests of consumers;

(e)   promoting competition in the provision of services within subsection (2);

(f)   encouraging an independent, strong, diverse and effective legal profession;

(g)   increasing public understanding of the citizen's legal rights and duties;

(h)   promoting and maintaining adherence to the professional principles.

(2)   The services within this subsection are services such as are provided by authorised persons (including services which do not involve the carrying on of activities which are reserved legal activities).

(3)   The "professional principles" are—

(a)   that authorised persons should act with independence and integrity,

(b)   that authorised persons should maintain proper standards of work,

(c)   that authorised persons should act in the best interests of their clients,

(d)   that persons who exercise before any court a right of audience, or conduct litiga-tion in relation to proceedings in any court, by virtue of being authorised persons should comply with their duty to the court to act with independence in the inter-ests of justice, and

(e)   that the affairs of clients should be kept confidential.

The job of the LSB is to oversee the regulation of the legal profession. It does not itself deal directly with complaints about lawyers, but it has the job of ensuring that there are adequate regulations in place. In 2013, the Ministry of Justice announced a review into the regulation of the legal profession.[6] The Bar Standards Board (BSB) and Bar Council suggested that the LSB, which had kick-started reforms to the regulation of the legal services, could now be abolished, because the regulatory systems are working well.

The Solicitors Regulation Authority

There are three main elements to the work of the Solicitors Regulation Authority (SRA). First, it sets the standards for solicitors in order to give the public confidence in the profession. The SRA defines its primary tasks in doing this as follows:

- We set the standards for qualifying as a solicitor.

- We monitor the performance of organisations that provide legal training.

- We draft the rules of professional conduct, particularly to make sure they protect the interests of clients.

- We provide authoritative guidance and rules to solicitors on ethical issues, laws and regulations that affect solicitors' work.

- We administer the roll (register) of solicitors.

[6] Ministry of Justice, *Review of Legal Services Regulation* (Ministry of Justice, 2013).

- We provide information to the public about solicitors, their work and the standards the public is entitled to expect.
- We set requirements for solicitors' continuing professional development.[7]

Its second role is to protect consumers and to protect the public interest by regulating the profession. It lists the features of this role as follows:

- We monitor solicitors and their firms to make sure they are complying with the rules.
- We exchange information with other regulators and law enforcement agencies in order to protect the public.
- We investigate concerns about solicitors' standards of practice and compliance with the rules, where necessary taking regulatory action such as reprimanding the solicitor.
- When necessary, we close down solicitors' firms so as to protect clients and the wider public, and returning papers and monies to their owners.
- We refer solicitors to the independent Solicitors Disciplinary Tribunals and deal with the prosecutions.
- We run a compensation fund to help people who have lost money as a result of a solicitor's dishonesty or failure to account for money they have received.[8]

Its third role involves consulting with the public and legal profession to ensure that the latter provides a good service.

All solicitors who practise law are required to hold a practising certificate issued by the SRA. This must be renewed each year, by means of an application that confirms that there is appropriate insurance in place[9] and that the solicitor has undertaken the necessary continuing professional development (CPD). It is a crime to practise as a solicitor without such a certificate.

The SRA regulates the work that solicitors perform. It has produced the SRA Code of Conduct 2011, which is regarded as subordinate legislation[10] in that its production is required and authorised by an Act of Parliament; although it is not produced by Parliament itself, it is produced with Parliament's authority. Solicitors who carry on investment business are subject not only to the SRA Code of Conduct, but also to the Financial Services and Markets Act 2000.

The Solicitors Disciplinary Tribunal

The Solicitors Disciplinary Tribunal (SDT) deals with allegations of serious breaches of the rules.[11] Appeal from the Tribunal lies to the High Court. The Tribunal comprises

---

[7] Solicitors Regulation Authority, *What We Do* (Solicitors Regulation Authority, 2013).

[8] SRA (n. 7).   [9] SRA, *Indemnity Insurance Rules* (SRA, 2012).

[10] *Westlaw Services Ltd v Boddy* [2011] EWCA Civ 929.

[11] R. Able, *Lawyers in the Dock: Learning from Attorney Disciplinary Proceedings* (Oxford University Press, 2009).

50 members, 32 of whom are solicitors and 18, lay members. The Tribunal was created under the Solicitors Act 1974 and is a statutory tribunal. Its primary role is to adjudicate on allegations of breaches of professional rules.[12]

The Bar Standards Board

The Bar Standards Board (BSB) has a similar role to that of the SRA, but in relation to barristers. It describes its primary roles as follows:

- Setting the education and training requirements for becoming a barrister;
- Setting continuing training requirements to ensure that barristers' skills are maintained throughout their careers;
- Setting standards of conduct for barristers;
- Monitoring the service provided by barristers to assure quality;
- Handling complaints against barristers and taking disciplinary or other action where appropriate.[13]

The Bar Tribunals and Adjudication Service

The Bar Tribunals and Adjudication Service (BTAS) organises hearings in instances of complaints against barristers.

Other regulators

Other approved regulators that can be involved in regulating the work of people who perform legal work include:

- the Master of the Faculties;
- the Council for Licensed Conveyancers (CLC);
- the Chartered Institute of Legal Executives (CILEx);
- the Chartered Institute of Patent Agents (CIPA);
- the Institute of Trade Mark Attorneys (ITMA); and
- the Costs Lawyer Standards Board (CLSB).

The Legal Ombudsman

The Legal Ombudsman was established by the Office for Legal Complaints (OLC) under the Legal Services Act 2007 and began accepting complaints on 6 October

---

[12] The Solicitors Disciplinary Tribunal (Appeals and Amendment) Rules 2011, SI 2011/2346, and the Solicitors Disciplinary Tribunal (Appeals) (Amendment) Rules 2011, SI 2011/3070, govern its procedures.
[13] Bar Standards Board, *What We Do* (BSB, 2013).

2010. The Legal Ombudsman provides a free complaints resolution service to members of the public, very small businesses, charities, and trusts.

The Legal Ombudsman can deal with complaints about the following types of lawyer (and, generally, those working for them):

- barristers;
- costs lawyers;
- legal executives;
- licensed conveyancers;
- notaries;
- patent attorneys;
- probate practitioners;
- registered European lawyers;
- solicitors; and
- trademark attorneys.

The Legal Ombudsman can hear a case only after complaints have been made to the barristers' chambers. The Ombudsman explains its service in the following way:

> The Legal Ombudsman resolves complaints about legal services. It may be that your lawyer has failed to do what they agreed, has been slow in responding, or increased their charges without explaining why. Perhaps you think you've been unreasonably refused a legal service or have been pressured to accept a service you didn't want.
>
> We will investigate your complaint and look at all the facts to reach a fair outcome. We are independent, impartial and we don't take sides. If we decide the service you received was unreasonable, we can make sure your lawyer or law firm puts it right.[14]

The Ombudsman is primarily focused on poor service rather than misconduct. Professional misconduct should be dealt with by the BSB or the SRA.

Discussion of the complaints procedures

This system of complaints was introduced under the Legal Services Act 2007. Previously, the Law Society itself had handled complaints. The review by Sir David Clementi found that there were concerns about the volume of complaints and the Law Society's handling of them.[15] As already noted, the current system is not fully independent regulation, but something of a 'halfway house'.[16] The Law Society appoints

---

[14] Legal Ombudsman, *Here to Help* (Legal Ombudsman, 2013).
[15] Clementi (n. 1), ch. 3.
[16] A. Boon, 'Professionalism under the Legal Services Act 2007' (2010) 17 International Journal of the Legal Profession 195.

the SDT, which is predominantly staffed by lawyers, but the independent LSB will oversee the regulation of the profession. This might be seen as 'reinvigorating' the legal profession by providing external focus. Alternatively, it may be seen as the state threatening to control professional work.[17]

There has been some interesting work on the kind of lawyers who have behaved wrongly. Perhaps surprisingly, age is an important factor, with older lawyers more likely to commit wrongdoing. It may be that older lawyers are likely to be in more senior positions and so are less likely to be supervised.[18] Characteristics such as pride and inability to make mistakes are also linked. Commonly, lawyers accused of wrongdoing argue that they were seeking to achieve justice. Whether that is an attempt to justify in retrospect what they did or whether it stems from a genuine belief that they know better than the rules is a matter for debate. Common too is an attitude that clients are lucky to have got such good advice from lawyers and are ungrateful for the work that lawyers do. One can imagine that years of working hard for clients whom the lawyer perceives to be richer, but less talented, than himself or herself might build up an attitude that might make it easier for the lawyer to engage in fraud.

Self-regulation

A notable feature of the regulatory bodies is that the professions are largely self-regulating. The Solicitors Regulation Authority and the Bar Standards Board were set up by the professions to organise regulation. Although they are separate from the professional bodies, they are responsible to them. By contrast, other professions are overseen by bodies selected by the government and over which the professions have no control. It should be noted, however, that the Legal Services Board is an independent body with oversight of the regulation of the profession. It was created under the Legal Services Act 2007. In the run-up to that legislation, there was considerable speculation that the legal profession might lose its ability to self-regulate. The LSB can be seen as a compromise whereby an independent body oversees the regulation, while the professions regulate themselves. Another way of seeing this is as a veiled threat: the professions will regulate themselves, but they will be watched. If they do not do the job adequately, external regulation will take place.

Looking at the issue from the perspective of the Bar, Ruth Deech makes the case for self-regulation, while recognising that it carries dangers:

> Self regulation used to be totally appropriate because of the relatively small size of the Bar, its concentration in London and a few other centres, and the constant surveillance by peers, judges and solicitors. This obviated the need for outside regulation. Now self regulation has a bad name. Self regulation, if left unchecked, can become self interest. That is the risk that must be guarded against. We need appropriate

---

[17] Boon (n. 16).   [18] Able (n. 11).

checks and balances in place to ensure that self regulation does what is necessary to reinforce independence, that is, organise the profession to ensure that its members genuinely support the rule of law and the proper administration of justice.[19]

The division between the SRA/BSB and the LSB has caused concern for some.[20] The exact relationship between these bodies will emerge over time. The more interventionist the LSB, the harder it will be for the profession to claim that it is self-regulating.
A number of reasons are given in favour of self-regulation.[21]

1. A profession can be governed by principles and rules made by people who have technical skill and knowledge of how the profession works in practice.

2. The intimate knowledge of the profession means that changes can be made quickly in response to changes in professional practice.

3. Enforcement and monitoring is easier if undertaken by those who work in the same areas as those being assessed. Less work has to be done to explain to the regulators the reasons why certain actions have been taken and regulators will easily be able to spot inappropriate practices. There will also be greater trust if the regulator is a fellow professional.

4. Changes can take place more easily because there is no need to work with third parties if amendments to regulations are required.

Why does independence matter?[22] It is because it enables clients and organisations to challenge the government of the day; it is because it secures the interpretation and application of legislation by persons who have no conflicting loyalties.[23] Independence is inseparable from the enforcement of human rights.

Another mark of being a professional is self-governance. Most professions—perhaps all—have professional bodies that seek to create rules that govern how its members should act. Of course, not all of these are ethical principles. Rules governing how a person should dress in court are not really an ethical issue. However, while deciding that the professions determine the professional codes and deal with breaches of those codes is part of the autonomy that is seen as a hallmark of professionalism, it may also be seen as an inappropriate lack of control. Allowing lawyers to be the legislators, prosecutors, judges, and juries for any breach of lawyers' professional ethics may lead some to raise an eyebrow. Many workers would like the idea of making

---

[19] R. Deech, 'How the Legal Services Act 2007 has affected regulation of the Bar' (2011) 11 Legal Information Management 89, 91.

[20] S. Patel, C. Howarth, J. Kwan, and P. McDonald, *Reform of the Legal Profession* (Wilberforce Society, 2012).

[21] C. Decker and G. Yarrow, *Understanding the Economic Rationale for Legal Services Regulation* (Regulatory Policy Institute, 2010).

[22] G. Turriff, 'The consumption of lawyer independence' (2010) 17 International Journal of the Legal Profession 283.

[23] The Law Society of Upper Canada, *Task Force on the Rule of Law and the Independence of the Bar* (The Law Society of Upper Canada, 2006), para. 1.

their own rules, and then deciding how and when to enforce them. This is especially ironic in the case of lawyers, who are involved in a legal system applying to others who have very little control over the promulgation and enforcement of the law.

However, the issue is not straightforward, as we shall see. If it is alleged that a lawyer handled a case badly, does anyone apart from another lawyer have the skill to determine whether the first lawyer gave bad advice? A layperson is simply not in a position to know whether the lawyer's advice on the interpretation of a contract, for example, was negligent or not. Further, if the government takes on the role of investigation, it may pick on lawyers who are effective in bringing litigation against the government itself or who stand up for the rights of unpopular individuals, rather than seek out wrongdoing. While professional regulation brings with it dangers, so too does leaving regulation to the government.

There are two major problems with self-regulation. First, there is an incentive for the regulator to entrench the profession's monopoly: if the regulator of the legal profession *is* the legal profession, it will be in its own interests to restrict who can become a lawyer and who can carry out legal work.[24] Second, there is the problem of perception: self-regulation can create the appearance of lawyers 'looking after their own'.

The traditional model of regulation has required a clear separation between the regulator and the regulated. However, there is some support for 'responsive regulation'. Julian Webb and Donald Nicolson describe this in the following way:

> Responsive regulation is fundamentally concerned with developing...a positive conception of trust, drawing on a recursive relationship between the actors. This requires that regulation is grounded in 'reflexive' relationships characterised by integrity, flexibility and participation in decision-making, by diffusion of authority and less top-down administration.[25]

The SRA Code of Conduct

The SRA has produced the SRA Handbook, the latest version of which appeared in April 2013.

Follow the Code

The Handbook explains its aim as follows:

> This Handbook sets out the standards and requirements which we expect our regulated community to achieve and observe, for the benefit of the clients they serve and in the general public interest.

---

[24] A. Shaked and J. Sutton, 'The self-regulating profession' (1981) 48 The Review of Economic Studies 217.

[25] J. Webb and D. Nicolson, 'Institutionalising trust: Ethics and the responsive regulation of the legal profession' (1999) 2 Legal Ethics 148, 149.

It goes on to set out in more detail:

> We are confident that the contents of this Handbook, coupled with our modern, outcomes-focused, risk-based approach to authorisation, supervision and effective enforcement will
>
> - benefit the public interest;
> - support the rule of law;
> - improve access to justice;
> - benefit consumers' interests;
> - promote competition;
> - encourage an independent, strong, diverse and effective legal profession;
> - increase understanding of legal rights and duties; and
> - promote adherence to the professional principles set out in the Legal Services Act 2007.

This Handbook provides a code of ethical conduct for solicitors. This new code departs from the style of previous codes in a striking way: it seeks to rely on principles-based regulation rather than rules-based regulation.

Principles-based regulation

Principles-based regulation can be contrasted with rules-based regulation, the latter being based on setting down detailed rules with which people are expected to comply carefully. Critics complain that rules-based regulation involves 'nit-picking bureaucracy in which compliance with detailed provisions is more important than...the overall outcome'.[26]

A particular concern is that rules-based regulation leaves professionals making ethical decisions simply to 'follow the rules' rather than actually to try to find out the best solution to the problem at hand. As Nick Smedley argues: '[P]ages and pages of rules can create a passive, dependent culture. The focus shifts to filling in the form correctly, rather than thinking positively and creatively about how to meet the highest standards of conduct and service.'[27]

The SRA Handbook instead prefers principles-based regulation (sometimes known as 'outcomes-based regulation', or OFR). This sets out principles that are to be followed and outcomes to be achieved, but leaves the detail of what the principles

---

[26] J. Black, *The Rise, Fall and Fate of Principles-Based Regulation*, LSE Law, Society and Economy Working Paper 17/2010 (November 2010), online at http://ssrn.com/abstract=1712862, 3.

[27] N. Smedley, *Review of the Regulation of Corporate Legal Work* (Law Society, 2009), 3.

mean for a particular situation with a particular client for the lawyer. To quote Nick Smedley again:

> Principles-based regulation, as advocated by the LSB in its draft Business Plan, focuses more on outcomes, allowing the regulated community latitude to achieve stated goals. The idea is to instil a culture of personal and corporate responsibility, maturity and commitment to higher standards.[28]

Charles Plant, chair of the SRA Board, summed up the approach in this way:

> OFR amounts to a shift in emphasis from prescriptive, rigid rules to flexible, outcomes-focused requirements…the way the legal services market is evolving demands that regulation should focus more on the quality of clients' experience—and less on prescribing the approach that firms should take.[29]

Supporters of the new principles-based regulation claim that it allows a solicitor to find the solution to an ethical dilemma that best fits the relationship with a client. For example, what might resolve the dilemma in a case involving an elderly confused client might not be appropriate if the client were an experienced business person. We might be happy to allow the business person to consent to allow a solicitor to act in a case involving a conflict of interest, but not a vulnerable client.

They also acknowledge that there is a danger that a rules-based approach can produce an absurd result if applied without thought to the particular case. Bronwen Still gives the example of a rule saying that solicitors must pay clients any interest earned on money held on their behalf.[30] She argues that if the amount of money were tiny, it might be absurd to require the lawyer to send off a cheque for a few pence. Indeed, in the case of large company, it may cost the company more to deal with the cheque than the value of the cheque itself.

The SRA Code of Conduct is structured by means of certain outcomes that a solicitor should achieve. These outcomes are supported by 'indicative behaviours'. These are seen as examples of ways in which the outcomes might be achieved. A solicitor who follows the indicative behaviour can be safe in the knowledge that he or she is behaving properly, but a solicitor may depart from the indicative behaviours if doing so would better promote the outcomes in the particular case.

A notable feature of the new Code is the lack of detailed guidance. That is deliberate. The aim is for solicitors to think about how the outcomes can be achieved for each client. What might achieve the outcome for one client may not achieve the outcome for another.

---

[28] Smedley (n. 27), 3.

[29] C. Plant, 'Our proposals for alternative business regulation', Speech delivered at *The Lawyer*'s conference on alternative business structures (8 November 2010), online at www.sra.org.uk/sra/news/plant-abs-proposals-speech.page

[30] B. Still, 'Outcomes-focused regulation: A new approach to the regulation of legal services' (2011) 11 Legal Information Management 85.

It is easy to exaggerate the difference between a rules-based approach and an outcomes-based approach. It might be pointed out that some of the 'outcomes' are very specific and look like rules. For example, under the complaints procedure, one outcome is that clients must be notified of their right to complain to the Legal Ombudsman. That looks very much like a rule. Similarly, the outcomes requiring that there is no conflict of interest, breach of a solicitor's undertaking, or breach of confidentiality look rather like rules, even if expressed as outcomes.

The ten Principles

The Handbook opens with ten Principles that underpin the SRA Code of Conduct.

Follow the Code

You must:

1. uphold the rule of law and the proper administration of justice;
2. act with integrity;
3. not allow your independence to be compromised;
4. act in the best interests of each *client*;
5. provide a proper standard of service to your *clients*;
6. behave in a way that maintains the trust the public places in you and in the provision of legal services;
7. comply with your legal and regulatory obligations and deal with your regulators and ombudsmen in an open, timely and co-operative manner;
8. run your business or carry out your role in the business effectively and in accordance with proper governance and sound financial and risk management principles;
9. run your business or carry out your role in the business in a way that encourages equality of opportunity and respect for diversity; and
10. protect *client* money and *assets*.

The SRA explains: 'We expect you to act in accordance with the Principles in everything you do; for example, when dealing with clients, or the SRA.'[31] It also acknowledges that, in some cases, these Principles will conflict. In such a case, the following advice is offered: 'Where two or more Principles come into conflict, the Principle which takes precedence is the one which best serves the public interest in the particular circumstances, especially the public interest in the proper administration of justice.'[32]

---

[31] Solicitors Regulation Authority, *Outcomes-Focused Regulation at a Glance* (SRA, 2011).
[32] SRA (n. 31), para. 2.2.

Outcomes and indicative behaviours

Having set out the ten Principles, the Handbook then proceeds to discuss particular issues. In broad terms, these are described as:

- You and your client
- You and your business
- You and your regulator
- You and others[33]

It does so by setting out objectives and indicative behaviours.[34] The guidance sets out the difference between these:

> Outcomes we require which, when achieved, benefit users of legal Services and the public at large. These Outcomes are mandatory and, when achieved, will help ensure compliance with the Principles in the particular contexts covered by the various chapters in the Code. We recognise that these mandatory Outcomes may be achieved in a variety of ways depending on the particular circumstances, and we have supplemented the mandatory Outcomes with non-mandatory 'Indicative Behaviours' to aid compliance. The Indicative Behaviours which we set out are not exhaustive: the Outcomes can be achieved in other ways. We encourage firms to consider how they can best achieve the Outcomes taking into account the nature of the firm, the particular circumstances and, crucially, the needs of their particular clients.[35]

In short, the outcomes must be achieved. The indicative behaviours are good ways, but not the only ways, of achieving these outcomes.

Examples of the outcomes and indicative behaviours will be given throughout this book. But to give an example of why the Code is structured in this way, the following is an example.

Follow the Code

Outcome 1.1 requires:

> you treat your *clients* fairly

Indicative Behaviour 1.3 requires:

> …ensuring that the *client* is told, in writing, the name and status of the person(s) dealing with the matter and the name and status of the person responsible for its overall supervision

---

[33] SRA (n. 31), 12.   [34] SRA (n. 31), 12.   [35] SRA (n. 31), 12.

Nearly always, informing the client in writing who is dealing with the matter and who is responsible for overall supervision will be part of treating a client fairly. But you could imagine cases in which that might not be appropriate. If the client has been dealing with the lawyer for years and knows very well who is dealing with the case, he or she may not need to be told. A client who cannot read may not need the advice in writing, preferring it instead in another form. By making this an indicative behaviour, the Code allows solicitors to use common sense to ensure that clients know what they need to know.

 What would you do?

An ethical dilemma arises and your partner instructs you to act in a way that clearly breaches one of the indicative behaviours in the Code. You discuss this with the partner; he says that is the way in which the firm has always dealt with this issue and no one has complained. How will you satisfy yourself that you are acting in line with the Code?

What would they do?

This 'What would you do?' scenario is accompanied by a podcast in which current law students debate the issues and articulate their own responses to the ethical questions that it raises. The podcast is available online at www.oxfordtextbooks.co.uk/orc/herringethics/

Issues around codes

There has been quite some debate over what a lawyer's ethics code should try to do.

How detailed the guidance should be

The debate between principles-based regulation and rules-based regulation high-lights the central problem. The more detailed the rules are, the greater the risk that lawyers following the 'letter of the rules' will not, in fact, achieve an ethical result.[36] On the other hand, if a code seeks to highlight general principles, it will be vague and some think that it will lose its value.[37] John Flood has expressed the concern that large law firms are manipulating the UK's principles-based regulatory system to promote

---

[36] A. Crawley and J. Bramall, 'Professional rules, codes, and principles affecting solicitors (or what has professional regulation to do with ethics?)', in R. Cranston (ed.) *Legal Ethics and Professional Responsibility* (Oxford University Press, 2005).

[37] D. Edmonds, 'Training the lawyers of the future: A regulator's view', Lord Upjohn Lecture (19 November 2010), online at www.legalservicesboard.org.uk/news_publications/speeches_presentations/2010/de_lord_upjohn_lec.pdf

their own narrow self-interests.[38] He has suggested that large law firms have sought to 'exploit' the principles-based approach 'to arrogate power to themselves' and to 'escape considerable, though not all, regulatory oversight'.[39]

As Donald Nicolson argues:

> Detailed ethical codes undermine ethical evaluation. They tend to replace ethical decision-making with mindless conformity to rules and inadvertently suggest that compliance with the code is sufficient for moral behaviour because all possible ethical dilemmas have been considered by the experts.[40]

A further problem with detailed ethical codes is that they can quickly become out of date, with new technologies and new practices changing what might be regarded as standard behaviour. Without regular updating, detailed codes can come to be seen as irrelevant.[41] The benefit of more generalised principles is that they will require less updating.[42]

Are codes about enforcement?

The traditional approach to regulation has been to lay out a set of rules and then to provide a system for dealing with complaints made by the public. John Briton and Scott McLean have set out some of the difficulties with such a 'complaints-driven' approach, which can be summarised as follows.[43]

1. The complaints-driven approach focuses on the conduct of individual lawyers. It involves the punishment of individuals who breach the ethical codes. However, this ignores the fact that lawyers are influenced by the culture of the firms in which they work. As Briton and McLean put it, a complaints-driven approach identifies and deals with the '"bad egg" lawyers, but leaves incubator law firms off limits'.[44]

2. Complaints-driven processes are highly selective in their application. Briton and McLean argue that lawyers working in the areas of family law, personal injury, conveyancing, or probate are many times more likely to be the subject of complaints as compared with those who work in commercial litigation, banking, or construction law. Yet there is no reason to believe the latter groups are more ethical than the former.

---

[38] J. Flood, 'The landscaping of the legal profession: Large law firms and professional re-regulation' (2011) 59 Current Sociology 507.   [39] Flood (n. 38), 508.

[40] D. Nicolson, 'Mapping professional legal ethics: The form and focus of the ethics' (1998) 1 Legal Ethics 51, 64.

[41] D. Morgan, 'Doctoring legal ethics: Studies in irony in legal ethics and professional responsibility', in R. Cranston (ed.) Legal Ethics and Professional Responsibility (Oxford University Press, 2005).

[42] Nicolson (n. 40).

[43] J. Briton and S. McLean, 'Incorporated legal practices: Dragging the regulation of the legal profession into the modern era' (2008) 11 Legal Ethics 241.

[44] Briton and McLean (n. 43), 242.

3. Complaints-driven processes focus on minimum standards. They punish conduct that falls well below the line of acceptable standards, but do nothing to promote behaviours of the highest standard.

4. Complaint-driven processes are reactive. They respond to wrongs only once they have happened, but they do not prevent bad conduct from occurring in the first place. It is true that responding to complaints can be seen as providing a deterrent, but that is a narrow focus to prevention.

Another point that could be added to these is that complaints-driven models usually rely on clients bringing complaints. There are two difficulties with this. The first is that it does not deal with cases in which clients do not have the capacity to complain: when the clients are those with mental illness, for example. Second, it does not deal with unethical conduct that does not harm an identified client, but which is more generally contrary to the public good. Then, there may be no individual with sufficient interest to make the complaint.

One view is that codes should set out what behaviour is unacceptable and should lead to sanctions. Another view is that codes should also provide guidance in cases in which there is no clearly wrong answer, but two permissible alternatives. In such cases, the code might offer guidance to indicate what will be the most ethical course of action, even though taking the less desirable action will not be bad enough to warrant censure. In other words, is the code designed simply to stop the worst kind of behaviour or is the code also to promote the ideal behaviour?[45]

One of the problems that can arise with professional codes generally is that part of them gets ignored. Everyone in the profession overlooks the detail of particular provisions and the enforcers overlook the failure to comply.[46] It may be that the requirement has become obsolete or is simply too burdensome to be realistic and may even be widely accepted as an error. This is a very familiar aspect of regulation and occurs in many walks of life. Good practice is for those overseeing codes to check regularly whether there are obsolete provisions of this kind that need to be rejected. However, the existence of these ignored and unenforced provisions is problematic. There may be provisions on which there is no consensus whether the regulation is, in effect, a 'dead one'.[47] This lack of consensus may mislead lawyers to believe that they will not get into trouble for behaving in a particular way when they will. Worse, it might lead to a lessening of respect for the code if 'comply with the parts with which it makes sense to comply' becomes the norm.

[45] N. Moore, 'The complexities of lawyer ethics code drafting: The contributions of Professor Fred Zacharias' (2011) 48 San Diego Law Review 335.

[46] F. Zacharias, 'What lawyers do when nobody's watching: Legal advertising as a case study of the impact of underenforced professional rules' (2002) 87 Iowa Law Review 971.

[47] J. Sahl, 'Behind closed doors: Shedding light on lawyer self-regulation—What lawyers do when nobody's watching' (2011) 48 San Diego Law Review 447.

One code for all lawyers?

There is an issue over the extent to which it is possible to produce one set of guidance that applies to all solicitors. The practices of the lawyer who focuses on domestic violence cases for little or no pay are a world away from those of the lawyer in the city with large businesses as clients, negotiating deals worth millions of pounds. Both will face profound ethical dilemmas in their work, but those dilemmas will be of a very different kind. The kinds of protections that an individual client seeking advice on his or her welfare entitlements needs from the code are utterly different from the protections needed by a client who is an international corporation.[48]

Indeed, in his review, Nick Smedley suggested that the kind of regulation promoted by the SRA was largely irrelevant for large firms.[49] He suggested creating a 'Corporate Regulation Group' within the SRA, which could then produce guidance tailored to the needs of commercial practice.[50] One issue that the specific guidance could address is how ethical principles work in the international arena in which there are competing understandings of ethical principles.[51] Opponents of this suggestion argue that such an approach would lead to the fragmentation of the solicitors' profession. Solicitors should accept one code for all, even if some will find portions of the code more relevant than others. The idea of a separate code for commercial law firms would not be as revolutionary as it sounds, however: large law firms already arrange their own legal practice courses (as we shall see later in this chapter).

The legal status of codes

There has been discussion of the codes in the case law and the following points appear to be well established.

- Simply because conduct is prohibited by the code does not mean that the behaviour is illegal.[52] The codes set out 'professional conduct', not legality.[53]
- A judge can decide that provisions of a code are in error. In *Thai Trading Co. v Taylor*,[54] a provision under the Solicitors Practice Rules was said to be inapplicable after the court decided that the case law underpinning them should be overruled.

---

[48] C. Sampford and S. Parker, 'Legal regulation, ethical standard-setting and institutional design', in S. Parker and C. Sampford (eds) *Legal Ethics and Legal Practice: Contemporary Issues* (Oxford University Press, 1996).   [49] Smedley (n. 27).

[50] R. Lee, 'Liberalisation of legal services in Europe: Progress and prospects' (2000) 30 Legal Studies 186.

[51] L. Etherington and R. Lee, 'Ethical codes and cultural context: Ensuring legal ethics in the global law firm' (2007) 14 Indiana Journal of Global Legal Studies 6.

[52] *Picton Jones v Arcadia* [1989] 1 EGLR 43.   [53] *Giles v Thompson* [1993] 3 All ER 321.

[54] [1998] 2 WLR 893.

- It seems that a distinction may be drawn between the core codes and supplementary guidance, with the core codes having a stronger status than supplementary guidance.[55]

- Breach of a code could be evidence of negligence. However, it does not follow that because a lawyer has breached a code that therefore he or she was negligent. That said, if conduct did breach the code, a lawyer would face an uphill task claiming that the breach was reasonable.

Digging deeper

A good ethical lawyer will need to:

1. be able to identify that there is an ethical issue that needs addressing;

2. be equipped to determine what is the best response to the ethical issue; and

3. have the character and determination to carry that decision through.

The ethical codes primarily focus on the second of these skills.[56] A person is likely to consult the code only if he or she thinks that there is an issue on which direction is needed.

The first skill, identifying that there is an ethical problem, is one that is difficult to teach. Some believe that everyone has a 'conscience'—that is, a kind of inner voice that will warn them that what they are doing is wrong. But not everyone is convinced by that.

Notably, the third skill is one that is little dealt with in the code. Perhaps most cases of wrongdoing by lawyers have been ones in which lawyers know that they are doing the wrong thing, but do it anyway.[57]

The Bar Council Code of Conduct

The Bar Council Code of Conduct (the Bar Code) is notably shorter than the SRA Code. This is perhaps unsurprising. Barristers do not have to handle clients' money and their contact with clients is less direct. There are therefore fewer issues with which to deal.

Follow the Code

The Bar Code, para 105, explains:

> A barrister must comply with this Code which (save as otherwise provided) applies to all barristers whenever called to the Bar.

---

[55] *Garbutt v Edwards* [2005] All ER (D) 316.

[56] R. Moorhead, V. Hinchly, C. Parker, D. Kershaw, and S. Holm, *Designing Ethics Indicators for Legal Services Provision* (Legal Services Board, 2012).

[57] L. Levin, 'Misbehaving lawyers: Cross-country comparisons' (2012) 15 Legal Ethics 357.

The general purpose of the Code is said, in para 104, to be the following:

> The general purpose of this Code is to provide the requirements for practice as a barrister and the rules and standards of conduct applicable to barristers which are appropriate in the interests of justice and in particular:
>
> (a) in relation to self-employed barristers to provide common and enforceable rules and standards which require them:
>   (i) to be completely independent in conduct and in professional standing as sole practitioners;
>   (ii) to act only as consultants instructed by solicitors and other approved persons (save where instructions can be properly dispensed with);
>   (iii) to acknowledge a public obligation based on the paramount need for access to justice to act for any client in cases within their field of practice;
> (b) to make appropriate provision for:
>   (i) barrister managers, employees and owners of Authorised Bodies; and
>   (ii) employed barristers taking into account the fact that such barristers are employed to provide legal services to or on behalf of their employer.

The general principles

Just like the SRA Code, the Bar Code has some key principles.

Follow the Code

The Bar Code, para 301, reads:

> A barrister must have regard to paragraph 104 and must not:
>
> (a) engage in conduct whether in pursuit of his profession or otherwise which is:
>   (i) dishonest or otherwise discreditable to a barrister;
>   (ii) prejudicial to the administration of justice; or
>   (iii) likely to diminish public confidence in the legal profession or the administration of justice or otherwise bring the legal profession into disrepute;
> (b) engage directly or indirectly in any occupation if his association with that occupation may adversely affect the reputation of the Bar or in the case of a practising barrister prejudice his ability to attend properly to his practice.

The Bar Code then goes on to deal with detailed provisions governing the practice of the Bar. We will examine these at the appropriate points throughout this book. Notably, these do not rely on the same distinction between 'outcomes' and 'indicative behaviours' as the SRA Code of Conduct; rather, they present the more traditional approach of setting out what conduct is or is not permitted.

Alternatives

We have grown accustomed to the idea of professional bodies publishing ethical guide-lines, but there are alternatives. We could simply leave ethical matters to the individual autonomy of the lawyer concerned. Should that lawyer behave clearly unethically, he or she would be subject to punishment, but otherwise ethical issues would be matters of indi-vidual conscience. In favour of such a view would be the argument that on many matters of ethical behaviour there are a range of acceptable views and that it would be wrong for the profession to presume a single ethical stance.[58] Further, such an approach would rec-ognise that the ethical thing to do will depend so much on the particular circumstances of the case that generalised guidance is not very helpful. Finally, it can be argued that ethical issues need careful thought and balancing of principles. Encouraging lawyers to think that ethical dilemmas are resolved by means of following rules is encouraging lazy thinking.[59]

These are strong points. However, if people are to be punished for acting unethi-cally, they are entitled to know what the profession will regard as 'unethical'. Second, some practitioners may have no clear intuitive sense of what is the right thing to do and believe that, in such a case, guidance should be offered by the professional bodies. This is especially so given the general lack of ethical education provided both gener-ally and especially in law schools. Third, it is important that the public has complete confidence in the legal profession. The existence of a code marks the profession's com-mitment to ethical practice and gives the public reassurance that lawyers take their ethical obligations seriously.

A rather different approach is to allow clients and lawyers to set out the ethical prin-ciples that will govern their relationship. Indeed, there is some evidence that, in com-mercial practice, some large companies require lawyers acting for them to agree to an ethical code.[60] This may have an attraction for a company that sells itself as being, for example, 'green' or as having an ethical approach. It will want those who act on its behalf to follow the same approach to preserve its reputation. It also has the benefit for interna-tional companies of ensuring that, wherever they are in the world, their lawyers are fol-lowing the same guidance. There is, of course, no problem with a firm agreeing to taken on heightened obligations beyond those set out in the professional codes. The problem will arise where the agreement between the firm and client permits conduct that would otherwise breach the professional code. As we shall see in this book, there are several ethi-cal principles under which the consent of a client means that the code is not breached. An example would be confidentiality: if the client consents to the disclosure of confidential material, there is no breach of ethics. However, breach of other principles cannot be justi-fied by claims that the conduct was required by the client. So, obviously, it is no defence to an allegation that a lawyer lied to the court if the lawyer claims that the client required

---

[58] W. Simon, 'Ethical discretion in lawyering' (1988) 101 Harvard Law Review 1083.
[59] Nicolson (n. 40).
[60] C. Whelan and N. Niv, 'Privatizing professionalism: Client control of lawyers' ethics' (2012) 80 Fordham Law Review 2577.

him or her to do so. Andrew Boon has raised another concern.[61] He worries that, under principles-based regulation:

> Firms may have a very different practice on a particular ethical issue than that of a neighbouring firm and divergence could magnify over time. The risk here is that the common ground of professional ethics is lost, with each firm becoming an 'ethical silo'.[62]

There has been an interesting shift in the role of regulation. In the past, the primary role of the regulator was to issue guidance and to handle complaints from the public about lawyers who breached the guidance. There have been two tensions here. The first is the extent to which the regulators should deal with cases in which the complaint is not that the behaviour is unethical as such, but rather that the lawyer has simply done a bad job. Traditionally, regulators have seen complaints of negligent work as a matter to be dealt with by suing in the courts. However, the division between conduct that is unethical and that which is negligent is now coming under pressure. Second, there is a tension over the extent to which regulators are meant to ensure compliance with the guidance or whether their role is simply to respond to complaints from the public.[63]

With this in mind, it might be questioned whether it is helpful to have separate codes for barristers and solicitors. Might it be more helpful to have codes based on categories of work?[64]

Complaints about solicitors

A client who is unhappy about the way in which the lawyer has treated him or her is likely to start by making a complaint to the law firm itself. The SRA Code requires that all complaints are dealt with fairly and promptly.

Follow the Code

O 1.9 clients are informed in writing at the outset of their matter of their right to complain and how complaints can be made;

O 1.10 clients are informed in writing, both at the time of engagement and at the conclusion of your complaints procedure, of their right to complain to the Legal Ombudsman, the time frame for doing so and full details of how to contact the Legal Ombudsman;

O 1.11 clients' complaints are dealt with promptly, fairly, openly and effectively;

---

[61] Boon (n. 16).   [62] Boon (n. 16), 213.

[63] L. Haller, 'Professional discipline for incompetent lawyers? Developments in the UK and Australia' (2010) 17 International Journal of the Legal Profession 83.

[64] Patel et al. (n. 20).

When a lawyer faces a disciplinary tribunal, there is considerable discretion as to how the case is dealt with. The case law does provide some limited guidance, which can be helpful. The following are some of the key principles to emerge.

- Where a lawyer makes a genuine and honest mistake on a matter of professional judgement, it is unlikely that this will result in disciplinary proceedings.[65] If the decision that the lawyer made was one that no reasonably competent solicitor could have made, however, it could be inferred that it was not a genuine mistake because the lawyer could not have properly addressed the issue.

- If a finding of misconduct is reached, then adequate reasons must be given for this finding.[66]

- Sometimes, conduct by a lawyer outside his or her professional work was so serious as to undermine the confidence in the profession and so could be subject to professional sanctions.[67]

Able argues that it is not really ignorance of the rules that is the problem.[68] It is also notable that apologies and an assessment of character play relatively little role.[69]

Barristers

Surprisingly, barristers had no effective complaints system until 1997. Since 2006, the Bar Standards Board has dealt with complaints. This now operates under the Legal Services Board.

All chambers now operate an internal complaints procedure. The head of chambers has the responsibility for setting up such a procedure and ensuring that it operates successfully.

Bar Standards Board complaints procedure

A disappointed client now has an alternative remedy to launching proceedings against a barrister. Clients can complain to the BSB about inadequate professional service and may be awarded up to £15,000 in compensation, although compensation is limited to the loss that is recoverable at law. The case is heard by a disciplinary tribunal. If the tribunal dismisses the complaint, then the client can complain to the Legal Ombudsman, who has the power to award compensation.

---

[65] *Connelly v Law Society* [2007] EWHC 1175.
[66] *Quinn v Bar Standards Board*, 23 February 2013.
[67] *Afolabi v Solicitors Regulation Authority* [2012] EWHC 3502 (Admin).
[68] Able (n. 11).
[69] F. Bartlett, 'The role of apologies in professional discipline' (2011) 14 Legal Ethics 49.

The complaint may be heard by a three- or five-person disciplinary tribunal. This is chaired typically by a Queen's Counsel (QC) or a judge. The panel will also contain a barrister and a layperson. The most serious sentence that a three-person panel can impose is a suspension for up to three months. A five-person tribunal can suspend barristers for any period of time or strike them off (disbar them).

The tribunal will focus on whether or not there has been professional misconduct—defined as the barrister not adhering to the Code. It cannot cover complaints that are not covered by the Code, for example simply that the advice given was wrong.

The BSB gives the following as an example of how it might handle a complaint:

A litigant in person in a family case complained to the BSB that opposing counsel in the case had lied to the Court. The complainant said that the barrister had deliberately given false information about the history of the case and had not given the Court important financial statements.

Our Assessment Team looked at the complaint first to see if there was evidence of a possible breach of the Code of Conduct. The Assessment Team then passed it to our Investigation and Hearings Team for a formal investigation to be carried out.

Evidence was gathered as part of the investigation, including the comments of all relevant people involved and transcripts of hearings. That evidence showed that the barrister appeared to have breached the Code of Conduct and those breaches were serious. The investigation file was then sent to a barrister member of the Professional Conduct Committee for a report, with recommendations on future action, to be prepared for presentation to the full Committee. At the Committee meeting, the Committee discussed the case and agreed that:

- there was evidence that the barrister had misled the Court;
- there were reasonable prospects of securing a finding of professional misconduct in front of a Tribunal; and
- the regulatory objectives would best be served by taking disciplinary action.

The Committee also took the view that the charges were serious, and if proved, the barrister might be suspended from practice for more than three months. The Committee therefore referred the case to a 5 person Disciplinary Tribunal on two charges of misleading the court contrary to paragraph 302 of the Code.

Following the necessary preparation by the BSB and the service of formal charges on the barrister, an independent Disciplinary Tribunal was convened by the Council of the Inns of Court (COIC). The Tribunal considered all the documentary and oral evidence including all information that the barrister put forward. The Tribunal found the charges proved on the basis that it was sure beyond a reasonable doubt that the barrister had misled the court about the history of proceedings and that crucial financial statements had not been presented to the Court. This meant that the complainant's ability to present her case to the Court had been adversely affected. The Tribunal suspended the barrister from practising for 18 months and ordered the barrister to pay the costs of the hearing.

Scandal!

An enquiry was put in place to investigate the way in which the BSB dealt with complaints about the behaviour of barristers. The LSB found, in 2013, that complaints had lain unresolved for years. There were some cases going back a decade. The investigation found that two in three of those who complain to the BSB think that they are treated unfairly.[70]

The structure of the barristers' profession

Chambers

Barristers can practise only as sole practitioners. Traditionally, barristers cannot set up a company and operate through that, at least while purporting to act as barristers. That is still the general rule, but through alternative business structures (considered later in this chapter), they may now be able to do so. Most barristers are self-employed and the significance of that is set out in the Bar Code.

Follow the Code

The Bar Code, para 104(a), requires barristers:
(i)   to be completely independent in conduct and in professional standing as sole practitioners;
(ii) to act only as consultants instructed by solicitors and other approved persons (save where instructions can be properly dispensed with).

It is, however, common for barristers to combine in chambers. There is no need for them to do this and they can operate alone, but most choose to join chambers. By combining with other barristers, they can share the costs of rent, training, and marketing. Typically, a QC will head a chambers, but this is not compulsory. Often, a chambers will have several QCs, but most will be junior counsel. The average size of chambers is around 30 barristers. Most will also have pupil barristers, who are training. There are also often door tenants, who can practise from the building, but are not formally members of the chambers. In England and Wales, there are around 300 sets of chambers.

It is common for chambers to employ a chambers clerk. Despite its name, this is a senior and generally well-paid position. The clerk—in bigger chambers, supported by

---

[70] Legal Services Board, *Developing Regulatory Standards* (Legal Services Board, 2013).

a team of assistants—arranges the day-to-day work of the chambers. Most importantly, the clerk receives briefs and allocates them between barristers. It is a little-known secret that it is very important for barristers to develop a good relationship with the clerks! Some chambers employ a professional chambers manager.

Barristers and briefs

Barristers have traditionally been forbidden from acting directly for clients, but can do so if briefed by a solicitor. Historically, this can be seen as the deal between the professions: only barristers can advocate in court, but they can do so only if briefed by a solicitor. While the attraction of this arrangement is evident from the point of view of the professions, some clients feel that they are being made to pay twice. Further, they find that the person representing their case in court is someone whom they have met only briefly (excuse the pun!) and with whom they have not had the chance to develop a relationship of trust.

There are arguments in favour of this division. It offers the client a second opinion from an expert who is not influenced by knowing the client personally and who will offer a fresh look, of the kind that a court will take.

In recent years, direct access to barristers has gradually increased. Now, it is possible for members of the public to instruct barristers themselves. However, there are important restrictions: this can happen only if the barrister has had more than three years' call and has attended a training course on dealing with the public, keeping records, and money-laundering regulations. The direct-access barristers must be registered with the Bar Council. Further, certain matters cannot be dealt with by direct access—notably, criminal proceedings, family cases, and immigration issues.

Although the ban on public access to barristers has been lifted a little, as will be seen from these exclusions many important issues cannot be dealt with in that way. Further, barristers are not permitted to hold client funds and cannot issue proceedings or serve documents. This limits the kinds of matters that a client might want to instruct a barrister to do. Where direct access is used, it is typically used to obtain advice (counsel's opinion) on a particular matter or to engage in advocacy for a small-scale piece of litigation.[71]

Licensed access to the Bar can be claimed in two ways: first, by members of a professional body who are automatically given access to the Bar, which includes members of the Institute of Chartered Accountants in England and Wales (ICAEW), for example; second, individuals or bodies with specialist knowledge can apply to the BSB and seek a licence to have direct access. Some police forces have done this. Where barristers are doing licensed access work, there is no need for a special training, although there are restrictions on when they can undertake advocacy.

---

[71] J. Flood and A. Whyte, 'Straight there, no detours: Direct access to barristers' (2009) 16 International Journal of the Legal Profession 131.

Unlicensed access is permitted for any person. However, the barrister must be satisfied that it is not in the client's best interests to use a solicitor, and that the barrister and client can complete any necessary court work themselves.

The guidance from the Bar Council includes the following list of factors to consider when determining whether a client would be better off using a solicitor:

- Complexity of the case

- Nature of the lay client (some lay clients may be better suited to dealing with a barrister directly than others)

- Capacity of the lay client to carry out the facets of the case that the barrister cannot (correspondence with the Court, filing of documents etc)

- Availability of the barrister related to the probable length of the case

- Whether the administration of justice requires a solicitor

- Whether the client, for whatever reason, is unable to communicate easily with the barrister and therefore, for example, requires an interpreter. The need for an interpreter to be instructed in the case would greatly increase the likelihood that the case would not be suited to the public access scheme.

- However, each case should be considered individually[72]

Crime, family, and immigration work cannot be done on this basis. To do unlicensed work, barristers must have practised for three years since finishing pupillage and completed a training course. Although quite a number of barristers have completed the course, for complex cases and those involving non-professional clients, most barristers prefer a client to be represented by a solicitor.

It would certainly be wrong to say that the barristers' and solicitors' professions have now fused. The gates have been opened, however, and with alternative business structures becoming popular, the professions are likely to grow ever closer in the future.

Becoming a Queen's Counsel

As a barrister gains experience and reputation, he or she may seek to become a QC. This is sometimes known as 'taking silk'. This is usually after at least ten years' practice. QCs can typically ask for higher rates of pay and take on only more complex cases. In particularly complex cases, a QC may be assisted by a junior barrister. Originally, QCs were appointed in an informal process, involving discussions with the judiciary. Now, there is a more open applications process. Applicants must apply anonymously, and include references from judges and clients. Applications for silk are then considered by a panel. There is a hefty fee for the application. Notably, since the process has become more open, a larger number of women and black and minority ethnic (BME)

---

[72] Bar Council, *Public Access Work: Guidance for Barristers* (Bar Council, 2010), para. 44.

applicants have been appointed, although they are still underrepresented. That issue will be discussed further in Chapter 14.

McKenzie friend

If someone is not entitled to legal aid and cannot afford a lawyer, one option is to use a 'McKenzie friend', who can act as an advocate on the person's behalf. Usually, this will be someone with some legal knowledge, but who is not a trained lawyer. Before someone can act as a McKenzie friend, he or she needs the leave of the court. The Court of Appeal has confirmed that there is a presumption in favour of allowing a McKenzie friend, but if it is an unsuitable person, leave may be refused.[73] In *Re F*,[74] leave to appoint a McKenzie friend was refused because the person wishing to act was a campaigner against the whole family justice system, who had breached confidentiality in other cases and who failed to understand the role of a McKenzie friend. Where a McKenzie friend cannot be found, a person can act alone.

Alternative business structures

Solicitors typically operate through a partnership or a company. These firms often employ not only solicitors, but also support staff, paralegals, and trainee solicitors. Traditionally, a solicitors' firm has not been permitted to offer services other than legal services. For example, a firm could not set itself up as both a firm of solicitors and an estate agent. If a firm had been keen to do this, it would have needed to create two separate businesses that could be closely connected, but which would officially have had to be kept separate. Where there are close links, there are concerns that conflicts of interests can arise, and lawyers need to act carefully. For example, the close links between solicitors and claims firms have been said by some to create ambiguities for clients. In the Legal Services Act 2007, however, the law was changed to provide much more flexibility and to permit the creation of 'alternative business structures' (ABSs). These now mean that a single body can provide legal, accountancy, and other services.[75] Under ABSs, lawyers can now work alongside other professionals, and, indeed, even non-lawyers can own and manage firms. This means that not only might a firm of solicitors now employ an accountant and offer 'one-stop shop' legal and accountancy services, but also that non-legal groups, such as supermarkets, could employ lawyers and offer legal services—hence the nickname 'Tesco law'.

---

[73] *Mackenzie friend, Re O (Children) (Hearing in Private: Assistance)* [2005] EWCA Civ 759, [2006] Fam 1. [74] 14 May 2013.

[75] Boon (n. 16).

As will have been clear from that brief introduction, the ABS can cover a wide range of bodies. At the one extreme, they can be sophisticated services for commercial clients, combining a range of specialist professional services;[76] at the other end, they can be high-street names offering basic legal services to individuals—perhaps particularly aimed at people who would not be familiar with legal services.

The idea of non-lawyers owning legal services has not been welcomed by everyone.[77] It will pose a challenge to the attorney–client privilege (see Chapter 5) because the information given will not be restricted to a lawyer and a client. Prima facie, a lawyer is not permitted to disclose information given by a client; if the lawyer is under a manager who is a non-lawyer, then he or she may be expected to disclose the paperwork. In an ABS, the best course of action is to request the client's permission to share the information with other staff in the firm as necessary. However, a client may well be reluctant to consent to that. Further difficulties can arise with regards to conflicts of interest. The basic rule is that a firm cannot work for two clients who have conflicting interests. However, with ABSs involving a range of different professionals and particularly being owned by a range of bodies, it will become very hard for them to ensure that there are no conflict difficulties.

Lawyers may, however, welcome a new source of investment and may be able to open up new markets by providing a range of services. It is even possible that ABSs could be listed on the stock exchange and a market open up in ownership of them.

All ABSs must be approved by the Legal Services Board, although the LSB has authorised the Law Society to give approval on its behalf.[78] Once approved, non-lawyers can be involved in a professional, managerial, or ownership activity, including as partners. They cannot, of course, practise as lawyers. The ABS has proved popular, with 65 applications being made within the first two weeks of applicants being accepted. External investors may be attracted by the opportunity to invest in commercial firms, especially given their record of reliable and high profitability.

A smaller law firm may be attracted by the benefit of being linked to a well-known household brand name or simply a national group.[79] National chains, such as Face2Face Solicitors[80] and High Street Lawyer,[81] have been launched.

The client may gain from this too: greater competition may increase investment in law firms, resulting in improvement to the range of services offered. It is, however, likely that there will be a decline in the number of independent high-street firms. Reardon draws

---

[76] A. Perlman, 'Toward a unified theory of professional regulation' (2003) 55 Florida Law Review 97.

[77] K. Reardon, 'It's not your business! A critique of the UK Legal Services Act of 2007 and why nonlawyers should not own or manage law firms in the United States' (2012) 40 Syracuse Journal of International Law and Commerce 155.

[78] Legal Services Act 1997, s. 27 and Sch. 10.

[79] N. Jarrett Kerr, 'Alternative business structures: The long pregnancy' (2011) 11 Legal Information Management 82.

[80] www.face2facesolicitors.net/   [81] www.highstreetlawyer.com/

attention to the opticians market, in which, despite some big-name players, small independent opticians seem to have managed to survive.[82] There is, however, a real fear that the marketing, brand, and economic power of the large firms will offer a challenge with which small firms will not, in the long term, be able to compete.

Legal education

At the heart of professionalism is the claim that there are special skills and knowledge. It is therefore essential that all those who practise professionally as lawyers have been educated and trained to the appropriate level.

There are currently four educational elements required of all practising lawyers:

1. the qualifying law degree (QLD) or a one-year conversion course (the Graduate Diploma in Law, or GDL);
2. the vocational training year (the Legal Practice Course, or LPC, or the Bar Professional Training Course, or BPTC);
3. working as a trainee solicitor for two years or as a pupil barrister for one year (pupillage); and
4. continuing professional development (CPD) post-qualification.

We will consider each of these in turn.

The qualifying law degree

A solicitor or barrister must complete a full-time law degree, or a degree in another subject and then the graduate diploma course (commonly known as the 'conversion course'). There is another route and that is to qualify as a member of the Chartered Institute of Legal Executives (CILEx) and then to take the solicitors' vocational course.

The law degree, if it is to count for the professional bodies, has to be a qualifying law degree (QLD). It requires coverage of the six pillars:

- tort;
- crime;
- land;
- equity and trusts;
- public law; and
- European law.

This is controversial for several reasons, as we shall now see.

---

[82] Reardon (n. 77).

Which subjects are on the list?

First, there is disagreement about which subjects are or are not on the list.[83] For example, why is personal property not included, or the law of property or family law? Why is commercial law, which is important for many practising lawyers, not required? The great Peter Birks was highly critical of insistence on the foundational subjects:

> The greatest absurdity which will now be continued for the best part of a decade is the combination of a list of compulsory subjects and the impossibility of substitution. It means in effect that nearly half the time available must be clogged up with courses pitched at the most superficial level. There is so much that has to be done in each compulsory module that superficiality is inevitable. Look for example at Public Law, and calculate the time available for administrative law or human rights. A law school which wants to give depth a priority over breadth is crippled by these prescriptions, for no reason at all beyond a bureaucratic refusal to contemplate a more flexible system. If, for example, someone has done company law, commercial law, family law and labour law, no case whatever can be made for worrying about the omission of some part of the so-called foundations.[84]

For the purposes of this book, a key question is whether legal ethics should be a compulsory subject on the law degree.

Recent history on legal education has been heavily influenced by the Ormrod Report of 1971,[85] the Benson Report of 1979,[86] and the Marre Committee Report in 1989.[87] One debate that runs through these reports is the division between the academic year and the vocational year. Interestingly, the reports acknowledged that ethical issues were important for lawyers. The Benson Report states:

> It is essential that throughout their training students should be impressed with the importance of maintaining ethical standards, rendering a high quality of personal service, maintaining a good relationship with clients, providing information about work in hand for clients, avoiding unnecessary delays, maintaining a high standard in briefs and preparation for trial, promptly rendering accounts with clear explanations and attending to other matters mentioned elsewhere in this report.[88]

The Marre Report specifically acknowledged the need for 'an adequate knowledge of professional and ethical standards'[89] but it was unclear at what stage of the legal education this was to be imparted.

---

[83] R. Huxley-Binns, 'What is the "Q" for?' (2011) 45 The Law Teacher 294.

[84] P. Birks, 'Compulsory subjects: Will the seven foundations ever crumble?' (1995) 1 Web Journal of Current Legal Issues 1, 7.

[85] Justice Ormrod, *Report of the Committee on Legal Education* (Lord Chancellor's Department, 1971).

[86] R. Benson, *The Royal Commission on Legal Services* (Lord Chancellor's Department, 1979).

[87] The Committee on the Future of the Legal Profession, *A Time for Change* (General Council of the Bar and the Law Society, 1988).   [88] Benson (n. 86), para 39.47.

[89] Committee on the Future of the Legal Profession (n. 87), para. 12.21.

How law is to be taught

Another issue of controversy surrounds whether law degrees should be taught using the positivist approach towards the law—that is, the view that law can be learned by looking at the legislation and cases alone. Critics argue that we must understand the social, political, and moral context within which the law operates in order to come to a full comprehension of the law.

There is a tension among universities and even among academics over the extent to which legal study at degree level at university should be designed to prepare someone to be a lawyer. Clearly, the profession's main aim is that law degrees produce competent lawyers. However, academics seek academic respectability: wanting to engage in theoretical, interdisciplinary, and critical work. If academic lawyers are seen simply as people who teach rules to students, they will not be held in high esteem in the wider academic community. Anthony Bradney rejects the view that the law degree is about preparing people to be professional lawyers.[90] He has a grander aim: the fulfilment of human flourishing. Contrast that with the view of Stephen Mayson:

> [T]he starting point for considering changes to professional legal education must be the needs of the employment market for qualified lawyers and, in particular, those parts of the market that offer employment to the greatest number of trainees and newly qualified lawyers.[91]

Clearly, students must be part of the discussion. Their payment of fees arguably gives them a greater stake in the content of the course. Those seeking 'value for money' will seek a degree that best places them in the market to get the career that they want. 'Commercial awareness' came top in a study of what solicitors are looking for in graduates, yet few university courses teach that, at least in their compulsory courses.[92] Others emphasise the importance of the use of information technology in the modern commercial world, yet that is rarely a major part of a law degree.[93] However, it should be noted that only 60 per cent of law graduates go into legal practice, so ensuring that the degree provides a broad range of skills that might be used in a range of occupations seems sensible. Only just over half of qualified lawyers have a law degree.

---

[90] A. Bradney, 'English university law schools, the age of austerity and human flourishing' (2011) 18 International Journal of the Legal Profession 59.

[91] S. Mayson, *The Education and Training of Solicitors: Time for Change* (Legal Services Institute, 2010), 4.

[92] C. Strevens, C. Welch, and R. Welch, 'On-line legal services and the changing legal market: Preparing law undergraduates for the future' (2010) 45 The Law Teacher 328.

[93] C. Strevens, 'The changing nature of the legal services market and the implications for the qualifying law degree' (2011) 1 Web Journal of Current Legal Issues 1.

The vocational year

The vocational year comprises a one-year course: the Bar Professional Training Course (BPTC) for barristers and the Legal Practice Course (LPC) for solicitors.[94] These are designed to improve the quality of knowledge and skills needed for a practical lawyer. Their development might be seen as acknowledgement that the academic law degree was not providing the complete skill set required to practise.

The aim of vocational training has been said by the Solicitors Regulation Authority to be to:[95]

1. research and apply knowledge of the law and legal practice accurately and effectively

2. identify the client's objectives and different means of achieving those objectives and be aware of

   – the financial, commercial and personal priorities and constraints to be taken into account

   – the costs, benefits and risks involved in transactions or *courses of action*

3. perform the tasks required to advance transactions or matters

4. understand where the rules of professional conduct may impact and be able to apply them in context

5. demonstrate their knowledge, understanding and skills in the areas of:

   – Professional Conduct and Regulation

   – the core practice areas of Business Law and Practice, Property Law and Practice, Litigation and the areas of wills and administration of estates and taxation

   – the core skills of Practical Legal Research, Writing, Drafting, Interviewing and Advising, and Advocacy.

Students should also be able to transfer skills learnt in one context to another;

6. demonstrate their knowledge, understanding and skills in the three areas covered by their choice of electives, and

7. reflect on their learning and identify their learning needs.

The overarching aims of the BPTC are to:

- prepare students of the Inns of Court for practice at the Bar of England and Wales;

- prepare students for pupillage; and

- enable students of the Inns from overseas jurisdictions to acquire the skills required for practice at the Bar of England and Wales, thereby assisting them to undertake further training or practice in their home jurisdictions.

---

[94] P. Knott, 'Becoming a lawyer: Entry level training for the legal profession' (2010) 19 Nottingham Law Journal 42.

[95] SRA and BSB, *Legal Practice Course Outcomes* (SRA and BSB, 2011), 2.

Specific objectives of the course are to:

- bridge the gap between the academic study of law and the practice of law;
- provide the foundation for the development of excellence in advocacy;
- inculcate a professional and ethical approach to practice as a barrister;
- prepare students for practice in a culturally diverse society;
- prepare students for the further training to be given in pupillage;
- equip students to perform competently in matters in which they are likely to be briefed during pupillage;
- lay the foundation for future practice, whether in chambers or as an employed barrister; and
- encourage students to take responsibility for their own professional development.

In recent years, a group of major commercial firms has created a City LPC that focuses on preparing graduates to work in a commercial setting. This has proved somewhat controversial. The setting up of different training for different kinds of legal practice may be seen as a challenge to the unity of the legal profession.

Training and pupillage

The training stage involves a period of training working with a professional. For a barrister, this is a one-year pupillage; for solicitors, a two-year traineeship.[96]

Continuous professional development

Much CPD within the legal profession takes the form of lawyers remaining up to date with the latest developments in the law and procedure.[97] Although lawyers must attend CPD sessions, there is little attempt to ensure that they have understood what they have heard.

The place of ethics in legal education

As already indicated, teaching ethical principles has traditionally played a lowly part in legal education. The kindest way of putting it might be that it has been seen as a consistent theme in all topics and so as not requiring explicit articulation.

There are a number of reasons why ethics have played a relatively small part in legal education.[98] First, there is general feeling that ethics cannot be taught. If a person

---

[96] J. Ching, 'The significance of work allocation in the professional apprenticeship of solicitors' (2012) 34 Studies in Continuing Education 57.

[97] J. Ching, 'Solicitors' CPD: Time to change from regulatory stick to regulatory carrot?' (2011) 3 Web Journal of Current Legal Issues 3.

[98] J. Hodgson and N. Peck, 'How "vocational" do law schools want to be? A brief comparison of England and the USA' (2010) 19 Nottingham Law Journal 45.

is of a dishonest disposition, then there is no point teaching him or her about honesty. For many ethical issues, our consciences or instincts will tell us what to do and encouraging people to follow that is more reliable than setting down rules. Teaching ethics is therefore in danger of teaching the obvious.

Second, for some, lawyers' ethics are a matter of practice. They elide into issues such as speaking nicely to clients and negotiating well, and so are better matters for the professional training period than a law degree.

Third, there is, as will be apparent in this book, a danger of reducing ethical analysis to a set of rules. Ethical responses must be sensitive to the particular contexts and individuals involved. It may be more ethical to encourage lawyers to seek a solution to dilemmas that works for the good of the particular client in the particular context than to require them to follow abstract rules.

Fourth, there may be a question whether ethics is even appropriate to the profession. Lawyers are meant to be competitive, individualistic, ruthless, legalistic, authoritative; asking them to be moral might, in fact, be dangerous. It invites controversy: whose ethics and whose morals are we going to teach? It is interesting that writing on legal ethics, such as this book, generally avoids the controversial and focuses on the 'legal' issues, such as duties of confidentiality. What of love? Fear? Altruism? Joy? Where do these fit in with legal ethics?[99]

Support for the importance of ethics in legal education may come from a range of points of view. Brownsword suggests the following groups of supporters.[100]

1. The *legal idealist* sees law as inevitably and unavoidably moral. Legal argument must, in its nature, involve moral argument, because law grows from and is shaped by moral principles. It is simply impossible to teach or to understand law in an amoral context.

2. The *intersectionist* sees that there are some cases in which law and moral issues intersect, and that an understanding of ethics is necessary for those cases. This, if you like, is a more moderate version of the legal idealist.

3. The *contextualist* believes that the law can be understood only in its broad context. This includes the economic, political, and social realities within which the law operates; it also operates with the ethical principles prevalent in society.

4. The *liberal* argues that law degrees should give lawyers a broad education, with an understanding of the law, but also an ability to critique it—and that this requires an understanding of moral principles.

---

[99] A. Boon and J. Levin, *The Ethics and Conduct of Lawyers in England and Wales* (Hart, 2008), 166.

[100] A. Brownsword, 'Ethics in legal education: Ticks, crosses and question marks' (1987) 50 Modern Law Review 529.

Alternative view

Is it really possible to teach ethics 'in the classroom'? The world of a practising solicitor or barrister is a mystery to many students, and indeed many lecturers. It is one thing to decide what is the right thing to do within a classroom, when we have plenty of time to think, but in a high-pressure, fast-moving environment, it is far from straightforward. Further, the cultural pressures generated by the expectations of those senior to us and of the firm in general can have a powerful effect. Might it not therefore be better to delay ethics training until someone has worked for, say, a year with a firm? Or is that an argument for training both during a degree and beyond?

The delivery of ethics

If we accept that ethics should be included in a law degree, in what way should it be taught?

1. Should ethics be a stand-alone subject or included in every topic? The argument for keeping it separate is twofold. First, some topics, such as confidentiality, apply across the board, whether we are talking about family law, land law, or contract law. Unless it is given its own designated place, it may slip between the cracks and no subject will cover it, or it will become highly repetitive. Second, there is a danger that some of the broader tensions between lawyers' ethics may not be articulated. For example, the distinction between the family lawyers and commercial lawyers may never be explored if they are treated separately. On the other hand, there are dangers that if legal ethics are taught as a stand-alone topic, they will not be treated as seriously as a 'hardcore legal subject', such as contract law. They may even be 'relegated' to a sideline or as part of the general introduction to a law degree. This need not happen. More significantly, legal ethics may be seen as isolated from real practice. The solution is obvious: we need *both* approaches. Legal ethics should both be studied as a subject in its own right *and* integrated into the syllabus generally.

2. It is easy to reduce lawyer's ethics to a set of rules—'Thou shalt not'—and weaken the significance of a truly ethical approach. Deborah Rhode has warned against ethics courses becoming 'unethics...the careful delineation of precisely how far the lawyer can go without disbarment, with copious suggestions on how to do things lawyers ought not to be doing'.[101]

   There is a particular danger of this given the emphasis on commercialisation. If firms want to do everything that they can to make money and make themselves as attractive as they can to clients, there is a danger that legal ethics will be perceived

---

[101] D. Rhode, *Access to Justice* (Oxford University Press, 2004), 34.

as a barrier to those goals. The temptation is therefore to restrict ethical limitations to as narrow a band of cases as possible, so 'liberating' the lawyer to increase profit and do what the client wants.

3. There is also a danger that, by reducing ethics to rules, we rob people of ethical judgements. Some of the most unethical conduct that we have seen lawyers commit has been technically within the rules, but should have been clearly immoral. The issue here is to ensure that students realise that the rules on 'lawyers' ethics' are not meant to supplant the basic principles of behaving properly. A study of ethics should not rob someone of ethical common sense.

4. One of the difficulties is how to deal with morally controversial topics. It is understandable that universities and professions do not want to be seen clearly to take sides on a controversial issue. You do not see, for good reason, a law faculty proclaiming that it opposes the right to die and supports the right to life of a foetus—in part, no doubt, because there would be no agreement among the faculty members on such a matter. However, there is no real problem here: not many lecturers seek to turn students into clones of themselves![102] Lecturers are more likely to want to encourage students to think about and articulate the different views that can be taken. So too with ethics.

Some of these issues feed through into the style of teaching legal ethics. This tends not to be the old-fashioned way in which core subjects are often taught: setting out key definitions and central legal principles, and key cases and statutes. Rather, hypothetical scenarios are given, and students are then encouraged to discuss and explore these.

This practice has several benefits. First, students need to think through their ethical analyses and not assume that 'Everyone would agree...'. For example, I remember giving a group of students a scenario in which a professional, after a busy day at work, went home and discussed her clients with her husband. Interestingly, there was one group of students who were shocked and thought that there could be no question but that this was completely wrong. Another group were astonished that anyone would think there was anything wrong with this scenario. (This latter group contained many students who experienced this as normal home life!) At least one benefit of the exercise was that the two groups came to realise that we cannot always assume 'Everyone thinks...' on an issue.

Second, that same scenario revealed another issue. As the discussion developed, it became clear that more information was required to determine the answer. If all that the lawyer was telling her husband was that a client came in wearing a wild orange suit, no one thought that there was anything wrong with this. Similarly, if the lawyer was telling her husband information that would help the husband's business, all agreed that this would be wrong. So it became clear that much would depend on the precise circumstances.

---

[102] What an awful thought!

A third benefit of this approach is that it can bring home to students the strength of feelings. Some might see some of the rules of ethics as technical, but hearing from others the impact of a breach is powerful. I remember hearing a student describe her experience of a doctor telling her mother what the student had disclosed and discussing the impact on her life. Suddenly, the rules on protection of confidentiality did not seem so dry after all!

Another approach is using role play. There is some evidence that persuading people to act out ethical behaviour encourages people to act in that way. It also helps them to appreciate and discuss how behaving in the ethically appropriate way can be challenging. This can take place in the classroom, but more significantly as part of the traineeship that the professions offer. One of the roles of the close supervision in the first year or two of practice is to ensure that ethical standards are kept up.

Role play also encourages 'self-reflection'. Why did people act as they did? What were their true motivations? Was there a more ethical alternative? Encouraging lawyers to ask themselves these questions is good practice. Where universities offer clinical practice or pro bono work, this can perform this role too.[103]

Perhaps it is worth ending this debate over reform of legal education with a reference to the views of Lord Neuberger of Abbotsbury:

> There is real reason for doubting whether there is that much wrong. UK lawyers enjoy a high worldwide reputation. Places on our university law degrees, at both undergraduate and postgraduate levels, are highly sought after. Research and publications of academics in our universities are of high value and enjoy international recognition. Our courts and our substantive law are prized throughout the world—not only by those who seek to litigate in our courts, but also by those who seek our judges and lawyers out to assist them in the development of their laws and justice systems.[104]

The Legal Education and Training Review

In 2013, a major review of legal education and training was produced.[105] The Legal Education and Training Review (LETR) summarised its main findings as follows:

Quality

- strengthen requirements for education and training in legal ethics, values and professionalism, the development of management skills, communication skills, and equality and diversity;
- enhance consistency of education and training through a more robust system of learning outcomes and standards, and increased standardisation of assessment;

---

[103] D. Nicolson, ' "Education, education, education": Legal, moral and clinical' (2008) 42 The Law Teacher 145.

[104] Lord Neuberger of Abbotsbury, 'Lord Upjohn Lecture 2012: Reforming legal education' (2013) 47 The Law Teacher 4, 6.

[105] Legal Education and Training Review, *Setting Standards* (LETR, 2013).

- place greater emphasis on assuring the continuing competence of legal service providers through a system of continuing professional development that will require practitioners more actively to plan and demonstrate the value of continuing learning;

- require regulators to gather and make available key data and information that will reduce information gaps, support decision-making by prospective entrants, consumers and employers, and increase the effective market regulation of LSET.

Access and mobility

- establish professional standards for internships and work experience;

- enhance quality and increase opportunities for career progression and mobility within paralegal work, by encouraging regulatory and representative bodies to collaborate in the development of a single voluntary system of certification/licensing for paralegal staff, based on a common set of paralegal outcomes and standards;

- provide higher quality and more accessible information on the range of legal careers and the realities of the legal services job market;

- support and monitor the development of higher apprenticeships at levels 6–7 as a non-graduate pathway into the regulated sector.

Flexibility

- expect regulators to co-operate in setting outcomes for LSET to ensure equivalence of baseline standards;

- clarify systems for accreditation of prior learning and transfer between professional routes, and ensure that these do not create unnecessary barriers to progression;

- remove requirements in training regulations that unduly restrict the development of innovative and flexible pathways to qualification, including the more effective integration of classroom- and workplace-learning.[106]

The Legal Services Board has announced that a period of consultation will take place on how to implement these reforms. It is seeking responses particularly on five principles:

   i.   Education and training requirements focus on what an individual must know, understand and be able to do at the point of authorisation

  ii.   Providers of education and training have the flexibility to determine how best to deliver the outcomes required

 iii.   Standards are set that find the right balance between what is required at entry and what can be fulfilled through ongoing competency requirements

  iv.   Obligations in respect of education and training are balanced appropriately between the individual and entity, both at the point of entry and ongoing

---

[106] LETR (n. 105), 121.

v. Education and training regulations place no direct or indirect restrictions on the numbers entering the profession[107]

It is too early to know quite what reforms will emerge from the LETR and the further consultations, but the following points seem to be clearly emerging.

1. There is a need to provide better training on some of the practical skills that people need in the profession, such as communication skills.

2. It is important that lawyers are trained in ethics.

3. There needs to be flexibility so that training can match the kind of work that a lawyer might undertake. So someone seeking a career in commercial law does not necessarily need the same training as a person intending to work in criminal law.

4. Ensuring the education and training process produces a diverse profession.

Conclusion

It is essential that the legal profession is well regulated. The public must have confidence that lawyers will treat them well and that the clients will be compensated if the lawyers do not. Lawyers need to have clear guidance regarding what is or is not expected of them. Lawyers play a central role in the legal system, and if that is to flourish, it is important that lawyers perform the role that they should.

However, the regulation of the legal profession is difficult. It can be used by government to control lawyers and to make sure that they do not cause the authorities too much trouble. On the other hand, there are complaints that the codes are more concerned with maintaining the reputation of the legal profession than promoting the interests of clients.[108]

 Further reading

The nature of regulation is discussed in the following works:

R. Able, *Lawyers in the Dock: Learning From Attorney Disciplinary Proceedings* (Oxford University Press, 2009).

A. Boon, 'Professionalism under the Legal Services Act 2007' (2010) 17 International Journal of the Legal Profession 195.

S. Patel, C. Howarth, J. Kwan, and P. McDonald, *Reform of the Legal Profession* (Wilberforce Society, 2012).

[107] LSB, *Proposals on Draft Guidance on Education and Training* (LSB, 2013), 12.

[108] D. Rhode and A. Woolley, 'Comparative perspectives on lawyer regulation: An agenda for reform in the United States and Canada' (2012) 80 Fordham Law Review 2761.

R. Pearce and E. Wald, 'Rethinking lawyer regulation: How a relational approach would improve professional rules and roles' [2012] Michigan State Law Review 513.

D. Rhode and A. Woolley, 'Comparative perspectives on lawyer regulation: An agenda for reform in the United States and Canada' (2012) 80 Fordham Law Review 2761.

N. Smedley, *Review of the Regulation of Corporate Legal Work* (Law Society, 2009).

B. Still, 'Outcomes focused regulation: A new approach to the regulation of legal services' (2011) 11 Legal Information Management 85.

C. Strevens, 'The changing nature of the legal services market and the implications for the qualifying law degree' (2011) 1 Web Journal of Current Legal Issues 1.

C. Whelan and N. Niv, 'Privatizing professionalism: Client control of lawyers' ethics' (2012) 80 Fordham Law Review 2577.

Legal education is considered in these works:

A. Brownsword, 'Ethics in legal education: Ticks, crosses and question marks' (1987) 50 Modern Law Review 529.

J. Hodgson and N. Peck, 'How "vocational" do law schools want to be? A brief comparison of England and the USA' (2010) 19 Nottingham Law Journal 45.

Lord Neuberger of Abbotsbury, 'Lord Upjohn Lecture 2012: Reforming legal education' (2013) 47 The Law Teacher 4.

D. Nicolson, '"Education, education, education": Legal, moral and clinical' (2008) 42 The Law Teacher 145.

M. Robertson, L. Corbin, and K. Tranter, *The Ethics Project in Legal Education* (Routledge, 2010).

4 The lawyer–client relationship

⊚ Key issues

- What is the nature of the relationship between a lawyer and a client?
- When can a lawyer refuse to act for a client?
- What restrictions are there on a lawyer attracting business?

Introduction

This chapter will explore the relationship between a lawyer and a client. We are not here considering the specific details of what a lawyer is legally required to do, but rather more broadly examining what is the nature of the lawyer–client relationship. Specific issues concerning matters such as confidentiality and conflicts of duty will be discussed in the chapters to come. This chapter will concentrate on questions such as: what kind of relationship will a good lawyer try to have with his or her client? Is the lawyer to be a friend? An adviser? Or is the lawyer to be the most dedicated servant doing everything possible to help the client?

People go to a lawyer for various reasons. But many clients are seeking an advocate: someone who will stand up for them and argue their case, and make sure that they protect the clients' rights. Clients seek someone who will make sure that the client is not being taken advantage of and fight the client's corner. Whether you want a professional to draft a will, to organise your company's insolvency, or to sue for damages on your behalf, you want someone focused on your interests and who will 'have your back'.

Hence, for many commentators, the relationship between the lawyer and the client is marked by the notion of 'partisanship'. A lawyer is not meant to be neutral, ensuring there is a fair outcome; rather, he or she is meant to represent the client's case and ensure that the client gets the best outcome possible. A lawyer is not meant to use cases to pursue his or her own agenda, but to enable the client to do what he or she wants. As we shall see, however, not everyone agrees that the lawyer should be simply a 'hired gun' doing everything that he or she can in order to achieve what the client wants. Some argue that lawyers do have obligations to the greater good and to the justice system generally.

The professional codes

The professional codes reflect the competing claims on a lawyer.

Follow the Code

The Bar Council Code of Conduct (the Bar Code) states that:

302. A barrister has an overriding duty to the Court to act with independence in the interests of justice: he must assist the Court in the administration of justice and must not deceive or knowingly or recklessly mislead the Court.

303. A barrister:

(a) must promote and protect fearlessly and by all proper and lawful means the lay client's best interests and do so without regard to his own interests or to any consequences to himself or to any other person (including any colleague, professional client or other intermediary or another barrister, the barrister's employer or any Authorised Body of which the barrister may be an owner or manager)

[...]

The Solicitors Regulation Authority (SRA) Code of Conduct puts the promotion of the interests of the client at the heart of a lawyer's ethical responsibilities.

Follow the Code

SRA Code of Conduct, Outcome 1.2, reads:

you provide services to your *clients* in a manner which protects their interests in their matter, subject to the proper administration of justice

Solicitors must therefore put the clients' interests before their own. Of course, that is not quite as self-disinterested as it might at first appear: doing well for a client will result in fees being paid and new work arriving.

Yet the principles as set out in the professional codes of practice have at their heart two key ambiguities.

- What does it mean to promote a client's interests?
- What is the significance of the words 'subject to the proper administration of justice' in the Solicitors Code? And how are barristers meant to balance their duties under paragraphs 302 and 303?

These questions need to be explored further.

Who defines a client's interests?

First, what exactly does it mean to promote your client's interests? In particular, who decides what those interests are? If a client asks you to complete the legal side of buying a house, and you determine that the house is an awful one and that the client should not buy it, are you acting in that client's interests if you complete the transaction? According to Andrew Boon and Jennifer Levin, the 'modern view' is that lawyers should empower clients 'by treating them as individuals and allow them to reach their own decision'.[1] This emphasises the principle of **autonomy**.

 Definition

> **Autonomy** involves allowing people to make their own decisions and to be free to carry out those decisions. This is commonly subject to the caveat that a person should not be allowed to exercise his or her autonomy in a way that unfairly harms others.

The principle of autonomy could be used to say that it is not the job of the lawyer to impose on the client the lawyer's view of what is best. The job of the lawyer is to give the necessary information to the client and enable the *client* to decide. So, in the example of the client buying an undesirable house, the lawyer might properly point out to the client the problems with the property, but the lawyer should recognise that whether or not to buy is a decision for the client and should seek to implement the client's wishes.

Boon and Levin put the reasonable case for autonomy well:

> People should be allowed and enabled to make as many decisions as possible for themselves, exercising free will. They should not be seen as passive recipients of advice or assistance, but as consumers. As such, they have a right to obtain what they want in a form which is appropriate to the circumstances. Professional help may be needed, and in some cases may be essential, to achieve this, but sufficient information should be given to allow clients to make their own informed decisions on their own interests.[2]

Even adopting such an approach, there may be a role for the lawyer to issue warnings. A lawyer may make it clear that he or she is willing to implement the instructions of the client, but warn that the course of action that the client is pursuing carries dangers. They may even be a case for urging a client not to follow a course of action.[3]

Some advocate a 'modern' approach, involving a dialogue between the client and lawyer. As Robert Dinerstein puts it: 'Client-centred relationships entail shared decision-making responsibility and mutual participation by lawyer and client. By avoiding the trap of either lawyer or client-dominance, these relationships provide

---

[1] A. Boon and J. Levin, *The Ethics and Conduct of Lawyers in England and Wales* (Hart, 2008), 183.

[2] Boon and Levin (n. 1), 184.

[3] R. Uviller, 'Calling the shots: The allocation of choice between the accused and counsel in the defense of a criminal case' (2000) 52 Rutgers Law Review 719.

greater opportunities for facilitating a wise client decision in a supportive atmosphere.'[4] The client in this model is the decision maker and the lawyer is an adviser, and perhaps counsellor. Such a view rejects **paternalism**.

 Definition

> **Paternalism** involves one person making a decision for someone else, based on what the first person thinks is best for that other person. Typically, it involves an expert making a decision for someone whom they feel is less informed about the issue.

A paternalistic model, which is clearly rejected by the 'modern view', is that the clients provide the information to the lawyers and outline their problems, but it is the lawyers who make the decision as to how best to respond and tell the clients what to do. Few would adopt this view now, but its rejection is at the heart of the current approach. It used to be argued that, because the lawyer has the knowledge, skill, and experience in matters to which the law relates, the lawyer is in the best position to make the decision. The lawyer can best assess what is best for the client, who may not fully understand all of the issues, and who may be affected by emotion and unable to make a more detached assessment.

Paternalism for lawyers, while deeply untrendy, is not entirely without merit. A client is seeing a lawyer because of that lawyer's expertise. The client would not see a lawyer if the client were able to make the decision on his or her own. Further, many clients are caught up in the excitement and emotion of the dispute, and so cannot take the longer-term, detached view of the lawyer. The difficulty with paternalism is that it fails to recognise that, on many issues, a diverse range of views is acceptable. While the paternalistic view might have some attraction in cases in which the client is adamant in pursuing a course of action that virtually everyone would agree is foolish, it is less straightforward in most cases, in which a range of responses to the client's proposal is possible. In such a case, surely it is for the client, not the lawyer, to make the decision on what should happen?[5]

While most commentators support autonomy-based approaches and paternalism is typically rejected, it may be questioned what the practice is on the ground. While we talk of lawyers advising their clients of options and letting the clients make the decisions, that may be something of a fiction. If a client seeks to draw up a will and the lawyer recommends that a trust be set up in the will, while officially the client may agree with this, it may be questioned to what extent he or she is making a choice. Few clients buying a house with a solicitor will appreciate what the detailed terms of the conveyance are; they will

---

[4] R. Dinerstein, 'Client-centred counselling: Reappraisal and refinement' (1990) 32 Arizona Law Review 501.

[5] D. Luban, 'Paternalism and the legal profession' (1981) Wisconsin Law Review 454, 457; D. Luban, 'Partnership, betrayal, and autonomy in the lawyer–client relationship: A reply to Stephen Ellmann' (1990) 90 Columbia Law Review 1004, 1036.

sign where the lawyer tells them, trusting the lawyer to have drafted the contract well. The point is simply that we must not get too carried away with talk of 'autonomy' and should recognise that, especially for lay members of the public, even if they do make a decision, they will usually decide what their lawyer tells them to decide!

Balancing the interests of clients and others

The second issue left unresolved in the professional codes is that the duty to promote the interests of the clients sits alongside duties to the 'proper administration of justice'. The question of the extent to which this is a limitation on the duty to promote the interests of a client is one of the major debates in legal ethics. The following case may highlight the issue.

 Scandal!

In 2010, *The Guardian* ran a story on Nick Freeman, a solicitor who specialises in driving offences.[6] He has had a series of successes, enabling celebrities including David Beckham and Ronnie O'Sullivan to defend against charges for driving offences. The newspaper described Freeman as 'one of Britain's wealthiest lawyers'. It claimed that he is known as 'Mr Loophole' because of his success in finding technical legal reasons why a person should not be convicted for a driving offence. The article acknowledged that his work is controversial and asked: 'Is Freeman a freedom fighter at a time when some speed cameras are bringing in tens of thousands of pounds a week in fines, or a man who manipulates the law in favour of the rich and famous?'

To some commentators, a lawyer such as 'Mr Loophole' is simply doing his job. He is seeking out every possible argument to promote the best interests of his clients. Critics will reply that, in some cases, he is subverting the proper administration of justice by finding technical ways out of what should be a conviction. Supporters will respond that if these 'technicalities' should not allow someone to be acquitted, the fault lies with the law, not the lawyer. Indeed, it is often owing to errors by the police or authorities that these technical arguments succeed. In these cases, we should not blame the lawyer if we think any acquittal inappropriate, but rather the authorities who have failed to follow the legal guidelines.

We will now explore in more detail the different ways in which commentators have described the relationship between lawyers and their clients. We will start by looking

---

[6] N. Rose, 'The "loophole lawyers" who help clients beat motoring charges', *The Guardian*, 24 August 2010, online at www.theguardian.com/law/2010/aug/24/loophole-lawyers-motoring-charges

at those who have turned to other kinds of legal relationship in an attempt to find an analogy for the relationship between a lawyer and a client. Many commentators have concluded that none of these quite describes the lawyer–client relationship and so we need to develop a unique model.

Agency

To some, a lawyer should be seen as an agent of the client. The term 'agent' here is used to refer to a particular kind of legal relationship in which an agent must act under the direction of a 'principal'. Typically, a principal will use an agent to perform a task that the principal cannot do himself or herself. The principal might, for example, ask an agent to sign a contract or to deliver goods at his or her request. The agent has a task to perform, but is given some latitude as to how to do it. The agent must sign the contract on Wednesday 1 April, but precisely when to sign, how to travel to the meeting place, and what pen to use is left to the agent.

One can see that this model does capture some aspects of the role of a lawyer. The client instructs the lawyer to prepare, for example, a ten-year lease for a commercial premises, but leaves the precise details to the lawyer. However, many people feel that it downplays the role of the lawyer too much. Lawyers are often expected to advise and to challenge in a way that an agent is not. Further, lawyers are bound by ethical codes and duties to the court, rather than simply able to 'do as they are told' by their principals.

Contractual relationship

The 'contractual relationship' model suggests that the client–lawyer relationship is defined by the terms of the contract between the parties. The parties reach agreement over the nature of their relationship. One consequence of this approach is that we cannot say very much about the general relationship between lawyers and clients, because it all depends on what the particular parties have agreed.

Again, this is undoubtedly part of the story. A lawyer is bound by the contract with his or her client and it can shape the relationship. However, the problem with it as an overarching theory is that there are some central aspects of the lawyer–client relationship that are *not* subject to contract. These are set by professional ethics and by the law. Further, in most contracts between lawyers and clients, there is little that deals expressly with the ethical side of their relationship.

Digging deeper

There is, however, an argument that, especially in the international corporate law market, law firms have become increasingly market-orientated.[7] The claim is that because the

---

[7] D. Rhode, *In the Interests of Justice: Reforming the Legal Profession* (Oxford University Press, 2000), 9.

competition for international corporate legal services has become fierce, this impacts on ethical obligations. Milton Regan argues that companies 'want litigators who will press for every advantage and counselors who will exploit every regulatory loophole, not lawyers who feel bound by nebulous duties that supposedly arise from being an officer of the court'.[8]

A study by Christopher Whelan and Neta Ziv found that 'corporate clients, and in particular global corporations, are gaining influence and control over lawyers' practices at a scope significantly above and beyond what had been customary in the past'.[9] The corporate clients, they find, are demanding terms in contracts dealing with matters such as confidentiality and conflict of interest that have traditionally been seen as set by the standards of the profession, rather than as matters for negotiation between lawyer and client.[10] Hence Whelan and Ziv talk of 'privatising professionalism'. Interestingly, they note that this does not always lead to 'lower standards' and can cover, for example, requiring law firms to meet diversity standards or not to use coercive tactics in litigation.

The fiduciary model

Some commentators turn to the fiduciary model. A 'fiduciary' is given special legal obligations to look after the interests of a 'beneficiary'. A common example is a trustee of a fund, who looks after it for the good of those entitled to it. This model sees the solicitor as looking after the affairs of the client much as a trustee looks after the affairs of the beneficiary. It has some benefits as a model for the lawyer–client relationship. It acknowledges the expertise of the solicitor, and emphasises the obligation to take care of the interests of the beneficiary and to ensure that there is no conflict with the solicitor's own interests. The law governing fiduciary obligations also has strict rules about not benefiting from one's position as a fiduciary. These seem to match neatly the similar obligations that lawyers have towards their clients.

There is another aspect of the fiduciary model that may fit well with some aspects of the lawyer–client relationship: that is, that the lawyer normally conducts the day-to-day business without having to involve the client. The client, in a conveyancing case, for example, will typically leave all of the paperwork to the lawyer and not expect to

[8] M. Regan, 'Taxes and death: The rise and demise of an American law firm', in A. Sera (ed.) *Studies in Law, Politics and Society: Law Firms, Legal Culture, and Legal Practice* (Emerald Group Publishing, 2010), 108.

[9] C. Whelan and N. Ziv, 'Privatizing professionalism: Client control of lawyers' ethics' (2012) 80 Fordham Law Review 2577, 2579.

[10] E. Davis, 'The meaning of professional independence' (2003) 103 Columbia Law Review 1281, 1281. See also R. Painter, 'The moral interdependence of corporate lawyers and their clients' (1994) 67 Southern California Law Review 507, 520.

have to confirm everything that the lawyer does. This captures the position in a fiduciary relationship in which the fiduciary is not expected to obtain the beneficiary's permission for every act.

Critics will say that the fiduciary model promotes too paternalistic a model of a lawyer. Commonly, fiduciaries are appointed to look after the affairs of those unable to look after them themselves (for example children). It might be possible to make the model less paternalistic by suggesting that while the fiduciary must promote the well-being of the client, the definition of 'well-being' is determined by the client. Whether that is adequate to give sufficient respect to the autonomy of the client is open to debate.

Some commentators would combine a fiduciary and a contractual model. Lord Walker, in *Hilton v Barker Booth and Eastwood*,[11] stated:

> A solicitor's duty to his client is primarily contractual and its scope depends on the express and implied terms of his retainer.... The relationship between a solicitor and his client is one in which the client reposes trust and confidence in the solicitor. It is a fiduciary relationship.

We shall now look, in no particular order, at some of the leading authors, and consider the ways in which they have sought to express the relationship between lawyers and clients.

The 'standard conception'

Up until the end of the twentieth century, there was widespread support for the so-called 'standard conception' of lawyers' ethics. Support for this has waned somewhat, but it still has its supporters and is one of the primary theories explaining the lawyer–client relationship.

The standard conception is based on three principles: partisanship; neutrality; and non-accountability. As Bradley Wendel explains:

> Lawyers adhering to the standard conception are directed to seek to protect or advance the legal rights of their clients—partisanship; not to consider their own views of the moral merits of their clients' positions—neutrality; and to rest assured that they will not be subject to justified moral criticism by observers—non-accountability.[12]

These principles are seen to trump other claims that morality may otherwise impose. We will briefly describe these three themes.

Partisanship

Partisanship captures the notion that the lawyer acts to ensure that the client is able to do what he or she wants. In short, the lawyer is on the client's side.

---

[11] [2005] 1 All ER 651.

[12] B. Wendel, 'Three concepts of roles' (2011) 48 San Diego Law Review 547, 548.

⊙ Application

You are acting for a cleaner, who is alleging sex discrimination against her employers. They claim that defending the claim is putting huge financial strain on the company and that there is a risk it will go under if you continue with your claim. They plead with you to abandon the case. But, under the partisanship model, your responsibility is to represent your client's interests and to focus on her. You are not to be swayed by concerns for others in deviating from the course that best promotes your client's well-being.

Neutrality

Neutrality reminds lawyers that their role is not promote their own views, but those of their clients. They are to be neutral as to whether they approve of what the client is doing. They may inform the clients of different issues to take into account, but it is not their job to persuade the clients to adopt particular solutions.

Non-accountability

The idea of non-accountability is closely linked to neutrality and makes the job of the lawyer easier for some. Lawyers may negotiate deals that they think are unfair or even immoral, but it is not their job to decide on such matters and they are not responsible for the decisions of their clients. They may be representing a defendant to a criminal charge whom they suspect is guilty, but again it is not for them to judge. The lawyer is to receive the instructions of the client and to put those into effect, in so far as the law and professional ethics allow. This notion of non-accountability helps some lawyers to sleep at night.

Justifications for the standard conception

The standard conception model has been justified in several ways.

1. Tim Dare argues that the legal system has determined who has which legal rights.[13] Most people cannot understand the law and need lawyers to explain it to them. This means that lawyers have power. The standard conception model ensures that lawyers do not misuse that power:

   [T]he principle of neutrality recognises that it is not up to lawyers to determine what we will do as a community, what rights we will allocate and to whom. The complexity of the procedures upon which a pluralist community such as ours must rely, means that lawyers do have tremendous power in this regard. Their legal expertise means they are better placed than any other group of citizens to work in, and with, our legal

---

[13] T. Dare, 'Mere-zeal, hyper-zeal and the ethical obligations of lawyers' (2004) 7 Legal Ethics 24.

and political institutions. The principle of neutrality recognises this power and its potential for abuse. It guards against the possibility that someone might be denied rights allocated by a legal system because its lawyers find those rights or their allocation to that person morally objectionable.[14]

His point is that if we do not require lawyers to use all legal routes open to a client, this allows the lawyers to decide when the public interests or moral values mean that clients should exercise their rights.

2. In his controversial book, *A Modern Legal Ethics*, Daniel Markovits argues in favour of the standard conception.[15] He justifies this by means of 'democratic legitimacy'. He argues that the whole point of a law is to find a way of mediating between an individual's own values and the public norms needed to govern how to deal with disagreements between people. For the law to be acceptable, individuals need to be able to participate in and engage deeply with the legal system. A partisan lawyer can do that. He or she can assure the client that the best arguments, in terms of the law, can be put forward. Only in this way will individuals feel that they can own and engage with the legal system.[16] This means that lawyers have a very special place in the legal system, one of such importance that it justifies their violating normal principles of morality.

3. Stephen Pepper also promotes the standard conception, but in a somewhat different way from Markovits.[17] For Pepper, autonomy is a central value. People are allowed to pursue their own good unless there is a legal obligation not to act in that way. Lawyers should see themselves as allowing individuals to do that: to seek their own preferences, subject only to legal restrictions. For Pepper, the basic function of the legal profession is to provide 'access to law for those who are not sufficiently knowledgeable or sophisticated to provide it for themselves'.[18] He writes:

The client often wants or needs to understand what the law is in order to evaluate options and make decisions about his or her life, and the most common function of lawyers (across specializations and areas of practice) is to provide that knowledge.[19]

The non-accountability principle helps to protect the public image of lawyers and helps to salve the conscience of lawyers. It means that people should not assume that because a lawyer represents a client, that lawyer approves of what the client has done. It has further advantages because it helps to ensure that even the most unpopular client receives representation.

---

[14] Dare (n. 13), 25.

[15] D. Markovits, *A Modern Legal Ethics* (Princeton University Press, 2010).

[16] It might be questioned, however, how lying and cheating lawyers will engender ownership and engagement.

[17] S. Pepper, 'The lawyer's amoral ethical role: A defense, a problem, and some possibilities' (1986) 11 American Bar Foundation Research Journal 613.

[18] S. Pepper, 'Integrating morality and law in legal practice: A reply to Professor Simon' (2010) 23 Georgetown Journal of Legal Ethics 1011, 1013.   [19] Pepper (n. 18), 1014.

4. Charles Fried, in an influential article, has claimed that the lawyer should act as a friend.[20] Just as a friend is morally justified in preferring the claims of a friend over the claims of other people, so a lawyer should put the interests of his or her clients above those of others:

> What is special about legal counsel is that whatever else may stop the pornographer's enterprise, he should not be stopped because he mistakenly believes there is a legal impediment. There is no wrong if a venture fails for lack of talent or lack of money— no one's rights have been violated. But rights are violated if, through ignorance or misinformation about the law, an individual refrains from pursuing a wholly lawful purpose. Therefore, to assist others in understanding and realizing their legal rights is always morally worthy.[21]

There is also some disagreement between supporters of the standard conception model over how far lawyers should go to promote their client's case. Some have argued in favour of 'hyper-zeal'. This requires lawyers to do everything permitted by the law to promote the client's case. Lawyers must never act illegally, but any other tactic, however dastardly or ethically dubious, is permitted. Daniel Markovits defends a 'modem legal ethics' that pervasively requires lawyers to lie (to deceive others) and to cheat (by which he means take advantage of rules, in a way that they were clearly not intended to be used).[22] Lawyers, it is said, must use 'fearless advocacy'.[23]

There are two primary arguments in favour of this hyper-zeal. The first is that it is the most likely to achieve justice. If each side of the argument uses every legal tool at its disposal, then the best case on either side of the argument is being made and that gives us the best chance of obtaining justice. If either side does not put forward every available argument, then the system of justice becomes impaired. The second is that if the client is permitted by the law to use certain arguments or tactics, then it is not for the lawyer to pick and choose which to use. If we find a particular tactic unfair, the fault lies not with the lawyer who uses it, but with the legal system that permits it.

Other supporters of the standard conception have argued that a better version of the standard conception is simply to require 'mere zeal'. In other words, although the lawyer should strive to make the best case for the client, the lawyer does not have to use every tactic or argument, especially where there may be a strong ethical objection to doing so. Tim Dare explains:

> His professional obligation is to zealously pursue the client's legal rights. He is to be partisan in the sense that he must bring all of his professional skills to bear upon the task of securing *his* client's rights. But he is under no obligation to pursue interests that go beyond the law.[24]

---

[20] C. Fried, 'The lawyer as friend: The moral foundations of the lawyer–client relationship' (1976) 85 Yale Law Journal 1060.

[21] Fried (n. 20), 1062.   [22] Markovits (n. 15), 17.

[23] Y. Ross, *Ethics in Law: Lawyers' Responsibility and Accountability in Australia* (LexisNexis Butterworths, 2001), 432.   [24] Dare (n. 13), 34.

The argument is that those in favour of the standard conception explain why the law has given the clients certain rights that the lawyer should assist in protecting, but that this does not permit the lawyer to use all tactics. So, applying Dare's approach, there would be no difficulty in a lawyer defending a claim against a client by asserting that the claim has been brought too late under the Limitation Act 1980, which requires certain cases to be brought within a particular time. This is asserting a right given by the law. However, seeking to delay proceedings to put financial pressure on the other party is not asserting a particular legal right. Dare's approach places much weight on what may or may not be regarded as a legal right. One response is that one has a legal right to do anything apart from that which is forbidden by the law, which is what the supporters of hyper-zeal would claim.

Objections to the standard conception

Opponents of the standard model may take several tacks. One is to note that, generally, supporters of the standard model assume that the current legal system promotes justice and that the lawyer's role is justified by the good of the system. However, is the current system just? Can such claims be made when many of the best lawyers, at least the best-paid lawyers, work not for the weakest or most vulnerable in society, but for the richest and most privileged? And when those lawyers often seem to help the rich and most privileged become even richer and more advantaged, often at the expense of the most vulnerable? The weakest and poorest are unable to access legal advice. If the current legal system fails to operate fairly, then a lawyer cannot justify what would be otherwise immoral activity by pointing to the goodness of the system in which he or she is playing a part.

So this view of the role of the lawyer as neutral and partisan is not accepted by everyone. It can be seen as letting lawyers off the hook too easily. Donald Nicholson and Julian Webb go further, objecting to the 'anaesthetization of moral conscience' promoted by the standard conception.[25] It seems to place no moral restrictions on what a lawyer can do. The lawyer may play a significant role in achieving a result that is harmful to the public interest, or is unjust or harms others, yet be able to deny any responsibility. These concerns lead some to argue that the relationship with a client has to be put alongside a lawyer's responsibilities to the greater good and the justice system. Rhode considers that a lawyer should not 'simply retreat into some fixed conception of role that denies moral accountability for public consequences or unduly privileges clients' and lawyers' own interests', but should work within a framework that, '[a]t its most basic level...requires lawyers to accept personal responsibility for the moral consequences of their professional actions'.[26]

---

[25] D. Nicolson and J. Webb, *Professional Legal Ethics: Critical Interrogations* (Oxford University Press, 2000), 194–7.   [26] Rhode (n. 7), 67.

A different angle of criticism of the standard conception is that it requires the lawyer to operate in a cold, abstract way in relation to a client. The lawyer is to be uninvolved and neutral towards the case—yet this may not be possible or psychologically healthy for a lawyer. Certainly, it seems unrealistic.[27]

Critics of Pepper's view that autonomy justifies the standard conception have queried whether autonomy is the only value.[28] Generally, as a society, we do seek to give people the freedom to act as they wish, but we also uphold other values, such as protecting the vulnerable or promoting communal values. Why should the lawyer be tied to the promotion of autonomy rather than one of these other values? Further, as Simon has queried, just because you respect someone's freedom to live their life as they wish, that does not mean that you are obliged to help others do what they want.[29] That is right. It is one thing to say: 'I know my friend visits prostitutes. I disapprove, but he should be free to act as he wishes.' It is another to say: 'I know my friend visits prostitutes and I disapprove, but believe I should drive him to the red light district to help.' Leaving people to do what they want is different from helping them do it. Pepper's response to these points might be that it is not for the lawyer to decide which decisions of his or her clients to support and which not to. He is happy to see the lawyer informing the client of relevant moral principles, but argues that ultimately it is for the client to decide.

David Luban is critical of those who put a lawyer's moral obligations in terms of being a role.[30] He argues that the 'common morality' that applies to everyone should prevail over any role morality:

> The implication this conclusion carries for the moral responsibility of lawyers should be reasonably clear: if a client's choice is morally wrong and promotes none of the values that make autonomy important, then 'interference with client autonomy' is simply not an objection to moral activism. There may be other reasons for carrying out the client's wish: its moral wrongness may be too slight to override the presumption in favor of professional obligation, or the interests of other people may be badly damaged by the lawyer's refusal, or the case may be one in which the weight of professional obligation is very strong (as in criminal defense), or the lawyer's own livelihood or reputation may be so badly damaged by the refusal as to excuse her participation. These are good reasons; the client's autonomy is no reason at all.[31]

The standard conception model promoting zeal may have ready application in a case involving litigation, but it has little resonance in non-litigious work or cases in which

---

[27] R. Mortensen, 'The lawyer as parent: Sympathy, care and character in lawyers' ethics' (2009) 12 Legal Ethics 14.

[28] D. Luban, 'The Lysistratian perspective: A response to Stephen Pepper' (1986) 11 American Bar Foundational Research Journal 637.

[29] W. Simon, 'Role differentiation and lawyers' ethics: A critique of some academic perspectives' (2010) 23 Georgetown Legal Ethics 987.

[30] Luban (n. 28).   [31] Luban (n. 28), 667.

the lawyer is assisting a client who is using mediation. In Chapter 10, we shall explore the growing use of mediation and alternative dispute resolution (ADR). These often promote the parties cooperating together to find a solution. The aggressive style promoted by the standard conception does not fit at all well with this.

This last argument leads into a final complaint made against the standard conception: it assumes that lawyers want to win their cases at all costs—but do clients want their lawyers to cheat and lie to get the best possible result? Leaving aside any moral objections that a client may have, the dispute may be part of an ongoing relationship and there is a danger that a client may 'win the battle but lose the war' if he or she is seen to have used underhand and unfair tactics.[32] It is by no means obvious that clients want to win their cases at all costs.

Alternatives to the standard conception

If the standard conception is not used, what should replace it?

Bradley Wendel

Bradley Wendel believes that it is important to recognise the range of calls upon lawyers.[33] He suggests that they serve many masters: fiduciaries in relation to their clients, but officers of the court too. They owe duties to promote the interests of their clients, but obligations to the wider society. He argues that many commentators take one aspect of the role of a lawyer (for example fidelity to the client) and emphasise it to the exclusion of others:

> What many of these arguments have in common is evaluative monism: the belief that a single, impersonally justified value can serve as a polestar for any moral agent's deliberation about her ethical responsibilities. Monism requires the analysis of apparently different values in terms of some comparative value, or higher-order conceptual category that permits the ranking of options in relation to one another in an impersonal manner, i.e., without reference to the circumstances of a particular agent.[34]

He rejects monism, and believes instead that the values of lawyers are plural and incommensurable. These cannot be ranked or weighed against each other: 'Instead, my argument is that the lawyer seeking to act ethically must take account of different value claims that may not be comparable with one another in an impersonally rational, mathematical, or algorithmic manner.'[35]

---

[32] N. Cahn, 'A preliminary feminist critique of legal ethics' (1990–91) 4 Georgetown Journal of Legal Ethics 23.

[33] B. Wendel, 'Value pluralism in legal ethics' (2000) 78 Washington University Law Quarterly 113, 120.   [34] Wendel (n. 33), 122.

[35] Wendel (n. 33), 122.

This recognition of the different claims that they may face and that these are not directly comparable can lead to two lawyers responding appropriately to the same dilemma in different ways. We cannot criticise either if they are both reflecting a competing moral claim. Wendel notes:

> Just as neither a nun nor a mother can be criticized for failing to realize the virtues particular to the other, so is it possible that two or more types of lawyers may exist, each of which exemplifies competing but incompatible virtues.[36]

Just as the concept of beauty does not lead us always to pick one work of art as better than another, so morality should not lead us to think that one approach is better than another. Note that Wendel is not saying that any response to an ethical dilemma is right and that there are no wrong answers; rather that we need to be open to the fact that different moral principles can be reflected in contrasting responses. Some responses, however, may not reflect any moral principle and these will not be justified.[37]

Critics of Wendel's approach might argue that it fails to provide clear guidance to lawyers. Indeed, he acknowledges that, in some situations, a range of alternative courses of actions may be justified.

William Simon

William Simon is critical of the standard conception.[38] He argues that lawyers are part of the legal system and that, in seeking to determine what ethical principles should govern their actions, we should look at the moral foundation of the legal system: that is, justice. All that a lawyer does should therefore be aimed at this higher goal. A lawyer cannot, then, argue that legal ethics allow him or her to promote the interests of a client if doing so will lead to injustice.

Simon is aware of the predictable riposte: that by vigorously pursuing and presenting a client's case, the lawyer is promoting justice. A just result in a case is most likely to be found, supporters of the standard conception often argue, if both sides present the best possible arguments. Simon accepts that, in some cases, that must be so. However, in plenty of cases, it will not. For example, if the representative of the other side is doing a poor job or if the law is not just, then justice will not be achieved by the lawyer striving for his or her own side.

Ethics of care

In Chapter 1, we saw some of the broader arguments promoted by an ethics of care. This can be used to promote a particular approach to client–lawyer relationships. This approach would say that the relationship should be a caring one. So rather than encouraging lawyers to be 'neutral' and 'non-accountable' for their clients, it urges lawyers

---

[36] Wendel (n. 33), 123.   [37] Wendel (n. 12).   [38] Simon (n. 29).

to enter into relationships of care with them. Nicolson and Webb argue that lawyers should 'take into account the real life situation of their clients, including all their needs, desires and interests, and the possible impact of their actions on third parties, the general public and the environment'.[39] They should be 'engrossed' in the client.[40]

The practical consequences of this kind of approach are several. First, a lawyer may decide that it is not possible to enter into a caring relationship with a particular client, in which case that lawyer should not act for that client. A victim of child abuse may feel that he or she cannot act for a convicted paedophile, for example. This application would go against the standard conception, which urges lawyers to be willing to take on all clients. An ethic of care is therefore more sympathetic to **cause lawyers**.

 Definition

> Andrew Boon defines **cause lawyers** as 'qualified, licensed practitioners, dedicating most of their time, whether in private practice or in non-governmental agencies, to pursuing political goals through action for clients representing one side of an issue or cause'.[41]

Second, because a caring relationship is at the heart of lawyering, it questions the assumption that the lawyer must follow the instructions of the client. Reid Mortensen, applying an ethic of care in this context, suggests that the lawyer should see his or her role as that of a 'good parent'.[42] This might involve talking through the issues with a client, trying to influence the client, and seeking a mutually acceptable outcome. It is not necessarily 'caring' simply to accept what a client wants. Not all ethics of care supporters will necessarily agree with this. A caring relationship is not necessarily a 'warm one'. It may, in some contexts, be caring to be cold and detached: a person receiving an intimate medical examination, for example, may want the person doing the examination to be somewhat detached and depersonalised. This point suggests that an ethics of care does not necessarily lead to a 'cuddly' relationship between a lawyer and a client; there may be some cases in which a more detached one is more caring.

Third, an ethic of care will recognise that both the client and the lawyer will owe caring responsibilities to other people. The principles underpinning the standard conception have prevented lawyers from carrying out their positive role. This is not to say that supporters of an ethic of care do not recognise the principle of loyalty—namely, a duty to uphold a client's interests; it is just that this is tempered by 'integrity'—that is, an acceptance of moral responsibility for the actions taken on behalf of clients. Similarly, they promote the importance of candour between a lawyer and client, but argue that there is also a duty of candour between a lawyer and a

---

[39] Nicolson and Webb (n. 25), 197.   [40] Mortensen (n. 27).
[41] A. Boon, 'Cause lawyers and the alternative ethical paradigm: Ideology and transgression' (2007) 4 Legal Ethics 250, 253; A. Sarat and S. Scheingold (eds) *Cause Lawyering and the State in a Global Era* (Oxford University Press, 2001).   [42] Mortensen (n. 27).

third party.[43] This vision accepts that the lawyer–client relationship needs to be viewed in the context of the other obligations and relationships with which they are both living.[44]

Fourth, one of the most powerful aspects of an ethics of care approach is that it recognises that a lawyer's work is not often adversarial. As we shall see in Chapter 10, ADR and negotiation have become common forms of resolving issues. These typically involve the parties working together to find an acceptable solution. The values promoted by an ethics of care fit in far better with these than those promoted by the standard conception of the lawyer–client relationship. Clients may want a result that enables them to retain a good relationship with the other side, or others who care about the other side. Winning at all costs and using any tactics to succeed may not be in the client's best interests, broadly understood.

Finally, it should not be forgotten that the relationship between a lawyer and a client will vary enormously depending on the circumstances of the case. The lawyer advising a widow on the probate of her husband's estate is going to have a different kind of relationship with the client from a lawyer advising a large commercial firm on a takeover bid. What will constitute a 'caring relationship' will depend very much on the needs and characters of those involved.

Critics of an ethics of care approach will be concerned that ethics of care can lead to a 'collapse into situational ethics'. At the heart of the approach, as mentioned in Chapter 1, is the argument that the solution to an ethical dilemma is that which will promote caring relationships. What precisely that will involve will depend on the characters, abilities, and relationships of the parties involved. The approach therefore tends to reject abstract moral principles, in favour of a careful analysis of the particularities of the case. But critics say that is problematic in the context of legal ethics, because it fails to provide any proper guidance to lawyers. It makes drafting professional code and regulation of lawyers difficult, if not impossible.

That objection is a powerful one, but there are two options open to an ethics of care supporter. One is to emphasise that the approach does provide a clear guiding principle—'Do that which promotes caring relationships'—even if the application of that principle creates difficulties. The other is that a supporter could be happy with the approach taken in the SRA Code of Conduct, which provides some indicators of behaviour that typically promotes caring relationships, even while accepting that the circumstances of the case may provide a good reason to act differently.

The differing models

We will now consider some hypothetical situations that will bring out the differences in approach.

---

[43] Although not if that conflicts with loyalty.

[44] T. Glennon, 'Lawyers and caring: Building an ethic of care into professional responsibility' (1991–92) 43 Hastings Law Journal 1175.

What would you do?

You are a solicitor and a client asks you to draft a contract. The client indicates that he will breach the contract midway through its course and asks you to make sure that, if he does so, he will not suffer any bad consequences. Can you advise the client?

This issue is not straightforward. You might argue that it is for the other side's solicitor to make sure that the contract is drafted in such a way that there are no serious consequences if it is breached. If the other side is happy with a contract with no serious consequences in the event of a breach, that is their choice. The solicitor is doing nothing wrong in following this course of action.

A second point to make is that a breach of contract is not a criminal offence. Very respectable people breach contracts. As long as they pay damages for the harm caused by the breach, it is hard to see what is particularly wrong. Advising a client on the damages that he or she must pay and negotiating about what the contract should say would happen if the client were to be in breach is unobjectionable.

You might think that the answer all depends on who the other party to the contract is. Is he or she advised by a lawyer? Is he or she vulnerable?

 What would you do?

A client tells a solicitor that his father has died without making a will, but that he is going to 'create' one. The client is seeking advice on how to make it appear realistic. Can the solicitor advise the client?

That seems a straightforward case: the client is proposing a fraud and it is undoubtedly a criminal offence. No theory of lawyers' ethics would support the solicitor advising the client in this instance.

 What would you do?

A client sees a solicitor, explaining that his wife is desperate to commit suicide because she is facing a terminal illness. She has asked him to find her tablets so that she can do so. The client seeks advice on whether the police tend to prosecute such cases, and if they do, what sentence he is likely to receive.

Some would argue that giving such advice might be seen to encourage the client to commit the offence of assisting suicide. On the other hand, the advice sought is readily available in textbooks, and guidance on prosecution policy has been issued by the Director of Public Prosecutions and is available on its website. It seems odd that it could be seen as unethical to give such advice, if it is readily available elsewhere.

> Perhaps the line to draw is that a lawyer can set out what the law is, but cannot go beyond this to encourage or facilitate an offence. Or perhaps the fact that the client has chosen to seek a lawyer rather than look it up on the Internet indicates he is looking for more than information?

A lawyer, it goes without saying, must not commit a criminal offence and so must be very careful of saying anything that could encourage or assist an offence. It is essential to be aware that it itself is a clear criminal offence to aid, abet, counsel, or procure a criminal offence.

Key statute

Under the Serious Crime Act 2007, s. 44:
(1) A person commits an offence if—
  (a) he does an act capable of encouraging or assisting the commission of an offence; and
  (b) he intends to encourage or assist its commission.
(2) But he is not to be taken to have intended to encourage or assist the commission of an offence merely because such encouragement or assistance was a foreseeable consequence of his act.

So telling a client 'This would be a crime, but you won't get caught if you...' would risk the lawyer committing an offence under the Serious Crime Act 2007, s. 44. However, the lawyer who says 'It would be an offence if you do X, so you should do Y' is, if anything, discouraging an offence.

In Chapter 15, we will explore further how different perspectives on legal ethics can lead to different responses in particular situations.

Advertising

Traditionally, lawyers were not allowed to advertise legal services. It was seen as unprofessional and beneath their status. It has now become more familiar. Advertising can inform customers of what services are available. Perhaps the best known are those that ask something like 'Have you been involved in an accident?', before informing people of legal services that might help them obtain compensation. These are primarily directed at people who might not have thought of making a claim otherwise, but might now do so, having read the advertisement. Other advertisements might be designed to persuade a client to come to one firm over another, emphasising the first firm's experience, or size, or ethos.

There are restrictions on advertising. The Bar allows barristers to advertise including photographs of the barrister, statements about the work of the barrister, and charging rates. But there are limitations: advertisements must comply with the British Code of Advertising, Sales Promotion, and Direct Marketing. Further, paragraph 709.2 of the Bar Code states:

> Advertising or promotion must not:
>
> (a) be inaccurate or likely to mislead;
>
> (b) be likely to diminish public confidence in the legal profession or the administration of justice or otherwise bring the legal profession into disrepute;
>
> (c) make direct comparisons in terms of quality with or criticisms of other identifiable persons (whether they be barristers or members of any other profession);
>
> (d) include statements about the barrister's success rate;
>
> (e) indicate or imply any willingness to accept instructions or any intention to restrict the persons from whom instructions may be accepted otherwise than in accordance with this Code;
>
> (f) be so frequent or obtrusive as to cause annoyance to those to whom it is directed.

Solicitors are also permitted by their code to advertise. Publicity must not be misleading and must be 'sufficiently informative to ensure that *clients* and others can make informed choices'.[45] The advertising must not be likely to 'diminish the trust the public places in you and in the provision of legal services'.[46] Some forms of advertising are prohibited, including unsolicited approaches to member of the public, for example by 'cold calling' on the telephone, or approaching people in a hospital or at a scene of an accident. If fees are mentioned, any estimated fees must not be 'pitched at an unrealistically low level'.[47]

The 'cab-rank rule'

One of the best-known rules governing the rules between a lawyer and a client is the 'cab-rank rule'. This rule applies only to barristers. It requires a barrister to take on every client if he or she has the time and skills necessary to act for that client. The rule is set out in the Bar Code.

---

[45] SRA Code, O 8.1.   [46] SRA Code, O 8.1.   [47] SRA Code, IB 8.7.

Follow the Code

The Bar Code, para 602, requires that:

A self-employed barrister must comply with the 'Cab-rank rule' and accordingly except only as otherwise provided in paragraphs 603 604 605 and 606 he must in any field in which he professes to practise in relation to work appropriate to his experience and seniority and irrespective of whether his client is paying privately or is publicly funded:

(a)   accept any brief to appear before a Court in which he professes to practise;
(b)   accept any instructions;
(c)   act for any person on whose behalf he is instructed;

and do so irrespective of (i) the party on whose behalf he is instructed (ii) the nature of the case and (iii) any belief or opinion which he may have formed as to the character, reputation, cause, conduct, guilt or innocence of that person.

The cab-rank rule makes it clear that a barrister should not refuse instructions and must accept any brief, regardless of his or her own views. Paragraph 602 accepts that there are exceptions and these are included in the subsequent paragraphs. These explain that a barrister may refuse a case if he or she would be 'professionally embarrassed' (para 603). This would include cases in which a barrister lacks experience or competence to handle the matter, has other professional commitments that prevent him or her handling the case appropriately, or will put himself or herself in a conflict of interest by taking on the case.

The justification for the rule

The justification for the cab-rank rule is that it ensures that unpopular clients can receive the representation of a lawyer. The Bar Standards Board (BSB) has also argued that:

It also brings significant benefits to the public in specialist areas, such as commercial and regulatory law, where its absence would create a real risk that major players (e.g. banks) could demand exclusivity, depriving potential opponents of much of the talent available at the Bar.[48]

The rule is therefore not designed to promote the interests of barristers, but rather of clients.

It does, however, carry one important benefit for barristers:[49] it means that a barrister can represent an unpopular client without being criticised by the general public

[48] M. McLaren, C. Ulyatt, and C. Knowles, *The 'Cab Rank Rule': A Fresh View* (Bar Standards Board, 2012).   [49] McLaren et al. (n. 48), para. 17.

or colleagues for doing so. It is appreciated that the barrister has no choice but to accept the next client and that, if a barrister is representing a client, no one assumes that therefore the barrister approves of the client.

The rule has certainly received judicial support. Many judges have spoken of the importance of the rule, of whom Lord Hobhouse is typical:

> It is fundamental to a just and fair judicial system that there be available to a litigant (criminal or civil), in substantial cases, competent and independent legal representation... the professional rule that a barrister must be prepared to represent any client within his field of practice and competence...underwrite...this constitutional safeguard.[50]

The cab-rank rule in practice

There has been a lively debate over whether the cab-rank rule is followed in practice. The Flood/Hviid Report suggested that it was widely ignored.[51] The exceptions are sufficiently vaguely drafted to mean that it is unlikely that a barrister could not find a way around representing a client whom he or she really did not wish to represent. However, the BSB rejects this claim and denies that the rule is widely ignored.[52] Flood and Hviid note that the cab-rank rule has not been used as the basis of a disciplinary finding by the BSB. They suggest:

> ...that it is not really a rule but more a principle masquerading as one; it is unenforceable and there is no evidence to show that it has ever been the subject of enforcement proceedings; it applies only to a small, select group of lawyers, and finally the exclusion and exemptions from the rule virtually emasculate it.[53]

Notably, in the empirical research carried out by Flood and Hviid, although there were anecdotal reports of other barristers not following the cab-rank rule, there were, perhaps unsurprisingly, no barristers willing to admit openly that they breached the rule. They did note that, in 1974, the Bar Council had to appeal for assistance from Queen's Counsels (QCs) to defend Irish Republican Army (IRA) bombers, because there were difficulties in finding barristers to take the briefs. The Bar Council criticised Flood and Hviid for not finding concrete examples with which to back up their claims.[54]

 Alternative view

One of the reasons that Flood and Hviid give for dispensing with the rule is that they suggest that, nowadays, a barrister can gain welcome publicity from representing a notorious criminal. It is very unlikely that an unpopular figure would, in fact, struggle

---

[50] *Medcalf v Mardell* [2002] UKHL 27, [51] and [52].

[51] J. Flood and M. Hviid, *The Cab Rank Rule: Its Meaning and Purpose in the New Legal Services Market* (Legal Services Board, 2013).   [52] McLaren et al. (n. 48).

[53] Flood and Hviid (n. 51), 24.   [54] S. Kentridge, *Bar Council Response* (Bar Council, 2012).

to find legal representation.[55] Indeed, in *Hall v Simons*,[56] Lord Steyn said of the cab-rank rule:

> [I]ts impact on the administration of justice in England is not great. In real life a barrister has a clerk whose enthusiasm for the unwanted brief may not be great, and he is free to raise the fee within limits. It is not likely that the rule often obliges barristers to undertake work which they would not otherwise accept...

Similarly, although solicitors do not have a rule like the cab-rank rule, if a client is willing to pay their fees, it is unlikely that many lawyers will want to turn the work away, however unsavoury the client may be.

Solicitors and client choice

Generally, solicitors can choose which clients to accept.

Follow the Code

Chapter 1 of the SRA Code states:

You are generally free to decide whether or not to accept instructions in any matter, provided you do not discriminate unlawfully.

At one time, the idea that clients had a right to a free choice of solicitor was seen as an important principle. However, that has not appeared as a specific right in the most recent version of the Code. In part, this is recognition that legal aid regulations now greatly restrict the freedom that a client has over choice of solicitor. Clients can use only those approved by the Legal Aid Agency as experts in the field. Similarly, those with legal expenses insurance can face restrictions on which solicitors they are able to use. Most obviously, the rate of fees charged by solicitors will mean that many clients cannot afford them. The conflict of interest rules also limit choice. In short, there are now so many restrictions on freedom of choice, that it seems inappropriate to claim it as a grand principle.

---

[55] J. Flood, *Response to the Bar Council and Bar Standards Board Responses to the Flood-Hviid Report on the Cab Rank Rule for the Legal Services Board* (April 2013), online at http://ssrn.com/abstract=2258707

[56] [2000] 3 All ER 673, 680e.

Who is the client?

Normally, a solicitor should have no difficulty in identifying the client: it will be the person with whom the solicitor has entered into a contract. Good practice recommends that a lawyer must write to the client, having agreed to act for the client, setting out the terms of the contract (the retainer). This should make it clear what the solicitor is expected to do and what fees will be paid. We discuss this further in Chapter 7, where we will also discuss the circumstances in which a lawyer may owe duties to someone who is not the client.

Referrals

The issue of referrals arises in cases in which a firm of solicitors has an arrangement with, for example, an estate agency that it will recommend the estate agency to its clients. You can imagine if a solicitor were to have such an arrangement with the leading firm of estate agents in his or her area, this could be a lucrative source of clients. At one time, referrals of this kind were forbidden. The concern was that it would create a dangerously close relationship between the solicitor and the referrer. In the example just given, for example, a solicitor acting for a client referred by the estate agent may uncover a problem with the title being purchased. The best advice might be to recommend that the client pull out of the deal. However, it would be in the interests of the estate agent for the purchase to go so that the agent could receive its commission. This would put the solicitor in a position of conflict of interest and the danger is that the importance of maintaining a good relationship with the estate agent may override the solicitor's duties to the client.[57]

A major limitation on referral fees has been introduced by section 56 of the Legal Aid, Sentencing and Punishment of Offenders Act 2012, which prohibits the payment of fees to a solicitor in relation to 'prescribed legal business'. This is defined in section 56(4) as follows:

"Prescribed legal business" means business that involves the provision of legal services to a client, where—

(a) the legal services relate to a claim or potential claim for damages for personal injury or death,

(b) the legal services relate to any other claim or potential claim for damages arising out of circumstances involving personal injury or death, or

(c) the business is of a description specified in regulations made by the Lord Chancellor.

The Code offers further guidance to solicitors.

---

[57] A. Higgins, 'Referral fees: The business of access to justice' (2012) 32 Legal Studies 109.

Follow the Code

The SRA Code of Conduct requires that:

O 6.1 whenever you recommend that a *client* uses a particular *person* or business, your recommendation is in the best interests of the *client* and does not compromise your independence;

O 6.2 *clients* are fully informed of any financial or other interest which you have in referring the *client* to another *person* or business;

O 6.3 *clients* are in a position to make informed decisions about how to pursue their matter;

O 6.4 you are not *paid* a *prohibited referral fee.*

Ending a relationship with a client

A solicitor is entitled to cease to act for a client. Indeed, there may be cases in which the solicitor ought to do so.

Follow the Code

The Code's Indicative Behaviour (IB) 1.7 says that a solicitor should consider:

whether you should decline to act or cease to act because you cannot act in the *client's* best interests.

It should not, however, be thought that the right to 'drop a client' is unlimited. Indicative Behaviour 1.26 states that a solicitor should not cease to act for a client without good reason and without reasonable notice. Where there is litigation, the solicitor needs the leave of the court.

 Key case

R v Ulcay [2007] EWCA Crim 2379

A solicitor sought to adjourn a criminal case because he needed more time to prepare the case. The court refused the adjournment and the solicitor (and barrister) applied to withdraw from the case. The court refused to allow him to do so. He could appeal against the refusal to adjourn if he wished to do so, but he could not drop the client.

Good reasons justifying terminating a retainer would clearly arise if there were a conflict of interest (see Chapter 6), or if a solicitor were to feel that the case involved issues outside his or her expertise and that this meant the solicitor could not provide good advice. It might even arise if a solicitor were to feel so busy that he or she could no longer act appropriately for the client. Perhaps the most common reason for terminating a retainer is that the client has not paid the lawyer as required.

It seems that the regulation for barristers is somewhat stronger. The Bar Code sets out the circumstances in which a barrister may withdraw if there is professional embarrassment.

Follow the Code

The Bar Code, para 608, sets out when a barrister must cease to act for a client:

A barrister must cease to act and if he is a self-employed barrister must return any instructions:

(a)   if continuing to act would cause him to be professionally embarrassed within the meaning of paragraph 603 provided that if he would be professionally embarrassed only because it appears to him that he is likely to be a witness on a material question of fact he may retire or withdraw only if he can do so without jeopardising the client's interests;

(b)   if having accepted instructions on behalf of more than one client there is or appears to be:
   (i)   a conflict or risk of conflict between the interests of any one or more of such clients; or
   (ii)   risk of a breach of confidence;
   and the clients do not all consent to him continuing to act;

(c)   if in any case funded by the Legal Services Commission as part of the Community Legal Service or Criminal Defence Service it has become apparent to him that such funding has been wrongly obtained by false or inaccurate information and action to remedy the situation is not immediately taken by the client;

(d)   if the client refuses to authorise him to make some disclosure to the Court which his duty to the Court requires him to make;

(e)   if having become aware during the course of a case of the existence of a document which should have been but has not been disclosed on discovery the client fails forthwith to disclose it;

(f)   if having come into possession of a document belonging to another party by some means other than the normal and proper channels and having read it before he realises that it ought to have been returned unread to the person entitled to possession of it he would thereby be embarrassed in the discharge of his duties by his knowledge of the contents of the document provided that he may retire or withdraw only if he can do so without jeopardising the client's interests.

Paragraph 609 sets out when a barrister may withdraw from a case:

Subject to paragraph 610 a barrister may withdraw from a case where he is satisfied that:
(a)   his instructions have been withdrawn;
(b)   his professional conduct is being impugned;
(c)   advice which he has given in accordance with paragraph 607 or 703 has not been heeded; or
(d)   there is some other substantial reason for so doing.

It should be noted that if a trial is ongoing, leave from the court will be required. In *R v Ulcay*,[58] Sir Igor Judge stated that '[t]he absence of what [the barrister] would regard as sufficient time for the purpose of preparation did not constitute an exception' allowing him or her to withdraw from a case. However, the Court of Appeal accepted that a client who changed his or her instructions could put the court in an impossible position. Clearly, changing representation mid-trial severely slows down the trial process and there is a fear that clients will use doing so to delay matters. The courts therefore tend to require convincing reasons for allowing a change of representation mid-trial.[59]

Conclusion

This chapter has explored the nature of the relationship between a client and a solicitor. In conclusion, it is worth noting that while there has been much debate, there is also considerable consensus. Most people agree that the lawyer should give especial attention to the interests of the client. Most people also agree that there are limits to how far the lawyer should go to promote the interests of a client. The dispute is really over how much attention the lawyer is required to give to the interests of others and greater societal interests, and over how far the lawyer is expected to go to promote the client's interests. One difficulty in responding to the debate is that lawyers deal with a broad range of clients, from experienced business people to individuals barely able to cope with life. Expecting a single approach to all client relationships is not realistic.

 Further reading

> T. Dare, 'Mere-zeal, hyper-zeal and the ethical obligations of lawyers' (2004) 7 Legal Ethics 24.
>
> R. Dinerstein, 'Client-centred counselling: Reappraisal and refinement' (1990) 32 Arizona Law Review 501.
>
> J. Flood and A. Whyte, 'Straight there, no detours: Direct access to barristers' (2009) 16 International Journal of the Legal Profession 2.
>
> C. Fried, 'The lawyer as friend: The moral foundations of the lawyer–client relationship' (1976) 85 Yale Law Journal 1060.
>
> T. Glennon, 'Lawyers and caring: Building an ethic of care into professional responsibility' (1991–92) 43 Hastings Law Journal 1175.
>
> D. Luban, 'Paternalism and the legal profession' (1981) *Wisconsin Law Review* 454.

---

[58] [2007] EWCA Crim 2379, [41].   [59] *R v Iqbal (Naseem)* [2011] EWCA Crim 1294.

D. Luban, 'Partnership, betrayal, and autonomy in the lawyer-client relationship: A reply to Stephen Ellmann' (1990) 90 Columbia Law Review 1004.

R. Mortensen, 'The lawyer as parent: Sympathy, care and character in lawyers' ethics' (2009) 12 Legal Ethics 14.

D. Nicolson and J. Webb, *Professional Legal Ethics: Critical Interrogations* (Oxford University Press, 2000).

S. Pepper, 'The lawyer's amoral ethical role: A defense, a problem, and some possibilities' (1986) 11 American Bar Foundation Research Journal 613.

S. Pepper, 'Counselling at the limits of the law: An exercise in the jurisprudence and ethics of lawyering' (1995) 104 Yale Law Journal 1545.

S. Pepper, 'Integrating morality and law in legal practice: A reply to Professor Simon' (2010) 23 Georgetown Journal of Legal Ethics 1011.

D. Rhode, *In the Interests of Justice: Reforming the Legal Profession* (Oxford University Press, 2000).

W. Simon, 'Role differentiation and lawyers' ethics: A critique of some academic perspectives' (2010) 23 Georgetown Legal Ethics 987.

E. Wald, 'Loyalty in limbo: The peculiar case of attorneys' loyalty to clients' (2009) 40 Saint Mary's Law Journal 909.

B. Wendel, 'Value pluralism in legal ethics' (2000) 78 Washington University Law Quarterly 113.

B. Wendel, 'Three concepts of roles' (2011) 48 San Diego Law Review 547.

C. Whelan and N. Ziv, 'Privatizing professionalism: Client control of lawyers' ethics' (2012) 80 Fordham Law Review 2577.

Confidentiality

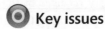

Key issues

- Lawyers have a special obligation not to disclose information that their clients have given them.
- The principle of confidentiality is subject to many exceptions, most notably where there is the consent of the client.
- Legal professional privilege means that lawyers must not disclose to third parties information about legal advice given or documents prepared for litigation.

Introduction

It is not difficult to state the principle of confidentiality: you must keep your client's information confidential. However, the devil is in the detail and the subject is far more complicated than it looks at first sight. It is, of course, a principle that is adopted by all professions and, indeed, it is part of general ethics. However, there is especial protection given to communications between lawyers and clients by what is known as 'legal professional privilege'. This plays a central role in establishing trust between a client and a lawyer. Clients often seek legal advice about intimate issues or issues of great financial importance to them. If we want people to receive good advice, clients must feel free to be completely open with their lawyers, without fear that the information they provide will be disclosed to others.

The protection of lawyer–client communications

The ethical basis of the principle of confidentiality can be presented in a number of ways, as follows.

- A client has a right of privacy. This right to protection of private life is now seen as a fundamental human right.[1]

---

[1] *Morgan Grenfell v Special Commissioners of the Inland Revenue* [2002] UKHL 21; *R v Secretary of State for the Home Department, ex p Daly* [2001] UKHL 26.

- Lawyers have a special obligation flowing from their position in society and the trust imposed on them by their clients to keep information private. This flows from their professional and fiduciary position. Lord Scott has declared that confidentiality is a 'central pillar' of legal ethics.[2]

- It is an implied term in a contract between a lawyer and a client that the lawyer will keep the client's information confidential.

- The information given to the lawyer is property, received by the lawyer as a fiduciary, and the fiduciary must account for gains made using the information.[3]

- There is a public interest in ensuring that discussions between clients and lawyers are kept confidential. It is in society's interests that people be able to obtain the best possible legal advice. Protecting confidentiality helps to ensure that this happens. In *Bolkiah v KMPG*,[4] Lord Millett stated that:

> It is of overriding importance for the proper administration of justice that a client should be able to have complete confidence that what he tells his lawyer will remain secret. This is a matter of perception as well as substance. It is of the highest importance to the administration of justice that a solicitor or other person in possession of confidential and privileged information should not act in any way that might appear to put that information at risk of coming into the hands of someone with an adverse interest.

You do not need to choose between these different explanations for why lawyer–client communications should be protected. Indeed, when combined, they provide a powerful basis for the principle that lawyers should not disclose the secrets imparted to them.

The law of confidentiality applies to anyone who receives information that he or she knows or has agreed is confidential. The law as it applies to lawyers is therefore but an application of the general rules relating to confidentiality.[5] However, there are two particular aspects of the law relating to lawyer–client communications which are special, as follows.

1. There is an assumption that all information given by a client to a lawyer is confidential. Once it is shown that the client passed on information to the lawyer, there is little room for the lawyer to argue that it was not protected by confidence. In other circumstances (such as discussions between friends), a key question is often whether the person receiving the information realised that it was meant to be confidential.

---

[2] *Three Rivers District Council v Governor and Company of the Bank of England (No. 6)* [2005] 1 AC 610, [34], *per* Lord Scott.

[3] *Boardman v Phipps* [1967] 2 AC 46. Although the view that confidential information can be treated as property has fallen into disfavour: *Douglas v Hello! Ltd (No. 3)* [2005] EWCA Civ 595.

[4] [1999] 2 AC 222, 240.

[5] See generally R. Toulson and C. Phipps, *Confidentiality*, 2nd edn (Sweet and Maxwell, 2006).

2. The doctrine of **legal privilege** means that communications between lawyers and clients, and documents prepared for the purposes of litigation, must not be disclosed to others—even to a court—without the consent of the client. For communications in other relationships, disclosure can be required in a range of circumstances.

 Definition

A client will rely on breach of confidence if claiming that the lawyer wrongfully disclosed information to others (or is about to do so). The client will rely on **legal privilege** if he or she has been asked to hand over information, but does not want to do so and it is covered by the privilege.

Digging deeper

The principle of confidentiality fits well into an adversarial model of justice, in which each side is seeking to win, by fair means or foul. Clients can be completely open with their lawyers and lawyers can select from what they are told the best pieces of evidence to present to the court. While, of course, a lawyer must never deceive the court or other lawyers, confidentiality allows the lawyer to keep hidden information that might affect the outcome of the trial. Those who oppose the adversarial approach may question the significance of confidentiality. The move in the Civil Procedure Rules towards a less adversarial and more cooperative approach may not be entirely consistent with the traditional approach to confidentiality. We will discuss this new approach to litigation further in Chapter 9.

Professional guidance

Professional guidance contains some clear direction on the importance of keeping clients' information confidential.

Follow the Code

The Bar Council Code of Conduct (the Bar Code), para 702, requires that:

Whether or not the relation of counsel and client continues a barrister must preserve the confidentiality of the lay client's affairs and must not without the prior consent of the lay client or as permitted by law lend or reveal the contents of the papers in any instructions to or communicate to any third person (other than another barrister, a pupil, in the case of a Registered European Lawyer, the person with whom he is acting in conjunction for the purposes of paragraph 5(3) of the Registered European Lawyers Rules or any other person who needs to know it for the performance of their duties) information which has been entrusted to him in confidence or use such information to the lay client's detriment or to his own or another client's advantage.

> **Follow the Code**
>
> Under the Solicitors Regulation Authority (SRA) Code of Conduct, Outcome 4.1:
>
> > you keep the affairs of *clients* confidential unless disclosure is required or permitted by law or the *client* consents

Notably, solicitors must make sure that all of their staff keep client information confidential. This applies not only to existing clients, but also to previous and even deceased ones.[6] It should also be noted that although these provisions make it clear that confidentiality must be preserved, they leave it to the law to set out when confidence can be breached and the precise definition of 'confidentiality'.

Confidentiality

A client could make an application to a court for breach of confidence if there were a breach, or anticipated breach, of confidence. These applications have become well known in recent years, with celebrities and politicians seeking to obtain injunctions, or even super-injunctions, to prevent the press from publishing photographs or stories about their love lives. It is rare for such an application to be made in respect of a lawyer. The most common scenario in the case law is that in which a claimant is objecting to a solicitor acting for a rival because the claimant is concerned that the solicitor will disclose information that he or she holds about the claimant to the rival.

As already indicated, a breach of confidence claim can be seen as a claim brought for breach of contract, a tort, breach of fiduciary duty, and a breach of human rights. It seems that the precise nature of the claim will not affect the essential elements of it.[7] Indeed, the courts tend to speak generally of giving a remedy for breach of confidence without explicitly detailing the precise legal nature of the claim.

If X wishes to claim that Y breached confidence by disclosing information, it must be shown that:

1. the information is of a confidential nature;

2. it was imparted to Y in circumstances that justified imposing a duty of confidence; and

3. Y had used or disclosed, or threatened to use or disclose, the information without X's consent.[8]

---

[6] *Bolkiah v KPMG* [1999] 2 AC 222, 235D, *per* Lord Millett.

[7] See *Parry-Jones v Law Society* [1969] 1 Ch 1, 7A–7B.

[8] J. Powell and R. Stewart, *Jackson & Powell on Professional Liability*, 7th edn (Sweet and Maxwell, 2012), ch. 2.

These are the general factors that apply whenever a breach of confidence claim is made. In cases involving clients seeking to prevent their lawyers from disclosing information, the first and second criteria will be proven automatically. Once it is shown that the client gave the information to a lawyer in the context of that relationship, it will be presumed that the information is confidential and that circumstances will impose a duty of confidence. But that assumption will follow only if material is imparted to a lawyer inside the confines of client–lawyer relationship. If someone were to announce something at a party at which a lawyer was present, that would be protected by confidence only if it was made clear at the time that it was confidential or if it was clear from its nature that it was. If however, in a private conversation after dinner between a celebrity and lawyer, the celebrity were to disclose that she had recently been diagnosed with cancer, this would probably be taken to be confidential. The nature of the information and the fact that it was a conversation between only two people would indicate that confidentiality was expected.

 Alternative view

It might be questioned whether all information passed between a client and a lawyer within their professional relationship should be confidential. Generally, a duty of confidence does not apply to information that is trivial.[9] So would it really be a breach of confidence if a lawyer were to tell a friend about the client's extraordinary coloured socks or to repeat a joke that a client had told him or her? Similarly, if the client were to disclose during a meeting a fact that was widely reported in the media, would the lawyer be doing anything wrong in repeating it? Indeed, it has been suggested by one commentator that the legal responsibility to keep confidences should be the same as that for everyone, and should apply only where the material is sensitive and it is clear that it is meant to be kept secret.[10] Nevertheless, the safest course of action for lawyers is not to disclose anything said to them in their professional capacity, without the consent of the client to do so. One reason for this is that facts that might appear trivial may not, in fact, be so, or the lawyer may be mistaken over how well known a certain fact is.

To succeed in obtaining an injunction to prevent a disclosure, it must be shown that the risk of this happening is not fanciful, although it does not need to be a substantial risk.[11] The issue can arise if a former client is concerned because a

---

[9] *Attorney General v Guardian Newspapers (No. 2)* [1990] 1 AC 109, 282D, *per* Lord Goff.

[10] R Aviel, 'The boundary claim's caveat: Lawyers and confidentiality exceptionalism' (2012) 86 Tulane Law Review 1055.

[11] *Re Z* [2009] EWHC 3621 (Fam).

solicitor is now advising a rival. In *Koch Shipping Inc v Richards Butler (A Firm)*,[12] a case involving a solicitor now advising a rival, Tuckey LJ set out the general approach:

> In these days of professional and client mobility it is of course important that client confidentiality should be preserved. Each case must depend upon its own facts. But I think there is a danger inherent in the intensity of the adversarial process of courts being persuaded that a risk exists when, if one stands back a little, that risk is no more than fanciful or theoretical. I advocate a robust view with this in mind, so as to ensure that the line is sensibly drawn.

On the facts of that case, it was found that there was no risk. A similar conclusion was reached in *Re T and A (Children)*,[13] in which a local authority sought care orders in respect of children. A firm of solicitors was instructed to represent the children at the hearing as guardian ad litem. The father opposed this, because the firm had acted for him in a series of criminal charges, although this was several years ago. The judge rejected the claim because the particular solicitor involved in the care case was not in the criminal department of the firm and the partner who had acted for the father had no recollection of his case. There was no danger of a breach of confidentiality. The court refused, therefore, to bar the firm from acting as guardian.

There are plenty of other cases in which the courts *have* been persuaded that there is a non-fanciful risk of disclosure and have prevented the lawyer from acting for a rival to an existing client.[14] These cases often also involve conflicts of interests and are discussed in detail in Chapter 6.

 Scandal!

In 2013, a novel was published under a pseudonym (Robert Galbraith). Several months after publication, it was leaked to the press that the author was J. K. Rowling,[15] the author of the Harry Potter novels. It transpired that her solicitors had leaked her identity. She was reported as saying that she had assumed she could expect 'total confidentiality' from her lawyers and was 'very angry' at what had happened. Of course, the sales of the book rocketed, and so she could not expect legal damages and she had not lost financially. Nevertheless, the firm of solicitors was highly apologetic. One of its partners had told his wife's best friend, who had let it slip to a journalist.

---

[12] [2002] EWCA Civ 1280, [23].   [13] [2000] Lloyd's Rep PN 452.
[14] *Ball v Druces & Attlee (A Firm)* [2002] PNLR 23.
[15] BBC News, 'JK Rowling "anger" at legal firm over pseudonym leak', 18 July 2013, online at www.bbc.co.uk/news/entertainment-arts-23366660

Legal professional privilege

Legal professional privilege is different from the doctrine of confidentiality, although closely associated with it. Legal professional privilege is a rule that neither lawyers nor clients can be ordered by a court to disclose communication between them in relation to work done by the lawyer in the giving of legal advice or preparing for litigation. The privilege therefore covers two kinds of material and can be distinguished as:[16]

- *legal advice privilege*, which covers all communications between a lawyer and a client concerning the giving and receiving of legal advice; and
- *litigation privilege*, which covers all communications between a lawyer and someone else connected to the preparation for litigation.

So, in a criminal trial, the defendant's solicitor cannot be called to give evidence about anything that the client has said unless the client has consented to removal of the privilege. If a defendant has admitted to the lawyer that he or she committed the crime, the lawyer cannot be required to disclose that admission of guilt if the privilege has not been waived. Note that this applies only to communications in the context of a lawyer–client relationship. If a friend from schooldays were to bump into a lawyer at a party and confess a crime, the privilege would not apply: the discussion would not have involved the giving and receiving of legal advice.

Litigation privilege applies to communications between a lawyer and someone else. So if, for the purposes of a personal injury claim, a doctor were asked to prepare a medical report on a client, that report would be protected by the privilege and its disclosure could not be ordered.

The privilege was justified by Lord Scott in *Three Rivers District Council v Bank of England (No. 6)*.[17] He explained:

> [I]n the complex world in which we live there are a multitude of reasons why individuals, whether humble or powerful, or corporations, whether large or small, may need to seek the advice or assistance of lawyers in connection with their affairs; they recognise that the seeking and giving of this advice so that the clients may achieve an orderly arrangement of their affairs is strongly in the public interest; they recognise that in order for the advice to bring about that desirable result it is essential that the full and complete facts are placed before the lawyers who are to give it; and they recognise that unless the clients can be assured that what they tell their lawyers will not be disclosed by the lawyers without their (the clients') consent, there will be cases in which the requisite candour will be absent. It is obviously true that in very many cases clients would have no inhibitions in providing their lawyers with all the facts and information the lawyers might need whether or not there were the absolute assurance of non-disclosure that the present law of privilege provides. But the dicta to which I have referred all have in common the idea that it is necessary in our

---

[16] *Three Rivers District Council v Governor and Company of the Bank of England (No. 6)* [2005] 1 AC 610, [105].   [17] [2004] UKHL 48, [3].

society, a society in which the restraining and controlling framework is built upon a belief in the rule of law, that communications between clients and lawyers, whereby the clients are hoping for the assistance of the lawyers' legal skills in the management of their (the clients') affairs, should be secure against the possibility of any scrutiny from others, whether the police, the executive, business competitors, inquisitive busy-bodies or anyone else.[18]

Legal advice privilege exists 'solely for the benefit of the client'.[19] The significance of this is that, as Lord Hoffmann pointed out in *Morgan Grenfell*:[20] 'If the client chooses to divulge the information, there is nothing the lawyer can do about it.' A lawyer cannot plead professional client privilege for his or her own benefit.

We will explore a little further the two kinds of privilege.

Communications between lawyer and client

Legal professional privilege covers communications between a lawyer and a client, but it applies only to advice on legal matters. That restriction was considered in the following case.

 Key case

Three Rivers District Council v Bank of England (No. 6) [2004] UKHL 48

The Bank of England was preparing a submission to the Bingham Inquiry into the collapse of the bank BCCI. In preparing its response, it sought the advice of a firm of solicitors, Freshfields, and of counsel. The central question in the case was whether or not the work of the solicitors and counsel was protected by legal advice privilege. To the surprise of many, the Court of Appeal held that it was not.[21] In the Court of Appeal, Lord Phillips clearly sought to restrict the scope of legal advice privilege: 'The justification for litigation privilege is readily understood. Where, however, litigation is not anticipated it is not easy to see why communications with a solicitor should be privileged.'[22]

The House of Lords, however, took a different view.[23] It noted that solicitors generally gave their clients advice on a wide range of issues, and on their rights, liabilities, and obligations. It would be wrong to restrict the privilege to cases in which litigation was envisioned or only to matters that were focused on this law in a narrow sense. The privilege in this case covered legal rights, liabilities, and obligations, and so was inclusive

---

[18] At [34].

[19] *R (on the Application of Prudential Plc & anor) v Special Commissioner of Income Tax & anor* [2013] UKSC 1, [22], *per* Lord Neuberger.

[20] *Morgan Grenfell v Special Commissioners of the Inland Revenue* [2002] UKHL 21, [37].

[21] *Three Rivers District Council v Bank of England (No. 5)* [2004] 3 WLR 1274.   [22] At [39].

[23] *Three Rivers District Council v Bank of England (No. 6)* [2004] UKHL 48.

LEGAL PROFESSIONAL PRIVILEGE

of the advice sought. Lord Carswell quoted with approval the dicta of Taylor LJ in *Balabel v Air India*,[24] who had stated that the privilege covered 'advice as to what should prudently and sensibly be done in the relevant legal context'.

As this case makes clear, the legal privilege extends beyond classic legal advice.[25] It can cover cases in which the lawyer is giving general legal advice about what the law requires. In *Nederlandse Reassurantie Groep Holding NV v Bacon and Woodrow*,[26] it was held to cover advice from solicitors on the commercial wisdom of a transaction. This was held to be covered because the advice was in the context of the solicitors generally acting as legal advisers for the whole transaction. This suggests that where a firm is giving legal advice, the courts will not be willing to separate out which parts of the advice are legal and which are not; the advice generally will be covered if it is, broadly speaking, legal in nature.

Communications between lawyers and third parties

Communications between lawyers and third parties are protected only if they are in connection with litigation. The full requirements were summarised by Lord Carswell in *Three Rivers (No. 6)*:[27]

[C]ommunications between parties or their solicitors and third parties for the purpose of obtaining information or advice in connection with existing or contemplated litigation are privileged, but only when the following conditions are satisfied:

(a) litigation must be in progress or in contemplation;

(b) the communications must have been made for the sole or dominant purpose of conducting that litigation;

(c) the litigation must be adversarial, not investigative or inquisitorial.

The privilege applies to documents if the dominant purpose was litigation, even if they had other purposes.[28] In *AXA Seguros SA de CV v Allianz Insurance*,[29] a report prepared into a highway that was said to be damaged by a hurricane was primarily for purposes of assessing the insurance claim. It was true that there was a reasonable prospect of litigation, but the dominant purpose for preparation of the document was assessment of the claim rather than with litigation in mind.

Legal professional privilege afforded 'a very high degree of protection' by the law.[30] This was shown in *Bates v CC of Avon and Somerset*,[31] in which a warrant was issued

---

[24] [1988] Ch 317, 330; quoted at [59].
[25] G. Sisk and P. Abbate, 'The dynamic attorney–client privilege' (2010) 23 Georgetown Journal of Legal Ethics 201.   [26] [1995] 1 All ER 976.
[27] *Three Rivers District Council v Bank of England (No. 6)* [2004] UKHL 48, [102].
[28] In *Collidge v Freeport PLC* [2007] EWHC 645.   [29] [2011] EWHC 268 (Comm).
[30] *SC BTA Bank v Shalabayev* [2011] EWHC 2915 (Ch).   [31] [2009] EWHC 942 (Admin).

to search the premises of man who had previously acted as an expert in court proceedings, but was now suspected of possessing indecent images of children. The warrant was quashed because it was not possible to have reasonable grounds to believe that there was no material on the computer protected by privilege. This case shows how strongly the court will protect privileged information.

Section 10 of the Police and Criminal Evidence Act 1984 defines, for the purpose of that legislation, what is covered by legal privilege.[32]

Key statute

Police and Criminal Evidence Act 1984, s. 10, lists:
(a) communications between a professional legal adviser and his client or any person representing his client made in connection with the giving of legal advice to the client;
(b) communications between a professional legal adviser and his client or any person representing his client or between such an adviser or his client or any such representative and any other person made in connection with or in contemplation of legal proceedings and for the purposes of such proceedings; and
(c) items enclosed with or referred to in such communications and made—
   (i) in connection with the giving of legal advice; or
   (ii) in connection with or in contemplation of legal proceedings and for the purposes of such proceedings, when they are in the possession of a person who is entitled to possession of them.

There is a crucial exception in section 10(2): 'Items held with the intention of furthering a criminal purpose are not items subject to legal privilege.'

Alternative view

The argument in favour of legal advice privilege is that, if people are to be able to access legal advice, they need to feel able to be completely open with a lawyer and free of the fear that what they say will be made public. This argument is not beyond question. One issue is whether this is any truer than with other professions. Why is legal advice different in this regard as compared with, say, psychiatry? Patients should be open with their psychiatrists and there is a public interest that they are. Certainly, there is little evidence that people go to other professionals less, or are less open with them, because these professionals do not have as strong a protection as lawyers have.[33]

---

[32] This is said to reflect the common law as stated in *R v Bowden* [1999] 4 All ER 43.

[33] See D. Shuman and M. Weiner, 'The privilege study: An empirical examination of the psychotherapist–patient privilege' (1982) 60 North Carolina Law Review 893, 894; J. Auburn, *Legal Professional Privilege: Law and Theory* (Hart, 2000).

Who can plead the privilege?

The privilege applies not only to solicitors and barristers, but also allied legal professionals such as patent agents, licensed conveyancers, and authorised advocates and litigators.[34] However, a lively controversy has surrounded whether privilege should attach to non-lawyers. The issue came to a head in the following case.

 Key case

R (Prudential Plc & anor) v Special Commissioner of Income Tax & anor [2013] UKSC 1

A firm of accountants gave legal advice concerning tax matters. The (then) Inland Revenue sought disclosure of the documents relating to that advice under section 20 of the Taxes Management Act 1970. The accountants sought to rely on legal advice privilege as a defence. In short, they argued that it would be unfair to a client that if that client were to consult a lawyer, the advice would not have to be disclosed, but if he or she were to consult an accountant on the same issue, it would. The central issue for the Supreme Court was whether legal advice privilege could be relied upon by accountants.

The majority (seven to two) held that legal advice privilege did not apply to accountants. The majority emphasised that the privilege had been restricted to lawyers for a long time. The majority accepted that the arguments in favour of a person seeking and receiving legal advice applied equally to whether he or she was seeking the advice from a lawyer or another professional. They even accepted that the principled arguments for restricting the privilege to lawyers were weak. However, any change to the traditional approach might have unforeseen consequences. The current position was clear and well understood. If the privilege were extended, it was hard to foresee what the consequences would be; there would be uncertainty over which professions or occupations would be covered. The issue raised matters of policy that were better left to Parliament.

Lord Sumption produced a powerful dissent. He emphasised that the privilege was the privilege of the client and was based on the public interest in promoting access to legal advice. That required absolute confidence, but did not depend on the status of the adviser. He saw no principled reason why a person seeking legal advice over tax who was consulting an accountant should be treated any differently from one seeking that advice from a lawyer.

Cynics will see the decision in *Prudential* as designed to give lawyers the upper hand as compared to accountants in the lucrative tax advice market.

---

[34] Courts and Legal Services Act 1990, s. 63.

In *Walter Lilly v Mackay*,[35] Akenhead J held that a claims company that employed no barristers or solicitors was not entitled to rely on the privilege, even though it was engaged in dispensing legal advice.

In *Akzo Novel Chemicals v European Commission*,[36] it was decided that, in relation to proceedings in the European Court of Justice (ECJ), in-house lawyers were not entitled to legal advice privilege in relation to communications with their employers. The decision applies only to European law and it is by no means certain that English courts will follow it in cases under English law.[37] The decision was met with strong criticism from academics.[38] A common criticism is that clients should be entitled to protection of confidentiality regardless of whether they are seeking advice from an in-house or external lawyer. The reasoning of the ECJ, however, is that privilege is necessary to help a person to obtain *independent* legal advice and that in-house lawyers are not in a position to give independent advice. In-house lawyers would strongly disagree and claim that the whole point of their role is to give independent advice to their employers.[39] It is not clear that in-house lawyers are pressured to be less independent than external lawyers, especially in the current climate in which lawyers wish to maintain as many clients as possible.

One interesting question arising from the *Prudential* decision is how it will operate in an alternative business structure (ABS).[40] These are firms comprising a range of professionals dealing with clients and offering a spectrum of expert advice (see Chapter 3). The whole idea is that a client may be in a room at a meeting receiving advice from lawyers, accountants, and other professionals, all at the same time. Will these communications be privileged in relation to the lawyer, but not the accountant? The Legal Services Act 2007, section 190, is designed to deal with this eventuality: as long as the accountant is giving legal advice and is acting under the supervision of a lawyer, the legal privilege will apply.[41]

---

[35] [2012] EWHC 649 (TCC).

[36] C-550/07 P *Akzo Nobel Chemicals Ltd v European Commission* [2011] 2 AC 338.

[37] Indeed, current precedent indicates that in-house lawyers are protected by the privilege: *Alfred Compton Amusement Machines Ltd v Customs and Excise Commissioners (No. 2)* [1974] AC 405.

[38] For example, F. Rizzuto, 'The Akzo ruling of the Court of Justice and the private enforcement of European Union competition law: Two steps back, one step forward' (2010) 3 Global Competition Litigation Review 121; C. Long, 'Akzo and the debate on in-house privilege in the European Union' (2011) 8 International Law and Management Review 1.

[39] A. Higgins, 'ECJ confirms no privilege for in-house counsel: *Azko Nobel v European Commission*' (2011) 30 Civil Justice Quarterly 113.

[40] M. Stockdale and R. Mitchell, 'Legal professional privilege and alternative business structures' (2012) 33 Company Lawyer 204.

[41] Section 190(4) and under the common law privilege preserved by s. 190(7).

Exceptions to privilege and confidentiality

Lord Neuberger in *Prudential*[42] explains that legal professional privilege is strongly protected:

> Where legal professional privilege ('LPP') attaches to a communication between a legal adviser and a client, the client is entitled to object to any third party seeing the communication for any purpose, unless (i) the client has agreed or waived its right, (ii) a statute provides that the privilege can be overridden, (iii) the document concerned was prepared for, or in connection with, a nefarious purpose, or (iv) one of a few miscellaneous exceptions applies (eg in a probate case where the validity of a will is contested).

As is clear from this quote, only in very exceptional circumstances can the privilege be breached.[43]

Consent/waiver

The right to confidentiality and/or legal privilege rests with the client. This means that the client is entitled to waive that right. Clients may agree that information can be disclosed so that the press can be informed of their position. Another common situation is that client may decide to use his or her communications with the lawyer as evidence in the trial.

Generally, a waiver of confidentiality will be express, but it can also be implied.[44] A common example will be where the document is put into the public domain. Similarly, when privileged documents are sent to the other side's solicitor, there is a presumption of waiver. However, that is not so where the document was clearly confidential and sent by mistake; in that instance, the material cannot be used in litigation.

It is generally thought that a person can waive privilege in a document for one purpose, but not another.[45] It is less clear whether it is possible to waive privilege in relation to a part of a document. There is clearly some concern in doing so in that, if only part of a document can be used in evidence, it may be misleading if the document cannot be seen as a whole. This last point can mean that if a single document can be properly understood only in the context of a series of documents, than a waiver of one will be seen as a waiver of all.[46] So if a report of an expert witness is given to the other side and privilege waived, that waiver applies to background material in the report.[47] However, a court may be persuaded that only part of a document needs to be

---

[42] At [17].   [43] *R v Derby Magistrates' Court, ex p B* [1995] 4 All ER 526

[44] *MAC Hotels Ltd v Rider Levett Bucknall UK Ltd* [2010] EWHC 767 (TCC).

[45] *Balu v Dudley Primary Care Trust* [2010] EWHC 1208 (Admin); *Berezovsky v Hine* [2011] EWHC 1904 (Ch).

[46] C. Passmore, 'The dangers of waiving privilege' (1997) 147 New Law Journal 931.

[47] *Clough v Thameside and Glossop Health Authority* [1998] 2 All ER 971, 977.

disclosed if the court is confident that the rest of the document is separate from it and does not affect its meaning.[48]

Care must be taken by clients giving evidence that they do not unintentionally waive privilege, as the following cases show.

 Key case

R v Seaton [2010] EWCA Crim 1980

At a trial, a defendant was asked why his explanation of events differed from that given in a witness statement prepared by his solicitor. He explained that the solicitor had not recorded what he had said correctly. He claimed to have consistently maintained the same explanation of the events and that any inconsistency was the result of errors by his lawyers. The prosecution wished to call the solicitor to give evidence. The issue of legal professional privilege was raised.

It was held that, by referring to what passed between him and his solicitor, the defendant had waived legal professional privilege. Although the communications were privileged, the privilege belonged to the client, and he was free to waive it if he so wished. The solicitor could not rely on the privilege if the client had waived it.

 Key case

Re D (A Child) [2011] EWCA Civ 684

A mother was a defendant to care proceedings. During the investigations, she had changed her story about how the injuries had occurred. Initially, she claimed that the father accidentally harmed the child, but later she claimed that he harmed the child in a fit of temper. In a witness statement, she explained that she had changed her story after attending a number of meetings with her lawyers. The local authority wanted to question the lawyers about what had been said in the meetings. The lawyers relied on professional privilege.

The Court of Appeal found that the mother had waived her privilege. She had argued that she had been advised neither to the privilege nor the consequences of waiver, and so it would be unfair to find that she had waived the privilege. However, the Court of Appeal held that waiver could take place even where the client did not appreciate the significance of the waiver.

The Court explained that the judge had to balance the fairness between both parents and, ultimately, the best interests of the child. The judge had to determine the facts relating to the injury. Because the mother had said that she changed her story following legal advice, the Court was required to understand more precisely the nature of the advice and why it led to her changing her story.

---

[48] *Brennan v Sunderland City Council* [2009] ICR 479 (EAT).

As these cases show, a client has to be very careful, when making reference to legal advice, not to introduce that advice as evidence and thereby waive privilege.

The criminal activity exception

Section 10(2) of the Police and Criminal Evidence Act 1984 states that the privilege does not apply to 'items held with the intent of furthering a criminal purpose'—but there is an ambiguity in that provision: whose intent is being referred to? This ambiguity was the subject of the following case.

 Key case

Francis and Francis v Central Criminal Court **[1989] AC 346**

Mrs G retained a solicitor to purchase a house, using money given to her by a relative. Neither she nor or her solicitor realised that the money being used to buy the house came from drug trafficking. The police sought an order requiring the solicitors to hand over all of the documents relating to the transaction. The solicitors refused. In the court case, the police relied on s. 10(2) of the 1984 Act, arguing that the intent referred to could be anyone's intent, and did not need to be the intent of the solicitor or the client; if there were someone with a criminal intention in relation to the property, that would be sufficient.[49] Their Lordships agreed. If someone were seeking to use the communication for fraud, the privilege would be lost, even if it were a third party acting through an innocent client.

In order to invoke section 10(2), there must be strong evidence of criminal fraud. This is because section 10(2) operates as an exception to the established rule that the material should not be disclosed. Difficult cases can arise in which there may be a mixture of purposes relating to the item. Here, the courts will try to ascertain whether the dominant purpose of the creation of the document was a criminal one, in which case it will not be protected, or whether the dominant purpose was the provision of legal advice, in which case it will be.[50] This is particularly relevant where a client is seeking legal assistance over 'sharp practice' or something bordering on illegality. In such a case, Lord Justice Schiemann in *Barclays Bank v Eustice*[51] thought that clients should be encouraged to seek advice on matters that they feared were bordering on illegality and that this was a particularly strong argument for upholding privilege in

[49] The decision is criticised in L. Newbold, 'The crime/fraud exception to the legal professional privilege' (1990) 53 Modern Law Review 472.
[50] *Barclays Bank v Eustice* [1995] 4 All ER 511.   [51] [1995] 4 All ER 511.

such a case. Hence it has been said that the fraud exception should be applied 'with caution'.[52]

Interestingly, in *Re McE*,[53] Lord Phillips questioned whether the fraud exception was properly described as an exception. This was because criminal communications could not be seen as part of the giving of legal advice and so could not claim the privilege in the first place. Further, the whole point of the privilege was to enable the administration of justice, and criminal communications went against the principle underpinning the privilege.

The Children Act 1989

In *Re L*,[54] the House of Lords held that a special exception to the rule on legal professional privilege applied to reports prepared for child protection litigation under the Children Act 1989.[55]

 Key case

Re L (Police Investigation: Privilege) [1996] 2 FLR 731

The House of Lords considered a case in which the mother had been accused of administering drugs to her child. Child protection proceedings were commenced. The mother's solicitor commissioned a report from a consultant on how methadone was given to the child. The report indicated that it had been administered by the mother, which she denied. The police learned of the existence of the report and sought a copy. The solicitors refused to supply it, relying on legal professional privilege. The House of Lords held that the privilege between solicitor and client did not apply to reports prepared by third parties for the purposes of litigation for care proceedings under the Children Act 1989.

Note that this case is looking only at third-party reports in child protection cases. The communications between client and solicitor in general are still protected even in cases brought under the Children Act 1989.

The decision in *Re L* is notable because their Lordships held that the privilege did not apply at all to expert reports prepared under the Children Act 1989. It might have been expected that even if the privilege did not apply, there was still a need to balance the importance of protecting the privilege with the importance of protecting the child. However, their Lordships held that the report was simply unprotected.

---

[52] *Group Seven Ltd v Allied Investment Corp Ltd* [2013] EWHC 1509 (Ch).
[53] [2009] UKHL 15.   [54] *Re L (Police Investigation: Privilege)* [1996] 2 FLR 731.
[55] R. Langdale and R. Miller, 'Professional ethics: Counsel acting in family proceedings' [2010] Family Law 718.

Unfortunately, the issue is clouded by comments made their Lordships. They declined to express a view on whether or not a court order was needed before disclosure. The fact that a court order may be required implies that some kind of protection applies to such a report; otherwise, it would automatically have to be handed over with all other paperwork. Lord Jauncey also referred to the rule applying 'where the welfare of the child is involved'.[56] This seems to suggest that there may be cases in which the welfare of the child does not require the disclosure of a report. Again, there is an implication that such reports do have a vestige of protection even in Children Act cases.

But why is it that Children Act cases are treated differently from all other proceedings? The simple answer is that their Lordships held that this was a special rule relating to the Children Act 1989. It was explained that care proceedings are not adversarial, but are investigative. This makes them different from other litigation. However, the dissenting judges were sceptical. Lords Nicholls and Mustill pointed out the Children Act 1989 contains no provision stating that the normal rules of legal professional privilege do not apply. Lord Nicholls also doubted whether there was a clear division between solicitor–client privilege, which was protected, and litigation privilege in relation to third-party reports. Lord Nicholls even questioned whether the judgment in *Re L* was complaint with the rights under Article 6 of the European Convention on Human Rights, protecting the right to a fair hearing, in that it interfered with a parent's opportunity to obtain legal advice. Further, while the majority said that such proceedings are not adversarial, it is not clear that parents who are threatened with the removal of their children will not see the proceedings in that way. However, clearly, the majority of their Lordships thought that the need to take effective measures to protect children overrode all of these concerns.

Disclosure in the public interest

Where the claim rests in confidentiality alone, it is well established that the disclosure can be justified where there is a strong public interest. Where, however, legal professional privilege applies, it seems—although it is not beyond question—that a general public interest is insufficient to justify disclosure. Remember that the privilege applies to communications concerning the seeking of legal advice or communications connected to litigation; confidentiality alone will apply where the client is talking to the lawyer about issues, but is not seeking advice. An example might be where the client discloses to his solicitor that he is having an affair, over a glass of wine after their meeting: in that instance, confidentiality alone applies.

If it is a 'confidentiality alone' case, the court will need to weigh up the interest in maintaining confidence and the public interest in favour of disclosure.[57] The case law on this is fairly complex and the cases rarely involve solicitors, so we will not go into the detail on the case law. A couple of points of are worth emphasising, however.

---

[56] At 741.   [57] *Attorney General v Guardian Newspapers Ltd (No. 2)* [1990] 1 AC 109, 282E–F.

First, the courts have said that they will look at the public interest, not at what the public is interested in. Publication of gossip about a celebrity's sex life is unlikely to promote the public interest, however much interest there may be among the public. Publication of a political scandal, however, may well promote the public interest.

Second, the courts will also take into account whether a non-public disclosure (for example disclosure to the police) will be just as effective in promoting the public good, in which case disclosure to the media may not be justified. So if a client admits to a solicitor outside the context of legal professional privilege that he is abusing his child, breaching confidence by disclosing that to the police might well be justified; breaching confidence by telling the tabloid newspapers might not.[58]

 Alternative view

So it seems that you cannot rely on the general public interest to justify a breach of legal privilege. Indeed, the privilege has been described as 'absolute'.[59] Some commentators have questioned that.[60] If, during the seeking of advice, it were to become clear that a client was operating a highly dangerous factory, putting hundreds of lives at risk, should the lawyer not disclose? Certainly, doctors are permitted to disclose medical secrets if lives are at risk.[61] Should lawyers be treated differently?

In *JSC BTA Bank v Ablyazov*,[62] a bank sought disclosure from a solicitor of details of a client's address and telephone number, after the client had been held in contempt of court. The court refused the order, relying on the principle of protection of legal professional privilege. Because the whereabouts of the client were unknown, the order could not be enforced. This case shows the strength of the privilege, especially because the information about which disclosure was sought was not particularly sensitive.

 What would you do?

You are defending a man charged with theft. He informs you that he is HIV positive. He tells you that he keeps his HIV status a secret from his boyfriend because he does not want to 'dampen their sex life'. The boyfriend later consults you about drafting a will.

---

[58] *W v Egdell* [1990] All ER 835.   [59] *R v Derby Magistrates' Court, ex p B* [1995] 4 All ER 526.
[60] Powell and Stewart (n. 8), ch. 5; M. Brindle and G. Dehn, 'Confidence, public interest and the lawyer', in R. Cranston (ed.) *Legal Ethics and Professional Responsibility* (Oxford University Press, 1995).   [61] *W v Egdell* [1990] All ER 835.
[62] [2012] EWHC 1252.

Should you tell him about his partner's HIV status? If not, is there anything else that you might do?

What would they do?

This 'What would you do?' scenario is accompanied by a podcast in which current law students debate the issues and articulate their own responses to the ethical questions that it raises. The podcast is available online at www.oxfordtextbooks.co.uk/orc/herringethics/

Statute

Occasionally, a statute will permit a breach of legal professional privilege. Perhaps the most remarkable exception is Part II of the Regulation of Investigatory Powers Act 2000, which allows covert surveillance of privileged communications between lawyers and clients in cases involving serious crime. The legislation was challenge in *Re McE*[63] as a breach of human rights, but the challenge failed.

A less remarkable, but more common, situation is that in which the Law Society or Solicitors Regulation Authority requires solicitors to disclose their documents as part of an inspection to ensure compliance with accounting rules. In such a case, confidentiality or privilege provides no defence,[64] although if the lawyer believes that, as a result, the client may face prosecution (for example because such disclosure will reveal fraud), the lawyer can apply to court for direction on how to act.

Client–solicitor litigation

Another exception to confidentiality is where the client sues a solicitor. In that event, a solicitor can use as a protection material that would otherwise be covered by confidence. It would be hard for a solicitor to defend an allegation of negligence, for example, if he or she were not able to rely on material that would otherwise be protected by confidentiality. The explanation for this rule was said, in *Lillicrap v Nalder and Son*,[65] to be that, in suing a solicitor, the client waives privilege in relation to all of the documents relevant to the suit.[66] That is an interesting explanation in that it may mean that if a solicitor is suing a client, the argument will not apply, because only a client can waive the privilege.

Mediation

Mediation is discussed in Chapter 10. In short, it is a process whereby the parties discuss the issues around their disagreement, with the help of a third party, and seek to reach agreement. Are the discussions of the parties protected by confidentiality? Of

---

[63] [2009] UKHL 15.   [64] *Parry-Jones v Law Society* [1969] 1 Ch 1.
[65] [1993] 1 All ER 724.   [66] Confirmed in *Hellard v Irwin Mitchell* [2012] EWHC 2656 (Ch).

course, these discussions are not protected by legal professional privilege, because no lawyer is involved.[67] So any protection will rest in confidentiality. Ideally, the mediator will make it clear at the start whether or not the contents of the mediation are to be treated as confidential or not. If it is decided that they are not to be confidential, then anything said can be referred to by the parties in any subsequent litigation. If it is decided the mediation is to be confidential (which is common), then prima facie the discussions are protected by confidentiality. Some doubt surrounds the position if the parties make no decision about confidentiality. Although there is no definitive answer, it might be thought that, generally, parties to mediation would expect confidentiality.

In *Farm Assist Ltd v Secretary of State for the Environment, Food and Rural Affairs*,[68] although the parties had agreed that the mediation was confidential, it was held that the mediator could be called to give evidence when a party claimed that it had agreed to the settlement reached at mediation only as a result of economic duress. It was held that confidentiality could be breached if necessary in the interests of justice. In this case, this was not an attempt to challenge the underlying dispute, but the circumstances surrounding the settlement.

Another point made in *Farm Assist* was that the mediator could rely on confidentiality. Even if both parties wished the mediator to reveal what happened during the mediation, the mediator could, on the terms of the agreement that the parties reached, refuse based on confidentiality.

Joint retainers

When two clients instruct a solicitor together, then all information must be given to both.[69] So if a husband and wife instruct a solicitor to prepare wills, it is assumed that confidential information provided by one can be disclosed to the other. This is perhaps best understood as an example of implied waiver, but it is sometimes presented under a separate heading.

Duty to disclose

So far, in this chapter, we have been looking at cases in which a lawyer must not disclose a client's information. However, there are some circumstances in which a lawyer is positively required *to* disclose it.[70]

First, a lawyer has a duty to disclose all relevant information about the case to the client.

---

[67] Occasionally, a lawyer will act as a mediator, but then his or her role will not be the giving of legal advice.   [68] [2009] EWHC 1102 (TCC).

[69] *R (Ford) v Financial Services Authority* [2011] EWHC 2583 (Admin).

[70] R. Aviel, 'When the state demands disclosure' (2011) 33 Cardozo Law Review 675.

Follow the Code

The SRA Code of Conduct, Indicative Behaviour (IB) 4.4, requires that:

where you are an individual who has responsibility for acting for a *client* or supervising a *client's* matter, you disclose to the *client* all information material to the *client's* matter of which you are personally aware, except when:

(a) the *client* gives specific informed consent to non-disclosure or a different standard of disclosure arises;

(b) there is evidence that serious physical or mental injury will be caused to a person(s) if the information is disclosed to the *client*;

(c) legal restrictions effectively prohibit you from passing the information to the *client*, such as the provisions in the money-laundering and antiterrorism legislation;

(d) it is obvious that privileged documents have been mistakenly disclosed to you;

(e) you come into possession of information relating to state security or Intelligence matters to which the Official Secrets Act 1989 applies;

Notice the five important exceptions to this duty under the SRA Code. Perhaps the most common is where the information is confidential to another current or former client. In such a case, the consent of that current or former client must be obtained before there can be disclosure.[71] Should that client refuse consent, then the best course of action is for the solicitor to refuse to act for either of the two clients. This issue is discussed further in Chapter 6.

The money-laundering legislation is another major requirement for disclosure and this is discussed in Chapter 13.

◎ Application

You are a solicitor who has been instructed by a husband and wife who are buying a house together. The husband informs you that he has a problem with internet pornography, but that he has not told his wife about it. The wife tells you that her business is about to go bust, but she has not told her husband.

You are required to disclose information relevant to the issue on which you have been instructed. The husband's issue is not relevant to the purchase and should be kept confidential. However, what the wife has said should be disclosed—and you should tell the wife that you are required to disclose it.

[71] S. Mize, 'Should the lawyer's duty to keep confidences override the duty to disclose material information to a client?' (2012) 12 Legal Ethics 171.

Against privilege

As we saw at the start of this chapter, the courts have claimed strong reasons in favour of legal professional privilege and lawyer–client confidentiality. The arguments tend to rest on the importance of obtaining sound legal advice to the general rule of law, and the requirement that clients are able to be completely open with their lawyers to that end.

It should not be thought, however, that these assumptions are without question. First, it might be queried whether the obtaining of legal advice is necessarily a good thing. A company might be seeking to find out what are the best ways of avoiding paying tax or the most onerous conditions that it can place on consumers, while still remaining within the law.[72]

Second, it might be queried whether clients need the protection of legal privilege in order to be completely open. A client facing a serious criminal conviction will do anything to be acquitted. The client will reveal all of the facts in a hope that the lawyer will find a loophole that can be used in the client's defence. Is it really believable that a client will not be open for fear that a lawyer might, at some time in the future, be forced to declare what was said? Notably, clients of other professionals do not receive the same protection, but there is no evidence that they are less open with them. For example, psychiatrists do not find patients reluctant to reveal things for fear that a court may subsequently require them to disclose the information.[73]

Third, even if you think that such a fear will deter clients, do clients actually know the law? In other words, is it the privilege that is really protecting them or their trust in the lawyer? I suspect that many clients will be surprised that their lawyers cannot be ordered to reveal what the client has said to them. Even if clients were to know this, they may suspect that there were ways in which a lawyer could ensure that the truth would be revealed to the authorities. In other words, it is trust in the lawyer that might matter more than the legal requirement.

Even leaving aside these points, there are concerns that privilege can be misused. Andrew Higgins has found evidence of companies using privilege to retain information that they do not wish to be known to shareholders or the public.[74] So if a company fears that it may face scandal and that there will be calls for it to produce documentation, the company can consult a lawyer and then claim that the paperwork is all protected under legal privilege.

Enron and other financial scandals in particular have raised the dark side of confidentiality.[75] Claims were made that lawyers were aware of some of the improper

---

[72] A Higgins, 'Legal advice privilege and its relevance to corporations' (2010) 73 Modern Law Review 371.

[73] F. Zacharis, 'Rethinking confidentiality' (1989) 74 Iowa Law Review 351.

[74] A. Higgins, 'Corporate abuse of legal professional privilege' (2008) 27 Civil Justice Quarterly 37.

[75] T. Bost, 'Corporate lawyers after the big quake: The conceptual fault line in the professional duty of confidentiality' (2008) 19 Journal of Business, Entrepreneurship and the Law 335.

goings-on, but were reluctant to report anything or to raise concerns for fear of breaching client confidentiality. Interestingly, in his discussion of the Enron incidents, Bost concludes that lawyers need to imagine their role as a 'trusted counsellor' rather than simply as an 'implementer or transaction engineer'.[76] The lawyer needs to provide 'candid advice' and 'a moral discourse with her client'. However, that role can be achieved only if the client can be completely open. For Bost, the lessons of the scandal are not less confidentiality, but rather a change in the nature of the lawyer's role. We discuss this further in Chapter 2.

A rather different concern is that lawyers do not take client confidentiality seriously enough. There is routine use of email to convey sensitive material, despite its vulnerability to hacking.[77] Further, there is casualness among some lawyers about disclosing confidential information to friends and colleagues by way of telling amusing stories. As David Chavkin notes, even lecturers on professional ethics regularly use cases that they have experienced in practice as examples in class, despite the fact that doing so, technically, will involve a breach of confidence.[78]

A more cynical view is that confidentiality protects lawyers from scrutiny over what they do. The public does not learn of what lawyers are told and what their advice is, because it is protected by client confidentiality.[79] Notably, because the legal privilege does not apply to other professionals, there have been complaints from accountants and other professionals that this gives lawyers an unfair advantage in the competition for business.[80]

 Scandal!

The American case of *State v Macumber*[81] is often cited as an example of where confidentiality was taken too far. It involved a case in which a man was charged with murder and was facing the death penalty. Another person, who had since died, had confessed to his lawyers that he had committed the murder, but the lawyers were prevented from disclosing this information to the court. Cases such as these raise concerns that confidentiality leads to 'a kind of moral blindness to the real issues of potential conflict and abuse that a broad and unqualified claim to confidentiality can mask'.[82]

---

[76] Bost (n. 75).

[77] R. Bolin, 'Risky mail: Concerns in confidential attorney–client email' (2013) 81 University of Cincinnati Law Review 7.

[78] D. Chavkin, 'Why doesn't anyone care about confidentiality? (And, what message does that send to new lawyers?)' (2012) 25 Georgetown Journal of Legal Ethics 239.

[79] D. Nicolson and J. Webb, *Professional Ethics, Critical Interrogations* (Oxford University Press, 1999), 255.

[80] A. Boon and J. Levin, *The Ethics and Conduct of Lawyers in England and Wales* (Hart, 2008), 221.

[81] 112 Arizona 569, 544 PZd 1084 (1976).

[82] C. Wolfram, *Modern Legal Ethics* (West Publishing, 1999), 24.

Conclusion

In this chapter, we have explored the requirement that lawyers keep clients' information private. Lawyers are put in a special position by the doctrine of legal professional privilege, which offers especial protection to communications between clients and lawyers, and to documents prepared for the purposes of litigation. Although there are some circumstances in which the privilege does not apply, these are fairly limited. Generally, a client can be completely open with his or her lawyer, fairly confident that these discussions will not be made public without the client's consent. This is seen by many as central to a sound legal system: people must be able to get independent legal advice; access to good legal advice is possible only if there is a promise of confidentiality. That is what the law seeks to provide.

 Further reading

The detail on the law on confidentiality can be found in the following works:

J. Auburn, *Legal Professional Privilege: Law and Theory* (Hart, 2000).

M. Brindle and G. Dehn, 'Confidence, public interest and the lawyer', in R. Cranston (ed.) *Legal Ethics And Professional Responsibility* (Oxford University Press, 1995).

A. Higgins, 'Legal advice privilege and its relevance to corporations' (2010) 73 Modern Law Review 371.

A. Higgins, 'ECJ confirms no privilege for in-house counsel: *Azko Nobel v European Commission*' (2011) 30 Civil Justice Quarterly 113.

R. Toulson and C. Phipps, *Confidentiality*, 2nd edn (Sweet and Maxwell, 2006).

Work on legal professional privilege is found among the following:

J. Auburn, *Legal Professional Privilege: Law and Theory* (Hart, 2000).

M. Stockdale and R. Mitchell, 'Legal professional privilege and alternative business structures' (2012) 33 Company Lawyer 204.

The following discuss some of the theoretical issues concerning confidentiality:

R. Aviel, 'When the state demands disclosure' (2011) 33 Cardozo Law Review 675.

R. Aviel, 'The boundary claim's caveat: Lawyers and confidentiality exceptionalism' (2012) 86 Tulane Law Review 1055.

T. Bost, 'Corporate lawyers after the big quake: The conceptual fault line in the professional duty of confidentiality' (2008) 19 Journal of Business, Entrepreneurship and the Law 335.

G. Chavkin, 'Why doesn't anyone care about confidentiality? (And, what message does that send to new lawyers?)' (2012) 25 Georgetown Journal of Legal Ethics 239.

A. Higgins, 'Corporate abuse of legal professional privilege' (2008) 27 Civil Justice Quarterly 37.

S. Mize, 'Should the lawyer's duty to keep confidences override the duty to disclose material information to a client?' (2012) 12 Legal Ethics 171.

F. Rizzuto, 'The *Akzo* ruling of the Court of Justice and the private enforcement of European Union competition law: Two steps back, one step forward' (2010) 3 Global Competition Litigation Review 121.

G. Sisk and P. Abbate, 'The dynamic attorney–client privilege' (2010) 23 Georgetown Journal of Legal Ethics 201.

F. Zacharis, 'Rethinking confidentiality' (1989) 74 Iowa Law Review 351.

6 Conflicts of interests

 Key issues

- Lawyers should not put themselves in a position in which their own interests conflict with those of a client.
- Lawyers should not act for two clients whose interests conflict.
- An exception to the no conflict rule may be permitted if the firm can create an 'informational barrier'.

Introduction

Successful lawyers have many clients. This can be a problem because a central principle of traditional legal ethics is that lawyers must put the interests of their clients first. But what may be in the interests of one client may not be in the interests of another. If that is the case, which client should the lawyer prefer? There is no correct answer to that question. A lawyer in such a situation will inevitably end up acting against the interests of one client. Professional ethics therefore requires lawyers to avoid getting into such a position in the first place. A lawyer should avoid being in a position in which there is a conflict, or even a risk of conflict, between what is in the interest of one client and what is in the interests of another client. Similarly, a lawyer should avoid being in a position in which there is a conflict between his or her own interests and those of a client. The **conflicts of interests principle** is one of the central pillars of professional ethics. It has been suggested that the avoiding of conflicts is 'a keystone of the profession'.[1]

 Definition

The **conflicts of interests principle** requires that lawyers should avoid situations in which their duties to one client conflict with their duties to another client or their own interests.

---

[1] C. Kindregan, 'Conflict of interest and the lawyer in civil practice' (1976) 10 Valparaiso University Law Review 433.

The basic principles

The no conflict rule is, in fact, made up of two principles.

1. You must not put yourself in a position in which your own interests conflict with those of a client. This is called 'own interest conflict' in the Solicitors Regulation Authority (SRA) Code of Conduct.

2. You should not put yourself in a position in which the interests of one client conflict with the interests of another client. The Code calls this a 'client conflict'.

This chapter will explore what the application of these principles means in practice. It will also explore what lawyers should do if things go wrong and they find themselves in a position in which the conflict has arisen.

The reason behind these principles in their basic form is readily understood: as a client, you would not want a solicitor acting for you who would be better off if you were to lose your case; nor would you want a barrister to be arguing for you while also advising your adversary. In either case, you would feel that the lawyer was not putting your interests first. But notice that the rules are all about avoidance: the real wrong is the lawyer acting against the interests of the client; the rule against conflict is about the lawyer *avoiding* being in a position in which he or she is tempted to do that. It is also about perception. The rule prevents people suspecting that lawyers are not promoting their clients' interests because they are influenced by their own interests.

The professional codes

The SRA Code of Conduct

The SRA Code is clear.

Follow the Code

The SRA Code of Conduct, Chapter 3, states:

> You can never act where there is a conflict, or a significant risk of conflict, between you and your *client*.

> If there is a conflict, or a significant risk of a conflict, between two or more current *clients*, you must not act for all or both of them unless the matter falls within the scope of the limited exceptions set out at Outcomes 3.6 or 3.7.

The Code goes further and requires solicitors to put in place steps to ensure that a conflict does not arise unintentionally.

Follow the Code

SRA Code of Conduct, Outcome 3.1, reads:

> you have effective systems and controls in place to enable you to identify and assess potential *conflicts of interests*.

These systems should mean that a solicitor should not act for a client if the solicitor's ability to act in the best interests of the client is impaired by the following interests of the solicitor or anyone in his or her firm:

(a) any financial interest;

(b) a personal relationship;

(c) the appointment of you, or a member of your *firm* or family, to public office;

(d) commercial relationships; or

(e) your employment.[2]

The Code gives some examples of personal conflict, including:

> in a personal capacity, selling to or buying from, lending to or borrowing from a *client*, unless the *client* has obtained independent legal advice;

> advising a *client* to invest in a business, in which you have an interest which affects your ability to provide impartial advice.[3]

The Code is clear that there are exceptions to the no conflict rule and we will look at these later in this chapter.

The Bar Council Code of Conduct

The Bar Council Code of Conduct (the Bar Code) explains the no conflict principle as an exception to the 'cab-rank rule' (see Chapter 4).

Follow the Code

The Bar Code, regulation 603, requires that a barrister must not agree to act for a client:

> If there is or appears to be a conflict or risk of conflict either between the interests of the barrister and some other person or between the interests of any one or more clients (unless all relevant persons consent to the barrister accepting the instructions);

---

[2] SRA Code of Conduct, Outcome 3.2.

[3] SRA Code of Conduct, Indicative Behaviours (IBs) 3.8 and 3.9.

If a conflict arises once a barrister has accepted instructions, then regulation 608 applies.

Follow the Code

Under Bar Code, regulation 608:

A barrister must cease to act and if he is a self-employed barrister must return any instructions:

[...]

(b) if having accepted instructions on behalf of more than one client there is or appears to be:

    (i) a conflict or risk of conflict between the interests of any one or more of such clients; or

    (ii) risk of a breach of confidence;

and the clients do not all consent to him continuing to act;

This is reinforced by regulation 606.4.

Follow the Code

Under Bar Code, regulation 606.4:

In cases involving several parties, a barrister must on receipt of instructions and further in the event of any change of circumstances consider whether, having regard to all the circumstances including any actual or potential conflict of interest, any client ought to be separately represented or advised or whether it would be in the best interests of any client to be jointly represented or advised with another party.

It might seem at this point that the 'no conflict' principle should not be a difficult one to understand or to apply. However, it seems to be far more difficult to apply in practice than in theory. In one recent case, the court noted that the solicitor's conduct was 'bedevilled by a massive conflict of interest'.[4] The following case is an example of a blatant conflict of interest that the solicitor overlooked.

Key case

Hilton v Barker Booth & Eastwood [2005] 1 All ER 651

Ian Hilton was a builder who was approached by Neil Bromage with a proposal that Hilton buy some commercial property to redevelop. Hilton, a builder, was keen to

---

[4] *Cherrilow Ltd v Osmond Solicitors* [2011] EWHC 3443 (QB), [12].

get into the commercial property business and agreed. Hilton agreed to buy the property, develop it, and then sell it on to Bromage. He consulted the defendant solicitors. They did not tell Hilton that they had acted previously for Bromage when he was imprisoned for fraud; nor, even more importantly, did they tell Hilton that they were acting for Bromage in this deal and that they were lending Bromage the deposit. The contracts were entered into and, later, Bromage failed to complete the contracts. This caused serious loss to Hilton, who sued the solicitors for breach of contract.

To the surprise of many commentators, Hilton lost before the Court of Appeal on the basis that there was an implied term in the contract between Bromage and the solicitors that the solicitors would not reveal confidential information that they held about Bromage. This argument was rejected by the House of Lords. Had the ruling in the Court of Appeal been upheld, it would have created a serious inroad into the conflicts of interest principle. Lord Walker was clear that the case involved an unacceptable breach of the principle of conflict of interest. His assessment that the Court of Appeal judgment was 'contrary to common sense and justice' was strongly worded. The error in the Court of Appeal reasoning was straightforward: even if the contract with Bromage prevented the solicitor from revealing information about Bromage to another client, it did not justify the solicitors agreeing to act for Hilton. They could have explained to Hilton that professional ethics meant that they could not act for him, without having to reveal any confidential information.

In *Bolkiah v KPMG*,[5] Lord Millett confirmed the no conflict rule as part of the legal regulation of lawyers. It would mean that a former client could object to a solicitor taking on a new client, who was a rival:

> My Lords, I would affirm this as the basis of the court's jurisdiction to intervene on behalf of a former client. It is otherwise where the court's intervention is sought by an existing client, for a fiduciary cannot act at the same time both for and against the same client, and his firm is in no better position. A man cannot without the consent of both clients act for one client while his partner is acting for another in the opposite interest. His disqualification has nothing to do with the confidentiality of client information. It is based on the inescapable conflict of interest which is inherent in the situation.

One notable point in these statements is that the rule against conflict is not simply a repetition of the protection of confidence; the rule against conflict applies even if there is no question of the misuse of confidential information.

---

[5] [1999] 2 AC 222, 234.

The ethical basis for the principle

We have already mentioned one basis for the conflict of interest principle. A client is entitled to expect a lawyer to give impartial advice and to recommend a course of action that is best for the client. That ensures that clients are given the best chance to make their own decisions and so maximises their autonomy. The principle ensures that a lawyer is not put into the position of having to make an impossible choice between two clients, and making a decision that will harm one and benefit the other.

This reflects the special position of trust that exists between a lawyer and his or her client. The client needs to feel free to be completely open with the lawyer so that the best and most accurate advice can be given. If clients fear that information they give might be used to help another client or the lawyer himself or herself, clients will be less open, and that will harm the provision of legal advice generally.

Although, as already noted, the rule against conflicts of interest is separate from the confidentiality principle (see Chapter 5), they are connected. If a lawyer is advising two clients on a matter, there is a risk that information gained from one client will be used to advise the other client. A lawyer will be in a very difficult position if client A is proposing to engage in a course of action that the lawyer knows will be disastrous, because of information that he or she has gained from client B. The lawyer will be in an impossible position: he or she must choose either to give bad advice to client A or to breach confidentiality to client B. It is better to avoid being in that position in the first place.

From what has been said so far, you might think that the ethical case in favour of the no conflict principle is straightforward. But it is not. First, we will discuss the practical problems around the principle, and then we will consider the problem in finding a remedy.

The problem of the real world

The no conflict principle can be hard to apply in the real world! In any lawyer–client relationship, conflict is inevitable. There are plenty of examples.

- A lawyer wants to make money from a case, but that is not in the client's interests!
- The lawyer needs to have a life and cannot spend every available hour working on their clients' cases. That is not necessarily in their clients' interests either.
- The law firm must have in place procedures to ensure that the firm works efficiently and these procedures are not necessarily in the interests of each client.[6]

---

[6] See *Heron v TNT Ltd* [2013] EWCA Civ 469, which raised, but did not resolve, the question of whether a conditional fee created an unacceptable conflict of interest.

- A lawyer must divide up his or her time in an appropriate way between clients, delegating suitable work to juniors. That division of work can create conflicts between the interests of clients and the lawyer.

In short, the client–lawyer relationship is riddled with conflict and it is artificial to pretend that it is not. The idea that the lawyer should avoid all conflicts of interests is idealistic and unrealistic. It might be better to say that we should ensure that no *improper* conflicts should be permitted.

The practical problems around the conflicts of interest rule are particularly acute for large firms.[7] As Daniel Bussel argues:

> As law firms have grown in size and reach, and as institutional clients have adopted the practice of engaging lawyers from a variety of firms on a case-by-case rather than general retainer basis, the rule has become increasingly out-of-touch with the realities of modern law practice.[8]

Indeed, the City of London Law Society Working Party complained that the conflict rules caused real problems for commercial firms, especially because continental firms did not face the same strict rules on conflicts. According to the report, 'English and Welsh solicitors are in a uniquely disadvantageous position in comparison with lawyers in continental Europe.'[9]

The practical problems surrounding conflicts of interest have become especially acute for commercial firms, which have been employing ever larger numbers of people, interacting with an expanding range of professional groups, and becoming increasingly international.[10] This means that if a company seeks advice from a large law firm, it is almost inevitable that there will be someone on the firm's staff who is, or was, dealing with a rival to the new client.[11] Indeed, Harry McVea reports one partner of a large city firm saying: 'We apply our own standards and manage conflicts through Chinese Walls.'[12] The reference to 'Chinese walls'—the term 'informational barriers' is now preferred—will be explained shortly. But some city firms especially feel that the current approach to conflicts does not appreciate the reality of the commercial world. Some create their own regulations on conflicts, which they ask all clients to accept.[13]

---

[7] M. Regna and P. Heenan, 'Supply chains and porous boundaries: The disaggregation of legal services' (2010) 78 Fordham Law Review 2137.

[8] D. Bussel, 'No conflict' (2012) 25 Georgetown Journal of Legal Ethics 207, 208.

[9] City of London Law Society, *Report of Working Party on Review of Conflict Rules* (City of London Law Society, 2000), 3.

[10] J. Griffiths-Baker and N. Moore, 'Regulating conflicts of interest in global law firms: Peace in our time?' (2012) 80 Fordham Law Review 2541.

[11] Griffiths-Baker and Moore (n. 10); J. Loughrey, 'Large law firms, sophisticated clients, and the regulation of conflicts of interests in England and Wales' (2011) 14 Legal Ethics 45.

[12] H. McVea, '"Heard it through the grapevine": Chinese walls and former client confidentiality in law firms' (2000) 59 Cambridge Law Journal 370.

[13] C. Whelan and N. Ziv, 'Privatizing professionalism: Client control of lawyers' ethics' (2012) 80 Fordham Law Review 2577.

So maybe we should be much more relaxed about conflicts of interests? Remember that lawyers are used to putting their own views to one side and working fearlessly for their clients. That is part of what the lawyer's job is all about. Should a lawyer not be able to act for client A one day and client B the next? We need the rules on confidentiality and the rule that lawyers must promote their clients' best interests, of course, but we must allow firms to act for multiple clients.

One response to the argument that we can trust lawyers to deal with the problems raised by a conflict of interest is that it may be psychologically inaccurate. People are not as good at compartmentalising their thinking as they might think. Examining the evidence from neuroscience, Paul Thagard writes:

> Decision makers who have acquired interests at odds with their official responsibilities have no way of knowing whether their decisions emanate from the biases they have acquired from personal interests instead of from good reasoning that takes their responsibilities into account. People are incapable of knowing whether they are acting appropriately or out of a conflict of interest. Hence morally objectionable factors such as personal relationships can intrude into official decisions without much possibility of detection. People naturally have personal goals that may conflict with their professional responsibilities, but lack a mental mechanism to detect such divergences.[14]

Interestingly, he concludes his article by suggesting that rather than disallow conflicts, it might be better to encourage people to disclose their conflicts and to be more open about the pressures that they face. Lawyers may, by being more open, educate themselves to take appropriate account of the conflicts that they face. Further, by opening the decisions up to outside scrutiny, others can check that the lawyer is being fair between clients. It is this kind of thinking that is behind, for example, the rule that members of Parliament (MPs) must make public any interests that they have in outside bodies. It is also worth noting that other psychologists note that, sometimes, when faced with a conflict between our own interests and the interests of another, we give much more weight to the interests of the other, especially if we are in a close relationship with that person.[15]

Digging deeper

One issue that emerges from this discussion is that the essential wrong is not simply being in a conflict of interest, but the wrongs that may emerge from being in that position: a beach of confidence; making a profit from a fiduciary position; not giving a client the best advice.[16] But is the potential for harm a sufficiently good reason for not allowing a conflict, especially if conflicts are an inevitable part of legal practice?

[14] P. Thagard, 'The moral psychology of conflict of interest: Insights from affect neuroscience' (2007) 24 Journal of Applied Philosophy 373, 373–4.

[15] J. Gore and S. Cross, 'Conflicts of interest: Relational self-construal and decision making in interpersonal contexts' (2011) 10 Self and Identity 185.

[16] E. Haavi Morreim, 'Taking a lesson from the lawyers: Defining and addressing conflict of interest' (2011) 11 The American Journal of Bioethics 33, 34.

One justification for the current position is that if we were to do away with the current no conflicts approach and instead penalise acting improperly in the face of a conflict, we would face some very difficult questions. For example, how will we know whether the lawyer improperly used information gained from one client to assist another? Richard Epstein suggests that the purpose of the conflicts rule is 'to separate the lawyer from temptation so that the breach will not have to be remedied after it occurs, when it is so difficult to identify both the source of the leak and the consequences that flow from it'.[17]

In other words, it is very difficult to know whether a lawyer has handled a situation of conflict appropriately. It is much easier, and clearer, simply to say that a lawyer should never get into a position of conflict in the first place.

Another justification is to rely on public perception. It is important that lawyers are seen to be above reproach. The no conflict principle means that there is no hint of suspicion that lawyers are not putting their clients first.[18]

The question remains whether these are strong enough to justify the practical problems created by the principle.[19]

The remedy

A second problem with the ethical basis for the principle concerns the remedy: if there is a conflict of interest, the lawyer must stop acting for the client. Fair enough? Well, maybe not for the client. He or she will need to find a new lawyer: a new person to trust; a new person to spend time instructing and getting to know. All of that takes time and, as always, time with lawyers means money. In short, it might seem that the costs and burdens of the no conflict rule fall on the client rather than the lawyer. True, the lawyer will lose out by not gaining an extra client, but in terms of being out of pocket, it is the client who pays.

Cory J, in a dissenting judgment in a Canadian case, *MacDonald Estate v Martin*,[20] has stated: 'The requirement of change imposed upon a client is, on balance, a small price to pay for maintaining the integrity of our system of justice.' Nevertheless, the client who is out of pocket may not see it that way. This may explain why (as we shall see) there are exceptions that allow a client to consent to the existence of the conflict so that the lawyer can continue acting—although it should be borne in mind that the financial cost of changing solicitors is a strong incentive to a client to give consent.

---

[17] R. Epstein, 'The legal regulation of lawyers' conflicts of interest' (1992) 60 Fordham Law Review 579, 590.

[18] K. McMunigal, 'Rethinking attorney conflict of interest doctrine' (1992) 5 Georgetown Journal of Legal Ethics 823.

[19] J. Macey and G. Miller, 'An economic analysis of conflict of interest regulation' (1997) 82 Iowa Law Review 965.   [20] (1991) 77 DLR (4th) 249, 261.

What is a 'conflict of interest'?

When we talk about a 'conflict of interest', what is meant exactly? It has been inter-preted widely. The word 'interests' includes not only financial interests, but also per-sonal interests. A lawyer should be wary of, for example, working for his wife's or her husband's ex-spouse. Unless the divorce had been particularly amicable, the lawyer might be put into a position in which his or her emotional feelings and professional duties are in too much of a conflict.

We will explore here some of the ambiguities surrounding the term 'conflict of interests'.

Own interests

It is generally agreed that it is harder to justify a situation in which a client's interests conflict with those of a lawyer than one in which the conflict is with another client. Cases of conflict with a lawyer's own interests will arise where he or she is buying or selling his or her own property to a client, or lending the client money, or advising on a venture from which the lawyer or the lawyer's family will profit.[21] This is not to say that a solicitor cannot do these things with a client; rather, the solicitor must reveal the interests to the client and the client must receive appropriate independent advice.

The no conflict rule applies when the client's interests conflict not only with those of the lawyer, but also the lawyer's family or someone with whom the solicitor has an intimate relationship.[22]

A tricky situation can arise if the solicitor discovers that the client has a claim against the solicitor. The most obvious scenario would be where a solicitor discovers that he or she has been negligent in handling a client's affairs and that the client may have a claim against the solicitor. In such a case, there is a conflict of interest and the solicitor must make the client aware of the potential claim.

The following is a fairly clear case of a personal conflict of interest.

 Key case

Solicitors Regulation Authority v Dennison [2012] EWCA Civ 421

A firm of solicitors used a company to provide medical reports for clients. One of the partners in the firm owned one third of the shares in the company. He told neither his partners, nor the clients. He made substantial profits from this arrangement. The Solicitors Regulation Authority (SRA) decided that he had to be struck off, given the dishonesty. The tribunal found it very serious and the Court of Appeal agreed with his suspension.

---

[21] *Cobbetts LLP v Hodge* [2009] EWHC 786 (Ch).

[22] *Richards v Law Society* [2009] EWHC 2087 (Admin), in which a client was entering a transac-tion with the children of the solicitor.

What interests are covered?

The fact that the principle extends beyond financial interests can create problems. What if there is a conflict between the moral views of a lawyer and those of his or her client? For example, imagine that a pro-choice pressure group asks a devout Catholic lawyer to represent it in a case seeking to liberalise the law on abortion. What should the lawyer do? There is no straightforward answer to this. It may be that lawyers in this situation should ask themselves whether their own beliefs will mean that they will not able to act as strongly in the clients' interests as they should; if the answer is that they will not, they should not act. Some lawyers do not find it difficult to put their own views to one side and throw themselves into fighting for the client, despite strongly disagreeing with the client's views. These lawyers may legitimately feel that there is no conflict of interest. If, however, they decide that their moral convictions will inhibit their representation, they should recommend that the client finds an alternative lawyer. It might be worth adding that, similarly, a lawyer who feels passionately in agreement with a client might be in a position in which he or she cannot offer dispassionate advice.

An easy issue arises if there is a conflict between a solicitor's professional obligations and what a client was to do. Then, clearly, the professional obligation must win out. An obvious example would be if a client were to instruct a lawyer to lie in court. The lawyer must refuse to do that. That is not the lawyer putting his or her personal beliefs above the client's interests (which would be impermissible); rather, it is the lawyer putting his or her duty to the court and justice generally above the clients' interests (which is permissible).

A risk of conflict?

Conflict can arise not only with the interests that a lawyer (or another client) has, but also with the interests that the lawyer (or another client) may acquire in the future. So if a solicitor is hoping to buy shares in a company and a client seeks advice in a deal involving that company, the solicitor should not act. Although there is no direct conflict of interest, the solicitor has clear plans to acquire an interest. This is a relatively easy case. But what if the lawyer had only been considering buying shares in the company? Is only a vague possibility of a conflict sufficient to bring the principle into play? In *Marks & Spencer plc v Freshfields Bruckhaus Deringer*,[23] the court held that the conflict must be more than a mere theoretical possibility. It was held that only if there were a reasonable apprehension of a possible conflict would the courts intervene:

> This is in no sense an indication of what may happen, as to which I have no idea whatever, but it cannot be assumed that the arrangements between the parties involved will be on a friendly basis. It is not right that a solicitor is entitled to wait in a takeover situation until it is clear whether the bid is going to be a friendly or a

---

[23] [2004] EWHC 1337 (Ch).

hostile one before he decides whether or not to act. It is said against the judge that he was speculating as to what might happen in the future.[24]

In *Bolkiah v KPMG*,[25] Lord Millett added to this analysis:

> I prefer simply to say that the court should intervene unless it is satisfied that there is no risk of disclosure. It goes without saying that the risk must be a real one, and not merely fanciful or theoretical. But it need not be substantial.

Notably, the International Bar Association (IBA) maintains that a conflict exists if 'there is a significant risk that the representation of one or more clients will be materially limited by the lawyer's responsibilities to another client, a former client, a third person or by a personal interest of the lawyer'.[26] This suggests that, in other countries and in the international sphere, a more relaxed approach is taken about the degree of risk of conflict that is required before a lawyer cannot act.

 Scandal!

Even the most senior of lawyers can fall foul of the no conflict principle. In *R v Bow Streeet Magistrate, ex p Pinochet*,[27] a challenge was made to the decision of the House of Lords that General Pinochet did not have immunity from arrest. The challenge was on the basis that one of the Law Lords was an unpaid director and chair of Amnesty International, a charity that had been involved in the appeal. The case was about bias and it was argued that, because the judge was connected with the charity that was joined in the appeal, he should not have been involved in the case. This was even though there was no financial gain or even personal gain that could be obtained. At the heart of the case was the point that justice must be seen to have been done. Although there were no suggestions that the judge in this case had been influenced by his support for Amnesty International, it may have appeared to others that he was.

 Alternative view

Is the conflict of duty based on an unrealistic expectation? Very often, a lawyer has to balance his or her own interests and the interests of his or her clients. A lawyer may have two urgent cases and deal with them both well, but a degree of balancing is likely to have taken place: running an efficient office and ensuring that burdens on employees are not too heavy will both be in tension with offering the best possible service to clients. As

---

[24] At [26].   [25] [1999] 2 AC 222, 237A.

[26] International Bar Association, *Conflicts of Interest* (International Bar Association, 2012).

[27] [2000] AC 119.

> Boon and Levin argue: 'It is naive for any professional—whether a doctor, lawyer or social worker—to maintain that they always put the interest, or the best interests, of the patient, client or child first.'[28] With that in mind, might it be better to talk about ensuring that there is not *too much* of a conflict of interest, rather than chasing the impossible ideal of ensuring that there is no conflict of interest at all?

How direct must the conflict be?

The rule applies to what might be called 'indirect conflicts'—that is, situations in which there is a conflict of interest not in relation to the issue on which the client is seeing the lawyer, but in regard to a related matter. There is a balance to be drawn here. Clearly, if a lawyer is advising client A on the purchase of a house from client B, then the lawyer cannot advise client B on the sale without the consent of both parties. However, if client B approaches the solicitor to advise on an unrelated matter, say an employment issue, there may be no relevant conflict. As this example shows, just because a lawyer is advising client A in a case against client B, it is not always not permissible for the lawyer to act for client B. The lawyer can do so in regard to an unrelated matter. Of course, whether a matter is unrelated or not may be open to debate in borderline cases. The best advice in such a situation, if there is any ambiguity, is to get the consent of all parties.

Who is a client?

There is, of course, no difficulty with a lawyer advising a client whose interests conflict with those of a third party who is not a client. Indeed, they almost inevitably will, but that raises the question of who is a client? Say, for example, that a managing director of a company is seeking advice on a matter relating to the company.[29] The lawyer has no conflict of interest with the company, but does with the managing director. Should that prevent the lawyer from acting? There is no easy answer to such a question.[30] It should be recalled that part of the purpose of the rule is to ensure that there is no *apparent* conflict of interest and it might be thought, in such a case, that the appearance arises. No doubt the safest course of action is not to act where the issue is dubious.

New clients

The rule against conflict of interest is particularly relevant when a new client approaches a solicitor or a barrister. Then, the lawyer is under a duty to consider whether there is

---

[28] A. Boon and J. Levin, *The Ethics and Conduct of Lawyers in England and Wales* (Hart, 2008), 199.

[29] See *Newcastle International Airport Ltd v Eversheds* [2012] EWHC 2648 (Ch), in which that issue arose.

[30] W. Simon, 'Whom (or what) does the organization's lawyer represent? An anatomy of intra-client conflict' (2003) 91 California Law Review 57.

an actual or potential conflict of interests with an existing or previous client. If there is, the lawyer must not act for the new client, unless he or she can rely on one of the exceptions that we will consider shortly. Notice that the professional codes require the lawyer to take positive steps to consider whether there is a conflict of interest. Simply claiming ignorance—saying 'I did not realise there may be a conflict'—may not be a defence if reasonable consideration of the question would have revealed it.

Tricky issues can arise if the firm takes on a new client and only later discovers that there is a conflict of interest with a previous client, particularly if the firm holds confidential information from the previous client that is relevant to the new client. The ideal solution is to obtain the consent of the previous client to disclosure.[31] If the previous client refuses to allow disclosure, then the firm should inform the new client that it will not be able to use the confidential information in advice, and then put in place informational barriers (at which we look later in the chapter) to ensure that there is no breach of confidence.

The following case provides a good example of these principles being applied.

 Key case

Re Z [2009] EWHC 3621 (Fam)

A husband and wife were divorcing. The husband sought an order to prevent the wife from instructing her current solicitor on the basis that, nine years previously, the husband had sought the advice of the firm (albeit another partner) in connection with his marriage. The solicitor had then acted for the husband for a year. The wife's solicitors were prepared to put in place undertakings that the partner dealing with the wife's case (Mrs F) would not discuss the case with her colleagues.

Bodey J, in granting the order, concluded that the firm of solicitors had information that was confidential to the husband and that there was a risk the partner would receive it that was not 'fancy or theoretical'. He accepted that the proposed undertaking would deal with deliberate disclosures, but could not deal with inadvertent disclosures. This was especially because Mrs F was a senior partner and in regular contact with others in her firm.

Interestingly, Bodey J saw the case as involving a conflict between two interests:

[F]irst, there is the interest of the client in being able to have the fullest confidence in the solicitor whom he instructs, for which purpose there should be no risk or perception of risk that confidential information would be disclosed to anyone else. Second, there is the interest in the freedom of the solicitor to be able to take instructions from any member of the public, together with the interest of members of the public to be able to instruct solicitors of their choice whenever there is no real need for constraint.[32]

---

[31] Although care needs to be taken: asking a previous client for consent may involve making disclosure about the new client's plans and therefore may need the consent of the new client.

[32] At [20].

He went on to emphasise that a number of factors may be relevant in deciding whether the lawyer could act:

The picture may change, for example, according to how long ago and for how long the former solicitor acted for the former client; the precise nature of the work done by the former solicitor for the former client and the precise nature of the work being done or proposed to be done by the former solicitor (or the firm which he or she has joined) for the new client; how many individuals who acted for the former client have moved to the firm about to represent or representing the new client; how many people will be working on the case at the new solicitors; where the former solicitor's files of the former client are kept and who can access them; whether the firm against which objection is taken has already been working on the relevant matter for a period of time before the former solicitor joins it having represented the former client; and whether effective 'information barriers' can be made. Permutations and nuances of detail as to factors like these are considerable and vary from case to case, a point which has to be borne in mind when considering dicta from the various authorities to which I have been referred, each having a factual matrix quite different from this case.[33]

In that case, Mrs F emphasised that she had no recollection of her dealings with the husband. Bodey J placed little weight on this, saying that memories could arise unexpectedly, and also noting that the solicitor had got to know what kind of person the husband was and his 'sensitivities and feelings'. This last point is interesting because it shows that the court is not only concerned about factual information gained from one client that can be used by another, but also with what might be called 'emotional information'.

Application

You are consulted by Mrs Jones, who wants to divorce her husband. Several years ago, your firm acted for Mr Jones in a business transaction. There is here a potential conflict of interest. The information that your firm learned about Mr Jones's business may be useful if you are acting for Mrs Jones.

You should first seek permission from Mr Jones to act for his wife. If he refuses, then the only possibility will be to put in place arrangements (an informational barrier) to ensure that those who advised him on the business will not be in contact with the lawyer advising Mrs Jones. Even then, the court may take some persuading that the barrier will be secure. The safest course of action is to advise Mrs Jones to find another solicitor.

---

[33] At [28].

Exceptions

The professional codes and the courts are clear that there are exceptions to the principle that a lawyer must not be in a position in which there is a conflict of interest. Ian Ferguson suggests that lawyers are inclined to think of ways of fitting the case within an exception, rather than to seek to comply with the central principle.[34] That is not surprising, because lawyers want to have as many clients as possible!

We shall now explore the exceptions.

Consent and common interest

A lawyer may act in a position in which there is a conflict of interest in certain circumstances if all of the parties consent. This exception derives from the fact that the principle is seen as a matter of implied agreement between the parties. In *Clark Boyce v Mouat*,[35] Lord Jauncey of Tullichettle explained:

> There is no general rule of law to the effect that a solicitor should never act for both parties in a transaction where their interests may conflict. Rather is the position that he may act provided that he has obtained the informed consent of both to his acting. Informed consent means consent given in the knowledge that there is a conflict between the parties and that as a result the solicitor may be disabled from disclosing to each party the full knowledge which he possesses as to the transaction or may be disabled from giving advice to one party which conflicts with the interests of the other. If the parties are content to proceed upon this basis the solicitor may properly act.

The SRA Code of Conduct sets out when a solicitor may, with the consent of clients, act for both: that is, where there is a common interest and where the clients are competing for the same objective. The Code sets out the detail.

Follow the Code

The SRA Code of Conduct, Outcome 3.6, requires that:

> where there is a *client conflict* and the *clients* have a *substantially common interest* in relation to a matter or a particular aspect of it, you only act if:
>
> (a) you have explained the relevant issues and risks to the *clients* and you have a reasonable belief that they understand those issues and risks;
> (b) all the *clients* have given informed consent in writing to you acting;
> (c) you are satisfied that it is reasonable for you to act for all the *clients* and that it is in their best interests; and
> (d) you are satisfied that the benefits to the *clients* of you doing so outweigh the risks.

---

[34] I. Ferguson, 'A proposal to rethink the conflict of interest rules', *The Firm*, 3 October 2013.
[35] [1994] 1 AC 428, 435.

Outcome 3.7 requires that:

where there is a *client conflict* and the *clients* are *competing for the same objective*, you only act if:

(a) you have explained the relevant issues and risks to the *clients* and you have a reasonable belief that they understand those issues and risks;

(b) the *clients* have confirmed in writing that they want you to act, in the knowledge that you act, or may act, for one or more other *clients* who are *competing for the same objective*;

(c) there is no other *client conflict* in relation to that matter;

(d) unless the *clients* specifically agree, no individual acts for, or is responsible for the supervision of work done for, more than one of the *clients* in that matter; and

(e) you are satisfied that it is reasonable for you to act for all the *clients* and that the benefits to the *clients* of you doing so outweigh the risks.

The two exceptions cover cases in which, despite a potential conflict of interest, there are shared interests or objectives. Examples may be: a husband and wife who want to enter linked wills; a friendly takeover by one company of another; two brothers charged with a crime, which they both deny, claiming that they were sat together watching television at home at the time of the alleged offence. In all of these cases, although one can imagine circumstances arising under which the interests might diverge, the parties currently have similar objectives, so it makes sense for them to use one lawyer to advise them both. If they were to seek legal advice separately, they would be given the same advice by two different lawyers and have to pay twice. An obvious example in which the exception could be relied upon is in group litigation.[36]

When deciding whether it is reasonable to act for the clients, solicitors should consider whether the clients will be prejudiced by not being represented separately and whether the lawyer can represent both clients even-handedly. If there is a real risk that they cannot be so represented, the lawyer should not act for both.[37]

One very relevant factor is whether the clients are sophisticated users of legal services.[38] If they are, the solicitor is likely to believe reasonably that there is no risk of conflict. So, two companies seeking advice on a joint venture may appropriately use a single solicitor.

There is some concern over the exception. If a client is asked by a solicitor to consent to a conflict arising, there will be pressure on the client to agree. If the client has to change solicitors, this may incur extra expenses and require them to re-establish a

---

[36] C. Needham, 'Advance consent to aggregate settlements: Reflections on attorneys' fiduciary obligations and professional responsibility duties' (2011) 44 Loyola University Chicago Law Journal 511.   [37] SRA Code, IB 3.5.

[38] SRA Code, IB 3.6.

relationship of trust.[39] This may well be why the requirements, where there is a common interest, make it relatively easy for solicitors to act in a position of conflict. Not allowing the solicitor to carry on acting will lead to expense for clients and loss of income for lawyers.

 Alternative view

Boon and Levin refer to an 'increasing tendency' to use the rule against conflict 'cynically and ethically as a litigation tactic'.[40] They refer to practices under which litigants seek to complain about the other person's solicitor of choice by means of allegations of conflict of interests. This generates cost and inconvenience for the other party. A common example is family cases, in which there have been reports of husbands visiting all of the solicitors in the area for initial advice, to make it hard for the wife to access legal services.

Informational barriers

The rule against a conflict of interest can restrict business, especially those working in commercial law. If you are advising a major bank and a competitor bank also seeks your advice, you will be turning away big money if the no conflict principle means that you have to refuse to act on its behalf. It is not surprising that big firms have sought ways in which to avoid this. A common one is to erect 'informational barriers' (formerly known as 'Chinese walls'). This is a fairly long-standing practice that enables the firm to segregate collections of employees and to guarantee that one part of the firm will not communicate with the other.[41]

Harry McVea explains:

Typically, the 'wall technique' consists of detailed monitoring of the transfer of personnel from one side of the wall to the other; on-going educational and training programmes; disciplinary sanctions in the event of a breach occurring; and, on some occasions, even physical compartmentalism, with different departments being housed in separate buildings.[42]

The informational barrier is normally made up of the following elements.

- *Physical separation* Those working for one client will be restricted to one part of the office and not allowed into the part in which the lawyers are working for the rival. The extent to which this is possible will depend on the nature of the firm.

[39] D. Bassett, 'Three's a crowd: A proposal to abolish joint representation' (2001) 32 Rutgers Law Journal 387.   [40] Boon and Levin (n. 28), 205.
[41] J. Griffiths-Baker, *Servicing Two Masters: Conflicts of Interest in the Modern Law Firm* (Hart, 2002).   [42] McVea (n. 12), 283.

- *Separate records* Computer-stored information and files of one client must not be accessible by those working for the rival. The physical paper copies should be kept in a place not accessible by the other group of lawyers. The computer records should be password protected.

- *Restrictions on communication* Lawyers and other staff working for one client should be trained not to communicate information about the case to those working for the other client. The training will remind them that information that might seem trivial or even funny might in fact, unknown to them, be relevant.

- *Management control* There should be in place oversight of the procedures to make sure that they are being complied with and ongoing training to ensure that everyone knows what is required.

Where a firm is working for two clients who are ongoing rivals, the informational barriers may need to be in place on a permanent basis.

The courts have not been as supportive of the informational barriers as some firms would wish. As the following case indicates, the courts may take some convincing that the informational barrier is effective.

 Key case

Bolkiah v KPMG [1999] 1 All ER 517

This case involved a firm of accountants (KPMG), but the court confirmed that the same rules apply to solicitors. KPMG was auditor of an agency of the government of Brunei. The agency was chaired by Prince Jefri. KPMG also advised the prince in his personal commercial affairs. The Prince stopped being chair and the Brunei government asked KPMG to undertake an investigation into its affairs. Because the Prince had ceased to be a KPMG client two months earlier, the firm accepted the work. There was a conflict of interest and so the firm created an informational barrier. That meant that the staff working for the government were completely separate from those who had worked with the Prince. The Prince objected and sought an injunction to prevent KPMG working for the government. The House of Lords agreed with the Prince. Given the potential conflict of interest, KPMG could accept the work from the government only if the Prince agreed. The informational barrier did not prevent the possible leakage of confidential information.

Lord Millett emphasised that the duty was to 'keep the information confidential, not merely to take all reasonable steps to do so'.[43] He went on:

It is in any case difficult to discern any justification in principle for a rule which exposes a former client without his consent to any avoidable risk, however slight, that information which he has imparted in confidence in the course of a fiduciary relationship may come into the possession of a third party and be used to his disadvantage. Where in addition the information in question is not only confidential but also privileged, the case for a strict

---

[43] At 527.

approach is unanswerable. Anything less fails to give effect to the policy on which legal professional privilege is based. It is of overriding importance for the proper administration of justice that a client should be able to have complete confidence that what he tells his lawyer will remain secret. This is a matter of perception as well as substance. It is of the highest importance to the administration of justice that a solicitor or other person in possession of confidential and privileged information should not act in any way that might appear to put that information at risk of coming into the hands of someone with an adverse interest.[44]

He added: 'The court should intervene unless it is satisfied that there is no risk of disclosure. It goes without saying that the risk must be a real one, and not merely fanciful or theoretical. But it need not be substantial.'

Concluding his speech, Lord Millett described the burden on a firm of solicitors of showing that there is no risk of confidential information being inadvertently passed on as being 'heavy'.

Notably, this case does not suggest that it is impossible to create an informational barrier that will mean there is not a risk of a conflict or disclosure.

Interestingly, Lord Millett suggested that, to be effective, the informational barrier would need to be 'an established part of the organisational structure of the firm'.[45] Where the firm has regularly used informational barriers and the principles behind them have been well integrated into the way in which the firm works, and where its restrictions are second nature to the staff, the court may be more persuaded that they are effective.

The decision was followed in *Marks & Spencer v Freshfields Bruckhaus Deringer*,[46] in which Freshfields solicitors had been advising Marks and Spencer on many issues. They were approached by a group including Revival Acquisitions Limited and Philip Green, which were interested in taking over Marks and Spencer. The firm wanted to act for the group, but Marks and Spencer objected. The Court of Appeal confirmed that the principle against conflicts applied even though it was not yet clear whether any takeover would be welcomed or not. There was a clear potential for a conflict to arise and that was sufficient to bring the principle into play.

The Court of Appeal supported the conclusion of Collins J:

So far as confidential information is concerned, it is obviously a huge amount of confidential information within Freshfields in relation to Marks and Spencer's affairs through acting for it over the years, some of which may be material to the bid, if only to be discarded. I cannot see, even with a firm the size of Freshfields, that effective information barriers can be put in place given the very large number of people involved, even on the two matters. There must be very many Freshfields people with

---

[44] At 529   [45] At 527.   [46] [2004] EWCA Civ 741.

knowledge of Marks and Spencer's confidential information. In those circumstances I am satisfied that the Chinese Walls cannot be or be seen to be sufficient.[47]

Again, the Court is not saying that the informational barrier can never be effective, but that considerable care will be required for the court to permit it.

There are several reasons to treat the *Marks and Spencer* decision with care. First, it should be noted that there was an application by the former client to prevent the firm from acting. The Court was not saying that, if the former client had agreed to the use of the proposed barrier, it would have been unethical for Freshfields to use it.

Second, Marks and Spencer had been a major client of Freshfields, and many of the firm's solicitors had at some time or other been involved in its work. That was a major reason for doubting whether the informational barrier could be effective. Even if information gained in the future might not leak, it was hard to believe that information that was gathered from past engagement with the firm would not be present in the minds of the solicitors working for the other client. In cases in which the previous client's dealings with a firm were limited to only a few individuals, it may be easier to establish an effective barrier.

Third, this was hardly a friendly takeover bid and the possibility of a conflict arising was by no means fanciful.

Despite these comments, it must be accepted that the courts have taken quite some persuading that informational barriers are effective. In *Re A Firm of Solicitors*,[48] the Court of Appeal relied on the test of whether 'the ordinary man in the street' would anticipate a breach of confidence or some likelihood of mischief. Applying that to the informational barrier proposed in this case, it was found that the man in the street would not be reassured. This is interesting because it emphasises that we are looking not only at whether there is in fact a risk of leakage of confidential information or a conflict of interest, but also at whether there is a *perception* that this might occur. In *Supasave Retail Ltd v Coward Chance (a firm) & ors*,[49] Sir Nicolas Browne-Wilkinson VC said: 'Experience in this court demonstrates that the maintenance of security on either side of Chinese walls in the context of the City does not always prove to be very easy. I think it is a very difficult task.'

Interestingly, it is not only judges who have been sceptical of the effectiveness of the informational barriers. The distinguished Professor L. C. B. Gower, in his report *Review of Investor Protection*, claimed that he had 'never met a Chinese wall that did not have a grapevine trailing over it'.[50]

The reluctance of the courts to uphold informational barriers has certainly caused some disquiet among the larger firms. They argue, as noted earlier, that clients in the commercial world need large law firms with a range of specialist expertise. It is increasingly difficult for a firm to ensure that there is no member of staff who has not worked for a rival. And with a concentration of skills, it is hard for a client to

---

[47] Quoted at [26].   [48] [1992] 1 All ER 353.   [49] [1991] Ch 259, 270.
[50] Part II, Cmnd. 9125, at para. 4.13.

find a firm that is not currently working for a rival. Finding a way of enabling firms to work for clients who have conflicting interests is essential. Despite the complaints of the large firms, however, it should be emphasised that if both clients are happy with the proposed informational barrier, the issue is unlikely to come to the Solicitors Regulation Authority or the courts. So informational barriers are very much in use, especially in large firms, and commercial clients seem confident in this regard.

For some, the increasing size and diversity of law firms makes a case for being stricter about the standards expected. Sopinka J, a Canadian judge, has said in relation to Canadian developments that, '[w]hen the management, size of law firms, and many of the practices of the legal profession are indistinguishable from those of business, it is important that the fundamental professional standards be maintained and indeed improved'.[51]

 Alternative view

Small firms are notably less happy with the use of informational barriers than big firms. It is much easier for large firms to use them; small firms may face similar problems, but on a smaller scale, and for them the no conflict rules bite hard.

Merging firms

Particular difficulties with the no conflict principle can arise when a solicitor changes firms, or when two firms merge. A lawyer can find that, in the previous job, he or she was acting for one client, but the new firm acts for a rival. While it seems harsh, the principle of no conflict means that the new firm must cease to act for the client, unless it can be established by the firm that there is no reasonable prospect of a conflict or breach of confidence.[52]

In *Koch Shipping v Richard Butler*,[53] a solicitor left one firm to join Richard Butler. She had been representing a client who was one party to an arbitration involving a client of Richard Butler. The Court of Appeal was convinced that an effective informational barrier was created. The case involved a single 'solicitor of integrity', who had given an undertaking not to discuss the case with anyone handling the same case in the new firm. She worked in a different part of the firm's building from those dealing with the case. The client was very keen to continue using Richard Butler. Tuckey LJ concluded that any risk of breach of confidence was fanciful.

---

[51]   *MacDonald Estate v Martin* (1991) 77 DLR (4th) 249, 255.
[52]   This was shown in *Re A (Firm of Solicitors)* [1995] 3 All ER 482.
[53]   [2002] EWCA Civ 1280.

Conflict arising between existing clients

What if a firm is acting for two people who were not previously in conflict, but between whom a conflict arises unexpectedly? In that case, the lawyer can act for only one client. In the United States, this has been called the 'hot potato' doctrine:[54] as soon as the conflict arises, the lawyer must drop one client—quickly! There is little guidance on which client the lawyer should select.[55] Sadly, this is likely to be based on a commercial assessment of which client will bring in the most money to the firm in the long term. A better approach, however, might be to consider which client is in the best position to find alternative advice. A common example may be where a lawyer has acted for a husband and wife in drafting their wills and a conveyance, and then later they seek a divorce. The lawyer cannot act for both, but could act for one if there is no problem with confidential information as a result of the earlier dealings.

It has been suggested that this is not strict enough. Especially in personal matters, a client may develop a relationship of trust, and it may been seen as a breach of trust for the lawyer to act for the other side. As Boon and Levin point out, even if information as such is not shared, knowledge of a person's personality and how he or she copes with stress can be used, or perceived to be used.[56] A better rule may be that if the lawyer has been acting for both clients and their interests are now in conflict, then the lawyer can act for neither, unless an effective informational barrier can be erected.

Criminal cases and clients

Criminal law is one area in which a solicitor may end up representing two clients in conflict. Imagine, for example, that two brothers are charged with a burglary. They seek legal advice and tell their solicitor that, in fact, they were both at home watching television at the time. In such a case, it might appear that there is no conflict of interest; indeed, they are backing each other's stories up. The solicitor might therefore take on both clients. Problems can arise, however, as the case develops. Let us say that one brother's car is spotted by an eyewitness near to the scene of the crime. Suddenly, a conflict of interest may arise.[57] Criminal lawyers sometimes refer to these as 'cut-throat cases' in which each defendant then tries to blame the other. In a case such as this, the solicitor can clearly not act for both defendants. Indeed, if there has been confidential information acquired from both, the solicitor may not be able to act for either.

---

[54] J. Leubsdorf, 'Conflicts of interest: Slicing the hot potato doctrine' (2011) 48 San Diego Law Review 251.

[55] M. Conaglen, 'Fiduciary regulation of conflicts between duties' (2009) 125 Law Quarterly Review 111.

[56] Boon and Levin (n. 28), 199.   [57] *R v Morris* [2005] EWCA 1246.

In *R v MH*,[58] two men were charged with sexual offences against the same woman. A barrister agreed to act for both men. Because they were being tried separately, the court held that there was no danger of there being a conflict between them and that the barrister could act for both. There may be a small question mark over that decision. An issue might arise as to which defendant should be tried first. There might, in such a situation, be a benefit for one client to be tried second, so that lessons could be learned from the first case.

Buyer and seller

Rarely is it appropriate for a solicitor to act for both the buyer and seller of a piece of property. The SRA Code of Conduct gives as examples of indicative behaviours complying with the Code:

declining to act for *clients* where you may need to negotiate on matters of substance on their behalf, for example negotiating on price between a buyer and seller of a property;[59]

declining to act where there is unequal bargaining power between the *clients*, for example acting for a seller and buyer where a builder is selling to a non-commercial *client*;[60]

These indicate that it may be appropriate for a lawyer to act for both buyer and seller where the terms have been agreed by the parties and they are both commercial entities.

Special regulations apply where a solicitor acts for the buyer, seller, and/or borrower in a conveyancing matter.

Follow the Code

The SRA Code of Conduct allows a solicitor to act for both a borrower and lender in relation to a conveyance in the following circumstances, as set out under Indicative Behaviour (IB) 3.7:

(a) the mortgage is a standard mortgage (i.e. one provided in the normal course of the lender's activities, where a significant part of the lender's activities consists of lending and the mortgage is on standard terms) of property to be used as the borrower's private residence;

(b) you are satisfied that it is reasonable and in the *clients'* best interests for you to act; and

(c) the certificate of title required by the lender is in the form approved by the *Society* and the Council of Mortgage Lenders.

---

[58] [2008] EWCA Crim 2644.   [59] SRA Code, IB 3.3.   [60] SRA Code, IB 3.4.

This is best understood on pragmatic terms. If a client is buying a house, then his or her solicitor will undertake a wide range of legal checks and investigations to ensure that the client understands what he or she is buying and whether there are any legal encumbrances that affect the law. The money lender, which will be using the land as security for the loan, will want exactly the same checks to be done. Rather than using two sets of solicitors to duplicate the work, it makes a lot of sense for the one solicitor to do the checks on behalf of both parties. The difficulty comes in relation to the advice given to the client over the terms of the mortgage. The regulations cited above indicate that where the mortgage is of a standard form and is from an established lender, it is assumed that the risk to the client of entering into an exploitative deal is lessened.

The issue has become much more debatable now that there are increased worries over borrowing and when inappropriate mortgages are sometimes being taken out. Where a person is keen to buy a house and a mortgagee is keen to lend, the role of the solicitor as adviser becomes more important.

The interests of the purchaser and borrower do not always align. In *National Home Loans Corp v Giffen Couch and Archer*,[61] the solicitor failed to inform the lender that the purchaser was in arrears with its existing mortgage. The case turned on the precise instructions given to the solicitors. The solicitors were instructed to report on the title to the land and to undertake a bankruptcy search. This they did faultlessly. They had not been asked to report or comment on the personal creditworthiness of the borrower. In *Mortgage Express v Bowerman*,[62] the solicitors realised that the lender had been told that the property was worth £220,000, but the purchaser was paying £150,000. When there was a default on the loan, the property sold for only £96,000. Lord Bingham took the view that, when investigating title, if a solicitor were to discover facts that a reasonable solicitor would realise would have a material bearing on the valuation of the security, he or she had a duty to point this out. The claim succeeded, although it should be added that the purchase price is confidential to the purchaser and so the solicitor would need him or her to consent to the disclosure.

Family cases

Another area of work in which conflicts of interest can give rise to difficulties are family cases. It might seem obvious that, where spouses are divorcing, a solicitor cannot act for both the husband and wife. But what if they approach a solicitor having already reached an agreement as to their property, which they wish to be formalised in the law? This would seem to fall into the category of 'two clients with mutual interests' and so be permissible, as long as the rule outlined earlier in this chapter is complied

---

[61] [1997] 3 All ER 808.   [62] [1997] 4 All ER 582.

with and in particular both parties give written consent. If a solicitor does accept such a case, he or she must be alert to conflicts arising, for example if it appears that one party is acting under undue influence or that there has been deceit. Remember that the solicitor must prove the lack of significant conflict. It is therefore not surprising that many solicitors refuse to act on such a basis.

For the avoidance of doubt, it is a very different matter if a solicitor offers to act as a mediator, rather than a lawyer, between two parties.

 Alternative view

It has been suggested that we should be more open to the idea of a lawyer acting as a 'lawyer for the family', so that a family in difficulty can seek legal advice and that the lawyer's duty is to the family. This might be argued by those who suggest that family breakdown cases can be very expensive and that the costs are effectively doubled if each side needs a lawyer.[63] It is supported too by those who argue that family law should not be seen as a 'husband vs wife' dispute and that the couple should be encouraged to cooperate. Giving each 'side' a solicitor encourages the parties to see the dispute as a 'battle'.

Special care must be taken when a solicitor is acting for a child. It is important to be clear who is instructing the lawyer: is it the parent, as litigating friend, or is it the parent in his or her own right, or is it the child? If the litigation friend is used (as it would be if a child were seeking personal injury damages, for example), then the solicitor should be aware that the friend must be instructing the solicitor in the best interests of the child. If the solicitor decides that this is not the case, then the solicitor can apply to the court to remove the person as litigation friend.

In relation to family cases, a child can bring litigation in his or her own right, without a litigation friend. The solicitor can accept the child as a client only if the child has sufficient understanding of the issues and is able to give instructions. The solicitor then has a duty to represent the child's instructions. This makes the solicitor's role clearly different from a guardian for a child in litigation, whose duty is to represent to the court a view as to what is in the best interests of the child. If the solicitor determines that the child lacks the capacity to give instructions or to understand the issues, the solicitor must act in the best interests of the child. This may be accomplished by informing the police, or the local authority, or other family members.

---

[63] R. Tur, 'Family lawyering in legal ethics', in S. Parker and C. Sampford (eds) *Legal Ethics and Legal Practice: Contemporary Issues* (Clarendon Press, 1995).

What would you do?

You are acting for a mother whose child is the subject of care proceedings. The local authority is planning to have the child removed from her care. The mother instructs you to defend the proceedings. She tells you that, although she has not harmed this child, several years ago, when known by a different name, she was convicted of harming another child. The local authority is unaware of this conviction and the mother tells you that you must not inform the local authority.

Group litigation

Sometimes, a lawyer is instructed by a group of people to bring a class action. That might, for example, arise should a group of people claim to have been badly affected by a prescription drug. While they have a common claim, a conflict of interest can arise. Indeed, in some cases, it may be difficult to know whose instructions are to be taken. There is some protection offered in these cases. The court needs to give leave to the group to join as parties and it is permissible for some to comprise a representative group of the others. Under the Civil Procedure Rules, it is possible for a group litigation order to be made, which sets up a register establishing the court and judges' management of the cases. We will explore these issues further in Chapter 9.

Conclusion

One leading American lawyer has said that the law on conflict of interest is 'arcane, a subspecialty whose interpretation can seem as abstruse as explicating the Dead Sea Scrolls'.[64] But is that right? The basic principle that a lawyer must not put himself or herself in a position in which the client's interests conflict with the lawyer's own or those of other clients is not hard to understand. What has created the difficulty are the myriad attempts by lawyers to get around this principle and to exploit the exceptions to it. So the central principle of the chapter is clear: a lawyer should not act where there is, or may be, a risk of a conflict of interest between a client and the lawyer or another client. The difficulty has been how to put that into practice.

 Further reading

> D. Bassett, 'Three's a crowd: A proposal to abolish joint representation' (2001) 32 Rutgers Law Journal 387.
>
> D. Bussel, 'No conflict' (2012) 25 Georgetown Journal of Legal Ethics 207.

[64] S. Gillers, 'Conflicts: Risky new rules' (1989) Sept American Law 39, 41.

R. Epstein, 'The legal regulation of lawyers' conflicts of interest' (1992) 60 Fordham Law Review 579.

J. Gore and S. Cross, 'Conflicts of interest: Relational self-construal and decision-making in interpersonal contexts' (2011) 10 Self and Identity 185.

J. Griffiths-Baker, *Servicing Two Masters: Conflicts of Interest in the Modern Law Firm* (Hart, 2002).

J. Griffiths-Baker and N. Moore, 'Regulating conflicts of interest in global law firms: Peace in our time?' (2012) 80 Fordham Law Review 2541.

C. Kindregan, 'Conflict of interest and the lawyer in civil practice' (1976) 10 Valparaiso University Law Review 433.

J. Leubsdorf, 'Conflicts of interest: Slicing the hot potato doctrine' (2011) 48 San Diego Law Review 251.

J. Loughrey, 'Large law firms, sophisticated clients, and the regulation of conflicts of interests in England and Wales' (2011) 14 Legal Ethics 45.

K. McMunigal, 'Rethinking attorney conflict of interest doctrine' (1992) 5 Georgetown Journal of Legal Ethics 823

H. McVea, '"Heard it through the grapevine": Chinese walls and former client confidentiality in law firms' (2000) 59 Cambridge Law Journal 370.

M. Regna and P. Heenan, 'Supply chains and porous boundaries: The disaggregation of legal services' (2010) 78 Fordham Law Review 2137.

P. Thagard, 'The moral psychology of conflict of interest: Insights from affect neuroscience' (2007) 24 Journal of Applied Philosophy 373.

7   Fees

 Key issues

- How do lawyers decide how much a client should pay?
- What are the ethical obligations relating to fees?
- What role does legal aid play?
- What will be the impact of cutbacks in legal aid?

Introduction

I well remember my second interview for a job as a trainee solicitor, during which one of the first questions I was asked was: 'What is the primary purpose of a law firm?' My incoherent reply mentioned achieving justice, making the world a better place, and doing good for clients. The partner interviewing me was unimpressed: 'It's making money', he replied. The interview was very short. Indeed, it ended with the partner saying to me: 'You are not the kind of person we want working for this firm. Go and be a social worker.'

I was, no doubt, naive. If making money is not the sole purpose of a law firm, it is an important one. The issue of fees is certainly important for clients. The advice and services of a lawyer come at a hefty price. Yet those seeking legal advice are often in a vulnerable position. They need the advice of an expert to avoid a catastrophic outcome, to achieve a dearly held goal, or to find resolution for an intractable problem. They will pay anything to receive help. But because they are desperate, there is a fear that they will be taken advantage of by the lawyer. The lawyer may charge an excessively high rate or may undertake more work than is necessary. Further, the client is often utterly ignorant of the law and cannot know whether his or hers is an easy case requiring a brief letter, or a complex one involving many hours of research. Is the will that the solicitor has produced one simply printed off a databank of standard form wills, or has it been carefully crafted by an expert?

Lawyers are sensitive on the question of costs. To maintain the high charges applied to their work, they fiercely protect the monopoly of solicitors and barristers over legal work, and control entry into these professions. This means that there is a restricted number of lawyers and hence that there is a limited market. That helps to keep fees high. Lord Woolf's review of civil procedure, in a pointed understatement, concluded that he doubted whether controlling costs was a central concern of the legal profession.[1] That is

---

[1] Lord Woolf, *Access to Justice: Interim Report to the Lord Chancellor on the Civil Justice System in England and Wales* (Lord Chancellor's Department, 1995), 13.

putting it politely. The Civil Procedure Rules require the costs to be proportionate to the nature and value of the case.[2] That is a fine-sounding principle, but it is hard to define when costs are 'proportionate'.

It is not difficult to find cases in which the costs of the case have got out of hand.

 Scandal!

The report of the Legal Ombudsman[3] included the following case summary:

Miss D needed a lawyer to help oversee divorce proceedings, which included both financial matters and issues around access to her child. Little did she know it would end in tears and considerable worry over her family's welfare, not to mention an invoice for £4,000 worth of photocopying.

The first law firm that Miss D instructed turned out to be very poor. Although she'd already accrued some costs using them, she decided to pay the outstanding bill and then use a different firm. Miss D settled on a second firm after shopping around for what she thought would be an affordable, reputable divorce specialist.

She met with the firm and discussed costs. She was conscious of the fact that she had recently been made redundant and that her husband had considerably greater funds to draw on given his high paying job. However, she needed to get the best outcome for her and her child. So, despite having used much of her redundancy money on the first law firm Miss D borrowed money from friends and used credit cards to pay the second firm.

Miss D explained that once this money had gone she had nothing else; so, everything would need to be achieved within the specified budget. The law firm agreed to act on behalf of Miss D under this arrangement.

Unfortunately, court proceedings dragged on and Miss D's money was quickly swallowed up. Miss D asked the firm to stop since she simply couldn't afford any further work. Despite this, the firm continued acting without her consent before eventually hitting her with an invoice for £15,000.

Miss D did not have this money. She complained to the firm but they rejected it, even using aggressive letters to insist she would have to pay the outstanding costs. Miss D was so distressed, she worried more than ever about her child's welfare given her dwindling funds and growing debt.

Finally, Miss D brought her complaint to us. We investigated and agreed that the firm had acted unreasonably, particularly in continuing to accrue costs when they had specifically been asked not to do any more work. An investigator also discovered, after going through an itemised bill, that the firm's costs included an enormous £4,000 for photocopying.

The firm contested the investigator's remedy, which was for the firm to waive the outstanding £15,000, and so it went to an ombudsman decision. The ombudsman agreed the firm should waive the final bill and they were ordered to do so.

---

[2] CPR 1.1.

[3] Legal Ombudsman, *What Were the Complaints about?* (Legal Ombudsman, 2013).

The most common kind of complaint to the Office for Legal Complaints and the Legal Ombudsman involves fees. For the Legal Ombudsman, 8.27 per cent of complaints concerned excessive fees and a further 8.39 per cent related to a lack of clear information about fees.[4] Indeed, the Ombudsman says that a complaint about fees is 'a staple of my work diet'.[5] However, the Ombudsman, in his 2013 report, recognised that out-of-control fees were not entirely the fault of lawyers. Talking about divorce cases, he said:

> A high proportion of the problems we encountered were the result of consumers having unrealistic expectations of what could be achieved in a divorce or pushing their own costs higher because of a desire to punish their former partner rather than achieve a reasonable settlement.[6]

Not everyone would accept this analysis. In divorce cases especially, the lawyer must realise that the client's heart may rule his or her head. It is the role of the lawyer to stop the client acting disastrously.

There is a widespread feeling that the issue of costs has not been adequately addressed by the legal profession. Boon and Levin point out that the 1999 Law Society Guide on Solicitors' Ethics had as its first listed principle the power of the solicitor to require payments on account.[7] If that is seen as the starting point of legal ethics, it is not surprising that lawyers have a bad reputation. Of course, the most recent codes do not start with fees—but there is little in them that restricts fees. The Solicitors Regulation Authority (SRA) Code of Conduct emphasises the importance of explaining fees to clients,[8] but contains little that seeks to ensure that the fees charged are reasonable. The Bar Council Code of Conduct (the Bar Code), meanwhile, is explicit.

Follow the Code

The Bar Code, para 405, states that:

> a self-employed barrister may charge for any work undertaken by him (whether or not it involves an appearance in Court) on any basis or by any method he thinks fit provided that such basis or method:
> (a) is permitted by law;
> (b) does not involve the payment of a wage or salary.

---

[4] Legal Ombudsman (n. 3).

[5] Office for Legal Complaints, *Annual Report and Accounts, for the Year Ending 31 March 2013* (Office for Legal Complaints, 2013).

[6] Office for Legal Complaints (n. 5), 15.

[7] A. Boon and J. Levin, *The Ethics and Conduct of Lawyers in England and Wales* (Hart, 2008), 241.

[8] Indicative Behaviour 1.14.

The fact that professional codes make no attempt to limit fees to a reasonable sum is striking. As noted earlier, it is important to recognise the power imbalance at play, with clients often in a weak position, at least outside the commercial context. The issue cannot be left to the market to determine. There must be more done by the profession to indicate appropriate levels of costs. There should also be a fair and accessible way of reviewing fees to ensure that there has been no overcharging.

There is no doubt that some firms make huge sums of money. Even given the financial crisis of recent years, the profits made by the large firms are substantial. For example, Freshfields made profits of £548 million in 2012–13, a 2.4 per cent increase on the previous year. Its turnover was £1,221 million, an increase of 7.2 per cent. The profit for each equity partner was £1.39 million.[9] However, these kinds of profits are rare. Indeed, many smaller firms are in financial difficulties. In 2013, a survey by the Solicitors Regulation Authority (SRA) found around 1,200 firms in financial difficulty.[10] That is some 10 per cent of solicitors firms.

Sources and forms of funding

When a client is thinking about the costs of using a lawyer, it important to remember that the costs that a client might face are not only the costs of the lawyer, but also the court costs, general disbursements (for example fees for instructing an expert report), and potentially the costs of the other side.

There are three primary ways in which lawyers charge fees. First, there is the hourly rate. Here, the client pays a fixed sum per hour spent by the lawyer on the case. The lawyer will record (typically in blocks of five or six minutes) how long he or she spends on the case and, at the end, will calculate the total time spent.

Second, there may be a fixed fee for certain transactions. Here, the lawyer will agree in advance a fixed sum for a particular task. This is normally used in non-contentious business, such as conveyancing or drafting a will, in which the lawyer can predict how long the work will take with a reasonable degree of confidence.

Third, some lawyers charge an 'uplift' in addition to the standard way of assessing methods (normally the hourly rate or fixed fee). The enhancement of the fee will be justified by claiming that the matter was particularly delicate or complex, or needed to be performed at speed.

A fourth method is the contingency fee, under which agreement the lawyer is paid nothing if the case is lost, but is paid a percentage of the proceeds if the client wins.

---

[9] K. Hall, 'Modest profit increases at Linklaters and Freshfields', *Law Society Gazette*, undated, online at www.lawgazette.co.uk/71659.article

[10] J. Hyde, 'SRA survey exposes 1,200 firms in financial difficulty', *Law Society Gazette*, 18 September 2013, online at www.lawgazette.co.uk/practice/sra-survey-exposes-1200-firms-in-financial-difficulty/5037705.article

We will explore some of these options further. We will also be looking at the different ways of funding these costs throughout this chapter, but it is helpful to summarise them here.

1. *Personal funding* The client will fund the case from his or her own savings or borrowings.

2. *Civil legal aid* The client's costs will be paid for through the legal aid scheme. This is a state-run system that covers costs only for those on low incomes and only for certain kinds of litigation.

3. *Legal expenses insurance* Some people take out an insurance policy that, if they ever need to use a lawyer, will cover the expenses. There may be restrictions in the policy over what kinds of costs will be covered.

4. *Contingency fee* This is an agreement between the lawyer and client under which if the client recovers damages, then a percentage of the proceeds will be given to the lawyer. Most agreements state that if the case is lost and no damages are recovered, then the lawyer will not be paid ('no win, no fee').

5. *Conditional fee system* Here, the agreement is that the lawyer will be paid a basic fee (at a lower rate than might normally be received), but if damages are recovered, then the lawyer will receive an extra reward by way of an enhanced fee (normally higher than what might be paid otherwise).

6. *Third-party funding* An external investor may fund the litigation in return for a cut of any damages recovered.

We will be exploring these different forms of funding as the chapter develops.

Ethics and fees

There is something a little odd about lawyers' ethics and fees. At the heart of lawyers' ethics is the principle that the lawyer must put the client's interests first. However, requiring payment for services is not obviously in a client's interests. Indeed, the existence of fees creates an inevitable tension between the lawyer's wish to advance the client's cause and the natural wish to make a good profit from the case.[11]

The standard approach to the dilemma is that the lawyer is completely open about how he or she will charge costs and then the client has the choice whether or not to consent to those costs. This approach means that the lawyer's obligations concerning costs focus on disclosure at the start of the process; it is for the client to decide how high he or she wishes the costs to go. Hence at the heart of the professional guidance is the importance of clarity in relation to fees.

---

[11] R. Moorhead, 'Filthy lucre: Lawyers' fees and lawyers' ethics—What is wrong with informed consent?' (2011) 31 Legal Studies 345.

Follow the Code

The SRA Code of Conduct, Indicative Behaviour (IB) 1.14, requires:

> clearly explaining your fees and if and when they are likely to change

Some guidance on what this might mean has been offered by the Ombudsman.

 **Application**

The Legal Ombudsman requires that lawyers draft an introductory letter as follows:

To make the letter explicit about services offered and costs, it should include information on:

- why the customer has decided to engage the lawyer;
- the course of action the customer has chosen;
- what work will (and won't) be carried out;
- the standards and timescales for the work;
- the likely costs of the case based on the information within the letter.[12]

Richard Moorhead argues that the empirical data suggests that the 'informed consent' model is 'deeply flawed'.[13] Clients rarely appreciate how costs are building up or how much a case will cost. The hourly billing rate does not really give clients a clear indication of what expenses the work will involve. Indeed, lawyers will typically warn clients that, in many areas of work, it is not possible to give an exact figure. Moorhead argues that, in simply relying on the informed consent of the client, we ignore the reality that there is an 'ethic of greed' that governs legal practice. That may be putting it too strongly, but naturally lawyers want to make money and any ethical analysis must openly acknowledge that. Indeed, if legal services are to be provided commercially and at a high quality, then a profit must be made. Moorhead acknowledges this, but adds that 'there is significant public interest in ensuring such profits are not exploitative and that the distributional concerns exacerbated by high fees are countered'.[14]

Indeed, one of the concerns about the cutbacks in legal aid work is that even more lawyers will cease working for legally aided clients or that the quality of advice will be very poor. If law is to attract the best graduates and enable them to pay back their graduate loans, profits must be made.[15] In short, the market requires high fees.

---

[12] Legal Ombudsman, *An Ombudsman's View of Good Costs Service* (Legal Ombudsman, 2012), 8.
[13] Moorhead (n. 11).   [14] Moorhead (n. 11), 349.
[15] G. Hadfield, 'The price of law: How the market for lawyers distorts the justice system' (2000) 98 Michigan Law Review 953.

However, the problem with a market model is that it is difficult for a client to know who the best lawyer is, and the appearance of high fees and swanky offices can be used as the basis for that assessment. Ironically, appearances matter, and this drives up costs.

The difficulty in ensuring that fees are fair and proportionate is great. Part of the problem is that, in litigation especially, it is genuinely hard to know what the outcome will be or how long the case will take to prepare. A lawyer cannot, with confidence, guarantee a victory. Until all of the evidence is established, the case for the other side is heard, attempts to settle the case are made, and the judge has ruled on the points of law, prediction of outcome is a risky business. But the risks and costs of the inherent uncertainty usually fall on the client. Unless there is contingency fee arrangement (see below), the lawyer will be paid whatever the outcome. So, when a question arises about whether more work should be done to prepare a client's case, the lawyer has every incentive to do that work. It is probably rare for a lawyer deliberately to work unnecessary extra hours on a client's case just to make more money, but it must be common for borderline calls to be made in favour of doing so.[16]

Contingency fees

Contingency fee arrangements were first permitted under the Conditional Fee Agreements Order 1995.[17] The regulation governing them changed dramatically in 2013. The details of the regulations governing conditional fees are now found in the Conditional Fee Arrangements Order 2013.[18]

There are two permitted contingency fee systems in England and Wales.

Conditional fee agreements

A **conditional fee agreement** (CFA) means that the client pays nothing to the lawyer if the case is lost, but if the case is won, then a client must pay the normal fee of the lawyer plus an 'uplift' or 'success fee'.[19]

---

[16] C. Tata, 'In the interests of commerce or clients: Which comes first? Legal aid, supply, demand, and "ethical indeterminacy" in criminal defence work' (2007) 34 Journal of Law and Society 498.

[17] SI 1995/1674.   [18] SI 2013/689.

[19] R. Moorhead and R. Cumming, *Damage-Based Contingency Fees in Employment Cases: A Survey of Practitioners*, Cardiff Law School Research Paper Series No. 6 (December 2008).

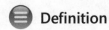 **Definition**

The Courts and Legal Services Act 1990, s. 58, defines the **conditional fee agreement** as follows:

(2) For the purposes of this section and section 58A—

(a) a conditional fee agreement is an agreement with a person providing advocacy or litigation services which provides for his fees and expenses, or any part of them, to be payable only in specified circumstances;

[…]

One way of thinking about this is that the lawyer gets a bonus if he or she wins the case. But if he or she loses the case, the lawyer is penalised by getting no pay. This uplift or success fee can never be more than 100 per cent of the standard fee;[20] so the most that a lawyer can claim is twice his or her standard rate.[21]

An important change introduced in 2013 is that this success fee cannot be recovered from the other side. Normally, if a party loses a case, it must pay the other party's legal costs. Previously, that could include the success fee. However, section 44 of the Legal Aid, Sentencing and Punishment of Offenders Act 2012 means that, in future, success fees will not be recoverable.

'Damages-based agreements'

Damages-based agreements (DBAs) have only recently been permitted in the UK.[22] Like CFAs, if the case is lost, the client pays the lawyer nothing. However, the difference arises if the case is won. Under a DBA, the lawyer's fee is a percentage of the client's damages. In some cases in which there is a large award of damages, the client may end up paying more under a DBA than he or she would have done under a CFA. However, in cases in which only a small award of damages is made, the client ends up paying less.

 Definition

The Ministry of Justice has defined **damages-based agreements** as follows:

A damages-based agreement ('DBA') is a private funding arrangement between a representative and a client whereby the representative's agreed fee ('the payment')

---

[20] The client may, in addition, face costs for disbursements, as discussed in Moorhead (n. 11).

[21] Conditional Fee Agreements Order 2013, art. 5. For a broader discussion on what percentages should be used, see J. Swett, 'Determining a reasonable percentage in establishing a contingency fee: A new tool to remedy an old problem' (2010) 77 Tennessee Law Review 653.

[22] Legal Aid, Sentencing and Punishment of Offenders Act 2012.

is contingent upon the success of the case, and is determined as a percentage of the compensation received by the client.[23]

The DBA is available only in limited areas, including (most importantly) personal injury claims, contentious business matters, and in employment tribunals. The percentage that can be used is capped at 25 per cent for personal injury work[24] and 50 per cent for other work.[25] The agreement must explain the reason for the figure chosen.[26]

The operation of contingency fees

Under either CFAs or DBAs, if the client loses, he or she does not need to pay the lawyer any fees, but may be liable to pay the costs of the other side.[27] To make these arrangements attractive, therefore, clients will typically take out an after-the-event (ATE) legal expenses insurance policy, which will pay out the costs that the client is due to pay the other side if the case is lost. If the client wins the case, he or she cannot (since April 2013) claim the expense of this insurance as part of his or her legal costs.[28] This change will make CFAs slightly less attractive because they are no longer free to clients, who will at the very least have to cover the insurance premium.

The problems with the old system were well demonstrated by Lady Justice Smith in *Rogers v Merthyr Tydfil CBC*:[29]

> However, I do not think it was the intention of Parliament that would-be claimants should be able to litigate weak cases without any risk whatsoever to themselves. But it seems to me that this is what is happening. ATE premiums are set on the basis of a high expected failure rate at trial. Even cases that are assessed at a prospect of success of only 51% receive ATE insurance. Thus the premiums have to be significantly higher than they would be if a more rigorous standard were applied. Often no premium has to be paid upfront. If the case is lost the premium is rarely paid. That practice inevitably increases the premiums even further. If the case is won, the premium is in principle recoverable from the liability insurer and, as this court has held in the instant case, if it was necessary for the claimant to take out ATE insurance and the solicitor has acted reasonably, the whole premium will be recovered.[30]

---

[23] Ministry of Justice, *Explanatory Memorandum to the Damages-Based Agreements Regulations 2013* (Ministry of Justice, 2013), 2.

[24] Damages-Based Agreements Regulations 2013, SI 2013/609.

[25] Damages-Based Agreements Regulations 2013, reg. 4.

[26] Damages-Based Agreements Regulations 2013, reg. 3.

[27] Although not in personal injury cases.

[28] Legal Aid, Sentencing and Punishment of Offenders Act 2012, ss 44 and 46; Conditional Fee Agreements Order 2013. There are exceptions for diffuse mesothelioma claims, publication/privacy proceedings, and insolvency work.

[29] [2006] EWCA Civ 1134.   [30] At [127].

For the lawyer, the contingency fee offers enhanced payment if the case is won, but no payment if the case is lost. Clearly, the lawyer will hope, if a case is lost and so no payment for his or her work is received, to be able to offset this loss through the enhanced payments received in those cases that he or she wins.

Notably, contingency fees are not permitted in all areas of work. They are not permitted in family law cases or criminal cases. Family law cases are typically understood not as involving a 'winner' and a 'loser', but as an attempt to find an agreement over the fairest way of dividing the family assets or of finding the most appropriate arrangements for the children. Because there is no winner and loser, the contingency fee system does not work. Further, we would not want to give lawyers any incentive to discourage couples from reaching an amicable settlement.

There is an obvious benefit for clients in these arrangements: whatever happens, they will not be out of pocket. If the case is lost, the expenses will be borne by the lawyer. If the case is won, then the client will receive the damages, even if somewhat depleted because of the lawyer's cut. The standard contract proposed by the Law Society contains the following term explaining to clients what will happen if they win:

> If you win your claim, you pay our basic charges, our expenses and disbursements and a success fee together with the premium for any insurance you take out. You are entitled to seek recovery from your opponent of part or all of our basic charges and our expenses and disbursements, but not the success fee or (save for clinical negligence cases) any insurance premium. If your claim is for clinical negligence and you have taken out a costs insurance policy, then, if you win, you may be able to recover from your opponent that part of the insurance premium which relates to the risk of having to pay for expert reports.[31]

There is, of course, a cost to the client: the percentage fees that the lawyer will receive are likely to be significantly more than would result if the lawyer were paid on an hourly basis. From the lawyer's point of view, this is essential. Lost cases will lead to a net loss to the lawyer and they need to recoup that cost by charging more for the cases that are won.

If a fee is charged unlawfully, the solicitor will not be able to recover the fee, or even disbursements.[32] However, if the money has been paid over, it cannot be reclaimed.[33] That is because the contract is not enforceable, but that does not mean that it is void. So the solicitor cannot get the money, but if he or she has it already, he or she can keep it.

Contingency fees, be their CFAs or DBAs, are controversial and have generated lively debate over whether they are desirable or not.

---

[31] Law Society, *New Model Conditional Fee Agreement* (Law Society, 2013), 2.
[32] *Re Trepca Mines* [1963] Ch 199.
[33] *Aratra Potato v Taylor Joynson Garrett* [1995] 4 All ER 695.

In favour of contingency fees

There are a number of arguments that are used in favour of contingency fees, as follows.

1. Lawyers are encouraged to be reasonable with their time and hence with client's costs. Under the normal billable hour system, a lawyer has an incentive to take on cases that have little chance of success or to spend unreasonable numbers of hours dealing with a case. The lawyer is paid by the hour, regardless of the outcome. However, under a contingency fee arrangement, if the hours of work exceed the cap, the lawyer is not going to get paid. He or she has an incentive to win the case, but not to do so at the expense of putting in an absurd number of hours.

2. Contingency fees open up access. Many clients will be unable to afford litigation on the normal basis of payment. They cannot afford to pay a lawyer's fee, especially if the case is lost. Contingency fees make litigation affordable because fees are payable only if the client wins the case and obtains damages. In a sense, it is a 'no loss' scenario for the client.[34] As David Luban has put it: 'Contingency fee arrangements allow individuals who might otherwise be unable to afford legal vindication of their rights to gain access to justice. Such fee arrangements aid in fulfilling the fundamental ideal of equality before the law.'[35] It should not be only the rich who can go to court and assert their rights.

   This argument is convincing only if you think that opening up litigation to a broader range of people is a good thing. Supporters will argue that it enables people to exercise their legal rights. If you think that litigation is a bad thing, naturally you will oppose contingency fees as a device to encourage litigation.[36] It could be argued that contingency fees will allow *too many* people to sue, but perhaps those who think this should target their criticism at the law that gives people rights, not at those exercising their rights or at fee structures enabling them to exercise their rights. If people are misusing the law, we should put in place provisions to prevent vexatious litigation. Excessive or vexatious litigation should not be an argument against contingency fees.

3. Some supporters of contingency fees suggest that they should simply be seen as a form of loan. The lawyer loans his or her services based on the security of the client's claim. The success fee can be seen as payment of interest on the loan.[37] Another model sees the success fee as a form of insurance premium. The success fee is, in effect, a kind of risk-spreading device. These kinds of arguments seek to

[34] E. Zamir and I. Ritov, 'Notions of fairness and contingent fees' (2011) 74 Law and Contemporary Problems 1.

[35] D. Luban, 'Speculating on justice: The ethics and jurisprudence of contingency fees', in S. Parker and C. Sampford (eds) *Legal Ethics and Legal Practice: Contemporary Issues* (Oxford University Press, 1995), 116.

[36] Luban (n. 35).   [37] Luban (n. 35).

reassure those who view contingency arrangements with suspicion by suggesting that they are really no different from standard financial arrangements.

4. A less obvious argument in favour of contingency fees is that they help high-street law firms. Firms that traditionally relied on legal aid have struggled since the cutbacks and yet they provide a crucial service. It may be that contingency fees offer a new set of work for these firms and improve their provision.

Against contingency fees

The arguments that are used against contingency fees can be summarised as follows.

1. Perhaps the most common argument against contingency fees is that they encourage litigation.[38] The client has nothing to lose by bringing the case and can therefore be persuaded to bring an action even if it has little merit.[39] Such litigation may have broader costs, as listed by an Australian law reform body:

   The costs include those of overcautious practices adopted by manufacturers and service providers to minimise the risk of liability, increased insurance premiums, and increased legal costs and payouts. They also include the economic impact of inhibiting product innovation and development, and withdrawing goods and services from the market.[40]

2. The contingency fee creates a conflict of interest between the lawyer and the client. Because the lawyer's fee is fixed, he or she does not have an incentive to 'pull out every stop' to win the case. Indeed, the best outcome for the lawyer is to win the case, while doing the minimum necessary work. This problem is less of an issue with CFAs than it is with DBAs. A similar issue is that, as the odds of winning a case shorten, a lawyer may become increasingly keen to cut his or her losses and end the litigation, which may not necessarily be in the best interests of the client.

   While these are good points, it should be recalled that hourly fees also create conflicts. The real question is therefore whether the conflicts created by the contingency fee are significantly worse than the conflicts created by other fee structures.

3. There is a concern that, with contingency fees, lawyers have a strong interest in their client winning; otherwise, they will not be paid. This may put pressure on lawyers to use unethical, or even illegal, tactics to win a case. This must be a

---

[38] This claim is rejected in R. Moorhead, 'An American future? Contingency fees, claims explosions and evidence from employment tribunals' (2010) 73 Modern Law Review 752.

[39] This was disputed in M. Glanter, 'The day after the litigation explosion' (1986) 19 Maryland Law Review 463. See further L. Brickman, *Lawyer Barons: What Their Contingency Fees Really Cost America* (Cambridge University Press, 2011).

[40] Law Reform Commission of Victoria, *Restrictions on Legal Practice*, Access to Law Discussion Paper No. 23 (Law Reform Commission of Victoria, 1991), 26.

concern, although, as David Luban points out, there is little evidence that this kind of improper activity is commoner in contingency fee cases than it is in others.[41]

4. The contingency fee system, it is said, does not work well when the client has an extremely strong case.[42] The client in a contingency fee arrangement is paying over the odds, precisely to have a protection in the event that he or she loses the case. However, if the client is guaranteed a victory, he or she does not need this protection and is, in effect, paying over the odds. The difficulty is that whether a case is extremely strong or not is often difficult to tell at its outset, when the fee arrangements are being negotiated.

 What would you do?

A client comes to see you with a personal injury case. It is quickly apparent that she has an extremely strong case. For such cases, you normally recommend a contingency fee, giving you an extra bonus if you win, but no costs for the client if you lose. You realise that, in this case, if the client were charged on an hourly basis, she would almost certainly end up paying less.

Claims companies

The conditional fee arrangements have been adopted by claims companies, which advertise widely, encouraging people to bring claims. These are not firms of lawyers and are not subject to any professional conduct regulation.[43] In some circles, they are known as 'ambulance chasers', suggesting that they run after injured people hoping to sign them up to bring claims. They sell their own insurance packages and even arrange loans. As Boon and Levin argue:

> Many of the claims they handled were of small value (and doubtful legality) and the costs, both legal and insurance, far outweighed the value of the claim to the client but made a lot of money for the claims companies.[44]

---

[41] H. Kritzer, 'Seven dogged myths concerning contingency fees' (2002) 80 Washington University Law Quarterly 739.

[42] T. Friehe, 'Contingent fees and legal expenses insurance: Comparison for varying defendant fault' (2010) 30 International Review of Law and Economics 283.

[43] Compensation (Regulating Claims Management Services) Order 2006, SI 2006/3319.

[44] Boon and Levin (n. 7), 248.

Key case

Sharratt v London Central Bus Co (No. 2) [2004] EWCA 575

The Accident Group, a claims company, brought several cases against the London Central Bus Company. All of the cases were settled and damages were agreed. These ranged from £1,000 to £3,500. The costs ranged from £2,100 to £4,800. The insurance premium had been between £840 and £997. The solicitors had paid a subsidiary of the Accident Group a fee of £310 (plus VAT) for 'investigations'. The primary issue was which of these costs could be recovered from the bus company. It was held that the insurance premiums were not reasonable, given the risk and value of the claims. Further, that the premiums covered services that included insurance. Judge Hirst, approved by the Court of Appeal, reduced the recoverable premiums to £450, and he also held that the payments by the solicitors to the Accident Group could not be referred because, in reality, they were a referral fee.

 Alternative view

Although claims companies have a bad press, it is important to put them in their social context. They often direct their advertisements to those who would not normally consider seeking legal advice and who would find going to a solicitor's office intimidating. By making the idea of bringing a legal action stress-free and user-friendly, they may be enabling groups whose legal rights normally go unenforced in the courts to seek remedies.

Speculative fees

A lawyer may be willing to accept a case on a speculative basis—that is, the basis that if the case is lost, no fees will be payable. If the case is won, the client will pay the standard fees, or the other side will be ordered to do so. You will see why lawyers have not generally been willing to take cases on this basis. The lawyer takes the risk of not recovering his or her costs if the case is lost; if the case is won, he or she gets only the normal fee.

This arrangement is thought to be rare, although it is lawful.[45] It might be used by a lawyer working for a charity or non-governmental organisation (NGO) that he or she wishes to support.

---

[45] *Thai Trading Company v Taylor* [1998] 3 All ER 65.

Insurance

Sometimes, people take out legal expenses insurance. This is not common, but is sometimes included as an aspect of other kinds of insurance, such a car or house insurance. Some foresee a growth in this market.[46] People are now used to the idea of taking out insurance in case unexpected costs arise. With the restrictions on legal aid and high legal costs, it is possible that people will increasingly see a benefit in taking out legal expenses insurance.[47] One difficulty with the insurance model, however, is that the insurance company will need to restrict what kinds of cases will be covered and, in effect, which lawyers can be used.

Commission

Lawyers are commonly asked to recommend a service or product. In such a case, a lawyer may be offered a commission by a company for recommending its services. Can the lawyer accept such payment? It is forbidden in the case of financial services products under the SRA Financial Services (Scope) Rules 2013. For other matters, it is allowed, but is subject to strict regulation.

Follow the Code

The SRA Code of Conduct, IB 1.20, requires:

where you receive a *financial benefit* as a result of acting for a *client*, either:
(a)   paying it to the *client*;
(b)   offsetting it against your fees; or
(c)   keeping it only where you can justify keeping it, you have told the *client* the amount of the benefit (or an approximation if you do not know the exact amount) and the *client* has agreed that you can keep it

The starting point is therefore that any commission that a solicitor earns belongs to the client, but the client can agree that the solicitor can keep it. There may be some concerns, however, about whether the client understands precisely what is happening when the solicitor asks if he or she can retain the commission.

One view is that solicitors should, when advising clients, give disinterested advice and that the passing on of a commission, even one that the solicitor has only a hope

---

[46] L. Visscher and T. Schepens, 'A law and economics approach to cost shifting, fee arrangements and legal expense insurance', in M. Tuil and L. Visscher (eds) *New Trends in Financing Civil Litigation* (Edward Elgar, 2010).
[47] J. de Mot and M. Faure, 'Legal expenses insurance and the free rider problem', online at https://biblio.ugent.be/input/download?func=downloadFile&fileOId=1071903&recordOId=1070897

of retaining, improperly influences the solicitor. An absolute bar on the retention of commissions might therefore ensure that the highest standards are retained.

Hourly fees

Hourly fees are the commonest fee arrangements. These are straightforward: the client simply pays the lawyer for each hour of work that he or she does. The agreement between the lawyer and client will set out the hourly rate that is to be paid. Typically, the more senior the lawyer, the higher the hourly rate the client must pay.[48] Some law firms explain that there may be an 'enhancement' (that is, an increase) to the fee if the work involves a particularly large sum of money or is particularly sensitive. If, for example, the client wishes the work to be done very quickly, or if it involves a high-profile client and the firm needs to handle the publicity that comes with the work, it may require an extra fee.

Understandably, clients prefer a fixed-fee basis, because that means that they know exactly how much the litigation will cost. With an hourly rate, they will find out how much the case will have cost in terms of lawyers' fees only when the case is finished. As the Legal Ombudsman has noted:

> Take an obvious example of the sort of thing we see. People going to see a solicitor may be told that it is not possible to put a price on what the whole service may cost but the lawyer will charge, say, £210 per hour plus VAT, with fees and disbursements being extra. Even for someone familiar with the law, that provides almost no useful information about how much they can expect to pay and little indication on what options they have to keep costs down. An hourly pricing rate with no limit makes it almost impossible for the consumer to challenge the bill. Nor does it provide any useful information to allow them to compare the cost of one lawyer with another.[49]

Critics claim that fixed costs tie a lawyer's hands. It can be impossible to know in advance what twists and turns a case will take. A lawyer may end up in the invidious position of having to decide whether to pursue a further line of enquiry for which there will be no pay or to leave it. Further, lawyers using a fixed fee are likely to set the fee at somewhere above the average fee for such work and those whose cases are straightforward will therefore be paying more than they would under an hourly rate. These arguments lead some to say that, in fact, overall the hourly rate is preferable for clients.

In one survey, the lawyers interviewed greatly preferred hourly fees over contingency fees.[50] It was seen to be a proper reward for the effort put in by the lawyer, whereas payment under contingency fees involved luck.

---

[48] D. Webb, 'Killing time: A limited defence of time-cost billing' (2010) 13 Legal Ethics 39.

[49] Legal Ombudsman, *Costs and Customer Service in a Changing Legal Services Market* (Legal Ombudsman, 2012), 6.   [50] Moorhead (n. 11).

Barristers typically work on fixed fees for advice or drafting, but use a daily rate for court work. Traditionally, barristers have argued that their fees are negotiated by their clerks, and are 'honoraria' and not legally enforceable. This was used to explain why a lawyer could not be sued for his or her work. Because they were not officially paid and there was no official contract involved, it was inappropriate for barristers to be liable in tort law. However, the immunity from suit for tort liability was removed in joined cases *Arthur JS Hall v Simons; Barratt v Ansell*,[51] and it is now acknowledged that barristers can enter into binding contracts.[52]

Both barristers and solicitors undertaking legal aid work are normally paid a fixed sum. Indeed, in some areas of work, solicitors are paid a fixed sum for a block of cases.

Although the hourly rate is readily understood by lawyers, it is less well understood by clients. One survey found that most clients could not recall the agreed hourly rate and did not understand what work had been done in their case. While the solicitor may be painfully aware of all of the work that has gone into the client's case, most of this is invisible to the client, who will focus on the outcome and the total bill.[53]

Duncan Webb summarises some of the main arguments in favour of hourly fees:

> Time-based billing is transparent, can be communicated up-front, and clients can compare the pricing of lawyers. The actual process of billing can be at least partially automated, dispensing with a high degree of discretion in billing. It also enables clients to track what lawyers have done for them in the form of an itemised list of work. A further advantage for the lawyer is that the risks are placed on the client rather than the lawyer (as opposed to any success-based fee where the lawyer undertakes some risk). Of course, given its prevalence, both lawyers and clients understand how it works.[54]

There is no doubt that hourly billing does rely on a degree of trust. A lawyer might explain that it took an hour to draft a carefully worded letter, but the client has to take the lawyer's word for that. Lawyers are encouraged in many firms to record their time as they go. They will note the time at which they start working on a file and then note the time at which they finish. This is seen as more reliable than trying to remember, weeks later, how long it took to write a particular document—although it has been suggested that, in fact, it is common for solicitors to complete time sheets some time after the event.[55]

Critics will also question the apparent fairness of hourly billing: is each hour of a lawyer's time equal? The hour of the exhausted lawyer on a Friday afternoon may not be equal to his or her hour fresh to work on Monday morning. A lawyer may spend an hour composing a letter, but during that hour may have popped out for a cup of coffee, checked the Internet for last night's sports results, and joked with a colleague. While some firms do have a slot on time sheets for, in effect, 'wasted time', it is

---

[51] [2000] 3 All ER 673.   [52] Courts and Legal Services Act 1990, s. 61.
[53] Moorhead (n. 11).   [54] Webb (n. 48), 44.   [55] Webb (n. 48).

inevitable that some lawyers will clock down an hour on the client's file even if their minds were not fully on that file for the whole hour.

A further problem is that, for ease, most firms ask lawyers to fill in their time sheets in blocks of five or six minutes. In part, this is to make the job of calculating the fee to be paid easier, but also means that the lawyer does not have to keep to a 'to the minute' check on the clock. What this means is that a letter that took only two minutes to write may be rounded up and clocked in at six minutes, for example. That may seem like a minor matter, but if the charging rate is £200, a six-minute block calculates out at £20, whereas two minutes should be only £6.66 (if charged by the minute). An old joke captures this well. A lawyer dies and goes to heaven. At the gates, he is asked by the angel how old he is. 'I'm 64', he replies. 'That's odd,' the angel replied, 'because, according to your time sheets, you're 107!'

Another common concern is 'over-servicing'. This refers to a lawyer spending longer on a matter than might strictly be necessary. A lawyer seeking to make sure that he or she puts in as many billable hours as possible may be tempted to spend an inordinate amount of time researching the law on a particular issue or drafting a document. That is so especially if he or she does not have other billable work at hand. The problem is that it would be hard to challenge this: the lawyer has done the work; the complaint is that, in effect, that he or she has been too diligent.

 ## Application

Most solicitors record their time as they go. Every six minutes, they note down which file they have been working on. When the case is complete, the firm's costs lawyer will add up the total number of hours worked on the case and draft a bill accordingly. Many firms, in their retainer or in practice, allow some finessing at this point, where appropriate. It may be that the bill is reduced because the lawyer accepts that he or she should not have spent as long as he or she did on the case, or because a trainee spent time on the case, but made some errors, which should not be charged to the client. Such reduction is rare. The firm may also give itself scope to increase the fee if, given the importance of the work and the outcome, the total bill looks too low.

 ## Scandal!

Christine Parker and Adrian Evans tell of a case in which a lawyer included in his fees 12 minutes for his secretary wrapping a box of chocolates to be given to the secretary of a doctor who had helped to correct a report, and another 12 minutes in which the lawyer and the secretary discussed the purchase of the box of chocolates![56]

---

[56] C. Parker and A. Evans, *Inside Lawyers' Ethics* (Cambridge University Press, 2007).

Court assessment

One way of tackling costs is through court procedures. We will be exploring these in detail in Chapter 9. It is notable that the Civil Procedure Rules (CPR) open with a rule on costs.

Key statute

CPR 1.1 ('The overriding objective') explains that:

(1) These Rules are a new procedural code with the overriding objective of enabling the court to deal with cases justly and at proportionate cost.
(2) Dealing with a case justly and at proportionate cost includes, so far as is practicable –
    (a) ensuring that the parties are on an equal footing;
    (b) saving expense;
    (c) dealing with the case in ways which are proportionate –
        (i) to the amount of money involved;
        (ii) to the importance of the case;
        (iii) to the complexity of the issues; and
        (iv) to the financial position of each party;
    (d) ensuring that it is dealt with expeditiously and fairly;
    (e) allotting to it an appropriate share of the court's resources, while taking into account the need to allot resources to other cases; and
    (f) enforcing compliance with rules, practice directions and orders.

One important way of restricting costs in the litigation area is that the court can be required to assess the costs. The two most common situations in which this will arise are when:

- the court has to determine whether the loser of the case has to pay the winner's costs, and if, so how much; and
- a client seeks an assessment of the lawyer's costs before having to pay them.

Looking first at what happens when a case is lost, CPR 44 explains that 'the general rule is that the unsuccessful party will be ordered to pay the costs of the successful party'. That presumption does not apply in relation to proceedings in the Court of Appeal in family matters or probate proceedings. It is only a presumption and will not automatically be followed, as the CPR make clear.

Key statute

CPR 44.3 states:

[...]

(4) In deciding what order (if any) to make about costs, the court will have regard to all the circumstances, including –
    (a) the conduct of all the parties;

(b) whether a party has succeeded on part of its case, even if that party has not been wholly successful; and

(c) any admissible offer to settle made by a party which is drawn to the court's attention, and which is not an offer to which costs consequences under Part 36 apply.

(5) The conduct of the parties includes –

(a) conduct before, as well as during, the proceedings and in particular the extent to which the parties followed the Practice Direction – Pre-Action Conduct or any relevant pre-action protocol;

(b) whether it was reasonable for a party to raise, pursue or contest a particular allegation or issue;

(c) the manner in which a party has pursued or defended its case or a particular allegation or issue; and

(d) whether a claimant who has succeeded in the claim, in whole or in part, exaggerated its claim.

(6) The orders which the court may make under this rule include an order that a party must pay –

(a) a proportion of another party's costs;

(b) a stated amount in respect of another party's costs;

(c) costs from or until a certain date only;

(d) costs incurred before proceedings have begun;

(e) costs relating to particular steps taken in the proceedings;

(f) costs relating only to a distinct part of the proceedings; and

(g) interest on costs from or until a certain date, including a date before judgment.

[...]

 Key case

King v Daily Telegraph Group [2005] 1 WLR 2282

The case was a libel case with a 100 per cent success fee. The claimant had no money and no relevant insurance. The newspaper group was in the position that even if it were to win, it would not get its costs paid because the claimant could not pay. The costs were estimated to be likely to exceed £1 million, while the damages at most would be £150,000. In fact, the defendant newspaper would save money by losing the case early and be better off than if it were to continue the case and win. Lord Justice Brook noted that the case was more valuable to the client's lawyers than to the claimant. The solution was to make an order under CPR 44.8 to determine the recoverable costs and to cap them.

Where costs are to be ordered at the end of the case, the court will use the standard or the indemnity basis. The indemnity basis is used where there is culpability or abuse of process by the paying party; otherwise, the standard basis is used. The key difference between the two methods of assessment is that if there is any doubt over reasonableness, it is resolved in favour of the paying party if the standard basis is used, but in favour of the receiving party where the indemnity approach is used.

Where a client is challenging his or her own solicitor's costs, the key issue will be reasonableness of the fees. It is rare for a client to require assessment of the costs bill. In part, this is because, unless the bill is reduced by more than a fifth, the costs of the assessment will fall on the client.[57] Also, many clients will not be aware of the option. The client only needs to be told of the option if the solicitor's firm is planning to sue for its costs.

Whether the new CPR have led to reduced costs is a matter for debate. A common view is that the procedures have focused lawyers' minds on ensuring that costs remain reasonable and proportionate. This general change in attitude may be more effective than the Rules themselves, which we will examine further in Chapter 9.

The significance of the CPR should not be exaggerated. Most cases do not get to the litigation stage and so the Rules cannot affect them.

Solicitors Regulation Authority review

A review of costs by the Solicitors Regulation Authority (SRA) is another option for a client seeking to challenge the propriety of his or her bill. However, this is permitted only in certain circumstances—that is, where the issue is non-contentious, where there is no business agreement, and where the bill is for less than £50,000.[58] The SRA will assess what would be a fair and reasonable charge for the work. Notably, it cannot increase the bill, nor can it reduce it; it can only declare what would be reasonable. That said, a solicitor would presumably be very reluctant to insist on a bill that the SRA had declared unreasonable.

The SRA will normally require the client who is challenging the bill to pay 50 per cent of the costs, plus VAT, plus disbursements, in advance, although this can be waived. This provision seems designed to ensure that the review is not used simply as a means of delaying payment.

Legal proceedings to recover fees

At its heart, the legal relationship between a client and solicitor is governed by contract. The client is required to pay the fees under the contract. So a lawyer can enforce payment through breach-of-contract proceedings. The normal rules of contract apply. Lawyers typically seek to avoid having to bring proceedings to enforce fees by asking

---

[57] Solicitors Act 1974, s. 70(9).
[58] Solicitors (Non-contentious Business) Remuneration Order 2009, SI 2009/1931, c. 9(c).

for payments on account. It is very common for lawyers at least to ensure that all disbursements are paid for by clients in advance, so that even in the worst-case scenario the lawyer will not be out of pocket.

Apart from the usual methods of enforcement under contract law, the lawyer can also rely on the 'solicitor's lien'. This allows the solicitor to keep any property (including paperwork) until the bill is paid. The solicitor must inform the client of this at the start of the case. This can be a powerful negotiating tool, because the paperwork can be very important, and is often essential if the client wants to move on to another solicitor.

The solicitor must wait one month from presenting the bill before suing on it, unless the court gives leave. In relation to contentious matters, section 61 of the Solicitors Act 1974 states that leave of the court is required before proceedings for fees are brought.

Client funds

There is complex and important guidance dealing with cases in which a solicitor looks after clients' funds. Indeed, in the 1999 Law Society Guide, more than 260 pages were spent on the issue.

This is not surprising. A major source of solicitors' malpractice has been inappropriate dealings with money held by lawyers on behalf of clients. It is important for a range of transactions that solicitors do hold their clients' money and so clients must have full confidence that their funds will be dealt with appropriately. The rules are found in the Solicitors Act 1974 and the Solicitors' Accounts Rules 1998 (SAR). Their technicality means that they cannot be covered here in detail, but we will outline the main themes.

The primary aim of the rules is to prevent solicitors from acting fraudulently or improperly profiting from their clients' money. The rules are designed to see not only that no wrongdoing is done, but also that handling of money is transparent so that there can be no perception of wrongdoing.

Separate accounts

At the heart of the rules is the principle that client accounts and office (solicitors) accounts be kept separate. These two must both be kept separate from any trust money that a solicitor holds. A fundamental principle is that a solicitor cannot use the money in one account for purposes of others. So, obviously, a solicitor cannot pay the firm's electricity bill out of money held in the clients' account. The rules set down the detail regarding precisely what money can be used for what purposes. If a client suffers loss as a result of a breach of the accounts rules, then he or she may receive payments from the Solicitors Indemnity Fund.[59]

---

[59] Solicitors Act 1974, s. 37.

Inspection

The SRA has the power to order that accounts be inspected under SAR 6. Confidentiality is not a reason to refuse to disclose the books. Annual accounts prepared by an independent accountant must be disclosed to the SRA.

Interest on clients account

A complex issue is what happens to interest that is earned on the client account. The difficulty is that the client account will typically contain money from a range of clients, with differing sums and held for differing lengths of time. The interest, however, might be significant. It is clear that a solicitor cannot profit from the interest and so is not allowed to keep the money. Any doubt on this was confirmed in *Brown v IRC*,[60] in which the (then) Inland Revenue wished to charge a solicitor tax on interest earned on client accounts. The House of Lords was clear that the interest did not belong to the solicitors and so could not be taxed.

Rule 24 of the Solicitors' Accounts Rules 1991 states that solicitors shall account to clients for interest earned on deposits in client accounts. There is a de minimis rule under which sums of £20 or less relating to interest do not need to be paid. There are similar rules when sums of money are held for very short periods of time. It is thought, in these cases, that the administrative costs in working out tiny sums of interest are not worth the effort and expense of returning them to the client. However, as Boon and Levin point out, added together over the course of a year, these small sums might be significant.[61] Some jurisdictions, including Canada, require the payment of these small sums into a fund for charitable purposes.

Legal aid

In 2013, drastic cuts to the provision of legal aid came into effect. In this section, we will explore the impacts of these cuts and why so many lawyers are deeply concerned at what has happened.[62]

Legal aid was first introduced in England and Wales in 1949. It was intended to ensure that there was access to justice for the poor, as well as the rich. It provides funds for those who cannot afford to obtain legal advice or to litigate in cases in which they have a reasonable reason for doing so.

---

[60] [1965] AC 244.   [61] Boon and Levin (n. 7), 261.
[62] S. Cobb, 'Legal aid reform: Its impact on family law' (2013) 35 Journal of Social Welfare and Family Law 3.

The problem with the previous regime

The cuts can be traced back to the Comprehensive Spending Review in October 2010, which set the Ministry of Justice a target of cutting spending by 23 per cent: from £9.3 billion to £7.3 billion. The legal aid budget, sitting at £2.1 billion, was an obvious target for the Ministry. It sought to save £450 million per annum from the legal aid budget.[63] Early on, it was decided that relatively little could be done to cut the criminal legal aid budget because of the right of criminals to a fair trial, protected by the European Convention on Human Rights.[64] This meant that civil legal aid bore the brunt of the cuts, and especially housing, benefits, employment, immigration, and social welfare law.

The government did not, however, put its case solely in terms of saving money. It also argued that people were too ready to litigate. By denying them easy access to lawyers, they could be encouraged to mediate and to resolve their disputes amicably. We will be exploring the issues surrounding mediation in Chapter 10.

The cuts

There were three ways in which the cuts operated:

- cuts to the scope of legal aid—that is, what kinds of cases are covered;
- assessments of financial eligibility—that is, how poor someone has to be before he or she is entitled to legal aid and how much, if at all, he or she must contribute; and
- cuts to legal aid fees—that is, the amount that legal aid will pay to lawyers and experts.

The budget cuts were intended to bring around a 100 per cent reduction in legal aid welfare benefit, clinical negligence, and employment cases, an 83 per cent reduction in family cases, and a 36 per cent reduction in housing cases. It was estimated that, of those who would have done so under the old, some 623,000 people a year would no longer receive legal advice or representation under the new regime.[65]

The case for cuts

The starting point for the case in favour of cuts was its expense. David Lammy MP, the legal aid minister, reported that spending on legal aid, both criminal and civil, had

---

[63] Ministry of Justice, *Impact Assessment: Cumulative Legal Aid Reform Proposals* (Ministry of Justice, 2010).

[64] S. Hynes, 'Austerity justice' (2013) 21 Journal of Poverty and Social Justice 97.

[65] Ministry of Justice, *Legal Aid Reform: Scope Changes, Impact Assessment* (Ministry of Justice, 2010), 16; Hynes (n. 64).

risen from £1.5 billion in 1997 to £2 billion in 2004.[66] The legal aid budget per capita was 17 times that of the United States and four times that of the Netherlands.

These are striking statistics. However, as Cookson points out, in fact, in the past ten years, legal aid as a proportion of gross domestic product (GDP) had fallen.[67] Further, the international comparison is somewhat misleading. It is not possible to compare the legal aid budget in the UK directly with that of other countries. In part, that is because the work done by lawyers in the UK is sometimes done by other professionals in other countries, paid for by the state, but outside the legal aid budget. Also, the UK has an adversarial system of justice, which makes it very different from other systems in which state officials, court officials, or even judges do some of the work that lawyers perform in the UK.

The case for the cuts was also justified on the basis that the use of lawyers and courts was not appropriate to deal with some cases. People seeking advice on benefits could receive this from voluntary organisations such as Citizens Advice, rather than by using expensive lawyers. Couples who were separating could use mediation, rather than the legal system, to resolve their disputes.

The case against the cuts

Human rights

Access to justice is a fundamental aspect of the rule of law. The availability of legal aid shows that access to justice is not just a theoretical concept. It makes nonsense of legal rights if people cannot afford to find out what rights they have or take steps to enforce those rights.[68] It is the most disadvantaged in society who most need access to their legal rights.[69] As Liz Curran and Mary Anne Noone argue:

> Without knowledge about human rights and legal rights, without the confidence to exercise those rights and without the capacity or capability to seek or find help it is unlikely that people will realise their rights and accordingly access to justice is placed in question.[70]

Many of those who are legally aided and using the courts suffer from mental ill-health problems, have learning difficulties, are addicted to alcohol or other substances, or have limited English. The idea that they will be able to mediate their problems or find

---

[66] J. Flood and A. Whyte, 'What's wrong with legal aid? Lessons from outside the UK' (2006) 25 Civil Justice Quarterly 80.

[67] G. Cookson, *Unintended Consequences: The Cost of the Government's Legal Aid Reforms* (King's College London, 2011).

[68] Flood and Whyte (n. 66).

[69] R. Smith, 'Human rights and access to justice' (2007) 14 International Journal of the Legal Profession 261.

[70] L. Curran and M.-A. Noone, 'Access to justice: A new approach using human rights standards' (2008) 15 International Journal of the Legal Profession 195, 196.

other sources of help is extraordinary.[71] For such cases, it is possible that, under section 10 of the Legal Aid, Sentencing and Punishment of Offenders Act 2012, a grant of legal aid will be made if the case is exceptional.

The idea that legal aid can, in some cases, be seen as a human right has some support.[72] Article 47 of the European Charter of Fundamental Rights and Freedoms states: 'Legal aid shall be available to those who lack sufficient resources in so far as such aid is necessary to ensure effective access to justice.' Under the European Convention on Human Rights, the issue falls as part of the right to a fair hearing under Article 6.

In the leading judgment, the European Court of Human Rights stated:

> The question whether the provision of legal aid was necessary for a fair hearing had to be determined on the basis of the particular facts and circumstances of each case and depended inter alia upon the importance of what was at stake for the applicant in the proceedings, the complexity of the relevant law and procedure and the applicant's capacity to represent him or herself effectively.[73]

It is almost inevitable that there will, in the future, be cases brought by litigants who have been unable to present their cases owing to a lack of legal aid in which human rights issues will be key.

 Key case

Re T (Children) [2012] UKSC 36

In this case, there were claims that the grandparents were involved in the abuse of their grandchild. The grandparents were a retired fisherman and bookkeeper with a modest income, but not low enough for legal aid. They were joined as parties to care proceedings and borrowed £55,000 to fund their defence of the allegations. At the hearings, it was found that the allegations were entirely without foundation and the grandparents were completely exonerated. They were left with a legal bill that it would take them more than 15 years to pay off. The Supreme Court, while sympathising with the grandparents' position, held that the local authority (which had acted appropriately) could not be ordered to pay their costs. The fact that couples of very modest circumstance will have to go into great debt, or may simply be unable, to defend themselves against allegations of child abuse is hard to justify. The Supreme Court raised the question of whether the denial of legal aid breached the couple's rights under Article 6.

---

[71] House of Commons Justice Committee, *Third Report: Government's Proposed Reform of Legal Aid* (House of Commons, 2011), online at www.publications.parliament.uk/pa/cm201011/cmselect/cmjust/681/68102.htm

[72] Smith (n. 69).

[73] *Steel and Morris v UK* [2005] ECHR 103, 120. See also *Airey v Ireland* [1979] ECHR 3.

False economy

Although the government has declared that the cutbacks in the legal aid budget will save the £450 million required, this has been questioned. One problem is the difficulty of calculating the overall costs to the government of the limitations on legal aid. The National Audit Office has confirmed as much: 'The Ministry's Finance Directorate does not have sufficient visibility of the costs of policy proposals, affecting its ability to monitor their financial implications centrally.'[74]

There are several stages to the argument that the legal aid cuts will not result in as many savings as may be hoped. First, there is the concern that, by denying legal aid, costs will be passed on to other areas of public expenditure.[75] The claim is that if people cannot access remedies to their problems through the courts, this will produce problems in other areas of government expenditure, such as housing or welfare. The family law group Resolution has argued:

> This is essentially a false economy, as the weaker partner is left with an inadequate settlement and is pushed into reliance on benefits, shifting the costs to other areas of public spending. This will ultimately place a greater burden on the public purse.[76]

Resolution goes on to express concern that cuts in legal aid will lead to damaging results for children, with long-term social consequences. Graham Cookson estimates that there will be £136 million in 'knock-on' costs to other parts of government expenditure as a result of the legal aid cutbacks.[77] These include the need to provide extra funding for alternative sources of legal advice, increased reliance on welfare payments, and increasing burdens on health and housing services.

A second argument is that if people are not able to access legal advice and representation, they will seek to represent themselves in court.[78] That will lead to delays and expenditure for the court system, and costs to the judiciary. This will especially arise in cases in which, had people sought legal advice, it could have been explained to them that their claim was misconceived, or the lawyer could have recommended a better route to resolve the problem. Now, the unadvised litigant will have to institute proceedings and appear before a judge to receive that advice. The President of the Family Division has warned of huge delays as people attempt to litigate cases themselves.[79] He suggests, from his experience of litigants in person, that cases that could be resolved in an hour were both parties represented will now take a day or longer.

---

[74] National Audit Office, *Ministry of Justice: Financial Management Report HC 187 Session 2010–2011* (National Audit Office, 2011), 8.

[75] A. Buck and M. Smith, 'Back for the future: A client-centred analysis of social welfare and family law provision' (2013) 35 Journal of Social Welfare and Family Law 95.

[76] Resolution, *Cuts to Legal Aid Leave 200,000 People at Risk of Marital Purgatory* (Resolution, 2013).

[77] G. Cookson, 'Analysing the economic justification for the reforms to social welfare and family law legal aid' (2013) 35 Journal of Social Welfare and Family Law 21.

[78] K. Williams, *Litigants in Person: A Literature Review* (Ministry of Justice, 2011).

[79] P. Wall, 'The President's Resolution Address 2012' (2012) 42 Family Law 742.

Not only will the result be increased costs, but there is also evidence that litigants in person often fail to achieve full justice for themselves.[80]

A third issue is that the government may have underestimated the number of people who, even under its proposals, will be entitled to claim legal aid. In particular, there may be significant numbers of people who, in family cases, are victims of domestic violence or are vulnerable, and so are entitled to be regarded as exceptional and entitled to legal aid. Similarly, there have been suggestions that the government has not appreciated the number of people with mental health problems who may thus fall within an exception and be entitled to legal aid. Jo Miles and colleagues estimate that 71 per cent of those eligible for legal aid for family problems under the old system reported mental health problems and so may still be able to obtain legal aid.[81]

Criminal law

While the government has not been able to restrict access to legal aid to defend a criminal trial, it has introduced a tendering process based on a set figure.[82] This will have the effect of severely restricting the choice of lawyers for criminal defendants. With contracts going to the lowest bidder, there are concerns over the quality of representation. A group of leading academics wrote to the press saying:

> Those firms lucky enough to secure a contract—the government plans to reduce the number from about 1,600 to 400—will receive a guaranteed share of the work however well or badly they represent their clients. Since contracts will be awarded to the lowest bidder—and bids will have to start at least 17.5 per cent lower than existing average costs—the quality of legal representation will be an early casualty. Suppliers will have a strong financial imperative to do as little work as possible, and to persuade clients to plead guilty irrespective of the merits of their case.[83]

Family law

The largest cutbacks in terms of money will be in family law cases. The Legal Aid, Sentencing and Punishment of Offenders Act 2012 has drastically restricted access to legal aid in family law cases. There will be no legal aid in private cases (for

---

[80] C. Bevan, 'Self-represented litigants: The overlooked and unintended consequence of legal aid reform' (2013) 35 Journal of Social Welfare and Family Law 1, 43.

[81] J. Miles, N. Balmer, and M. Smith, 'When exceptional is the rule: Mental health, family problems and the reform of legal aid in England and Wales' (2012) 24 Child and Family Law Quarterly 320.

[82] A. Edwards, 'Will defendants survive changes to criminal legal aid?' (2011) 86 Criminal Justice Matters 30.

[83] Law Society, 'Leading academics warn legal aid cuts "could have devastating effects"', online at www.lawsociety.org.uk/news/stories/leading-academics-warn-legal-aid-cuts-could-have-devastating-effects/

example in disputes over contact or residence, or financial disputes) unless the claimant falls into an exceptional category. These include cases in which the applicant is the victim of domestic violence, cases involving a forced marriage injunction, cases involving allegations of child abuse, cases in which a child is party to proceedings, or cases in which there are exceptional circumstances.[84] In public law cases, legal aid will be available for parties to the proceedings, but this will be restricted to a fixed fee. This means, for example, that if a father is seeking contact with his child, while in the past (subject to his means) he could have obtained legal aid to obtain legal advice and representation, this will not now be available, unless he is the victim of domestic violence. He will need to negotiate the issue with the mother or represent himself in court. The most that he might get is £150 for mediation and legal help.

However, the effectiveness of these provisions is questionable. There are exceptions on the restrictions to legal aid. Much will depend on the extent of the exceptions. First, there is the exclusion for cases in which 'there has been, or is a risk of, domestic violence'.[85] There will be great difficulties in proving this. The government has suggested that those claiming to be victims will be interviewed by telephone, but need to provide evidence, for example that they have obtained a court order. However, critics point out that many victims of domestic violence do not seek help until the violence has escalated to extreme levels.

The cuts in legal aid have been described by a leading expert on family law and policy as 'savage'[86] and 'breathtaking'.[87] Two other reasons appear in the government's justification for the cutbacks in relation to family law cases. One is that litigation should not be available for things that are a result of personal choice.[88] The argument appears to be that if someone chooses to divorce, he or she cannot expect the state to fund the litigation that results from this decision. John Eekelaar argues that the reasoning is 'bizarre to the point of incoherence'.[89] As he points out, a person may be a victim of fraud as a result of his or her choice, but that is no reason for not giving legal aid to protect that person's rights. In any event, many family disputes do not result from choice, for example a parent being prevented from seeing his or her children by the other parent.

[84] R. Hunter, 'Doing violence to family law' (2011) 33 Journal of Social Welfare and Family Law 343. See Legal Aid, Sentencing and Punishment of Offenders Act 2012.

[85] Legal Aid, Sentencing and Punishment of Offenders Act 2012, Sch. 1, para 12(1).

[86] M. MacLean, 'Family law in hard times' (2011) 33 Journal of Social Welfare and Family Law 309.

[87] Hunter (n. 84).

[88] Ministry of Justice, *Proposals for the Reform of Legal Aid in England and Wales: Consultation Paper* (Ministry of Justice, 2010), para. 4.19.

[89] J. Eekelaar, '"Not of the highest importance": Family justice under threat' (2011) 33 Journal of Social Welfare and Family Law 317, 319.

Digging deeper

One of the most striking things about the government's justifications for the cutbacks in legal aid is its failure to appreciate what legal aid in family law cases is actually spent on. The government's justifications give the impression that family lawyers spend their time litigating cases. In fact, very few family law cases are resolved through the courts. The proposals seemed to be based on a false image of what family lawyers do. Joan Hunt, looking at contact disputes, notes that, of cases in which there were concerns over child abuse or neglect, domestic violence, substance abuse, or mental illness, only 51 per cent had been to court.[90] Among those, where the non-resident parent complained that the resident parent had prevented contact, only 19 per cent litigated. So litigation is already very rare. The contact cases that will be shifted from the courts to mediation by the reforms are not trivial cases in which couples have litigated 'for fun', but rather are the most serious of an already serious category of cases. As Hunt puts it: 'Parents go to court, therefore, not because they see this as a simple way of dealing with contact difficulties, but because, in most cases, they are desperate and cannot think what else to do.'[91] Telling them that they should mediate will not do much good.

Conclusion

Richard Moorhead concludes:

> Many lawyers structure their billing arrangements to put their own financial interests before those of their client. That a significant proportion also do *not* charge in this way suggests that it is possible to charge the client on a more equitable and ethical basis. If it is possible, those lawyers who do not charge transparently and simply have to answer the question: why not? The only plausible explanation that they might rely on is that clients are adequately informed of the charges, understand them, understand there are alternatives and choose to stay with their particular firm because they are persuaded of the need to do so on the basis that these extra costs are justified on quality or access to justice grounds.[92]

This is a somewhat harsh indictment of the fees that lawyers charge their clients. One theme that emerges from this chapter is the difficulty of finding a way of structuring fees. The difficulty is the unknowns at the start of a legal case. The fact that the costs of a legal case usually cannot be predicted in advance means that it is impossible to provide a clear estimate of costs in advance of a case.

This chapter has also discussed the debates surrounding legal aid. At one time, an English lawyer could declare, with a reasonable degree of confidence, that a person's

---

[90] J. Hunt, 'Through a glass darkly: The uncertain future of private law child contact litigation' (2012) 33 Journal of Social Welfare and Family Law 379.
[91] Hunt (n. 90), 383.   [92] Moorhead (n. 11), 364.

poverty should never be a reason why he or she is unable to access the courts to enforce his or her rights. Now, that cannot be said. Many who previously would have been entitled to legal advice must now make do with advice from non-lawyers or informal means of resolving their disputes. To supporters of the cutbacks, this will lead to cheaper and less acrimonious resolution of disputes. To critics, it means that the most vulnerable in society will be left with second-class justice. The courts will be forums in which the rich can entrench their power, while the poor will be left with their rights ignored and unenforceable.

Further reading

The following works consider the impact of the legal aid cutbacks:

C. Bevan, 'Self-represented litigants: The overlooked and unintended consequence of legal aid reform' (2013) 35 Journal of Social Welfare and Family Law 1.

A. Buck and M. Smith, 'Back for the future: A client-centred analysis of social welfare and family law provision' (2013) 35 Journal of Social Welfare and Family Law 95.

G. Cookson, *Unintended Consequences: The Cost of the Government's Legal Aid Reforms* (King's College London, 2011)

G. Cookson, 'Analysing the economic justification for the reforms to social welfare and family law legal aid' (2013) 35 Journal of Social Welfare and Family Law 21.

L. Curran and M.-A. Noone, 'Access to justice: A new approach using human rights standards' (2008) 15 International Journal of the Legal Profession 195.

J. Eekelaar, '"Not of the highest importance": Family justice under threat' (2011) 33 Journal of Social Welfare and Family Law 317.

J. Flood and A. Whyte, 'What's wrong with legal aid? Lessons from outside the UK' (2006) 25 Civil Justice Quarterly 80.

J. Hunt, 'Through a glass darkly: The uncertain future of private law child contact litigation' (2012) 33 Journal of Social Welfare and Family Law 379.

R. Hunter, 'Doing violence to family law' (2011) 33 Journal of Social Welfare and Family Law 343.

S. Hynes, 'Austerity justice' (2013) 21 Journal of Poverty and Social Justice 97.

M. Maclean, 'Family law in hard times' (2011) 33 Journal of Social Welfare and Family Law 309.

J. Miles, N. Balmer, and M. Smith, 'When exceptional is the rule: Mental health, family problems and the reform of legal aid in England and Wales' (2012) 24 Child and Family Law Quarterly 320.

K. Williams, *Litigants in person: A literature review* (Ministry of Justice, 2011).

The following works discuss the position of fees generally:

G. Hadfield, 'The price of law: How the market for lawyers distorts the justice system' (2000) 98 Michigan Law Review 953.

R. Moorhead, 'Filthy lucre: Lawyers' fees and lawyers' ethics—What is wrong with informed consent?' (2011) 31 Legal Studies 345.

R. Smith, 'Human rights and access to justice' (2007) 14 International Journal of the Legal Profession 261.

C. Tata, 'In the interests of commerce or clients: Which comes first? Legal aid, supply, demand, and "ethical indeterminacy" in criminal defence work' (2007) 34 Journal of Law and Society 498.

L. Visscher and T. Schepens, 'A law and economics approach to cost shifting, fee arrangements and legal expense insurance', in M. Tuil and L. Visscher (eds) *New Trends in Financing Civil Litigation* (Edward Elgar, 2010).

D. Webb, 'Killing time: A limited defence of time–cost billing' (2010) 13 Legal Ethics 39.

These works consider contingency fees:

T. Friehe, 'Contingent fees and legal expenses insurance: Comparison for varying defendant fault' (2010) 30 International Review of Law and Economics 283.

H. Kritzer, 'Seven dogged myths concerning contingency fees' (2002) 80 Washington University Law Quarterly 739.

D. Luban, 'Speculating on justice: The ethics and jurisprudence of contingency fees', in S. Parker and C. Sampford (eds) *Legal Ethics and Legal Practice: Contemporary Issues* (Oxford University Press, 1995).

E. Zamir and I. Ritov, 'Notions of fairness and contingent fees' (2011) 74 Law and Contemporary Problems 1.

Negligence and lawyers

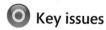 **Key issues**

- To whom does a lawyer owe a duty of care?
- When is a duty of care breached?
- Is the law on negligence for lawyers different from the general law on negligence?

Introduction

As we saw in Chapter 3, lawyers are regulated by their professional bodies. A client with a complaint about a lawyer can apply to the relevant regulatory body. Negligent work may well breach the professional codes.

Follow the Code

The Solicitors Regulation Authority (SRA) Code of Conduct, para 2.9, requires:

> You should…provide a proper standard of client care and of work. This would include exercising competence, skill and diligence, and taking into account the individual needs and circumstances of each client.

Outcome 1.5 requires that:

> the service you provide to *clients* is competent, delivered in a timely manner and takes account of your *clients'* needs and circumstances;

However, that may not provide a sufficient remedy. A finding of malpractice will not necessarily lead to the client being granted any monetary compensation, or at least not necessarily to compensation sufficient to meet his or her loss. A finding of malpractice will generally not be made in a case of 'genuine professional judgment',[1] even if that was a faulty judgement. For some cases, clients need to turn to the courts

---

[1] *Connolly v Law Society* [2007] EWHC 1175 (Admin).

and sue the lawyer in tort for negligence, or possibly for breach of contract. But it is a brave person who sues a lawyer.

As we shall see, a claimant seeking to sue a lawyer will face an uphill task.[2] Cynics will say that lawyers will stand up for each other and for the reputation of the legal profession, meaning that the law is designed to make it nearly impossible to establish negligence against lawyers. Supporters of the current approach will say that lawyers are highly trained professionals and that it would be surprising if there were many cases of negligence. Further, it is important for the law to recognise that interpreting law is not an exact science and that, in exercising professional legal judgement, a range of possible views is acceptable. It would be unfair if a lawyer were to be found negligent simply because the advice that he or she gave was not the same as the advice that another lawyer would give.

If a claimant wishes to sue a lawyer, there are three primary routes: the law of contract; the law of fiduciary duty; and the law of negligence. We will start by looking at the law of contract.

Contract

If a client were to wish to sue a solicitor on the basis of the law of **contract**, the following questions would arise.

 Definition

A **contract** is a formal agreement by two parties under which one offers something in exchange for something else. Typically, goods or services are exchanged for money. Should the goods or services not be as promised, a claim for breach of contract can be brought.

Is there a contract?

In many cases, whether or not there is a contract is very clear. There will be a letter from a solicitor setting out the terms and conditions under which he or she is acting (known as the 'retainer'), which the client must sign. However, it is possible for a contact to be made orally, rather than in writing, and a contract can even be inferred from conduct.[3] So if a lawyer starts to act as if he or she is someone's lawyer, then it may be assumed that there is a contract between the lawyer and that person, even if they have not explicitly agreed to be in a lawyer–client relationship.

---

[2] A detailed discussion of the law is found in J. Powell and R. Steward, *Jackson and Powell on Professional Liability*, 6th edn (Sweet and Maxwell, 2007). For a discussion of tort law generally, see K. Horsey and E. Rackley, *Tort Law* (Oxford University Press, 2013).

[3] *Groom v Crocker* [1939] 1 KB 194.

Generally, the courts will be reluctant to imply a contract to provide legal services from conduct, unless the facts are clear. In *BDG Roof-Bond Ltd v Douglas*,[4] a firm regularly acted as solicitors for a company. The firm was asked by a client to arrange for the sale of his 50 per cent shareholding in the company. It was held that the firm was not acting for the company in that transaction. The simple point was that no one from the company had explicitly instructed the firm to work on this transaction. All that the solicitors had done was explicable as acting for the shareholder.

Lawyers will want to be clear with whom they are contracting. This is particularly an issue if the director of a company is seeking advice. The lawyer will want to know whether he or she is representing the company or the director, or both.[5] The retainer will seek to set this out clearly. However, a lawyer will need to be careful that, having set out a contract with person A, he or she does not start to act as a lawyer for person B and then create an implied contract with that second person. This is most likely to happen in a case involving a company and its directors, but could also occur where a lawyer is advising a client and that client's spouse then seeks advice as well.

With barristers, there is rarely a contract between the client and barrister; it is the solicitor, if anyone, who enters into the contract. A client who is seeking to sue a barrister is most likely to use negligence. But it is now possible for clients, in certain circumstances, to instruct a barrister directly (see Chapter 4) and in those cases a contract may be established between the client and the barrister.

What are the terms of the contract?

In easy cases, the retainer will set out the terms of the contract between the lawyer and the client.[6] The contract should set out what the lawyer is promising to do. A solicitor might, for example, be expected to advise on a very specific issue and so cannot be sued for breach of contract for failing to advise on other issues. A solicitor who is asked to convey a house may not be acting in breach of contract if he or she fails to tell the client that he or she is paying too much for the house. If the contract makes it clear that the lawyer is simply ensuring that the legal requirements for the sale are complete, he or she will have done what is required and so will not breach the contract. However, in agreeing to act for a purchaser, the lawyer will be taken to have agreed to do all of the things that are normally done by lawyers in connection with the purchase of a house (for example completing the relevant searches and registrations), even if those are not spelt out in the retainer.

It is for this reason that the solicitor will want to set out in the retainer what he or she is expected to do. If nothing is set down in writing, the court will expect the solicitor to advise on all issues on which a reasonable solicitor might advise in the

---

[4] [2000] PNLR 397.

[5] *Edenwest Ltd v CMS Cameron McKenna (A Firm)* [2012] EWHC 1258 (Ch).

[6] *Bristol and West Building Society v Fancy and Jackson (A Firm)* [1997] 4 All ER 582, 604j–605b, *per* Chadwick J.

circumstances. So, for example, if a lawyer is instructed to draft a will and there is no written agreement setting out his or her obligations, the court may well infer that the solicitor has undertaken to advise on relevant tax issues relating to the will: that is what solicitors typically do.[7] The courts tend to take the view that if the solicitor decides not to clarify his or her obligations, he or she cannot complain if the court implies reasonable terms into the contract.[8]

Underpinning the contract will be a general duty that the lawyer will act with the 'reasonable care and skill' of a normally competent practitioner in performing professional tasks.[9] This requirement will be read into any contract in which a solicitor undertakes to advise on a certain issue or to perform a certain task, even if the contract does not say so explicitly. This general requirement is helpful because it is not normally possible in a contract to set out all of the things that a solicitor may be required to do in a particular case.

There is lively debate over whether a solicitor can contract out of this general liability. There is no doubt that he or she can increase the obligation. In *Zwebner v The Mortgage Corp Ltd*,[10] the firm of solicitors foolishly undertook that all documents would be properly executed before completion of the mortgage. Through no fault of its own, the firm was not able to execute all of the documents, but because it had promised that it would do so, the firm was liable for breach of contract.[11] Such a case is unusual. Usually, the courts will assume that lawyers are promising to use a reasonable degree of care and skill to achieve a result, rather than guaranteeing a particular result, unless the wording precludes any other interpretation.[12] The court will find it hard to believe that a solicitor intended to enter a contract meaning that he or she would be liable even if not at fault.[13]

 Key case

Midland Bank Plc v Cox McQueen [1999] PNLR 593

A bank instructed solicitors to obtain the signature of Mr and Mrs Duke to a mortgage and to explain its implications. Mr Duke attended with a woman whom he said was Mrs Duke, but she was not. The bank sued the solicitors in negligence. The claim failed on the basis that the solicitors had acted reasonably in assuming that the woman was

---

[7] See *Hurlingham Estates Ltd v Wilde Partners* [1997] 1 Lloyd's Rep 525, in which solicitors had not made it clear that they were advising on the tax consequences of a commercial transaction and so were held to be doing so.

[8] *Griffiths v Evans* [1953] 1 WLR 1424, 1428, *per* Denning LJ.

[9] *Midland Bank v Hett, Stubbs Kemp* [1979] Ch 384.   [10] [1998] PNLR 769.

[11] See, for another example, *Platform Funding Ltd v Bank of Scotland Plc* [2008] EWCA Civ 930.

[12] *Barclays Bank Plc v Weeks Legg Dean (A Firm)* [1999] QB 309.

[13] *Midland Bank plc v Cox McQueen* [1999] PNLR 593; *UCB Corporate Services Ltd v Clyde Co (A Firm)* [2000] PNLR 841.

Mrs Duke. The Court of Appeal rejected the argument that the solicitors had an absolute duty to obtain Mrs Duke's signature. Lord Woolf MR stated:

> If commercial institutions such as banks wish to impose an absolute liability on members of a profession they should do so in clear terms so that the solicitors can appreciate the extent of their obligation which they are accepting...Unless the language used in a retainer clearly has this consequence, the courts should not be ready to impose obligations on solicitors which even the most careful solicitor may not be able to meet.[14]

Rather than increase the potential liability, it is more likely that a solicitor will add in terms to the contract limiting liability, so that he or she will not be liable even if he or she fails to exercise reasonable care and skill. In many cases, these clauses will be ineffective. This raises some general issues of contract law and will not be covered in detail, but there are three main reasons why such clauses may not be effective.

1. The *contra proferentem* rule will mean that any term limiting a person's liability will be construed strictly. This means that if the clause is ambiguous and could mean either X or Y, the interpretation that is most favourable to the client will be taken.

2. Under the general principles of contractual interpretation, the courts will be reluctant to believe that a solicitor was saying that he or she could act below the standard of reasonable care and skill without contractual liability.

3. Under the Unfair Contract Terms Act 1977 and the Unfair Terms in Consumer Contracts Regulations 1999,[15] such exclusion clauses may be struck down if found to be unreasonable or unfair.

Further, any provision that exempts a solicitor from liability for negligence or breach of contractual duty is void under the Solicitors Act 1974.

Key statute

Under the Solicitors Act 1974, s 60(5) and (6):

(5) A provision in a contentious business agreement that the solicitor shall not be liable for his negligence, or that of any employee of his, shall be void if the client is a natural person who, in entering that agreement, is acting for purposes which are outside his trade, business or profession.

(6) A provision in a contentious business agreement that the solicitor shall be relieved from any responsibility to which he would otherwise be subject as a solicitor shall be void.

---

[14] At 848.   [15] SI 1999/2083.

Section 60 applies only where the solicitor is contracting with an individual acting outside his or her trade or business. So it does not apply to a business client. It also applies only to contentious business.

Digging deeper

A literal reading of section 60 of the 1974 Act might suggest that it applies only to removal, and not restrictions, of liability. So a clause saying that a lawyer will not be liable for a breach of contract is clearly caught. But what about a clause saying that liability will not exceed £10,000?[16] In part, the issue is dealt with by Outcome 1.8 of the SRA Code of Conduct, which forbids exclusion of liability below the minimum level of insurance cover held by the solicitor. The wording of that provision might suggest that the SRA believes that limitations above the level of insurance might be justified.

Fiduciary duties

Another route for suing a lawyer would be to sue for breach of a fiduciary duty. A solicitor owes fiduciary duties to their clients. Indeed, in *Re Van Laun*,[17] Cozens-Hardy MR stated that the relationship between a solicitor and his or her client has been described as 'one of the most important fiduciary relations known to our law'.

Many cases of breach of fiduciary duty can be dealt with under contract law or even tort law. In *Bristol and West Building Society v Mothew*,[18] the Court of Appeal considered that the term 'fiduciary duty' should be limited to those duties peculiar to fiduciaries breach of which attracts different legal consequences from the breach of other duties. In other words, claims of breach of fiduciary duty should be used where tort or contract law liability does not arise.

The most significant fiduciary principles include the following.

1. *Undue influence*[19] If a client makes a gift to a solicitor, there will be a presumption of undue influence, meaning that the gift is voidable and must be returned at the request of the client. That presumption is rebuttable. So a client who is a successful businessman who gives his solicitor tickets to Wimbledon may be shown to have genuinely wanted to give a gift, but the burden will be on the solicitor to show that the gift was valid.

2. *Conflict of interest* If a solicitor has an interest in an issue over which he or she is advising a client, the solicitor must disclose all known facts, including his or her interest.[20] This was discussed further in Chapter 6.

---

[16] A. Horrocks and S. Brake, 'Limitations of liability in solicitors' retainers' (2007) 23 Professional Negligence 108.

[17] *Re Van Laun* [1907] 2 KB 23, 29.   [18] [1998] Ch 1.   [19] *Liles v Terry* [1895] QB 679.

[20] *Swindle v Harrison* [1997] 4 All ER 705, 732.

3. *No profit* A solicitor must not gain a benefit from his or her position as a solicitor, save as per the fees agreed with a client. In particular, if the solicitor holds money from a client, he or she cannot seek to keep interest earned on that money.[21] This principle would also cover obtaining bribes or commission from his or her position as a solicitor.[22] This was discussed further in Chapter 7.

The basic principles of negligence

You may have already studied the law of negligence, in which case you will be familiar with much of this material. If you have not, you are likely to be learning much more about negligence later in your studies, but for now, the key principles will suffice, focusing on the special rules applying to lawyers.

In order to bring a claim of negligence against a lawyer, the client will need to show three things:

- that the lawyer owed the client a duty of care;
- that the lawyer breached that duty of care; and
- that the breach of duty caused the client a loss.

There has been some dispute over whether a client can sue in tort if there is a contract. In *Henderson v Merrett Syndicates Ltd*,[23] the House of Lords resolved the issue, at least in terms of professionals and their clients, by answering this question: 'Yes.' So it is no defence to an action in tort against a lawyer that the claim could have been brought under contract law.

That said, faced with a choice of suing either in tort or for breach of contract, contract law normally offers the better deal. The damages tend to be higher, establishing the scope of the duty is easier, and liability for breach of contract can arise even where there is no negligence by a solicitor. This means that tort law tends to be used if the claimant cannot establish that there was a contract between himself or herself and the solicitor.

A good example of when tort may be used is *Crossan v Ward Bracewell Co*,[24] in which the claimant was charged with reckless driving and consulted a firm of solicitors. The firm told him that he could represent himself or use its services, in which case he would need to pay £50 on account of costs. The firm failed to tell him about applying for legal aid or about seeing whether his insurers would pay his costs. He decided to represent himself and pleaded guilty. Although there was no contract between the parties, by discussing methods of funding with the claimant, the firm owed him a duty of care. It was found liability in negligence for failing to inform him

---

[21] *Brown v Inland Revenue Commissioners* [1965] AC 244.
[22] *Islamic Republic of Iran v Denby* [1987] 1 Lloyd's Rep 367.
[23] [1995] 2 AC 145.   [24] (1989) 5 PN 103.

adequately about funding options. Another example is where a lawyer acts for no fee: in such a case, there may be no contract, but still a duty of care in tort.[25]

Perhaps the most significant situation in which tort will be used is where the solicitor is advising a client, but a third party suffers a loss as a result of that advice. We shall be discussing this later. If the third party wishes to sue the solicitor, they will need to sue in negligence.

Establishing a duty of care

Establishing a duty of care in the law of tort has proved a highly contentious issue. The case law does not provide a consistent view. There appear to be two primary schools of thought: one believes that there is an overarching set of principles that determine when there is a duty of care; the other suggests that there is only a set of ad hoc decisions, based on particular scenarios, and that one cannot draw out a general principled approach. In each set of circumstances, the court decides whether or not there is a duty of care.

The first approach—the principled approach—is emphasised in four leading cases: *Smith v Bush*;[26] *Caparo v Dickman*;[27] *Spring v Guardian Assurance Plc*;[28] and *Marc Rich Co v Bishop Rock Marine Co Ltd*.[29] These suggest that, when determining whether there is a duty of care, the court will consider three factors: foreseeability; proximity; and justice and reasonableness.

- The *foreseeability* test asks whether it was foreseeable that the defendant might harm the victim by his or her actions.

- The *proximity* test considers whether the defendant and victim were 'neighbours'— that is, whether they were close, be that physically close or in a relationship.

- The *justice and reasonableness* test asks whether it would be just and reasonable to impose a duty of care.

In *Murphy v Brentwood District Council*,[30] *Henderson v Merrett Syndicates Ltd*,[31] *White v Jones*,[32] and *Williams v Natural Life Ltd*,[33] it was argued that the key overarching principle is whether there is a voluntary assumption of responsibility by the defendant towards the claimant.

The second view—the ad hoc approach—is exemplified by *Customs and Excise Commissioners v Barclays Bank Plc*,[34] in which the House of Lords found that there was no single factor or set of factors to be taken into account when deciding whether there was a duty of care. Instead, a court should focus on the detailed circumstances of the case and the relationship between the parties.

---

[25] *Throwley Homes v Sharratts* [1998] NPC 57. [26] [1990] 1 AC 837.
[27] [1990] 2 AC 605.   [28] [1995] 2 AC 296.   [29] [1996] AC 211.
[30] [1991] 1 AC 398.   [31] [1995] 2 AC 145.   [32] [1995] 2 AC 207.
[33] [1998] 1 WLR 830.   [34] [2006] UKHL 28.

Fortunately for us, we do not need to get into the detail of this complex area of the law. In a straightforward lawyer–client situation, there will definitely be a duty of care in tort owed by a lawyer to his or her client, whatever approach is taken. There used to be an immunity that prevented claimants from suing lawyers who were acting as advocates. This applied to solicitors and barristers. It was, however, abolished by the House of Lords in *Hall v Simons*.[35] We will explore the immunity later in the chapter.

The difficult issue is whether a lawyer owes a duty of care to a person who is *not* a client. On that question, a series of cases set out the law, which we shall examine next.

Duty of care to third parties

When a lawyer gives advice to, or acts for, a client, sometimes that can foreseeably impact upon others. On the basis of the first principle, it might be thought unlikely that a lawyer would be liable for losses caused to third parties. A lawyer gives advice to a client, but cannot foresee how that advice may be used, and it seems unreasonable to expect the lawyer to be responsible for all those who may come to rely on the advice. Indeed, it is why a lawyer will generally not owe a duty of care to a third party.

On the other hand, there are circumstances under which although one person is officially the client of a lawyer, it is appreciated that the advice given will be acted upon, or will impact upon, others. The most obvious case might be that in which a mother seeks legal advice on a housing problem on behalf of her family. Added to this are the points that lawyers are typically insured and so it will not be too harsh to render them financially liable for any loss. Further, there is an understandable lack of sympathy for well-paid professionals who do not do their jobs properly and who, as a result, cause loss to others. These points combine to mean that courts have been more willing than might be expected to find a duty of care between a lawyer and a third party.

There are two main hurdles to finding a duty of care owed by a lawyer to a non-client. The first is that, generally speaking, the law does not attach liability to statements of a person that cause economic loss. However, professionals can be liable for such statements. In *Hedley Byrne v Heller*,[36] the House of Lords approved of the dissenting speech of Denning LJ in *Candler v Crane Christmas*.[37] Denning J had suggested that where professionals, such as accountants or lawyers, are making reports or giving advice on which people other than their clients are likely to rely, a duty of care may arise. He restricted the duty to third parties whom the professional knew were going to rely on the advice. So that would not apply in a case in which a client passed on a lawyer's legal advice to a friend about whom the solicitor did not know. But it might apply if the solicitor had been consulted by someone who had made it clear that he or she was going to pass the advice on to an identified person. Denning J rejected any

---

[35] [2000] 3 WLR 543.   [36] [1964] AC 465.   [37] [1951] 2 KB 164.

argument that this was unduly burdensome because the professional holds himself or herself out as having special knowledge and skill, and can be expected to apply that special knowledge and skill.

The duty is owed, then, not only to the client, but also to third parties who the lawyer knows will be influenced to rely on the advice. This clearly covers a person who is seeking advice on behalf of a group, or a situation in which advice is given to one company, but the lawyer is aware that companies owned by the same shareholder will act on that same advice. The most notable discussion of this issue was in *White v Jones*.

 Key case

White v Jones [1995] 2 AC 207

Mr Barratt had a terrible row with his adult children. He went to see his solicitors and asked them to redraft his will so that the children got nothing. He signed the will, but later was reconciled with his children. He contacted his solicitors and instructed them to prepare a new will, leaving £9,000 to each child. The solicitors were extremely slow to fulfil this instruction and Mr Barratt died before the new will was prepared.

The House of Lords confirmed the obvious point that the children did not have a contract with the solicitors and could not sue for breach of contract. The executors (standing in the shoes of Mr Barratt) *did* have a contract with the solicitors and so could sue for breach of contract—but they would not be entitled to any damages, because they had not lost any money. So the only hope for the children was that a claim could be brought in negligence.

The majority agreed that the children could bring a claim in negligence, although they did not precisely agree why. Lord Goff, giving a leading judgment, placed much weight on justice. It would be unfair if a professional who had been negligent, broken a contract, and caused an entirely predictable loss could escape all legal liability. Lord Goff's preferred line of reasoning was to say that the solicitors had assumed responsibility towards the beneficiaries by agreeing to draft the will and so owed a duty of care. Lord Browne-Wilkinson, also in the majority, argued that the case came within the category of a 'special relationship' within which a duty of care could be found. The client was seeking the change to the will on behalf of all of his family and so the duty of care was owed to all. Lord Nolan applied the *Caparo* three-part test (considered earlier in this chapter) and also relied on the idea of assumption of responsibility to justify a finding of a duty of care.

Although there has been lively debate over which of the speeches of the majority in *White v Jones* should be seen as definitive, later cases have adopted Lord Goff's speech as providing the central plank of the reasoning.[38]

---

[38] *Carr-Glynn v Frearsons (A Firm)* [1999] Ch 326, 335D; *Worby v Rosser* [2000] PNLR 140, 149B; *Corbett v Bond Pearce (A Firm)* [2001] 3 All ER 769, 775, [18].

Lord Goff specifically left the exact scope of the ruling for later cases to decide. An analysis of *White v Jones* itself and of later cases that have developed the doctrine reveals the following points of detail.

- The duty arises the moment at which the solicitor agrees to draft the will. He or she does not need to have actually started work on the will.[39]

- The duty owed to the beneficiaries will match that owed to the client and will certainly not be any higher.[40] In other words, the beneficiary can claim in tort only if the deceased could have established a breach of contract or tort.

- There is some ambiguity over whether the beneficiaries need to be clearly identified. What would happen if, for example, the client simply told the solicitor that he wished to change his will, but did not provide details, or made a general remark about making a will to provide for his relatives? This was discussed in *White v Jones* without any definitive view emerging. It seems, at the very least, that there needs to be an identified group of people who could benefit.[41] So if it was clear that the testator was going to change the will to benefit some of his children, it might not matter that it was unclear which children were going to benefit. However, if there was a vague statement that 'other people' would benefit, that would be insufficient. In *Feltham v Freer Bouskell*,[42] Charles Hollander QC said obiter that a beneficiary could sue for a percentage of a gift if he or she could show that there was a chance of his or her being given a gift.

- The *White v Jones* doctrine can be applied only if there is a settled decision by the testator to make the will.[43] So if, in the case, the deceased had said that he wanted to discuss his will with his lawyer because he was uncertain whether it needed changing, it is unlikely that the claim would succeed.

- The beneficiary will not be able to use a tort claim if the executors of the deceased estate can recover damages.[44] In such a case, the executors must bring any claim. That might arise if the claim concerned simply the recovery of legal expenses connected to a negligently drafted will.

- It seems that the doctrine can apply beyond the context of wills. It can also apply to a case in which a lawyer is asked to arrange a transfer of money to a third party,[45] and presumably to any transaction designed to benefit an identified third party. In *Dean v Allin and Watts*,[46] the borrower retained the defendant firm of solicitors to give effect to a secured loan. The loan was not secured and the lender lost out. It

---

[39] This is clear from *White v Jones* itself.

[40] *Cancer Research Campaign v Ernest Brown Co* [1998] PNLR 592.

[41] In *Gibbons v Nelsons* [2000] PNLR 734, Blackburne J held that a duty of care was owed to an unidentified intended beneficiary only where the solicitor knew of the benefit that the testator wished to confer and the class of persons that he or she wished to benefit.

[42] [2013] EWHC 1952 (Ch).   [43] *Trusted v Clifford Chance* [2004] EWHC 151.

[44] *Worby v Rosser* [2000] PNLR 140.   [45] [1995] Ch 223.   [46] [2001] EWCA Civ 758.

was held that there was a duty of care owed to the lender. The solicitor knew that the security for the loan was for the benefit of the lender.[47] Another good example is *Penn v Bristol and West Building Society*,[48] in which a husband instructed solicitors to sell a house that he owned with his wife. The husband forged his wife's signature and the sale went through. It was held that the solicitors owed the wife a duty of care. They knew that the house was jointly owned, but failed to check that she approved of the sale.

In Chapter 11, we will be discussing in more detail the extent to which a lawyer owes obligations to third parties.

There is little authority on whether a barrister owes third parties a duty of care. It is likely that the court will follow the *White v Jones* line of cases. In *Mathew v Maughold Life Assurance Co Ltd*,[49] a barrister was instructed by a company specialising in tax avoidance schemes. The barrister was aware that the advice was for the benefit of Mr and Mrs Mathew, clients of the company. Leonard J held that the barrister owed Mr and Mrs Mathew a duty of care because he was aware that the advice was to be relied upon by them. The issue was not considered on appeal.

Breach of the duty

It must be shown that the lawyer breached the duty of care. This turns on whether or not he or she showed the degree of care and skill reasonably expected of a lawyer in his or her position. In *Midland Bank v Hett, Stubbs Kemp*,[50] Oliver J emphasised that a solicitor should not be judged by the standard of a 'particularly meticulous and conscientious practitioner . . . The test is what the reasonably competent practitioner would do having regard to the standards normally adopted in his profession'.

The Supreme Court in Canada suggested that this can be broken down into the following elements:

The obligations of a lawyer are, I think, the following: (1) To be skilful and careful; (2) To advise his client on all matters relevant to his retainer, so far as may be reasonably necessary; (3) To protect the interest of his client; (4) To carry out his instructions by all proper means; (5) To consult with his client on all questions of doubt which do not fall within the express or implied discretion left to him; (6) To keep his client informed to such an extent as may be reasonably necessary, according to the same criteria.[51]

---

[47] For a detailed analysis, see C. Holbech, 'Professional negligence: *White v Jones* liability in context of wills, trusts and tax', online at www.9stonebuildings.com/publications/profneg_bulletin.pdf

[48] [1996] 2 FCR 729.   [49] (1984) 1 PN 142.

[50] [1979] Ch 384, 402–3. This dictum was approved by the Court of Appeal in *Martin Boston Co v Roberts* [1996] 1 PNLR 45, 50.

[51] *Tiffin Hldg Ltd v Millican* (1964) 49 DLR (2d) 216, *per* Riley J, approved by the Supreme Court of Canada in (1967) 60 DLR (2d) 469.

It is crucial to recognise that the scope of the duty is limited by the terms of the retainer. This will typically set out precisely on what the solicitor is required to advise and what it is that he or she is expected to do.

A lawyer will never be liable simply for failing to win a case. In *Greaves & Co (Contractors) Ltd v Baynham Meikle & Partners*[52] (a case involving consulting engineers), Lord Denning MR stated:

> Apply this to the employment of a professional man. The law does not usually imply a warranty that he will achieve the desired result, but only a term that he will use reasonable care and skill. The surgeon does not warrant that he will cure the patient. Nor does the solicitor warrant that he will win the case.

Nevertheless, there will be some cases in which a failure to provide what the solicitor promised will almost automatically lead to a finding of negligence. So a lawyer who says that he or she will produce a will and produces a defective will is almost inevitably negligent.

It is therefore very unlikely that a lawyer will be taken to have to do more than exercise reasonable care and skill. In *Platform Funding Ltd v Bank of Scotland Plc*,[53] Rix LJ summarised the current law:

> (1) that the default obligation is one limited to the taking and exercise of reasonable care; (2) that it requires special facts or clear language to impose an obligation stricter than that of reasonable care; (3) that a professional man will not readily be supposed to undertake to achieve a guaranteed result; and (4) that if he is undertaking with care that which he was retained or instructed to do, he will not readily be found to have nevertheless warranted to be responsible for a misfortune caused by the fraud of another. It follows from the jurisprudence and from these conclusions to be derived from them, however, that it is not possible to support a blanket approach whereby, even in the absence of an express warranty, a professional's responsibility is nevertheless always limited to the taking of reasonable care.

The general requirement is that the solicitor should act as a reasonably competent practitioner. That does not require the solicitor to act perfectly.[54] In *Fletcher Son v Jubb, Booth Helliwell*,[55] Scrutton LJ quoted with approval a statement by Tindal CJ in *Godefroy v Dalton*[56] that the solicitor 'is not answerable for error in judgment upon points of new occurrence, or of nice or doubtful construction, or of such as are usually entrusted to men in the higher branch of the profession of the law'.

We will now explore some particular issues raised by the case law.

---

[52] [1975] 1 WLR 1095, 1101.   [53] [2008] EWCA Civ 930, [36].
[54] *R Thew Ltd v Reeves (No. 2) (Note)* [1982] QB 1283, 1287D.   [55] [1920] 1 KB 275, 286.
[56] (1830) 6 Bing 460.

Knowledge of the law

Lawyers are not expected to know all of the law.[57] However, they may be liable for failure to look up and research areas with which they are not familiar. In *Copeland v Smith*,[58] the Court of Appeal said that a reasonable advocate would keep himself or herself up to date with the law. The Court mentioned reading the general law reports—that is, the Weekly Law Reports and the All England Law Reports. However, since that case, there has been a proliferation of electronic databases and it may be insufficient simply to read the official law reports.

The courts are generally unsympathetic to solicitors who make mistakes of the law. In *Dean v Allin Watts (A Firm)*,[59] solicitors were liable for failing to appreciate that section 2 of the Law of Property (Miscellaneous Provisions) Act 1989 applied to an equitable change by deposit of title deeds. The textbooks had disagreed on the issue, but it was held that a reasonably competent solicitor would know at least that the issue was debatable and would have explained the uncertainty over the law to the client.

In assessing negligence, the solicitor must be judged on the facts as they appeared at the time. So if the advice was reasonable at the time, the solicitor is not negligent because later events show it to be wrong.[60] An example might be where a solicitor recommends that a client sue someone over a personal injury, but months later it becomes clear that the person being sued has no money to pay any damages and so that suing him or her will be fruitless. Although by then it is clear that it would have been best not to commence proceedings, the solicitor will not be negligent if he or she gave sound advice based on the facts known at the time proceedings were commenced.

It has been held that if a solicitor acts in line with standard practice, he or she will not be negligent if it is subsequently held by a court that the standard approach is incorrect. The solicitor was acting as a 'reasonable solicitor' would have done at the time and so will not be liable.[61] It may be that there are limits to this. If a practice was popular, but exposed a client to a foreseeable and avoidable risk, and could not rationally be defended, then a solicitor may face liability even if he or she was acting in a way that many solicitors would. It must be very rare that such a finding would be made, however.[62] More likely is a case in which there is a range of practices among solicitors and one such school of thought is dangerous. It seems that, in such a case, the court will be more open to finding it unreasonable to have followed the risky approach.[63]

---

[57] *Fletcher Son v Jubb, Booth Helliwell* [1920] 1 KB 275.   [58] [2000] 1 WLR 371.

[59] [2001] Lloyd's Rep PN 605.

[60] *Duchess of Argyll v Beuselinck* [1972] 2 Lloyd's Rep 172, 185, col. 1, *per* Megarry J.

[61] *Simmons v Pennington* [1955] 1 WLR 183.

[62] *Patel v Daybells (A Firm)* [2001] EWCA Civ 1229, which accepted the argument in principle, although the solicitors in that case were found not to be negligent.

[63] *G&K Ladenbau (UK) Ltd v Crawley De Reya* [1978] 1 WLR 266.

The SRA Code of Conduct sets out the requirements of the solicitor's profession, as does the Bar Council Code of Conduct (the Bar Code) for barristers. If a lawyer follows the good practice laid down in the appropriate code, it would be extraordinary if a court were to find the lawyer to have acted negligently. Of course, ultimately, it is for the court, rather than the Solicitors Regulation Authority or Bar Council, to determine whether an action is negligent. Nevertheless, it would be very surprising if it were found to be unreasonable to follow the guidance of a professional body. By contrast, if a lawyer has acted in a way that is contrary to professional guidance, it may be easy for a court to determine that he or she was negligent.[64]

Lawyers and specialisation

Lawyers are to be judged by the standards of a competent solicitor in whatever specialisation they hold themselves out as having. So if a solicitor holds himself or herself out as being a tax specialist, he or she will have to exercise the skill expected of a reasonably competent tax specialist.[65] However, if he or she holds himself or herself out as being a general solicitor and not having specialist tax skills, then the levels of tax advice expected will be lower.[66] However, a solicitor may also be liable if he or she advises on a matter on which he or she should have sought counsel's advice, or should have sought advice from an expert.[67] In relation to barristers, in *Moy v Pettman Smith*,[68] Lord Carswell expressed the test for negligence as being whether the advice fell within the range of that to be expected of reasonably competent counsel of the defendant's seniority and experience.

Perhaps surprisingly, there is relatively little guidance on the standard to apply to a trainee solicitor, legal executive, or paralegal. Possibly, under the standard approach adopted in tort law, these would need to show the standard of skill expected of a reasonable person of their standing.[69] It may be that a firm would be negligent for asking an unqualified member of staff to do a job that a solicitor should have done, if doing so caused the client loss.[70] In *Balamoan v Holden*,[71] it was held that a one-man firm was liable when work was delegated to an unqualified member of staff. The resulting advice given was below the standard of a reasonable solicitor and the client was entitled to damages.

The burden of proof

The breach of duty must be proved on the balance of probabilities. In a case of barrister's negligence, in *Rondel v Worsley*,[72] Lord Reid stated that 'the onus of proving

---

[64] *Johnson v Bingley Dyson Furey* [1995] NPC 27.
[65] *Matrix Securities Ltd v Theodore Goddard* [1998] PNLR 290.
[66] *Balamoan v Holden Co* [1999] NLJ Prac 898.   [67] *Ireson v Pearman* (1825) 3 BC 799.
[68] [2005] 1 WLR 581, [62].
[69] The Australian High Court decision *Shigeva v Schafer* (1984) 5 NSWLR 502 took this line.
[70] *Balamoan v Holden Co* [1999] NLJ Prac 898.   [71] [1999] NLJ Prac 898.
[72] [1969] 1 AC 191, 230F.

professional negligence over and above errors of judgment is a heavy one'. This was approved in the case of solicitors in *Martin Boston Co v Roberts*.[73] The quote from *Rondel* might be read as suggesting that the burden of proof is higher than the standard one in tort law, showing whether it is more likely than not that this was negligence. However, it is suggested that this would be a misreading. The better reading may be that the courts are emphasising that they must be persuaded that the case is one not only of an error of judgement, but also of negligence. Given the respect due to lawyers, a court will need good evidence that a professional was negligent.

It is important to recognise that negligence and blame are not the same thing. In *Sykes v Midland Bank Executor Trustee Co Ltd*,[74] Salmon LJ, in affirming the finding of negligence, observed that 'the degree of blame in the present case was slight'. A solicitor who has just heard that his or her mother is seriously ill may be distracted and do a bad job. He or she will be negligent even if no moral censure attaches to that finding.

Practical advice

Sometimes, a solicitor may be asked to advise on practical matters that are not legal issues. A client may ask a lawyer how to save his or her marriage, for example. In such circumstances, where the lawyer is not purporting to give an expert opinion, it is very unlikely that he or she will be liable in negligence.[75] At least, he or she will not be required to show any more skill on such an issue than that of an ordinary person.

Settlement

In *Moy v Pettman Smith*,[76] a claimant sued a barrister who had advised a client to reject an offer to settle a case. The barrister justified that advice on the basis that considerably more money could have been obtained if later leave had been given to introduce medical evidence. As events transpired, leave was not granted and the client had to settle for less than the original offer. In the Court of Appeal, Latham LJ upheld a finding of negligence. Notably, this was not on the basis that the advice itself was negligent, but on the failure to explain the basis of the advice (and particularly the importance of obtaining leave). The House of Lords allowed the appeal. The barrister had acted as a reasonable practitioner. Clearly influencing their Lordships was a fear that, otherwise, counsel would become defensive and would recommend acceptance of low offers, for fear of being found negligent if the case were to work out against the client. This decision means that it is now going to be difficult for a client to show that a lawyer was negligent in advising on a settlement.

---

[73] [1996] 1 PNLR 45, 50D.   [74] [1971] 1 QB 113, 126.
[75] For example, *Bryant v Goodrich* (1966) 110 SJ 108.   [76] [2005] UKHL 7.

Following the instructions of a client

A lawyer who fails to follow the client's instructions is likely to be found to be negligent.[77] This puts the lawyer in a difficult position when a client wants to engage in a foolish action. Anthony Lincoln J[78] has explained that a lawyer has a duty to advise on the risks of the proposed course of action, but that, at the end of the day, the matter is one for the client: 'It was the duty of the solicitor to inform and advise, ensuring that the information and advice was understood by the client. It was not part of his duty of care to force his advice on the client.'

In *Middleton v Steeds Hudson*,[79] a husband wanted to give his wife a very generous sum of money on their divorce to settle her claim for financial support. The solicitors informed him that his offer was far more generous than a court was likely to order. The husband was insistent that he wanted to make his offer. The solicitors carried out his wishes, but he later sued, saying that they should have insisted that he make a reasonable offer. The claim failed. The solicitors had been entirely correct in informing him that his offer was generous, but ultimately leaving the decision to him. In cases in which clients were seeking to pursue unwise courses of action, Johnson J explained that the solicitors either had to follow their clients' instructions or refuse to act.

Solicitors following the advice of a barrister

The traditional view has been that if a solicitor properly instructs a barrister and follows his or her advice, the solicitor will not be liable in negligence, however mistaken counsel's advice was. It seems that this view is not followed strictly. In *Davy-Chiesman v Davy-Chiesman*,[80] May LJ said that it was the ordinary rule 'that save in exceptional circumstances a solicitor cannot be criticised where he acts on the advice of properly instructed counsel'. But he qualified this statement:

> However, this does not operate so as to give a solicitor an immunity in every such case. A solicitor is highly trained and rightly expected to be experienced in his particular legal fields. He is under a duty at all times to exercise that degree of care, to both client and the court, that can be expected of a reasonably prudent solicitor. He is not entitled to rely blindly and with no mind of his own on counsel's views.[81]

In *Locke v Camberwell Health Authority*,[82] the Court of Appeal explained:

(1) In general, a solicitor is entitled to rely upon the advice of counsel properly instructed.

(2) For a solicitor without specialist experience in a particular field to rely on counsel's advice is to make normal and proper use of the Bar.

---

[77] *Re Graham Oldham (A Firm)* [2000] BPIR 354; *Fraser v Gaskell* [2004] EWHC 894.
[78] *Dutfield v Gilbert H Stephens and Sons* [1988] 18 Fam Law 473 at 473.
[79] [1998] 1 FLR 73.   [80] [1984] Fam 48, 63E.   [81] At 63F.
[82] [2002] Lloyd's Rep PN 23, 29.

(3) However, he must not do so blindly, but must exercise his own independent judgment. If he reasonably thinks counsel's advice is obviously or glaringly wrong, it is his duty to reject it.[83]

Barristers

In *Rondel v Worsley*,[84] Lord Upjohn expressed the view that counsel would be liable for negligence only if he or she were to commit 'some really elementary blunder'. However, this seems overly generous. In *Saif Ali v Sidney Mitchell Co*,[85] Lord Wilberforce put the matter in this way:

> Much if not most of a barrister's work involves exercise of judgment—it is in the realm of art not science. Indeed the solicitor normally goes to counsel precisely at the point where, as between possible courses, a choice can only be made on the basis of judgment, which is fallible and may turn out to be wrong. Thus in the nature of things, an action against a barrister who acts honestly and carefully is very unlikely to succeed.

Lord Diplock explained that not every error would be negligence, but only 'such errors as no reasonably well-informed and competent member of that profession could have made'.[86]

Whether these dicta allow us to conclude that it is harder to prove negligence against a barrister than against a solicitor or other professional is open to doubt. There seem to be no particularly good reasons why a barrister should not have to live up to the same standard of care that is expected of ordinary professionals. It is suggested that the best reading is that the courts are emphasising that counsel are likely to be instructed on cases in which the law and its application are complex. As long as they use reasonable skill in making their judgements, they will not be negligent, even if it later turns out that they were wrong.

If a barrister is sued for his or her performance in court, Lord Steyn explained in *Hall v Simons*:[87]

> [C]ourts will take into account the difficult decisions faced daily by barristers working in demanding situations to tight timetables. In this context the observations of Sir Thomas Bingham M.R. in *Ridehalgh v Horsefield* [1994] Ch. 205 are instructive. Dealing with the circumstances in which a wasted costs order against a barrister might be appropriate he observed, at p.236:

> 'Any judge who is invited to make or contemplates making an order arising out of an advocate's conduct of court proceedings must make full allowance for the fact that an advocate in court, like a commander in battle, often has to make decisions quickly and under pressure, in the fog of war and ignorant of developments on the other side

---

[83] At 254.   [84] [1969] 1 AC 191, 287A–B.   [85] [1980] AC 198, 214f–g.
[86] At 218D and 220D, applying *Ridehalgh v Horsefield* [1994] Ch. 205 and *Re A Barrister (Wasted Costs Order) (No. 9 of 1999)* (2000) 16 PN 122.   [87] [2000] 3 WLR 543, 549.

of the hill. Mistakes will inevitably be made, things done which the outcome shows to have been unwise. But advocacy is more an art than a science. It cannot be conducted according to formulae. Individuals differ in their style and approach. It is only when, with all allowances made, an advocate's conduct of court proceedings is quite plainly unjustifiable that it can be appropriate to make a wasted costs order against him.'

For broadly similar reasons it will not be easy to establish negligence against a barrister. The courts can be trusted to differentiate between errors of judgment and true negligence. In any event, a plaintiff who claims that poor advocacy resulted in an unfavourable outcome will face the very great obstacle of showing that a better standard of advocacy would have resulted in a more favourable outcome.

Loss caused by breach of the duty

Demonstrating loss caused by breach of the duty is a less straightforward requirement than may at first appear. First, it must be shown that the loss occurred because of breach of the duty. This requirement of causation (did the breach cause the loss?) can raise some complex issues. Did the client lose the case because of the negligence or would he or she have lost the case anyway?

Second, the loss must be 'within the scope' of the lawyer's duty. This will be explained further shortly, but it captures the idea that someone may owe a duty of care to protect someone else against one kind of loss, but not another. So a taxi driver may owe a business person a duty of care not to drive carelessly and so injure him or her. But a taxi driver may not undertake a duty to ensure that the business person arrives on time at a meeting and so does not lose out on an important deal. So if a taxi driver crashes a taxi and, as a result, injures the passenger, the taxi driver will be liable for compensation for the injuries; if he or she crashes the taxi and so the passenger misses a meeting, the taxi driver will not be liable for the lost profits, because that was not the kind of risk for which the driver was accepting responsibility.[88] Similarly if a lawyer negligently advises a wife on her divorce and, as a result, her husband becomes infuriated with and assaults her: the duties undertaken by the lawyer in negotiating a divorce settlement do not extend to protecting the wife from her husband's violence.[89]

Third, only certain kinds of losses are covered by the law.[90]

Looking at the first issue, the court will determine what would have happened if the lawyer had not been negligent. Imagine, for example, that a client is buying a house and the lawyer negligently fails to check whether there are any rights of way

---

[88] There may be a case in which a business person employs a driver specifically with the instruction to reach a destination by a particular time, in which event the driver appreciates the significance of the duty and requires higher payment. Then, perhaps, a greater obligation can be found.

[89] It would be different if a victim of domestic violence were to seek legal help to protect her and, owing to the lawyer's negligence, no protection was put in place and she were to suffer further violence.

[90] See, e.g., *Nitrigin Eireann Teoranta v Inco Alloys Ltd* [1992] 1 WLR 49, in which pure economic loss was not recoverable.

over the property before the client completes the purchase. The client, to succeed in a claim of negligence, would need to show that, had the lawyer performed the check and found the right of way, the client would not have bought the house, or would at least have negotiated a lower price. If the court concludes that even if the solicitor had completed the checks, the client would have proceeded with the purchase at the agreed price, then the negligence has not caused a loss.

The requirement of causation can be particularly difficult in a case in which the claimant is not a client of the solicitor. The claimant would need to show that the claimant relied on the solicitor's advice in a way that caused the claimant loss. In *AJ Fabrication (Batley) Ltd v Grant Thornton*,[91] a creditor sued a liquidator for failing to sue the directors of a company within the required time limit. The creditor wished also to sue the liquidators' solicitor. However, there had been no communication between the creditor and the solicitors. Astill J held that although the creditor had relied upon the liquidators doing their job properly, it had not relied on the solicitors.

The removal of immunity

At one time, a client could not sue a lawyer acting as an advocate, because that was seen as an 'abuse of process'. That immunity has been definitively abolished by *Hall v Simons*.

 Key case

***Arthur JS Hall & Co (a firm) v Simons* [2000] 3 WLR 543**

Three cases were heard by the House of Lords. They were all cases of clients suing their solicitors in which the court had struck out the applications on the basis of the immunity and abuse of process. One case involved a lawyer who, it was said, had failed to advise a client about the liability of other parties, leading to an inappropriate negotiated settlement. In another, there was alleged negligent advice in valuing a home in a family law case. In the third, an application for ancillary relief was settled following allegedly inappropriate cases. The House of Lords refused to strike out the claims in any of the three cases.

Unfortunately, there was some disagreement in the reasoning used. All of the members of the House of Lords agreed that the immunity should be abolished as a general rule, but that it could still apply in some cases.

---

[91] [1999] PNLR 811.

In relation to criminal proceedings, there was a concern that suing a solicitor for negligence would, in effect, be used to reopen the criminal case. If a defendant were convicted of a crime, then allowing him or her to sue the solicitor for negligently presenting the case could easily become a way of a defendant trying to have the case reheard and to prove his or her innocence. While accepting this danger, however, Lords Steyn, Browne-Wilkinson, Hoffmann, and Hutton all seemed to keep the door open for negligence proceedings following a criminal conviction. Lord Hoffmann explained that there may be exceptional circumstances in which 'the issue can be tried without a risk that the conflict of judgments would bring the administration of justice into disrepute'.[92]

In relation to civil cases, their Lordships were open to a claim in negligence being brought against an advocate, as long as it was not an abuse of process, designed to reopen the previous litigation. Lord Hoffmann disagreed and thought that the immunity should never apply in civil cases. It seems that the others thought that, in a case in which it was simply being used to reopen resolved litigation, then the court could refuse to hear the application.

The immunity for barristers and advocates from claims for negligence has been abolished.[93] This was confirmed in *Jones v Kaney*,[94] which also removed the immunity for expert witnesses. However, a court may find a negligence claim against an advocate to be an abuse of process where it is done in an attempt to reopen a previous court decision, especially in criminal cases. So where the claimant is simply stating that he or she lost the case (or was convicted), but would have won (or been acquitted) had the lawyer done a better job, that looks like an attempt simply to say that he or she should have won the case and is likely to be an abuse of process.

The kinds of cases of alleged negligence that are likely to be seen as not an abuse of process and so able to be heard include those in which the defendant's conviction has been quashed and so there is no question of reopening the original trial. This was mentioned by several of their Lordships in *Hall v Simons*. Lord Hoffmann gave as another example a claim that an advocate had failed to pursue an appeal on a point of law. Again, such a claim could be considered without reopening the original trial. It is generally thought that, in civil cases, the courts will be less willing than in criminal cases to find that a negligence suit is an abuse of process.

---

[92] At 552.

[93] Although the immunity from suit has been removed, the advocate retains protection for defamation proceedings in respect of statements made in court.

[94] [2011] UKSC 13.

Alternative view

Mark Davies has expressed concern over the response of courts to allegations of negligence against lawyers.[95] He notes that, in his sample of negligence proceedings against barristers, only 10 per cent succeeded, while looking at the same time period at cases of negligence against solicitors, he recorded 50 per cent. While he accepts that it cannot be shown that courts favour barristers over solicitors or over other professionals, Davies notes the danger that this might appear to others to be the case.

Conclusion

This chapter has explored the circumstances in which a barrister and solicitor can be sued in negligence or for breach of contract. In general, a client is going to face an uphill battle in suing a solicitor or barrister. In relation to a breach of contract, it can be difficult to establish the breach of reasonable skill. In relation to negligence, proving breach of a duty of care and the causation of a loss is problematic. In part, these difficulties are understandable. In difficult cases, the law is often uncertain and its application is a matter of judgement. It would therefore be unfair if lawyers were too readily found to be negligent.

 Further reading

M. Davies, 'Not an impartial tribunal? English courts and barristers' negligence' (2010) 13 Legal Ethics 113.

A. Horrocks and S. Brake, 'Limitations of liability in solicitors' retainers' (2007) 23 Professional Negligence 108.

J. Powell and R. Steward, *Jackson and Powell on Professional Liability*, 6th edn (Sweet and Maxwell, 2007).

---

[95] M. Davies, 'Not an impartial tribunal? English courts and barristers' negligence' (2010) 13 Legal Ethics 113.

Litigation

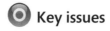

Key issues

- What is the purpose of litigation?
- What approach towards litigation should a lawyer take?
- How should lawyers deal with plea bargaining?
- What are the ethical issues surrounding cross-examination?

Introduction

When the public thinks of lawyers, it probably imagines them engaging in litigation: issuing writs; pleading with a jury; or shouting 'Objection!' to the judge. Advocacy and litigation are seen as at the heart of the legal professions, and they are areas in which the professions have a well-established monopoly: solicitors, in the conduct of litigation; and the barristers, in advocacy.

But this image of lawyers immersed in litigation is far from the whole truth. First, many lawyers are involved in non-contentious work, such as negotiating contracts, merging companies, or drafting leases, in which there is no expectation that the issue will arrive at court. The lawyer is helping the client to reach a particular goal, rather than litigating against another person. Many lawyers will never in their careers be involved in issuing a writ, let alone setting foot in a court.

Second, even if the case does involve clients in a dispute, lawyers are far more likely to settle the issue through negotiation and alternative dispute resolution (ADR) rather than to go to court. Even if the matter starts down the litigation route, it is far more likely to settle than to reach a final hearing before a judge. We discuss the issues around negotiation and ADR in Chapter 10.

Third, there is a growing wariness about litigation. It is seen as costly and unwieldy. It rarely leaves the parties satisfied. Litigation is increasingly recognised as a last resort. Governmental and professional pressures seek to reduce court cases to a minimum— or, to the more cynical, to restrict them to the preserve of the wealthy.

Despite these points, there are some cases in which litigation is inevitable. Criminal cases, in which a defendant pleads 'not guilty', for example, or civil cases in which all attempts to settle have proved futile. Only then might the television image of the lawyer become a reality.

This chapter will not focus on the detailed regulation surrounding litigation procedure, which is complex and often frankly tedious. Instead, we will pick out the main issues of ethical significance. Before doing so, we will explore the issues around litigation: what exactly are lawyers doing when they litigate?

Theories of litigation

In an ideal world, no one would ever wrong anyone else. There would be no disputes or, if there were any, they would be quickly resolved over a mug of hot chocolate. Sadly, we do not live in an ideal world. People do behave wrongly and harm others. Society needs a way of righting these wrongs. We need to ensure that those who have lost out as a result of the wrong behaviour of others are compensated, and that those who have behaved very badly are held to account for what they have done and, if necessary, are punished. This is what litigation is about. As Neil Andrews has put it, litigation is about making 'order out of chaos'.[1] Without it, we would live in a world in which the strong would oppress the weak with no consequences. Those wronged could get justice only by taking things into their own hands. Vigilantism would be the order of the day.

Litigation will, however, achieve its goal of producing an ordered society only if it is seen to be fair. Neil Andrews suggests four pillars of a good civil justice system:

- access to legal advice and dispute resolution systems;
- equality and fairness between the parties;
- a focused and speedy process; and
- adjudicators of integrity.[2]

Digging deeper

Imagine a legal system that resolved disputes between citizens by means of a judge tossing a coin. That would provide swift and clear resolution. It might even satisfy all four of Neil Andrews' pillars, but would it be a good civil justice system? Notice that Andrews is seeking to define what is a fair procedural system; he is not talking about the content of the law. So while this is not an argument against his approach, notice how well coin-tossing satisfies his requirements: might there be a conflict between a sophisticated content of the law and a system that is, for example, speedy and fair?

---

[1] N. Andrews, *Fundamental Principles of Civil Procedure: Order out of Chaos In Civil Litigation In A Globalising World* (Springer, 2012).
[2] Andrews (n. 1), 2.

Is litigation good?

As already noted, there is considerable doubt over the benefits of litigation. Procedural and funding measures are used to restrict access to litigation because it is assumed to be a 'bad thing'. With less legal aid, increased procedural pressure to settle, and the growth of mediation, only the richest and most determined of clients will get to have their day in court. Many lawyers regard a negotiated settlement as clearly preferable to a case fought out in court.

While most people seem to approve of this shift away from litigation, Professor Hazel Genn argues against it.[3] She claims that civil justice is a 'public good' and that it should not be seen as only about private issues. She explains that the civil law and its enforcement:

> ...play a part in the sense that we live in an orderly society where there are rights and protections, and that these rights and protections can be made good. In societies governed by the rule of law, the courts provide the community's defence against arbitrary government action. They promote social order and facilitate the peaceful resolution of disputes. In publishing their decisions, the courts communicate and reinforce civic values and norms.
>
> Most importantly, the civil courts support economic activity. Law is pivotal to the functioning of markets. Contracts between strangers are possible because rights are fairly allocated within a known legal framework and are enforceable through the courts if they are breached.
>
> Thriving economies depend on a strong state that will secure property rights and investments.[4]

Against her view is the argument that disputes over civil matters, such as a breach of contract, are really personal matters. Let us consider an example. Bob the builder fails to complete Maureen's extension by the time agreed in their contract. This looks like a private matter: the rest of us are not really affected by the dispute. It does not really matter to the rest of us how Maureen and Bob resolve it. Genn argues, however, that having some kind of formal legal system to resolve such disputes is of public importance: without some form of resolution, Maureen may seek to extract revenge on Bob. There is a broader point too, that if contracts are not enforced and people are free to breach contracts without consequence, then this will have harmful consequences for society. So although there is not a public interest in a single dispute, there is a public interest in how such disputes are resolved generally.

One response to Genn's argument is that although there is a public interest in having these disputes resolved (we do not want people in dispute to resort to violence or vigilantism), the mechanism of that resolution (be that negotiation, mediation, tossing a coin, or litigation) is not important. So, as long as there is some mechanism for

---

[3] H. Genn, 'What is civil justice for? Reform, ADR, and access to justice' (2012) 24 Yale Journal of Law and the Humanities 397.   [4] Genn (n. 3), 400.

holding contract breakers to account and resolving disputes, it does not matter if we are shifting away from litigation to other (cheaper) forms of resolution.

Supporters of Genn's argument have replies to this. One is that the other forms of resolution depend on there being a well-articulated and functioning civil justice system. It is only the threat of the costs of litigation that enables negotiation to succeed. The principles of the legal system in civil litigation give the lawyers the tools and guidance that they need to litigate. Further, mediation and ADR do not guarantee the enforcement of rights in the way that litigation purports to. Access to justice, Genn argues is 'an essential element in the rule of law'. If people have no access to courts to enforce their legal rights, we should give up the pretence that they have such rights. It should also be noted that litigation leads to clearly established rules on which people can rely in future cases to resolve their disputes; mediation does not provide such rules.[5]

Lord Neuberger has echoed some of these concerns in his comments on the efforts to discourage litigation and to make civil litigation efficient:

> Citizens are bearers of rights; they are not simply consumers of services. The civil justice system exists to enable them to secure those rights. It does not exist to merely supply a service, which like a bar of chocolate may be consumed.[6]

In a justifiably famous article, Owen Fiss writes against the prevailing wisdom that it is better to settle than to litigate.[7] He argues that:

> Consent [to settle] is often coerced; the bargain may be struck by someone without authority; the absence of a trial and judgment renders subsequent judicial involvement troublesome; and although dockets are trimmed, justice may not be done. Like plea bargaining, settlement is a capitulation to the conditions of mass society and should be neither encouraged nor praised.[8]

In the current times of 'austerity' measures, there may be a further issue. Given that the civil justice system costs the government significant sums of money, is it not entitled to cut back the funding of civil litigation in order instead to fund essential services (and thereby support the rights) of others? Some might say that, in an ideal world, we would have a well-funded civil litigation scheme, but sadly we cannot afford it. So even if Profession Genn is right to talk of the public benefits of private litigation, are these benefits sufficient to justify the expense? Whether you accept that kind of argument depends on how important you think some of the rule-of-law arguments are, particularly in comparison with some of the other claims on the government's costs.

There is some evidence that those seeking the advice of lawyers, rather than a community service such as Citizens Advice, are more likely to end up litigating.[9] However,

---

[5] F. Cross, 'In praise of irrational plaintiffs' (2000) 86 Cornell Law Review 1.

[6] Lord Neuberger, 'Justice in a time of economic crisis', 18 October 2011, online at www.judiciary. gov.uk/media/speeches/2011/mr-speech-justice-in-age-internet-13102011

[7] O. Fiss, 'Against settlement' (1984) 93 Yale Law Journal 1073.   [8] Fiss (n. 7), 1074.

[9] P. Pleasence, H. Genn, N. Balmer, A. Buck, and A. O'Grady, 'Causes of action: First findings of the LSRC Periodic Survey' (2003) 30 Journal of Law and Society 11.

it cannot be concluded from this that lawyers are more litigious. It may well be that people seek the advice of lawyers only over more serious matters that are more likely to end up in court.[10]

Adversarial litigation

In England and Wales, the adversarial system is at the heart of litigation. Under this approach, each party finds the evidence to support its case and presents it to the court; the judge then decides who wins based on the issues raised.[11] In fact, we are so familiar with this form of litigation that it is easy to forget that other jurisdictions have a very different approach to legal disputes.

Supporters of the adversarial system of litigation tend to justify this approach by means of two arguments.[12]

1. The best way in which to discover the truth is to hear the best evidence and the best arguments that either side can bring, and then to decide between them.

2. Each litigant has freedom to choose how to present his or her case and what evidence to bring. That is part of his or her freedom of autonomy.

Neither approach is without its critics. The first argument has a number of problems. It assumes that each side will, indeed, present the best case. If one side presents the best case and the other a very weak case, however, it is unlikely that justice will be done. Both sides have a strong incentive to hide evidence and to mislead the court. That hardly sounds like a route to discovering the truth. As Gavin Lightman, an experienced barrister, points out:

> [S]uccess turns very much on the performance on the day. If (as often happens) a party or his witness for any reasons 'has a bad day' (or under-performs as a witness) or his counsel (*e.g.* because of lack of preparation or ability or misjudgment) lets him down, his prospects are placed at the greatest risk. He has had 'his day in court'. He cannot obtain a 'replay'.[13]

A further important point is that this first argument in favour of adversarial litigation assumes that the two sides to the argument will present all of the necessary evidence, but there may be interests of others whose arguments are not taken into account. In a family law case, hearing the arguments of the mother and father will not necessarily enable the judge to determine what is best for the child.

[10] Pleasence et al. (n. 9).

[11] E. Sward, 'Values, ideology, and the evolution of the adversary system' (1989) 64 Indiana Law Journal 301.

[12] D. Barnhizer, 'The virtue of ordered conflict: A defense of the adversary system' (2000) 79 Nebraska Law Review 657.

[13] G. Lightman, 'The civil justice system and the legal profession: The challenges ahead' (2003) 17 Civil Justice Quarterly 235, 239.

The second argument, which seems currently to be more in vogue,[14] has problems of its own. If we want the law to be determined by justice and rights, is it appropriate for these to be sidetracked by respecting autonomy and allowing the parties to present the arguments that they want to present? To consider again the example of the family case, if neither parent decides to present arguments in terms of what is best for the child and simply present arguments based on their own rights, surely that is not a reason for the judge to ignore the child's interests? Or if a claimant decides not to pursue his or her rights for some reason, is that a sufficient reason for the judge not to take those rights into account? More fundamentally, should a person be able to choose not to seek justice because he or she has esoteric views on what arguments will persuade a judge? These concerns are especially strong if Professor Genn is correct and achieving justice in private disputes is in the public interest.

Ellen Sward picks up on some of these issues, and is concerned that a process that emphasises solely the parties' rights is in danger of promoting individualism and not giving sufficient weight to communal interests:

> In an individualistic system of litigation, that creative force is helpful to the case-by-case development of legal doctrine: the common law. But individualism untempered by communitarian values can lead to unremitting selfishness, including an utter lack of concern for the consequences of one's action.
>
> That selfishness could completely counter any creative value that individualism promoted. Communitarian ideals can result in a society that is caring and supportive of its members, ensuring that none goes without basic needs.[15]

As she suggests, there is a real concern that adversarial litigation will overemphasise the interests of the two parties in dispute. If communitarian interests are to be given weight, then the judge must ensure that not only these interests are considered.

David Barnhizer argues that the adversarial system has the advantage of ensuring that a range of views are heard before courts.[16] He argues that the adversarial system:

> ...is about obtaining and protecting shares of power for specific interests. One undeniable reality of existing in a society with so many competing demands is that without widespread advocacy for the competing interests, those already in possession of power will dominate the sources and levers of power. While it is easy to argue that such a condition is unfair and even immoral—and it is often both—the vital point is that it is inevitable. There is no way to avoid the continual struggle for power and dominance in complex human political systems. While we can take steps to improve the process, we cannot 'fix' the legal system or the roles of lawyers in that system. We cannot alter basic human nature through teaching people to be 'nice' and cooperative.[17]

The key point here is that there are many views or interests in society. If, in a trial, we do not allow the party to decide how to present its own case and what arguments to

---

[14] Sward (n. 11).   [15] Sward (n. 11), 331.   [16] Barnhizer (n. 12).
[17] Barnhizer (n. 12), 659.

use, then someone else must make that decision. As we shall see shortly, under the inquisitorial system, that 'someone else' will be the judge. But then the concern is that courts will hear only a narrow set of standard arguments. Allowing parties to present their own cases as they wish promotes diversity.

Another arguable benefit of the adversarial system is that it gives the judge a clearly defined role. He or she must choose between the arguments presented. If he or she were expected to think of arguments that others might make or arguments based on the interests of the wider community, this would likely impose an intolerable burden on the judge.

Digging deeper

Gavin Lightman suggests that we can draw an analogy between litigation and cricket:

> English institutions have tended to reflect the traditions and values of upperclass England. English civil procedure has always reflected the values and traditions of the English sport of cricket most markedly in the adversary system of justice, and not only in the sense that both are slow and boring. In summary, each side prepares its team for the contest. One side in turn goes in to bat (*i.e.* address the court and call its witnesses) and faces the bowling of the other side (*i.e.* the cross-examination of its witnesses); then the other side takes its turn at the wicket, calling its witnesses. Each side then has the opportunity in final speeches to make its case and unmake that of its opponent. Throughout, an independent third party umpire, selected on grounds of his relative expertise and experience, watches, listens, and enforces the rules, and at the end of the game gives his decision as to the winner.[18]

Do you think that presentation of litigation is an argument in favour of it or against it?

Inquisitorial adjudication

As a contrast to the adversarial litigation in England and Wales, let us consider an approach based on inquisitorial adjudication, used in France for example. The following are the key elements of an inquisitorial adjudication.

- The judge is responsible for the gathering of evidence, rather than (under the adversarial system) the two parties. The judge will direct lines of inquiry to be followed and witnesses to be interviewed.
- The parties may recommend courses of action, but ultimately this is left to the judge.
- The judge is an active participant in the preparation for the trials.

---

[18] Lightman (n. 13), 237.

- The judge then, during the trial, may determine that further information will be required to resolve the dispute.

Opponents to inquisitorial adjudication claim that, under such an approach, the judge loses impartiality. They also suggest that it impedes a party's autonomy. If someone wants to present a particular set of evidence to the court or to pursue a particular line of inequity, he or she may be prevented from doing so if the judge does not think it helpful.

While adversarial litigation and inquisitorial litigation are seen as competing alternatives, there is perhaps less difference than is sometimes imagined. In adversarial litigation, a judge is in fact free to raise an issue that has not been raised by the advocates, even though it is rare for judges to do so.[19] In the inquisitorial system, the judge will rely on advice from the parties as to which lines of enquiry to follow.

Criminal litigation

Funding

Article 6 of the European Convention on Human Rights recognises that a person has a right 'to defend himself in person or through legal assistance of his own choosing or, if he has not sufficient means to pay for legal assistance, to be given it free when the interests of justice so require'. This is closely related to the right under Article 5 to a 'fair and public hearing...including an adequate defence'.

There is strict control over representation of criminal cases in England and Wales. Criminal prosecutions are nearly always brought by the Crown Prosecution Service (CPS). The CPS decides whether to charge a suspect and then prepares the litigation. The CPS employs solicitors and barristers as case workers, and sometimes instructs private practitioners as advocates.

For the defence, clients use private solicitors. A few defendants can afford to instruct their own solicitors and they can do so in the normal way; many need to rely on legal aid. The Legal Aid Commission oversees the provision of legal aid in criminal work. There is currently much uncertainty over its provision. In 2012, it was announced that a new scheme would be introduced involving a system of competitive tendering, so that firms would bid for a package of cases, with the lowest bid obtaining the contract. However, in the summer of 2013, that decision was reversed.[20] The argument that persuaded the Justice Secretary was that cost alone should not determine who provides representation under the legal aid system. The Law Society argued that it was important that people be able to select the solicitor of their choice. Awarding the

---

[19] A. Frost, 'The limits of advocacy' (2009) 59 Duke Law Journal 447.
[20] BBC News, 'Legal aid U-turn over price competition plan', 5 September 2013, online at www.bbc.co.uk/news/uk-23967908

contract for all of the legal work in a particular town to a particular firm, as had been envisioned, would have the effect of requiring legal aid clients to use that one firm.

It remains to be seen quite how the new system will operate. One thing is clear: there will be further cuts in the money paid for legal aid, an area in which funding is already seen by many lawyers as very low. This will exacerbate a growing trend towards fewer and fewer firms undertaking criminal legal aid work. The Carter Review of legal aid had already led to a significant reduction in the number of firms and barristers doing criminal legal aid work.[21] This will fall even further with the extra cuts and it is likely to mean that, in any event, there will be few firms between which a defendant relying on legal aid can choose.

Investigation

A fully contested criminal trial is rare following an arrest. It may be that, following investigation, it is decided not to charge the defendant. For the year ending September 2012, 386,857 'out of court' disposals were given—most commonly, cautions.[22] A caution is an official warning about the defendant's conduct, which is recorded. In more trivial cases, an informal warning might be given. In the year ending September 2012, 1,471,304 accused were proceeded against. Where proceedings are brought, the police gather the evidence and the accused can conduct his or her own investigation. The prosecutor is relatively partisan, because his or her job is to establish the case for the prosecution. This is in marked contrast to the continental inquisitorial system, under which the judge oversees the gathering of evidence and the preparation of the case. Jacqueline Hodgson complains that, in an inquisitorial system, '[t]he accused is simply a witness in the overall investigation and so there is little expectation that she conduct her own enquiries and present an equal and opposite case to that of the prosecution.[23] She is concerned by suggestions that England should move away from adversarialism, and require more cooperation between the defence and prosecution:

> The result has been the attenuation of defense rights and new pressures on the defense to co-operate in the investigation and assembly of evidence against them; this weakens the presumption of innocence and requires the suspect to account for herself in the absence of full knowledge of the case against her. It has also led to a narrowing of the separation between the police and the prosecution, and so between investigation and prosecution—and even case disposal. This brings advantages such as better-prepared cases and more accurate charging decisions, without the dangers of supervision and mutual dependence as seen in France and elsewhere. However, it

[21] Lord Carter, *Legal Aid: A Market-Based Approach to Reform* (Department for Constitutional Affairs, 2006).

[22] Ministry of Justice, *Criminal Justice Statistics 2013* (Ministry of Justice, 2013).

[23] J. Hodgson, 'The future of adversarial criminal justice in 21st century Britain' (2010) 35 North Carolina Journal of International Law and Commercial Regulation 320, 341.

also risks compromising the independence of the CPS as their role becomes entwined with that of the police, and increasingly, the court.[24]

We now turn to the major ethical issues that arise in criminal cases, which can be summarised as follows.

The decision to prosecute

Decisions to prosecute are generally made by the CPS, which is headed by the Director of Public Prosecutions (DPP) and is a government-funded body. It would be wrong, however, to say that all prosecution decisions are made by the CPS, because most commonly the decision is made by the police or another enforcement agency (such as HM Revenue and Customs, or HMRC) not to prosecute. Prosecutors are bound by the CPS Code for Prosecutors,[25] as well as by the professional guidance.

The decision to prosecute by the CPS is governed by its Code for Prosecutors, and there is a two-part test for determining whether a prosecution should be brought, as follows.

- Is there evidence that offers a realistic prospect of conviction?
- Does the public interest require a prosecution?

Donald Nicolson and Julian Webb note that this does not require the prosecuting lawyer to believe in the defendant's guilt.[26] It is possible to imagine a case in which a prosecutor decides that there is a good chance of a conviction even though he or she personally thinks that the defendant is innocent. Nicolson and Webb argue that 'lawyers should decline to prosecute unless convinced beyond reasonable doubt of the defendant's guilt', because 'it is dangerous to trust the court always to get it right when the consequences of unjustified convictions are serious'.[27]

However, not everyone will agree with that view. It is understandable that the Code does not refer to the prosecution lawyer's own beliefs, because that reflects the principle of neutrality that we discussed in Chapter 3. It is not the job of the lawyer, the traditional approach states, to judge the client's case, but rather only to present the arguments. It may be argued that the Code does, in fact, cover the case in which the prosecutor believes that the defendant is innocent (although liable to be convicted) when it states that the prosecutor must be convinced that it is in the public interest for there to be a prosecution. If he or she believes that the defendant is innocent, it is hard to see how that will be so. Richard Young and Andrew Sanders, however, argue that if there is good evidence against a defendant, the court should determine the guilt of the accused, and it is not for the prosecutor to

---

[24] Hodgson (n. 23), 342.

[25] Crown Prosecution Service, *The Code for Prosecutors* (Crown Prosecution Services, 2013).

[26] D. Nicolson and J. Webb, *Professional Legal Ethics: Critical Interrogations* (Oxford University Press, 2000).

[27] Nicolson and Webb (n. 26), 121.

impose his or her own views.[28] They note that prosecutors must realise that they may be mistaken in their assessment and that the ethical concerns a prosecutor may have can be mitigated by the fact that he or she must disclose relevant evidence to the defence, who can then make the relevant case.

The client who confesses guilt

Lawyers get rather fed up with being asked at parties: 'How can you represent a client whom you know is guilty?' While the question is an old chestnut, to which there is an established answer, nevertheless it raises some tricky issues.

The well-established answer is this. If a client confesses his or her guilt to the lawyer, the lawyer is not permitted to deceive the court. It is permissible to enter a 'not guilty' plea on the basis that the prosecution has not proved its case beyond reasonable doubt, but the lawyer cannot present evidence in court that his or her client did not commit the crime. So the central principle is that a lawyer must never knowingly lie to a court.

Follow the Code

The Bar Council Code of Conduct (the Bar Code), Principle 302, states that:

> A barrister has an overriding duty to the Court to act with independence in the interests of justice: he must assist the Court in the administration of justice and must not deceive or knowingly or recklessly mislead the Court.

 Alternative view

While that is a well-established approach to the thorny issue, it is not beyond questioning. If a lawyer knows that the client has committed the crime, should he or she not inform the court? Even by saying 'the prosecution has not proved its case', is the lawyer colluding in the acquittal of a person whom he or she knows to be innocent? The argument in favour of the current approach is that the lawyer, in requiring the prosecution to establish the case, is not deceiving the court. It is Parliament that has decided that a person should be guilty only if that is proven beyond reasonable doubt, and by asking that the prosecution prove its case, the lawyer is only ensuring that Parliament's will is upheld. Further, to make a disclosure to the court of what the client has said without the client's permission would be a breach of confidence (see Chapter 5). However, some might argue that these values are outweighed by the importance of ensuring that justice is done.

---

[28] R. Young and A. Sanders, 'The ethics of prosecution lawyers' (2004) 7 Legal Ethics 190.

What would you do?

You are acting for a client who you are sure has committed the offence with which he is charged. He seems to change his story every time you ask him what happened. When you ask him outright whether he committed the crime, he simply replies 'Well, that *is* the question' and avoids answering it.

The quality of defence lawyers

There is some concern over the quality of the defence system. A study in the 1990s found that:

> Almost all our respondents came to see criminal defence practices as geared, in cooperation with the other elements of the system, towards the routine production of guilty pleas. A minority of them found this to be a source of injustice for clients and of disillusionment for themselves, given their earlier expectations of the defence solicitor's role in an adversarial system.[29]

Whether this grim picture still represents a true picture may be open for debate. Certainly, criminal lawyers often believe their clients to be guilty and it can be difficult then for them to be motivated to make as strong a defence as possible. The criminal law is also seen as the less glamorous part of the profession. Its financial rewards are lower and some will regard it as less prestigious than, say, commercial law. In particular, given the plans to cut legal aid fees by a further 17.5 per cent,[30] it is going to be increasingly difficult for criminal lawyers to do an adequate job without making losses. So there are a range of forces pushing downwards on the quality of criminal defence work.

There is now a body of evidence that suggests that criminal aid lawyers are performing inadequately.[31] Devereux and colleagues conclude that a large number of them have low-level competency and act at an unacceptable level.[32] They tend to be very passive. Some studies report inappropriate attitudes held by criminal defence lawyers towards their clients: they approach clients with an assumption that they are guilty; they saw clients as not worthy of time or attention; they offered the minimum service required to obtain the legal aid payment.[33]

---

[29] M. McConville, J. Hodgson, L. Bridges, and A. Pavlovic, *Standing Accused* (Oxford University Press, 1994), 71.

[30] BBC News (n. 20).

[31] C. Baksi, 'Some criminal advocates "not up to the job"', *Law Society Gazette*, 25 February 2010.

[32] A. Devereux, J. Tucker, R. Moorhead, and E. Cape, *Quality Assurance for Advocates* (Legal Services Commission, 2009).

[33] D. Newman, 'Still standing accused: Addressing the gap between work and talk in firms of criminal defence lawyers' (2012) 19 International Journal of the Legal Profession 3.

These criticisms must be put into context. Those involved in defending the accused on legal aid are often the worst paid and claim that they are often looked down upon by other lawyers. To keep their businesses afloat is a daily struggle. They cannot afford to invest huge amounts of time and energy in any case. There is, of course, the danger of a vicious cycle here: the more poorly paid the work, the less likely it is to attract able lawyers. As the Law Society put it in 2010:

> For increasing numbers of lawyers, legal aid is no longer a viable business proposition or an acceptable career path. The rewards have become too low relative to what qualified professionals can reasonably expect...the government is compromising lawyers' ability to do a good job for their clients.[34]

Victims and witnesses

One of the failings of the adversarial criminal legal system is that as a result of the resources put into the prosecution and defence, it is easy for the others in the system to be ignored. In particular, victims and witnesses are often overlooked. Andrew Ashworth writes:

> The criminal justice system has moral dimensions other than the moral force of the law against those who do wrong. Among those other moral dimensions are that the rights of victims and witnesses should be respected, and that citizens who are suspected of, or charged with, offences must be dealt with in a way which respects their rights.[35]

It is generally thought that the criminal justice has, for too long, failed to protect the rights of witnesses and victims.

The focus on the criminal legal system

Richard Young and Andrew Sanders make the important point that, when thinking about the goals of the criminal system, it is easy to state that it should ensure the conviction of the guilty and the acquittal of the innocent.[36] However, these goals can be contradictory. Measures designed to enable the conviction of the guilty make it more likely that the innocent will be convicted too. The authors promote what they call the 'freedom model':

> It starts from the recognition that the criminal process involves many conflicting values, aims and interests, such as: convicting the guilty; protecting the innocent

---

[34] Law Society, *Access to Justice Interim Review 2010* (Law Society, 2010), para. 2.66. See also Law Society, *As New Report Finds Legal Aid Lawyers Paid Less than Sewage Workers, Law Society Says NO to More Fee Cuts* (Law Society, 2009); Law Society, *NAO Report Shows Lawyers Are Ready to Walk as Failing Legal Aid System Crumbles* (Law Society, 2009); Law Society, *Access to Justice Review: Final Report* (Law Society, 2010).

[35] A. Ashworth, 'Ethics and criminal justice', in R. Cranston (ed.) *Legal Ethics and Professional Responsibility* (Oxford University Press, 1995), 146.

[36] Young and Sanders (n. 28).

from wrongful conviction; protecting human rights by guarding against arbitrary or oppressive treatment; protecting victims; maintaining order; securing public confidence in, and cooperation with, policing and prosecution; and achieving these goals without disproportionate cost and consequent harm to other public services. Whilst politicians like to pretend that these goals are all equally achievable, the reality is that choices have to be made over which are to have priority and such choices inevitably express a particular ethical or philosophical standpoint. Our standpoint is that the overriding purpose of the criminal justice system in a liberal democracy should be the promotion of freedom.[37]

They argue that this makes prosecution valuable as a means to reduce the propensity to commit crime, and to reinforce law-abiding instincts and habits. By reducing crime and fear of crime, freedom is increased.[38]

One area in which this tension reveals itself is over the position of a prosecutor. The following passage from a lecture given by an American prosecutor to his colleagues captures the issue for some:

Although your true purpose is to convict the guilty man who sits at the defense table, and to go for the jugular as viciously and rapidly as possible, do not allow the jury to perceive your attempt. Hide your claws. You must never forget that your goal is total annihilation.[39]

Others see prosecutors as having a broader duty to justice. They should be as concerned with making sure that the innocent are acquitted as they are with ensuring that the guilty are convicted.

Rape

Perhaps the most dramatic and controversial of the cases that criminal advocates may face is when they are acting for men accused of rape. Of course, these issues can arise in other crimes, but the example of rape brings the issues clearly to the fore. Consider a case in which a woman has complained of being raped by the accused. He claims that the sex was consensual; the complainant denies that. The case comes to trial. How far should the lawyer for the defence go to push the victim to establish his or her case? Are there ethical limits on what information the lawyer might use, or what tactics he or she might employ?

David Luban highlights the dilemma:

To make it seem plausible that the victim consented and then turned around and charged rape, the lawyer must play to the jurors' deeply rooted cultural fantasies about feminine sexual voracity and vengefulness. All the while, without seeming like a bully, the advocate must humiliate and browbeat the prosecutrix, knowing that if she blows up she will seem less sympathetic, while if she pulls inside herself

---

[37] Young and Sanders (n. 28), 192.   [38] Young and Sanders (n. 28).
[39] Quoted in M. Frankel, *Partisan Justice* (Will and Wang, 1978), 32.

emotionally she loses credibility as a victim. Let us abbreviate all of this simply as 'brutal cross-examination'.[40]

Repeated questioning, constant interruption, demanding precise recollection of peripheral details, and closed questions are common techniques.[41] Everyone agrees that there must be some limits—for example the advocate must never mislead the court[42]—but beyond that there is little agreement over what ethical limits should be imposed.

In favour of strong cross-examination

These are some of the arguments raised in favour of an 'all out' cross-examination in rape cases.

1. In a criminal trial, the defendant is up against the full force and resources of the state. He or she is entitled to use every tool at his or her disposal to defend the case. It is the lawyer's duty to do all that he or she can to put the best case for the defendant.

2. In a rape case, it is often one person's word against another's. The jury can properly assess who is telling the truth only if the parties are rigorously tested. However unpleasant that it is, there is no alternative if we want to discover the truth.

3. Advocates use harsh cross-examination only because it works. If juries find the evidence elicited reliable and useful, is it proper for lawyer's ethics to prevent it from being used?

Against strong cross-examination

The following are some of the arguments raised against aggressive cross-examination in cases of rape.

1. Cross-examination that humiliates complainants will deter women from reporting crime.

2. Much of the cross-examination relies on 'rape myths'—that is, false beliefs about women and their consent to sex.[43] These include assumptions that women dressed in a particular way are consenting to sex with anyone, or that women who have had several sexual partners should be presumed to have consented on this occasion.[44] By relying on and reinforcing these myths, the lawyer is effectively misleading the court.[45]

---

[40] D. Luban, 'Partisanship, betrayal and autonomy in the lawyer–client relationship: A reply to Stephen Ellmann' (1990) 90 Columbia Law Review 1004, 1041.

[41] L. Ellison, *The Adversarial Process and the Vulnerable Witness* (Oxford University Press, 2001).

[42] Luban (n. 40).

[43] See, e.g., J. Temkin and B. Krahé, *Sexual Assault and the Justice Gap: A Question of Attitude* (Hart, 2008).

[44] R. Collier, '(Un)sexy bodies: The making of professional legal masculinities', in C. McGlynn (ed.) *Legal Feminisms: Theory and Practice* (Ashgate, 1998).

[45] O. Smith and T. Skinner, 'Observing court responses to victims of rape and sexual assault' (2012) 7 Feminist Criminology 298.

3. Conviction rates for rape are very low, with 6.5 per cent of reported rapes resulting in conviction.[46] The conviction rates of cases that reach trial are low, with 38 per cent of rape proceedings leading to a conviction as compared with 69 per cent of those relating to violence against a person.[47] Aggressive cross-examination techniques are seen to be impeding justice.

4. We need to recognise the vulnerability of rape victims: they have already experienced the trauma of rape and the aftermath police investigations can be traumatic. Victims are sometimes left with little guidance or support during trials. There is some recognition of this. In one case, a defendant represented himself. He wore the same clothes that he wore during the attack and cross-examined the victim for six days, leading to her hospitalisation.[48] Following this case, section 35 of the Youth Justice and Criminal Evidence Act 1999 provided that 'protected witnesses' (defined in section 34 to include rape victims) cannot be cross-examined by the accused, who will have to appoint an advocate lawyer to cross-examine.

5. The European Court of Human Rights may well be willing to accept that a trial could constitute torture and inhuman and degrading treatment under Article 3 of the Convention.[49] The vulnerability to this is particularly intense when the victim is a child.[50]

 Scandal!

In February 2013, Frances Andrade gave evidence against a music teacher, who she claimed had abused her when she was a child.[51] In her cross-examination, she was accused of lying. Her husband said that she had been devastated by the intense cross-examination. During the cross-examination, she complained that the trial felt like she was being raped all over again. Shortly after her cross-examination, she committed suicide. Her husband is reported to have said:

> There was a downward spiral in the course of the last year. She was dreading being a witness. She had to go on antidepressants, possibly her drugs were getting stronger and having no effect, but the court tipped her over the edge.

---

[46] Smith and Skinner (n. 45).   [47] Smith and Skinner (n. 45).

[48] P. Rock, *Constructing Victims' Rights: The Home Office, New Labour and Victims* (Oxford University Press, 2004), 346–52.

[49] P. Londono, 'Positive obligations, criminal procedure and rape cases' (2007) 2 European Human Rights Law Review 158; Temkin and Krahé (n. 43).

[50] R. Boyd and A. Hopkins, 'Cross-examination of child sexual assault complainants: Concerns about the application of s 41 of the Evidence Act' (2010) 34 Criminal Law Journal 149.

[51] P. Walker, 'Frances Andrade killed herself after being accused of lying, says husband', *The Guardian*, 10 February 2013, online at www.theguardian.com/uk/2013/feb/10/frances-andrade-killed-herself-lying

Legal protections

The Youth Justice and Criminal Evidence Act 1999, section 41, restricts the use of prior sexual history in rape cases unless:

- a written application was made before the trial; and
- one of four requirements was satisfied:
    - (a) relevant, but does not relate to consent; or
    - (b) relevant to proving consent and the 'sexual activity' occurred around the same time as the alleged events; or
    - (c) was too similar to the alleged events to be coincidental; or
    - (d) relates to questions raised during the victim's evidence-in-chief.

The purpose of this provision was to prevent evidence of past sexual experience from being used to argue that the complainant was 'promiscuous' and therefore consented to the act, but to allow it for other reasons, such as to argue that the complainant had lied in her evidence about having had no sexual experience.

The general consensus is that the legislation has not proved an effective bar on raising the victim's past sexual history. In one leading study, applications to introduce sexual history were made in 25 per cent of cases; in 75 per cent of such cases, that application was successful.[52] Despite the legal protections, Olivia Smith and Tina Skinner comment that:

> [V]ictims are routinely intimidated and asked about their sexual history, to discredit them and imply the presence of consent. This may involve the assumption that women with more sexual experience are more likely to make a false allegation, despite American research indicating evidence to the contrary.[53]

The bar applies only to 'sexual history' and that phrase is undefined.[54] Does it apply to questions about whether the complainant has ever been pregnant or had a boyfriend? Most significantly, the 1999 Act did not bar the use of past sexual history to form the basis of a reasonable belief in consent. So the argument 'She has a sexual history and so she must have consented to sex with me' is not permitted; the argument 'I knew she had a sexual history and so I believed she consented to sex with me' is permitted. The 1999 Act also introduced special measures, including using screens, giving evidence via video link, or emptying the public gallery, which can be helpful in some cases.

The issue of rape trial procedures and law is complex, and outside the scope of this book.[55] However, it reveals the problems with the criminal trial, which sees itself as a

---

[52] L. Kelly, J. Temkin, and S. Griffiths, *An Evaluation of New Legislation Limiting Sexual History in Rape Trials* (Home Office, 2006).

[53] Smith and Skinner (n. 45), 303.   [54] Smith and Skinner (n. 45).

[55] Ellison (n. 41); L. Ellison, 'Witness preparation and the prosecution of rape' (2007) 27 Legal Studies 171; L. Ellison and V. Munro, 'Reacting to rape: Exploring mock juror's assessments of complainant credibility' (2009) 49 British Journal of Criminology 202.

'two-horse race'—the prosecution versus the defence—with no scope for protection of the rights of the victim or the other. The lawyer for the prosecution focuses on presenting the case for the state and the defence lawyer presents the case for the defendant, but no one specifically represents the interests of the victim.[56] Louise Ellison argues that the problem is that that adversarial system encourages competition and combat.[57] She refers to advocacy manuals that speak of trials as battles between 'warriors', who must 'break' and 'butcher' the witness. This is exacerbated by the fact that, normally in criminal trials, the primary focus is on protecting the rights of the defendant, although we are beginning to see, in the European Convention, protection for the rights of victims. The difficulty is that, as the Stern Report emphasised, we need to ensure 'that every victim be treated with dignity',[58] but doing so in a way that allows the defendant full scope to make all of the arguments that he or she may wish to make remains problematic.

Plea bargaining

The official position is that plea bargaining is not permitted in the UK. You may have seen on American television shows the defendant offering to plead guilty to a lesser charge as long as he or she has a guarantee that he or she will not be sentenced for a certain period. That kind of deal is not officially permitted, but English law has been moving towards acceptance of plea bargaining. It has long been established that the courts are able to take into account whether the defendant entered an early plea and grant a lower sentence when he or she did so.[59]

Although, traditionally, a judge was forbidden from giving an indication what sentence might be imposed,[60] that has now changed. In *R v Goodyear*,[61] the Court of Appeal said that a judge could, if he or she so wished, indicate the likely maximum sentence if a defendant were to plead guilty.

 Key case

R v Goodyear [2005] EWCA Crim 888

The appellant sought an indication of what sentence would be imposed in the event of a guilty plea and the judge indicated that it was 'not a custody' case. The appellant pleaded

---

[56] J. Doak, *Victims' Rights, Human Rights, and Criminal Justice: Reconceiving the Role of Third Parties* (Hart, 2008); F. Raitt, 'Independent legal representation for complainants in rape trials', in C. McGlynn and V. Munro (eds) *Rethinking Rape Law: International and Comparative Perspectives* (Routledge, 2010).

[57] F. Wellman, *The Art of Cross Examination* (Touchstone, 1997).

[58] V. Stern, *The Stern Review: A Report by Baroness Stern CBE of an Independent Review into How Rape Complaints Are Handled by Public Authorities in England and Wales* (Home Office, 2010); The Cabinet Office, *The Government Response to the Stern Review: An Independent Review into How Rape Complaints Are Handled by Public Authorities in England and Wales* (Cabinet Office, 2011).

[59] Power of Criminal Courts (Sentencing) Act 2000, s. 152.

[60] *R v Turner* [1970] 2 QB 321.   [61] [2005] EWCA Crim 888.

guilty, but the judge imposed six months' imprisonment suspended for two years. The Court of Appeal rejected an argument that the judge had acted improperly in giving an indication of sentence. In particular, the Court rejected the argument that the indication amounted to putting improper pressure on the defendant. It recommended that the judge should give an indication of what would be the maximum sentence if a guilty plea were tendered. However—and this was the crucial point in this case—the judge was then bound by that indication. In this case, the judge should not therefore have imposed a custodial sentence.

The Court went on to give further guidance: counsel should seek an indication only if it had a written and signed authority from its client. The Court also reminded counsel that great care had to be taken in these cases. The lawyer was personally responsible for ensuring that the client realised that he or she should not plead guilty unless he or she *was* guilty. The Court of Appeal, however, was clearly opposed to a plea bargain under which a defendant would offer to plead guilty to a lesser offence than the one charged and receive a low sentence in return for not being charged with the more serious offence.

The Court of Appeal in *Goodyear* was insistent that giving an indication in advance of a likely sentence was not the same as a plea bargain. This is a somewhat puzzling distinction. As Daniele Alge comments:

This denial that advance indication of sentence has anything to do with plea bargaining is difficult to rationalise, other than on the narrowly conceived basis that a response to a request is just that, rather than a bilateral exchange of concessions in the stricter sense of a 'bargain'. But what is a formal, judicial indication of a light(er) sentence in exchange for a guilty plea, if not a plea bargain?[62]

It seems that what the Court of Appeal was saying was that an advance indication of sentence was not a plea bargain because: (a) there was no room for discussion or negotiation of a deal; and (b) there was no question of a defendant being convicted of a lesser offence after agreeing to plead guilty when originally charged with a more serious offence.

As mentioned by the Court of Appeal, a key issue of concern for the courts is whether improper pressure is being put on a defendant to plead guilty. In *R (on the application of M) v West London Youth Court*,[63] the magistrates stated that they were not going to accept jurisdiction for a burglary case because the severity of the circumstances meant that the case would need to be referred to a higher court, in which higher levels of punishment were available. However, they then added that they would

---

[62] D. Alge, 'Negotiated plea agreements in cases of serious and complex fraud in England and Wales: A new conceptualisation of plea bargaining?' (2013) 19 Web Journal of Current Legal Issues 1, 2.   [63] [2009] EWHC 1777 (Admin).

accept jurisdiction if the defendant were to plead guilty. The defendant thereupon changed his plea to guilty, leaving the case in the magistrates' court, with the lower powers of sentence. It was held that this did not place improper pressure on the defendant and that the defendant was appropriately sentenced.

What marks that case out is that the defendant had not previously indicated a willingness to plead guilty. The case therefore marks an extension from *Goodyear*, which had involved a defendant who was trying to decide whether or not to plead guilty.

Some commentators believe that, through these cases, we are witnessing a growing acceptance of plea bargaining. Mike McConville argues:

A fundamental re-legitimation of plea bargaining is under way, the effect of which is to obscure, behind a mask of professional ethics and classical moralism, a process based on a culture of extortionate relationships which extract crude cost/benefit actuarialism from everyone involved.[64]

In making that claim, he draws attention to *R v Cain*,[65] in which it was held that the reduction of sentence following a guilty conviction did not require remorse, but simply the fact of the guilty plea. It is the administrative convenience that is the driving force behind the reduction of sentence, rather than the demonstration of a change of heart. McConville sees this as open acknowledgement that economic savings and administrative convenience have become key features of sentencing decisions.

Plea bargaining or indicative sentencing can put the lawyer in a difficult position.[66] If a client has been pleading not guilty, but the judge then indicates what sentence will be given in the event of a guilty plea, how should the lawyer advise the client? The Royal Commission on Criminal Justice (RCCJ) sought to overcome this by seeing the issue as one for the client: 'We envisage that the procedure which we recommend would be initiated solely by, and for the benefit of, defendants who wish to exercise a right to be told the consequence of a decision which is theirs alone.'[67]

The line between informing a client of the consequences of his or her decision and recommending a decision is a fine, but crucial, one. It is, perhaps, an unrealistic one. Clients are bound to ask their lawyers' advice and seek an indication of what their chances at trial are. The lawyer is in a particularly difficult position where the client maintains innocence, but indicates a willingness to plead guilty to take advantage of the lower sentence. Is counsel who enters a guilty plea for a client in such a case misleading the court? Counsel would certainly be acting improperly in many cases if he or she were to enter a not guilty plea, knowing the client to be guilty. However, there is a difference. A not guilty plea can be entered on the basis that the prosecution has not proved its

[64] M. McConville, 'Plea bargaining: Ethics and politics' (1998) 25 Journal of Law and Society 562, 571.
[65] [1976] Crim LR 464.
[66] R. Lippke, *The Ethics of Plea Bargaining* (Oxford University Press, 2012).
[67] *Report of the Royal Commission on Criminal Justice* (HM Stationery Office, 1993), para 45.

case, and so the entering of the plea may not be deceiving the court if the defendant's case is that the prosecution has not proven its case. However, the guilty plea is a full admission of guilt. One solution to this is to argue that, in fact, it is the defendant who enters the plea personally and so the lawyer has no responsibility for it. It may be questioned whether that is sufficient to avoid the responsibilities that the barrister has as an officer of the court.

Supporters of plea bargaining are sceptical that anyone will plead guilty who has not committed a crime. By encouraging the defendant to plead guilty, however, the court is saving a huge public expense, and saving the victim and witnesses the stress of a trial.

Critics complain that plea bargaining can especially benefit defendants who are adroit at playing the system. A crafty accused will be able to manipulate the case to get a low sentence, while a less sophisticated accused will not. Their sentences may differ, even though their moral blameworthiness is similar.

There is also a real concern that people will plead guilty for fear of getting a longer sentence if the matter goes to trial, even if in fact a defendant is not guilty. It is, of course, difficult to know how many people plead guilty, who were in fact innocent, following an indication of sentence.[68]

Mike McConville is concerned too that there will be the creation of a 'guilty plea' culture, in which a non-guilty plea is seen as a failure.[69] Modern divorce lawyers do all that they can to get the parties to agree to a divorce and so avoid a contested divorce petition; the same may be happening with the parties to a legal trial. This may be particularly so given the political and economic climate in which there is pressure to obtain convictions and cost-efficiencies. The costs of a criminal trial can be huge; cost savings are welcomed in a climate in which cost-effectiveness and cost-efficiency are king and queen.

While the focus of the debate often concerns the defendants and the ethical dilemma that lawyers may face, there is an issue for prosecutors too, especially in a full plea bargain case.[70] If the defendant has committed a serious crime, is it right for the prosecutor to accept a plea for a lesser crime? Is that failing in his or her duty to aid the court in holding people to account for what they have done?

In 2009, the Attorney General announced a special set of procedures for plea bargaining in cases of serious and complex fraud.[71] The Serious Fraud Office (SFO) is given the power to, in effect, negotiate with defendants over pleas and sentence. This is interesting for two reasons. The first is to question why fraud cases should be subject to special treatment. The explanation for the cynic is that fraud trials are particularly prone to being lengthy and expensive. Therefore the cost-saving pressure

---

[68] S. Jones, 'Under pressure: Women who plead guilty to crimes they have not committed' (2011) 11 Criminology and Criminal Justice 77.   [69] McConville (n. 64).

[70] A. Stern, 'Plea bargaining, innocence, and the prosecutor's duty to "do justice"' (2012) 25 Georgetown Journal of Legal Ethics 1027.   [71] Alge (n. 62).

in that context is particularly strong. Second, it seems that we have here the kind of negotiating over sentence that is the classic plea bargain phenomenon.[72] Critics will point to *R v Innospec*,[73] in which Thomas LJ stated that the fine imposed was 'wholly inadequate', but that he felt bound by the terms of the agreement already reached with the SFO.[74]

Civil litigation

Civil litigation is now governed by the Civil Procedure Rules 1998 (CPR),[75] amended on multiple occasions. The civil litigation costs system has been comprehensively reviewed by Lord Justice Jackson, whose final report was published in 2010.[76] Many of his proposals are being gradually introduced by means of amendments to the rules. This book will not detail the regulations, but will highlight some of the key ethical issues that arise.

The basic structure of civil litigations is straightforward, comprising the following main stages.

1. Issue of a claim form

2. Service of process on the defendant (that is, a claim form)

3. Service of the parties' statements of case

4. Allocation of the claim to a case management track

5. Disclosure of documents

6. Exchange of witness and expert evidence

7. Listing for trial

8. Trial

9. Assessment of costs

Costs

Litigation is extremely expensive. The preparation of documents and gathering of evidence all take time, and as we know, for lawyers, time is money. For a litigant, the risk is doubled, because if he or she loses the case, not only will he or she face paying his or her own lawyer's bill, but also the other side's. This means that there is a constant fear of costs hanging over the litigation. Indeed, it means that, in relation to small sums of money, litigation is rarely worth the risk, stress, or cost.

---

[72] The power has been used in, e.g., *R v Innospec* [2010] Lloyd's Rep FC 462, *R v BAE Systems Plc* [2010] EW Misc 16 (CC), and *R v Dougall* [2010] EWCA Crim 1048.

[73] *R v Innospec* [2010] Lloyd's Rep FC 462.   [74] At [40].   [75] SI 1998/3132.

[76] R. Jackson, *Review of Civil Litigation Costs: Final Report* (HM Stationery Office, 2010).

◎ Application

The fear of costs can promote settlement. Imagine that you are seeking £1 million. The other side offers you £750,000. You might think that this is too far below what you are seeking—but remember the costs. If you carry on litigating, you may not win in court, in which case you will face a very heavy bill. You might win, but the judge might award you something close to the £750,000, in which case you might be liable for the costs after the offer was made, because you were not litigating reasonably. Suddenly, the £750,000 offer does not look so bad after all.

From that perspective, costs do not play an entirely negative role. But the issue is not straightforward: what if you had been injured in a car crash and needed £1 million to provide you with the care that you now needed? Should fears over costs pressure you into settling for £750,000? Should you not expect the law to give you the full costs to compensate you?

Also, the fear of costs will be greater for parties of limited means. The fears over costs may give the richer party a distinct advantage in litigation. A company, in which no single individual is going to suffer a loss, may be willing to endanger its finances in the lottery of litigation in a way that an individual would not. Indeed, it is a well-known tactic of richer litigants to drag the litigation out in an attempt to lead the other parties to run out of money and to settle. However, litigation tactics are unlikely to breach professional ethics, unless the costs are dragged out utterly unnecessarily.

Digging deeper

An innovation in Australia is interesting in this regard.[77] It requires that lawyers certify a reasonable prospect of success before proceedings are brought. The idea is to prevent people from using litigation not with an expectation of winning in court, but with the goal of pressurising the other party into settling. A party might sue a large company, aware that he or she has little chance of success, but hoping that the company will pay the party to 'go away' and avoid the bother of litigation. A company may defend a claim not with any hope of winning, but hoping that the claimant will run out of money or energy, or both. Requiring the lawyer to certify a reasonable prospect of success will hopefully deal with both of these issues. However, it does challenge the traditional model of professional ethics (see Chapter 3) and especially the notion of neutrality: traditionally, it is the job of the judge, not the lawyer, to decide whether a client has a strong case.

---

[77] P. Stewart and M. Evers, 'The requirement that lawyers certify reasonable prospects of success' (2010) 13 Legal Ethics 1.

Some commentators have sought to apply game theory to litigation.[78] Much is made of the 'prisoners' dilemma'. There are various versions of this theory, but it involves two prisoners charged with an offence who have to decide whether or not to talk to the police.

- If they both keep quiet, they will both walk free.
- If one keeps quiet and one implicates the other, the quiet one will go to prison for a long time and the other will walk free.
- If they both implicate each other, they will both go to prison for a medium length of time.

This model can be presented in terms of points, with the parties choosing either cooperation or defect. If there is cooperation, then each gets three points. If one defects and the other chooses cooperation, the defected gets five points and the cooperating party, none. If they both defect, they get one point each.

The point of these scenarios is that if there is cooperation, both parties will win out. However, if one cooperates and the other does not, the deserted loses. It is said that litigation and offering to settle can be a little like this: one can settle for a medium amount, or go for litigation and risk either winning the jackpot or losing out terribly.

Andrew Boon and Jennifer Levin suggest that the best strategy is that 'people should begin relationships by being cooperative; they should punish uncooperative behaviour in equal measure; and they should return to cooperation if they receive an "apology", provided that it offers future cooperative behaviour'.[79]

 Scandal!

In one case that attracted media attention, a judge was critical of a dispute over a leaking pipe that had generated costs of £225,000.[80] The costs incurred were held by the Court of Appeal to be 'disproportionate' to the importance of the issue at hand. The dispute centred on a builder who had banged a nail into a pipe, causing a flood, which led to damages of £21,000. Lord Justice Rix, in something of an understatement, described it as an 'unhappy story'.

[78] D. Baird, R. Gertner, and R Picker, *Game Theory and the Law* (Harvard University Press, 1994).

[79] A. Boon and J. Levin, *The Ethics and Conduct of Lawyers in England and Wales* (Hart, 2008), 357.

[80] N. Fagge, 'No-win, no-fee, no common sense: Judge's fury after five-year dispute over leaking pipe leads to £225,000 bill', *Daily Mail*, 19 December 2011, online at www.dailymail.co.uk/news/article-2075814/Judges-fury-225-000-legal-simple-dispute-private-schools-leaky-water-pipe.html

The Woolf Reforms

A major review of civil litigation was undertaken by Lord Woolf in 1996.[81] At the heart of his reforms was an aim to produce a civil litigation system that was available at a reasonable cost and understood by the public.[82] He found the current system to be marked by delays and excessive costs. Some cases moved too slowly through the system, causing extra expense and stress; others arrived at court inadequately prepared. Following the Woolf Report, the Access to Justice Act 1999 and the revised Civil Procedure Rules reformed civil procedures in England and Wales. These contained some key principles, including the following.

- Claimants had to clearly state their cases.[83]
- Defendants had to state their reasons for denying liability.[84]
- Protocols required the early release of information to enable the parties to gauge the strength of each other's cases and then to settle.[85]
- Timetables set out the exchange and disclosure of documents, including joint expert reports.
- Costs were to follow the event as a general result.
- In deciding what costs order to make, the court was to consider the conduct of the parties and offers to settle.[86]
- Fast-track procedures were put in place for smaller claims.

A major feature of the reforms was to encourage judicial case management. Judges were to take a more interventionist role in encouraging the parties to disclose evidence, to encourage settlement, and to ensure that costs were kept reasonable and that the case moved speedily through the courts.

A key principle was the idea of proportionality: the fees should match the sums involved, the importance of the case, the complexity of the issues, and the financial position of the parties. Cases valued at less than £5,000 were put on the small claims track; a fast track was available for those valued between £5,000 and £15,000; the multitrack, for those valued at £15,000 and over. The track on which a case was placed would depend on which court dealt with it and which timetable had to be maintained.

Another principle was to encourage the parties to cooperate in the conduct of proceedings[87] and to help judges to achieve the objectives. Parties were expected to disclose relevant documentation to each other and to work together to keep to timetables.

Generally, the CPR are seen as a success.[88] A MORI poll in 2000 found that 80 per cent of solicitors were happy with the CPR.[89] The Rules seem to have encouraged

---

[81] M. Zander, 'The government's plans on civil justice' (1998) 61 Modern Law Review 382.

[82] Lord Woolf, *Access to Justice* (Lord Chancellor's Department, 1996).   [83] CPR 3.4.

[84] CPR 16.5.   [85] CPR, Pt 31.   [86] CPR 44.   [87] CRP 3.1.4.2a.

[88] Civil Justice Council, *Annual Report* (Civil Justice Council, 2004).

[89] MORI, *Lawyers Endorse Woolf Reforms* (MORI, 2000).

more settlements and greatly improved the speed of litigation. There have been some dissenting voices, however. They have complained that the speedy timetables benefit those who can mobilise resources quickly (that is, bigger firms). Also, they have complained that, by requiring much expense earlier on in terms of disclosure and investigation, the costs may be greater in cases that may otherwise have settled earlier.[90] There have also been concerns that reducing costs encourages nuisance claims.[91]

The CPR do mark an interesting departure from some of the standard approaches to legal ethics.

1. They require a degree of cooperation between the parties in meeting the court timetables. This is at variance with the adversarial approach to litigation normally taken.[92]

2. The judge plays a more interventionist role, requiring the parties to comply with timetables and directions. This is at variance with the autonomy-based approach, which allows the parties to conduct litigation in the way in which they think fit.

3. The pressure to negotiate and settle is strong and explicit. This can be seen as a restriction on the access to a court hearing, which some people believe is an important aspect of access to justice.

Another aspect of the Access to Justice Act 1999 was that legal aid for civil cases was effectively swept away and replaced with 'no win, no fee' arrangements for most money claims. It also required people wishing to access legal aid to attempt mediation first, and settlement was promoted for all.[93] There was evidence of high satisfaction among those who volunteered to use the service, although they had nothing with which to compare it. There was, perhaps surprisingly, no evidence that the mediated cases were quicker.[94] Whether mediation is more costly or not than litigation is contentious and difficult to assess, because it is hard to know how quickly the case could have settled otherwise. The evidence suggests that claimants get significantly less compensation.[95] We discuss the issues around mediation and negotiation in Chapter 10.

The 'crisis in civil litigation'

There has been much talk of a 'crisis in civil litigation'. This led to the Woolf Reforms and has continued to produce ongoing reforms. However, Professor Genn argues that

---

[90] Zander (n. 81).

[91] T. Aldridge, 'Downside of procedural reform', *Solicitors Journal*, 29 March 2002, 1142.

[92] Lightman (n. 13).

[93] For example, M. Doyle, *Manchester Small Claims Mediation Scheme Evaluation* (Department for Constitutional Affairs, 2006).

[94] H. Genn, P. Fenn, M. Mason, A. Lane, N. Bechai, L. Gray, and D. Vencappa, *Twisting Arms: Court Linked and Court Refereed Mediation under Judicial Pressure* (Ministry of Justice, 2007).

[95] H. Genn, *Central London Country Court Mediation Scheme* (Department for Constitutional Affairs, 1998).

this 'crisis' did not emanate from real problems with how the system worked, but rather from government concerns about the cost of legal aid.[96] There is some merit in this argument. The government is not normally concerned with how rich people choose to waste their money; it is, on the other hand, very interested in reducing costs. Ironically, Genn notes that more effective policing and more extensive criminalisation put more pressure on the criminal legal aid budget.

Wealth

Even with the cost-reducing reforms to the civil procedure, there is no doubt that litigation is a rich person's game. In a strikingly blunt comment, a leading Queen's counsel (QC) has been quite open about the way in which litigation favours the well-off:

> The quality of solicitors and counsel varies as does the quality of wine from 'unfit to drink' to vintage. Vintage tends to be very expensive beyond the means of the ordinary litigant. Most must be satisfied with 'plonk'. Prospects of success of a case very much turn on the quality or lack of quality of preparation for trial. Cases are won and lost by reason of the quality of representation at the trial: hence the extravagant fees paid to litigation lawyers. Common experience reveals how unbalanced the legal process is at all three stages between the 'haves' and the 'have nots'. Tell it not in Gath but the scales of justice favour those who can afford to buy it.[97]

It is rare to hear this view so openly expressed from within the profession. The benefit of wealth should not be over-exaggerated. Even the very best QC cannot win a case in which all of the evidence points one way. However, it is in borderline cases in which the difference in resources can be seen to play a role.

Justice

One of the phrases that echoes in the reforms is the notion of 'access to justice'. Once we accept the rule of law as foundational to a democracy, this emphasises the importance of liberty, and promises justice and equality before the law. All citizens have their legal rights and access to the courts to enforce those rights. This is at the heart of the current debates around civil justice.

On the one hand, there is a view that if we accept access to justice, we must make sure that access to the courts is available for all. That means two things: we must offer legal aid to those who cannot afford legal advice; and we must restrict the costs of litigation so that it does not impose a huge burden on the legal aid fund or on individual citizens.

However, even this will not guarantee access to justice: many cases simply do not reach lawyers. There are, of course, some issues in which a person will almost inevitably involve a lawyer: a criminal case, for example. In others, whether a person will

---

[96] Genn (n. 3).   [97] Lightman (n. 13), 237.

think of seeking legal advice will depend on his or her educational background, financial and emotional resources, and so forth. It should not be forgotten that many of the cases that could theoretically lead to a legal solution are simply resolved informally. The bad job done by a plumber will not necessarily lead to a court case, but rather to someone telling his or her friends not to use that plumber. The cohabitants who split up may simply decide to go their separate ways. Even if the parties are aware that the issue could be taken to court, they may be too intimidated to seek legal advice or simply see that as too much bother.

Digging deeper

Jennifer Levin and Andrew Boon refer to the low recourse to courts as a 'blemish on contemporary society's claim to be just'.[98] This is a striking claim in an era during which it is much more common to hear claims that there is too much litigation.[99] There is a genuine issue here: would a society marked by widespread court attendance be a more just society? Or is the question whether a society in which people's rights are infringed with no recourse to court action a just one? Perhaps the answer in part lies in what happens when a person is wronged and the matter does not go to court. If there is an apology, an acceptance of responsibility, a reassurance that it will not happen again, and informal restitution, then that may be seen as an adequate expression of justice. However, if people's rights were being infringed without any concern by the wrongdoer because he or she knew that the other person would not take the matter to court, then that would be a mark of injustice.

Interestingly, there is some research to suggest that users of the civil justice system are often facing multiple problems in their lives. Their litigation may, in other words, be only the tip of an iceberg, rather than the thing that matters most to them. The following matters have been found to be linked to litigation.[100]

1. Family problems: divorce; domestic violence; disputes over children

2. Homelessness

3. Unfair police treatment

4. Mental ill-health

5. Consumer, employment, and money and debt problems

The researchers found that 73 per cent of respondents with justifiable problems fell into one of these clusters.

---

[98] Boon and Levin (n. 79), 364.

[99] G. Boehm, 'Debunking medical malpractice myths: Unraveling the false premises behind "tort reform"' (2005) 5 Yale Journal of Health Policy, Law, and Ethics 9.

[100] P. Pleasence, N. Palmer, A. Buck, and H. Genn, 'Multiple justiciable problems: Common clusters and their social and demographic indicators' (2004) 1 Journal of Empirical Legal Studies 301.

One response to such observations is that the courts should become multi-agency locations where a person can receive not only legal advice, but also personal counselling, debt advice, housing advice, employment advice, mental health assistance, mediation, and the like. This approach recognises that people need to be treated holistically: as individuals looking for solutions to all of the problems that involve their emotional health, their relationships, and their integration into society. This may involve a broad range of services. Simply providing, say, a small claims payment may not meet the deeper issues underlying the claim.

Advocacy

The job of an advocate is to present a client's case. It is not the advocate's role to present his or her own point of view. While **advocacy services** can be defined broadly, advocacy in its popular sense is normally restricted to court appearances.

 Definition

> Section 190(6) of the Legal Services Act 2007 defines **advocacy services** broadly as 'any services which it would be reasonable to expect a person who is exercising, or contemplating exercising, a right of audience in relation to any proceedings, or contemplated proceedings, to provide'.

Advocacy has traditionally been associated with the Bar. Indeed, until 1990, it was the preserve of the Bar. It was the job of the solicitors to deal with clients on a day-to-day basis and to prepare cases, but barristers were to appear in courts. Traditionally, the solicitor would sit behind a barrister in court to aid communication with a client and to offer any practical help needed. However, that has become rare, especially in legally aided work.

The Courts and Legal Services Act 1990 broke the monopoly of the Bar. Bodies can now apply to show that their members should have rights of audience if they have appropriate rules of conduct to ensure the proper administration of justice. Since 1993, the Law Society has been able to grant its members rights of audience in higher courts.

It might be thought that the monopoly of the Bar on advocacy in the higher courts is anachronistic, but it is possible to argue for it. Barristers are self-employed and not guaranteed a salary, unlike solicitors, who normally have a guaranteed income from their firms. Moving work from barristers to solicitors may make the Bar even more financially precarious. Further, newly qualified barristers need experience at the Bar and taking some of the more minor work to solicitors may impact on that. Barristers have special training in advocacy, while solicitors may not.

However, it has been argued that some solicitors can be skilled advocates. Those that have this skill should be encouraged to use it. A firm with an advocate solicitor can serve its client well, probably in a cheaper and more efficient way than by using a barrister. It is notable however, that in fact relatively few solicitors have taken up the chance of being an advocate.

Qualification

To be able to provide advocacy services in all courts, a barrister must have completed his or her education and been 'called to the Bar'. He or she must work from the office of a qualified person, and must have practised for three years.

Solicitors can apply for advocacy rights after three years' experience of advocacy. This can either be under regulation 4 of the Higher Courts Qualification Regulations if they have 'appropriate judicial or higher court advocacy experience', or they can apply to the Law Society and show that they are suitably experienced and qualified. Solicitor advocates must pass the 'Test of Evidence and Procedure in the Higher Courts' (there are separate ones for civil and criminal courts) and must then complete an appropriate course.

The practice of advocacy

Follow the Code

The Bar Code, para 701, makes it clear that a barrister:

must not undertake any task which:

(i)   he knows or ought to know he is not competent to handle;

(ii) he does not have adequate time and opportunity to prepare for or perform; or

(iii) he cannot discharge within the time requested or otherwise within a reasonable time having regard to the pressure of other work;

There is less regulation over the presentation of cases. In part, that is a recognition that advocacy often involves a matter of taste: whether a pithy focused speech will be more effective than a lengthy detailed analysis is hard to tell.

Scandal!

Roscoe Pound writes of a true case in which a barrister was indicted for murder when, while the barrister was speaking in court, a boy in the public gallery fell asleep in the court and broke his neck.[101] It was said that the barrister had committed murder by means of 'a certain dull instrument to wit a long speech of no value'!

---

[101]   R. Pound, *The Lawyer from Antiquity to Modern Times* (West, 1953), 27.

The Bar Code is clear on the merit of brevity.

Follow the Code

The Bar Code, para 701.1, states that a barrister:

> must in all his professional activities be courteous and act promptly, conscientiously, diligently and with reasonable competence and take all reasonable and practicable steps to avoid unnecessary expense or waste of the Court's time and to ensure that professional engagements are fulfilled;

The role of the advocate

There is an interesting academic debate over the role of the advocate.

- Some argue that an advocate has to argue zealously on behalf of the defendant.[102] This might include discrediting witnesses, known to the lawyer to be telling the truth, or introducing witnesses that the advocate knows will commit perjury.

- Others argue that the advocate's job is to help the judge (or jury) to make a wise, informed, impartial decision that will establish the truth.[103]

This is a reflection of the wider debate over the role of the lawyer that was discussed in Chapter 3, but it is worth returning to some of the issues and applying them in this context. As Daniel Markovits, supporting the argument for zealousness, states:

> Unlike juries and judges, adversary lawyers should not pursue a true account of the facts of a case and promote a dispassionate application of the law to these facts. Instead, they should try aggressively to manipulate both the facts and the law to suit their client's purposes. This requires lawyers to promote beliefs in others that they themselves (properly) reject as false. Lawyers might, for example, bluff in settlement negotiations, undermine truthful testimony, or make legal arguments that they would reject as judges. In short lawyers must lie.[104]

The differences between the two views are fewer than might be thought. Supporters of the first approach might well agree that the primary job of the advocate is to help the court to find the truth, but believe the best way of achieving that is to put forward the strongest possible case for the defendant. If the prosecutor puts forward the best case for the state, then that is a recipe for success. Monroe Freedman includes as one argument for his approach that the defendant is up against the massive power of the state and needs a 'champion against a hostile world'.[105]

---

[102] M. Freedman, 'Professional responsibility of the criminal defense lawyer' (1966) 64 Michigan Law Review 1469.

[103] J. Noonan, 'Professional ethics or personal responsibility' (1977) 29 Stanford Law Review 363.

[104] D. Markovits, *A Modern Legal Ethics* (Princeton University Press, 2012), 211.

[105] Freedman (n. 102), 1471.

The Bar Code is more in tune with the view that the primary duty is to the court. Paragraph 302 (quoted earlier in the chapter) makes it clear that a barrister has an overriding duty to the court. That duty requires him or her to assist the court in the administration of justice and not to deceive the court.

The advocate's duty to the witness

The cross-examination of a witness is a key skill of advocacy. The aim of cross-examination is to expose contradictions and flaws in the witness's account. The aim is to discover whether the witness is being entirely truthful. This can, on occasion, require strong cross-examination, or examination that involves entrapping a witness or confusing him or her. A popular method is using 'closed questions' to which the witness is required to answer 'yes' or 'no', or is given two answers from which he or she must choose. By clever use of these, the lawyer is able to present a particular picture of the case. We have seen earlier, in relation to the cross-examining of rape complainants, that the issue raises some complex issues. Here, we shall look at the issue of cross-examination more broadly.

The line between effective cross-examination and examination that is bullying or manipulative may be thin. In *Rondel v Worsley*,[106] Lord Reid said that:

> Every counsel has a duty to his client fearlessly to raise every issue, advance every argument, and ask every question, however distasteful, which he thinks will help his client's case. But...counsel...must not lend himself to casting aspersions on the other party or witnesses for which there is no sufficient basis in the information in his possession.

The Bar Code states three key principles.

Follow the Code

The Bar Code, para 708, states that a barrister:

[...]

(g)   must not make statements or ask questions which are merely scandalous or intended or calculated only to vilify, insult or annoy either a witness or some other person;

[...]

(i)   must not by assertion in a speech impugn a witness whom he has had an opportunity to cross-examine unless in cross-examination he has given the witness an opportunity to answer the allegation;

(j)   must not suggest that a victim, witness or other person is guilty of crime, fraud or misconduct or make any defamatory aspersion on the conduct of any other person or attribute

---

[106] [1969] 1 AC 191, 207.

> to another person the crime or conduct of which his lay client is accused unless such allegations go to a matter in issue (including the credibility of the witness) which is material to the lay client's case and appear to him to be supported by reasonable grounds.
>
> [...]

These three principles are relatively self-explanatory, but are not without ambiguity. As to the first, whether a question is annoying or whether it is probing may be a matter of opinion. Even the question 'Are you lying?' can be annoying.

As to the second, it is clear that a witness must be given the chance to refute any allegation that a barrister may want to make 'impugning' the witness's character. But what does 'impugning' mean? It is likely to be given a broad meaning, suggesting anything negative about a witness. As the obligation on the barrister is not onerous—he or she must simply raise it with the witness—it would seem reasonable to give it a broad reading.

The third principle requires the barrister to ensure that allegations of criminal or misconduct are raised only if they go to the matter at issue. That is likely to include whether the witness is credible, and if the defendant is adamant the witness is lying, that is likely to give the barrister reasonable grounds to believe that the witness many not be truthful.

A barrister is not permitted to train or encourage a witness. *R v Momodou*[107] held that while helping a witness to be familiar with the court proceedings is permitted, witness preparation is not. Telling the witness about the procedures of a trial and explaining the personnel of the court is permitted, but the line is crossed if the witness is told about what questions he or she will face and how to respond to them. A witness can be told in general terms about how to give evidence (for example to speak slowly), but not what to say. This is, of course, a fine line.[108]

While the tradition of cross-examination is well established as a method of testing the accuracy of a witness, it has been challenged by some psychologists. Tim Valentine and Katie Maras, in their analysis, conclude:

> A substantial body of research has demonstrated that eyewitness memory can be highly malleable. Eyewitness memory can be distorted by suggestion from information acquired after the relevant event was witnessed, by the style of questioning that a witness encounters or by repeated questioning.[109]

There are particular concerns over the cross-examination of children and vulnerable witnesses.[110]

---

[107] [2005] EWCA Civ 177.

[108] L. Ellison, '"Could you ask me that in a different way please?" Exploring the impact of courtroom questioning and witness familiarisation on adult witness accuracy' (2010) 11 Criminal Law Review 823.

[109] T. Valentine and K. Maras, 'The effect of cross-examination on the accuracy of adult eyewitness testimony' (2011) 25 Applied Cognitive Psychology 554, 564.

[110] S. O'Meill and R. Zajac, 'Disorder in the courtoom? Child witnesses under cross-examination' (2012) 32 Developmental Review 17.

Duty to court

What duties do litigators owe to the court? This issue is addressed in Chapter 13, but we will outline here some of the major issues.

Section 118(2) of the Legal Services Act 2007 states that litigators have a duty to the court 'to act with independence in the interests of justice'. This is reinforced in the professional codes.

Follow the Code

The first of the ten Principles of the SRA Code of Conduct is:

> You must uphold the rule of law and the proper administration of justice

In one influential article, David Ipp suggests that we can distil the primary duties to courts into four categories, as follows.[111]

- The general duty of disclosure owed to the court
- The general duty not to abuse the court process
- The general duty not to corrupt the administration of justice
- The general duty to conduct cases efficiently and expeditiously

As we have seen, regulation 302 of the Bar Code explicitly acknowledges the overriding duty of the barrister to the court to ensure that there is proper and efficient administration of justice. The precise nature and extent of these is unclear. Some are explicitly mentioned in the Bar Code.

Follow the Code

The Bar Code, para 708, states that a barrister:

[...]

(c) must ensure that the Court is informed of all relevant decisions and legislative provisions of which he is aware whether the effect is favourable or unfavourable towards the contention for which he argues;

(d) must bring any procedural irregularity to the attention of the Court during the hearing and not reserve such matter to be raised on appeal;

[...]

(f) must not make a submission which he does not consider to be properly arguable;

[...]

---

[111] D. Ipp, 'Lawyers' duties to the court' (1998) 114 Law Quarterly Review 63.

However, it is generally agreed that the duty is broader than the provisions of the Bar Code. Boon and Levin give the example of an advocate showing courtesy to the judge, which is not mentioned in the Code precisely, but would fall under the general duty to the court.[112]

A major point of contention is whether barristers must ever introduce evidence that they suspect to be false. A number of points could be made. Monroe Freedman would argue that the zealous advocate will do all that he or she can to win the case for the client, even introducing evidence that he or she believes to be false.[113] While this might sound remarkable, it might be said to be for the court to assess the truthfulness of the evidence. This leads on to a second point, which may be to question how many barristers deal with this issue in practice. Although a barrister might suspect, or fear, that a piece of evidence is false, he or she will rarely know it to be untrue. This might allow a barrister to introduce evidence suspecting it is false, but not seeing it as his or her job to assess its truth.

In *Re Mayor Cooke*,[114] it was held that:

> [I]t was part of [a lawyer's] duty that he should not keep back from the court any information which ought to be before it, and that he should in no way mislead the court by stating facts which were untrue...How far a solicitor might go on behalf of his client was a question far too difficult to be capable of abstract definition, but when concrete cases arose everyone could see for himself whether what had been done was fair or not.

In *Tombling v Universal Company Ltd*,[115] a barrister called a witness. In questioning him, the barrister brought out the fact that the witness was a prison governor. What did not emerge was that the witness was currently serving a sentence for a driving offence. The Court of Appeal did not allow an appeal. The Court of Appeal's response to what the barrister had done was interesting. Somerville LJ's criticism was mild: it would have been better if the barrister had not acted that way. For Denning LJ, the intention seemed to be the key factor, and here he assessed that the barrister had not intended to mislead the court. Singleton LJ was most critical, arguing that the barrister had forgotten his duty to the court.

A similar situation emerged in *Meek v Fleming*,[116] in which a barrister did not inform the court that his client, a police officer charged with assaulting a journalist, had been demoted for deception. The Court of Appeal this time determined that the barrister had deliberately set about structuring the evidence and examination so that the facts had not emerged, and that he had behaved wrongly in doing so.

---

[112] Boon and Levin (n. 79), 357.   [113] Freedman (n. 102).
[114] [1989] Times Law Reports 407, 407.   [115] [1951] Times Law Reports 289.
[116] [1961] 2 QB 366.

The following case positions the obligation to the court at a high level.

 Key case

Vernon v Bosley [1997] 1 All ER 614

A client had been awarded damages for nervous shock. After the draft judgment, the client's barrister was given documents from another court case, which showed that the client had largely recovered from the nervous shock injury. It was held that the barrister had a duty to inform the court of the new evidence.

The key point here was that the new information demonstrated to the barrister that the case he had earlier presented to the court was false. He had a duty to correct the false impression that he had earlier created.

A special set of obligations applies in family law cases involving children. The Bar Council has offered some clear guidance in such cases.

Follow the Code

The Bar Council's 2012 guidance, *Disclosure of Unhelpful Material Disclosed to Counsel in Family Proceedings (Children)*, states that:

4. Counsel should advise the client at the earliest opportunity:
   (i) Counsel's role is to represent the client and to present the client's case to the best of his or her ability;
   (ii) Counsel has a duty of 'full and frank' disclosure in respect of relevant material that is disclosed by the client and which impacts upon the welfare of the child;
   (iii) Counsel is not in a position to conduct a trial or proceedings whilst withholding or concealing relevant information from the parties and the Court;
   (iv) The duty of confidentiality to the client owed by Counsel and contained in paragraph 702 of the Code of Conduct may be overridden as permitted by law. In particular, any information which reveals a serious risk to the welfare of a child, or serious harm to a third party, may have to be disclosed even if Counsel's instructions are discontinued.

Conclusion

This chapter has considered the broad ethical issues that arise in relation to litigation. At the heart of many of these debates is the adversarial style of adjudication that is used in England. This imagines litigation as a battle between the two sides, with the judge as the adjudicator. While this approach has some benefits, it also has problems, as this chapter has shown. There are concerns that the interests of others, including witnesses and victims of crimes, can be overlooked. It also might permit practices that work against the aim of discovering the truth. We have seen, in recent years, a slight softening of the adversarial approach, with lawyers being encouraged to work more cooperatively to enable litigation to be economically efficient and speedy.

 ## Further reading

The following articles and books discuss issues around civil litigation generally:

N. Andrews, *Fundamental Principles of Civil Procedure: Order out of Chaos in Civil Litigation in a Globalising World* (Springer, 2012).

H. Genn, 'What is civil justice for? Reform, ADR, and access to justice' (2012) 24 Yale Journal of Law and the Humanities 397.

G. Lightman, 'The civil justice system and the legal profession: The challenges ahead' (2003) 17 Civil Justice Quarterly 235.

Lord Woolf, *Access to Justice* (Lord Chancellor's Department, 1996).

The following discuss issues around criminal litigation:

A. Ashworth, 'Ethics and criminal justice', in R. Cranston (ed.) *Legal Ethics and Professional Responsibility* (Oxford University Press, 1995).

J. Doak, *Victims' Rights, Human Rights, and Criminal Justice: Reconceiving the Role of Third Parties* (Hart, 2008).

J. Hodgson, 'The future of adversarial criminal justice in 21st century Britain' (2010) 35 North Carolina Journal of International Law and Commercial Regulation 320.

P. Londono, 'Positive obligations, criminal procedure and rape cases' (2007) 2 European Human Rights Law Review 158.

D. Newman, 'Still standing accused: Addressing the gap between work and talk in firms of criminal defence lawyers' (2012) 19 International Journal of the Legal Profession 3.

F. Raitt, 'Independent legal representation for complainants in rape trials', in C. McGlynn and V. Munro (eds) *Rethinking Rape Law: International and Comparative Perspectives* (Routledge, 2010).

O. Smith and T. Skinner, 'Observing court responses to victims of rape and sexual assault' (2012) 7 Feminist Criminology 298.

R. Young and A. Sanders, 'The ethics of prosecution lawyers' (2004) 7 Legal Ethics 190.

The following discuss plea bargaining:

D. Alge, 'Negotiated plea agreements in cases of serious and complex fraud in England and Wales: A new conceptualisation of plea bargaining?' (2013) 19 Web Journal of Current Legal Issues 1.

S. Jones, 'Under pressure: Women who plead guilty to crimes they have not committed' (2011) 11 Criminology and Criminal Justice 77.

R. Lippke, *The Ethics of Plea Bargaining* (Oxford University Press, 2012).

M. McConville, 'Plea bargaining: Ethics and politics' (1998) 25 Journal of Law and Society 562.

A. Stern, 'Plea bargaining, innocence, and the prosecutor's duty to "do justice"' (2012) 25 Georgetown Journal of Legal Ethics 1027.

These works consider the nature of litigation generally:

D. Barnhizer, 'The virtue of ordered conflict: A defense of the adversary system' (2000) 79 Nebrasksa Law Review 657.

D. Ipp, 'Lawyers' duties to the court' (1998) 114 Law Quarterly Review 63.

D. Luban, 'Partisanship, betrayal and autonomy in the lawyer–client relationship: A reply to Stephen Ellmann' (1990) 90 Columbia Law Review 1004.

E. Sward, 'Values, ideology, and the evolution of the adversary system' (1989) 64 Indiana Law Journal 301.

T. Valentine and K. Maras, 'The effect of cross-examination on the accuracy of adult eyewitness testimony' (2011) 25 Applied Cognitive Psychology 554.

10 Alternative dispute resolution

 Key issues

- Most lawyers spend far more time negotiating than they do in court.
- Increasingly, parties are encouraged to use alternative ways of resolving their disagreements rather than going to court.
- Much controversy surrounds whether alternative dispute resolution (ADR) is preferable to litigation.

Introduction

Anyone who thinks, after watching television crime shows, that a lawyer's day is typically spent in court is very much mistaken. Very few cases go to court. Most are resolved by negotiation, mediation, or other forms of **alternative dispute resolution (ADR)**. We will explore all of these in this chapter.

 Definition

Alternative dispute resolution (ADR) refers to the various ways of settling a dispute that avoid the parties going to court. It typically involves the parties negotiating a resolution themselves or through their lawyers. Sometimes, a third party, such as a mediator, can be brought in to resolve the disagreement.

The ethical issues raised by ADR are complex. First, there is the question of whether mediation and negotiation are to be encouraged. Many people assume that ending up in court is the worst possible outcome and that the more cases in which the parties reach agreement on their own, the better. There is said to be a sign in a US magistrate's office that reads: 'To sue is human; to settle, divine.' This is echoed by two leading American academics, who have written:

> A trial is a failure. Although we celebrate it as the centerpiece of our system of justice, we know that trial is not only an uncommon method of resolving disputes, but

a disfavored one. With some notable exceptions, lawyers, judges, and commentators agree that pretrial settlement is almost always cheaper, faster, and better than trial.[1]

But not everyone agrees. Some see grave dangers in ADR. Certainly, there are serious concerns about it, as well as undoubted benefits. We will explore these concerns later.

Second, there is an issue about the ethical standards that lawyers should use while negotiating. Lawyers acting in court are open to public scrutiny and assessment. There are reasonably clear rules that govern how they should behave. Judges will quickly spot whether or not lawyers have done their preparation properly, or if they are employing unethical tactics. By contrast, negotiation and mediation are undertaken in private, and thus are not subject to overt scrutiny. There are few clear ethical guidelines that apply to negotiation. Indeed, it perhaps not too cynical to suggest that one reason why lawyers are keen on settlement may be that it means they avoid public scrutiny and regulation.

The forms of ADR

The following are some of the ways in which a case might be resolved without going to court.

1. *Negotiation between lawyers* This refers to situations in which lawyers reach a settlement between themselves by discussing the issues. The clients are normally involved only when asked to approve the agreement that the lawyers have reached. The client will normally trust the lawyer to get the best deal possible.

2. *Negotiation between the parties* This refers to situations in which the discussions take place between the parties, in which instance the lawyers have relatively little to do. They may advise the clients on the legal position at the start of discussions or they may be asked to comment on the proposed settlement that the parties have reached. Of course, in some cases, clients will reach agreement without seeking the advice of lawyers at all.

3. *Mediation* The clients may seek the help of a mediator—that is, someone trained in helping parties to reach an agreement. The precise role of a mediator is somewhat controversial and will be discussed in detail later in this chapter. In England, the most popular model is to use a neutral mediator, whose primary role is to help the parties to reach an agreement, irrespective of the content of the bargain. In other words, the mediator should not express a view on whether the agreement is fair and should not seek to usher the parties towards the agreement that he or she thinks is best; rather, the role of the neutral mediator is simply to facilitate the parties' discussions and in doing so help them to reach an agreement. Other models

---

[1] S. Gross and K. Syverud, 'Getting to no: A study of settlement negotiations and the selection of cases for trial' (1991) 90 Michigan Law Review 319, 320.

give mediators a more interventionist role, encouraging the parties to reach a fair agreement. Sometimes, lawyers can act as mediators and can then give neutral legal advice while also facilitating consensus.

4. *Alternative adjudication* Alternative adjudication, or arbitration as it is sometimes known, is in some ways similar to court procedure. The parties ask an arbitrator to hear their arguments and to determine the best solution. Usually, such a hearing will be less formal than that which would take place in court. Arbitrators are sometimes preferred to courts because they are cheaper and less formal. Depending on the nature of the matter, the parties might ask lawyers to represent them at the arbitration.

The main variations between these four methods can be summarised as follows.

1. *The role of the third party* As already indicated, at one extreme is arbitration, in which the arbitrator determines the outcome much as a judge rules on a case. By contrast, in mediation, the mediator usually is not meant to impose, or even influence, a decision; the mediator is merely meant to help the parties to reach an agreement.

2. *The effect of the decision* Different processes will create results that are more or less binding. In arbitration, the parties typically agree that they will comply with the decision of the arbitrator, whereas mediated agreements are binding only in so far as the parties are happy to comply with them. Indeed, one of the aims of a mediated settlement is that the parties are equipped to review the agreement over time.

3. *The role of lawyers* The extent to which lawyers are involved may vary. In some systems, such as arbitration, solicitors may play a major role. In some forms of mediation, the use of lawyers is positively discouraged.

4. *The role of law* In some systems, the aim is to produce the result that best reflects the legal principles. Arbitrators will typically determine the result that reflects the law. When lawyers negotiate, they normally seek to agree on a solution similar to that which a court might reach. In mediation, by contrast, the mediator will expect to help the parties to reach the conclusion that they think is fair, which may or may not be what a judge would think appropriate.

Digging deeper

Although the different forms of ADR are offered as alternatives to litigation, the contrast is not that straightforward. Marc Galanter is critical of the description of negotiation as 'alternative dispute resolution', arguing that:

> [T]he negotiation of disputes is not an alternative to litigation. It is only a slight exaggeration to say that it *is* litigation. There are not two distinct processes, negotiation and litigation; there is a single process of disputing in the vicinity of

official tribunals that we might call *litigotiation*, that is, the strategic pursuit of a settlement through mobilizing the court process.[2]

As we shall see, predictions about litigation impact on negotiations, and what has happened in negotiations can impact on how the court resolves a dispute. Where it is very clear what a judge would order if a case were to go to court, this can be a powerful incentive on the parties to settle with an agreement along those lines, but without incurring the expense of going to court.

There is much pressure in the legal system to discourage the parties going to court. Court proceedings are expensive to the parties, and take up judicial and court time. Most lawyers will attest that finding a negotiated settlement with which both parties can live is preferable to fighting it out in the courtroom.

Even if the case is not settled and litigation is instigated, studies suggest between 60 and 80 per cent of cases settle.[3] Of course, many more settle even before litigation is started. The Civil Procedure Rules (CPR) encourage the parties to make sensible offers and to reach agreement. A study of the new CPR found that all involved agreed that the Rules now strongly encourage settlement.[4] In particular, the new rules governing costs (see Chapter 7) and single-expert reports created a strong incentive to settle.

This chapter will start by looking at the process of negotiation, which is the way in which lawyers resolve most disputes. We will then look at other forms of ADR, including mediation and, briefly, arbitration.

Negotiation

Negotiation is at the heart of a lawyer's job. Whether it is finding a mutually acceptable set of terms for a contract or determining what damages should be paid following injuries caused by a road traffic accident, negotiation is key. There are some areas of work in which standard forms make matters easier. In conveyancing, for example, there is standard documentation for buying a house that can be used with relatively little need for negotiation, other than over the price. Similarly, there are standard levels of award available for certain injuries and so there will be little to discuss about

---

[2] M. Galanter, 'Worlds of deals: Using negotiation to teach about legal process' (1984) 34 Journal of Legal Education 368, 398.

[3] J. Peysner and M. Seneviratne, *The Management of Civil Cases: The Courts and the Post-Woolf Landscape* (Department for Constitutional Affairs, 2005).

[4] S. Gibbons, 'Group litigation, class actions and collective redress: An anniversary reappraisal of Lord Woolf's three objectives', in D. Dwyer, *Civil Procedure: Ten Years On* (Oxford University Press, 2009).

those. But in other areas there will be plenty to debate. In commercial work, the lawyers will be involved in negotiating a contract tailored to the case, designed to meet
the needs of the parties. In a family case, the lawyers will seek to negotiate the set of
arrangements that will work best for the particular family.

Although negotiating is probably the most important part of a lawyer's job, the
area is largely unregulated. There are the general duties in the professional codes to
be honest and to treat third parties fairly, discussed in Chapter 11, but these are not
specific to negotiation. Indeed, neither professional code offers any specific guidance
on negotiation at all. The contrast between the extensive regulation of litigation and
the lack of guidance on negotiation is stark. A client claiming that his or her lawyer
had negotiated negligently or in breach of ethical principles would face a huge battle.

One explanation for this is that there are a wide range of theories about the best
way in which to negotiate: there may be few standards because there is little agreement over what good mediation involves. We will now look at some of the different
theories on how to negotiate.

Theories of negotiation

There are a number of issues that will impact on how the parties go about negotiating.

The approach to negotiation

There is a vast literature on negotiation strategy and it would not be possible to set out
all of the issues here. There are, however, two basic theories: win–lose approaches; and
problem-solving approaches.

The *win–lose approach* assumes that there is a finite asset that must be divided
between the couple. For example, if a divorcing couple has assets of £100,000, the
lawyers may need to negotiate how that sum is to be divided. In a commercial transaction, one company will be trying to get as large a sum in payment as possible in
payment for a product and the other, to pay as small a price as possible. In such a
negotiation, a gain for one side must be matched by a loss to the other. Obviously,
in the divorce case, the more the wife gets, the less the husband will get; the same
applies to the parties in the commercial transaction. It is a little like a game of tug of
war, with each side pulling as hard as it can and hoping to get as much as possible.
This approach, well captured in the book *Start with No*,[5] encourages a forceful, even
aggressive, style of negotiating, regarding the other side as an enemy to be exploited
for gain. That may sound harsh, but remember that a lawyer must strive to do his or
her best for the client. A lawyer who is kind to the other party and agrees a 'reasonable' settlement may not be doing his or her job. If you were choosing a lawyer, would

---

[5] J. Camp, *Start with No* (Crown Publishing, 2002).

you not rather have a negotiator striving to get the best possible settlement for you, rather than a negotiator who was trying to be fair to each side?

The *problem-solving approach* is somewhat different in that it focuses on the needs of the parties. In particular, this explores ways of meeting the needs or interests of *both* parties. In relation to our divorcing couple, it may be that the central wish of the wife is to be able to stay in the family house, while that of the husband is to be able to buy a flat of his own. The negotiators must then find a way of achieving both parties' goal. Exploring ways of meeting these needs may be more productive than looking at the dispute from a 'win–lose' perspective. The aim is to move away from seeing the matter in terms of a 'winner' and 'loser', towards seeing both parties finding a way in which to meet both of their needs. To consider another example, in a commercial transaction, if a suitable price cannot be found, it may help to explore what the parties really need. It may be that one company is suffering a cash flow problem and needs money quickly. That company may be happier with a smaller sum, if it is paid quickly. It may be willing to agree to that smaller sum if the other company were to introduce it to other clients. In such a case, both sides may feel that they have had a successful outcome.

Carrie Menkel-Meadow explains:

> This problem-solving model seeks to demonstrate how negotiators, on behalf of liti-gators or planners, can more effectively accomplish their goals by focusing on the parties' actual objectives and creatively attempting to satisfy the needs of both par-ties, rather than by focusing exclusively on the assumed objectives of maximizing individual gain.[6]

Supporters of the problem-solving approach often claim that the win–lose approach pitches the parties against each other as adversaries. This creates a competitiveness that can disguise from the parties the solution that may be apparent to an outside observer. The parties become so fixed on winning or losing that they lose sight of what they really want from the negotiations. In the literature, an example is commonly used of two children disputing the right to the last orange in a fruit bowl. Both are adamant that they want the orange and will not share it. When the parent intervenes, it transpires that one wants the skin for a recipe for orange cake and the other, the seg-ments to eat. There is an easy way in which both of them can have their desires met.

There is a danger of idealising the problem-solving approach, however. The exam-ple of the orange is homely, but reality is rarely that easy: usually, both children want to eat all of the orange! Going back to the divorcing couple, it is easy to pretend that finding the solution that gives the husband the flat and the wife the house is the answer, but in reality, the bigger the flat the husband gets, the less money there will be for maintenance payments to the wife. In a case involving money, a gain for one nearly always means a loss for another. We cannot skin money like we can an orange.

---

[6] C. Menkel-Meadow, 'Toward another view of legal negotiation: The structure of problem solv-ing' (1984) 31 UCLA Law Review 754, 767.

Nevertheless, there is no doubt that encouraging parties to think about what they really want from the solution can help them to get around some seemingly impassable problem. In particular, persuading the parties to think about whether they have each reached their goals can be more helpful than thinking about who has won or lost.

Imaginative solutions are often essential to successful negotiations. Sometimes, it is not the sum of money that is the central issue, but the packaging of it: if payments were to be made in advance, would a lower sum be acceptable? Would offering a childcare subsidy encourage the applicant to take the job? Would delaying the start of the contract by six months ease matters? Sometimes, it is not the content of the agreement, but how it will appear to others that lies behind the dispute. Perhaps the job applicant is willing to agree to take the new job even if there is a lower salary, but does not want others to know that he or she has done so. Giving the role a fancy job title might be the key to making the offer acceptable. These are just a few examples of the kind of imaginative thinking that a good lawyer negotiating a dispute needs to employ.

It is also important to realise that *people* are at the heart of any negotiations and that we cannot abstract the people from the problem. Indeed, there are dangers in negotiation of treating everything in a logical way and overlooking the emotional values that may be at play.[7] That is why much of recent writing on good negotiation has emphasised the importance of the value of empathy—that is, of being able to imagine yourself in the other party's shoes. Only then can you begin to imagine the kind of offer that the other party may find acceptable.

Some commentators draw a distinction between competitive and cooperative negotiators.

- *Competitive* negotiators will try to get the very best deal for their clients (or themselves). They will squeeze the other party for every last concession and reach agreement only when no more concessions can be made.

- *Cooperative* negotiators will seek to find an agreement that is reasonably fair to both parties. They will not push for every last penny if they feel that both parties can agree on a price that is reasonable.

A good example of a more cooperative approach is given in a leading work on negotiation theory written by Roger Fisher and William Ury, *Getting to Yes*.[8] This promotes a principled negotiation that seeks a result that fulfils three goals:

- a fair and reasonable agreement;

- an agreement that is sufficient in expression and operation; and

- an agreement that improves, or at least does not harm, the relationship between the parties.

---

[7] C. Menkel-Meadow, 'Negotiating with lawyers, men, and things: The contextual approach still matters' (2001) 17 Negotiation Journal 257.

[8] R. Fisher and W. Ury, *Getting to Yes: Negotiation Agreement without Giving In* (Random House, 2008).

It is also notable that the goal of a lawyer under this approach is not to get the largest amount of money for the client, but rather a fair and reasonable amount. But is that ethically supportable if lawyers are meant to do the best for their clients?

Boon and Levin have made an ethical case for problem-solving negotiation, which they call 'principled negotiation':

> Principled negotiation also promotes core ethical principles, such as promoting individual autonomy, beneficence, non-maleficence and justice. By seeking to meet people's needs, principled negotiation respects individual autonomy; by attempting the [sic] expand the 'negotiating pie', it supports beneficence; by not taking advantage of the other side, it respects the principle of non-maleficence; by identifying positive criteria for resolving distributional ideas, it seeks to do justice.[9]

This depends very much on what you regard the role of the lawyer to be (see Chapter 2). It is one thing to put fairness above self-interest if you are negotiating for yourself, but if you are acting for someone else, should you do so? Perhaps the answer is that the lawyer should discuss negotiation tactics with the client, or choose what will be best for the client, regardless of what is fair for the other side.

 What would you do?

You are a family law solicitor. You represent a husband who is divorcing his wife. The wife is looking after the couple's four young children. The husband instructs you to make sure that he pays as little as possible in maintenance, and to use every trick and pressurising tactic that you can. What do you do?

What would you do if you were acting for the wife and she were to ask you to get every last penny that you could for her and the children by using every trick and pressurising tactic that you could?

Would it be justifiable to have different tactics whether acting for the wife or the husband in this case?

What would they do?

This 'What would you do?' scenario is accompanied by a podcast in which current law students debate the issues and articulate their own responses to the ethical questions that it raises. The podcast is available online at www.oxfordtextbooks.co.uk/orc/herringethics/

---

[9] A. Boon and J. Levin, *The Ethics and Conduct of Lawyers in England and Wales* (Hart, 2008), 368, citing T. Beauchamp and J. Childress, *Principles of Biomedical Ethics* (Oxford University Press, 2001).

Empirical studies suggest that solicitors and barristers normally negotiate by means of a win–lose approach.[10] Each party sets out its 'maximum offer' and then there is an attempt to reach an agreement that falls somewhere between the two figures. The studies suggest that this is done with a low-level intensity.[11] Andrew Boon and Jennifer Levin argue that this is partly because this positional approach is familiar and recognised. Perhaps such an approach assists with reaching a solution rapidly? After each side posits its opening offer, all that is left to do is to find a suitable figure somewhere between the two. But it may be that as teaching on negotiation techniques and books on the issue proliferate, styles of negotiation may change. Indeed, there is some evidence that the style adopted depends on the kind of work on offer. Studies of family lawyers in particular found little evidence of confrontational negotiation techniques; many operate instead in ways that promote the well-being of children and seek not to exacerbate conflict.[12] The problem-solving approach seems to be used more often by family lawyers.

Digging deeper

You might think that the competitive style will lead to the best results for the client, but that is not necessarily so. Competitive negotiators more often find that negotiations simply break down: they push so hard for the best deal that the other party walks away. Competitive negotiators may not mind that result: they want a deal only if it is a bargain. That works well for the client only if it is not important for him or her to get a contract. Perhaps more to the point is that competitive negotiation can backfire, especially in cases involving long-term relationships. Where the matter under negotiation is part of an ongoing relationship between the parties, then it is in both parties' interests that they leave the negotiations feeling reasonably happy with the settlement. If one party feels hard done-by, then it is unlikely to return to the other party next time it wants to transact that type of business. In family cases, if the parents are going to have to cooperate and communicate in the future, that is most likely if neither party feels taken advantage of. In short, the maintenance of goodwill between the parties may be of greater value than obtaining every last penny.

One final and very important point is that many theories on negotiation assume that the parties are rational. It is, however, crucial in some cases to be aware of the psychological and relational issues involved.[13] If we go back to the two children arguing over the orange, the truth may be that neither of them even wants the orange,

[10] Menkel-Meadow (n. 7).

[11] Boon and Levin (n. 9), 372, referring to M. Murch, 'The role of solicitors in divorce proceedings' (1977) 40 Modern Law Review 625 and J. Morison and P. Leith, *The Barristers' World and the Nature of Law* (Open University Press, 1992).

[12] J. Eekelaar, M. McLean, and J. Beinart, *Family Lawyers* (Hart, 2000).

[13] D. Kolb and J. Williams, *The Shadow Negotiation: How Women Can Master the Hidden Agendas that Determine Bargaining Success* (Simon & Schuster, 2000).

but that they have fallen out over something else and the orange is simply a symbol of the disagreement.[14] Again, family lawyers will be familiar with bitter disputes over apparently trivial matters being masks for a deeper anguish between the parties. Good negotiators will exercise high levels of empathy and insight to see what is really at the heart of the dispute. Emotion may be more important than logic in such a case.

The importance of bargaining power

A key issue in negotiations is bargaining power. The person in the stronger position at the start of the negotiations is in a better position to get a good deal. This involves a consideration of his or her current position. What will be lost if he or she does not get a deal? What might be gained if he or she wins? An example would be a small manufacturer trying to persuade a large supermarket to stock its product. If the supermarket is making good profits and is happy with its current suppliers, it will feel that it is in a good position and so has little to gain from entering into a contract with the small manufacturer. The manufacturer will need to provide the supermarket with a really good reason to enter into the deal—perhaps an exceptionally low price. However, if the supermarket is in desperate need of a refreshing new look and the small manufacturer's product is very popular, then the supermarket may have much to gain from entering into the contract. It may well be willing to pay a higher price than it would otherwise.

So, at the start of the negotiation, a key issue is always what position the parties will be in should a deal not be reached and what position they will be in if it is. Where the party is currently in a good position and the deal will not put him or her in an obviously better position, there is little incentive for him or her to reach agreement. Where the party is in a bad position and the agreement will put him or her in a good one, he or she will be keen to reach an agreement. The party with the stronger bargaining power, with less incentive to get a deal, can normally get away with making extreme demands and need to make few concessions. A key job for lawyers is to be honest with clients about their bargaining strength, so that they can be realistic about what outcome to expect.

It should not be assumed that the bargaining position of the parties is the only relevant factor; the two lawyers may also have positions of power in relation to each other. They may well need to negotiate with each other on further matters in the future; there may be rivalry between the firms or the lawyers: these matters may affect the outcome of the negotiations.

The 'shadow of the law'

There is one way in which negotiation using lawyers can differ from other negotiations: the legal dimension. Imagine, for example, that you are negotiating with a builder over the price of a job. At the end of the day, if the negotiations break down,

---

[14] Menkel-Meadow (n. 7).

the builder will walk away and that will be that. But with negotiations involving law-yers, if those break down, the parties will not necessarily walk away because of the spectre of litigation. This has led to what is called 'negotiation in the shadow of the law'. In other words, the order that a court is likely to make will influence the parties' discussion. So if an offer of £3.2 million to settle a dispute is on the table, a client is likely to refuse it if the lawyer says: 'We can reject this offer and go to court, and I predict the court will order that we be given £6 million.' However, if the lawyer were to say 'We can reject this offer and go to court, but I can't see the court giving us more than £3.5 million—and that's only if we win and there will be around £300,000 in costs if we proceed to court', then the client will be tempted to accept the offer. We might therefore expect the results reached in lawyer negotiations to be similar to those that would emerge in court.

It is not only the predicted results that impact on the negotiations. The lawyers will typically conduct their negotiations on the basis of legal principles and language. They will focus on the factors that a court would take into account. This all means that lawyers have considerable power in negotiations because they will set the tone and scope of the discussions.

Rebecca Hollander-Blumoff explains further how predictions over what the court will order can influence the outcome of the negotiations:

> Economic theories of negotiation in the civil justice system share a premise: legal actors in the civil system will settle a case if the value of the settlement is greater than the expected value at trial, minus transaction costs. If the parties agree on the expected value at trial, all cases will settle. However, parties will not always agree, because they do not have perfect information, the law is uncertain, or both. If parties had complete information and the law was entirely predictable, so that litigants could calculate perfectly accurate figures for the expected value at trial, then all cases would settle because transaction costs could be saved for both sides by avoiding trial.[15]

It would be wrong to suggest that, inevitably, a negotiated settlement will match what a court would award. Some people may have strong incentives not to go to court, owing to the publicity or time involved. Others may find legal proceedings stressful. In such cases, the parties may be willing to agree to settle for much less than a court would award. In other cases, the law may be unclear, in which case it can provide little guidance.

The role of the lawyer

As already noted, in a case involving negotiation through lawyers, the lawyer will have a key role to play. One important job of a lawyer in negotiations can be to manage cli-ents' expectations. A client may be convinced that he or she is bound to win the case and be awarded millions of pounds in damages. If the client believes this, he or she is unlikely to settle for anything less than what he or she thinks the court will award. If

---

[15] R. Hollander-Blumoff, 'Just negotiation' (2010) 88 Washington University Law Review 381, 398.

that belief is based on an overinflated view of what a court is likely to award or of his or her chances of success, then it is crucial that the lawyer is realistic with the client about what to expect.

Much has been written about the barriers that prevent people from reaching sensible agreements. These range from overconfidence to risk aversion and even prejudice.[16] People tend to place an irrational weight on avoiding risks. For example, if offered a £100 prize or a 50 per cent chance of winning £200, studies suggest that most people take the £100, even though, in economic terms, they are equivalent. Interestingly, when faced with a definite £100 fine or a 50 per cent chance of a £200 fine, however, they will prefer to take the chance, hoping to avoid any loss.[17] Lawyers should be alert to these barriers, so that they can give clients good advice. This all means that although studies of negotiations often focus on the communications between the lawyers, the discussions between the lawyers and their clients can be just as important.[18]

One ethical issue is the extent to which the lawyer should encourage the client to agree to a proposed settlement. This reflects the broader discussions over the role of a lawyer at which we looked in Chapter 3. For those who see the role of the lawyer as being simply to follow the instructions of the client, the job of the lawyer may be to advise and inform, but to respect the decision of the client. Those who see a more interventionist role for a lawyer may see his or her job as being to put pressure on the client to accept a reasonable compromise.

Lying and negotiation

Perhaps the major ethical issue in relation to this topic is whether it is acceptable to lie during negotiations. Most people, at first thought, believe it clearly to be wrong to be deceptive in negotiations. However, lying is regarded by some to be an inevitable part of the process. Typically, in negotiations, one side will start with its 'best deal' and say that it 'could not possibly accept less', even if in fact it *would* be willing to do so. Is that very common practice unethical? One of the 'tricks' of negotiating is trying to find out the other party's real 'bottom line'. If lying is unethical, there are many unethical negotiators out there.[19]

Professor Welaufer is blunt: '[E]ffectiveness in negotiations is central to the business of lawyering and a willingness to lie is central of one's effectiveness in negotiations.'[20] Niccolò Machiavelli, as is well known, was positively enthusiastic about the

---

[16] B. Spangler, 'Heads I win, tails you lose: The psychological barriers to economically efficient civil settlement and a case for third-party mediation' [2012] Wisconsin Law Review 1435.

[17] Spangler (n. 16).

[18] R. Mnookin, S. Peppet, and A. Tulumello, *Beyond Winning: Negotiating to Create Value in Deals and Disputes* (Harvard University Press, 2000).

[19] A. Hinshaw and J. Alberts, 'Doing the right thing: An empirical study of attorney negotiation ethics' (2011) 16 Harvard Negotiation Law Review 95.

[20] G. Wetlaufer, 'The ethics of lying in negotiation' (1990) 76 Iowa Law Review 1219, 1221.

benefits of lying: '[Y]ou must be a great liar.... [A] deceitful man will always find plenty who are ready to be deceived.'[21]

That conclusion—that, to be a good negotiator, you must be a good liar—is uncomfortable for many lawyers. Indeed, the Bar Council Code of Conduct (the Bar Code) seems to forbid it.

Follow the Code

The Bar Code, para 708.1, requires that:

> A barrister instructed in a mediation must not knowingly or recklessly mislead the mediator or any party or their representative.

As the Bar Code indicates, lying is seen by many as a clear moral wrong. Sissela Bok, in her influential book *Lying: Moral Choice in Public and Private Life*, sets out the wrongs of lying.[22] Lying, she argues, undermines the trust that is essential for human interaction; it interferes in the freedom of others to make informed choices about how to live their lives and it undermines the integrity of the liar.

So is there any way in which lying in negotiations can be justified? It may be said that to describe negotiation 'bluffing' as lying is unfair because there is no real deception involved. Both parties know that what is being said is not literally true.[23] When one side presents its 'best offer', all those involved realise that it may not literally be the best offer that the party can make.

An analogy might be drawn with a fruit seller in a market shouting out that her oranges are the tastiest in the world. No one really believes such a statement; rather, they interpret it in the context within which it is made. Because of the context of the comment, the statement is not a lie, because it is understood to be a deliberate exaggeration. Similarly, when advertisers tell us that a particular beer 'reaches the parts other beers cannot reach', we know that they are not being serious and that it is an advertising 'puff'. It may be that we can say the same of negotiation. Some statements are not to be taken seriously as literally true. This argument is particularly convincing if we accept that parties to negotiation share the same understanding about bluffing strategies.[24]

If we accept that argument, then it may be necessary for us to draw a distinction between different kinds of 'lie'. We may readily agree that 'I could not accept anything

---

[21] N. Machiavelli, *The Prince* (trans. Robert M. Adams, W.W. Norton & Co, 1977), ch. XVIII.

[22] S. Bok, *Lying: Moral Choice in Public and Private Life* (Vintage, 1999).

[23] C. Provis, 'Ethics, deception and labor negotiation' (2000) 28 Journal of Business Ethics 145.

[24] A. Carr, 'Is business bluffing ethical?' (1968) 46 Harvard Business Review 143.

less than £100,000' is not to be taken as literally true—but other statements of fact during the negotiations might be. We might need to explore the 'rules of the negotiating game' to see which kinds of statement were generally understood to be puffs and which were generally understood to be taken as true.[25]

This still leaves a degree of uncertainty over quite where the line is on what is or is not proper. John Cooley notes that 'white lies' in fact permeate our social interactions.[26] From 'How nice to see you' to 'I love your new haircut', we use phrases that are not literally true in order to avoid hurting our friends' feelings and to ease social interactions. And this is not limited to chit chat: employment references inflate the qualities of the applicant; politicians seek to sell policies to a doubting public; and doctors try to paint a positive picture to seriously ill patients. With that in mind, if the lies in negotiations are only 'white lies' intended to oil the cogs of negotiation, perhaps we should not be too worried about them. Indeed, Cooley argues that negotiation and mediation nearly always involve deception.

 Alternative view

Not everyone agrees that deception is expected or required as part of negotiation.[27] An understanding based on complete honesty might lead to the best results. Indeed, there is some evidence that being very honest in negotiations produces better results for you than being dishonest.[28] Notably, if, during negotiation, an overt deception is uncovered, then that deceitful behaviour is regarded as unacceptable and negotiations often break down.[29] Similarly, if a party later finds out that it was deceived into accepting a settlement, this may impact on the long-term relationship between the parties, which, in some contexts, will harm the deceitful party. Perhaps the truth depends on context.[30] Is there a difference expected in negotiations between, say, divorcing spouses and business rivals? If so, who would you expect to be more honest?!

[25] D. Schmedemann, 'Navigating the murky waters of untruth in negotiation: Lessons for ethical lawyers' (2010) 12 Cardozo Journal of Conflict Resolution 83.

[26] J. Cooley, 'Defining the ethical limits of acceptable deception in mediation' (2004) 4 Pepperdine Dispute Resolution Law Journal 263.

[27] C. Provis, 'Ethics, deception, and labor negotiation' (2000) 28 Journal of Business Ethics 145.

[28] J. Banas and J. McLean Parks, 'Lambs among lions? The impact of ethical ideology on negotiation behaviors and outcomes' (2002) 7 International Negotiation 235.

[29] R. Croson, T. Boles, and J. Murnighan, 'Cheap talk in bargaining experiments: Lying and threats in ultimatum games' (2003) 51 Journal of Economic Behavior & Organization 143.

[30] For a review of the evidence, see R. Lewicki and R. Robinson, 'Ethical and unethical bargaining tactics: An empirical study' (1998) 17 Journal of Business Ethics 665.

Peter Reilly suggests a different response to the prevalence of lying:

> Good negotiators must therefore learn how to conduct extensive background research, to engage aggressively and relentlessly in asking questions and digging for answers, and to take other proactive steps to unearth or extract the most (and most accurate) information possible from all parties at the table.[31]

His approach starts with the assumption that people will lie and that we need to try to ensure that people minimise the risk of their being exploited. Our focus should be on training negotiators to find out the truth, rather than on combating lying.

Another ethical question arises where one party to the negotiations realises that the other is under a mistake. Unusually, the issue came before the courts in the following case.

 Key case

Thames Trains v Adams [2006] EWHC 3291

Mr Adams was an American citizen who had suffered serious injuries in a train crash in England, for which Thames Trains Ltd was liable. The solicitors for Thames Trains (TT) paid £9.3 million into court. Negotiations were ongoing over the final amount that should be paid. A solicitor for Adams, Ms C, told TT's solicitors that Adams sought a total of £10 million. TT's solicitors told Ms C that no further money was available. Ms C then told another solicitor in her firm to send a fax accepting the £9.3 million paid into court as a final sum. The fax was sent, but owing to an internal error at TT's solicitors, the fax was not received properly. TT's solicitors discussed the case with TT and decided to offer a further £500,000, bringing the total to £9.8 million. Ms C then accepted that offer and a consent order was prepared on those terms. TT's solicitors later found the fax and sought to set the consent order aside.

Nelson J heard the case. Under the terms of contract law, the fax was an offer, but one that had not been accepted. Instead, TT had made an alternative offer (for £9.8 million), which had been accepted and which thus created a contract. The question Nelson J held, however, was whether Ms C had behaved unconscionably in accepting the offer for £9.8 million, knowing that TT's solicitors must not have received, or had forgotten, her offer to settle for £9.3 million. In the end, he concluded that she had not. He noted that, when Ms C accepted the higher offer, she did not know for sure whether her colleague had sent the fax. She did not know for sure that she was taking advantage of a mistake. Further, she was not under a general duty to correct her opponent's misunderstanding.

---

[31] P. Reilly, 'Was Machiavelli right? Lying in negotiation and the art of defensive self-help' (2008) 24 Ohio State Journal on Dispute Resolution 481, 484.

> Perhaps the most helpful test in the judgment was given when Nelson J asked whether the reasonable person would have expected Ms C, acting honestly and responsibly, to tell TT of her earlier offer. He asked whether the conduct was 'deceitful' or 'sharp practice'. He thought not. He relied on three particular points. The first was that Ms C had not lied; she had simply remained silent. A second was that TT had not been entirely open in saying that no further money was available when, in fact, it was. Neither side was seeking to be entirely open with the other. The third factor was that the difference between the two figures was not vast, so it was not as if one party was gaining a huge sum of money by means of an obvious mistake.

There is clearly no general obligation on a lawyer to be completely open with the other side.[32] In *Ernst & Young v Butte Mining plc*,[33] Mr Justice Walker said:

> Heavy, hostile commercial litigation is a serious business. It is not a form of indoor sport and litigation solicitors do not owe each other duties to be friendly (so far as that goes beyond politeness) or to be chivalrous or sportsmanlike (so far as that goes beyond being fair). Nevertheless, even in the most hostile litigation (indeed, especially in the most hostile litigation) solicitors must be scrupulously fair and not take unfair advantage of obvious mistakes…. The duty not to take unfair advantage of an obvious mistake is intensified if the solicitor in question has been a major contributing cause of the mistake.

In that case, there was a crucial difference between misleading conduct, which would be seen as improper, and a failure to notify the other person of a fact about which he or she was mistaken, which would not.

Regulatory possibilities

There has been some discussion over whether we need a code of ethics for negotiation.[34] There is a real difficulty inherent to developing a regulatory regime for negotiations, however. First, there needs to be a consensus over the appropriate bargaining model and, as we have seen, that does not exist. Boon and Levin, for example, are critical of the current system:

> Trust is vital to cooperation and generally benefits markets by facilitating agreement and reducing transaction costs. The current situation, where there are no definitive rules of bargaining for lawyers, is inimical to an environment of trust. In each interaction, the protagonists are unsure what to expect, and this breeds excessive caution and results in poor solutions for clients in the long term.[35]

---

[32] *Thompson v Arnold* [2007] EWHC 1875 (QB).   [33] [1996] 1 WLR 1605, 1612.

[34] W. Steel, 'Deceptive negotiating and high-toned morality' (1986) 39 Vanderbilt Law Review 1387.

[35] Boon and Levin (n. 9), 384.

They suggest that we could apply the principle that the parties will be honest in relation to material facts and add to this the following three principles:

- to explore with clients their perceptions of their interests;
- to seek a settlement where that is in the client's best interests; and
- to seek a settlement which satisfied the client's interests as far as possible and which is fair and reasonable to both sides.[36]

The difficulty is probably the last factor. The line between an unfair deal and one that is good for one side is hard to draw. If a lawyer is instructed to get the best possible price, is he or she doing anything wrong? Imagine that someone is reluctant to sell a house, but will do so if the purchaser offers an extravagant price. Is he or she doing anything wrong? These questions show how hard it can be to determine what is 'fair' or 'reasonable'.

At the root of the problem is the difficulty in defining what is 'good' negotiation. Carrie Menkel-Meadow, supporting the problem-solving approach to negotiations, helpfully suggests the following questions that could be asked to determine the answer:

1. Does the solution reflect the client's total set of 'real' needs, goals and objectives, in both the short and the long term?

2. Does the solution reflect the other party's full set of 'real' needs, goals and objectives, in both the short and long term?

3. Does the solution promote the relationship the client desires with the other party?

4. Have the parties explored all the possible solutions that might either make each better off or one party better off with no adverse consequences to the other party?'

5. Has the solution been achieved at the lowest possible transaction costs relative to the desirability of the result?

6. Is the solution achievable, or has it only raised more problems that need to be solved? Are the parties committed to the solution so it can be enforced without regret?

7. Has the solution been achieved in a manner congruent with the client's desire to participate in and affect the negotiation?

8. Is the solution 'fair' or 'just'? Have the parties considered the legitimacy of each other's claims and made any adjustments they feel are humanely or morally indicated?[37]

These questions are helpful ones for negotiating lawyers to think about. Whether they could be formulated into clear rules that provide ethical guidance is less clear. It may be, however, that posing the guidance in the form of such questions is more helpful in this context than offering a vaguely defined set of rules.[38]

---

[36] Boon and Levin (n. 9), 383.   [37] Menkel-Meadow (n. 6), 755.
[38] See Hollander-Blumoff (n. 15).

Mediation

In mediation, the clients seek to resolve the dispute themselves, with the help of a third party, a mediator. This can be done without the involvement of lawyers at all. Sometimes, lawyers advise the parties before they enter into mediation; sometimes, they do so at the end. Mediation has become a popular form of resolving disputes, particularly in family cases.[39]

There are undoubtedly a wide range of reasons why there has been an increase in the use of mediation, including the following.

- *Cost* Mediation is sometimes regarded as a cheaper alternative than litigation. The government, in the area of family law especially, has been keen to cut back the legal aid bill and mediation may offer a cheaper way of dealing with such cases.

- *Lack of confidence in the court* The appeal of mediation is that the parties can resolve the dilemma themselves and that the state is not required to take a particular line on a controversial issue. Indeed, there may be more generally a feeling that, in hotly disputed cases, a mediated resolution is as likely to be a good outcome as one produced by a judge. This has been a particularly influential argument in family law, in which cases the courts have been criticised as being anti-men or anti-women. In the government's *Family Justice Review*, it was stated:

  Generally it seems better that parents resolve things for themselves if they can. They are then more likely to come to an understanding that will allow arrangements to change as they and their children change. Most people could do with better information to help this happen. Others need to be helped to find routes to resolve their disputes short of court proceedings.[40]

- *Long-term benefits* Where the parties are likely to have an ongoing relationship, mediation offers to give the parties the tools with which they can pursue a continued relationship in an amicable way.

Much support for mediation has come from the government, in the form of the cutbacks in legal aid, which were explored further in Chapter 7. However, the judiciary too has encouraged mediation. In *Day v Cook*,[41] Ward LJ concluded his judgment thus:

Finally, I ask in utter despair, and probably in vain, is it too much to expect of these parties that they seek to avail of this court's free ADR service so that a legally qualified mediator can guide them to a long overdue resolution of this dispute which reflects little credit to the legal profession?

[39] J. Lande, 'The revolution in family law dispute resolution' (2012) 24 Family Law Dispute Resolution 411.

[40] D. Norgrave, *Family Justice Review* (Department of Education, 2012), para. 104.

[41] [2002] 1 BCLC 1, [188].

The Civil Procedure Rules (CPR) allow judges to manage cases, and this includes 'encouraging the parties to co-operate with each other in the conduct of…proceedings'[42] and alternative dispute resolution (ADR) when 'appropriate'. This is backed up by the power of a judge to award costs for unreasonable conduct, which can include refusing to mediate.[43] In *Dunnett v Railtrack*,[44] the Court of Appeal took into account the fact that Railtrack had refused to attempt mediation to resolve the dispute when it decided not to award it costs, even though it had won the litigated case.[45]

What is mediation?

The government White Paper on divorce reform defines mediation as 'a process in which an impartial third person, the mediator, assists couples considering separation or divorce to meet together to deal with the arrangements which need to be made for the future'.[46] The core goal in mediation is:

> …to help separating and divorcing couples to reach their own agreed joint decisions about future arrangements; to improve communications between them; and to help couples work together on the practical consequences of divorce with particular emphasis on their joint responsibilities to co-operate as parents in bringing up their children.[47]

While these comments were made in the context of divorce, they can be applied generally to the idea of mediation.

While there is agreement that the basic idea of mediation is that a mediator helps the parties to reach an agreement, however, there is disagreement over exactly what role the mediator is to play.

The role of the mediator

It is striking how little control there is over mediation. There is no state regulation of mediators' training, accreditation, or performance.[48] There are the College of Mediators and the Family Mediation Council, but these neither regulate the profession nor control who can act as a mediator.[49] They provide general guidance and

---

[42] CPR 1.4(a).

[43] CPR 44.4(a). See also *Burchell v Bullard* [2005] EWCA Civ 358; *Rolf v De Guerin* [2011] EWCA Civ 78.   [44] [2002] EWCA Civ 302.

[45] J. Mason, 'How might the adversarial imperative be effectively tempered in mediation?' (2012) 15 Legal Ethics 111.

[46] Lord Chancellor's Department, *Looking to the Future: Mediation and the Ground for Divorce* (HM Stationery Office, 1995), para. 5.4.

[47] Lord Chancellor's Department (n. 46), para. 6.7.

[48] A. Boon, R. Earle, and A. Whyte, 'Regulating mediators?' (2007) 10 Legal Ethics 26.

[49] L. Webley, 'Gate-keeper, supervisor or mentor? The role of professional bodies in the regulation and professional development of solicitors and family mediators undertaking divorce matters in England and Wales' (2010) 32 Journal of Social Welfare and Family Law 119.

support for mediators, but no official regulation. One consequence of this is that there is little formal guidance on precisely what role the mediator should play. This has enabled a broad range of styles of mediation to develop. As Andrew Boon, Richard Early, and Avis Whyte note:

> As to approaches to the process of mediation, there are, as currently conceived, a range of perspectives on how mediation can or should be practised. Mediation practices can be seen as involving open or closed processes; a variety of models—facilitative, evaluative (including elements of arbitration), transformative (seeking education and empowerment), activist (substantial mediator involvement, including elements of conciliation), pragmatic (agreement orientated), bureaucratic (institutional setting), therapeutic, and narrative; and involving specific areas of expertise such as international, commercial, family oriented, and community based.[50]

The following are some of the main models that a mediator could choose to adopt.[51]

1. *Minimal intervention* This model requires the mediator to ensure that there is effective communication between the parties, but it is not the job of the mediator to influence the content of the agreement.[52] So even if the mediator believes that the parties are reaching an agreement that is wholly unfair to one side, the mediator should not try to correct the balance. At the heart of this model is the notion that the agreement should be the parties' own decision. If the agreement seems fair to them, then it is not for anyone else to declare it unfair.

2. *Directive intervention* Under this model, the mediator might provide additional information and seek to influence the content of the agreement if the proposed agreement is clearly unfair to one side or the other. He or she may try to persuade one or both parties to change their views, and may attempt to persuade the parties to agree to the arrangements that the mediator believes are most suitable. The mediator may seek to change the way in which the parties view each other or their dispute.[53] It is still the parties who find the solution, but the mediator helps the parties to see the problems in a way that facilitates their resolution.

3. *Therapeutic intervention* This model sees the mediator focusing on the relationship between the parties. It promotes the belief that the dispute is merely a symptom of a broken relationship. The time spent in mediation may not therefore focus on the actual issues in dispute, but rather on trying to improve the parties' relationship

---

[50] Boon et al. (n. 48), 27.

[51] C. Menkel-Meadow, 'The many ways of mediation: The transformation of traditions, ideologies, paradigms, and practices' (1995) 11 Negotiation Journal 217; S. Imperati, 'Mediator practice models: The intersection of ethics and stylistic practices in mediation' (1997) 33 Willamette Law Review 703.

[52] K. Stylianou, 'Challenges for family mediation' (2011) 31 Family Law 874.

[53] J. Bush and R. Folger, 'Transformative mediation and third-party intervention: Ten hallmarks of a transformative approach to practice' (1996) 13 Mediation Quarterly 26.

generally. This view is influenced especially by the perception that the issue of dispute is often a symptom of an underlying relationship problem, rather than the real problem itself. This kind of approach is most useful in cases involving people in a close relationship, such as neighbours, family, or co-workers.

4. *Bureaucratic mediation* This is a highly formalised style of mediation, with strict rules about the kind of information that can be used and the style of discussion. This might be used in a school setting or in the workplace, for example. It is hoped that the formality will keep the parties calm and will encourage settlement. It keeps the discussions bounded and focused on the issue at hand. Some court-based settlements may operate in this way, with the judge guiding the parties towards a solution and playing the role of mediator.

5. *Activist mediation* In this model, the mediator comes to the case with a clear agenda and a degree of expertise. The parties expect the mediator to find the solution with them, with the agenda in mind. A good example will be a religious couple who ask a religious leader to resolve their dispute. They hope that the religious leader will use religious principles to work through the issues to find a solution. Clearly, this is only acceptable when the parties know that this is happening, because it blurs the line between mediation and arbitration.

6. *Community mediation* Community-controlled mediation typically involves quite a number of community members. It will appear more like a meeting than a private mediation. This is normally used when the dispute is seen as harming the community and there are communal interests involved. There are concerns about who takes a leading role in this approach, with self-appointed community leaders often seen to be exercising power over vulnerable members.

7. *Pragmatic mediation* This type of mediation tends to be 'on-the-spot peacemaking', and occurs when someone steps in to help parties to resolve an immediate situation and to find a resolution.

In England and Wales, the model of minimalist intervention is the most often used.[54] Resolution, the solicitors' organisation promoting non-contentious approaches to family law, explains this standard model to the public in the following way:

> Mediators are trained to help resolve disputes over all issues faced by separating couples, or specific issues such as arrangements for any children. A mediator will meet with you and your partner together and will identify those issues you can't agree on and help you to try and reach agreement.
>
> Mediators are neutral and will not take sides, so they cannot give advice to either of you. They will usually recommend that you obtain legal advice alongside the mediation process and will guide you as to when this should happen.[55]

---

[54] UK College of Family Mediators, *Mediation* (UK College of Family Mediators, 2000), para. 42.
[55] Resolution, *Alternatives to Court* (Resolution, 2013), 1.

It is important to realise that, under this model, the mediator is not powerless to prevent an unfair agreement being reached.[56] Commonly, before commencing mediation, a mediator will hold a 'screening meeting' to ascertain whether or not mediation is suitable. If the mediator decides that the parties were not in a fair bargaining position (for example one had been violent to the other in the past), then he or she may refuse to go ahead with the mediation. Similarly, if during the mediation the mediator is concerned that one party is taking advantage of the other, the mediator is free to stop the mediation and to encourage the parties to seek legal advice.

Although this minimalist model is still the standard one, it has been questioned. There is some evidence that the goal of non-intervention is rarely achieved in practice.[57] We will discuss this issue shortly. Some commentators believe that there is gradual change in attitudes over the role of mediators and that they are becoming increasingly interventionist, at least on key principles.[58] So a mediator in a family case might encourage the parties to put the interests of the child first and to decrease the bitterness of the family dispute.[59] There may therefore be some basic cultural norms of which it is legitimate for the mediator to remind the parties.[60] What is not permissible is for the mediator to seek to impose his or her own norms on the couple.[61] However, this view is based on our being able to draw a reasonably clear line between which norms are social and which are personal. One suggestion is that as long as the mediator is open about what norms he or she is bringing to the discussion and the couple accept this, the mediator is acting appropriately.[62]

One important aspect of mediation is that it is designed to be forward-looking.[63] In other words, the focus is on how the parties can move forward and find a solution to their problems. Hence, in the family law context, the mediator does not encourage the parties to look back at which of them were to blame for the breakdown of the relationship, but rather to look to the future and work out who is going to care for the children. A similar attitude is found in employment disputes, in which the focus

[56] E. Waldman, 'Identifying the role of social norms in mediation: A multiple model approach' (1997) 48 Hastings Law Journal 703.

[57] R. Bush and J. Folger, *The Promise of Mediation: Responding to Conflict through Empowerment and Recognition* (Jossey-Bass Publishers, 1994); D. Kolb, *When Talk Works: Profiles of Mediators* (Jossey-Bass Publishers, 1994); S. Engle Merry and N. Milner (eds) *The Possibility of Popular Justice: A Case Study of American Community Justice* (University of Michigan Press, 1993).

[58] B. Wilson, 'Do mediators care?' (2009) 39 Family Law 201.

[59] M. Stepan, 'Mediation is moving on' (2010) 40 Family Law 545.

[60] S. Belhorn, 'Settling beyond the shadow of the law: How mediation can make the most of social norms' (2005) 20 Ohio State Journal on Dispute Resolution 981.

[61] See the discussion in Stepan (n. 59).

[62] S, Imperati, D. Brownmiller, and D. Marshall, 'If Freud, Jung, Rogers, and Beck were mediators, who would the parties pick and what are the mediator's obligations?' (2007) 43 Idaho Law Review 645.

[63] J. Poitras, 'The paradox of accepting one's share of responsibility in mediation' (2007) 23 Negotiation Journal 267.

is on how the employer and employee can work together in the future rather than on getting too tied up with who said what to whom. Indeed, some mediators claim that focusing on the past prevents the couple from moving on to the future.[64] This can provide a clear distinction between mediation and legal proceedings, in which typically the primary role of the court is to establish the facts of the case before it can determine how the parties should move on.

We can now consider the arguments over the benefits and disadvantages of mediation.

The case in favour of mediation

The following are some of the arguments used to support mediation.

1. A key argument in favour of mediation is that there is no 'right answer' to a particular dispute. If the parties reach a solution that is right for them, no one else should be able to regard their agreement as the wrong one. It could be said to be none of the state's business to seek to interfere in the arrangement that the parties have reached. Supporters of litigation might think that courts can ascertain the facts and provide the correct answer. But that is rather old-fashioned, as Carrie Menkel-Meadow argues:

   If late-twentieth century learning has taught us anything, it is that truth is illusive, partial, interpretable, dependent on the characteristics of the knowers as well as the known, and, most importantly, complex. In short, there may be more than just two sides to every story.[65]

   Alex Wellington argues that ADR is consistent with the basic tenets of liberalism—in particular, the importance of state neutrality over concepts of the good life, the respect for autonomy, and the importance of tolerating different ways of life and values.[66] We should prefer the parties using their own values and understandings of fairness to a privileged judge using his. Indeed, in the context of family law, the House of Lords itself has accepted that, in many cases, a variety of solutions could be appropriate and that there is not necessarily a right or wrong one.[67] If that is so, should not the solution to which the parties agree be preferred over one imposed on them? Indeed, Menkel-Meadow goes further and questions whether courts are a good way in which to ascertain facts: 'Binary, oppositional presentations of facts in dispute are not the best way for us to learn the truth; polarized debate distorts the truth, leaves out important information, simplifies complexity, and obfuscates rather than clarifies.'[68]

---

[64] Poitras (n. 63).

[65] C. Menkel-Meadow, 'The trouble with the adversary system in a postmodern, multicultural world' (1996) 38 William and Mary Law Review 5, 23.

[66] A. Wellington, 'Taking codes of ethics seriously: Alternative dispute resolution and reconstitutive liberalism' (1999) 12 Canadian Journal of Law and Jurisprudence 297.

[67] *Piglowska v Piglowski* [1999] 2 FLR 763, HL.   [68] Menkel-Meadow (n. 65).

There are three key issues here. The first is whether it is correct that there is no right answer for a court to declare. If there is not, then the solution reached by the parties is likely to be as good as the solution that would be reached by anyone else.

If, however, you do not accept this and believe that it is possible to state that some solutions are better than others, then the second key issue is whether there is a good reason to believe that the court is more likely to find a better solution than the parties in mediation.

Third, even if you accept that some solutions are better than others and that the court is more likely than the parties to find a better solution, there is still the issue of whether the state, through the courts, should be able to impose the right answer (or *a* right answer) on the parties. The law might want to impose a right answer on the parties because there are interests either of third parties, or of the state itself, which justify its doing so.[69] So, for example, many argue that mediation is not acceptable in family cases because it does not adequately protect the interests of the child: there is nothing to prevent the parents from reaching an agreement in mediation that does not promote the interests of the child. However, such an argument would need to demonstrate that allowing judges to resolve disputes over children has a better chance of promoting children's interests than letting parents reach their own decisions.

2. Supporters of mediation claim that the solutions agreed by the parties are more effective than court orders in the long term.[70] There are three aspects to the argument that mediation produces more effective results. The first is that, because the parties have reached the agreement themselves, they will more easily be able to renegotiate it together if difficulties with the agreement subsequently arise.

Second, the solution reached through mediation will be one that the parties can tailor to their particular lifestyles rather than a formula applied by lawyers or judges to deal with 'these kinds of cases'.

Third, it is argued that, because mediation can be hard work and emotionally exhausting, the parties will therefore feel more committed to the agreement than if it had been given to them by a judge. In fact, there is some dispute over whether mediated settlements do last well, with one study finding that only half of all mediated agreements were intact six months after they were reached.[71]

---

[69] Or even that there are rights that the divorcing couple have themselves, which they should not be permitted to negotiate away during the process of mediation.

[70] HM Government, *Parental Separation: Children's Needs and Parents' Responsibilities* (HM Stationery Office, 2004), para. 2. For a discussion of the evidence against this proposition, see Eekelaar et al. (n. 12).

[71] G. Mantle, *Helping Families in Dispute* (Ashgate, 2001). For other studies finding no evidence that mediated agreements were longer-lasting than court orders, see, e.g., J. Walker, *Picking up the Pieces: Marriage and Divorce Two Years after Information Provision* (Department for Constitutional Affairs, 2004).

3. Mediation enables the parties to communicate more effectively. The mediators can take the parties in dispute and give them the tools with which to communicate with each other, which may be essential if they are in an ongoing relationship. Opponents of mediation argue that lawyers can filter out particularly offensive communications and so, in fact, reduce bitterness, while mediation, by contrast, can increase bitterness, especially where it fails. The questions are: are parties helped by mediation or does the process of mediation exacerbate bitterness; and does litigation make the parties enemies of each other?[72] The answer to both questions is: in some cases, it does, and in some cases, it does not. We simply do not yet know which outcome is the commonest.

4. Mediation gives time for all issues that are important to the parties to be discussed. It has been a complaint of the legal process that it 'transforms' the parties' disputes: their arguments are put into legal terminology and some issues that might be of concern to them are ignored.[73] This argument can include a claim that mediation can tackle the emotional issues involved in divorce. The mediation process can not only help to resolve the dispute, but perhaps also help the parties to come to terms with their feelings about one another and begin the post-breakdown healing process.[74] This might be why, in successful mediation, parties report high levels of satisfaction with the result.[75]

5. Mediation saves costs—or at least the government certainly hoped that mediation would save costs. By using only one mediator rather than two lawyers, and with the hourly rate for mediators being generally less than that for lawyers, savings could be made. In fact, whether or not mediation saves money depends on the success rate of mediation. The present research indicates that, in the context of family law, if all couples were required to attend state-subsidised mediation, it would be likely to lead to increased, not reduced, costs.[76] This is because of the extra costs involved where mediation fails. The Newcastle study (based on people volunteering for mediation) suggested that only about 39 per cent of mediations were wholly successful; 41 per cent were partially successful and 20 per cent failed.[77] For the 20 per cent of totally failed mediations,[78] there are inevitably greater costs than if the parties had gone to lawyers to begin with, without using mediation. If mediation is partly successful, the parties still need to consult lawyers to resolve the remaining issues. But asking a lawyer to resolve 50 per cent of a dispute does not mean incurring only 50 per cent

---

[72] Mason (n. 45).

[73] A. Sarat and W. Felstiner, *Divorce Lawyers and their Clients* (Oxford University Press, Oxford University Press).

[74] C. Richards, 'Allowing blame and revenge into mediation' (2001) 31 Family Law 775.

[75] L. Teitelbaum and L. Dupaix, 'Alternative dispute resolution and divorce: Natural experimentation in family law', in J. Eekelaar and M. MacLean (eds) *A Reader on Family Law* (Oxford University Press, 1994).

[76] Walker (n. 71), 134.   [77] Walker (n. 71), 134.

[78] The success rate would be likely to be significantly lower if mediation were forced on all divorcing couples, because the survey covered those who had volunteered to participate in mediation.

of what the costs would have been had he or she been asked to resolve the whole of the dispute. This is because it is the gathering together of all of the facts and information that takes up most of a lawyer's time, and this will need to be done whether the lawyer is resolving all or only a part of a dispute. So resolving 50 per cent of a dispute may cost 75 per cent of what the fee would have been for resolving all of a dispute, in which case it is not clear that mediation actually saves costs.[79] Even if the mediation is completely successful, there are some who believe the costs will be greater.[80]

An important study looking at the comparative costs of mediation and solicitor-based negotiation found that mediation could cost between 65 per cent and 115 per cent of the solicitor-based negotiation.[81] The study suggested that if the success rate for mediation were to fall below 60 per cent (which the evidence suggests it is very likely to do), there would be no savings. A more recent study found that 59 per cent of cases were wholly or partially successful for mediation.[82] A study looking at the outcomes for non-family cases found the settlement rate among small claims cases that proceeded through mediation to be 82 per cent. This is impressively high, but in fact that represented only 34 per cent of cases that were referred to mediation at one venue and 10 per cent at another. In other words, while many cases were referred to mediation, only a small number were able to be taken on, although where they were there, there was a good success rate.[83] Although a definitive answer is not yet available, it seems that there are some categories of case in which mediation offers a cheaper solution, but that this cannot be assumed to be true in all kinds of case.

The case against mediation

The following are some of the arguments against mediation.

1. Some opponents of mediation argue that it is, in fact, impossible for a mediator to be purely impartial.[84] A mediator can influence the content of the agreement, through explicit as well as indirect means, such as body language or the way in which he or she responds to one party's proposal.[85] For example, one party might make a proposal and whether the mediator immediately asks the other party what

---

[79] G. Davis, S. Clisby, and Z. Cumming, *Monitoring Publicly Funded Family Mediation* (Legal Services Commission, 2003) found that 57 per cent of their sample stated that their partner was not keen to resolve the legal disputes and compromise.

[80] Davis et al. (n. 79), 5.

[81] G. Bevan and G. Davis, 'A preliminary exploration of the impact of family mediation on legal aid costs' (1999) 11 Child and Family Law Quarterly 411.

[82] House of Commons Public Accounts Committee, *Legal Services Commission: Legal Aid and Mediation for People Involved in Family Breakdown* (HM Stationery Office, 2007).

[83] Advice Services Alliance, *Small Claims Mediation: Does It Work?* (Advice Services Alliance, 2006).

[84] C. Piper, 'Norms and negotiation in mediation and divorce', in M. Freeman (ed.) *Divorce: Where Next?* (Dartmouth, 1996).

[85] R. Dingwall, 'Divorce mediation: Should we change our mind?' (2010) 32 Journal of Social Welfare and Family Law 107.

he or she thinks about the proposal or asks the first party to expand on the proposal might have a profound effect on the course of the negotiation. Piper, in her study of mediation, notes that a mediator would not repeat what one party had said and would move on if that party were to be introducing what the mediator believed to be 'non-relevant matters'.[86] Scott Jacobs found three ways in which a mediator, often unintentionally, can influence the course of the discussion: by asking questions (for example asking a party 'Do you think that's fair?'); in summarising the discussions that the parties have (inevitably, highlighting some points and glossing over others); and in the provision of information.[87] He accepts that mediators may be unaware that subtly, but significantly, these can influence the course of the discussions.

If the mediator does directly or indirectly affect the content of the agreement, then there are concerns that mediation will become, in effect, adjudication in secret.[88] The mediator will act like a judge, but without having to give any reasons for a decision or to be publicly accountable for the outcome.

2. One powerful criticism of mediation is that mediation can work against the interests of the weaker party. Weakness in the bargaining position may stem from three sources, the first among which is a lack of information, coupled with the inability to verify presented information. Because mediators have less effective methods of checking facts compared with the disclosure mechanisms used by lawyers,[89] it is likely to work against the interests of the more honest party. A party's lack of personal expert knowledge may also impede its bargaining position. For example, if one party is a trained accountant and the other has an aversion to figures, then, when the parties discuss financial issues, there might be an inequality of power.

The second weakness in the bargaining process may result from a lack of negotiation skills. One party may regularly take part in negotiations in the course of his or her work and may be trained to push for an agreement, while the other may not.

The third weakness can be psychological. Women, it is argued by some, are generally naturally conflict-averse.[90] They may more readily agree to a settlement rather than argue, partly as a result of being socially conditioned to avoid conflict.[91] There is also an argument that women generally may put greater value on things that are not material in value and/or that they may have lower self-esteem.[92] One survey of

---

[86] Piper (n. 84).

[87] S. Jacobs, 'Maintaining neutrality in dispute mediation: Managing disagreement while managing not to disagree' (2002) 34 Journal of Pragmatics 1403.

[88] C. Izumi, 'Implicit bias and the illusion of mediator neutrality' (2010) 34 Washington University Journal of Law and Policy 71.

[89] P. Parkinson, *Family Law and the Indissolubility of Parenthood* (Cambridge University Press, 2011).

[90] J. Doughty, 'Identity crisis in the family courts? Different approaches in England and Wales and Australia' (2009) 31 Journal of Social Welfare and Family Law 231.

[91] Walker (n. 71) argues that women are more concerned than men with keeping the relationship amicable.

[92] P. Bryan, 'Killing us softly: Divorce mediation and the politics of power' (1992) 40 Buffalo Law Review 441.

the research concluded that, generally, women were not putting their own interests first in mediation and therefore were losing out to men, who were.[93] However, these points are controversial and there is, in fact, much debate over whether women do better or worse when using mediation.[94]

There are particular concerns about using mediation in family law cases in which the relationship has been characterised by violence.[95] In such cases, mediators themselves accept that mediation is unsuitable because cooperation and proper negotiations can take place only where there is no abuse or fear of abuse.[96] The concern is whether the mediators can always ascertain those cases in which there has been domestic violence.[97] Particularly difficult are cases in which the parties do not regard themselves as victims of domestic violence.[98] In a recent study of mediation, it was found that mediators used a variety of techniques to put domestic violence issues to one side.[99] It may be that increased awareness of domestic violence issues and improved training can improve the response to violence among mediators.[100] These are powerful points, but we may need to consider whether litigation offers a better protection for victims of domestic abuse.[101]

3. Perhaps most fundamentally there is an issue about whether, if you believe that people have legal rights, we should have a system that does not guarantee their enforcement. Lord Dyson, a Supreme Court judge, has asked:

> Can it be right that parties who have exercised their right to go to court can be forced to sit down with the individual they believe to have wronged them to try to find a compromise which would probably leave them worse off than had they had their day in court? Leaving aside any human rights issues then, in my view, this simply cannot be right...[102]

When discussing the benefits of mediation, supporters emphasise the benefits of allowing the parties to bring their own values to the dispute. But that can be seen

---

[93] S. Tilley, 'Recognising gender differences in all issues mediation' (2007) 37 Family Law 352.

[94] Menkel-Meadow (n. 65).

[95] F. Kaganas and C. Piper, 'Domestic violence and divorce mediation' (1994) 16 Journal of Social Welfare and Family Law 265.

[96] Where mediators detect a clear imbalance of power that they cannot counter, they should terminate the mediation.

[97] R. Ballard, A. Holtzworth-Munroe, A. Applegate, C. Beck, and J. Connie, 'Detecting intimate partner violence in family and divorce mediation: A randomized trial of intimate partner violence screening' (2011) 17 Psychology, Public Policy, and Law 241.

[98] Davis et al. (n. 79), 5, found that 41 per cent of women and 21 per cent of men in their sample stated that fear of violence made it difficult to resolve issues in their case.

[99] T. Trinder, A. Firth, and C. Jenks, '"So presumably things have moved on since then?" The management of risk allegations in child contact dispute resolution' (2010) 24 International Journal of Law, Policy and the Family 29. [100] Parkinson (n. 89).

[101] M. Moffitt, 'Three things to be against ("settlement" not included)' (2009) 78 Fordham Law Review 1203.

[102] Lord Dyson, *Mediation in the English Legal Order Six Years after Halsey* (Ministry of Justice, 2010), 11.

as undermining the importance of law and legal rights. If the law has decided that a consumer should have a right to a certain remedy in a particular case, should we not insist on the law's values being upheld? This is a particular concern if the prejudices of the parties or their ignorance are used as ways of denying one of the parties his or her rights.

4. There are concerns over whether mediation affects the interests of third parties. Mediation allows the couple to find a solution that works for them; in a court, however, the judge can consider the interests of other people involved and even the interests of the wider community. A particularly telling point on this concerns children's interests on separation. In mediation, the parents might agree on the solution that they think is best, but that is no guarantee that the solution will work well for the children. As Martin Richards explains:

> [W]hile mediation may do much to help parents reach agreements and set up work-able arrangements for children, it cannot protect children's interests. It must rely on the information about children that the parties bring to the sessions. Necessarily this information will be presented in the light of parental perceptions, hopes, fears, anxieties, and guilt. In most cases this will serve children's interests well enough, but it cannot be termed protection as it is not based on an independent view.[103]

Certainly, there seems little in mediation that will ensure that the rights of children are protected. The argument applies not only to children; a court can also take into account the interests of the environment or the general good, which will be over-looked in mediation.[104]

5. There are doubts whether mediators have the expertise to consider the complex tax and financial issues that may have to be dealt with in some cases.[105] For example, even experienced solicitors struggle with the valuation and sharing of pensions on divorce, and most seek expert advice. To expect mediators and the couple to deal with such issues themselves is to expect too much.

 What would you do?

Do you think that there are some kinds of case that are better suited to mediation than others? Do you think that you would like to mediate if you were in dispute? Why? If you were a mediator, what approach would you take to mediation?

---

[103] M. Richards, 'But what about the children? Some reflections on the divorce White Paper' (1995) 4 Child and Family Law Quarterly 223, 224.

[104] R. Baruch Bush and J. Folger, 'Mediation and social justice: Risks and opportunities' (2012) 27 Ohio Journal of Dispute Resolution 1.

[105] R. Dingwall and D. Greatbatch, 'Family mediators: What are they doing?' (2001) 31 Family Law 379.

Lawyers and mediation

Lawyers can interact with mediation in many ways. They can, of course, recommend that their clients use mediation if they are in an intractable dispute, although it seems rare that lawyers choose to do so.[106] Lawyers may be asked by clients either before or during mediation for some general advice as to their legal rights. Alternatively, a lawyer might be consulted after mediation and be asked to put the agreement reached into the form of a court order.

Lawyers may feel uncomfortable advising clients in this way. Without fully ascertaining the facts and receiving all of the documentation, a lawyer may feel that he or she cannot give adequate advice. Yet that will involve the kind of detailed investigations that mediation is, in part, designed to avoid. Lawyers advising in these contexts will want to be very careful in explaining what kind of advice they are giving.

Occasionally, lawyers can be involved by sitting in on mediation, or at least by being regularly consulted during its course. Mediators complain that this decreases the chance of a settlement and there is some evidence in support of that argument.[107] Lawyers may respond that their involvement saved the client from accepting an unfair mediated agreement.

In an interesting analysis, John Lande suggests that mediation will play an increasing role in lawyers' practice.[108] He foresees 'liti-mediation' under which mediation becomes 'the normal way of ending litigation'. He foresees that a broad range of styles of mediation will be available, often specialised for particular kinds of cases, and that lawyers will need to assist their clients in selecting and being involved in the mediation.

Mediation and confidentiality

Mediation is based on trust. Each side is expected to be fully open with the other. To assist this, the content of the discussions and all information disclosed in mediation is protected by the rules of confidentiality, and cannot be disclosed without the consent of both parties.[109] There is, of course, an exception where the mediation discussions reveal a risk to children, in which case the potential harm to a child can justify interference with confidentiality.[110]

---

[106] L. Mulcahy, ' Can leopards change their spots? An evaluation of the role of lawyers in medical negligence mediation' (2001) 8 International Journal of the Legal Profession 203.

[107] J. Poitras, A. Stimec, and J.-F. Roberge, 'The negative impact of attorneys on mediation outcomes: A myth or a reality?' (2010) 26 Negotiation Journal 9.

[108] J. Lande, 'How will lawyering and mediation practices transform each other?' (1997) 24 Florida Law Review 839.

[109] *Practice Direction (Family Division: Conciliation)* [1992] 1 WLR 147.

[110] *Re D (Minors)* [1993] Fam 231.

 **Application**

> It is especially important, if mediation breaks down and the matter then becomes subject to litigation, that you remember the importance of confidentiality. You cannot rely in the litigation on matters that have been spoken about in mediation. This can be very frustrating, especially if you know that the other side is lying, because of what was said in mediation.

Collaborative law

Collaborative law is an approach that has been adopted and developed by quite a number of firms of solicitors. It is growing in popularity. It is perhaps best seen as a middle path between mediation and negotiation through lawyers. At its heart is a rejection of litigation as a helpful way of resolving financial disputes and the development of the following four principles.

- There is to be an open, but privileged, sharing of advice and information with the other participants.

- There is to be a face-to-face four-way meeting (two clients, each with their lawyer) designed to reach an agreement.[111] The parties may also be assisted by other professionals, such as an accountant.

- The negotiations are interest-based. This means that the process begins by identifying the interests of the parties and then negotiations seek to find a solution to meet those interests. This differs from the orthodox approach in which each party sets out what it wants.

- The clients and lawyers commit to resolving issues without going to court. Participants sign a formal participation agreement, including that the lawyers will not represent the parties in any litigation if the negotiations break down.

Users of the collaborative approach claim a success rate of over 85 per cent and increased rates of satisfaction from clients, although there is not yet sufficient data to confirm this.[112] There is much that is attractive about this model, which in a way formalises what was common practice in the past. It has received support from the judiciary, being described in *S v P (Settlement by Collaborative Law Process)*[113] as designed 'to provide as much encouragement as possible to people to resolve their difficulties in this civilized and sensible way'.[114] Unsurprisingly, it is family law that has led the way in the use of collaborative law.

---

[111] K. Wright, 'The evolving role of the family lawyer: The impact of collaborative law on family law practice' (2011) 23 Child and Family Law Quarterly 370; G. Bishop, S. Kingston, S. Max, and P. Pressdee, 'Collab lite: No substitute for the real thing' (2011) 41 Family Law 1556.

[112] Bishop et al. (n. 111).   [113] [2008] 2 FLR 2040.

[114] For further discussion, see P. Tesler, *Collaborative Family Law* (William Morrow, 2011).

The focus of collaborative law is on the objectives of each of the parties and seeking to find a solution that meets as many of these objectives as possible.[115] Where helpful, other professionals can be brought in to give specialist advice. A divorcing couple, for example, might bring in a pensions expert to advise on that issue.

Collaborative law is not without its critics. There have been concerns that people feel under considerable pressure to reach an agreement. The process is about putting the client in charge of the settlement, with the lawyer being a facilitator of that. If a party is particularly meek, or attaches great significance to one issue and is willing to sacrifice anything for that issue, his or her interests may not be adequately protected. Katherine Wright's study found cases in which agreements were reached that the lawyers agreed they would have urged their clients not to agree to in a traditional negotiation approach.[116] Solicitors using collaborative law can be put in a difficult position if they feel that their clients are not negotiating effectively or are agreeing to a settlement that is to their disadvantage.

Resolution defines collaborative law in the following way:

> Under the collaborative law process, each person appoints their own collaboratively trained lawyer and you and your respective lawyers all meet together to work things out face to face. Both of you will have your lawyer by your side throughout the process and so you will have their support and legal advice as you go.
>
> You and your lawyers sign an agreement that commits you to trying to resolve the issues without going to court and prevents them from representing you in court if the collaborative process breaks down. That means all are absolutely committed to finding the best solutions by agreement, rather than through court proceedings.[117]

Collaborative law shares many of the advantages of mediation, without some of its disadvantages. By being outside the court system, it can progress at the speed that the parties wish and focus on the issues closest to their hearts. It is private. The parties can tailor solutions that work for their lives. It has the benefits of legal advice, ensuring that the parties know their legal positions. Further, with a lawyer representing each party, there is perhaps less chance of one party taking advantage of the other. A major disadvantage, of course, is costs: with both parties receiving and paying for legal advice, collaborative law is currently available only to wealthier clients.

Arbitration

Arbitration has been increasing in popularity in recent years, especially in commercial cases. Essentially, it involves the parties reaching a contract under which they agree to take their dispute to a third party (an arbitrator) and to be bound by his or her

---

[115] G. Voegele, L. Wray, and R. Ouskytt, 'Collaborative law: A useful tool for the family law practitioner to promote better outcomes' (2007) 33 William Mitchell Law Review 971.

[116] Wright (n. 111).   [117] Resolution, *Collaborative Law* (Resolution, 2013), 1.

decision. Often, the parties, when entering a contract, will agree in advance that if a dispute arises, the issue will be resolved by arbitration. London has been increasingly recognised as one of the world's leading centres for arbitration.

The attraction to companies of this approach is that it offers a cheaper form of dispute resolution. It also enables the parties to determine their own rules for the arbitration. The arbitrator could apply English law to determine the resolution, but often the parties will use their own, or internationally developed, principles. This can be particularly helpful in international disputes, in which the worry may be that litigation in a range of countries may be recommended if there is a dispute, creating considerable expense.

An added benefit of arbitration is that the dispute can be kept private and confidentiality can be preserved. The parties can also select as an arbitrator an expert in their field. This may be particularly beneficial in a highly specialised area (such as intellectual property). The parties may believe that an expert, familiar with the commercial realities, will be better equipped to find an appropriate resolution than a judge. A further benefit is that the parties can limit rights to appeal and therefore that arbitrated settlements may be more final than litigated ones.

Despite these advantages, there are some disadvantages. The arbitrator has no power to compel third parties to disclose documents or to attend the arbitration; a judge's powers in relation to a third party are far more extensive. Specialist arbitrators can become very busy and so delays can result from that. Further, the lack of coercive powers of an arbitrator can mean that a party to arbitration who is determined to be uncooperative can cause severe delays and costs. There are fewer sanctions available to an arbitrator than there are to a judge in such a situation.

Arbitration is governed by the Arbitration Act 1996. This is a complex piece of legislation and we cannot go into the detail of it here. The key points to note are that section 9 makes it clear that if a party seeks to bring court proceedings over breach of the arbitration agreement, the court can stay the proceedings and require the parties to arbitrate. Under section 24, the court does have the power to remove an arbitrator who has abused his or her position or in the event of his or her incapacity. There is also a general duty under section 33 that the arbitration tribunal acts fairly and impartially.

Conclusion

The cost, publicity, stress, and time involved in litigation have all meant that clients are often keen to avoid going to court. It is not surprising therefore that the vast majority of cases are resolved by negotiation through lawyers. In some areas, lawyers are being avoided altogether and the parties are seeking to use mediation to resolve their disputes. These forms of alternative dispute resolution (ADR) are marked by the lack of clear regulation governing them. As we have seen, there is little agreement over the ethical principles that govern those negotiating or mediating. One thing is clear, however: the issues covered in this chapter are perhaps the most important in this book. We need to get better at negotiating and mediating in an ethical and successful way.

 ## Further reading

On mediation:

R. Baruch Bush and J. Folger, 'Mediation and social justice: Risks and opportunities' (2012) 27 Ohio Journal of Dispute Resolution 1.

S. Belhorn, 'Settling beyond the shadow of the law: How mediation can make the most of social norms' (2005) 20 Ohio State Journal on Dispute Resolution 981.

A. Boon, R. Earle, and A. Whyte, 'Regulating mediators?' (2007) 10 Legal Ethics 26.

J. Bush and R. Folger, 'Transformative mediation and third-party intervention: Ten hallmarks of a transformative approach to practice' (1996) 13 Mediation Quarterly 26.

R. Field, 'Exploring the potential of contextual ethics in mediation', in F. Bartlett, R. Mortensen, and K. Tranter (eds) *Alternative Perspectives on Lawyers and Legal Ethics* (Routledge, 2011).

S. Imperati, 'Mediator practice models:T intersection of ethics and stylistic practices in mediation' (1997) 33 Willamette Law Review 703.

C. Izumi, 'Implicit bias and the illusion of mediator neutrality' (2010) 34 Washington University Journal of Law and Policy 71.

J. Lande, 'How will lawyering and mediation practices transform each other?' (1997) 24 Florida Law Review 839.

T. Trinder, A. Firth, and C. Jenks, ' "So presumably things have moved on since then?" The management of risk allegations in child contact dispute resolution' (2010) 24 International Journal of Law, Policy and the Family 29.

On negotiation:

A. Hinshaw and J. Alberts, 'Doing the right thing: An empirical study of attorney negotiation ethics' (2011) 16 Harvard Negotiation Law Review 95.

R. Hollander-Blumoff, 'Just negotiation' (2010) 88 Washington University Law Review 381.

C. Menkel-Meadow, 'Toward another view of legal negotiation: The structure of problem solving' (1984) 31 UCLA Law Review 754.

C. Menkel-Meadow, 'The trouble with the adversary system in a postmodern, multicultural world' (1996) 38 William and Mary Law Review 5.

M. Moffitt, 'Three things to be against ("settlement" not included)' (2009) 78 Fordham Law Review 1203.

B. Spangler, 'Heads I win, tails you lose: The psychological barriers to economically efficient civil settlement and a case for third-party mediation' [2012] Wisconsin Law Review 1435.

W. Steel, 'Deceptive negotiating and high-toned morality' (1986) 39 Vanderbilt Law Review 1387.

On collaborative law:

G. Voegele, L. Wray, and R. Ouskytt, 'Collaborative law: A useful tool for the family law practitioner to promote better outcomes' (2007) 33 William Mitchell Law Review 971.

K. Wright, 'The evolving role of the family lawyer: The impact of collaborative law on family law practice' (2011) 23 Child and Family Law Quarterly 370.

11 Third parties

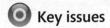

Key issues

- What obligations do lawyers owe to third parties?
- Do lawyers owe duties to the opposing side in litigation?
- What is the role of the lawyer when suing someone who is not represented?
- When can a lawyer be liable for incurring the other side's legal costs?

Introduction

At the heart of lawyers' ethics is the principle that a lawyer must act on his or her client's behalf. But do lawyers ever owe obligations to other people? That question is the focus of this chapter. When, and to what extent, do lawyers owe duties to people who are not their clients?

There are some who argue that the sole responsibility of a lawyer is to advance the interests of the client.[1] Such an approach would suggest that no special obligations are owed to third parties beyond the normal laws that apply to anyone. As we shall see, that view is not really tenable, and there are certainly situations in which lawyers have extra obligations to third parties, although the extent of these is controversial.

It need hardly be said that, in their dealings with third parties, lawyers must comply with the general law. Fraud is fraud whether committed by a solicitor following a client's instructions or by a person deceiving elderly people into handing over their savings. So lawyers owe the same duties to third parties not to commit crimes against them and not to commit wrongs under the civil law as does anyone else. Here, however, we are primarily interested in when an obligation is owed to a third party by the lawyer as a lawyer, and how he or she is to balance the claims of third parties and those of the client.

---

[1] T. Schneyer, 'Moral philosophy's standard misconception of legal ethics' [1984] Wisconsin Law Review 1529.

General principles: unfair advantage

Solicitors must put the interests of their clients first. The professional codes make that clear.

Follow the Code

Principle 4 of the Solicitors Regulation Authority (SRA) Code of Conduct requires the solicitor to:

> act in the best interests of each *client*;

Paragraph 303 of the Bar Council Code of Conduct (the Bar Code) states that:

A barrister:
(a) must promote and protect fearlessly and by all proper and lawful means the lay client's best interests and do so without regard to his own interests or to any consequences to himself or to any other person

However, the codes also make it clear that solicitors do owe some duties to third parties.

Follow the Code

Chapter 11 of the SRA Code tells solicitors to ensure that they do:

> not take unfair advantage of those you deal with and that you act in a manner which promotes the proper operation of the legal system

This is a general duty applying to solicitors in the course of their professional activities. It is an important limitation on the relationship between client and solicitor. A solicitor cannot seek to promote the client's interests in a way that takes unfair advantage of others. This obligation is stricter than the basic law. It means that a solicitor should not follow a client's instructions to mislead others, even if technically that is not fraud.

The Bar Code is less explicit. It contains general prohibitions against bringing the profession into disrepute.

Follow the Code

The Bar Code, para 301, requires that:

A barrister...must not:
(a) engage in conduct whether in pursuit of his profession or otherwise which is:
    (i)   dishonest or otherwise discreditable to a barrister;

(ii)   prejudicial to the administration of justice; or

(iii) likely to diminish public confidence in the legal profession or the administration of justice or otherwise bring the legal profession into disrepute;

[...]

This would undoubtedly cover a barrister who takes unfair advantage of a third party. But notice that the duty is expressed as a duty to the general justice system and the reputation of the profession, rather than as an obligation to third parties.

Legal professionals must strike an appropriate balance between the obligations to promote their clients' interests and their obligations to third parties. This chapter will explore how such a balance should be struck.

Correcting mistakes of third parties

Thames Trains v Adams[2] and *Thompson v Arnold*[3] suggests that solicitors need not correct mistakes made by the other side. Indeed, they are able to take advantage of them. However, Indicative Behaviour (IB) 11.7 of the SRA Code suggests that 'taking unfair advantage of an opposing party's lack of legal knowledge where they have not instructed a *lawyer*' would be a breach of professional ethics. So while it may be permissible to take advantage of the mistake made by a client's lawyer, if the client is unrepresented, a lawyer should not seek to gain unfair advantage from that. It is, however, only indicative behaviour and flows from the general obligation not to take unfair advantage of others. Indeed, if the opposing party is a barrister representing himself or herself, it might not be thought unfair to fail to disclose or correct a mistake of law.

 Alternative view

If you know that the other side is mistaken as to the law, you will realise that a settlement is going to be reached that is based on a mistake and which will not reflect legal principles. Is a lawyer really to stand by and let a member of the public enter into an agreement based on an error made by a fellow professional? In other professions, that would seem bizarre. We would not expect a doctor to keep quiet when realising that his colleague has made an error. One answer to this is that no great injustice is done in a case in which a member of the public has been wrongly advised, because the client can sue his or her solicitor. However, this response might be thought to overlook the difficulties and expense involved in suing a lawyer.

---

[2] [2006] EWHC 3291.   [3] [2007] EWHC 1875.

Threatening to bring a hopeless application

It is generally thought permissible for a solicitor to undertake litigation on behalf of the client even if it has a small chance of success, and even if it will cause expense and inconvenience to another person. However, there are limits to this. The SRA Code gives examples that are indicative of taking unfair advantage of someone.

Follow the Code

SRA Code, IB 11.8, gives as examples of inappropriate behaviour:

demanding anything for yourself or on behalf of your *client*, that is not legally recoverable, such as when you are instructed to collect a simple debt,

demanding from the debtor the cost of the letter of claim since it cannot be said at that stage that such a cost is legally recoverable

There is a blurry line here between making a claim that one knows is very weak and making a claim when you know that the loss will not be recoverable. The line is perhaps drawn as making a claim for which there is no legal basis (which would be improper) and making one for which there is a legal basis, but which the lawyers know will be difficult to prove. In *Gee v Shell UK*,[4] it was said to be in breach of professional ethics for an employer's solicitors to write to employees saying that they would be liable for costs in the case because in only exceptional cases would costs be awarded.

Offensive behaviour

Under the 1999 Solicitors' Code, solicitors were told not to write offensive letters or to behave offensively in their professional capacity.[5] There is no similar provision in the current guide, but it may be implied from IB 11.9 that the following would be indicative of unethical behaviour:

using your professional status or qualification to take unfair advantage of another *person* in order to advance your personal interests

This covers cases in which a solicitor might seek to use his or her position as a solicitor to intimidate others. For example, if the solicitor has a dispute with a neighbour over a hedge and tries to use his or her position as a solicitor to harass or intimidate that neighbour, that would breach ethical obligations. It does not clearly forbid writing

---

[4] [2002] EWCA Civ 1479.   [5] Regulation 17.01.

rudely worded letters, however—although that might also fall within the general principle that solicitors must act with integrity.

In *Ernst and Young v Butte Mining Co*,[6] Robert Walker J stated that:

> Heavy, hostile commercial litigation is a serious business. It is not a form of indoor sport and litigation solicitors do not owe each other duties to be friendly (so far as that goes beyond politeness) or to be chivalrous or sportsmanlike (so far as that goes beyond being fair). Nevertheless even in the most hostile litigation...solicitors must be scrupulously fair and not take unfair advantage of obvious mistakes...

 Scandal!

Rosaline Wilson won an equal pay claim against her local council with the help of her lawyer. She managed a team of care workers and was paid £6.50 per hour. She saw an article about a lawyer, Stefan Cross, who was bringing claims for people who were paid too little under the equal pay legislation. She consulted Cross and she was awarded £32,000; after her lawyer's fees and tax, she ended up with £18,000—some £13,000 more than the council had offered her to settle out of court.

A victory for justice and an example of good lawyering, you might think. But not everyone thought so. A spokesperson for the local government said:

> Councils have been hamstrung in their ability to deliver on equal pay because of no-win no-fee lawyers who have not served any useful purpose and instead have clogged up the tribunal system, causing severe delays to claims and costing taxpayers more money in bureaucracy.[7]

The unions complained that the cases upset carefully negotiated deals that had ensured better pay for all of the council workers, not only those who consulted lawyers.

Cynics said that the lawyer had made huge sums of money by bringing claims on behalf of low-paid workers. There were reports that he had acted for 30,000 such claimants. The local authorities lost huge sums of money and it was claimed that, as a result of all of the litigation, councils could employ fewer people.

Is this a case in which the lawyer was not taking proper account of his obligation to the greater good? Should the lawyer have considered the impact of the litigation on the other workers, or on council finances more generally? Or was the lawyer's job to ensure that the client got the money to which she was entitled?

---

[6] [1997] 2 All ER 471, 480.

[7] BBC News, 'Lawyers "are hampering equal pay"', 2 January 2008, online at http://news.bbc.co.uk/1/hi/uk/7168337.stm

Undertakings

An undertaking is a special binding promise that a solicitor can make.[8] Usually, undertakings are made to other lawyers, other professionals, or respected third parties. Undertakings are taken extremely seriously within the legal profession and breach of an undertaking is always a serious matter.

> ### Follow the Code
>
> The SRA Code of Conduct is clear, requiring in Outcome 11.2 that a solicitor must:
>
> perform all *undertakings* given by you within an agreed timescale or within a reasonable amount of time

These undertakings play an important role in solicitors' work. Much work in conveyancing is workable only if there is reliance on undertakings made by solicitors to banks and to the solicitors for the other side. Undertakings can be made orally or in writing.

Breach of an undertaking

A breach of an undertaking will prima facie be professional misconduct. Compensating for breaches of undertakings creates a substantial charge on the Solicitors Indemnity Fund. A solicitor will face blame even if it is not his or her fault that the undertaking is not honoured. A solicitor should not make an undertaking if there is a possibility that it will not be complied with. It should be recalled that 'there is no obligation to give or receive an *undertaking* on behalf of a *client*'.[9]

> **Key case**
>
> ### *Udall v Capri Lighting* [1988] QB 907
>
> A solicitor undertook to secure charges over the property of directors of a company in favour of Udall. In return, the plaintiff [now claimant] adjourned the judgment summons that he had obtained. The charges were not executed. Judgment was entered against the company, which then went into liquidation, and so the judgment could not be enforced and the charges could not be executed. It was accepted by the Court of Appeal that the solicitor had not acted dishonourably and was unable, despite his best endeavours, to implement the undertaking. Nevertheless, the undertaking had been breached. This was

---

[8] K. Hamer, *Professional Conduct Casebook* (Oxford University Press, 2012), ch. 64.
[9] SRA Code of Conduct, Chapter 11.

prima facie misconduct, although the Court accepted that a solicitor 'may be able to give an explanation for his failure to honour his undertaking which may enable the Court to say that there has been no misconduct in the particular case'.[10] The Court confirmed that normally, if an undertaking was not fulfilled, the court, under its inherent jurisdiction, would order implementation of the undertaking. If, as in this case, that was not possible, the court could order compensation to be paid. The case was remitted to the first-instance judge to determine whether compensation should be ordered. Where there has been professional misconduct, 'although the jurisdiction is compensatory and not punitive, it retains a disciplinary slant' acting 'to enforce honourable conduct on the part of the Court's own officers'.[11]

It is important to notice that, in *Udall*, the Court of Appeal made it clear that the courts would not enforce every undertaking. However, generally, once an undertaking is given, the courts will seek to ensure that it is enforced or compensation is paid. A solicitor may be found to have breached an undertaking even though he or she was not blameworthy. An undertaking can be enforced by a court even if the undertaking was made by mistake,[12] or if the client tells the solicitor not to perform it.[13]

If there is a question mark over the interpretation of the undertaking, it will be construed in the way in which it would be reasonably understood by the recipient in the circumstances in which it was received.[14]

 ## Application

You must take great care in making undertakings. It is normally better to use phrases such as 'use reasonable endeavours to produce' rather than to promise that you will produce. If you do make an undertaking, you must ensure that you honour it. In the SRA Code, ensuring that there is an effective record of all undertakings made and when they have been discharged is recommended as behaviour indicative of complying with the Code.[15]

Who is bound by an undertaking?

One important aspect of the rule on undertakings is that if given by a member of a firm, all partners in the firm are liable for each other's undertakings. This applies only to undertakings that are given by a solicitor while made in the usual business of the firm, with its ostensible authority.[16]

---

[10] At 920.   [11] At 921.   [12] *Dotesio v Biss (No. 2)* (1912) 56 Solicitors Journal 736.
[13] *The Gertrude* [1927] WN 265.   [14] *Reddy v Lachlan* [2000] Lloyd's Rep PN 858.
[15] Indicative Behaviour 11.5.   [16] *United Bank of Kuwait v Hammoud* [1988] 1 WLR 1051.

A different issue is the extent to which a solicitor can be responsible for a breach of an undertaking given by a solicitor in another firm. That situation was discussed in the following case.

 Key case

Twinsectra Ltd v Yardley [2002] UKHL 12

Sims and Roper, a firm of solicitors, was acting for Yardley. The firm undertook to pay money received as a loan to Yardley, solely for the purposes of buying a property. Sims paid the money to Paul Leach, a solicitor also acting for Yardley, after Yardley had promised that the money was to be used for acquiring a property. Leach then handed the money to Yardley without ensuring that it was to be used to buy property. No property was bought and the loan was not repaid. The lender sued Leach for breach of the undertaking.

A major issue before the House of Lords concerned whether there was a breach of a trust and so the breach of the undertaking was discussed only briefly. But the question was whether a solicitor who acted in a way that he or she knew would cause another solicitor to breach an undertaking could be said to have acted wrongly. It was clear that their Lordships believed that Leach had behaved badly, but it was not clear quite what he had done wrong in terms of his professional obligations. Lord Hoffmann held that Leach had acted wrongfully, because he knew of the undertaking. Lord Hutton held that Leach had taken a 'blinkered approach to his professional duties as a solicitor', but added that he was not dishonest. Interestingly, Lord Mustill, dissenting, attached great weight to the fact that Leach knew of the undertaking and held that he was an accessory to the tort of wrongful interference in the breach of contract.

Only Lord Mustill, dissenting, was clear in that case that the solicitor had acted in breach of legal and ethical guidelines. The rather relaxed view of the majority has, however, been criticised. Andrew Boon and Jennifer Levin suggest that 'the majority of their lordships appeared to expect a rather low level of competence from a solicitor in this case'.[17]

Enforcing undertakings

A person seeking to enforce an undertaking has three primary options:

- to bring a claim against the lawyer directly for breach of contract, if a contract could be shown, which will be rare;

---

[17] A. Boon and J. Levin, *The Ethics and Conduct of Lawyers in England and Wales* (Hart, 2008), 269.

- more commonly, to ask the court to exercise its inherent supervisory injunction; or
- to apply to the Law Society to enforce the undertaking.

As already noted, the court will often enforce the undertaking either by requiring the solicitor to act in the way promised or, if that is impossible, by requiring the solicitor to pay compensation.

The following case is a dramatic example of that.

 Key case

Clark v Lucas [2009] EWHC 1952 (Ch)

A firm of solicitors was acting for the seller of property. It undertook to redeem a charge over the property following completion of the sale. The firm failed to do that and was required to pay the amount due under the charge. The judge made the order even though the sum due under the charge was twice the sale price of the property. The solicitors argued that they should be liable to pay only the cost of damages caused to the purchaser. However, the judge ordered that the firm pay such sum as enabled the terms of the undertaking to be met.

A solicitor may seek to make a case against enforcing the undertaking. It will not be sufficient simply to argue that circumstances have changed since the undertaking was made.[18]

Digging deeper

Note that when the court is exercising its inherent jurisdiction to enforce undertakings, it states that its primary purpose is not to enforce the legal rights of clients, but to ensure 'honourable conduct' by solicitors.[19] This suggests that the wrong done by a breach of an undertaking is to the justice system as a whole, rather than to the client individually. Is that a sensible way of viewing things? One benefit is that it enables the court to require compliance even in cases in which loss to an individual cannot be identified.

Contacting opposing party

As a general rule, a solicitor should not directly contact the opposing party if he or she is represented by a solicitor or licensed conveyancer. Communications from a

---

[18] *Hole & Pugsley v Sumption* [2009] EWHC 1952.
[19] *John Fox v Bannister King Rigbeys* [1988] QB 925, 928B, *per* Nicholls LJ.

solicitor to the opposing side should be made through his or her solicitor. The SRA Code makes this clear.

Follow the Code

The SRA Code of Conduct, IB 11.4, indicates that a lawyer will be meeting his or her obligations by:

> ensuring that you do not communicate with another party when you are aware that the other party has retained a *lawyer* in a matter, except:
> (a) to request the name and address of the other party's *lawyer*; or
> (b) the other party's *lawyer* consents to you communicating with the *client*; or
> (c) where there are exceptional circumstances;

Of course, a client can contact the other side directly if he or she so wishes, subject to the normal criminal law. There are exceptional cases in which a solicitor can make direct contact, for example where the other solicitor is not passing on messages. The rule is based on the principle that solicitors should not pressurise individuals and should respect their fellow professionals.

Difficult issues can arise where the party is represented by an unqualified person. If a solicitor believes that the unqualified person is undertaking prohibited acts (such as probate or conveyancing services) while unqualified, then that person should be reported to the Law Society. If he or she is advising as a legitimate adviser, such as a McKenzie friend,[20] then dealing with the unqualified person may be permitted. In doubtful cases, it may be best to send communications to the individual, but to offer to deal with the representative at his or her request.

Unrepresented parties

With the cutbacks in legal aid, it is likely that the courts will see increasing litigants in person (LiPs)—that is, people representing themselves, without legal advice. Many solicitors dislike dealing with unrepresented parties. There is a concern that they will be expected to provide legal advice for both sides, or that the case will become lengthy and expensive, with the unrepresented party raising irrelevant issues and making legally invalid claims. There can be also some difficult issues involved in balancing acting in the best interests of the client and dealing fairly with an unrepresented party.

Clearly, a basic obligation may be to encourage the party to seek legal advice. Further, there is an obligation not to take unfair advantage of the lack of understanding of the unrepresented party.

---

[20] *McKenzie v McKenzie* [1970] 3 All ER 1034.

A good example of the dangers that a solicitor can face if opposed by a litigant in person is the following.

 Key case

Dean v Allin and Watts [2001] EWCA 758

Mr Dean, a car mechanic, was persuaded to make a loan to a company called Citizen Homes. The company's solicitors held a meeting that the company and Mr Dean attended. The solicitor made it clear that he could not act for Mr Dean, but offered to hold deeds for him and discussed the transaction. Dean relied on the defendant's solicitor for advice in relation to a loan that he was making to the defendants. The solicitor had realised that the claimant was unrepresented and had not advised him to obtain independent legal advice. The solicitor was found liable to pay damages.

It is, however, important to appreciate the basis for this decision. The Court of Appeal rejected an argument that there was an implied contract of retainer between Dean and the solicitor. The solicitor had made it clear that he was not acting for Mr Dean. Further, the Court rejected a claim that the solicitor had explicitly told Dean that there was good security for the loan. That would have made it an easy case. The basis for the liability was that the solicitor had a duty of care to advise Dean that the deposit of the deeds was inadequate security.

It will be interesting to see how far this develops. The Court emphasised that the loss to the claimant was foreseeable, and that there was proximity between the solicitor and Dean: they had been involved in face-to-face communication. Further, the solicitor had known that Dean was relying on his advice. Perhaps the key feature was the failure by the solicitor to recommend that the unrepresented party seek independent advice. In *Hemmens v Wilson Browne*,[21] the fact that the solicitor had recommended that the unrepresented person seek independent advice was a key factor in finding no liability.

 Alternative view

In New South Wales, Australia, a rather different approach is taken towards the obligations of lawyers to an unrepresented third party. In *Serobian v Commonwealth Bank of Australia*,[22] McFarlane JA stated:

> Where, as here in the case of the respondent, a party is represented by competent and experienced lawyers and is opposed by litigants in person, the party and its lawyers have

---

[21] [1995] Ch 223.   [22] [2009] NSWSC 1312, 1321.

a duty to assist the court to understand and give full and fair consideration to the submissions of the litigants in person. In particular such a party must refer the court to evidence in the proceedings that is relevant to those submissions. This duty is accentuated where, again as here, the party is a substantial institution accustomed to litigating cases involving issues such as are involved in the present case, often against litigants in person.

Many English lawyers would be horrified by the idea that they may be expected to provide the court with evidence and assistance to help to advance the case of the other side.

The Law Society has issued special guidance in a Practice Note to assist solicitors dealing with LiPs.[23] It emphasises that solicitors should not take unfair advantage of LiPs and gives four examples of wrongful behaviour:

bullying and unjustifiable threats;
misleading or deceitful behaviour;
claiming what cannot be properly claimed;
demanding what cannot properly be demanded.[24]

Solicitors are encouraged to remain measured and calm when dealing with LiPs.

On the other hand, this does not mean that a solicitor should not do the best that he or she can for his or her own client. The Practice Note states:

Conversely, knowing and using law and procedure effectively against your opponent because you have the skills to do so, whether that be as against a qualified representative or an unrepresented LiP, would not in itself be deemed to be either taking 'unfair advantage' or a breach of the SRA Code.[25]

The Note explains that a solicitor may be asked by a court to assist an LiP in understanding proceedings. However, it says that a solicitor should not assist if doing so conflicts with the interests of his or her client. Indeed, the Note says:

However, it is important that any dealings with a LiP intended to give constructive guidance are carefully considered and properly explained to your own client so as not to give rise to the impression that you are advising the opposing party. You should also consider whether you will carry the cost of any additional work or time involved in assisting the LiP, or seek to recover any additional costs you incur from your own client. If such a scenario is likely to arise, you should discuss it with your client in advance. You may also provide guidance as to what would and what would not amount to recoverable costs during proceedings.[26]

---

[23] Law Society, *Practice Note: Litigants in Person* (Law Society, 2012).
[24] Law Society (n. 23), para. 31.   [25] Law Society (n. 23), para. 32.
[26] Law Society (n. 23), para. 33.

The Note gives examples of the kind of help that it might be appropriate to give:

> Where it is necessary that the attention of an opposing party be drawn to a particular procedural rule a web-link could be provided for the LiP.
>
> Where legal argument is advanced it may save court time and be a matter of courtesy to provide a link or copy of any authority where an opposing solicitor would normally only require a citation. However, you are not obliged to provide information that your opponent would already be expected to have in their possession.
>
> It is sensible to avoid the use of technical language or legal jargon in your communications with a LiP . . .[27]

In addition, a solicitor may be required to prepare all of the necessary bundles of documents for the court.

 What would you do?

You are representing a company that is being sued by a former employee. You suspect that the employee has a good case, but he is representing himself. He is not using his best arguments and is presenting the evidence in a muddled way. The claimant is not showing the courts the documents that best support his case. Your client is very unhappy with you spending any time helping the employee.

What would they do?

This 'What would you do?' scenario is accompanied by a podcast in which current law students debate the issues and articulate their own responses to the ethical questions that it raises. The podcast is available online at www.oxfordtextbooks.co.uk/orc/herringethics/

Tort duties to third parties

In Chapter 8, we explored the circumstances in which a lawyer may owe a duty of care to a third party. It will be recalled that, generally, a lawyer does not owe a duty to a third party, but that, following *White v Jones*,[28] if a lawyer is instructed by a client to do an act that is intended to benefit an identified third party, fails to act appropriately, and as a result the third party foreseeably suffers a loss, that third party may be able to sue for the loss that has occurred. The detail of the law is discussed in Chapter 8, but it is worth making a couple of points here relating specifically to the issues raised in this chapter.

---

[27] Law Society (n. 23), para. 34.   [28] [1995] 2 AC 207.

The first is to note the limited nature of the tort duty. A solicitor does not owe a duty of care to any third party to whom he or she negligently causes harm. The *White v Jones* duty arises only where the third party is identified and it is clear to the solicitor that the client is instructing him or her to act primarily in order to benefit the third party.

Second, the duty of care is parasitic on the lawyer–client relationship. In *White v Jones*, the argument that won the day in the House of Lords was that it would be unjust if a lawyer could breach a contract with a client, cause loss, and yet not be liable in law. The claim could be brought only because the executors could not bring a claim for breach of contract. Indeed, where the client can bring a claim, the third party cannot.[29] This reveals that the driving force behind the duty of care to the third party is that it is a mechanism for giving effect to the obligations in the lawyer–client contract. It is recognition that a client may want to instruct a solicitor to perform an act for the benefit of a third party, and that the law should recognise that and protect the client's expectations. Only very occasionally will the duty be owed to a third party independently of the interests of the client. The following case is an example of that rare instance.

 Key case

Al-Kandari v Brown [1988] 1 All ER 833

The case involved a bitter family dispute. The father wanted to see his children, but the mother objected, concerned that he would remove the children from the country. The solicitor for the husband undertook to keep the husband's passport and not give it to him. Relying on that, the mother allowed the father to see the children. However, owing to the negligence of the solicitor, the father was given his passport and removed the children.

The father's solicitors were sued by the mother and she succeeded. The normal principle that solicitors do not owe special duties of care to non-clients could be departed from in this case. In giving the undertaking, the solicitors had 'stepped outside their role as solicitors for their client and accepted responsibilities towards both their client and the plaintiff and the children'.[30]

Al-Kandari is unusual. The next case reflects the more common line that lawyers do not owe duties to third parties.

---

[29] *Worby v Rosser* [2000] PNLR 140.   [30] At 843.

Key case

Gran Gelato Ltd v Richcliff Ltd [1992] Ch 560

Gran Gelato purchased an underlease from Richcliff. Grant Gelato's solicitors sent enquiries to Richcliff's solicitors in order to prepare the contact. One of the questions concerned whether there were any rights affecting the superior lease that would impact on the underlease. Richcliff told his solicitors to answer 'Not to the lessor's knowledge'. In fact, there were such rights. Richcliff was found liable for misrepresentation, which had caused loss to Gran Gelato. However, the solicitors were not liable. The court explained that 'in normal conveyancing transactions solicitors who are acting for a seller do not in general owe to the would-be buyer a duty of care when answering inquiries before contract or the like'.[31] The solicitors relied on what the client had said and that was sufficient.

It is notable in this case that the claimant had a remedy for the loss that it suffered, against Richcliffe. This made it easier to find that Richcliffe's solicitors did not owe Gran Gelato a duty of care. It should be noted that key to the court's approach was that the solicitors had reason not to believe their clients.

Gran Gelato was referred to with approval by Lord Goff in *White v Jones*[32] and by the Court of Appeal in *Dean v Allin Watts (A Firm)*. It is a decision that is not without its critics. In *McCullagh v Lane Fox Partners Ltd*,[33] it was suggested that *Gran Gelato* was restricted to conveyancing cases and may not apply outside that context, but that view has not been supported in other cases.[34]

Third parties and fees

The old rule that fees could be paid only by a client himself or herself has passed and now third-party supporters of litigation can pay. Commonly, this includes trades union insurance companies, charities, or pressure groups. For example, the Christian Legal Centre,[35] a pressure group, has funded litigation brought by Christians who believe that their religious rights have been improperly infringed.

It is important that, where a third party is paying for the legal costs of a client, the solicitor appreciates that his or her duty is owed to the client, *not to the person who pays costs*. If, for example, the client were to decide to stop the litigation, the solicitor must respect those instructions, whatever the funder wishes.

[31] At 571.
[32] [1995] 1 AC 207, 256D. See also *Memery Crystal v O'Higgins* [1997] 7 CL 457 (QBD).
[33] [1996] PNLR 205.
[34] In *First National Commercial Bank Plc v Loxleys* [1997] PNLR 211, the court even seemed to think that the issue was open to argument in the conveyancing context.
[35] www.christianconcern.com/christian-legal-centre

However, there are some duties owed to the funder. The solicitor must give information to the funder about how the fees will be paid and calculated. Further, there may be an arrangement between the parties that the solicitor keep the funder informed of progress. The solicitor should do that only with the client's consent.

This can all become artificial in some cases involving insurance, in which in practice the insurance company runs and manages the case. In many cases, the client agrees that the solicitor may receive instructions from the insurance company. The idea that the solicitor receives instruction from the client becomes rather theoretical. In *Chapman v Christopher*,[36] an insurance company was held liable to pay the costs of the other side, even though it was an individual who was officially the losing side to the claim. The court recognised that the reality was that the insurance company was instructing the solicitor.

Wasted costs orders

One way in which it might be said the law recognises a duty to other parties is through the wasted costs order. Under the Civil Procedure Rules, a lawyer may be ordered personally to pay the costs of the opponent or of his or her own client. This can create a clash between the solicitor's own interests and those of the client. The situation would arise if a client were to ask a solicitor to undertake an unnecessary or hopeless task. The solicitor may be aware that if he or she were to do so and as a result the other side incurred costs, he or she could become personally liable.

The jurisdiction for a **wasted costs** order is found under section 51(6) of the Supreme Court Act 1981.[37]

 Definition

> In section 51(7) of the Supreme Court Act 1981, **wasted costs** are defined as costs incurred by a party as 'a result of any improper, unreasonable or negligent act or omission on the part of any legal or other representative or any employee of such representative'.

---

[36] [1998] 2 All ER 873.   [37] Amended by the Courts and Legal Services Act 1990.

A solicitor can be required to pay personally any costs run up as a result of such work, be that work for his or her own client or the work of the other side. In appropriate cases, the order can require the lawyer to pay a portion of the costs.[38] There is no need for anyone to apply for a wasted costs order; the court can decide to make one on its own initiative.[39]

The following leading case provides some helpful guidance.

 Key case

Ridehalgh v Horsefield [1994] 3 All ER 848

Six different cases involving wasted costs orders were brought to the Court of Appeal for guidance. They all involved wasted costs orders against a solicitor or a barrister.

The Court of Appeal issued some important guidance on the meaning of the words 'improper', 'unreasonable', and 'negligent' in section 51(7) of the Supreme Court Act 1981.

- 'Improper' conduct was conduct that was a significant breach of a substantial duty imposed by a code of professional conduct, or conduct that would be considered improper according to the consensus of professional opinion.

- 'Unreasonable' conduct was conduct designed to harass the other side, rather than to advance the resolution of the case.

- 'Negligent' conduct was a failure to act with the competence reasonably expected of a member of the profession.

However, the Court added: 'A legal representative is not to be held to have acted improperly, unreasonably or negligently simply because he acts for a party who pursues a claim or defence which is plainly doomed to fail.'[40] It was therefore not correct to see the jurisdiction as requiring lawyers to 'filter out' unmeritorious cases. It was accepted that it was not always easy to tell if a case was simply hopeless or whether it amounted to an abuse of process. If the case were borderline, a solicitor should decide in favour of legal representation.[41]

These cases demonstrate that it is not an easy task to obtain a wasted costs order. They are reserved for the worst kinds of practice. A wasted costs order will not be made simply because the litigation was doomed to fail; it must be shown that the litigation was an abuse of process.[42] The following was one such example.

---

[38] CPR 46.8; Practice Direction 46.   [39] CPR 5.3; Practice Direction 46.   [40] At 852.
[41] *Patel v Air India Ltd* [2010] EWCA Civ 443.   [42] *Harley v McDonald* [2001] UKPC 18.

Key case

Tolstoy v Aldington [1996] 2 All ER 556

There was a lengthy and successful libel action brought by Lord Aldington against Count Tolstoy. Tolstoy lost the action, but his solicitors agreed to apply to have the judgment set aside based on fraud. The lawyers agreed to act with no fee, and indeed Tolstoy became bankrupt. The court found the application hopeless and an abuse of process. Lord Aldington sought a wasted costs order against the solicitor. This was successful. The circumstances were 'at least potentially vexatious'. It was an attempt to attack a court judgment and Rose LJ thought that no solicitor could have acted reasonably in bringing the proceedings. It was true that a barrister had signed the statement of claim, but that did not exonerate the solicitors from their duty to exercise their own judgement. The solicitors could not reasonably be said to be seeking to further the ends of justice.

An abuse of process would occur were the litigation to be brought with no hope of winning, but with some ulterior motive, such as causing a delay before payment needed to be made,[43] or putting bargaining pressure on the other side.[44]

Even in cases in which the litigation is unarguable, the court will consider whether it would be fair to penalise the lawyers with a wasted costs order. In *R v Westminster LBC, ex p Geehan Butler*,[45] the lawyers had had to prepare the application at great speed given the urgency of the issue. Although the application was not arguable, it would be unfair in the circumstances to make a wasted costs order.

In *R (on the application of B) v Secretary of State for the Home Department*,[46] applications brought by the lawyers were described as 'nonsense' and it was said that no lawyer 'knowing anything about the law, would have put forward the argument'. The lawyers had breached their duty to the court. The lawyers were punished by their firms and had apologised, and the court took no further action, but that was the kind of case in which a wasted costs order might have been made.

One issue that wasted costs orders are designed to address is where the costs of litigation become out of proportion to the issue at hand. In *C v C*,[47] a couple was divorcing. Offers to settle were made and rejected. By the end of the case, the costs were £60,000 for the wife and £70,000 for the husband, but the assets that the couple owned were very limited. Virtually all of their assets had been taken up with the divorce case, at the end of which the wife was awarded £20,000. It was not surprising that a wasted costs order was made.

---

[43] *Morris v Roberts (Inspector of Taxes) (Wasted Costs Order)* [2005] EWHC 1040 (Ch).

[44] *Flower Hart (A Firm) v White Industries (Qld) Pty Ltd* (1999) 163 ALR 744, Federal Court Australia.

[45] [1995] COD 204, *per* Dyson J.   [46] [2012] EWHC 3770 (Admin).

[47] [1994] 2 FLR 34.

As well as showing improper, unreasonable, or negligent conduct, it is necessary to show that this causes costs.[48] A lawyer may behave badly and cause delay and inconvenience, but a wasted costs order can be made only if costs are incurred as a result of that behaviour.[49]

A major practical problem that can face a court in deciding whether to make a wasted courts order is that much of the evidence on which a solicitor may seek to rely to defend a claim for wasted costs is protected by professional privilege. This was highlighted in the following case.

 Key case

Medcalf v Mardell [2002] 3 All ER 721

Two barristers were alleged to have amended a notice of appeal to include an allegation of fraud. However, it was said, those allegations had no evidence to support them. The other side investigated and rebutted the allegations, incurring costs.

The case went to the House of Lords, but does not provide major guidance on the jurisdiction. That was because the barristers were unable to provide evidence to justify their advice because they were bound by professional privilege not to disclose it. Their Lordships held that a wasted costs order should be made only if it would be fair. Here, because they could not introduce evidence that could justify their actions, it would not be fair to find the barristers liable to pay costs. Their Lordships accepted that, in some cases, even though professional privilege applied, the court could conclude that if the lawyers had a defence, other material could be used to establish it. However, in this case, they could not be sure that was so.

The privilege argument in that case would not be an issue in cases in which the client claimed wasted costs against his or her own lawyer, but it is an issue in a case such as this in which the client is seeking costs against the lawyers for the other side. If, because of the fact that the evidence is privileged, it is not possible to assess clearly whether a wasted costs order should be made, the lawyer should be given the benefit of the doubt.[50]

In deciding whether it is fair to make a wasted costs order, the court can take into account the personal circumstances of the lawyer.[51]

Problems with wasted costs orders

While wasted costs orders do provide a powerful incentive against utterly pointless litigation, concerns have been raised in relation to them. First, as was said by the

---

[48] *Kilroy v Kilroy* [1997] PNLR 67.
[49] *Re A (A Child) (Wasted Costs Order)* [2013] EWCA Civ 43.
[50] *Myers v Elman* [2008] EWHC 3664 (QB).
[51] *R (on the application of Hide) v Staffordshire CC* [2007] EWHC 2441 (Admin).

Court of Appeal in *Ridehalgh v Horsefield*,[52] wasted costs orders are particularly relevant in cases involving the legal representatives of recipients of legal aid, who were in a vulnerable position. Because the clients were not in a financial position to pay the costs of the other side, there would be a temptation to seek payment from their lawyers. Indeed, empirical studies suggest that most cases involving wasted costs are made in cases involving legal aid lawyers.[53] It would seem unfair if lawyers involved in legal aid work were far more likely to suffer a wasted costs order than privately funded lawyers—especially because privately funded lawyers are more likely to be in a position to be able to afford any wasted costs order.

Second, there are concerns that the size of the wasted costs order can too easily get out of proportion! In *C v C (Wasted Costs Order)*,[54] the proceedings over the wasted costs order themselves generated costs of £150,000, which was far in excess of the amount of the alleged wasted costs in the original proceedings.

Third, as already indicated, there are real problems with the fact that professional privilege protects crucial evidence in many cases. This leaves the courts with the unenviable—some might say impossible—task of considering whether it is possible that the privileged evidence would provide an explanation for what the lawyers did, such that a wasted costs order should not be made.

Hugh Evans summarises these concerns:

> [L]awyers should not be deterred from pursuing their clients' interests by fear of incurring a personal liability to their clients' opponents; that they should not be penalised by orders to pay costs without a fair opportunity to defend themselves; that wasted costs orders should not become a back-door means of recovering costs not otherwise recoverable against a legally-aided or impoverished litigant; and that the remedy should not grow unchecked to become more damaging than the disease.[55]

But that needs to be weighed against the need to protect litigants from being prejudiced by unjustifiable conduct in litigation and the need to protect the integrity of the justice system from claims being brought with ulterior motives. These are not easy to balance.

Broader ethical issues

The issues discussed in this chapter resonate with the issues relating to the role of a lawyer that we discussed in Chapter 3. How zealous should a lawyer be in pursuit of his or her client's interests? Should that zeal be tempered by concern for the interests of others? Or should lawyers owe duties to treat all people fairly and should their clients be no more than a first among equals?

---

[52] [1994] Ch 205.
[53] H. Evans, 'The wasted costs jurisdiction' (2001) 64 Modern Law Review 61.
[54] [1994] 2 FLR 34.   [55] Evans (n. 53), 70.

As noted in Chapter 1, there are some who argue that lawyers should do all that they can to promote the interests of their clients. There are others who argue that lawyers are not required to do anything for their clients and that, even beyond the law and professional rules, lawyers may refuse to follow clients' requests.[56] That debate was discussed in detail in Chapters 1 and 3. The issues are clearly relevant here. On the one hand, there are those who argue that lawyers must act with all legitimate zeal to ensure fulfilment of their clients' legal entitlements. If the law has granted a person a certain legal right, it is not for his or her lawyer to seek to refuse to enforce it because the lawyer thinks that would be unfair to the other side. If the law grants a building society the right to repossess a house because the owner has failed to pay the mortgage, the lawyer should not refuse to act because he or she believes that he or she owes obligations to the owner. If the lawyer believes that the building society should not be allowed to repossess, the problem lies with the law, not with the clients. So a lawyer should use every tool that the law provides to promote the building society's case, however unfair others might see that to be. This might be taken further: a lawyer may believe that the client has little chance of success, but ultimately it is for the court to make that decision. If the client demands that a lawyer bring the claim, are we to criticise the lawyer for doing so when the claim is groundless?

A different view would be that the lawyer has duties to the justice system and society more generally. We will discuss these in Chapter 13. While the lawyer's primary responsibility is to promote the interests of the client, he or she is not required to do so in a way that involves undermining the principles of justice. In acting for a client, the lawyer does therefore have obligations to ensure that the other side is dealt with fairly and that the interests of justice generally are pursued in the case.

We have already explored these debates in Chapters 1 and 3, and so will not repeat them all here. However, there are some points that are especially relevant to the issues in this chapter.

The 'zeal' model works well when all sides are represented by top-quality lawyers. Remember the argument that if the lawyers for both sides put forward the best arguments and produce the best evidence for the case, the judge has the best chance of reaching the ideal decision. This is seen as justifying the zeal approach. If a lawyer is not putting forward the very best case for his or her client, he or she is, in effect, impeding justice. As Bradley Wendel argues:

> So a lawyer who, on grounds of conscience, refuses to press a client's legal entitlements is sabotaging the very mechanism that allows us to manage value conflicts without falling into a war of all against all. The moral activist is not merely self-righteous. She is reckless and irresponsible toward a political settlement that we all need.[57]

---

[56] D. Nicolson and J. Webb, *Professional Legal Ethics: Critical Interrogations* (Oxford University Press, 1999).

[57] B. Wendel, *Lawyers and Fidelity to Law* (Princeton University Press, 2010), 221.

However, this argument works only when both sides are receiving the best advice.[58] Obviously, when one side is able to put forward its very best arguments and the other is able to put forward only a few of its weakest arguments, it is unlikely that justice will be done. Hence we might find an argument suggesting that the zeal approach is less suitable where the other side is unrepresented, or even when the other side is represented by a bad lawyer! But this argument may be in danger of proving too much. Lawyers who charge huge fees purport to offer a better service. Typically, this is that they will put a better case than cheaper lawyers. If expensive lawyers have to help out the cheaper lawyers to ensure that there is justice, they will lose the reasons why they can charge higher frees. Alternatively, one response might be that if the other side does not have good legal advice, the answer is to ensure that it does, not to require your own lawyer to act with less than full zeal.

One argument used to promote the zeal approach is that it means that people can access legal advice. The problem is that, increasingly in our society, access to legal advice is restricted, especially as a result of cutbacks in legal aid. If the primary basis of the zeal approach is to enable access to the law for all, the reality as things now stand in England is that it does not.[59] As Donald Nicolson puts it:

> [A]sserting formal rights to a lawyer simply reinforces the privileges of those rich enough to afford one and who in any event are already favoured *by* the content of law and their superior resources in using it to pursue their interests.[60]

One way of combating this is to say that a lawyer advising a client owes duties to ensure that the other side receives *some* basic advice. However, you might feel that this is not the best way of ensuring that everyone gets good access to legal advice.

The traditional approach encourages the perception that the lawyer is the 'tool' of the client. The lawyer follows instructions and does his or her best to implement the client's instructions. Ted Schneyer draws an analogy with a taxi driver.[61] The taxi driver's job is to drive the client to where he or she wants to go; it is not the driver's place to question whether the client is up to any good when going there. Many lawyers would feel uncomfortable with this analogy: they are not just 'taxi drivers'.

Conclusion

At first sight, the question 'Does a lawyer owe duties to the other side?' demands a clear answer: 'No'. A lawyer's duties are to promote the interests of his or her own client. However, as this chapter shows, the issue is not as straightforward as that. There are circumstances in which duties *are* owed to third parties. However, they are

---

[58] D. Luban, 'Misplaced fidelity' (2012) 90 Texas Law Review 673.

[59] D. Nicolson, 'Afterword: In defence of contextually sensitive moral activism' (2004) 7 Legal Ethics 249.

[60] Nicolson (n. 59), 250.   [61] Schneyer (n. 1).

limited, and the law and ethical codes struggle to ensure that even when these are imposed, they are not used to undermine the relationship between lawyer and client, or to ensure that the lawyer never acts against the best interests of the client.

 Further reading

H. Evans, 'The wasted costs jurisdiction' (2001) 64 Modern Law Review 61.

K. Hamer, *Professional Conduct Casebook* (Oxford University Press, 2012).

D. Luban, 'Misplaced fidelity' (2012) 90 Texas Law Review 673.

D. Nicolson, 'Afterword: In defence of contextually sensitive moral activism' (2004) 7 Legal Ethics 249.

T. Schneyer, 'Moral philosophy's standard misconception of legal ethics' [1984] Wisconsin Law Review 1529.

B. Wendel, *Lawyers and Fidelity to Law* (Princeton University Press, 2010).

Business ethics

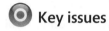

 Key issues

- What are business ethics?
- What is the significance of corporate accountability?
- What does corporate citizenship involve?
- How do businesses take ethical issues into account?

Introduction

This chapter will discuss business ethics—that is, what ethical approach business people should take to the running of businesses.

Definition

Business ethics is the application of ethical principles to commercial activities.

Business ethics are relevant to lawyers for three main reasons. First, commercial clients will be advising businesses and it is helpful to understand the attitudes they have towards ethical issues. Second, as we shall see, the debates highlight the question of who is the client when advising a business. Third, lawyers in their practices are increasingly themselves acting as businesses. This is especially so with the advent of alternative business structures (ABSs—see Chapter 3). Further, many lawyers work in-house and are employed by a company. This can create a tension between legal ethics and business ethics.

The financial disasters of the early part of the twenty-first century were seen by many as caused by a collapse of ethical standards. The pursuit of economic gain had become the sole focus of businesses, with no weight being placed on the wider societal good, or on standards of honesty and transparency. Similarly, severe pollution, the exploitation of workers in the developing world, and an extensive use of bribes all call out for better business ethics. This outright focus on profits sits uneasily for lawyers with their commitment to professionalism and, officially at least, to the greater good.

Scandal!

Christine Parker and Adrian Evans have described some of the wrongdoing in the Enron collapse in the following terms:

In the last weeks before Enron's collapse, and when it was already obvious that the regulator would be investigating Enron and multinational accounting firm Arthur Andersen's audit of Enron, an in-house Arthur Andersen lawyer wrote a memo reminding colleagues who had worked on Enron audits of Arthur Andersen's document retention policy. This policy required the destruction of notes and working papers used to prepare audits. Arthur Andersen's lead partner responsible for Enron then organised the urgent disposal of tons of Enron-related documents. The same lawyer also wrote another email suggesting changes to a draft file record on an Enron matter, to delete any further reference to the fact that Arthur Andersen had legal advice that Enron's disclosure in that matter might be misleading. Arthur Andersen was later convicted of the crime of obstruction of justice and then acquitted on appeal. Arthur Andersen, previously one of the 'big five' multinational accounting firms, collapsed as a result of its involvement with the Enron scandal.[1]

We explored in Chapter 1 the general nature of ethics and we will not repeat those points here. Instead, this chapter will focus on the particular issues that arise when ethical principles are applied in the context of business. The topic of business ethics is huge and covers a wide range of issues. This chapter will focus on just some of the general themes.[2]

Why business ethics matters

As already mentioned, the financial crisis of recent years has brought the issue of business ethics into the limelight. There are many reasons why business should not be run simply under the regulation of law and for the maximisation of profit. Companies play a major role in modern society. They exercise considerable power and influence. Companies employ many workers and manufacture products that are in daily use. Few people, if any, are able to avoid having any dealings with companies. If you believe it to be important for society to reflect ethical values, then it is difficult not to appreciate the significance of ethical principles for business. Further, we have seen that business can, if run solely for immediate profit, cause huge harm to society, the environment, and disadvantaged groups. It may be that some people will take the

---

[1] C. Parker and A. Evans, *Inside Lawyers' Ethics* (Cambridge University Press, 2007), 219–20.
[2] See A. Crane and D. Matten, *Business Ethics*, 3rd edn (Oxford University Press, 2010) for a detailed discussion.

view that the good achieved by businesses maximising their profits exceeds the social harms, but they will need to work hard to make a case for that. What is clear is that, at the very least, real ethical issues are raised about the approach that companies take to these social concerns.

There is a further argument to be made: that a body of consumers will take into account ethical practices when choosing what to buy. The growth of Fairtrade products, the existence of 'ethical banks', and an emphasis on green credentials can all be seen as evidence that the ethical practices of companies matter to consumers, investors, and staff. So even if you take the view that it is right for businesses to focus on profit-generation, there may be a business case for taking ethical concerns seriously.

The traditional view has been that companies are created to produce money and to be economically productive. Famously, in 1970, Milton Friedman wrote an article in the *New York Times* entitled 'The social responsibility of business is to increase its profits'.[3] His article became a classic text and comprised three central points.

1. Human beings have moral responsibility for their actions, but companies cannot. Companies are created by humans and their decisions are made by people. The humans involved are responsible for what is done. The company cannot control its actions (it has no power, save that exercised through the people who run it) and so cannot have moral responsibility.

2. The primary responsibility of directors and managers is to act in the interests of the shareholders. They must comply with the law, but outside that limitation they must not seek to act for the good of others, or the good of society. Friedman goes so far as to suggest that doing so would amount to 'theft' from shareholders.

3. It is the job of the state, not companies, to tackle social issues and problems. Indeed, Friedman suggests that it would be wrong if companies were to seek to identify and rectify social issues. There is a danger that, in doing so, they would undermine democracy. Business people lack the skills and democratic mandate to seek to change society.

These three points are highly controversial. They raise key issues in relation to business ethics and it is worth addressing them separately.

Is a company a moral agent?

The notion of 'corporate responsibility' assumes that we can attach responsibilities and ethical obligations to a corporate entity. But does it make sense to

---

[3] M. Friedman, 'The social responsibility of business is to increase its profits', *New York Times Magazine*, 13 September 1970, 122–5.

do so? For lawyers, this is perhaps less problematic than it is for philosophers. Company law clearly establishes that a company is a 'legal person'. A company can enter into a contract, commit a tort, and be convicted of a crime just like anyone else. Even if all of the directors and shareholders die, the company remains as a legal entity. A company is therefore separate from the shareholders or directors.

However, simply because it is a legal person does not mean that a company is a moral person and can be subject to ethical responsibilities. The argument that a company cannot have moral agency is based on the claim that it cannot make decisions. It is the decisions of the directors and, to a lesser extent, the shareholders and employees that determine what a company does. A company cannot do anything or change its behaviour except through the actions of these 'real' people. Hence, it is argued, we can blame directors, employees, or shareholders for what a company does, but it is a fiction to blame the company itself. Indeed, it is sometimes said that notions of corporate responsibility can wrongly be used to shield individuals from blame.

At first, that seems a highly convincing argument. However, there are counter-arguments. Companies have clear rules about which actions or decisions belong to the company, and for which actions the company has no responsibility. The company's articles of association will define who makes decisions on behalf of the company and imposes control, if any, on those people. The argument therefore goes that we are able to identify the actions and intentions of a company because the rules of the company define what those are.[4]

Some commentators argue that companies do have lives of their own. Its 'internal decision-making structure' gives a company its own identity. Indeed, the decision of a company may not, especially in a larger corporation, be the decision of a single person, but rather a collective decision. It might, for example, be one reached through compromise and consultation. Further, the people making that decision are not making it on their own behalf, but within the structure of the company and for the aims set out in the company's articles. So the moral responsibility cannot fairly be set at the feet of an individual in the company for two reasons: first, because it is rarely a single person's decision; and second, because that decision is made within the confines of the rules of the company structure. If the individuals cannot be held responsible for the decision, then it should be the company that is.

Another argument in favour of holding companies morally to account is that they can develop an **organisational culture**.

---

[4] P. French, 'The corporation as a moral person' (1979) 16 American Philosophical Quarterly 207; P. French, *Collective and Corporate Responsibility* (Columbia University Press, 1984); P. French, *Corporate Ethics* (Harcourt Brace, 1995).

 Definition

> Edgar Schein has proposed that **organisational culture** can be defined as:
>
> > …a pattern of shared basic assumptions that the group learned as it solved its problems of external adaptation and internal integration, that has worked well enough to be considered valid and, therefore, to be taught to new members as the correct way to perceive, think, and feel in relation to those problems.[5]

The notion of an organisational culture is that companies develop a set of beliefs and values that influence all those involved with the company. This is not merely a reflection of the beliefs and values of the members, because the culture of the company itself impacts on the values of those within it.

Digging deeper

As this discussion suggests, the precise relationship between a company, its shareholders, and its directors is complex. There is a sense in which the shareholders 'own' the company, in that, ultimately, if the company were to come to an end, they would be entitled to the company's assets, or if someone were to want to buy the company, he or she would pay the shareholders. However, this is a limited kind of ownership because shareholders are not responsible for the debts of the company or for damage that it causes to others. There is a similar tension in regard to the directors and managers of the company. They are given power to make decisions for the company, but this is limited by a 'fiduciary duty'. This means that they must make only decisions that promote the well-being of the company. They could not, for example, give a large portion of the company's assets to a charity.[6] As this brief discussion illustrates, the exact balance of power and the nature of responsibilities between the shareholders, the directors, and the company itself is complex and not always clear.[7]

 Alternative view

Cynics argue that this ambiguity surrounding the nature of a company and its relationships with its shareholders and directors is deliberate, enabling rich people to use corporate identity for their benefit. Where convenient, they will claim that the assets of the company are not theirs, but belong to the company. But on other occasions, when helpful, they will claim ownership of the company's assets.

---

[5] Quoted in B. Tharp, *Defining 'Culture' and 'Organizational Culture': From Anthropology to the Office* (Hadworth, 2012), 4.

[6] Company law does permit small charitable donations by companies.

[7] A detailed discussion can be found in a textbook on company law, such as L. Sealy and S. Worthington, *Cases and Materials on Company Law* (Oxford University Press, 2013).

A good example is the case of *Prest v Petrodel*,[8] in which a couple were divorcing. The husband, who appeared very wealthy, claimed that all of his money in fact belonged to a company and that his own assets were limited. This, he argued, meant that he could pay his wife very little on their divorce.[9] No doubt if the company had owed debts, he would have been keen to include them in an assessment of his wealth in this context.

The law has acknowledged that a company, as an entity itself, has legal responsibility. A good example is found in the criminal law.

Key statute

Under section 1 of the Corporate Manslaughter and Corporate Homicide Act 2007:

The offence
(1) An organisation to which this section applies is guilty of an offence if the way in which its activities are managed or organised—
  (a) causes a person's death, and
  (b) amounts to a gross breach of a relevant duty of care owed by the organisation to the deceased.
(2) The organisations to which this section applies are—
  (a) a corporation;
  (b) a department or other body listed in Schedule 1;
  (c) a police force;
  (d) a partnership, or a trade union or employers' association, that is an employer.
(3) An organisation is guilty of an offence under this section only if the way in which its activities are managed or organised by its senior management is a substantial element in the breach referred to in subsection (1).
(4) For the purposes of this Act—
  (a) "relevant duty of care" has the meaning given by section 2, read with sections 3 to 7;
  (b) a breach of a duty of care by an organisation is a "gross" breach if the conduct alleged to amount to a breach of that duty falls far below what can reasonably be expected of the organisation in the circumstances;
  (c) "senior management", in relation to an organisation, means the persons who play significant roles in—
    (i) the making of decisions about how the whole or a substantial part of its activities are to be managed or organised, or
    (ii) the actual managing or organising of the whole or a substantial part of those activities.

---

[8] [2013] UKSC 34.
[9] Ultimately, the Supreme Court bypassed this argument by finding that the company held the property on trust for him and so that it could be redistributed to his wife.

The moral aim of the company

Companies can be contrasted with charities, the primary aim of which must be to benefit those outside the charity. Indeed, if an employee or trustee of a charity were to make gains (over and above normal remuneration), that would be likely to be illegal. Companies are different: they are designed to make profits. Some commentators go further. In a controversial book, Joel Bakan referred to companies' 'pathological pursuit of profit and power'.[10] This dramatic phrase captured his argument that the company is compelled in its nature to be a self-interested entity. The company's DNA, if you like, is set out in its articles of association and in the regulations of company law. These compel the company to act in a self-interested way, typically for the good of its shareholders.

Let us assume for the moment that a company is designed for the economic good of its members. How are we to define 'members' for these purposes? This is one of the key debates in business ethics: the 'shareholder versus stakeholder' debate.

The shareholder interest

The shareholder interest view argues that the primary obligation of the company is to promote the interests of the shareholders. They are the owners of the company[11] and have invested their money into it. The company started and continued only because of their investment. It is their investment that will be lost if the company does not succeed. The primary obligation of the company, it is said, must be to reward the shareholders for their investment, without which the company would not have come into being. Supporters argue that this obligation is created via a contract between the shareholders and the company. The company promised, at its creation, to put the interests of the company first. Employees work for the company and must be paid their wages, but they do not gain any greater interest in the company any more than a person working for an individual would gain an interest in his or her employer's wealth.[12] Alternatively, it is said that seeking to ensure that the company makes a profit, and hence has dividends to pay shareholders, is for the good of all of the company. If a company seeks to take account of the interests of employees and, for example, pay them wages above market rate, there is a danger that the whole company will lack economic viability. Keeping the company's focus on profit-making is good for all involved in the company in the long run.

The stakeholder interest

According to the stakeholder theory,[13] all those who have a substantial relationship with the company can be regarded as stakeholders. The company must have as its

---

[10] J. Bakan, *The Corporation: The Pathological Pursuit of Profit and Power* (Robinson Publishing, 2005).

[11] Although that is debatable: L. Stout, *The Shareholder Value Myth: How Putting Shareholders First Harms Investors, Corporations, and the Public* (Berrett Koehler Publishers, 2012).

[12] G. Sollars, 'The corporation as actual agreement' (2002) 12 Business Ethics Quarterly 351.

[13] R. Freeman, *Strategic Management: A Stakeholder Approach* (Pitman, 1984).

primary purpose the good of these stakeholders. This includes not only the shareholders, but also the directors, the employees, and the company's suppliers. Supporters of the stakeholder theory sometimes draw a link with the state: just as the government does not owe duties only to those who pay taxes, but rather to all citizens, so a firm should be seen as responsible for more than those who invested money in it.

The stakeholder model sees the company more in terms of a family. It will help its members, sometimes generously. One difficulty with the model is clarifying who exactly is a 'stakeholder'. Freeman has suggested that anyone who 'can affect or is affected by the achievement of the organization's aims' is a stakeholder.[14] That could cover a very broad set of people. Andrew Crane and Dirk Matten suggest that '[a] stakeholder of a corporation is an individual or group which either: is harmed by, or benefits from, the corporation; or whose rights can be violated or have to be respected by the corporation'.[15] This would certainly take the definition beyond those who might obviously be regarded as stakeholders—that is, employees, shareholders, customers, and suppliers—to include also consumers, competitors, and the government.

Supporters of the stakeholder view will note that although shareholders will argue that they have an interest based on their position as stakeholders, their claim in essence is one based on contract. That is the same basis as an employee or supplier. Imagine, for example, that the company is considering sacking an employee. Doing so will increase profits and that will mean more money for shareholders. Not sacking the employee will mean less money, but maintain the stakeholder contract. Note, however, that the obligation to increase profits for shareholders is essentially a contractual obligation. Is it any different from the obligation to employ the worker? More discussion would be needed to determine why it is that the contract with the employee should be broken, rather than the contract with the shareholders.

There is a second, related, issue. When we say that 'the interests of the group', be that stakeholders or shareholders, should be the purpose of the company, which interests are we to take into account? Is it only the economic interests that matter? Or might other kinds of interest (for example reputational or moral standing) be considered? In either event, who decides what is or is not in the interests of the group? Thomas Jones and Wu Felps, for example, have argued that stakeholder happiness should be used as a measure, rather than wealth.[16] That might, for example, permit the use of company money to achieve altruistic goals.

According to Crane and Matten, although in the past the issue of social responsibility was controversial, 'it is by now fairly widely accepted that businesses do indeed have responsibilities beyond simply making a profit'.[17] Supporters of the ideal that companies do owe a broader responsibility to society rely on the notions of corporate social responsibility (CSR) and sustainability. We will now explore these further.

---

[14] Freeman (n. 13), 46.   [15] Crane and Matten (n. 2), 49.

[16] T. Jones and W. Felps, 'Stakeholder happiness enhancement: A neo-utilitarian objective for the modern corporation' (2013) 23 Business Ethics Quarterly 349.

[17] Crane and Matten (n. 2), 51.

Corporate social responsibility

The notion of **corporate social responsibility** (CSR) has become a key concept in business ethics. Interestingly, 96 per cent of large companies in one survey referred to CSR in their companies' annual report.[18]

 Definition

> Lord Holme and Richard Watts define **corporate social responsibility (CSR)** as 'the continuing commitment by business to behave ethically and contribute to economic development while improving the quality of life of the workforce and their families as well as of the local community and society at large'.[19]

Holme and Watts' definition contains a number of issues that need to be addressed.

Interestingly, one commonly provided reason why companies should support CSR is that doing so is in a company's own interests. It can create a larger number of customers and increase the loyalty of those customers, while social irresponsibility may lead to unwanted bad publicity and a loss of custom. Corporate social responsibility can encourage good employees to work for the company. One survey found that more than 50 per cent of global business leaders gave 'having a better brand reputation' as their primary reason for engaging in CSR.[20]

If this is the justification for CSR, it may be argued that it is really nothing very different from the traditional argument that the company must put its own economic interests first. Indeed, it has some worrying implications. It means that firms can ignore CSR if no one will find out about the breach and so there will be no reputational damage, or if the reputational damage will not be as great as the cost of behaving responsibly. Indeed, it is not surprising that Friedman argues that if firms simply engage in CSR for reasons of self-interest, then this is profit maximisation in disguise.[21] In fact, more recent studies have questioned whether CSR really does benefit a company—at least sufficiently to justify the money involved.[22]

Those seeking to find a moral justification for CSR argue that the activities of companies can cause significant social and environmental problems. The most obvious of these is environmental pollution, but they may include broader social

---

[18] T. Cooper, R. Hayward, and L. Neuberger, *A New Era of Sustainability: UN Global Compact–Accenture CEO Study* (United Nations, 2010).

[19] Lord Holme and R. Watts, *Making Good Business Sense* (World Business Council, 2010), 3.

[20] *The Economist*, 'A special report on corporate social responsibility', 17 January 2008, online at www.economist.com/node/10491077   [21] Friedman (n. 3).

[22] M. Orlitzky, 'Corporate social performance and financial performance: A research synthesis', in A Crane, A. McWilliams, D. Matten, J. Moon, and D. Siegel (eds) *The Oxford Handbook of Corporate Social Responsibility* (Oxford University Press, 2008).

and economic harms. This creates a duty that the company should do what it can to correct these wrongs. It is also pointed out that companies have substantial resources and, like anyone in society with significantly greater resources than others, they have an obligation to help those in their community who are less well off. Perhaps the strongest argument is that companies are able to operate and make profits because of the way in which society is organised. The provision of public transport enables a company's workers to come to work; the education system provides training for its employees; the clean atmosphere ensures the health of its staff, and so on. Because companies gain greatly from societal provision, they should pay back into society.

If we accept the notion of CSR, it is helpful then to separate these responsibilities into four categories, as Andy Carroll has done:

- *economic responsibilities* include the obligations to do pay shareholders a return on their investment and to pay employees fairly;
- *legal responsibilities* are the responsibilities imposed by the law;
- *ethical responsibilities* are responsibilities to do what is right, which might include a company choosing to reduce its greenhouse gas emissions or to ensure that all workers are paid a 'living wage'; and
- *philanthropic responsibilities*, which covers acts done to benefit society, not linked to what the company is doing, and might include a gift from a company to help survivors of a natural disaster.[23]

Carroll argues that the economic and legal responsibilities are required by the state. Ethical responsibilities are expected, but philanthropic responsibilities are simply desired. The reason why this is a helpful structure is that it helps to separate out those responsibilities that are mandatory and those that are voluntary. A company should receive no credit for fulfilling its legal responsibilities. We should expect it to do nothing less. A company that pays the taxes due on its profits, for example, should not really claim to be acting in a particularly praiseworthy way. However, the approach acknowledges that companies may undertake ethical responsibilities and while we should expect this of companies, they are not required to do so. Philanthropic responsibilities are beyond what is required of a minimally decent company and, arguably, only these really deserve fulsome praise.

Sustainability

The theme of sustainability has become a major one in business ethics. It ties in with a wide range of environmental issues: pollution; behaviours linked with climate change; waste disposal; the erosion of local cultures and environments. It is notable that many

---

[23] A. Carroll, 'The four faces of corporate citizenship' (1998) 100 Business and Society Review 1.

large firms now have a sustainability statement. To consider just one representative example, WholeSoy Co's sustainability statement reads as follows:

> At WholeSoy, we believe that sustainability is a journey and not a destination. We strive to operate in a manner that gives back to the planet that we call home. We prioritize the quality of the relationships we have with our customers, our employees, and our partners and vendors. It is this combination of respectful relationships and positive actions toward the planet that makes WholeSoy unique. We continue to integrate the broader meaning of the word 'sustainability' into every aspect of our business and try to make changes each and every day that will benefit the global community.[24]

Most large companies have a statement of this kind.

Closely tied to this is the idea of 'sustainable development'. The British government describes the term as follows:

> The goal of sustainable development is to ensure all people throughout the world are able to satisfy their basic needs, while making sure future generations can enjoy the same quality of life.
>
> Sustainable development recognises the interconnections between society, the environment, and economy—and aims to use a holistic approach to find solutions that deliver benefits for all of these whilst minimising negative impacts. Our long term economic growth relies on protecting and enhancing the environmental resources that underpin it.
>
> ...The past 20 years have seen a growing realisation that the current model of development is unsustainable.
>
> Our way of life is placing an increasing environmental burden on the planet through:
>
> - the consequences of unavoidable climate change
>
> - increasing stress on resources and environmental systems from the way we produce, consume and waste resources
>
> - increasing loss of biodiversity, from the rainforest to fish stocks.
>
> We are also living in a world where over a billion people live on less than a dollar a day, more than 800 million are malnourished, and over two and a half billion lack access to adequate sanitation. A world disfigured by poverty and inequality is unsustainable.
>
> Unless we reconcile these contradictions, we face a less certain and less secure future. It is in our long-term best interests to make a decisive move towards more sustainable development.[25]

It should be emphasised that the notions of sustainable development and sustainability are far from concrete. Andrew Crane and Dirk Matten suggest that they represent an 'elusive and widely contested concept—and one which has also been subject to a vast array of different conceptualizations and definitions'.[26]

---

[24] Online at www.wholesoyco.com/about-us/sustainability-statement/item/sustainability-statement
[25] Online at http://sd.defra.gov.uk/what/   [26] Crane and Matten (n. 2), 33.

The unifying feature of the definitions is a concern about protecting the planet (widely understood) for future generations. It covers environmental, social, cultural, and economic factors. This breadth can be justified because often these factors go together. A particular environment can be preserved only if certain social or cultural practices are preserved. Economic considerations may be key to ensuring long-term protection for the environment. This has led to support for what John Elkington has described as the 'triple bottom line'.[27] Companies should be interested in economic goals, but uphold environmental and social values too.

Environmental concerns are generally well understood. They rest on the fact that many natural resources are finite. Bio-systems are of limited capacity. Simply using the resources up with no thought of their replenishment will lead to long-term economic and social disaster, even if producing short-term gain. Non-renewable resources, such as oil, steel, and coal, need to be treated with care and will not last forever. Renewable resources, such as sunshine, wind, and tides, are to be preferred.

There is also increased interest in the idea of economic sustainability. A model of rapid economic expansion may not be possible as a long-term goal. For a company, or even a country, choosing the course of highest productivity may not, in the long term, be the most effective. Gradual, steady, long-term growth may be preferable to a short sharp burst of gain, followed by a collapse. This could be seen as having even a direct application. Crane and Matten suggest that:

> Corporations that attempt to avoid paying corporate taxes through subtle accounting tricks might be said to behave in an unsustainable way: if they are not willing to fund the political institutional environment (such as schools, hospitals, the police, and the justice system), they erode one of the key institutional bases of their corporate success.[28]

Drastic tax avoidance certainly produces short-term gains, but as Crane and Matten indicate it can be argued that these could be outweighed by the resulting long-term harms.

In the international setting, these themes are reflected in the eight Millennium Development Goals (MDGs) agreed by the United Nations:

- eradicating extreme poverty and hunger;
- achieving universal primary education;
- promoting gender equality and empowering women;
- reducing child mortality rates;
- improving maternal health;
- combating HIV/AIDS, malaria, and other diseases;

---

[27] J. Elkington, *Cannibals with Forks: The Triple Bottom Line of 21st Century Business* (Capstone, 1999).   [28] Crane and Matten (n. 2), 35.

- ensuring environmental sustainability; and
- developing a global partnership for development.

Although stated as being goals for government, it will be apparent that companies and businesses have a major role to play in achieving the MDGs.

 What would you do?

A company seeks your advice. It is building a new factory. It has become clear that the factory will pollute a nearby river, but at a low rate (0.05 grams per litre). Preventing the pollution will be expensive. You know that the firm will be committing a crime if it pollutes the river, but that the enforcement agency does not enforce the pollution regulations unless the violation is greater than 0.075 grams per litre.[29] Do you inform the company that it will not be prosecuted because its level of pollution is too low?

What would they do?

This 'What would you do?' scenario is accompanied by a podcast in which current law students debate the issues and articulate their own responses to the ethical questions that it raises. The podcast is available online at www.oxfordtextbooks.co.uk/orc/herringethics/

A UN survey in 2010 reported that 93 per cent of chief executive officers (CEOs) saw sustainability as important to their companies' future success.[30] However, the report went on to list some key actions needed if sustainability were to be promoted and adopted more fully:

1. **Actively shaping consumer and customer awareness, attitudes and needs.** To create a market for sustainable products and services, CEOs see the need to increase the provision of consumer information and set clear standards, as well as direct government incentives and investment in areas such as energy, transport and public infrastructure.

2. **Generating new knowledge, skills and mindsets for sustainable development.** Although businesses believe that formal educational institutions and business schools need to do more, CEOs also recognize the need to increase their own efforts to engender the right skills and mindsets in their managers and future leaders.

---

[29] The example is taken from S. Pepper, 'The lawyer's amoral ethical role: A defense, a problem and some possibilities' (1986) 11 American Bar Foundational Research Journal 613.

[30] Cooper et al. (n. 18).

3. **Leading the creation of an investment environment more favorable to sustainable business.** CEOs need to be more proactive in engaging with investors to ensure that the value of sustainability activities can be demonstrated through traditional metrics such as cost reduction and revenue growth.

4. **Embedding new concepts of value and performance at the organizational and individual levels.** Businesses will need to measure both positive and negative impacts of business on society, track and manage sustainability's impact on core business drivers and metrics, and embed sustainability in individual performance frameworks for managers across their organizations (e.g., through remuneration packages).

5. **Creating a clearer and more positive regulatory environment for sustainability.** To avoid the unintended consequences of regulation, build trust and provide a more informed basis for policymaking, businesses should adopt a more proactive and collaborative approach with governments to seek out genuine opportunities for business and societal benefit.[31]

Corporate accountability

The term **corporate accountability** is often used to encourage a more rigorous holding to account of corporations.

 Definition

Moses L. Pava defines **corporate accountability** in this way:

[C]orporate accountability is primarily a form of ethical communication directed toward those parties who are affected by corporate activities and effects. Corporate accountability represents a corporation's social responsibility to explain its actions (past, present, and future) in an accessible, reasonable, and meaningful way to the society in which it operates.[32]

The organization War on Want argues that:

The globalisation of the world's economy means corporations have gained more and more power. Too often, multinational companies harm local communities, damage the environment and violate workers' rights in the course of doing business—and there is no effective way of holding them to account when they do.

---

[31] Cooper et al. (n. 18), 12.

[32] M. Pava, 'Corporate accountability', in R. Kolb (ed.) *Encyclopaedia of Business Ethics and Society* (Sage, 2008), 11.

Business is ethically unequipped to deliver for people and the environment. In the modern world, companies should be required to serve the interests of society as a whole—not just rich shareholders.

[...]

War on Want's Corporate Accountability campaign has been challenging Governments who set the rules of the world economic game to end the economic oppression that people in the developing world face. We want to reduce the power of those who use the unfair rules—corporations. The link between the poverty that millions of people in developing countries suffer and the lack of effective rules on corporations is clear.[33]

At the heart of corporate accountability is the notion that companies should be answerable for their actions.[34]

Digging deeper

One reason in favour of corporate accountability is that companies are increasingly performing the tasks that used to be performed by government. Companies are now regularly used to provide health care, personal care, and even prison services. When the government engages in such activities, there is a wealth of regulations and restrictions with which it must comply, not least of which is that the activities must ensure protection under the Human Rights Act 1998. However, when performed by a company, without specific intervention, the regulations are far fewer.[35]

There are genuine concerns that companies are able to escape their responsibilities and that the profit-based approach to business ethics does not take corporate responsibilities seriously. A powerful example is Naomi Klein's book *The Shock Doctrine*, which argues that large corporations have been able to take advantage of disasters and crisis to make substantial sums of money for themselves.[36] Looking at examples such as the Iraq War, the terrorist attacks of 9 September 2001 ('9/11'), and the Indonesian tsunami, she charts how, in the aftermath of these events, large companies made huge gains. While not without its critics,[37] there is a popular view that governments have lost control over large corporations and have no power to rein them in. A striking example may be the ability of apparently large and successful companies to avoid paying any tax at all, or to set for themselves the amount of tax that they think they should pay. At the heart of this is a crisis about democracy. If we believe that people should control their lives and determine through elections the rules that bind society, then something has gone wrong if many of the most important decisions that affect people's lives are not taken by politicians in Parliament, but by business

[33] War on Want, *Corporate Responsibility* (War on Want, 2013), 1.
[34] D. McBarnet, A. Voiculescu, and T. Campbell, *The New Corporate Accountability: Corporate Social Responsibility and the Law* (Cambridge University Press, 2009).
[35] *YL v Birmingham CC* [2007] UKHL 27.   [36] N. Klein, *The Shock Doctrine* (Penguin, 2008).
[37] A. Rugman, *The End of Globalisation* (Random House, 2000).

people in boardrooms. Corporate accountability can therefore be seen as essential for the democratic process.

It is easy to complain about the lack of accountability for companies; it is harder to produce a suitable way of responding to the issues. One popular solution has been auditing—that is, requiring companies to produce social, ethical, and environmental audits.[38] While this itself will not produce change, opening up to public scrutiny what the company is doing in these areas and the extent to which it is, or is not, meeting its ethical obligations will enable others to put pressure on the company to improve. The hope is that transparency will lead to greater awareness of what companies are doing and enable them to be better held to account.

Corporate citizenship

The term **corporate citizenship** has been used to capture some of the themes that we have been discussing.

 Definition

Corporate citizenship can be defined as follows:

> Corporate Citizenship...involves corporations becoming more informed and enlightened members of society and understanding that they are both public and private entities. [...] They are created by society and derive their legitimacy from the societies in which they operate. They need to be able to articulate their role, scope and purpose as well as understand their full social and environmental impacts and responsibilities.[39]

The World Economic Forum has explained further:

> The aim of the corporation is to make profits for the shareholders...but another key purpose is to make real and lasting contributions to the communities in which it operates. Corporate citizenship is and has to be part of the company business model. The enterprise should be profitable and sustainable. It must balance the expectations of a wide range of stakeholders, including customers, suppliers, the communities in which it operates, governments and aid agencies, among others. The company has to maintain sustainable partnerships with governments at national, state and local levels. It does not seek to appropriate the role of government, but accepts that it has a major presence in the developing world and, because of this, is an important actor in many countries.[40]

---

[38] D. Owen and B. O'Dwyer, 'Corporate social responsibility: The reporting and assurance dimension', in A. Crane, A. McWilliams, D. Matten, J. Moon, and D. Siegel (eds) *Oxford Handbook of Social Corporate Responsibility* (Oxford University Press, 2008).

[39] M. McIntosh, D. Leipziger, K. Jones, and G. Coleman, *Corporate Citizenship: Successful Strategies for Responsible Companies* (Financial Times/Pitman, 1998), 16.

[40] World Economic Forum, *Corporate Global Citizenship* (World Economic Forum, 2012).

It must be admitted, however, that the precise meaning of 'corporate citizenship' remains unclear. To some commentators, it means little more than that companies should seek to assist in community projects. As Crane and Matten argue, if it is to have a particular meaning, the term 'corporate citizenship' needs to be understood in a broader and more precise way.[41]

At first sight, the term is a little odd. If we think about some of the basic rights of citizenship—such as to vote, or to receive financial support in times of hardship—they have little application to companies. However, the term 'citizenship' is helpful in two ways. First, it clearly places the company under the government. A company should not, in its public role, see itself as outside the normal regulations of society or beyond the control of the government. Like all citizens, it must respect the government and comply with the law. Further, it acknowledges that, as with all citizens, limitations may be put on their freedom, as required by the public good.

Second, the term 'citizen' places the company alongside other members of the society in a communal group. As they say, 'we are all in this together'. Citizens accept that, as members of the community, they pay their taxes and these taxes are used for the good of all; richer citizens accept that they will pay more taxes and that these will be used to assist disadvantaged citizens. The same kind of approach can be seen for companies.

Crane and Matten take the concept further, arguing that corporate citizens:

> ...enter the arena of citizenship at the point where traditional governmental actors start to fail to be the only counterpart of citizenship. Quite simply, they can be said to partly take over those functions with regard to the protection, facilitation and enabling of citizen's rights—formerly an expectation placed solely on the government.[42]

This approach places the corporate citizen alongside the government, with responsibilities towards other citizens.

It may be that much will depend on the nature and size of the company. Smaller companies may well fit better into the 'fellow citizen' category, while larger, more powerful, companies may fit into the social structure in the way that Crane and Matten suggest.

It is possible to find examples of companies taking on governmental-type roles. Many companies operate schemes to help unemployed people to find work, or provide special assistance to tackle homelessness. Some companies help in financing schools or training programmes. In the developing world, companies employing large numbers of staff often offer schools, medical centres, and transport to those communities in which they work.[43] In these examples, we see companies working in a quasi-governmental way.

---

[41] Crane and Matten (n. 2), 70.   [42] Crane and Matten (n. 2), 77.
[43] C. Whelan and N. Niv, 'Law firm ethics in the shadow of corporate social responsibility' (2013) 26 Georgetown Journal of Legal Ethics 153.

Application

As is clear from these discussions, you might decide that your role as a lawyer involves not only informing a company of its legal rights, but also reminding it of its obligations, both legal and moral. You will be aided in this when the company has a clear ethical policy to which you can refer. You might also remind the company of the business case for acting in a socially responsible way.

International responsibilities

There has been a lively debate over how ethical standards apply when company dealings take place between companies from different countries. An example will clarify the issue.

 What would you do?

You are sent to finalise a deal on behalf of a British company in a foreign country. Once there, you realise that it is common in that country to sweeten a deal with a bribe. That is expected, and indeed the deal will not proceed through the bureaucratic hurdles without a few bribes. The client is very keen to see that the deal goes through and is happy to pay the necessary bribes.

One view in a situation such as this is that one should follow the ethical standards of the country with which one is dealing. 'When in Rome, do as the Romans do', as the saying goes.[44] Conduct that would be immoral if performed in the UK must be judged in the context of the climate, standards, and values of the culture in which one is acting. If offering a bribe is permitted in the country in which one is dealing, then it is permissible to offer a bribe.

For some commentators, there is some truth in this approach: one should be culturally sensitive and not cause offence by means of one's actions, which means adopting cultural norms when visiting another country. So if, in a particular culture, it is polite only to eat with one's right hand, you should adhere to that norm. However, where the behaviour in question is morally repugnant to our own ethical standards, we should not follow that norm. So while eating with one's right hand is not objectionable in British culture and so one should follow the local custom, the giving of bribes is repugnant in the UK and should not be done.[45]

[44] R. Green, 'When is "everyone's doing it" a moral justification?' (1991) 1 Business Ethics Quarterly 75.

[45] The Bribery Act 2010 applies to bribery around the world and so, for a British citizen, conduct falling within this legislation would be criminal.

The issue can be reflected in attempts to produce universal declarations that are designed to produce values seen to transcend cultural differences. Hence the principles outlined in the United Nations' Universal Declaration of Human Rights and the United Nations Global Compact might be applied.

Example

The ten principles of the United Nations Global Compact are as follows.

Human Rights

Principle 1: Businesses should support and respect the protection of internationally proclaimed human rights; and

Principle 2: make sure that they are not complicit in human rights abuses.

Labour

Principle 3: Businesses should uphold the freedom of association and the effective recognition of the right to collective bargaining;

Principle 4: the elimination of all forms of forced and compulsory labour;

Principle 5: the effective abolition of child labour; and

Principle 6: the elimination of discrimination in respect of employment and occupation.

Environment

Principle 7: Businesses should support a precautionary approach to environmental challenges;

Principle 8: undertake initiatives to promote greater environmental responsibility; and

Principle 9: encourage the development and diffusion of environmentally friendly technologies.

Anti-Corruption

Principle 10: Businesses should work against corruption in all its forms, including extortion and bribery.

These principles are unpacked with further detail in the Compact.

Digging deeper

It is easy to be idealistic here. In a competitive market with different companies bidding for work, it is perhaps unrealistic that all will comply with UN standards. Indeed, there is a concern that if firms are willing to breach international standards and pay bribes, they will be likely to gain the contracts, but then feel less inhibited about breaking international guidance on environmental factors or the protection of workers. If the reality is that bribes will be paid, what moral good is being achieved by the virtuous companies refusing to do it?

A related issue is the extent to which, when engaging in international business deals, one should engage only with morally just governments and institutions. Again, that may be a particular problem when 'everyone is doing it'.

 What would you do?

Many textbooks on business ethics discuss the case of 'Italian tax mores'. Under Italian tax practice, firms are expected on their tax returns to take an initial bargaining position about their tax liability, rather than complete a full return. The Italian tax authorities will then make a counterproposal on the amount of tax that should be paid and negotiations follow. For American firms operating in Italy, this can be problematic. American securities regulations and standard accounting principles require tax returns to be complete and full. Indeed, the American guidance makes it clear that this applies to all tax returns completed by American companies across the world. As this scenario shows, the ethical dilemma here is not strictly about a clash between moral values, but more about a definition: what is a 'tax return'.

Sweatshops

A major contemporary issue is so-called 'sweatshop labour'. This term refers the use of labourers in developing countries who are employed at very low wages and in poor working conditions to create goods that are then sold in the developed countries, often at a high cost. The arguments are well entrenched. Opponents argue that Western firms take advantage of labourers who are paid small sums of money in bad conditions, when the firms could easily afford to pay more and improve conditions. Indeed, it is commonly argued that the firms seek out the lowest costs of production, with no thought of the impact on the workers, to ensure the highest profit.

But supporters see the issue differently. It can be argued that the sweatshops enable developing countries to gain inward investment—contracts that would never be won if the workers had to be paid a higher wage. Indeed, the sweatshops provide developing countries with a way in which to enable economic development.[46] The wages paid by the so-called sweatshops are often better than those paid by local employers and it can lead to a competition for staff, pushing wages up. Some have argued that sweatshop workers would be paid the minimum wage in the Western world. However, critics reply that the impact of that would be that firms would not use the workforces in the developing countries.

---

[46] I. Maitland, 'The great non-debate over international sweatshops' [1997] British Academy of Management Annual Conference Proceedings 240.

Some believe that there is clash here between idealism and practicality; some believe that it is a basic human right to be paid decently,[47] and that this could be little lower than the Western minimum wage and yet not impact on the employability of workers in the developing world.

Business ethics management

How can we ensure that businesses have an ethical dimension to their decision-making? Companies that try to ensure that they are acting ethically (or at least want to give the appearance that they are) typically create policies or practices designed to promote decisions that are made in compliance with ethical standards. These policies or practices can include the following.

Mission statements or value statements

Many companies seek to adopt a mission statement, which might include a reference to 'general good'.

Example

The following is the mission statement and vision of Coca Cola:

Our Mission

[...]

• To refresh the world...

• To inspire moments of optimism and happiness...

• To create value and make a difference.

Our Vision

Our vision serves as the framework for our Roadmap and guides every aspect of our business by describing what we need to accomplish in order to continue achieving sustainable, quality growth.

• **People:** Be a great place to work where people are inspired to be the best they can be.

• **Portfolio:** Bring to the world a portfolio of quality beverage brands that anticipate and satisfy people's desires and needs.

• **Partners:** Nurture a winning network of customers and suppliers, together we create mutual, enduring value.

---

[47] D. Arnold and N. Bowie, 'Sweatshops and respect for persons' (2003) 13 Business Ethics Quarterly 221.

- **Planet:** Be a responsible citizen that makes a difference by helping build and support sustainable communities.
- **Profit:** Maximize long-term return to shareowners while being mindful of our overall responsibilities.
- **Productivity:** Be a highly effective, lean and fast-moving organization.[48]

As with many companies, this example acknowledges that Coca-Cola seeks to make money and to be an economically successful company, while also seeking to achieve other goods.

While mission statements may be seen as indicating a commitment to ethical goals and improving the general good, whether they are any more than fine-sounding words and actually make a difference to what a company does may be questioned.

Codes of ethics

A code of ethics is a more concrete set of rules that seeks to govern what a company does.

Example

Vodafone's code of ethics includes the following:

...Each Relevant Officer must:

- act with integrity, including being honest and candid while still maintaining the confidentiality of Company information where required or in the Company's interests;
- observe, fully, applicable governmental laws, rules and regulations;
- comply with the requirements of applicable accounting and auditing standards and Company policies in the maintenance of a high standard of accuracy and completeness in the Company's financial records;
- adhere to a high standard of business ethics and not seek competitive advantage through unlawful or unethical business practices; and
- avoid conflicts of interest wherever possible. Anything that would be a conflict for a Relevant Officer will also be a conflict if it is related to a member of his or her family or a close relative.[49]

---

[48] Coca Cola, *Mission, Vision and Values* (2013), online at www.coca-cola.co.uk/about-us/coca-cola-mission-vision-statement.html

[49] Vodaphone, *Code of Ethics* (undated), online at www.vodafone.com/content/index/investors/about_us/governance/compliance_and_code_of_ethics.html

As this example shows, the code of ethics tends to be more precise than the mission statement. A breach of the code of ethics by an employee can be a serious matter and may even lead to dismissal.

Ethics managers

Some companies have individuals or committees who have responsibilities for upholding ethical standards within the company. One reason behind the creation of these posts is that they do provide the management with some protection if the company is found to be acting wrongly. A senior manager can claim that he or she expected the relevant ethics officer or committee to ensure that the company was complying with good practice, and so that he or she cannot be held responsible for any wrongdoing.

Ethics consultants and training

Some companies prefer to use an outsider to ensure control of business ethics. Environmental consultants have been particularly popular; training on ethics has been on the rise too. Even the US Army has been giving ethics training to its members. A survey in the UK found 71 per cent of large businesses arranging ethics training.[50]

Auditing and reporting

It is now common for companies to produce statements about matters such as sustainability and ethical practices in their annual reports. This symbolically emphasises the importance attached to these values, but can also provide a check on how well the company is living up to its ideals.

Lawyers and business ethics

This chapter has sought to highlight the complex ethical issues that business can raise. When lawyers act for business clients, they should not assume that companies are solely concerned with making money. As this chapter has shown, it has become increasingly common for companies to express an ethical dimension to their work. Lawyers may be asked to ensure that their clients abide by ethical standards.

---

[50] S. Webley, *Use of Codes of Ethics in Business* (Institute of Business Ethics, 2008).

Lawyers will need to tread carefully here. They should be aware of the practice of what Miriam Cherry and Judd Sneirson call 'greenwashing'[51]—that is, purporting to have ethical principles, but then ignoring them when necessary. They explain:

> By greenwashing, a corporation might increase its sales or boost its brand image through environmental rhetoric, but at the same time either pollute the environment or decline to spend money on the environment, employee welfare, or otherwise honor its commitments to other constituencies.[52]

However, a lawyer advised by a company should not assume that because the director wishes to ignore his or her ethical responsibilities, the company does. The directors are not the same as the company. A lawyer may find himself or herself unable to act if the instructions from the directors do not match the company's adopted ethical policy.

Increasingly, law firms may find themselves affected by business ethics in a different way. Christopher Whelan and Neta Niv have noted that, increasingly, businesses are requiring law firms to comply with the ethical standards that they have set for themselves.[53]

There is, however, also evidence that some companies use their lawyers to help them to dissipate blame. Richard Ackland has written:

> Boards of directors and senior directors have schemes that need implementation. Lawyers are hired to get the client over the line. When things go wrong, as they often do, the directors and executives invariably say, 'We acted on advice'. The standard retort of the advisers is; 'We were not given all the information, so the advice was necessarily limited'. This relatable formulation usually saves a lot of bacon.[54]

Conclusion

This chapter has explored the burgeoning issue of business ethics. The traditional view was that companies are solely interested in making money and that they do not owe obligations to anyone apart from their shareholders. Few business people would subscribe to that view today. There is a widespread acceptance that there are obligations to the environment and the broader societal good. How far these extend is much debated. Further, there is a concern that while companies will now commonly declare their intent for work to be sustainable and to be good corporate citizens, that may not work out in practice as well as it does in theory.

---

[51] M. Cherry and J. Neirson, 'Beyond profit: Rethinking corporate social responsibility and greenwashing after the BP oil disaster' (2011) 85 Tulane Law Review 983.

[52] Cherry and Neirson (n. 51), 984.   [53] Cherry and Neirson (n. 51).

[54] R. Ackland, 'Irresistible charms', *Business Review Weekly*, 29 September 2004, 50, cited in Parker and Evans (n. 1), 217.

Further reading

D. Arnold and N. Bowie. 'Sweatshops and respect for persons' (2003) 13 Business Ethics Quarterly 221.

J. Bakan, *The Corporation: The Pathological Pursuit of Profit and Power* (Robinson Publishing, 2005).

N. Capaldi, 'What philosophy can and cannot contribute to business ethics' (2006) 22 Journal of Private Enterprise 68.

A. Carroll, 'The four faces of corporate citizenship' (1998) 100 Business and Society Review 1.

M. Cherry and J. Neirson, 'Beyond profit: Rethinking corporate social responsibility and greenwashing after the BP oil disaster' (2011) 85 Tulane Law Review 983.

T. Cooper, R. Hayward, and L. Neuberger, *A New Era of Sustainability: UN Global Compact–Accenture CEO Study* (United Nations, 2010).

A. Crane and D. Matten, *Business Ethics*, 3rd edn (Oxford University Press, 2010).

A. Crane, A. McWilliams, D. Matten, J. Moon, and D. Siegel (eds) *Oxford Handbook of Social Corporate Responsibility* (Oxford University Press, 2008).

A. Marcoux, 'A fiduciary argument against stakeholder theory' (2003) 13 Business Ethics Quarterly 1.

D. McBarnet, A. Voiculescu, and T. Campbell, *The New Corporate Accountability: Corporate Social Responsibility and the Law* (Cambridge University Press, 2009).

C. McMahon, *Authority and Democracy: A General Theory of Government and Management* (Princeton University Press, 1994).

L. Stout, *The Shareholder Value Myth: How Putting Shareholders First Harms Investors, Corporations, and the Public* (Berrett Koehler Publishers, 2012).

C. Whelan and N. Niv, 'Law firm ethics in the shadow of corporate social responsibility' (2013) 26 Georgetown Journal of Legal Ethics 153.

13 Lawyers' social responsibilities

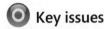 **Key issues**

- Do lawyers owe obligations to promote the public good?
- Are there social obligations that lawyers owe?
- What is the status of pro bono work?

Introduction

People say some nasty things about lawyers. Rodell once alleged: 'It is pretty hard to find a group less concerned with serving society and more concerned with serving themselves than the lawyers.'[1]

In this book, we have been especially looking at the obligations that a lawyer has towards his or her clients. In Chapter 11, we looked at the obligations that lawyers owe to third parties, in particular. In this chapter, we look more broadly at the responsibilities that lawyers have to society and the greater good.

Of course, many people believe that we all have responsibilities to the social good: to the environment; to those in society who are in especial need; and so on. The nature and extent of these are controversial, and we shall not discuss these. This chapter will focus instead on the obligations that it might be claimed lawyers have in their capacity as lawyers. That said, your beliefs about the extent to which people generally owe obligations to the community are likely to be reflected in what you think about the obligations of lawyers.

The theory

We have explored the general theoretical approaches to the relationship between lawyers and their clients in Chapters 1 and 3. The main positions will be familiar. There are those who argue that the lawyer's primary duty is to the client and that the lawyer must promote the interests of the client with utmost zeal. These people would argue strongly against the idea that lawyers owe a general duty to

[1] F. Rodell, 'Goodbye, to law reviews' (1936) 23 Virginia Law Review 38, 42.

the general good. Alternatively, as Bradley Wendel argues, some would say that lawyers should promote societal good, but that they should do this by promoting the interests of their clients with zeal.[2] Others yet will argue that lawyers owe a duty to society by virtue of their role as officers of the court and their place in the social justice system.

Rakesh Anand argues that lawyers have a special place in society. He is writing about the United States, but some would see the argument applying equally to England and Wales:

> [A]t the broad cultural level, the practice of law in America is a type of religious practice. It speaks to the deeper meaning of American life and marks an activity in and through which Americans move beyond themselves. Americans are a community committed to self-government under the rule of law. That commitment is as serious as any.
>
> If in America law is a cultural practice, then 'the lawyer' is the individual who serves that way of life (because his or her identity and substantive character is, by definition, a direct function of the field within which he or she operates). Given that this *modus vivendi* is built around the People, lawyers, correctly understood, are 'the People's people.' First and foremost, the role of the lawyer in the American democracy is to function as *their* representative.[3]

This role, Anand goes on to argue, requires lawyers to represent and affirm the rule of law. In practical terms, this leads to a strong focus by lawyers on protecting the legal interests of their clients. She rejects 'cause lawyering' (under which lawyers seek only to represent clients of whom they approve) and asserts that lawyers must not select clients. To her, the rule of law is about the same law applying equally to all, and the lawyer has an important role in that regard by ensuring that the best legal advice and representation is accessible by every client. In this way, Anand argues, as have others, that lawyers do have a duty to society, but that this duty requires them to focus on providing the best representation for their clients.

This argument will appeal to some, but has its difficulties. One problem is that it idealises the rule of law. It assumes that the legal system and society in question does indeed treat everyone equally and respects the rule of law. One of the arguments that cause lawyers often make is that they represent groups whose rights are typically ignored by the courts or society. They are, if anything, upholding the rule of law by supporting these groups. More cynically, it might be said that lawyers need to recognise their role as based not in an idealised system that promotes the rule of law, but in a flawed system that often privileges the rights of the rich and reinforces the advantages of the powerful. Their role does not therefore promote the rule of law.

    [2] B. Wendel, *Lawyers and Fidelity to Law* (Princeton University Press, 2010).
    [3] R. Anand, 'The role of the lawyer in the American democracy' (2009) 77 Fordham Law Review 1611, 1613.

The codes

The Bar Council Code of Conduct (the Bar Code) offers some recognition of an interest that is broader than that owed to a client.

Follow the Code

Under the Bar Code, para 302:

> A barrister has an overriding duty to the Court to act with independence in the interests of justice: he must assist the Court in the administration of justice and must not deceive or knowingly or recklessly mislead the Court.

There is a recognition here that the 'overriding' duty of a barrister is not to his or her client, but to the court, and to promote the administration of justice.

The Solicitors Regulation Authority (SRA) Code of Conduct has as the first three of its ten Principles not duties owed to clients, but rather duties to the broader good.

Follow the Code

The SRA Code of Conduct, Principles 1–3, require that a solicitor must:

1. uphold the rule of law and the proper administration of justice;
2. act with integrity;
3. not allow your independence to be compromised;

These are somewhat vague, but do make it clear that lawyers are expected to do more than simply promote their clients' interests.

Follow the Code

Another of the ten Principles expressed in the SRA Code of Conduct is:

6. behave in a way that maintains the trust the public places in you and in the provision of legal services;

There is a similar provision in the Bar Code.

Follow the Code

The Bar Code, para 301, requires that a barrister must not:

engage in conduct whether in pursuit of his profession or otherwise which is:
(i)   dishonest or otherwise discreditable to a barrister;
(ii) prejudicial to the administration of justice; or
(iii) likely to diminish public confidence in the legal profession or the administration of jus-
      tice or otherwise bring the legal profession into disrepute;

These may also be seen to involve an obligation to act in the public interest. But notice that they are presented as a requirement to protect the profession of barristers, rather than the interests of the public as a whole. These are not the same thing at all!

It is not clear quite what acting in a way that damages the profession might include. Clearly, criminal activities and those that clearly breach the ethics codes will. But how much further can this be taken? It presumably includes activities that are not, strictly speaking, illegal, but which might bring the profession into disrepute.[4] Andrew Boon and Jennifer Levin suggest that running a 'sex shop' would fall under this category.[5] Not everyone would agree with that suggestion. Indeed, that suggestion indicates a problem: on many issues, there is no community consensus on what is moral. If the 'sex shop' were designed to promote good sexual health and mutually respectful sexual behaviour, would that be undermining to the profession? Would a lawyer promoting gambling or payday loans be undermining the reputation of the profession? What about one belonging to the British National Party? One solution might be to say that if a majority of the population would think badly of the activity, this would be sufficient. However, that is not an easy test. Adultery might be thought of badly by a majority of the population, but are all barristers or solicitors who commit adultery bringing the profession into disrepute?! Even in relation to criminal activities, it might be questioned whether very minor offences, such as littering or speeding, would necessarily bring the profession into dispute. Why, even judges have been known to do such things!

Another interesting example comes from the Ladbroke Grove rail crash litigation. The solicitor for the victims produced a press release saying that their evidence would 'reveal shocking evidence of total mismanagement and utter callous disregard for safety' by the defendants (Railtrack and others). Railtrack complained to the Law Society that the overblown language brought the profession into disrepute. The Law Society concluded that the press release was 'regrettable', but had not breached professional rules.[6]

---

[4] Otherwise, the Code could simply have forbidden illegal behaviour.
[5] A. Boon and J. Levin, *The Ethics and Conduct of Lawyers in England and Wales* (Hart, 2008), 287.
[6] Boon and Levin (n. 5), 288.

Criminal law

Obviously, solicitors owe duties to the state to comply with the criminal law, as do any professionals. But there are some special offences designed to restrict solicitors' behaviour and these can be seen to reflect special obligations that lawyers owe to society.

Money laundering

Perhaps the best-known obligations imposed on lawyers by the criminal law are those surrounding money laundering. When criminals illegally obtain money, they sometimes pass it through various institutions so that the source of it appears to be respectable, which makes detection of its criminal roots difficult. Passing money through law firms is attractive to criminals attempting to launder money, because it is assumed that money transacted in by respectable firms of lawyers is clean. The principles of confidentiality also make lawyers a reliable resource for money laundering. Lawyers can become involved indirectly when buying houses or engaging in large commercial transactions. In the notorious Brink's-Mat gold bullion robbery, £30 million was laundered through solicitors. Of course, rarely are the lawyers aware that they are being used in this way.

Modern money laundering legislation is designed to prevent criminals from using lawyers as a means of laundering the proceeds of criminal activity. The law is found in the Proceeds of Crime Act 2002 and the Money Laundering Regulations 2007.[7] The Law Society has produced a guide for solicitors, which totals some 138 pages, indicating the complexity of the issue.[8]

The guide defines money laundering in the following way:

> Money laundering is generally defined as the process by which the proceeds of crime, and the true ownership of those proceeds, are changed so that the proceeds appear to come from a legitimate source. Under [the Proceeds of Crime Act 2002], the definition is broader and more subtle. Money laundering can arise from small profits and savings from relatively minor crimes, such as regulatory breaches, minor tax evasion or benefit fraud. A deliberate attempt to obscure the ownership of illegitimate funds is not necessary.[9]

There are two primary offences in the Proceeds of Crime Act 2002, which the Law Society guidance summarises as follows:

Section 327—concealing

A person commits an offence if he conceals, disguises, converts, or transfers criminal property, or removes criminal property from England and Wales, Scotland or Northern Ireland.

---

[7] SI 2007/2157.   [8] Law Society, *Anti-Money Laundering* (Law Society, 2012).
[9] Law Society (n. 8), para. 1.3.

Concealing or disguising criminal property includes concealing or disguising its nature, source, location, disposition, movement, ownership or any rights connected with it.

Section 328—arrangements

A person commits an offence if he enters into, or becomes concerned in an arrangement which he knows or suspects facilitates the acquisition, retention, use or control of criminal property by or on behalf of another person.[10]

Some of these terms need more definition.

Criminal property

 Definition

> The Proceeds of Crime Act 2002, section 340(3), defines **criminal property** as 'a person's benefit from criminal conduct or it represents such a benefit (in whole or in part and whether directly or indirectly)'.

Arrangement

The 2002 Act deliberately does not define an 'arrangement'. This leaves its interpretation open. The Law Society suggests a narrow interpretation, emphasising that:

- entering into or becoming concerned in an arrangement involves an act done at a particular time;
- an offence is committed only once the arrangement is actually made; and
- preparatory or intermediate steps in transactional work that does not itself involve the acquisition, retention, use, or control of property will not constitute the making of an arrangement under section 328.

In making this suggestion, the Law Society relies on *Bowman v Fels*,[11] in which it was held that the offence in section 328 does not cover or affect the ordinary conduct of litigation by legal professionals.

 Key case

Bowman v Fels **[2005] EWCA Civ 226**

The case involved a breakdown of a relationship. In acting for one party, the solicitor received paperwork dealing with the financial affairs of the parties, which indicated that the money had included costs of renovations to his home in his business accounts. That

---

[10] Law Society (n. 8), paras 5.4.2 and 5.4.3.   [11] [2005] EWCA Civ 226.

was unlawful tax evasion. The solicitor reported the matter to the National Criminal Intelligence Services (NCIS) under section 328, causing delay to the proceedings.

The Court of Appeal held that the solicitor had acted wrongly. Section 328 did not cover the 'ordinary conduct of litigation'. The solicitor, in dealing with the division of the couple's assets on separation, was engaged in routine legal work and not 'involved in an arrangement with criminal property'. Interestingly, Article 6 of the European Convention on Human Rights, which protects the right to fair trial, was brought in aid.

This is significant because, in many family cases (and indeed other kinds of cases), it will become clear that there is some, perhaps very minor, tax evasion. Because the regulations are not limited by sums involved, there could be serious delays if reports to the NCIS were to be required in each case in which there was suspicion that the activity was improper in routine legal practice.

So what constitutes an arrangement? The Law Society advises that:

[D]ividing assets in accordance with the judgment, including the handling of the assets which are criminal property, is not an arrangement. Further, settlements, negotiations, out of court settlements, alternative dispute resolution and tribunal representation are not arrangements.[12]

However, it interestingly warns solicitors that they may need to warn clients that they (the clients) will commit offences in their dealing with the property if it remains criminal property.

The Law Society gives examples of the kinds of transactions that are particularly likely to raise money laundering issues, including:

- complicated financial or property transactions;
- providing assistance in setting up trusts or company structures, which could be used to obscure ownership of property;
- payments that are made to or received from third parties;
- payments made by cash; and
- transactions with a cross-border element.

Application

The regulations are easy to use in straightforward cases. If a client is buying a house with cash and is not able to explain where the money has come from, the solicitor may suspect that it is from the proceeds of crime. In other cases, it will be less straightforward. If the money is a gift from 'my uncle in Russia' or 'a bonus from work', how much questioning is the solicitor required to do? The Law Society issues detailed guidance

---

[12] Law Society (n. 8), para. 5.4.3.

and can offer advice on such dilemmas. It is not appropriate here to go into all of the different scenarios. Perhaps the key point to emphasise for this book is that, given that we are dealing with a potential criminal offence, a solicitor in any doubt should report his or her suspicions. If the solicitor makes the report to the Serious Organised Crimes Agency (SOCA), then he or she has an automatic defence to any allegation of an offence. However, the disclosure has to be made before the solicitor has committed the offence. Where solicitors make such disclosure under section 337, they are not treated as being in breach of confidentiality or breach of contract.[13]

Solicitors will undoubtedly feel a tension here. There are no risks from making a disclosure and doing so will offer them complete protection from any criminal charge under the money laundering legislation. Not disclosing may be in the client's best interests, but carries a risk for the solicitor of a criminal conviction. This creates a clear conflict of interest. It is a conflict that is all the harder because if disclosure is made, it is unlikely that the client will want to continue using the solicitor; indeed, the solicitor may well feel that his or her relationship with the client has broken down and so that he or she should withdraw from the case.

Where there are concerns about a client, a solicitor should undertake 'customer due diligence'. Regulation 5 under the 2007 Regulations explains that this involves:

- identifying the client and verifying his or her identity on the basis of documents, data, or information obtained from a reliable and independent source;

- identifying, where there is a beneficial owner who is not the client, the beneficial owner and taking adequate measures, on a risk-sensitive basis, to verify his or her identity, until the solicitor is satisfied that he or she knows who the beneficial owner is (which will include understanding the ownership and control structure of a legal person, trust, or similar arrangement); and

- obtaining information on the purpose and intended nature of the business relationship.

Digging deeper

A tricky issue arises where a lawyer is considering making a disclosure. Should he or she inform the client? The lawyer must act carefully. There is an offence in section 333 of the Proceeds of Crime Act 2002 of 'tipping off'—that is, making a disclosure that 'is likely to preclude any investigation'. That may well be committed by a solicitor warning a client that a disclosure is likely. This offence, however, can be committed only by a solicitor regulated under the Financial Services Act 2012 and once the solicitor knows or suspects that the money laundering disclosure has been made. Its strict wording

---

[13] There are limited circumstances under which a lawyer prosecuted under section 328 can raise a defence that he or she did not make a disclosure owing to the rules of privilege, but this can operate under section 330(6) only if the information was not withheld for the intention of furthering a criminal offence. Many solicitors will prefer to make the disclosure than to hope that this defence will be found to apply.

therefore suggests that if there is a disclosure to the client before a disclosure has been made to the authorities, that is not an offence. However, that interpretation would seem to undermine the point of the section in this case. A court may decide that informing a client of a disclosure will be an ongoing statement and impede the investigation following a disclosure, and so be covered.

There is a separate offence in section 342 that applies if a disclosure is made, which is likely to prejudice the investigation, by someone who knows or suspects that an investigation is about to be undertaken. This too is an offence that could be committed by a solicitor who tells a client that a disclosure is about to be made to the SOCA. It seems clear that a solicitor who has decided that a disclosure must be made is safest simply not informing the client. Trickier are cases in which the solicitor is worried about the source of money and asks questions of the client. By expressing their concerns, such solicitors will reveal to well-informed clients that a disclosure to the SOCA may be made.

There are further requirements under the Money Laundering Regulations 2007 covering firms acting under the Financial Services Act 2012, but these will not be covered here.

 Application

Because money laundering is a serious criminal offence, you are always safest reporting suspicious activity. Remember that you will be judged in hindsight. What might appear simply a little odd in the moment might, in hindsight, appear to be an obvious case of money laundering.

Concerns about money laundering legislation

The money laundering regulations have raised concern among lawyers. Opponents argue that lawyers are being used to 'police' the enforcement of the law. The failure of the police and prosecution authorities to deal with the problem of locating criminal money means that the government turned to solicitors to do this 'police work' for them. Indeed, as can be seen from the above, a lawyer conscientiously seeking to comply with the law may feel the need in some cases to carry out extensive investigations into the source of money received by a client. This expense will ultimately fall on the client, with the peculiar consequence that clients will be paying for investigations into themselves. But this is just a reflection of what critics feel is the broader issue: that the legislation undermines the loyalty a lawyer owes to the client and the promise of confidentiality.[14]

---

[14] A. Odby, 'The European Union and money laundering', in I. Bantekas (ed.) *International and European Financial Criminal Law* (LexisNexis, 2006).

On the other hand, lawyers are being asked to be involved in transferring money and the like. They are not simply being asked to 'spy' on their clients. It is only when lawyers are handling money directly that they are told they must be confident that they are not facilitating a crime. This means that the potential conflict applies only in a relatively limited context and, supporters argue, can be justified in the name of the greater good that combating money laundering achieves.

Tax avoidance

Another area in which lawyers have special obligations is tax avoidance. Illegal tax evasion is unlawful and, of course, a lawyer must not be involved in it. However, tax avoidance, which involves seeking to make financial arrangements so that tax does not need to be paid, or so that less tax is paid than might otherwise be the case, is lawful.

Nevertheless, there is a duty under the Finance Act 2004 to disclose the details to HM Revenue and Customs (HMRC) of 'schemes or arrangements' that are not routine tax advice, and which are promoted or used by a professional to avoid tax. It is accepted that if a lawyer or accountant has found a way in which to avoid tax, the client can take advantage of that. However, by requiring disclosure of this to the authorities, any loophole can be closed, so that that method of tax avoidance cannot be used in the future.

There might be some debate over whether a lawyer advising a client of a scheme, or helping a client to put into effect a scheme devised by an accountant, will be a 'promoter'. Again, lawyers are likely to want to play it safe. Unless the lawyer's involvement is highly tangential, it is safest to disclose the scheme to HMRC.

Digging deeper

A rather odd aspect of the Finance Act 2004 requirements is that although section 314 states that the duty to disclose trumps the rules of confidentiality, this does not include privileged advice. It is arguable therefore that if the scheme could fall within professional privilege, which it probably would, it may not need to be disclosed. That interpretation, if correct, would rather negate the point of the legislation, at least as it applies to lawyers.

Duty to the court

As already mentioned, the professional codes emphasise the duty of the lawyers to the court. However, quite what this means is not clear. In *Copeland v Smith*,[15] Brooke

---

[15] [2000] 1 All ER 457, 462.

LJ noted that the court system is dependent on the assistance of advocates to the judiciary and that their assistance avoids 'having to incur the cost of legal assistance for judges'. Andrew Boon and Jennifer Levin somewhat acerbically comment: 'This particular collective duty therefore imposes a responsibility on clients to save the state money by paying their lawyers to inform the courts of its own laws!'[16]

Brooke LJ went on to suggest that the advocate needs to keep up to date with the cases found in the generalist law reports and not the specialist law reports. Notably, he was speaking in 2000, and it may well be that electronic databases have now become so widespread that his standard is too low. Further, in many areas of the law, advocates can be expected to have specialist knowledge and to read the specialist reports in their area.

Perhaps the most difficult issue surrounding this duty is the extent to which the lawyer has a positive duty to disclose information even if it assists the opponent. That issue was addressed in detail in Chapter 11.

Follow the Code

The Bar Code, para 708, states that the barrister:

[...]

(c) must ensure that the Court is informed of all relevant decisions and legislative provisions of which he is aware whether the effect is favourable or unfavourable towards the contention for which he argues;

(d) must bring any procedural irregularity to the attention of the Court during the hearing and not reserve such matter to be raised on appeal.

The Bar Code seems to put the standard quite high. It must cut against the grain for some advocates to have to inform the court of precedents that go against their clients' cases, but which their incompetent colleague had not found out. It may be some comfort to emphasise that this is a result of the duty to the court, rather than of a duty to the opponent.

Duties to the public

There is some debate over the extent to which it might be said that lawyers owe a duty to the state more widely. Imagine, for example, that a lawyer, in advising a client, came across information that indicated a major risk to public health or public finances. Is there a duty for the lawyer to act on that?

---

[16] Boon and Levin (n. 5), 295.

What would you do?

You are approached by a hospital trust, which is being sued by a patient for inadequate care at the hands of one of the trust's surgeons. As you investigate the case, it becomes clear that the whole department is linked with deaths to numerous patients. The trust does not want to intervene, because the surgeon is a powerful figure, but you are convinced that many patients are dying or suffering serious harm. The trust instructs you to defend the claim vigorously and to ensure that there is no adverse publicity.

Three approaches may be taken in such a case.

1. The principle of loyalty to the client and confidentiality mean that you *must not* disclose the risk to anyone without the client's permission.

2. The significant public interest in disclosure provides a reason why you *may*, if you wish, breach confidence and disclose.

3. The lawyer's duty to society generally means that you *must* disclose the serious risk to public well-being.

The financial scandals of recent years highlight the issue well. Some would say that lawyers for a number of institutions must have been aware of the precarious financial position of some of those institutions and yet no intervention was made, causing huge financial loss.[17] Critics claim that lawyers' misplaced sense of loyalty meant that they stood by while illegal activities took place and serious harm to the general good was done. As Gordon argues, it is surprising that lawyers want to see themselves as simply 'private agents for private parties'.[18] Their loyalty to clients need not be absolute and undivided. However, lawyers are paid, very well, by their clients and will want to present themselves as unswervingly dedicated to promoting their clients' interests, even where—perhaps especially where—that ignores conceptions of the public good.

This debate in part reflects much broader debates around allegations that we are witnessing an increasingly individualist society.[19] People are focusing more on their own interests and pursuing their own good, and are less willing to make sacrifices for

---

[17] See, for one example, W. Simon, 'The Kaye Scholer affair: The lawyer's duty of candor and the Bar's temptations of evasion and apology' (1998) 23 Law and Social Inquiry 243.

[18] R. Gordon, 'A collective failure of nerve: The Bar's response to Kay Scholer' (1998) 23 Law and Society 315.

[19] R. Pearce and E. Wald, 'The obligation of lawyers to heal civic culture: Confronting the ordeal of incivility in the practice of law' (2011) 34 University of Arkansas Little Rock Review 1.

community projects or for the wider good. Russell Pearce and Eli Wald have argued that lawyers have even contributed to this:

> [L]awyers as civics teachers have promoted the commitment to autonomous self-interest not only in the private dealings of clients but in culturally manufacturing autonomous self-interest as the dominant paradigm of public discourse and in the resulting erosion of relational self-interest as a countervailing influence. We assert that lawyers should instead draw upon the relational tradition found in professionalism and the lawyer's historic role to encourage public dialogue, help repair our civic culture, and suggest to clients relational means of pursuing their interests.[20]

They argue that lawyers, in their advice and practice, should encourage people not to seek their own self-interest above all, but to take account of the greater good and the interests of others.

This argument is developed further by Vivien Holmes and Simon Rice, who argue that lawyers need to appreciate that the world is increasingly interconnected:

> The world is connected as never before, and humanity's future is challenged as never before. In this context, the world needs lawyers to recognize the global effect of their conduct, and to take responsibility for it. This need becomes greater as legal practice increasingly operates away from, or outside, both formal regulation and 'rule of law' legal institutions. While an ethic of neutral partnership allows lawyers to avoid taking this responsibility, a contextual approach to legal ethics preserves and respects the lawyer–client relationship while requiring lawyers to take moral responsibility for the consequence of their work. The world cannot afford lawyers to do otherwise.[21]

Pro bono

If you were seeking to argue that lawyers *do* recognise the importance of working for the greater good, you could well point to the significant amount of **pro bono** work that lawyers do. This is typically presented as work for the poor or disadvantaged, who would not otherwise be able to afford a lawyer, or work for charitable organisations, undertaken without pay.

 Definition

The Joint Pro Bono Protocol for Legal Work, developed by the Pro Bono Coordinating Committee and endorsed by the leading professional bodies, defines **pro bono** work as:

> [L]egal advice or representation provided by lawyers in the public interest including to individuals, charities and community groups who cannot afford to pay for that

---

[20] Pearce and Wald (n. 19), 4.

[21] V. Holmes and S. Rice, 'Our common future: The imperative for contextual ethics in a connected world', in F. Bartlett, R. Mortensen, and K. Tranter (eds) *Alternative Perspectives on Lawyers and Legal Ethics* (Routledge, 2011), 121.

advice or representation and where public and alternative means of funding are not available.[22]

Legal work is pro bono legal work only if it is free to the client, without payment to the lawyer or law firm (regardless of the outcome), and provided voluntarily either by the lawyer or his or her firm.

The case for pro bono work

Pro bono work is seen by some as an essential aspect of being a lawyer.[23] As the respected Australian judge Justice Kirby has put it, pro bono is:

...the least that lawyers should do to maintain their own credibility and the credibility of the system of justice that they help to deliver...

...The bottom line is that law is not just a business. Never was. Never can be so. It is a special profession. Its only claim to public respect is the commitment of each and every one of us to equal justice under law.[24]

The argument is that if lawyers claim to be committed to the justice system, they must play their part in ensuring that justice is open to all. This is especially so because most lawyers are very well remunerated as a result of their position in the system.

Indeed, some have complained that, given the rich rewards that lawyers receive, not enough pro bono work is performed.[25] There have been calls for firms to encourage an ethos in which pro bono work is expected,[26] and even for it to be compulsory for lawyers to do pro bono work.[27] Other countries do that. In 2015, all applicants to the New York Bar will be required to complete 50 hours of pro bono work.[28] In *Van Der Mussele v Belgium*,[29] the European Court of Human Rights rejected a claim that compulsory pro bono work for Belgian pupil advocates was forced labour and so breached Article 4 of the European Convention on Human Rights.

---

[22] Pro Bono Coordinating Committee. *The Joint Pro Bono Protocol for Legal Work* (Ministry of Justice, 2013), para. 1.

[23] G. Bindman, 'What money could buy', in J. Robins (ed.) *Pro Bono: Good Enough?* (Legal Action Group, 2012).

[24] M. Kirby, 'Law firms and justice in Australia', Speech given at Australian Law Awards, Sydney, 7 March 2002, online at www.hcourt.gov.au/assets/publications/speeches/former-justices/kirbyj/kirbyj_award.htm

[25] D. Rhode, 'Pro bono in principle and in practice' (2003) 53 Journal of Legal Education 413, 417.

[26] R. Granfield, 'The meaning of pro bono: Institutional variations in professional obligations among lawyers' (2007) 44 Law and Society Review 113.

[27] E. Pearmaine, 'Is compulsory pro bono needed to fill the void left by legal aid cuts?', *The Law Society Gazette*, 21 January 2013, online at www.lawgazette.co.uk/analysis/is-compulsory-pro-bono-needed-to-fill-the-void-left-by-legal-aid-cuts/69069.article

[28] M. Fraser, 'Forced labour' (2013) 163 New Law Journal 11.

[29] App. No. 8919/80 [1983] ECHR 13.

Pro bono work provides the opportunity for the legal profession to show that its sense of social obligation is not lost. Indeed, it is notable that while pro bono work used to be seen as a matter of individual conscience, it has become increasingly well organised,[30] with the Law Society and Bar Council playing legal roles in pro bono work, suggesting that there is an acceptance that pro bono work is important for the public reputation and self-perception of the profession. As Lucy Scott-Moncrieff, President of the Law Society, has acknowledged:

> Pro bono is good for solicitors and enables them to show that they are genuinely committed to access to justice. It can build skills, experience, confidence and self-esteem. It brings lawyers into contact with many clients that they wouldn't otherwise meet and enables them to use their unique professional skills to make a high value contribution to helping others.[31]

Concerns about pro bono

It might be thought that pro bono work is so obviously good that no one could oppose it. However, it has raised a number of concerns. First, there is a problem in that some lawyers fear that, in their pro bono work, their duties may conflict with the interests of actual (or perspective) paying clients. This can impact on the kinds of pro bono work that lawyers are willing to undertake—the kind that current or future clients may find unobjectionable.[32]

Second, there is a concern that government encourages pro bono as an ideal simply to justify its restrictions on legal aid.[33] Certainly, there has been an increase in the amount of pro bono work being done since the cutbacks in legal aid, with some of the pro bono work being for clients who might previously have gained legal aid.

Third, cynics argue that lawyers are simply acting in self-interest and in an attempt to improve their public image, especially in the case of large commercial firms. That public image is used to justify excessive salaries and profits. It creates a positive vibe among employees, assists in recruitment, and even is a form of advertising to encourage clients to use the firm.[34] Indeed, it is interesting that some have made 'the business case' for pro

---

[30] S. Cummings, 'The politics of pro bono' (2004) 52 UCLA Law Review 18.

[31] L. Scott-Moncrieff, 'Lawyers view pro bono as the fabric of their business as 11th National Pro Bono Week kicks off', Press release, 5 November 2012, online at www.lawsociety.org.uk/news/press-releases/lawyers-view-pro-bono-as-the-fabric-of-their-business-as-11th-national-pro-bono-week-kicks-off/

[32] N. Spaulding, 'The prophet and the bureaucrat: Positional conflicts in service pro bono publico' (1998) 50 Stanford Law Review 1396.

[33] F. McLeay, 'The legal profession's beautiful myth: Surveying the justifications for the lawyer's obligation to perform pro bono work' (2008) 15 International Journal of the Legal Profession 249.

[34] J. Macy, 'Mandatory pro bono: Comfort for the poor or welfare for the rich?' (1991–92) 77 Cornell Law Review 1115.

bono work, although it is doubtful whether the tangential benefits are worth the cost of the pro bono work and that it can entirely be explained in commercial terms.[35]

 Alternative view

Neil Kinsella is openly cynical about pro bono work, asking:

Is there something rather distasteful about a top City lawyer who earns in a month what most people won't get in a year salving his or her conscience by attending a legal advice clinic every so often or setting up a small pro bono unit? Pro bono work can be like some foreign aid projects and cause more harm than good. Lawyers need to be careful about where and how they dispense their 'largesse'. Legal aid lawyers are angry or believe that city firms should 'stop meddling just to make [themselves] feel better' and keep out of legally aided areas.[36]

Pro bono work in practice

Pro bono work has become increasingly well organised and structured. For the Bar, the Bar Pro Bono Unit provides advice and representation for free. This is often done through the charity, the Free Representation Unit. It offers help to those who cannot obtain legal aid for their cases. The work attracts lawyers from a range of backgrounds. The Bar Pro Bono Unit claims that a third of Queen's counsel (QCs) offer help.[37]

The cutbacks in legal aid have presented a real challenge for these pro bono services.[38] It is likely that they will face increased use and it is unlikely that they will be able to supply services to all who approach them.[39] In 2012, LawWorks (a leading organisation of solicitors offering pro bono work) found that its workload increased by 29 per cent; the first half of 2013 saw a 69 per cent increase in calls to its helpline, as compared with the same period in 2012.[40] The Bar Pro Bono Unit claimed a 30 per cent increase in referrals during the same time period.

A survey by the Law Society in 2012 found that 61 per cent of solicitors said that they had undertaken pro bono work at some point in their career.[41] Some 40 per cent had done pro bono work in the year prior to the survey. The Law Society estimated

---

[35] McLeay (n. 33).

[36] N. Kinsella, 'Pro bono: good enough? Another vanity project?', in J. Robins (ed.) *Pro Bono: Good Enough?* (Legal Action Group, 2012), 73.

[37] Bar Society, *Barristers: The Bar Pro Bono Unit* (Bar Society, 2013).

[38] J. Wotton, 'Pro bono legal practice: New challenges', Speech at International Legal Forum, St Petersburg, 17 May 2012, online at www.lawsociety.org.uk/news/speeches/pro-bono-legal-practice-new-challenges/   [39] Wotton (n. 38).

[40] E. Reyes, 'LawWorks warning over pro bono surge', *The Law Society Gazette*, 15 July 2013, online at www.lawgazette.co.uk/71805.article

[41] Law Society, *Solicitors' Pro Bono Work* (Law Society, 2012).

that the value of pro bono work among private practice was some £511 million—around 2.6 per cent of the turnover generated by solicitors' firms.

Obligations to the Legal Services Commission

If a party is receiving legal aid, then his or her legal costs are paid by the Legal Services Commission. What duties does a solicitor owe to the Commission? It is not difficult to imagine circumstances in which the interests of the client and the Commission clash. A client will want everything done to pursue his or her case, whatever the expense; the Legal Services Commission will want to keep a tight rein on expenditure.

A long-standing principle is that legal aid clients should be treated in the same way as fee-paying clients. That is a fine-sounding principle, but is barely respected in practice. The Commission controls the costs and therefore what can or cannot be done by a solicitor.

At the heart of legal aid provision now is the contract between the Commission and the solicitor. There are restrictions as to which lawyers a legally aided client can use. He or she must choose one who has a contract with the Legal Services Commission to deal with the kind of case at hand; there may also be limits on the number of legal aid cases that a firm can take on: these all restrict the client's freedom to choose a lawyer. Further, legal aid work is permitted only if the Commission considers it to be 'reasonable' and of sufficient benefit to the client. We explore these issues further in Chapter 7.

Reporting other solicitors

Follow the Code

Outcome 10.4 of the SRA Code of Conduct requires of a solicitor:

> you report to the *SRA* promptly, serious misconduct by any person or *firm* author-ised by the *SRA*, or any *employee*, *manager* or *owner* of any such *firm* (taking into account, where necessary, your duty of confidentiality to your *client*);

There is therefore a positive obligation on the solicitor to inform the Solicitors Regulation Authority (SRA) of any serious misconduct by another solicitor. The solicitor can inform anonymously.

There are two main areas of ambiguity about this otherwise clear obligation. First, the reference is to 'serious misconduct'. That might suggest that minor breaches of the Code are not covered. Clearly, any solicitor should err on the side of caution, however, and report conduct that he or she thinks might be regarded as serious.

Second, there is the question over the reference to 'confidentiality'. The disclosure might involve the disclosure of confidential information about the reporting solicitor's client. Ideally, the consent of the client will be obtained, but it is not clear what the position is if that is not possible.

Conclusion

This chapter has explored the duties that a lawyer owes to the wider society. While the professional codes tend to focus on the duties to clients, there are some limited duties to the public good. These are found in the duties under the criminal law, and the broader duty to the court and justice system. We have also seen that lawyers recognise an obligation to the greater good by means of their pro bono work. However, this is not undertaken by every lawyer. It may well be that, in the future, the legal profession will seek to improve its public image by more explicitly emphasising its obligations to promote the greater good.

This issue can be put in terms of a crisis in professionalism. Professor Anthony Kronman, in his lament for *The Lost Lawyer*, cries out against what he sees as lawyers losing their public service calling and becoming obsessed with making money.[42] The sense of vocation and service to the community is lost, he argues, and has been replaced with blatant consumerism. Not everyone will be entirely convinced by Kronman's analysis, but it may be that such concerns do prick the conscience of many lawyers. His concerns are reflected in a British context in the remarks of Lord Phillips of Sudbury:

> Today, not many see solicitors as part of a profession anymore, and certainly not as serving a vocation. We are broadly indistinguishable from any other business committed first, second and third to 'the bottom line'. We have gone from making 'a good living' whereby one took the rough with the smooth to an occupation where, at the high-earning end, one can make a fortune, as many do.[43]

 Further reading

On the public role of lawyers, see:

R. Anand, 'The role of the lawyer in the American democracy' (2009) 77 Fordham Law Review 1611.

T. Dare, *The Counsel of Rogues? A Defence of the Standard Conception of the Lawyer's Role* (Ashgate, 2009).

---

[42] A. Kronman, *The Lost Lawyer: Failing Ideas of the Legal Profession* (Belknap, 1993).
[43] Lord Phillips of Sudbury, 'Tenuous links', in J. Robins (ed.) *Pro Bono: Good Enough?* (Legal Action Group, 2012), 13.

M. Freedman, 'A critique of philosophizing about lawyers' ethics' (2012) 25 Georgetown Journal of Legal Ethics 91.

R. Pearce and E. Wald, 'The obligation of lawyers to heal civic culture: Confronting the ordeal of incivility in the practice of law' (2011) 34 University of Arkansas Little Rock Review 1.

B. Wendel, *Lawyers and Fidelity to Law* (Princeton University Press, 2010).

On pro bono work, read:

G. Bindman, 'What money could buy', in J. Robins (ed.) *Pro Bono: Good Enough?* (Legal Action Group, 2012).

S. Cummings, 'The politics of pro bono' (2004) 52 UCLA Law Review 18.

M. Fraser, 'Forced labour' (2013) 163 New Law Journal 11.

R. Granfield, 'The meaning of pro bono: Institutional variations in professional obligations among lawyers' (2007) 44 Law and Society Review 113.

N. Kinsella, 'Pro bono: good enough? Another vanity project?', in J. Robins (ed.) *Pro Bono: Good Enough?* (Legal Action Group, 2012).

F. McLeay, 'The legal profession's beautiful myth: Surveying the justifications for the lawyer's obligation to perform pro bono work' (2008) 15 International Journal of the Legal Profession 249.

Lord Phillips of Sudbury, 'Tenuous links', in J. Robins (ed.) *Pro Bono: Good Enough?* (Legal Action Group, 2012).

Pro Bono Coordinating Committee, *The Joint Pro Bono Protocol for Legal Work* (Ministry of Justice, 2013).

D. Rhode, 'Pro bono in principle and in practice' (2003) 53 Journal of Legal Education 413.

W. Simon, 'The Kaye Scholer affair: The lawyer's duty of candor and the Bar's temptations of evasion and apology' (1998) 23 Law and Social Inquiry 243.

N. Spaulding, 'The prophet and the bureaucrat: Positional conflicts in service pro bono publico' (1998) 50 Stanford Law Review 1396.

H. Whalen-Bridge, 'Challenges to pro bono work in the corporate context: Means testing and the non-profit applicant' (2010) 13 Legal Ethics 65.

14

Gender, race, and diversity in the legal profession

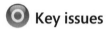

⊙ Key issues

- Why are women and minority groups so poorly represented in the profession, especially in the higher ranks?
- What can be done to improve the diversity of the profession?
- Why is diversity an important issue for the profession?

Introduction

One of the biggest issues facing the legal profession is diversity. Critics, with some justification, say that the legal profession—especially in its upper echelons—is male, white, heterosexual, able-bodied, and middle class. They are right. Of the judges on the Supreme Court in the UK, there is one woman and no members of ethnic minorities. There are complex reasons for this—and serious consequences. This chapter will explore these.

The legal profession as a whole is alert to the problems of diversity and has taken steps to address it. However, to date, the impact of these steps has been limited. The prejudicial stereotypes have proved hard to change and the ingrained legal culture creates barriers that are hard to shift.[1]

The meaning of diversity

Although the word 'diversity' is commonly used, its precise meaning is far from straightforward. There are three primary meanings of the word 'diversity'.

---

[1] E. Wald, 'A primer on diversity, discrimination, and equality in the legal profession or who is responsible for pursuing diversity and why' (2011) 24 Georgetown Journal of Legal Ethics 1079, 1081.

Formal diversity

Formal diversity requires that different groups should be represented in the legal profession according to their percentage of the general population. So, if 10 per cent of the population belongs to a particular group, we should expect 10 per cent of lawyers to belong to that group too. As Eli Wald explains:

> Formal diversity thus reflects the basic intuition that in a competitive, equal society, the diversity of the populace will and ought to be reflected in diversity in its educational system and in its various occupations and professions, at least in the sense that demographic changes and enhanced diversity in the populace lead to some increased, visible, and meaningful diversity in some occupations and professions, and that continued systematic under-representation of minorities requires attention and explanation.[2]

The argument tends to support the view that formal diversity should occur if there are fair selection and employment practices. We do not believe that some races or sexes have better legal abilities than others, and so if meritocratic standards were used, we would expect a diverse profession. The fact that there is not a diverse profession therefore indicates a flaw in the selection procedures. Our focus should consequently be on ensuring that the selection procedures are indeed fair. Success will be achieved when there is a match between the percentages of groups in the general population and those in the legal profession.

Formal diversity has been questioned by some commentators. One question relates to the assumption that all groups have the same desires and aims. There is considerable debate over this controversial issue. Does the fact that, for example, some racial groups seem to excel in certain sports reflect a natural ability for certain members of that race, or are there complex socio-economic explanations for it? Eli Wald notes that, in the United States, Jewish-Americans have a long and proud affinity with the legal professions, having a higher proportion of membership than might be expected based on a purely statistical approach.[3] Is that something that is bad? Some conclude that the fact that different groups and cultures make a particular profession popular or unpopular need not be a cause for concern, as long as no individual is excluded from the profession on the grounds of his or her race or background. The argument is that we should not want, or expect, men and women, or all racial or religious groups, to want to do the same kind of things. Others are more sceptical and believe that we should combat assumptions within groups that attract members disproportionately to one profession or another.

A second challenge to formal diversity is the difficulty of obtaining a 'level entry field'. If inequalities are found early in a person's life, then it might be difficult, if not impossible, to find an appropriate test or assessment that does not reflect the inequalities that are already there. In other words, if a university were to find that entry to law

---

[2] Wald (n. 1).   [3] Wald (n. 1).

degrees was not diverse despite a 'fair assessment', one conclusion would be that the test is not fair; another would be that applicants from disadvantaged backgrounds have not received a similar education and that this is reflected in test performance. If that is correct and applicants for a law degree or law job are already disadvantaged by what has happened before, it is possible to devise a fair system for assessing candidates? Or does a fair entry test need to ensure that those from disadvantaged educational backgrounds are not disfavoured by the test?

Substantive diversity

Emerging from some of the concerns over formal diversity have been arguments promoting **substantive diversity**.

 Definition

Eli Wald explains **substantive diversity** as follows:

> *Substantive diversity* denotes the idea that formal diversity, demanding equality in the opportunity to participate in the legal profession, is merely the first, necessary step in achieving the goals of diversity, but is insufficient. Rather, diversity efforts must also include elements of equality beyond mere opportunity to participate, including equal meaningful participation.[4]

This view sees equality not as something to be measured in terms of numbers, but rather as questions of participation in the profession, the quality of experience of people in the profession, and attitudes and values upheld by the profession. For example, it may be that equal numbers have been achieved, but only because the disadvantaged groups have to make considerably more effort to advance in the profession and at greater personal cost. It has been suggested that, even among firms with a roughly equal number of men and women, these firms are a 'man's world', with a culture and structure that makes life easier for men and harder for women.[5] Women succeed in so far as they can imitate men. Structural equality aims to ensure not only that the numbers are equal, but also that the structures within the professions do not prefer one gender or race over another.

---

[4] Wald (n. 1), 1083.

[5] P. Patton, 'Women lawyers, their status, influence, and retention in the legal profession' (2005) 11 William and Mary Journal of Women and the Law 173; R. Dinovitzer, N. Reichman, and J. Sterling, 'The differential valuation of women's work: A new look at the gender gap in lawyers' incomes' (2009) 88 Social Forces 819; J. Hersch, 'The new labor market for lawyers: Will female lawyers still earn less?' (2003) 10 Cardozo Women's Law Journal 1.

Diversity and attitude

Harold Patrick and Vincent Kuman argue that:

> The concept of diversity includes acceptance and respect. It means understanding that each individual is unique, and recognizing our individual differences. These can be along the dimensions of race, ethnicity, gender, sexual orientation, socio-economic status, age, physical abilities, religious beliefs, political beliefs, or other ideologies. It is the exploration of these differences in a safe, positive, and fostering environment. It is about understanding each other and moving beyond simple tolerance to embracing and celebrating the rich dimensions of diversity contained within each individual.[6]

It is notable that this definition seeks to involve not only a mix of races, sexes, and so on, but also an attitude of acceptance and respect for these differences. It involves *celebrating* the differences. This is not about numbers or even practices, but about the attitude that those in the firm have towards each other and towards diversity in general.

Why promote diversity?

Few people disagree that a diverse profession is a good thing, but why? Again, a range of arguments are used.

Benefits to the profession

One set of arguments focuses on the benefit to the profession itself. Justice O'Connor, an American judge, described the policy behind the University of Michigan's affirmative action plan to increase diversity in the following terms: 'The policy aspires to achieve that diversity which has the potential to enrich everyone's education and thus make a law school class stronger than the sum of its parts.'[7] A similar point could be made for the legal profession. If the legal profession is made up of people from a diverse range of cultural, religious, and socio-economic backgrounds, there will be a broad range of voices heard in debates. The law firm can provide lawyers who can understand where a wide range of clients are coming from.

There is, it has been argued a 'business case' for diversity, because it improves decision-making and makes firms attractive to clients. Whether such a business case is made out is debated.[8] Clare McGlynn is sceptical of those who argue that employing

---

[6] H. Patrick and V. Raj, 'Managing workplace diversity issues and challenges' (2012) 2 Sage Open 1, 3.

[7] *Grutter v. Bollinger* 539 US 306, 315–16 (2003) (internal citations omitted).

[8] L. Dickens, 'The business case for women's equality: Is the carrot better than the stick?' (1994) 16 Employee Relations 5; C. McGlynn, 'Strategies for reforming the English solicitors' profession:

a more diverse workforce is economically beneficial.[9] Not only is she sceptical that the case is made out, but she is also concerned that it will put pressure on women to provide the economic benefit that 'allowing them into the profession' should provide. Further, it reinforces the 'maleness' of firms with a focus on economic matters. It is fairness and justice, she argues, which should be at the heart of the case for diversity, rather than economic productivity.

Fairness

Others put the case of diversity in terms of fairness. The legal profession should make sure that those seeking to join it are treated fairly and, in particular, that no applicant or member of the profession is treated in a discriminatory way. Law firms should have an especial commitment to fairness as being central to the legal system. The Bar Standards Board put it this way:

> It is fundamental to a democratic society governed by the rule of law that there should be access to justice. The Bar has a special position in the legal system of England and Wales, and confidence in the legal system will be enhanced if the arrangements made for access to the Bar's services, and for access to practice at the Bar for aspiring barristers are seen to be fair and non-discriminatory, and to be open to all, regardless of social, economic or educational background or circumstances. This will lead, in time, to a more diverse Bar, which better reflects the diversity of society in England and Wales.[10]

Social good

A third case can be put in terms of the responsibilities of the profession to produce social good. Having a diverse legal profession increases social mobility and is a sign of a healthy society. Society must accept that current and past discrimination still has negative impacts on people, and that the law has a special commitment to combating the impacts of discrimination.[11]

A particular aspect of the social good is that the justice system must be seen to offer justice for all. This claim will be questioned if it appears to discriminate against particular groups and is not representative.

An analysis of the business case for sex equality', in U. Schultz and G. Shaw (eds) *Women in the World's Legal Professions* (Hart, 2002); K. Malleson, 'Justifying gender equality on the bench: Why difference won't do' (2003) 11 Feminist Legal Studies 1.

[9] McGlynn (n. 8).

[10] Bar Standards Board, *Guidelines on the Equality and Diversity Provisions of the Code of Conduct* (Bar Council, 2013), 1.

[11] T. Farrow, 'Sustainable professionalism' (2008) 46 Osgoode Hall Law Journal 51, 91.

Summary

Lord Neuberger described his own perspective, combining all three views, in the following way:

> The Bar can only flourish and retain public confidence if it is a diverse and inclusive profession. Diversity and inclusivity extend not only to gender, ethnic origin, physical ability, religious belief, and sexual orientation, but every bit as much to social, economic, and educational circumstances and background, and to age. Diversity and inclusivity are essential if a modern profession is to maximise its credibility and to contribute towards a fairer and more effective society.[12]

The current status of the profession in terms of diversity

In this section, we will examine how the professions currently perform in terms of diversity.

Gender

Solicitors

It was in 1919 that the Sex Discrimination (Removal) Act was passed and women were allowed to practise as lawyers. Undoubtedly, in the decades that have followed, there has been an increase in the proportion of women in the solicitors' profession, but still there are clear diversity problems.[13] Pascoe Pleasence and Nigel Balmer note, in their survey of the statistics, that in 2008 there were 112,433 women solicitors, a 332 per cent increase on the figures for 1978; women accounted for 62 per cent of assistant solicitors in private practice, yet only 24 per cent of partners were women.[14] In 2008, looking at solicitors who had been admitted between 10 and 19 years previously, while 77 per cent of men had reached the rank of partner, only 48 per cent of women had.[15] This suggests that although, at the point of entry, parity is being achieved, men still dominate in the higher levels of the profession.

Revealingly, in 2008 while 85 per cent of male solicitors were still working in law, only 72 per cent of the women were.[16] This indicates the worryingly high numbers of

[12] Bar Council, *Entry to the Bar Working Party: Final Report* (Bar Council, 2007), 36.

[13] U. Schultz and G. Shaw (eds) *Women in the World's Legal Professions* (Hart, 2002).

[14] P. Pleasence and N. Balmer, *Projecting Women's Future Participation in the Solicitor's Profession in England and Wales* (Legal Services Research Centre, 2009).

[15] J. Tomlinson, D. Muzio, H. Sommerlad, L. Webley, and L. Duff, 'Structure, agency and career strategies of white women and black and minority ethnic individuals in the legal profession' (2013) 66 Journal of Legal Resources 245.

[16] Pleasence and Balmer (n. 14).

women leaving the profession. Clare McGlynn, in her study of women in the legal profession, concludes that women are 'under-represented, underpaid and marginalised'.[17] This is true in academia too, where 'the experience of women academics is that they remain largely absent from the upper echelons of universities, at all levels are on average paid less than men and often occupy a marginalised role'.[18]

Bar

Of practising barristers in England in 2011–12, there were 10,117 men and 5,463 women. This means that the percentage split is 64.9 per cent men and 35.1 per cent women.[19] This may be set to improve slightly, given that 52.2 per cent of students enrolled in the Bar Professional Training Course (BPTC) in 2010–11 were women. In 2010–11, 41 per cent of registered pupils were women and 54 per cent were men, with 5 per cent of people not disclosing their gender.[20] These statistics indicate that while some work has been done to challenge problems with gender diversity at the point of entry into the profession, the profession as a whole is male-dominated. This is particularly so as one goes higher up the ranks. In 2011–12, a remarkable 88.2 per cent of Queen's counsel (QCs) were men.

Race

Solicitors

A major study commissioned by the Legal Services Board accepted that there was much improvement at the initial stages of the entry to the career of black and minority ethnic (BME) solicitors.[21] Between 1996 and 2006, the number of BME solicitors with practising certificates rose by 243.7 per cent. In 2008–09, 13 per cent of solicitors on the Roll are from BME groups.[22] However, again, as one rises up the ranks, the lack

---

[17] C. McGlynn, 'The status of women lawyers in the United Kingdom', in U. Schultz and G. Shaw (eds) *Women in the World's Legal Professions* (Hart, 2002).

[18] See also D. Nicolson, 'Demography, discrimination and diversity: A new dawn for the British legal profession?' (2005) 12 International Journal of the Legal Profession 201, 220.

[19] General Council of the Bar of England and Wales, *Annual Bar Barometer. 2007 to 2011/12* (Bar Council, 2013).

[20] Bar Council, *Pupillage Survey 2010/11: An Analysis of the Backgrounds of Pupils Registered in 2010/11* (Bar Council, 2012).

[21] H. Sommerlad, L. Webley, L. Duff, D. Muzio, and J. Tomlinson, *Diversity in the Legal Profession in England and Wales: A Qualitative Study of Barriers and Individual Choices* (Legal Services Board, 2012).

[22] The ethnic breakdown (where known) for BME solicitors with practising certificates as of 31 July 2009 was: African-Caribbean, 775; Asian, 6,859; Chinese, 1,251; African, 1,247; other ethnic origin, 2,066; white European, 89,718; the remainder of unknown ethnicity. See Law Society, *Diversity Monitoring* (Law Society, 2009), 10. See further Sommerlad et al. (n. 21).

of diversity becomes apparent. Only 4 per cent of partners are from an ethnic minority and only 0.5 per cent are black.[23] Further, BME solicitors are particularly likely to undertake legal aid work and lower paid areas of work.[24]

Bar

At the Bar, there are 1,594 barristers from a BME group, some 10.2 per cent of the profession.[25] This may be set to improve further, with a remarkable 42.4 per cent of students enrolling in the BPTC in 2010–11 being from BME groups. Notably, only 13 per cent of pupils at that time were from BME groups.[26] In part, this may reflect that a proportion of BME students on the BPTC were intending to practise overseas. Indeed, looking at the UK-domiciled students on the BPTC, 20 per cent were BME. Of those called to the Bar in 2010–11, 43.8 per cent were BME. There can be no doubt that a major influx of BME barristers is addressing a historic lack of diversity. Even looking at QCs, 5.2 per cent are BME, which, while lower than might be expected, is more reflective of the population than many other professions.[27]

Disability

Of practising barristers, 0.54 per cent report having a disability.[28] Among solicitors, 3.2 per cent of those with practising certificates report having a disability.[29] Those figures should be compared with the employed population of a whole, among whom 14 per cent report a disability.

Class

There is a well-established link between class and entry into the legal profession.[30] In 2007–08, 62 per cent of pupil barristers were drawn from the top two socio-economic groups.[31] Class can play a role throughout the process, from ensuring educational advantages at school and university, to selection for training contracts, and then promotion in the firm. A study in 1995 found that 10 per cent of

---

[23] J. Braithwaite, 'Diversity staff and the dynamics of diversity policy-making in large law firms' (2010) 13 Legal Studies 141.

[24] Tomlinson et al. (n. 15).

[25] General Council of the Bar of England and Wales (n. 19).

[26] J. Sauboorah and C. Carney, *Trends in the Profile of the Bar* (Bar Council, 2011).

[27] Sauboorah and Carney (n. 26).   [28] Sauboorah and Carney (n. 26).

[29] Law Society, *Diversity Profile of the Profession* (Law Society, 2013).

[30] A. Zimdars, 'The profile of pupil barristers at the Bar of England and Wales 2004–2008' (2010) 17 International Journal of the Legal Profession 117.

[31] Sauboorah and Carney (n. 26).

those with training contracts were employed in a firm that also employed a relative or family friend.[32] Knowing the right people, or having parents who know the right people, still helps.[33] Class can provide a person with the kind of etiquette, presentation skills, and aspects of personal appearance that can greatly benefit a person at interview.

Socio-economic background can impact on educational achievement from the earliest stages.[34] Of students on the BPTC, only 55 per cent were educated in state schools, compared with 93 per cent of children among the general population.[35] Graduates from Oxbridge are nearly seven times more likely to apply for the BPTC when compared with students at other universities.[36] Among the solicitors' profession, just under 60 per cent went to a state school.[37]

As Antony Dursi notes, it is easy to exaggerate the lack of social diversity at the Bar: 'The view that the Bar is still a male, public school, Oxbridge elite still pervades. In reality, the majority of pupil barristers are now normally women, state school educated and less than a third are Oxbridge graduates.'[38] While he argues that the situation is not as bad as the common perception, he acknowledges that there is still room for improvement.[39]

Complaints

One area in which there has been concern over diversity relates to complaints. A report looking at complaints between 2007 and 2011 found:

a) BME barristers are over-represented in the complaints process in relation to the outcomes of external complaints; BME barristers are more likely to have a complaint referred to disciplinary action, white barristers are more likely to have a complaint dismissed without referral to disciplinary action, and BME barristers are more likely to be subject to a disciplinary action outcome of upheld; even when controlling for differences in the subjects of the complaints.

b) BME barristers are over-represented in the complaints process in relation to internal complaints. There is no evidence that BME barristers were subjected to a larger proportion of internal complaints for any reason other than their ethnicity.

---

[32] Nicolson (n. 18).

[33] M. Blackwell, 'Old boys' networks, family connections and the English legal profession' [2011] Public Law 426.

[34] A. Dursi, 'Social mobility and the Bar' (2012) 46 The Law Teacher 283.   [35] Dursi (n. 34).

[36] Dursi (n. 34).   [37] Law Society (n. 29).   [38] Dursi (n. 34), 285.

[39] L. Ashton and L. Empson, *Differentiation and Discrimination: Understanding Social Class and Social Exclusion in the UK's Leading Law Firms* (Cass Centre for Professional Service Firms, 2011).

c) Male barristers were subject to a larger proportion of internal complaints than their proportion of the Bar although this difference on the basis of gender was not as pronounced as the difference on the basis of ethnicity.[40]

The report was not able to provide a reason for the statistics, although some have suggested that BME lawyers often seek to escape from the cultures of larger firms and are more likely to be practising alone, and that this can be linked with non-compliance.[41] The most striking statistic is that 74.5 per cent of complaints were made about male barristers. Given that male barristers make up 65.2 per cent of the Bar, that is notable, but seems to attract less concern.

Lesbian, gay, bisexual, and transgender (LGBT)

There is no doubt that matters have improved for lesbian, gay, bisexual, and transgender (LGBT) lawyers. The Law Society notes that 2.6 per cent of solicitors reported being lesbian, gay, or bisexual, with a further 6.6 per cent in the survey not wishing to report a sexual orientation. Just over 90 per cent reported being straight.[42] A survey in 2009 found that 96 per cent of gay men and 92 per cent of lesbians said that they were 'out' in their personal lives.[43] However, it was a different story in their professional lives, although age was a key factor. Only 15 per cent of 51–55-year-olds were out, while 60 per cent of those aged 25 and under were. Of the gay lawyers interviewed, 45.5 per cent said that they believed their sexual orientation had not impacted on their career, while 16.9 per cent thought that there had been a perceptible impact. The figures were slightly higher for lesbian lawyers, with 27.7 per cent feeling that there had been an impact on their career. Among gay lawyers, 26 per cent were able to be open to clients about their sexuality, while the figure for lesbian lawyers was 22 per cent. Clearly, for many LGBT lawyers, fear of prejudice means that they have to disguise their sexuality.

The report found particular problems facing LGBT lawyers wishing to adopt children. It also found that there was considerable variation between firms, with some more 'gay-friendly' than others. One respondent replied:

> I suspect that I would have had a more negative experience of being out in the workplace had I stayed at my training firm—my move was prompted partly by a growing awareness that I did not fit in. Although, as a trainee, I was afraid that being out would cause problems at work, my work actually benefits greatly by my being out

[40] Bar Standards Board, *Report on Diversity of Barristers Subject to Complaints* (Bar Standards Board, 2013), 2.

[41] L. Webley, 'What *Robinson v Solicitors Regulation Authority* tells us about the contested terrain of race and disciplinary processes' (2013) 16 Legal Ethics 236.

[42] Law Society (n. 29).

[43] InterLaw Diversity Forum, *Law Society Survey of LGB Solicitors* (Law Society, 2009).

(less distracted/anxious) and it has been very encouraging to have openly gay role models at senior levels in my current firm.[44]

Diversity and the judiciary

The problems of diversity are particularly apparent among the judiciary. A government report recently noted the following figures:

- 15 out of 17 Supreme Court judges and heads of division attended independent schools and went on to study at Oxford or Cambridge.

- Of 38 justices of appeal, 26 attended independent schools, eight attended grammar schools, two attended state comprehensive schools and two were schooled overseas; 28 then studied at Oxford or Cambridge.

- Of 114 High Court judges, 83 attended independent schools; 82 then went to either Oxford or Cambridge, 22 to other Russell Group universities and just three to other Universities. Of all the 169 judges, 33 went to the 11 major public schools.

- In 2011, 10 out of the 11 justices of the Supreme Court were white and male. For High Court judges, fewer than one in six (17 of 91 judges) are women and less than 5% are from black or minority ethnic (BME) backgrounds (four in total). Overall, of all judiciary roles, 22.3% are held by women and 5.1% are held by people from BME backgrounds.[45]

These worrying statistics not only reflect the lack of diversity at the top of the legal profession, but they also raise some important issues about the nature of justice and the judicial role, which are beyond the scope of this book.[46]

The Equality Act 2010

The Equality Act 2010 prohibits discrimination on the following grounds (known as 'the protected characteristics'):

- race (including colour, nationality, and ethnic or national origin);

- sex;

- pregnancy and maternity;

- disability;[47]

- sexual orientation;

---

[44] InterLaw Diversity Forum (n. 43), 22.

[45] HM Government, *Fair Access to Professional Careers: A Progress Report* (HM Government, 2012), 26.

[46] S. Kenney, *Gender and Justice: Why Women in the Judiciary Really Matter* (Routledge, 2012).

[47] According to section 6(1)(a) and (b) of the Equality Act 2010, 'a person has a disability if s/he has a physical or mental impairment which has a substantial and long term adverse effect on his/her ability to carry out normal day to day activities'.

- marriage and civil partnership;
- religion or belief;
- age; and
- gender reassignment.

The details of the legislation are beyond this book, so they will be covered only briefly.

The Act prohibits discrimination based on the protected characteristics in employment decisions. This includes offering people pupillage or training contracts.[48] The legislation covers both direct discrimination and indirect discrimination.

Key statute

Direct discrimination is defined in section 13 of the Equality Act 2010 as follows:

A person (A) discriminates against another (B) if, because of a protected characteristic, A treats B less favourably than A treats or would treat others.

This covers obvious cases in which an applicant for a job is not selected because of his or her sex or race. Less obvious is indirect discrimination.

Key statute

Indirect discrimination is explained in section 19 of the Equality 2010 as follows:

(1) A person (A) discriminates against another (B) if A applies to B a provision, criterion or practice which is discriminatory in relation to a relevant protected characteristic of B's.

(2) For the purposes of subsection (1), a provision, criterion or practice is discriminatory in relation to a relevant protected characteristic of B's if—

    (a) A applies, or would apply, it to persons with whom B does not share the characteristic,

    (b) it puts, or would put, persons with whom B shares the characteristic at a particular disadvantage when compared with persons with whom B does not share it,

    (c) it puts, or would put, B at that disadvantage, and

    (d) A cannot show it to be a proportionate means of achieving a legitimate aim.

This occurs where an apparently neutral provision is used that works in such a way that it disadvantages a particular group. An easy, if unrealistic, example is if chambers were to require all applicants to be at least 6 ft tall. That would, in effect, discriminate against women, even though the requirement does not specifically mention sex.

---

[48] Bar Council, *Guidelines on Equality and Diversity Provisions of the Code of Conduct* (Bar Council, 2012).

A more realistic example might be a requirement that applicants be available to attend social events in the evening. That might discriminate against those with childcare responsibilities, which might predominantly work against women. It is important to realise that we are talking about requirements that are more likely to work against one group than another. So, using the examples given, of course there are women taller than 6 ft and many women without caring responsibilities, but one might expect these requirements to work against women, on average.

The last example raises an important point, which is that indirect discrimination can be justified and therefore lawful. It will be justified if it can be shown that the requirement was justified as a proportionate means for achieving a legitimate aim. No doubt the chambers requiring all applicants to be 6 ft tall could not make that argument. The issue over the social events might also fail, although one could imagine that there might be cases in which it would be essential for a particular job that a worker be free in the evening. However, it is for the employer to show that the indirect discrimination is justified.

The Legal Services Board and Bar Standards Council, as public bodies, have a duty under the Equality Act 2010 to:

- eliminate unlawful discrimination, harassment, and victimisation;
- advance equality of opportunity between different groups; and
- foster good relations between different groups.

The Legal Services Board has produced guidance to the professional regulators on ensuring diversity.[49] This requires regulators to:

- gather a more comprehensive evidence base about the diversity characteristics of the legal workforce by ensuring that every individual is given an opportunity to self-classify against a broader range of characteristics (including age, gender, disability, ethnic group, religion or belief, sexual orientation, socio-economic background, and caring responsibilities);
- ensure the transparency of diversity data, including published summary data about some characteristics (age, gender, disability, ethnic group, socio-economic background, and caring responsibilities) at the level of individual regulated entities (where approved regulators regulate entities);
- collate diversity data to give an aggregate view of the diversity make-up of each branch of the profession;
- ensure that the data identifies seniority where appropriate, so that it can be used to track progress in relation to retention and progression; and
- evaluate the effectiveness and impact of existing diversity initiatives.[50]

---

[49] Legal Services Board, *Response Document and Accompanying Statutory Guidance Issued under Section 162 of the Legal Services Act 2007* (Legal Services Board, 2013).

[50] Legal Services Board (n. 49), para. 6.

Notably, this leaves much of the detail up to the regulators, but it does require data collection and monitoring, and the data must be published. This was controversial, but was justified by the Board as enabling regulators and consumers to compare firms, and as helping to raise awareness of the diversity issue.[51]

The professional bodies have accepted the importance of monitoring, because it:

- gives our policies credibility, among those in our workforce and those we may wish to recruit, our clients and prospective clients

- helps us to identify which policies and practices are effective and direct our resources to where they will have most impact

- enables us to identify where barriers exist that prevent the best use of all available talent

- can help to prevent costly discrimination claims by identifying possible problems early

- can help us to win business by evidencing our performance

- helps us to strengthen our reputation

- helps us to meet regulatory requirements, supports benchmarking exercises and our submission for the annual report on the Charter.[52]

The Bar Council says that attempts to improve diversity must be 'SMART':

Specific—i.e. clear, as opposed to vague statements or 'ideal scenario' wish lists.

Measurable—it should be clear how chambers will know when an action has been completed. Chambers may wish to use numbers, dates and times in order to achieve such clarity (e.g. ensure parental leave policy is included in chambers' induction pack for staff and barristers by a certain date).

Affordable—does chambers have sufficient resources to undertake the action?

Realistic—is it feasible in all the circumstances for chambers to undertake this action?

Timely—a clear deadline, by which each action must be completed, should be set.[53]

The Solicitors Regulation Authority Code of Conduct

The professional codes now include references to diversity.

Follow the Code

Principle 9 of the Solicitors Regulation Authority (SRA) Code of Conduct requires that solicitors must:

> run your business or carry out your role in the business in a way that encourages equality of opportunity and respect for diversity...

---

[51] Legal Services Board (n. 49), para, 8. [52] Legal Services Board (n. 49), para, 12.
[53] Bar Council Guidance (n. 48), 3.

The Code goes on to give more detailed guidance, by means of five Outcomes.

Follow the Code

Outcomes 2.1–2.5 of the SRA Code of Conduct require of solicitors that:

O(2.1) you do not discriminate unlawfully, or victimise or harass anyone, in the course of your professional dealings;

O(2.2) you provide services to *clients* in a way that respects diversity;

O(2.3) you make reasonable adjustments to ensure that disabled *clients*, *employees* or *managers* are not placed at a substantial disadvantage compared to those who are not disabled, and you do not pass on the costs of these adjustments to these disabled *clients*, *employees* or *managers*;

O(2.4) your approach to recruitment and employment encourages equality of opportunity and respect for diversity;

O(2.5) *complaints* of discrimination are dealt with promptly, fairly, openly, and effectively.

Indicative Behaviour (IB) 2.1 recommends an equality and diversity policy that covers:

(a) a commitment to the principles of equality and diversity and legislative requirements;

(b) a requirement that all *employees* and *managers* comply with the outcomes;

(c) provisions to encompass your recruitment and interview processes;

(d) details of how the *firm* will implement, monitor, evaluate and update the policy;

(e) details of how the *firm* will ensure equality in relation to the treatment of *employees*, *managers*, *clients* and third parties instructed in connection with *client* matters;

(f) details of how *complaints* and disciplinary issues are to be dealt with;

(g) details of the *firm's* arrangements for workforce diversity monitoring; and

(h) details of how the *firm* will communicate the policy to *employees*, *managers* and *clients*.

Training[54] and monitoring[55] are required in order to achieve diversity.

The Bar Council Code of Conduct

Under paragraph 408.1 of the Bar Council Code of Conduct (the Bar Code), chambers must appoint a senior member of chambers as an equality and diversity officer.

---

[54] SRA Code of Conduct, IB (2.2).   [55] SRA Code of Conduct, IB (2.3).

Follow the Code

Paragraph 408.1 of the Bar Code requires that the equality and diversity officer should be responsible for ensuring that:

- a written equality and diversity policy for chambers is adopted, implemented, then reviewed and kept up-to-date;

- all chambers policies and procedures (whether or not documented) are reviewed regularly to ensure that they comply with the equality and diversity policy and these guidelines and that records are kept of the outcome of reviews and of action taken in response;

- equality and diversity training is provided for all members of chambers and staff including clerks and that refresher courses are provided periodically once initial training has been given;

- advice is offered to the Head of Chambers, the senior clerk, the chair of the pupillage committee, members of the chambers management committee and individual members of chambers on equality and diversity issues, both in response to a request and whenever the Equality and Diversity Officer considers that equality and diversity issues arise;

- he or she is available to individual members or chambers staff to offer advice on equality issues and to provide an informal route, if requested, for the resolution of grievances; and

- monitoring data from pupillage, member or staff recruitment exercises, chambers membership, and the allocation of unassigned work is analysed regularly and that any actions necessary to remedy or investigate unfair outcomes are developed and added to chambers' equality action plan.

The Bar Council has produced guidance that should apply to all recruitment in chambers. This requires that there be objective selection criteria, based on the key requirements of the job. The guidance specifically says: 'Chambers should avoid criteria that are subjective, such as personality-based attributes, or behavioural attributes that cannot fairly be tested at some stage of the selection process.'[56] This is to avoid the concern that some barristers select applicants who are 'like me'. Chambers are encouraged to ensure that panels have representatives of all age groups. They should look at the data relating to appointments and consider whether the representation of different groups in those shortlisted for interview matched those of the applicants, and if not, why not.

Under paragraph 408.1(e) of the Code, chambers must regularly review: the number and percentages of barristers, pupils, and assessed mini-pupils from different groups; applications for assessed mini-pupillage, pupillage, staff, and membership of chambers; and the allocation of unassigned work. The Code is clear that this

---

[56] Bar Council, *Equality and Diversity Guidance* (Bar Council, 2013), 9.

includes collecting and analysing data based on race, disability, and gender. Chambers need to appoint a diversity data officer to do this.

The Code also includes provisions to ensure that those in disadvantaged groups are treated fairly once they are employed. Regulation 408.1(g) requires chambers to have a written anti-harassment code. The code must address harassing behaviour, which need not be intentional and need not be directed at the person. The Bar Council gives the following example of what might be considered to be harassment based on age:

> Chambers employs a former clerk, who retired at the age of 65, to carry out various administrative tasks. When he comes into the clerks' room, the clerks call him 'granddad' and make jokes about his free travel pass. He finds it humiliating to have his age constantly referred to in this way, but he feels that he has to go along with the 'joke' and says nothing.[57]

Chambers are also required to have a parental and adoption leave policy.[58] They need a flexible policy on the right of members to take a career break, to work flexible hours, or to work from home.[59]

Barriers to diversity

A report prepared for the Legal Services Board explains that:

> At each stage of the process of entry and progression, those from higher socio-economic backgrounds are at an advantage: attending a more academic school followed by a Russell Group university—which supply individuals with the knowledge of and contact with law firms; gaining work experience, often through contacts; and having similar social attributes to those in the profession, making them more appealing to firms. These advantages are likely to account for the over-representation of those from private schools in the profession, leading to the profession being perceived as having an elitist culture.
>
> The culture of the profession prevents women and ethnic minorities from progressing in the market due to the great emphasis placed on networking. Women and ethnic minorities often do not attend events due to their different cultural values, family commitments or reluctance due to the expectation for females to establish a demeaning role.
>
> Females from all social backgrounds face further obstacles to progression due to the lack of perceived flexibility, preventing them from meeting family commitments and possibly restricting their progression to partnership.[60]

As this quote indicates, there are a broad range of barriers to women and members of minority groups entering the legal profession.

We will explore here what these barriers might include.

---

[57] Bar Council (n. 56).   [58] Bar Code, para 408.1(h).   [59] Bar Code, para 408(j).
[60] R. Sullivan, *Barriers to the Legal Profession* (Legal Services Board, 2010), 21.

Expense

The training for the legal profession can undoubtedly be expensive. There are fees for the law degree and for the professional training course. There are, in addition, living expenses during that time. Most people starting out as a pupil or trainee solicitor will be on a relatively low salary and will already have accrued substantial debts. It is true that some of these costs can be mitigated by, for example, loans, scholarships, or awards from firms. Of course, for many, the financial rewards as the career progresses will pay back the initial expenses. However, there is no guarantee of that. There are dangers at various stages of the process. A student at university may not be offered a training contract; even after pupillage or the training period as a solicitor, there is no certainty that a person will be kept on. So the expenses come with no guarantee of a career. For example, in 2008, 7,000 people completed the LPC, but only 6,000 were given training contracts in the next year.[61] This risk is seen by some as a particular barrier for those whose families are not well off and so cannot provide help or support if things go wrong.

Work experience

It is commonly believed that work experience is important to success in being offered a training contract. One study found that 63 per cent of those who had undertaken vacation work were offered a training contract, but only 43 per cent of those who had not.[62] The difficulty is that work experience is not equally available to all. Students with parents, relatives, or friends in the profession are twice as likely to secure early work experience as those without.[63] Even being aware of the importance of work experience may reflect a person's background.

Perception

The Bar Council has referred to perception as a key barrier to diversity:

> So far as the social aspect is concerned, the Bar is perceived in many quarters as predominantly populated by those from socially, financially and educationally privileged backgrounds. Some people see it as disproportionately populated by those from public schools and Oxbridge. Like many perceptions, whether or not justified, it has a strong element of self-fulfilment.[64]

There is, of course, a problem here. The more a profession recognises that it has a problem with diversity and seeks publically to address it, the more it may be reinforcing

[61] Sullivan (n. 60).   [62] Sullivan (n. 60).

[63] H. Sommerlad, '"What are you doing here? You should be working in a hair salon or something": Outsider status and professional socialization in the solicitors' profession' [2008] Web Journal of Current Legal Issues 1.   [64] Bar Council (n. 12), 10.

the stereotype that it is seeking to combat and may, by deterring would-be applicants, even be exacerbating the problem. Hence bodies such as the Bar Council seek to promote a message that they represent a diverse profession, but wish to become more so.

One respondent talking about another lawyer to the Bar Council captured the common perception well:

> This is a school which is … you know, it's very expensive, you have to be of a certain class background to be able to send your children there. In the summer times, you know, you're going to the houses of MPs and whatever else … they can pull strings for you and open doors for you…. when you went to an exceptional school that … you are destined for great things and it makes doors … it's easier for doors to be opened for you because you're now sitting in front of someone in the City who may have gone to the same school as you … or gone to the same school as your father so as a result, the fact that you got a Third, we can ignore that.[65]

Choice

A controversial issue relates to choice. Some believe that women or BME lawyers make choices that restrict their career advancement. It may be the kind of work in which they choose to specialise or the types of firm for which they choose to work, or it may be a decision about work–life balance.[66]

Those who emphasise choice reject the argument that women and BME lawyers are disadvantaged as a result of structural or social pressures, or discrimination at the hands of other lawyers. Their lack of career progression is a personal choice, not a structural flaw in the profession, these people claim. A strong proponent of this view is Catherine Hakim, who has argued that women commit less to the 'demands of professional life' and hence have lower status.[67] In short, the lack of diversity lies in the hands of women and BME lawyers who *choose* not to make the necessary efforts to succeed.

That view is a very much minority one in academic circles, in which the gendered division of care work and expectations around mothering explain the decision of a woman to focus, say, more on care than work. The 'playing field' in the professional world is unequal owing to a range of disadvantages that are placed by society on women. What is described as a 'choice' is rather a reflection of an attempt to balance the competing demands on their work. Often, too, these choices are assumed, as Clare McGlynn suggests; motherhood is taken to mean a reduced commitment to work, in a way that it is not for fatherhood.[68]

---

[65] Bar Council (n. 12), 12.   [66] Sommerlad et al. (n. 21).

[67] C. Hakim, *Key Issues in Women's Work: Female Diversity and the Polarisation of Women's Employment* (Glass House Press, 2004).

[68] McGlynn (n. 8).

Legal culture

A less obvious barrier is legal culture. Edgar Schein has described an organised culture as:

> A pattern of shared basic assumptions that was learned by a group as it solved its problems of external adaptation and internal integration, that has worked well enough to be considered valid and, therefore, to be taught to new members as the correct way to perceive, think and feel.[69]

He explains that this can cover issues from what clothes are worn, the way people speak; assumptions about knowledge (e.g. of etiquette; traditions). This can be used to make those that are unfamiliar with these to feel like outsiders. As he notes members of the culture often do not realise the subtle ways that their traditions can exclude 'the outsider'.

The ways that legal culture can operate to disadvantage groups are many. Sometimes it is comments that are made. As one women barrister reported:

> I was told in no uncertain terms that the only suitable work for a woman at the Bar was either criminal, preferably doing...defending on rape case, or family; and as I had no interest in either I went into the civil service.[70]

A common complaint is that the life of a solicitor, and especially that of a partner, is based on a norm of white, married man, supported by a wife at home. Reports of lawyers being expected to be available 24 hours a day are common.[71]

This reveals itself in many ways: from what passes as acceptable 'banter', to assumptions about what work women should do, and an emphasis on social events arranged around 'male activities' (such as golf). Issues around the nature of 'networking' are particularly common in these discussions. One solicitor made the following comment to a group of researchers:

> I think that women find networking difficult because particularly, in areas like property and construction, you walk into a room and it's quite intimidating because it is pretty much full of men...I work in property and I recently went to a networking event which was at the—Club in London which still has rooms that women aren't even allowed in.[72]

A male Asian solicitor stated:

> It's a profession which drinks the whole time...and I am reluctant to go to an event which is alcohol dominated...Certain relationships, both internally within the firm and externally with clients, haven't developed or have deteriorated...I came here very self-assured and I still am...but do I think I can be the best at what I do? No...because I don't think I'll ever be able to build the relationships that people who are not Muslims will be able to build.[73]

[69] E. Schein, *Organizational Culture and Leadership* (Jossey Bass, 2004), 31.
[70] Bar Council (n. 12).   [71] Tomlinson et al. (n. 15).   [72] Tomlinson et al. (n. 15), 249.
[73] Tomlinson et al. (n. 15), 253.

Some authors have written of 'cultural masculinity', whereby the profession is 'male-shaped'.[74] One of the particular problems with culture is that often the professionals involved have no idea that the practice has an exclusionary effect. The idea that suggesting drinks after work creates an exclusionary environment will baffle some.

A particular aspect of the legal culture that can work against diversity is the 'work all hours' model. In one survey, many involved described working 12–14 hours a day on average, and in addition working weekends. Those who did not do this were seen as lacking commitment to their careers. But for those with children or other caring responsibilities, this kind of commitment is impossible.[75] As one respondent to the Bar Council report on improving access put it:

> It is almost impossible to arrange childcare whilst working at the Bar. I worked part-time at Lovells once I had my first child and stopped working when my second child was born. I intend to return to work but I am concerned that the hours are so unpredictable at the Bar it makes the cost of childcare very difficult to meet. I'm not sure I can afford to return to the Bar.[76]

Unclear promotion

Many have noted that women are badly represented at the top levels of the profession. Donald Nicolson writes:

> Overall, we see that, while women have been entering legal practice in large numbers and, while exceptional women have risen to the top, most tend to be located below the glass ceiling, and, in the solicitor's profession, constitute a 'reserve army' of relatively low paid, less permanent and expendable labour. In response, many choose to leave private practice for more favourable working conditions or the profession altogether or alternatively to forgo family plans.[77]

The figures bear this out. Less than 15 per cent of QCs are women and women are significantly underrepresented at partner level in firms of solicitors. As Nicolson indicates, there is a perception that if women wish to succeed at the top level, they must forgo having children.

These points highlight, among other things, a broader concern over the promotion methods within the profession. A common complaint is that promotion procedures lack transparency.[78] Whether it be appointment to partnership in a firm of solicitors or appointment to QC, there is much discretion left to senior lawyers in who is appointed. Cynics complain that the senior lawyers tend to appoint 'people like them'. There is here probably a subconscious fear of 'otherness'. There is among some

---

[74] Law Society, *Obstacles and Barriers to the Career Development of Woman Solicitors* (Law Society, 2010).
[75] Law Society (n. 74).   [76] Sommerlad et al. (n. 21), 31.   [77] Nicolson (n. 18), 281.
[78] Tomlinson et al. (n. 15).

a nervousness of being judged by the 'other'.[79] As one BME lawyer put it: 'If your face fitted, then you would be all right, and if it didn't, then you wouldn't.'[80]

Others complain about the lack of clarity. One woman who had eventually reached the level of partner explained the lack of clarity in her firm thus:

> The most challenging bit was getting put forward in the first place – that was an enormous frustration. You would discover after the event when people have been made up to partner that you hadn't and that there had been a process at some unknown time in the year that you hadn't been a part of. So there's no set structure, and there's no criteria that you can measure yourself against to know that you are approaching being able to have a discussion about being put forward.[81]

Stereotypes

There has been much study done on the stereotypes about women, BME, and other disadvantaged groups that impact on the workplace. Women, it is said, face a double bind: if they conform to the stereotype of being 'quiet, submissive, and sexy', they lack the steel needed to be an excellent lawyer; if they act in more assertive and confident ways, they are seen as being troublemakers with difficult personalities. One study found that senior figures in law firms commonly described women as being 'disloyal and under committed',[82] and as being as much interested in home life as in life in the office.[83]

It is clear that one barrier to diversity is prejudicial attitudes. Jonathan Sumption QC, now a justice of the Supreme Court, said:

> Clearly, the diversity of appointments is extremely sensitive to the profile of the higher reaches of the legal professions. My own impression—I can't say that it is more than an impression but it is based on a fair amount of experience—is that the quality of BME candidates entering the legal profession now has continuously increased over a number of years, just as the quality and number of women entering the legal profession continuously increased over a substantial period a generation ago.[84]

Implicit in what he is saying is that women and BME lawyers, in the past, were of lower quality, although he sees that as improving. There is a more widespread assumption that, if women or BME lawyers are appointed, this is to satisfy diversity needs and they are not of adequate quality. This can impact on women themselves. One female

---

[79] R. Graycar, 'Gender, race, bias and perspective: Or, how otherness colours your judgment' (2008) 15 International Journal of the Legal Profession 73.

[80] Tomlinson et al. (n. 15), 252.   [81] Tomlinson et al. (n. 15), 251.

[82] L. Barnes and K. Malleson, 'The legal profession as gatekeeper to the judiciary: Design faults in measures to enhance diversity' (2011) 74 Modern Law Review 245.

[83] E. Wald, 'Glass ceilings and dead ends: Professional ideologies, gender stereotypes, and the future of women lawyers at large law firms' (2010) 78 Fordham Law Review 2245.

[84] Quoted in Sommerlad et al. (n. 21), 12.

solicitor told the Law Society: 'We are limited by own perception of our self, we need more support to stand out ... We don't promote ourselves.'[85]

Another explains it in these terms:

> Women are exiting earlier and earlier, they are more conscious of the people ahead of them, senior women also making that choice. The combined effect of not seeing any inspirational women at partner level but seeing female partners who had 'given up' so much creates a lot of doubt.[86]

Not often raised as much in these debates, but an important point nonetheless, is the stereotypes that surround men too. There are assumptions in the office about how men are to behave and that being a man means that you will have 'male characteristics'.[87] This might explain the low rate of uptake of paternity leave among lawyers in England and Wales. Perhaps the men want to assert that they are able to 'leave home at the office door' and recognise the importance of the work that the firm is providing.

Practical steps to promote diversity

We will now focus on practical steps that might be taken to promote diversity in the legal workplace. Before looking at these, some of the difficulties in taking these will be addressed.

First, any understanding of diversity must be sensitive to the group in question and the setting.[88] Pursuing gender diversity raises different challenges to pursuing racial or religious diversity, and so on. Even more, the intersection of these identities can raise problems of its own. There are unique problems facing black women that are not necessarily resolved by simply taking measures against race and sex discrimination. Attempts to achieve racial diversity may result in only middle-class members of the racial group benefiting.[89] Steps taken to remedy lack of diversity can backfire and have unintended impacts.

Second, there can be serious difficulties relating to definitions. For example, seeking to achieve racial diversity immediately raises question about which racial groups are being discussed. The definitions of ethnicity, sex, sexual orientation, and disability are all replete with problems. To consider only one example, if you were to want to assess gender balance, would you include inter-sex conditions in your assessment? By seeking to ascertain only the numbers of men and women, are you perpetuating the

---

[85] Law Society (n. 74), 12.   [86] Law Society (n. 74), 13.

[87] R. Collier, 'Masculinities, law, and personal life: towards a new framework for understanding men, law, and gender' (2010) 33 Harvard Journal of Law and Gender 431.

[88] Wald (n. 1).

[89] It has been claimed that while attempts in the United States to increase racial diversity in law schools have achieved a degree of success, it is often the wealthier members of minority groups who have been represented.

view that there are only two sexes? Or with sexual orientation, is dividing people into 'gay' and 'straight' not a gross simplification of the diversity of sexual orientations that people may have? However, a study that sought to show sensitivity to these complexities would be in danger of becoming too complex.

A third issue relates to when diversity is sought. Typically, programmes encouraging diversity seek to increase diversity at the point of entry. However, one of the most notable things about the legal profession is that improvements in diversity at entry level are not matched by improvements higher up the profession.

A final issue relates to the fear that attempts to respond to diversity concerns will backfire. If coercive means are used to promote diversity (for example by imposing quotas requiring firms to appoint a certain proportion from disadvantaged groups),[90] those appointed may fear that they have been selected by virtue of their characteristic, rather than their ability. Others in the firm may regard them in the same way. If the system is seen as unjust, firms will seek to undermine the imposition. It is generally regarded as preferable to seek to remove the barriers that impede diversity, so that it will arise naturally and consensually.[91]

So what, practically, can firms do to promote diversity? There have been many suggestions.

Outreach

Much effort has been put into reaching members of unrepresented groups early in their studies. Organisations such as the Sutton Trust and the 'Pathways to Law' programme have sought to encourage pupils still at school to consider a law degree. The fear is that youngsters in some groups will be put off seeking to join the legal professions as a result of assumptions about the nature of the profession, because of a fear that they lack the ability, or simply because they lack of knowledge about how to successfully apply for a career in law. A study of BME lawyers found that many had felt ill-informed when embarking on their legal studies and career.[92] The expectations of parents seem to impact on their children's desires. One in five young people from average backgrounds, and one in eight young people from poorer backgrounds, currently aspires to be a professional. This is three times fewer than young people from professional backgrounds.[93]

There is a further issue here: that some disadvantaged groups will have been so disadvantaged through their education that their academic achievements to date are such that they would not, based on the standard criteria, be selected for places on a law degree or by a firm of lawyers. In other words, the disadvantages affect some at

---

[90] Braithwaite (n. 23).

[91] D. Rhode, 'From platitudes to priorities: Diversity and gender equity in law firms' (2011) 24 Georgetown Journal of Legal Ethics 1041.

[92] Law Society, *Ethnic Diversity in Law Firms: Understanding the Barriers* (Law Society, 2010).

[93] Sullivan (n. 60).

such an early stage that even by the time they are considering a legal career, they are doomed to fail. This has led to debates about the extent to which it might be possible to assess 'innate ability', so that even though someone may not have performed well at, for example, GCSE level, he or she may, with appropriate training, still make an excellent lawyer. It may even be questioned whether the unofficial requirement of a 2:1 result at degree level should be expected.

The legal profession might need to look again at what lawyers 'need' in terms of academic achievement to date, if that is affected by disadvantage. The suggestion that there might be a role for tests that assess innate ability, rather than taught skills, is controversial, however. First, some question whether tests for 'innate ability' can be created. Tests such as the National Admissions Test for Law (LNAT) in the UK and Law School Admission Test (LSAT) in the United States have been developed, but even these require a reasonable standard of education.

Second, some fear that emphasising 'innate ability' downplays the achievements of those who have excelled in standard education. If the legal profession declares that it is interested in innate ability rather than academic achievement to date, there is a danger that this will deter bright candidates who have excelled by traditional means. The trick may be for the legal profession to be open to those who can show ability under *either* the standard academic route *or* the alternative assessment, if such an assessment can be produced.

Financial support

As mentioned earlier, one barrier to the legal profession is the financial expense, and particularly the financial risk, to which law students are exposed.[94] There are already some bursaries and scholarships offered for those from deprived socio-economic backgrounds, but these are few and there is no doubt that some able candidates from disadvantaged groups are discouraged from seeking a legal career for economic reasons. One BME lawyer responding to a Bar Council survey said:

> I'd agree money is a big barrier, because I had the benefit of having a grant for most of my university education. And I got some money from the Local Authority when I started doing the [Common Professional Examination] CPE, and then I got sponsorship for my Law Society finals. So, I was really quite lucky in that I was basically funded by somebody else for almost the entire duration of my education. But I think if I had to do that now, I don't think I would do. When I've had some students sit in with me, the amount of debt that some of them have got, just to pay their way through a degree and then Law School, and then no guarantee of getting a training contract either. I just don't honestly think I would've made that decision. And it just really struck me how... and people who work hard and they're not going out living the life of Riley, but they've got a £15,000 debt easily. They're just really trying to pay it back.[95]

---

[94] Law Society (n. 92).   [95] Tomlinson et al. (n. 15), 249.

Recruitment

Recruitment is an obvious point at which to look when considering diversity. Ensuring fair recruitment strategies and practices has, of course, a key part to play in advancing diversity. Some City practices seek out students from BME and/or lower socio-economic groups, and develop diversity placement schemes to encourage applications and to help to ensure that applicants will perform their best during the recruitment process. Interestingly, despite these, a study of BME lawyers[96] found that nearly all believed that firms failed to have fair or transparent recruitment processes. There is still a widely held belief that there are hidden routes to obtaining training contracts available to those with good contacts or those who are 'in the know'. It was also commonly thought that people who could form a bond with a partner by, for example, having been to Oxbridge or sharing an interest in horse-riding were at a clear advantage. Notably, even if these assumptions are incorrect (and, of course, they might not be), the fact that they exist and may therefore deter those who do not fit the paradigm from applying is significant in terms of diversity.[97]

Entry standards

Making changes to the formal requirements of entry into the firm can help. One controversial suggestion is to think again about what we 'need for lawyers'. It seems obvious that a law firm will prefer a candidate with a first class law degree over one with a lower second. However, success in a law degree is not the same as success as a lawyer in practice. By requiring, say, a good 2:1 degree, is a firm setting a barrier that works against diversity? Of course, it may be that a good 2:1 is a necessary requirement for success as a lawyer, but not everyone is convinced of that.[98] The Legal Education and Training Review (LETR) opened up the possibility of finding, in the future, ways of entering the legal profession without having completed a degree.[99]

Diversity training

Training in diversity is sometimes promoted too. Diversity training carries the benefit that it demonstrates a firm's commitment to diversity. Indeed, some have suggested that it should be built into legal education.

---

[96] Law Society (n. 92).

[97] A. Cook, J. Faulconbridge, and D. Muzio, 'London's legal elite: Recruitment through cultural capital and the reproduction of social exclusivity in City professional service fields' (2012) 44 Environment and Planning 1744.

[98] R. Pearce and S. Nasseri, 'The virtue of low barriers to becoming a lawyer: Promoting liberal and democratic values' (2012) 19 International Journal of the Legal Profession 357.

[99] Legal Education and Training Review, *Setting Standards* (LETR, 2013).

It is generally thought that it is rare for there to be overtly racist or sexist attitudes expressed by senior lawyers when making appointment or promotion decisions. If there are such deep-seated attitudes, then it is unlikely that such attitudes could be changed by training. However, what diversity training can do is combat unconscious discrimination and raise awareness of the advantages of diversity. An understanding of cultural difference may help to raise awareness that, for example, a candidate who might appear timid is in fact demonstrating what he or she perceives to be due deference.

Monitoring

One way of combating diversity is to require firms to put in place strategies to measure diversity. This will make any lack of diversity clear to the members of the firm, which might itself encourage individuals in the firm to address the problem. Commonly, lawyers will claim that their firm has no diversity problems, although it is clear from the statistics that there are problems across the profession. This often occurs where the token representative from a disadvantaged group is regarded as evidence that there is no discrimination in the firm. Monitoring can also assist in ascertaining whether measures designed to address diversity have succeeded. The publication of the statistics can indicate a commitment to diversity.

As already mentioned, monitoring does carry with it problems. It tends to require a simplification of complex matters such as race and sex into 'tick boxes'. It can also impose extra bureaucracy and raises concerns that it is leading to explicit or implicit quotas. There is also concern that the data collected will be sensitive and there can be worries about how secure it is. Indeed, when the Bar Council promoted the use of monitoring by chambers, many barristers voiced precisely these concerns.[100] As we have seen, however, the Bar Council and Law Society have put in place requirements for monitoring for diversity.

Cultural changes

As mentioned already, some commentators see the major issue that needs addressing as being the culture of law firms. It is seen as being a hyper-competitive culture, with an undue focus on the making of profits and on aggressive styles of lawyering. Assumptions about what people should wear and in what social activities they should engage, and expectations around the cultivation of clients can all impact on diversity.[101]

---

[100] Legal Futures, 'Barristers express concern over equality and diversity monitoring', *Legal Futures*, 24 February 2011, online at www.legalfutures.co.uk/regulation/barristers/barristers-express-concern-over-equality-and-diversity-monitoring

[101] T. Brower and J. Jones, 'Dress and appearance codes in the workplace: Gender, sexuality, law and legal institutions' (2013) 32 Equality, Diversity and Inclusion 5.

It is perhaps the difficulty of identifying and challenging the cultural assumptions within firms that create barriers to diversity that is the biggest challenge. One might identify practices within a firm that appear to be exclusionary, but with what are they to be replaced? If, for example, the 'Christmas party' is seen as promoting a particular cultural identity, what will take its place? If alcohol-based events exclude some, we might replace these, but can events always be found that do not exclude some group or other? No doubt there are answers to these questions, but they require imagination.

 Alternative view

It is all very nice when academics talk about making firms 'family-friendly' and less focused on profits, but it is unrealistic in the real business world, where there is a genuine market for legal services and firms have to ensure economic viability to survive. Realistically, the culture of long hours and the importance of networking will remain with us.[102] Firms like employees who work hard and make lots of money for the firm. Is that discrimination—or economics?

Promotion

As mentioned earlier, one barrier to diversity is the lack of clarity in promotion procedures. Setting clear promotion criteria is key.[103] However, that is only part of the picture. Currently, informal criteria for promotion focus on billed hours and marketing. Some complain that these criteria are themselves a reflection of a macho culture. The quality of the work done may be more meaningful than 'billed hours'. The use of billed hours worked reinforces a long hours culture, which itself disadvantages women.

Mentoring

A common problem facing those seeking to improve diversity is that even where improvements are made in recruitment, women and BME lawyers leave the profession at far higher rates than white men. To combat this, many large firms are offering mentoring and support. This usually involves a partner or senior member of staff being asked to offer support and help to those at a disadvantage—although at least one report in the 2009 *Lawyer* magazine reported a finding that mentoring stigmatised women and suggested that they had 'special needs'.[104]

---

[102] D. Muzio and J. Tomlinson, 'Researching gender, inclusion and diversity in contemporary professions and professional organizations' (2012) 19 Gender, Work and Organization 455.

[103] Law Society, *International Women in Law Summit: Setting the Agenda for Change* (Law Society, 2012).   [104] Law Society (n. 103).

Flexible times

Another key barrier mentioned by women and BME lawyers is the focus on long work hours.[105] This has led some to argue that operating more flexible working practices might promote diversity. This, in particular, may help with the problem in low levels of promotion among women to the position of partner, which can become an issue at precisely the time a woman might be considering starting a family.

A Law Society report discussing flexible working made the following point:

> This research suggests that core competencies would not be affected by flexible work practice, as many participants could provide examples of how flexible working did not affect the level of service delivered to clients. However, there remains a 'disconnect' between expressed policies around flexible working and what is culturally acceptable. The implications of not embracing flexible work practices will be the continued exodus of talented and well-trained lawyers from firms that do not adapt to shifting expectations and priorities. Flexible working needs to become a genuinely acceptable choice, not one that currently equates to stepping off the career ladder.[106]

What is interesting about this quote is that it emphasises that it is not enough simply to introduce flexible working hours; it must also become culturally acceptable to take on flexible working. This is tied in with the 'billable hours culture'. As the report goes on to note, it is often incorrectly assumed that a lawyer billing many hours is working well:

> The billable hours structure could be a barrier to lawyers developing good management skills, especially if this was not accorded great importance. Participants identified that it adversely affected the way in which lawyers project manage caseloads, their clients and, most importantly, their teams. Several participants were critical of perceived poor levels of management skills within the profession. Lawyers commented on the lack of performance management or indeed active management of their individual career development.[107]

Quotas and positive action

In the face of these difficulties, some call for positive action—in other words, a positive attempt by the legal profession to ensure that there is diversity. It can include the following actions.

- *Quotas* It could involve, at the most extreme, a setting of quotas, so that a fixed percentage of entrants into the profession and a fixed percentage of prestigious positions are held by members of a particular minority group.

---

[105] L. Duff and L. Webley, *Qualitative Findings and Literature Review* (Law Society, 2004).
[106] Law Society, *Flexible Working and Solicitors' Work–Life Balance* (Law Society, 2010), 19.
[107] Law Society (n. 106), 20.

- *Diversity goals* These would not require professions to recruit a particular percentage of members of groups, but would encourage them to do so. The aim would be that if a firm is deciding between two similarly qualified applicants, it might choose the one needed to get closer to its diversity goal.

- *Encouraging application* One relatively uncontroversial approach is to target advertising towards less well-represented groups. The perception here is that advertising of jobs, scholarships, and the like can be focused on the groups representing the majority groups.

Most supporters of quotas accept that they are not a goal or an ideal. They are a remedy for discrimination and under-representation.[108] But the use of quotas is controversial. For some, the problem of diversity has proved so deeply ingrained and so difficult to tackle that the drastic measure of quotas is needed to combat it. Without quotas, the dominant legal culture will not change and therefore diversity cannot change. To others, the principle of appointment on merit is fundamental: we cannot depart from it. Once we do, there is the danger already mentioned earlier in this chapter that those BME and women lawyers appointed will be seen as not fully deserving of their appointments.

Donald Nicolson notes:

> No doubt, lawyers are likely to resist this argument by denying any obligation to act as 'social engineers' in order to remedy the consequences of social disadvantage for which they lack responsibility...and argue that as long as they avoid discrimination they must remain discriminating so as to maintain professional standards.[109]

However, he goes on to argue that:

> [P]rofessional incumbents benefit from the current unequal distribution of social goods and the role lawyers have played in helping to develop and apply a legal system which has expressly discriminated against women, allowed racial discrimination and upheld those relations of production and ownership which lie at the heart of class differences. Nor have they held back from acting for clients bent on using the law to ensure social oppression and exploitation.[110]

Other points that might be made include that even if one is focusing on merit, then there are still arguments that it is a desirable characteristic that a candidate from a disadvantaged background will be able to serve clients with a similar background, or that overcoming significant disadvantage to reach that position is evidence of strength of character. Indeed, Nicolson argues:

> [I]t can be argued that recruitment and promotion candidates who have had to overcome social disadvantages and possibly also discrimination in order to compete equally with more advantaged candidates are in fact more qualified than the latter,

---

[108] Wald (n. 1).   [109] Nicolson (n. 18), 202.   [110] Nicolson (n. 18), 202.

and that even those who are on paper less qualified may in fact have more potential and inherent ability. Accordingly, if the form of preferential treatment used is suitably gauged to reflect this fact, there need be no conflict with the merit principle and the need to maintain professional standards.[111]

No hope

Having looked through the things that might improve diversity, it is necessary to recognise that there are some commentators who are pessimistic about ever achieving diversity. They see the root problems of diversity as resting in past discrimination and present structural inequalities and social exclusion. In short, the roots of a lack of diversity are deep-seated within society, with a long history.[112] Law firms cannot expect to address all of these issues.

There seems little doubt that past and current disadvantage in society at large, and in the education system more specifically, makes it difficult for the legal profession to achieve diversity. These disadvantages have already prevented people from achieving the qualifications that they 'need' to enter the profession. This can lead some to throw their hands in the air and declare that the disadvantages are so engrained and so beyond the control of the legal profession that there is little that the profession can do. Similarly, if the culture of the group strongly discourages members from entering the legal profession, the hands of the profession are tied.

Another major social barrier to diversity is the failure of society to respond adequately to the issues around caring for children, those with disabilities, and other special needs.[113] In particular, the gendered assumptions surrounding care mean that, without much broader social support, women will be disadvantaged in the traditional workplace environment.[114] While it might be possible to reimagine a society that puts the importance of care of dependants at its heart and in which employment is worked around the assumption that workers will have caring responsibilities,[115] we are a long way from such a society.

Another grim response is that where we have seen an increase in women and BME lawyers, this has been because they have been willing to copy the characteristics of the standard 'white male' stereotype. By adopting the prevailing culture and 'playing the game', they have been able to reach the higher echelon.[116] But that may be seen as assimilation, rather than diversity. For the optimist, however, increasing the number of members of disadvantaged groups will itself ensure a change in the culture of lawyers.[117]

---

[111] Nicolson (n. 18), 203.   [112] Wald (n. 1).
[113] J. Herring, *Caring and the Law* (Hart, 2013).   [114] Muzio and Tomlinson (n. 102).
[115] Herring (n. 113).   [116] Sommerlad et al. (n. 21).   [117] Nicolson (n. 18).

What would you do?

You are the managing partner of a large firm of solicitors. You notice that most of the partners are white men. You wish to change the diversity of your firm. What steps could you take to improve its position?

Are women lawyers different?

A lively debate has arisen over whether women lawyers act differently and engage in law differently from men.[118] No one claims that all men act in a particular way and that all women act in a particular way. However, some argue that, generally speaking, there is a difference between the ways in which different genders behave as lawyers. More subtly, it is said that there are different styles of lawyering, one style associated with what are seen as traditionally masculine traits and another associated with what are seen as more feminine.

Carrie Menkel-Meadow has argued that women can lawyer differently.[119] She developed Carol Gilligan's writing, suggesting that women reason with an 'ethic of care', while men reason with an 'ethic of justice'. This, Menkel-Meadow suggested, was reflected in lawyering, because women would seek to avoid confrontation or aggressive lawyering, and to find instead a solution that reflected the interests of all of the parties. There would be more collaboration and less competition among women lawyers.[120] They would find ways of integrating home life and work life.[121] Some argue that men and women use different moral languages in dealing with moral problems, where ambition, reason, competitiveness, and aggression are seen as masculine, as compared with compassion or empathy, which are seen as more female. Men rely on abstract principles, while women approach solutions that seek relationships.[122]

Stephen Ellman lists three things that a lawyer using an ethic of care will consider when taking on a client:

First, the lawyer will want to consider the extent of client need, for caring lawyers will seek to respond to need when they recognize it. Second, she will want to listen to her own feelings of care for her potential client (or her lack of them), not only because her feelings can affect the quality of her work but also, and perhaps more

---

[118] Schultz and Shaw (n. 13).

[119] C. Menkel-Meadow, 'Portia redux: Another look at gender, feminism, and legal ethics', in S. Parker and C. Sampford (eds) *Legal Ethics and Legal Practice: Contemporary Issues* (Oxford University Press, 1995).

[120] C. Grant Bowman and E. Schneider, 'Feminist legal theory, feminist lawmaking, and the legal profession' (1998) 67 Fordham Law Review 249.

[121] Grant Bowman and Schneider (n. 120).   [122] Menkel-Meadow (n. 119).

fundamentally, because actually caring is part of honoring the ethic of care. Third, she will look to the caring, or uncaring, quality of her client and of the tasks he wishes her to perform, for helping another to act uncaringly is a blow to the values of care.[123]

This sort of claim is difficult to assess. It is certainly possible to point to some changes in the law and legal practice that have come about over the past 30 years or so at the same time as there have been more women in the profession.[124] For example, there is greater awareness of the significance of domestic violence; there has been an improvement in the law's response to sex and race discrimination; there is now a greater awareness of the importance of child care. There have been changes too in practice. Surveys of lawyers suggest that most lawyers recognise the importance of having empathy for a client and of seeking to negotiate an acceptable solution, rather than seeking litigation. However, whether these changes have occurred because women have entered the profession with a different style of lawyering, or whether these reflect broader social changes and the impact of feminist activism, is a matter for debate.

Those who support a difference in attitude between men and women lawyers might refer to the fact that there are certain areas of law in which there is a marked gender difference.[125] Family law and child protection commonly involve more women than men. Indeed, there, it might even be said that increased female participation in the profession is problematic, because it has reinforced the idea that certain areas of the law are primarily of female concern.[126]

Many people reject a clear binary divide. It is not difficult to find male lawyers who display empathy and female lawyers who are focused on profit. Even if it could be shown that women are more likely to display the 'feminine' style than men, it would be difficult to know whether that was the innate characteristic of women or whether it was socially learned behaviour.[127] As we mentioned earlier, some commentators have taken the view that many women who are successful lawyers have achieved their success by assimilating the traditionally male characteristics.[128] Others have focused on areas of law seen as traditionally for women. As one barrister commented to the Legal Services Board:

> You tend to find more women in family law. Criminal defence you tend to find women end up being pushed into sex offences.... I was specifically asked for in relation to

---

[123] S. Ellmann, 'The ethic of care as an ethic for lawyers' (1992) 81 Georgetown Law Journal 2665, 2667.

[124] H. Sommerlad, 'Can women lawyer differently? A perspective from the UK', in U. Schultz and G. Shaw (eds) *Women in the World's Legal Professions* (Hart, 2002).

[125] S. Parker and C. Sampford (eds) *Legal Ethics and Legal Practice: Contemporary Issues* (Oxford University Press, 1996).   [126] Sommerlad (n. 124).

[127] P. Hatamyar and K. Simmons, 'Are women more ethical lawyers? An empirical study' (2001) 34 Florida State University Law Review 784 found no evidence that women and men differed in their caring attitudes.   [128] Tomlinson et al. (n. 15).

rape cases and domestic violence cases because the defendants wanted to be seen having a female barrister because, of course, that meant they liked women and they wouldn't possibly beat a woman or rape a woman.[129]

What does seem to be reasonably well established is that women feel restricted in how they behave while at work. The qualities expected of them and the stereotypes against which they must work shape the personas that they adopt at work.[130] It might be added that some men may feel the same restrictions on them.[131]

Conclusion

The legal profession has a grim record on issues of diversity. Women, BME, LGBT, and disabled lawyers have all historically been marginalised in the profession. While great strides have been made to improve diversity at the entry level, there is still a significant lack of diversity at the upper end of the profession—no more so than the lack of judges from among disadvantaged groups. There are two particular difficulties facing the profession as it seeks to address diversity. The first is that many of the barriers facing disadvantaged groups are not created by the profession, but by the deeply ingrained socio-economic inequalities that exist in the broader society. The second major barrier is the legal culture of long hours and white masculine norms, which can be harder to challenge and change. If they do change, however, that will be good for all lawyers.

 Further reading

Articles discussing diversity in the legal profession generally include:

L. Ashton and L. Empson, *Differentiation and Discrimination: Understanding Social Class and Social Exclusion in the UK's Leading Law Firms* (Cass Centre for Professional Service Firms, 2011).

Bar Standards Board, *Guidelines on the Equality and Diversity Provisions of the Code of Conduct* (Bar Council, 2013).

M. Blackwell, 'Old boys' networks, family connections and the English legal profession' [2011] Public Law 426.

J. Braithwaite, 'Diversity staff and the dynamics of diversity policy-making in large law firms' (2010) 13 Legal Studies 141.

Law Society, *Ethnic Diversity in Law Firms: Understanding the Barriers* (Law Society, 2010).

---

[129] Sommerlad et al. (n. 21), 131.   [130] Sommerlad (n. 124).

[131] F. Bartlett and L. Aitken, 'Competence in caring in legal practice' (2009) 16 International Journal of the Legal Profession 241.

D. Nicolson, 'Demography, discrimination and diversity: A new dawn for the British legal profession?' (2005) 12 International Journal of the Legal Profession 201.

H. Sommerlad, L. Webley, L. Duff, D. Muzio, and J. Tomlinson, *Diversity in the Legal Profession in England and Wales: A Qualitative Study of Barriers and Individual Choices* (Legal Services Board, 2012).

R. Sullivan, *Barriers to the Legal Profession* (Legal Services Board, 2010).

J. Tomlinson, D. Muzio, H. Sommerlad, L. Webley, and L. Duff, 'Structure, agency and career strategies of white women and black and minority ethnic individuals in the legal profession' (2013) 66 Journal of Legal Resources 245.

E. Wald, 'Glass ceilings and dead ends: Professional ideologies, gender stereotypes, and the future of women lawyers at large law firms' (2010) 78 Fordham Law Review 2245.

E. Wald, 'A primer on diversity, discrimination, and equality in the legal profession or who is responsible for pursuing diversity and why' (2011) 24 Georgetown Journal of Legal Ethics 1079.

Work on gender issues within the legal profession includes:

R. Collier, 'Masculinities, law, and personal life: Towards a new framework for understanding men, law, and gender' (2010) 33 Harvard Journal of Law and Gender 431.

R. Dinovitzer, N. Reichman, and J. Sterling, 'The differential valuation of women's work: A new look at the gender gap in lawyers' incomes' (2009) 88 Social Forces 819.

S. Ellmann, 'The ethic of care as an ethic for lawyers' (1992) 81 Georgetown Law Journal 2665.

C. McGlynn, 'The status of women lawyers in the United Kingdom', in U. Schultz and G. Shaw (eds) *Women in the World's Legal Professions* (Hart, 2002).

C. Menkel-Meadow, 'Portia redux: Another look at gender, feminism, and legal ethics', in S. Parker and C. Sampford (eds) *Legal Ethics and Legal Practice: Contemporary Issues* (Oxford University Press, 1995).

D. Rhode, 'From platitudes to priorities: Diversity and gender equity in law firms' (2011) 24 Georgetown Journal of Legal Ethics 1041.

U. Schultz and G. Shaw (eds) *Women in the World's Legal Professions* (Hart, 2002).

H. Sommerlad and P. Sanderson, *Gender, Choice and Commitment* (Ashgate, 1998),

M. Thornton, *Dissonance and Distrust: Women and the Legal Profession* (Oxford University Press, 1996).

Works looking at diversity in the judiciary include:

K. Malleson, 'Justifying gender equality on the bench: Why difference won't do' (2003) 11 Feminist Legal Studies 1.

K. Malleson, 'Diversity in the judiciary: The case for positive action' (2009) 36 Journal of Law and Society 367.

Applying ethical theories

Key issues

- How should a lawyer balance his or her duties to a client and his or her duties to the general good?
- When acting for a company, whose interests should a lawyer promote?
- Is it possible to be a good person and a good lawyer?

Introduction

In this chapter, we will explore how the principles that we have been discussing will work out in particular cases. To present this, we will imagine how four lawyers might respond to three different scenarios, one taken from criminal law, one from commercial law, and one from family law. The four lawyers will represent different schools of thought on lawyers' ethics.

Before looking at the particular scenarios, the four (imaginary) lawyers will explain what they take as their starting points.

The general principles

Lawyer 1

At the heart of all lawyers' ethics is the principle that the lawyer must put the interests of the client first. Lawyers have a very particular job to do and that is to present the best case possible for their clients. The professional codes all refer to this.

> ### Follow the Code
>
> Principle 4 in the Solicitors Regulation Authority (SRA) Code of Conduct reads:
>
> You must…act in the best interests of each *client*;

Under para 303 of the Bar Council Code of Conduct (the Bar Code):

A barrister:

(a) must promote and protect fearlessly and by all proper and lawful means the lay client's best interests and do so without regard to his own interests or to any consequences to himself or to any other person.

Daniel Markovits captures the special role that lawyers have well:

Unlike juries and judges, adversary lawyers should not pursue a true account of the facts of a case and promote a dispassionate application of the law to these facts. Instead, they should try aggressively to manipulate both the facts and the law to suit their clients' purposes. This requires lawyers to promote beliefs in others that they themselves (properly reject as false)...

And unlike legislators, adversary lawyers should not seek to balance competing interests and claims so that all persons get what they deserve, Instead, they should strive disproportionately and at times almost exclusively to promote their clients' interests.[1]

There is a natural tendency for the lawyer to want to promote the social good or uphold moral standards. However, doing so is an error. That would be to step outside the carefully defined role of a lawyer. Margaret Simons, in an article, quotes from a lawyer whom she asked what role a lawyer would have if his client were to want to do something legal, but immoral. I would agree with that lawyer's response:

'I'm struggling to see where there would be a case where that actually arose.' He said 'The clients are entitled obviously to avail themselves of the full protection of the law and the lawyers are there to advance their clients' interests subject to the constraints of their professional duties, and in particular their duties to the court'...He said a lawyer might advise on the 'appropriateness' of different strategies, but it was wrong for a lawyer to make moral judgements. 'We don't take a moral stance and it's not up to us, as advocates for a client to take a moral stance. Ultimately that comes to a decision by the client, not the lawyer.[2]

So a lawyer must seek to put the interests of the client first, but what do we mean by 'interests' here? We must mean seek to promote what the client wants. In other words, we must enable the client to maximise his or her autonomy. Our society recognises that people should be free to live their lives as they wish, subject to the constraints of the law. Lawyers have a crucial role in ensuring that people are able to exercise their law-given freedom to make choices. Crucially, that is so however misguided or even immoral others may believe that to be.

---

[1] D Markovits, *A Modern Legal Ethics* (Princeton University Press, 2012), 3.

[2] M. Simons, 'Lawyers not moral judges', *The Sunday Age*, 4 August 2002, 3, quoted in C. Parker and A. Evans, *Inside Lawyers' Ethics* (Cambridge University Press, 2007), 16.

If a lawyer takes on the role of recommending a course of action or seeking to impose morality on the client, then whose values is that lawyer to use?[3] There is no good answer to that question, except that the client should choose the values that he or she wishes to follow. The lawyer must recognise that he or she is in a powerful position and that the client is likely to attach great weight to what the lawyer advises. That is why it is better not to try to impose a view on the client.

So the central principle is: the lawyer must promote the best interests of the client, as the client understands those interests to be.

Lawyer 2

While I agree with Lawyer 1 that the primary job of a lawyer is to promote the interests of the client, I think that he has made the mistake of assuming that this means that the lawyer must follow the client's instructions. There is all the difference in the world in doing what someone wants and doing what is in that person's best interests. Sadly, many of us want the things that are not good for us!

Lawyer 1 has quoted from the professional codes and these make it clear that a lawyer must act in the client's interests. Had they meant to require a lawyer to follow a client's instructions, they could have said so. There are some good reasons why a lawyer should not have to follow a client's advice. First, the client normally lacks legal expertise and so, in relation to a legal matter, will not have the understanding to make a decision. The client has come to the lawyer because the client lacks the ability to make the decision himself or herself.

Second, the client is often so caught up in the emotion of the issue that he or she cannot be expected to exercise the kind of dispassionate decision that a lawyer can make.

Third, the lawyer must accept responsibility for what he or she does. Acting in the way that promotes the client's interests is a good reason. That he or she simply did what as he or she was told provides no moral warrant at all. 'I was following orders' is not, and never has been, a good reason for acting in an immoral way.

Having made those points, of course, a lawyer will often decide that what the client wants is in his or her best interests, and the lawyer will always take into account the client's wishes in that regard.

Lawyer 3

I disagree with Lawyer 1 and Lawyer 2. The primary duty of a lawyer is not to the client, but to the justice system as a whole. Lawyer 1 cited Principle 4 of the SRA Code of Conduct, but what about the very first principle?

---

[3] J. Kirchmeier, 'Confession for the soul? A lawyer's moral advice to a guilty client about saving an innocent defendant' (2012) 10 Ohio State Journal of Criminal Law 219.

> ## Follow the Code
>
> Principle 1 of the SRA Code of Conduct reads:
>
> > You must uphold the rule of law and the proper administration of justice;

This makes it clear that the primary duty of a solicitor is to the administration of justice. It is true that following the instructions of the client or acting in the best interests of the client will help the lawyer to uphold the rule of law, but not always. Crucially, the SRA Code tells us what to do if there is a clash between the principles:

> ## Follow the Code
>
> Paragraph 2.2 of the SRA Code of Conduct reads:
>
> > Where two or more Principles come into conflict, the Principle which takes precedence is the one which best serves the public interest in the particular circumstances, especially the public interest in the proper administration of justice.

As this makes clear, the ultimate duty is always to promote the public interest, and especially the interest in promoting justice, which should be at the heart of lawyers' ethics.

Alvin Esau has captured my beliefs well:

[T]he wellspring of a lawyer's duties to clients and the public flows from the legal profession's unique role in society as the trustee for the forms of social order. The forms of social order include not only legislative, judicial and administrative forums, but also the process of private ordering through contract, and the negotiation and drafting of the constitutions of private organisations. Thus what the lawyer does in the privacy of the office may be seen as part of the public administration of justice because law is made and applied through lawyers counselling and planning... To keep all the forms of social order working fairly and with integrity is the obligation of the profession, and each lawyer must place that obligation above any particular client interest contrary to it. Loyalty to the fair process of law is primary and constrains lawyer behaviour on behalf of clients.[4]

---

[4] A. Esau, 'What should we teach? Three approaches to professional responsibility', in D. Buckingham, J. Bickenbach, R. Bronaugh, and B. Wilson (eds) *Legal Ethics in Canada: Theory and Practice* (Harcourt Brace, 1996), 178–9.

It might be said that such an approach is paternalistic, because it involves the lawyer telling the client what he or she should do. However, that is to misunderstand paternalism. As Julian Webb and Donald Nicolson argue:

> It is not paternalistic for a lawyer to tell the partner of a client who has approached the lawyer to make a will that the client has AIDS, even though disclosure is against the clients wishes. Interventions are paternalistic if they involve interference in what clients decide is good *for themselves* (what we will call their 'self-regarding choices'), as opposed to interventions which are designed to prevent clients harming others.[5]

The primary duty of the lawyer is to maintain and support the justice system, and to promote the wider good. In many cases, that will coincide with presenting the client's case, but not if doing so will undermine the lawyer's primary duty.

Lawyer 4

Lawyers' ethics need to be about promoting good, caring relationships. This means that lawyers should be trying to understand their obligations within their emotional and relational contexts.[6] My approach is built on applying an ethic of care to the issue. Parker and Evans set out three key aspects of an ethic of care in this context:

> First, the ethics of care encourages lawyers to take a more holistic view of clients and their problems. Thus lawyers following the ethics of care are likely to spend more time listening to and discussing the broader concerns of lawyers and the way that legal issues are likely to impact on other aspects of their lives and relationships...
>
> ...[S]econdly, the ethics of care emphasises dialogue between lawyer and client and participatory approaches to lawyers. The lawyer–client relationship is built on mutual trust and shared knowledge...the ethic of care puts a premium on the lawyer spending time listening to the broader concerns of the client so that the legal solution they offer fits in with the other aspects of the client's life...
>
> Thirdly, because the ethics of care asks lawyers (and clients) to see themselves within a network of relationships and to understand the feelings and experience of others within those relationships, they are likely to look for non-adversarial ways to resolve disputes and preserve relationships if possible.[7]

So, in my responses to the scenarios, I will be seeking to find a solution that promotes the best caring relationships between all those involved.

---

[5] J. Webb and D. Nicolson, *Professional Legal Ethics: Critical Interrogations* (Oxford University Press, 2000), 130.

[6] D. Prescott, 'The act of lawyering and the art of communication: An essay on families-in-crisis, the adversarial tradition, and the social work model' (2010) 7 Legal Ethics 126.

[7] C. Parker and A. Evans, *Inside Lawyers' Ethics* (Cambridge University Press, 2007), 34–5.

Criminal law

 What would you do?

You are acting for a defendant charged with a sexual assault against his ex-girlfriend. He tells you that she consented to the activity and that she is a liar, who is out to get revenge. He tells you to cross-examine as fiercely as possible, and to question her about her unusual sexual interests and establish that she has had a large number of sexual partners in the past.

At one point, you ask him to be utterly truthful with you about what happened and he replies: 'Well, I will tell you what to say at my trial. That is all you need to know.' You suspect that he may well be guilty of the offence.

Shortly before the trial, you approach the judge and ask for an indication of sentence if there is a guilty plea. The judge indicates that he is unlikely to send the defendant to prison if he pleads guilty. The defendant is not sure what to do.

There are three issues raised in this question:

- the cross-examination;
- the question marks over guilt; and
- the plea bargain issue.

The cross-examination

Lawyer 1

The client has issued clear instructions on how he wishes his defence to be conducted and the arguments that he wishes to make. It is not the lawyer's job to second-guess the client. It is paternalistic for the lawyer to decide how to argue a case or to direct the client how to act. After all, it is the client, not the lawyer, who will have to bear the brunt of any sentence. The lawyer's job is to enable the client to exercise his legal rights and to conduct his defence as he wishes.

It may be that, in relation to the cross-examination, you feel unhappy about doing that and you may even think that people should not be allowed to cross-examine in this way. The law, however, has addressed this issue and there are restrictions in section 41 of the Youth Justice and Criminal Evidence Act 1999. These mean that you will need the leave of the court to raise the prior sexual experience or that you must argue that the cross-examination falls outside the terms of section 41. You may think that the protections there are inadequate and that what Parliament has decided is inappropriate. But if the law allows you to cross-examine in this way and your client wants the cross-examination to take that form, you will be denying him his legal rights if you refuse to follow his wishes.

It is important that you remember your role in the litigation process. Your job is to present the case that your client wants you to make; it is the job of the judge to ensure the protection of the witness. Your job is to comply with the requests of your client, not to worry about the well-being of the witnesses.

Lawyer 2

The guiding principle, remember, is that you must act in a way that promotes the client's interests. The client has asked for a strong cross-examination of the witness, but is that the best way in which to present his case? You, as the lawyer, are best placed to decide what tactics will best advance the case of the client. There is a danger here that following the client's instructions will turn the jury against him. Sometimes, it is the job of a lawyer to protect a client against himself.

The dangers of simply following the instructions of a client were well acknowledged by Lord Templeman in *Ashmore v Corporation of Lloyd's*:[8]

> The parties and particularly their legal advisers in any litigation are under a duty to cooperate with the court by chronological, brief and consistent pleadings which define the issues and leave the judge to draw his own conclusions about the merits when he hears the case. It is the duty of counsel to assist the judge by simplification and concentration and not to advance a multitude of ingenious arguments in the hope that out of ten bad points the judge will be capable of fashioning a winner. In nearly all cases the correct procedure works perfectly well. But there has been a tendency in some cases for legal advisers, pressed by their clients, to make every point conceivable and inconceivable without judgment or discrimination.

So the central principle is to consider what form of cross-examination will best promote your client's case. Lawyer 1 is right to say that you must not be distracted by thinking about the interests of the witness. But Lawyer 1 is wrong to suggest that you must agree with the client about what is the best way in which to cross-examine the witness.

Lawyer 3

As mentioned in my introduction, the lawyer's primary duty is to promote justice. Rigorous cross-examination can promote justice in some cases, but not always. In this context, there are some good reasons why the administration of justice will not be promoted by a fierce cross-examination, as follows.

- Quite properly, evidence must be tested, but the form of cross-examination recommended by the client is simply abusive and unsettling. It will severely upset the witness without producing more reliable testimony.[9] There is ample evidence

---

[8] [1992] 1 WLR 446, 453.
[9] J. Temkin and B. Krahé, *Sexual Assault and the Justice Gap: A Question of Attitude* (Hart, 2008).

of victims of rape trials being cross-examined in a way that humiliates them, but which gets no closer to the truth.[10]

- The line of cross-examination proposed by the client promotes certain rape myths (which are untrue assumptions about women in the context of sexual relations). For example, it suggests that a woman with unorthodox sexual tastes will therefore be happy to have sex with anyone or that a woman with previous partners therefore consented to have sex with the defendant.[11] To rely on these untruths would be to encourage the jury to find an unjustifiable conviction. In effect, you are being encouraged to persuade the jury to rely on misleading evidence.

- This style of cross-examination will lead to women being deterred from reporting sexual assaults and will therefore undermine justice.[12]

These all point to the lawyer not cross-examining along the lines suggested by the client, but rather in a way that will help to produce the truth.

Lawyer 4

While the lawyer has an obligation to the client, a special obligation, you have a responsibility to be caring with all those with whom you come into contact. You also have a responsibility to yourself. So I would make the following observations on the issue of the cross-examination.

1. You need to discuss this proposed line of cross-examination with your client. Is it an approach with which you can both work? If you feel that this is improper, you need to talk it through with your client. You must not feel that your own wishes and feelings are not to be taken into account. Ultimately, if you are not able to find a result that works in your relationships, maybe it is best to end the relationship.

2. You must be alert to the emotional side of your client's request. Why does he want you to act in this way? Is he terrified by the trial or feeling angry? It may be that this is just a manifestation of emotional turmoil and not a genuine request. Perhaps suggesting counselling for your client would be a good idea.[13] You need to look after your client as a whole person, not only as a source of work and/ or money.

3. You must be caring towards the victim. You can cross-examine in a firm, but caring, way. Being caring does not always require a 'warm cuddly' approach; you can keep a professional distance, but respect the person and acknowledge her feelings. That is unlikely to involve asking the questions that the client has asked you to ask, but it can involve questions asked in a respectful, but determined,

---

[10] See Chapter 9.   [11] Temkin and Krahé (n. 9).   [12] Temkin and Krahé (n. 9).
[13] A. Melville and K. Laing, 'Closing the gate: Family lawyers as gatekeepers to a holistic service' (2010) 6 International Journal of Law in Context 167.

way seeking to ascertain the truth. In fact, treating a witness with dignity and acknowledging her emotions may well result in a trial that is more likely to ascertain the truth.

Admission of guilt

Lawyer 1

You may be concerned that the client has 'confessed' to committing a crime. It is true that a barrister must not mislead the court.

> **Follow the Code**
>
> The Bar Code, para 302, puts it thus:
>
> A barrister has an overriding duty to the Court to act with independence in the interests of justice: he must assist the Court in the administration of justice and must not deceive or knowingly or recklessly mislead the Court.

However, look carefully at what your client has told you. He has not confessed, but rather dodged the question. The instructions from the client are clear and there is no misleading the court; you simply have suspicions that he might have committed a crime. That provides you with no reason to depart from your client's instructions. It is the job of the jury or the court to decide whether your client is guilty or not, not yours.

Lawyer 2

As Lawyer 1 has said—and I agree—a lawyer should never deceive a client and so if the client has clearly stated that he committed the crime, then the lawyer cannot enter a 'not guilty' plea, except on the well-established basis that the prosecution has not proved its case. The facts in this case are not clear. It does not look like the client has actually confessed to the crime and it cannot be in his best interests to plead guilty. So a 'not guilty' plea must be entered.

Lawyer 3

It is a mistake to read the duty not to mislead the court as simply a negative one, only prohibiting an outright lie. As already mentioned, the duty to promote the administration of justice is at the heart of lawyers' ethics. Not only must a lawyer not deceive the court, but the lawyer also has a positive duty to assist the court in the administration of justice. So not only must the lawyer not lie, but you must also act in a way that best helps the court to find out the truth.

However, we need to be careful in this context. A lawyer's job is to present a client's case and that usually helps the court to ascertain the truth. When a lawyer presents a client's case, the lawyer is presenting what the client has said has happened, but it must be what the client genuinely says has happened. Here, there is sufficient ambiguity in what the client said that the lawyer must press the client and find out exactly what he means. It is correct that, as Lawyer 2 states, it is not the job of the lawyer to second-guess the client. However, Lawyers 1 and 2 seem to want to hide between the ambiguous statements as providing cover for making potentially untrue statements to the court. That is setting the standard of lawyers' ethics too low. Lawyers should strive for the highest standards. You can put forward a 'not guilty' plea in this case only when the client has made a clear confirmation to you that he did not commit the crime.

Lawyer 4

It is important to realise the lawyer–client relationship is one of trust. We often talk of the responsibilities that a lawyer has, but a client has responsibilities too. These include the obligation to be honest. Representing a client involves the lawyer engaging in hard work and being the front person for the client, but that will be a successful relationship only if the client is open and honest with the solicitor. In this case, it seems that the client is trying to avoid being open and honest with you. That cannot be the basis of a good lawyer–client relationship. You need to explain to the client that your relationship must be based on openness and honesty. If he cannot accept that, it is probably best for you to find another lawyer for him.

Plea bargain

Lawyer 1

Your key role here is to pass on the information that you have been given and to receive your client's instructions. Plea bargaining is, in general, something to be encouraged. It gives defendants a real choice and ability to exercise their autonomy. The trial is always a matter of chance, and giving clients the option to plead guilty and accept a lower sentence is to be encouraged.

We are told that the client does not know what to do. You must tread carefully here. Your job is not to make decisions for the client. That is a very dangerous route to go down. The best thing to do is to set out the options for your client and give him the legal information. But remember that your client is the boss and that he is the one who must make the decision.

Lawyer 2

The response of Lawyer 1 is astonishing. People pay lawyers large sums of money for their expert advice and assistance. It is crucial here that the lawyer steps up to the mark and advises the client as to the best course of action. The lawyer must be clear about what is on offer and seek to get the best deal for the client. Using your expertise, you must advise on the most likely outcome if the client pleads guilty and that if he pleads not guilty. Of course, you cannot guarantee a result, but it is your job to give a clear recommendation.

Lawyer 3

I strongly dislike plea bargains for two reasons. First, those who are guilty and accept them are not being given a lower sentence than justice demands. The sentence should reflect the gravity of the wrong done and the blameworthiness of the defendant. The fact that the defendant has saved the court time and the government money should not be a reason for lowering the sentence. The practice of plea bargaining elevates economic concerns over justice concerns and that is not acceptable.[14]

The second reason is that it pressurises clients who are not guilty into pleading guilty to get a low sentence, even though they may not have committed the offence. It is wrong to do anything that may lead an innocent person to plead guilty, which would lead to a profound injustice.[15]

So I wish that plea bargaining of any kind did not occur. In this case, however, it has happened and you have a duty to pass what the judge has said to the client. However, if your client does want to enter a guilty plea on this basis, you must be absolutely sure that he has committed the crime and is not pleading guilty for fear of something worse if he pleads not guilty.

Lawyer 4

What a stressful situation. This is going to keep you and your client up all night as you think through the different issues involved. You need to remember that there is a danger that, in caring for your client well, you will rack up huge legal fees and that would not be caring! With issues like these, you might need to advise your client to seek help from another trusted friend. Keep the conversations focused, but recognise the emotional turmoil involved. Encourage your client to think through his obligations to others as he decides. It is hard to see how pleading guilty is a caring thing to do in this context, given that he has previously said that he was not guilty, but it might be if it allows him to avoid prison and if the client is able, for example, thereby to keep on caring for his children. Remember that this is not only an issue about legal formalities, but also raises issues of emotional and family significance.

---

[14] See further the discussion on this in Chapter 9.

[15] S. Jones, 'Under pressure: Women who plead guilty to crimes they have not committed' (2012) 11 Criminology and Criminal Justice 77.

Commercial law

 What would you do?

You are instructed by Maria, who is the managing director of a large company, X Ltd. She instructs you to arrange for the takeover by X Ltd of another company, Y Ltd. You learn that, as part of the takeover, Maria will be paid £100,000. In your opinion, the price that X Ltd is paying for Y Ltd is very high, although you are not an expert on the issue. You are also concerned that Y Ltd is the major employer in a deprived area of the north east of England and that Maria has told you that, if the takeover goes ahead, she plans to shut down Y Ltd's factories in the north east.

Lawyer 1

A key ambiguity needs to be resolved before we can address this question: who is the client? You must follow your client's instructions and ensure that you follow only them. Fortunately, in this case, there is not too much of a difficulty. There are two options: either your client is X Ltd or it is Maria.

If your client is Maria, then you must follow her instructions. What she is instructing is not contrary to the law and does not involve a breach of the professional codes. It may be that you feel a little uneasy about what she has asked you to do, but this is why the principle of neutrality is so important. Your role is to help the client, Maria, to do what she wants to achieve.

It may be that your client is X Ltd. In fact, in this case, that would make no difference. Maria is the managing director of X Ltd and, as such, she presumably has authority to make decisions on behalf of the company. You might want to check in the company's articles of association that she has such authority, but it would be surprising if she, or at least the board of directors, did not.

Lawyer 2

It is unlikely that Maria is instructing you to act in her own capacity. She is asking you to do work for X Ltd, not her own private matters. I therefore assume that X Ltd is the client.

However, you must not assume that what Maria wants is what is good for the company. At the end of the day, the company is owned by the shareholders. It is their investment that enables the company to be formed and to operate. If the company fails, it is they who will lose out. You must therefore, as a company lawyer, have the good of the shareholders in mind too as of central concern. Some of the recent financial scandals have been a result of lawyers acting following the directions of the directors, while failing to think about the long-term benefits to the company and especially the interests of the shareholders.

It may well be that Maria has thought through the issues carefully and that the proposal is going to be a good one for the shareholders. However, it is important to make sure that this proposal is financially viable and that you have thought through the issues involved, so that if necessary you can confirm to the shareholders that this proposal appeared the best for the company as a whole. If, after deliberation, you determine that the proposed takeover is not in the interests of X Ltd, you must refuse to follow the instructions.

Lawyer 3

It is astonishing that Lawyers 1 and 2 have so calmly failed to mention what should be the key fact here: the impact of this decision on the wider social environment. Lawyers are citizens and, especially as lawyers, we have a duty to ensure that the public good is upheld. The loss of so many jobs in a deprived area of the country is a major social harm and lawyers must take that into account in determining their ethical obligations. I accept that the issues raised may be complex and that there may be no alternative other than the loss of these jobs, but the lawyer has responsibilities to take these into account. Lawyers ultimately owe their duties to the general good and the administration of justice, as I explained in my introductory comments.

There is another reason too why it is important to take these into account. As Lawyer 2 has said, it is wrong to see the company as simply the directors. However, it is also wrong to see the company as made up of only the directors and the shareholders. The company is made up of the directors, shareholders, employees, and suppliers, and even the wider local community. These are all seen as stakeholders in the company.[16]

We can see this with the increasing emphasis put on companies by the notion of **corporate social responsibility (CSR)**. You, as the company's lawyer, have a duty to advise the client not only of her rights, but also of her responsibilities.

 Definition

In a recent communication,[17] the European Commission puts forward a simpler definition of **corporate social responsibility (CSR)** as 'the responsibility of enterprises for their impacts on society' and outlines what an enterprise should do to meet that responsibility.

Although there is no 'one size fits all' solution and, for most small and medium-sized enterprises (SMEs), the CSR process remains informal, complying with legislation and

---

[16] See Chapter 12 for further discussion.

[17] European Commission, *Corporate Social Responsibility: A New Definition, a New Agenda for Action* (European Commission, 2011).

collective agreements negotiated between social partners is the basic requirement for an enterprise to meet its social responsibility.

Beyond that, enterprises should, in the Commission's view, have a 'process in place to integrate social, environmental, ethical human rights and consumer concerns into their business operations and core strategy', in close cooperation with their stakeholders. The aim is:

- to maximise the creation of shared value, which means to create returns on investment for the company's shareholders at the same time as ensuring benefits for the company's other stakeholders; and

- to identify, prevent, and mitigate possible adverse impacts that enterprises may have on society.

Important features of the new definition include the following.

- *Recognition of the importance of core business strategy* This is consistent with the approach taken by leading enterprises for which social responsibility and sustainability have become an integral part of the business model. The Commission's 2008 Competitiveness Report concluded that CSR is most likely to contribute to the long-term success of the enterprise when it is fully integrated into business strategy.[18]

- *Development of the concept of 'creating shared value'* This refers to the way in which enterprises seek to generate a return on investment for their owners and shareholders by means of creating value for other stakeholders and society at large. This links CSR strongly to innovation, especially in terms of developing new products and services that are commercially successful and help to address societal challenges.

- *Explicit recognition of human rights and ethical considerations, in addition to social, environmental and consumer considerations*

Your duty as a lawyer is to discuss these issues carefully with the client. You cannot act for your client in a way that will cause a serious social harm and which will breach the company's social responsibilities. You have a duty not to assist a client do an act that causes serious social harm.

Lawyer 4

I am very much drawn to the model of the company that Lawyer 3 adopts, with the notion of stakeholders. There is something in this, but it is too narrow. A company is made up of a network of relationships.[19] Before going on to critique it, Simon Marshall explains the main ideas of the stakeholder theory of companies:

---

[18] European Commission, *European Competitiveness Report* (European Commission, 2008).
[19] C. Williams and P. Zumbansen (eds) *The Embedded Firm: Corporate Governance, Labor, and Finance Capitalism* (Cambridge University Press, 2012).

Stakeholder theory holds, largely as a response to the kind of ethical controversies outlined in the preceding, that the primary responsibility of a corporation is not to maximise shareholder wealth, but instead to serve the interests of a range of stakeholders that make up the society in which it operates. These stakeholders are taken to include not merely the shareholders, but employees, lenders, suppliers, the local community and even 'society' at large. Though disagreements exist over exactly which stakeholders are to be considered legitimate, the idea that a corporation's objective should encompass the interests of non-shareholding groups is held as a fundamental step in establishing an ethically responsible business outlook.[20]

Under this kind of approach, the company must be run in a way that takes into account the responsibilities and relationships that the company has with all of its stakeholders. As a lawyer, you must enable the company to do this. In this case, this means that X Ltd will take on the relationships with the workers that Y Ltd has. This involves a duty to care for them and their communities. As Lawyer 3 has mentioned, it may be that the most caring thing is to close the factory as X Ltd proposes, but I doubt it. All those involved—the directors, shareholders, employees, and community leaders—should be invited to discuss the problems facing these two companies and to find an appropriate way in which to proceed.

Family law

 What would you do?

Susan seeks your advice. She has reached the following agreement with her husband, Jamil, through mediation.

1. They will divorce, after 15 years of marriage.
2. Their teenage daughter (Lea) will split her time between the two parents, living with Susan one week and Jamil the next week.
3. Jamil will keep the house, but pay Susan £100 per month.
4. Lea will look after their pet hamster.

Susan asks that you prepare the paperwork to put the agreement into the form of a court order. You are very worried. The parents live 200 miles apart and so Lea will need to undertake a long journey each week. You also learn that Lea wants to live only with her mother. You are also sure that Susan would get far more financially if the matter were to go to court. You raise these issues with Susan, and she replies that she and Jamil know what is best for their family, and asks you to complete the paperwork as requested. Susan seems unwilling to talk about the issues.

[20] S. Marshall, *Capitalism, Corporations and the Social Contract: A Critique of Stakeholder Theory* (Cambridge University Press, 2012), 2.

Lawyer 1

As you might expect, I am a great fan of mediation. Its genius lies in the fact that it puts the client in control. It allows each person to decide for himself or herself what is fair and just. It puts autonomy at the heart of the legal process. The point is this: you or I, or a judge, may have views on what are the key issues to be resolved in a family breakdown and what would be a fair outcome. Traditionally, it is the law that imposes on people a particular view of what issues are important and what results are fair. But how much better that the parties should decide for themselves which issues need to be resolved and what, for them, will be fair? There is a good example in this case and that is that they have decided what should happen to their hamster. A court would never resolve this issue. However, it is clearly a matter of great importance to this couple, and we should respect that and have it put into a court order.

Some people may be concerned that what is being agreed here is unfair to Jamil or Susan. Some lawyers may even seek to persuade their client to reject this agreement. But this is the life of Jamil and Susan not of the lawyer. The lawyer here can draft a quick (and cheap!) consent order to put before the judge in the terms agreed. The only issue of significance that you should address in this case is this question: what have the parties agreed? Fortunately, they seem have to set down their agreement with admirable clarity. Your job is straightforward.

Lawyer 2

The client has come to seek your legal advice and you need to promote the best interests of your client. In this context, you need to make an independent determination of whether the agreement is fair. At first sight, this agreement does not look fair. The amount of money awarded is far less than Susan might expect if the case were to go to court. You will need to apply the principles of family law, but courts will consider an equal split of the assets to be fair and will want to ensure that Susan has sufficient money to ensure that she can look after Lea.[21]

Lawyer 1 is mistaken in assuming that, because Susan and Jamil think the agreement is fair, the law must agree. That could lead to absurd results. The law has principles of fairness and justice that the parties cannot seek to put to one side. An employer cannot employ someone for £1 per hour, for example, because that is contrary to the minimum wage legislation. In any event, Susan has probably entered this proposed agreement without appreciating what her legal rights are. You need to sit down with Susan and take her through how a court would resolve this issue. As already mentioned, I expect that this will lead to her getting far more money than proposed. You need to ensure that her interests are promoted.

I am not completely against mediation. Family law has a degree of latitude on some matters and if the parties want to change some of the details of what the court would agree, then there is no problem with that. So, for example, normally if maintenance is

---

[21] For the detail of the law, see J. Herring, *Family Law*, 6th edn (Pearson, 2013), ch. 5.

to be paid, the court would order it to be paid monthly, but if Susan and Jamil decide it would work better for them if the sum were paid weekly, then of course there is no problem with that. Similarly, if what they had agreed were very close to what a court would order, it would be acceptable to go along with the arrangement that they have reached.

I fear that, in this case, Susan will need to fight in litigation to obtain her legal rights. You certainly cannot put her request into effect and turn their agreement into a court order. Hopefully, Jamil's lawyer will advise him of the legal position and the parties will be able to reach an amicable agreement more in line with the rights of the parties.

Lawyer 3

The scenario mentioned here highlights my deep concern with mediation. It assumes that disputes only involve the two parties involved. The responses of Lawyers 1 and 2 have made that same assumption. The obligation of the lawyer is to promote the interests of his or her client, I agree, but that is only a small part of the picture in this case.

First, no one so far has mentioned Lea, yet she is the most vulnerable person in this case. While family lawyers must act for their clients, they must always have the interests of the child(ren) at heart. Sometimes, it is possible to have children represented by their own lawyers, which can be a very effective way of ensuring that children are heard in family cases, but that is rarely possible owing to the expensive involved. However, where it is not possible, it is the responsibility of the lawyer of both parents to ensure that the interests of the children are protected. I would argue that this is part of the lawyer's primary duty to the administration of justice. In family cases, at the heart of the administration of justice are the interests of children.

Key statute

Section 1 of the Children Act 1989 provides:

> When a court determines any question with respect to—
> (a) the upbringing of a child; or
> (b) the administration of a child's property or the application of any income arising from it,
>
> the child's welfare shall be the court's paramount consideration.

In this case, the arrangement that Lea shall live with each parent one week and have a long journey in between looks potentially harmful to her, especially because she does not support this arrangement. You, as a family lawyer, have an obligation to stand up for Lea's interests and you cannot be party to an arrangement that harms a child.

Perhaps less straightforward is my objection to the financial arrangements that they have reached. These have left Susan with a tiny sum of money after a reasonably lengthy marriage. Jamil is receiving by far the largest portion. My concern is not only that this is unfair to Susan, as Lawyer 2 has pointed out, but also that this arrangement is not reflecting the broader legal and social principles. At the heart of the recent thinking of the family courts is that husbands and wives should be regarded as equal, and whether they have contributed to the marriage by means of earning money or looking after the children, they should receive an equal share of the assets generated during the marriage.[22] The fact that spouses should be seen as equal and that child care should be regarded as of equal value to earning money are important moral principles that the law is upholding and which are of social importance to the wider community. So the issue is not only about the two parties, but about conceptions of the general social good as well.[23]

There is one final issue here. The couple have reached an agreement about their hamster. That is really not a matter in which to involve the resources of the court and the judge's time. The lawyer, as an officer of the court, has a duty to ensure that the time of the court is not wasted on trivial matters. You should refuse to bring this to the court's attention, and leave it as a matter of note for Jamil and Susan.

Lawyer 4

In general, I would support the idea of people getting tougher and seeking to resolve their differences. I accept that the solution that might work for one couple in a family law case might not work for another. We should accept and encourage the finding of a resolution that works for the particular couple in the particular context.

However, we also need to be alert to the fact that relationships can be abusive, as well as empowering. One of the difficulties with mediation in a family law context is that it can involve a relationship marred by domestic violence. This can severely impact on the parties' bargaining power. Even if there is no domestic violence, the relationship may be marked by unequal power, with Susan expecting to accept everything that Jamil says. The parties' emotions must be considered too. There are high rates of depression among those who divorce.[24] Susan may be desperate to keep in regular contact with Lea and may agree to anything to enable that to occur. I cannot tell whether any of these factors is present in this case, but I recommend that you discuss these issues sensitively and carefully with Susan to understand whether she really has freely agreed to this arrangement.

It is crucial for a family lawyer to ensure that the result achieved will promote a good ongoing relationship between the parties. An arrangement that will produce ongoing discord will not be good for anyone. In this context, it is important that the arrangements concerning Lea are workable, and that they will promote good relationships between the parents and children. These do not look as though they will.

[22] *White v White* [2001] UKHL 9.
[23] J. Herring, 'Why financial orders on divorce should be unfair' (2005) 19 International Journal of Law Policy and the Family 218. [24] Herring (n. 21), 173.

Sometimes, in family cases, an equal division of time between parents is adopted because it is assumed that this is fair between the parents—but that should never be done at the cost of harming the family relationships.

With this last point in mind, I would strong encourage the parties to bring Lea into these discussions. She is a teenager and she clearly has strong views on what should happen. She is a member of the family and the decisions are going to impact on her.

In conclusion, it may be that the relationship between Susan and Jamil is so marked by violence that mediation is not possible. However, it may be that mediation can take place if the parties are advised and helped by a lawyer. I would recommend to Susan that she, Jamil, and Lea all sit down with legal advisers and a mediator, and try again to talk through these issues. Each party should respect the contribution of the other to the marriage and a resolution should be sought that will enable all three to move forward in healthy, fair relationships.[25]

Conclusion

This chapter has shown how lawyers might disagree on the correct response to complex ethical dilemmas. Indeed, each of the (imaginary) lawyers has relied on ethical approaches to justify sometimes wildly differing results. This chapter has shown how significant your starting principles are. Yet your ethical background rules what you regard as core moral values—and on these people profoundly disagree. This is because we have different views on what makes life valuable and what makes a good person. While appreciating this does not mean that complete agreement is possible, we might at least understand better why we may disagree.

[25] Sir Alan Ward, 'Professional responsibility when dealing with parental irresponsibility', in R. Cranston (ed.) *Legal Ethics and Professional Responsibility* (Oxford University Press, 1996).

Index